Perception and Its Modalities

Perception and Its Modalities

Edited by Dustin Stokes, Mohan Matthen,
and
Stephen Biggs

OXFORD
UNIVERSITY PRESS

OXFORD
UNIVERSITY PRESS

Oxford University Press is a department of the University of Oxford.
It furthers the University's objective of excellence in research, scholarship,
and education by publishing worldwide.

Oxford   New York

Auckland   Cape Town   Dar es Salaam   Hong Kong   Karachi
Kuala Lumpur   Madrid   Melbourne   Mexico City   Nairobi
New Delhi   Shanghai   Taipei   Toronto

With offices in

Argentina   Austria   Brazil   Chile   Czech Republic   France   Greece
Guatemala   Hungary   Italy   Japan   Poland   Portugal   Singapore
South Korea   Switzerland   Thailand   Turkey   Ukraine   Vietnam

Oxford is a registered trademark of Oxford University Press
in the UK and certain other countries.

Published in the United States of America by
Oxford University Press
198 Madison Avenue, New York, NY 10016

Library of Congress Cataloging-in-Publication Data

A copy of this book's Cataloging-in-Publication Data is on file with the Library of Congress

ISBN 978–0–19–983279–8 (hbk.); 978–0–19–983281–1 (pbk.)

1 3 5 7 9 8 6 4 2
Printed in the United States of America
on acid-free paper

{ CONTENTS }

{ ACKNOWLEDGEMENTS }

This volume comes, somewhat indirectly, out of a workshop on the senses organized in 2009 by the three editors jointly. The workshop was funded by an International Opportunities Fund grant from the Social Sciences and Humanities Research Council of Canada. It was held at the Institut Jean-Nicod in Paris, with organizational support from the then Director, Pierre Jacob, and David Landais, the local organizer. The three co-editors were all at the University of Toronto in 2009, and benefitted from the marvelous atmosphere for research provided by the Department of Philosophy. Stephen Biggs has received research support from Iowa State University, and Dustin Stokes from the University of Utah. Mohan Matthen continues to be supported by the Social Sciences and Humanities Research Council of Canada, the Canada Research Chairs program, and the University of Toronto. Our warm thanks to all.

{ ABOUT THE EDITORS }

Stephen Biggs is Assistant Professor in the Department of Philosophy at Iowa State University. He works generally in the areas of metaphysics and philosophy of mind. Recent research includes work on phenomenal consciousness, representationalism, and modality. For more information (including curriculum vitae and current research) see http://www.philrs.iastate.edu/stephen-biggs/.

Mohan Matthen is Professor and Canada Research Chair in philosophy, perception, and communication, in the Department of Philosophy at the University of Toronto. He works in the philosophy of perception and the philosophy of biology, and is currently researching issues concerning phenomenal content, audition, perceptual knowledge, and the relation between perception and memory. For more information (including curriculum vitae and current research) see http://web.mac.com/mohanmatthen/Site/Mohan_Matthen.html.

Dustin Stokes is Assistant Professor in the Department of Philosophy at the University of Utah. He works generally in the areas of philosophy of mind and cognitive science. His current research concerns the cognitive penetrability of perceptual experience, relations between sense modalities, and the role of imagination and imagery in practical and theoretical reasoning. For more information (including curriculum vitae and current research) see http://stokes.mentalpaint.net.

{ ABOUT THE CONTRIBUTORS }

Malika Auvray is Centre National de la Recherche Scientifique (CNRS) Researcher in cognitive sciences at the Institut Jean Nicod. Her main research interests involve sensory substitution and broader cross-modal interactions. She investigates the learning of sensory substitution devices and the involved mechanisms of distal attribution, challenges the distinction of sensory modalities through the examples of these devices, and collaborates on the development of several conversion systems. She has published more than thirty articles or book chapters on sensory substitution, multisensory perception, and cross-modal interactions.

Clare Batty works primarily in the philosophy of mind. Batty's current research is in the philosophy of perception and focuses on olfactory experience. Her publications include "A Representational Account of Olfactory Experience" (*Canadian Journal of Philosophy*), "Smelling Lessons" (*Philosophical Studies*), "Scents and Sensibilia" (*American Philosophical Quarterly*), and "What's that Smell?" (*Southern Journal of Philosophy*). She received her B. A. (Hons.) in philosophy from Simon Fraser University in 1999, and her Ph.D. from MIT in 2007. She is currently Associate Professor of philosophy at the University of Kentucky.

Tim Bayne is Professor of philosophy at the University of Manchester. He is the author of *The Unity of Consciousness* (Oxford University Press, 2010) and *Thought: A Very Short Introduction* (Oxford University Press, 2013), and is an editor of *The Oxford Companion to Consciousness* (Oxford University Press, 2009) and *Cognitive Phenomenology* (Oxford University Press, 2011). He is currently working on a textbook on the philosophy of mind.

Peter Carruthers is Professor of philosophy at the University of Maryland. His most recent book is *The Opacity of Mind: An Integrative Theory of Self-Knowledge* (Oxford University Press, 2011).

Roberto Casati is Tenured Senior Researcher with the French Centre National de la Recherche Scientifique (CNRS). He has worked on various research projects on philosophy of perception and has published articles in *Analysis, Proceedings of the Aristotelian Society, Studia Leibnitiana, Journal of Aesthetics and Art Criticism, Perception, Trends in Cognitive Science, Journal of Visual Language and Computing, Dialectica, Australasian Journal of Philosophy, Philosophical Studies, Philosophical Psychology, Behavioral and Brain Sciences*. This nonstandard spread reflects interdisciplinary interests, focusing on the psychological status of commonsense notions (such as that of object, event, colors, sounds, and holes and shadows). Main publications include *Shadows* (Vintage 2002, translated into seven languages), a few books with Achille C. Varzi: *Holes and Other Superficialities* (1994), and *Parts and Places* (1999), both published by MIT Press; *Unsurmountable Simplicities* translated into eight languages; and *The Planet of Disappearing Things*. He has collaborated with Jérôme Dokic of École des Hautes Etudes en Sciences Sociales (EHESS) on *La philosophie du son* (Chambon 1994).

Mazviita Chirimuuta is Assistant Professor in history and philosophy of science at the University of Pittsburgh. Trained both as neurobiologist and philosopher, her research and scholarship focus on the philosophy of neurobiology and perceptual science, including experimental work on vision and the development of novel theoretical/philosophical frameworks for understanding color. She has recently published articles on the topic of modeling and explanation in neuroscience and is currently preparing a monograph for the MIT Press, *Outside Colour: Perceptual Science and the Revision of Colour Ontology*.

Andy Clark is Professor of logic and metaphysics in the School of Philosophy, Psychology, and Language Sciences at Edinburgh University in Scotland. He is the author of *Being There: Putting Brain, Body and World Together Again* (MIT Press, 1997), *Mindware* (Oxford University Press, 2001), *Natural-Born Cyborgs: Minds, Technologies and the Future of Human Intelligence* (Oxford University Press, 2003), and *Supersizing the Mind: Embodiment, Action, and Cognitive Extension* (Oxford University Press, 2008).

Ed Cooke co-founded the website memrise.com in 2010 with the aim of making learning genuinely pleasurable. Before this, he wrote the book *Remember, Remember: Learn the Stuff You Thought You Never Could* (Viking, 2008), was a columnist for the *Times*, became a Grandmaster of Memory and trained Josh Foer to be US memory champion in a year. He holds degrees in cognitive science and philosophy from Oxford and René Descartes Universities, Paris.

Ophelia Deroy is Researcher at the Centre for the Study of the Senses and Associate Director of the Institute of Philosophy at the University of London. She specializes in philosophy of mind and cognitive sciences and has widely published on issues related to multisensory perception, sensory deficits, and synesthesia.

Jerome Dokic is Professor of cognitive philosophy at the École des Hautes Études en Sciences Sociales and a member of Institut Jean-Nicod in Paris. His research interests are perception, memory, imagination, and more recently epistemic feelings and metacognition. He has published many essays on these topics, including the books *La philosophie du son* with Roberto Casati (*Philosophy of sound*, Chambon, 1994), *L'esprit en mouvement. Essai sur la dynamique cognitive* (*Mind in motion. Essay on cognitive dynamics*, Center for the Study of Language and Information, Stanford, 2001), *Qu'est-ce que la perception?* (*What is perception?* Vrin, 2nd edition 2009), and *Ramsey. Truth and Success* with Pascal Engel (Routledge, 2002).

Robert Fendrich received his PhD in experimental psychology from the New School for Social Research in 1983, with a specialization in visual perception. He has been on the research faculty at Cornell Medical Center, Dartmouth College, the University of California at Davis, and Otto-von-Guericke University in Magdeburg, Germany. He is the author of more than forty papers published in refereed journals, which address topics such as the interactions between vision and eye motions, audio-visual perceptual interactions, visual attention, and blindsight. Currently, he is Visiting Scholar at Dartmouth College.

Matthew Fulkerson is Assistant Professor of philosophy at the University of California, San Diego. His research interests are in the philosophy of mind, perception, and psychology. He is the author of *The First Sense: A Philosophical Study of Human Touch* (MIT, 2014).

C. L. Hardin is Professor of philosophy, emeritus, at Syracuse University. He is the author of *Color for Philosophers* (Hackett, 1988, 1993) and co-editor of *Color Categories in Thought and Language* (Cambridge University Press, 1997).

Howard C. Hughes is Professor of psychology at Dartmouth College. His research is concerned with attention, spatial vision, eye movements, sensory-motor coordination, and polymodal integration. He has authored more than sixty journal articles and book chapters, and a book entitled *Sensory Exotica* (1999, MIT Press). The book describes the workings of a variety of "exotic" sensory modalities that humans do not posses (e.g., biosonar, electroreception, magnetoreception). *Sensory Exotica* was voted the "best book in biological sciences" by the Scholarly Division of the Association of American Publishers in 1999, and was reprinted in Italian in 2001.

John Kulvicki is Associate Professor of philosophy at Dartmouth College, New Hampshire. He is the author of two books on images and numerous papers on the philosophy of perception.

François Le Corre holds a master's degree in philosophy and a master's degree in cognitive science. He is currently a PhD student supervised by Roberto Casati at the Institut Jean Nicod (Paris, France) and at the Université Pierre et Marie Curie (Paris VI). His research addresses the question of the individuation of the senses, by examining two assumptions of the traditional conception of the senses: the assumption that humans have five senses and the assumption that the senses are separate modalities. To that matter, he pays close attention to recent ethnographic observations, crosslinguistics, psychological, ethnological, and neurological data.

Fiona Macpherson is Professor of philosophy and Director of the Centre of the Study of Perceptual Experience at the University of Glasgow. She is Co-director of the Centre for the Study of the Senses, Institute of Philosophy, University of London. She has been Visiting Professor at the Universities of London and Umea, and a research fellow at the Australian National University, Rosamund Chambers

Research Fellow at Girton College, Cambridge, and a research fellow at Harvard. She has published numerous papers in the philosophy of mind and perception in journals such as *Noûs* and *Philosophy and Phenomenological Research* and several edited volumes including *Hallucination* (MIT Press, 2013, with Dimitris Platchias), *The Senses* (Oxford University Press, 2009), *The Admissible Contents of Experience* (Wiley Blackwell, 2009, with Katherine Hawley), and *Disjunctivism* (Oxford University Press, 2008, with Adrian Haddock).

Erik Myin is Professor of philosophy at the University of Antwerp, where he is Head of the Centre for Philosophical Psychology. He has published papers on topics relating to mind and perception, and is, with Dan Hutto, co-author of *Radicalizing Enactivism: Basic Minds without Content* (MIT Press, 2013).

Matthew Nudds is Professor and Head of the Department of Philosophy at the University of Warwick.

Casey O'Callaghan is Associate Professor of philosophy at Washington University in St. Louis.

Mark Paterson is in the Department of Communication at the University of Pittsburgh and has an interest in blindness, touch, and the somatic senses. He is the author of *The Senses of Touch: Haptics, Affects and Technologies* (2007), and co-editor of *Touching Place, Spacing Touch* (2012). He has recently completed *Seeing with the Hands: Blindness and Philosophy after Descartes and Diderot* (in press), and his next contracted book is entitled *How We Became Sensorymotor* for Penn State University Press.

Vincent Picciuto is currently Adjunct Professor of philosophy at the United States Naval Academy in Annapolis. He earned his PhD from the University of Maryland in 2014.

Nicholas Shea is Interdisciplinary Philosopher of mind, and of psychology, cognitive science, and cognitive neuroscience. He came into philosophy via a master of arts degree at Birkbeck and a PhD at King's College, London. He then worked as Research Fellow in Oxford, based in the Faculty of Philosophy and Somerville College and affiliated with the Department of Experimental Psychology, before joining King's College London in 2012.

Barry Smith is Professor of philosophy and Director of the Institute of Philosophy. He is Founding Director of the Centre for the Study of the Senses, and The Arts and Humanities Research Council Leadership Fellow for the Science in Culture Theme. He edited Questions of Taste: The Philosophy of Wine (Oxford University Press, 2007) and co-edited *The Oxford Handbook of Philosophy of Language* (Oxford University Press, 2006) with Ernest Lepore.

Charles Spence received his PhD in experimental psychology from the Department of Psychology at the University of Cambridge in 1998. He is university Professor at the Department of Experimental Psychology at Oxford University and heads the Crossmodal Research Laboratory at the Department of Experimental Psychology, Oxford University. He has published over 500 articles in scientific journals over the last decade. He has been awarded the 10th Experimental Psychology Society Prize, the British Psychology Society: Cognitive Section Award, the Paul Bertelson Award, recognizing him as the young European Cognitive Psychologist of the Year, and the Friedrich Wilhelm Bessel Research Award from the Alexander von Humboldt Foundation in Germany. He is interested in all things multisensory.

Sarah E. Streeter graduated with honors from Dartmouth College in June 2012 with a major in neuroscience. She now works at AmeriCares, a global health and emergency response nonprofit organization devoted to providing disaster relief and emergency health care. She plans to attend medical school in the fall of 2014.

Karim Zahidi holds a PhD in mathematics and in philosophy. He lectures at the Department of Philosophy (University of Antwerp). He has published on decision problems in number theory, mathematical logic, decision theory, and philosophical psychology. His main research topics in philosophy are related to enactive approaches to perception and cognition.

Sorting the Senses

Stephen Biggs, Mohan Matthen, and Dustin Stokes

This volume is about the many ways we perceive. Contributors explore the nature of the individual senses, how and what they tell us about the world, and how they interrelate. They often represent competing views: for instance, some argue that perception uses the senses in concert while others are content, at least for present purposes, to leave unchallenged the traditional assumption that we perceive through discrete senses. And the methods deployed sometimes differ from one chapter to the next: some draw on the sciences and engineering while others rely upon conceptual analysis. Despite these differences, all the contributors agree that traditional theorizing about the senses is hampered by a neglect of the senses other than vision (based on the facile assumption that what goes for vision goes just as well for the other senses), and by the misconception that vision itself is a passive receptacle for an image thrown by a lens. In addition, many of the contributors believe that it is unduly restrictive to think of perception as a collation of content provided by individual modalities; they think that to understand perception properly, we need to build into our accounts the idea that the senses work together. The ambition of the volume is to begin to develop better paradigms for understanding the senses and thereby to move toward a better understanding of perception.

The push for change begins with recognizing the shortcomings of tradition. We introduce the volume, accordingly, by sketching some of those shortcomings and situating each contribution among the sketches. While we intend for the discussion to be informative in its own right, our sketches are offered to set the stage for the more detailed discussions presented by the chapters that comprise the volume.

Some shortcomings of traditional theorizing are easier for the philosopher to spot than others. For some are evident when one carefully describes the phenomenology of sense-perception. Others, however, are unearthed only when one considers philosophical issues in the light of results from the cognitive sciences.

As an example of a shortcoming that emerges from phenomenological description, consider this question: do we have auditory experience of sounds merely as coming from various directions, or do we hear some sounds as behind, farther away than, or partially occluded by others? Tradition tacitly assumes the former, on the grounds that sound impinging on the ear carries no mark of distance.[1] Reflection on our own auditory experience, however, makes clear that tradition is wrong: we often *do* hear some sounds as behind, farther away than, or partially occluded by others. With respect to distance, think of the sound of a train: it can sound not only as if it is approaching or receding, but also as if it is quite close by or distant. As for occlusion, think of the tap running in your kitchen sink, partially obscuring some of the conversation in the next room. Sounds are heard, then, as located in three-dimensional space.

As an example of a shortcoming that emerges only given empirical investigation, consider the nature of flavour. To the taster, it seems that flavour is a single composite quality of food, detected primarily by the tongue. The truth is more complex (Auvray and Spence 2008). Work by cognitive scientists has established that there are multiple sources of flavour perception, including not only taste receptors on the tongue (which account for the simplest taste components—salt, sweet, sour, bitter, and perhaps a couple more), but also olfactory receptors in the nasal tract (which react very differently when odorants emanating from the mouth flow over them in the retronasal, or opposite-to-sniffing, direction), and the trigeminal nerve, which is responsible for sensation in the face and for the motor control of biting and chewing. (It is the stimulation of the trigeminal nerve in the face that causes mint to have its characteristic coolness and chillies their characteristic heat—yet, the coolness and the heat are sensed *in the foods*, not in the face.) As well, of course, there is the complex experience of eating or drinking, of which flavour is only one part, with texture and mouth-feel as distinct but well-integrated components. Flavour, though experienced as if it were delivered in a single perceptual act of sampling, is actually a composite of outputs from all these sources.

Since recognizing the shortcomings of traditional theorizing often requires considering philosophical issues in light of results from the cognitive sciences, theorizing about the senses is inherently interdisciplinary: philosophers who ignore the sciences will not encounter many of the results that constitute problems for traditional theorizing, and scientists who ignore philosophy will not appreciate many of the problems that could drive significant research. For example, it is philosophically significant that flavour is experienced as a property of food, not as events in the body occasioned by food. And this makes good sense from an ecological point of view: flavour helps us identify foods and their characteristics, and is not used as a marker merely of the *experience* of tasting various foods. But how does this happen? How is it, for example, that the irritation of the trigeminal nerve caused by chillies is felt to belong to the food in one's mouth? (Actually, it isn't just a few philosophical problems that are of scientific interest: one could go

---

[1] This is largely only tacit, since audition hasn't been discussed very much until recently—but now see Pasnau (1999), Nudds (2001), O'Callaghan (2007), Nudds and O'Callaghan (2009), Bullot and Egré (2010). The conclusion, one should note, is transferred from Berkeley's discussion of the impossibility of seeing distance—which in turn is inferred from the fact that the retinal image is two-dimensional.

further and argue that without philosophy, scientists wouldn't have *any* problems to solve.)

We turn now to another glaring deficiency of the traditional view: it supposes that perceptual states reflect *just* the information available at the sensory receptors. In the case of vision, this information is supposed to be contained in the two retinal images; the nature of these images is supposed to be given in turn by geometrical optics and the theory of lenses, as investigated in a tradition that includes such landmark thinkers as Euclid, Ibn Haitham, and Johannes Kepler. Thus, philosophers from Berkeley down to A. J. Ayer (1956) supposed that visual awareness must be of a fusion of two planar distributions of coloured pixels. Since these images lack depth information—at least beyond the short distances in which there is detectable parallax displacement—any impression of depth or of object boundaries must come from learned associations. Thus, Berkeley held that there is no direct visual awareness of depth or distance (even at short distances, according to him) and that the appearance of depth must be added by the learned association of tactual ideas of distance with the inward turn of the eyes to fuse the two retinal images, by the parallax displacement of these two images, and with the "confused" character of visual ideas that come from afar.

Assumptions of this sort were strongly challenged by the Gestalt psychologists of the early mid-twentieth century (Kohler 1929; Koffka 1935). Through a series of cleverly constructed perceptual illusions, they showed that depth, size, and object unity are essentially and inextricably contained in visual percepts. They then speculated about principles of scene analysis, which would explain how the cues available in the retinal images account for the richness of visual percepts. Although the resulting Gestalt principles have been somewhat eroded by subsequent research, this work made a permanent contribution: it is now universally accepted that the perceptual system *interprets* sensory data in accordance with principles that enrich the information available to the sensory receptors. The image of the world that we receive through the senses incorporates the results of this interpretative process, which is largely beyond the control of the perceiver.

It is still an open question, nonetheless, exactly how the senses extract perceptual content from receptoral information. Three of the chapters in this volume explore new models. Andy Clark (Chapter 1) discusses "predictive coding", a model on which the perceptual system makes predictions about what it will encounter and compares these predictions with incoming information, adjusting as necessary when discrepancies are found. Mohan Matthen (Chapter 2) introduces a notion of active perception, which is a temporally extended process of deliberate probing of the environment, using bodily movement and interaction with objects of investigation. And Nicholas Shea (Chapter 3) investigates the interaction between learned associations and incoming data—he asks to what extent interpretation is shaped by past experience.

Another serious shortcoming of traditional theorizing about the senses is its strong commitment to the idea that all perception is modality specific.

The basic proposition underlying this commitment is that any sensory idea belongs to exactly one modality, which implies that there is no single sensory experience that is, say, audiovisual. Of course, visual and auditory experiences sometimes are coordinated, as when we see and hear a person speak. Tradition maintains, nonetheless, that the auditory experience is phenomenally distinct from the visual experience and hence should be treated as a separate entity. Relatedly, it implies that insofar as this and other perceptual experiences seem to the subject to be integrated wholes rather than mere aggregates of individual experiences, it is not because of the intrinsic nature of the experiences themselves, but rather, because of some further feature of the psychology in which they are embedded.

These assumptions are at play in Kant's discussion of the unity of apperception. Kant argues that a subject treats her visual and auditory experiences as belonging to herself and as being jointly informative about the world, and that this "treating as" is required for achieving the unity among the senses that one finds in perceptual experience. He would have proceeded differently had he taken perceptual experience to be a unitary product of information provided by the different sense modalities, rather than separate experiences that need then to be blended or added to one another. Although the view that perception is modality specific is a view about *experience*, it intimates that the senses themselves are discrete rather than integrated in virtue of their intrinsic natures. And it assumes, further, that (for example) the act of hearing and seeing a person speak must be post-perceptual. As we shall see in a moment, this is contestable.

One question that immediately arises from the modality specific perception view is this: what happens when a single quality is expressed in more than one modality? This puzzle expresses itself, for example, in Molyneux's Question:

> Suppose a man born blind, and now adult, and taught by his touch to distinguish between a cube and a sphere of the same metal, and nighly of the same bigness, so as to tell, when he felt one and the other, which is the cube, which is the sphere. Suppose then the cube and the sphere placed on a table, and the blind man made to see: Quaere, Whether by his sight, before he touched them, he could now distinguish and tell which is the globe, which the cube? To which the acute and judicious proposer answers: 'Not.' For though he has obtained the experience of how a globe, and how a cube, affects his touch; yet he has not yet attained the experience, that what affects his touch so or so, must affect his sight so or so . . . (Locke, *Essay Concerning Human Understanding* II, IX, 8)

If the visual idea of a globe is phenomenally distinct from the tactual idea, how is the man who is newly sighted supposed to identify the unfamiliar visual idea with the tactual one? The French philosopher, Denis Diderot, gave this problem an additional twist. The blind man takes the measure of a three-dimensional object by a temporally extended series of tactual impressions that unfolds as he feels it: how could such a temporal sequence of impressions be equivalent to the single idea that the sighted have of the same three-dimensional object?[2]

Though Molyneux's Question continues to be an open research problem (Held et al. 2011), several experiments challenge the modality-specificity of perception by identifying percepts naturally taken to be *multimodal*, for example, audiovisual. Consider the well-known "McGurk effect". In one demonstration (McGurk and MacDonald 1976), subjects see a video of a person saying "ga", alongside a synced audio track of a person saying "ba". They report *hearing* "da" (or a relevantly similar phoneme, such as "ta"). Plausibly, this is because their auditory experiences result from a subpersonal reconciliation of the visual and auditory stimuli—"da" is intermediate between "ga" and "ba" from the point of view of speech production. (Think of where in the mouth the closure occurs for these syllables.) Since subjects' *auditory* representations of speech result, to a significant degree, from the *visual* stimulus, that is, from the hearer's visual perception of how the speaker produces speech, one is tempted to describe this as a case where *two* senses essentially contribute to *one* percept (i.e., the subject's "da-experience"), and thus, a case where a single experience is audiovisual.

Consider next the "rubber hand illusion" (Botvinick and Cohen 1998). Here, a subject looks at a rubber-cast of a hand, while her own hand is hidden from her view. The rubber hand and her hidden hand are stroked in unison with a brush. Subjects report *feeling* the brush stroking the rubber hand. Thus, the feel of the brush on the subject's hand—obviously, she cannot feel the inanimate rubber hand being stroked—is location-shifted by vision. In other words, *visual* input affects subjects' representations of *tactile* stimuli. Again, one is tempted to describe subjects' experiences here as multimodal.

An advocate of the traditional view may respond that although the input to these perceptions is multimodal, the perceptions are nonetheless not cases of multimodal *experience*. Though they are caused by stimuli associated with (what are ordinarily taken to be) distinct sense organs, they are experiences characteristic of a single modality—audition in the case of the McGurk effect and touch in the case of the rubber hand illusion. Here, the respondent assumes that the sensory category an experience belongs to depends entirely on its phenomenal character, that is, what it is like to have it. It seems, phenomenally, to McGurk subjects that they hear a "da"; the "phenomenal character" of their perception is as if it is auditory. Thus, defenders of the traditional view take it to *be* auditory. The McGurk effect is simply an auditory illusion, they insist, a case where subjects *hear* "da" when "ba" is spoken. The genesis of the illusion has no bearing on its modality.

This discussion reveals that a lot can depend on whether we should give greater weight to the source of the information or to the phenomenal character of the resulting sense-impression. One might predict that ordinary ways of thinking

---

[2] See Diderot's *Letter on the Blind*, chapter 3 of Morgan 1977.

would favour the second alternative, since the first turns on a determination made by a cleverly designed experiment to which one would ordinarily have no access. Participating in such an experiment might persuade us that the sources of information used by speech perception are unexpectedly diverse, but it does not easily persuade us that we don't simply *hear* "da" or "ba" as the case may be. This brings out another problem for traditional theorizing: its criteria for *individuating* the senses face serious challenges, an issue we consider a little later.

Returning to multimodal perception, one might ask: what exactly is it that is multimodally perceived? In typical cases, there is no obvious answer. Consider a baseball player catching a ball (an example borrowed from Casey O'Callaghan). She sees the ball come into her glove, hears the sound of the ball making contact with the glove, feels the ball against her palm; she is also aware of her own bodily actions of reaching for and grabbing the ball. At first glance, this seems like a perfect example of a single occurrence being apprehended by many sense-modalities, each one an independent source of information, the whole being a sum of these independent contributions. Is there a single event or object here that is perceived by all modalities? One could argue that there is not. Vision engages the ball and its motion; audition picks up how the ball hitting the gloved hand disturbs the air; touch is concerned with how this collision affects the skin and muscles of the hand; bodily awareness monitors how the hand moves to grab the ball. These are four distinct events, constituting a single causal nexus, but arguably detected independently by different senses.

This is the sort of question that Casey O'Callaghan (Chapter 5) explores. He claims that multimodal perception is, in part, the unification of these distinct events into a coherent environmental whole. He concedes, for the sake of argument, that one could apportion these experiences to different modalities, but he questions whether the sum of single-modality experiences exhausts the total informational content of perceptual experience, given that the latter includes the connectedness and integration of the distinct event mentioned. Matthew Nudds (Chapter 6) takes a somewhat different tack: he explores how auditory and visual information can both be integrated in a single persistent material object, as in various "ventriloquism" effects, where seen objects are identified as sound *sources*. (Think of the ventriloquist's dummy, which is misidentified as the sound source because of its moving mouth.) Nudds's approach fits well with Matthen's line on active perception (Chapter 2), which identifies interactive multimodal perception as a method of arriving at this kind of source-identification. In other words, while O'Callaghan identifies coherent nexuses of events as the target of multimodal perception, Nudds and Matthen take the complementary view that multimodal perception targets the material objects that are the *sources* of nexuses of nonvisual sense-objects, such as sounds and smells.

However this may be, Charles Spence and Tim Bayne (Chapter 4) present evidence that indicates a significant limitation on multimodality: human subjects, they suggest, can never be perceptually aware of two modalities at the same time.

Of course, the system circulates among the modalities extremely fast and this is what accounts for the appearance, and possibly the functionality, of multimodality. Spence and Bayne maintain, however, that in any given very brief interval of time, one is aware only of ideas of one modality. (It is an open question how this works for flavour: is it impossible for us to be aware of taste and trigeminal stimulation simultaneously?) This calls into question the idea that there can be genuinely multimodal awareness: at the very least, there cannot be *simultaneous* multimodal awareness, if Spence and Bayne are correct. For in their view, multimodal awareness is a temporally extended collocation.

At the outset, we noted another deficiency of traditional theorizing about the senses: it all too often presupposes that theorizing about perception in general can proceed by studying only vision, and then taking claims about vision to generalize, with at most minor modifications, to nonvisual senses. Matthew Nudds and Casey O'Callaghan (2009) emphasize this point,

> Philosophical discussions of sensible and secondary qualities have focused upon color and color experience, while debates about perceptual content primarily concern the content of visual experience. (p. 1)
>
> While it might seem obvious in the case of vision that perceptual experience is *transparent* [i.e., that one is conscious of external objects, not of the experience itself *eds.*] or that space is required for objectivity, gustatory and olfactory experiences might tell otherwise. (p. 2)

The focus on vision is problematic at least because, in its thrall, philosophical theorizing has often suggested that all of the senses relate to knowledge and action in exactly the same way, that is, as vision does. Various scientific results suggest, however, that the senses differ in these regards. To correct the error, and to provide a much richer and more pluralistic account, we have contributors who provide analyses of touch (Fulkerson), audition (Kulvicki), olfaction (Batty), and flavour (Spence, Smith, and Auvray).

What can we learn from nonvisual perception? Consider, first, O'Callaghan's aforementioned question: what are the objects of the nonvisual senses? Interest in this question started with an influential paper by Robert Pasnau (1999). It is often taken for granted that audition picks up sounds, and that sounds are disturbances of the air. But, Pasnau argued, this cannot be right. For disturbances of the air are spatially pervasive: when the starter's gun is fired, the air throughout the stadium is disturbed. Yet the sound of the gun is heard as localized; it is heard as coming from the gun. So what is sound? What, in other words, is audition's target when we hear something? It is an event, says Pasnau—in this case, the firing of the gun. The disturbance of the air is simply the medium through which news of this event is conveyed to the ears of the competitors and spectators.

We noted earlier how the Gestalt psychologists had drawn attention to the objects of vision—material objects, not proximal stimuli. Pasnau's argument shows how thinking beyond proximal stimuli can render the senses heterogeneous. Vision may focus on persistent material objects; audition, however, is concerned (according to him) with events. What about the other modalities? A number of chapters in this volume address the issue. Matthew Fulkerson (Chapter 7) distinguishes touch from the modalities that deliver information about the subject's body by first noting that tactual properties are "bound" to external objects (as distinct from pains, itches, and the like) and then considering the role of active haptic exploration in detecting and binding these external properties. John Kulvicki (Chapter 8) argues (against Pasnau) that audition detects the sonorous properties of objects rather than the events that these properties result in. Clare Batty (Chapter 9) argues that olfaction is recognition-based rather than identification-based, that is, it is concerned with the *kind* of substance it is engaging with rather than with its location or boundaries. Charles Spence, Malika Auvray, and Barry Smith (Chapter 10) consider the multi-input character of flavour and argue that taste is *not* a discrete modality with input into flavour perception but is rather an integrated part of the flavour system.

These discussions of the nonvisual senses raise several interesting questions. For example, if one can sense flavours on the basis of input to multiple kinds of receptors, one wonders what else can be sensed. Picciuto and Carruthers (Chapter 11) ask a broadly related question: are the so-called inner senses genuine sense modalities? Humans are capable of higher-order representations of first-order perceptual states and cognitive states. And some have argued that calling this faculty a 'sense' is not mere metaphor. Picciuto and Carruthers proceed by first identifying a sense modality prototype (which we discuss later) and then analysing various inner sense theories accordingly. They conclude that in this light, at least some of the inner sense mechanisms posited by theorists *are* senses rightly so called.

One might suggest that in the face of the traditional overemphasis on vision, we should, as an antidote, just stop thinking about sight and seeing for a while to allow work on the other senses to catch up. But this is not a viable program. For the traditional conception of vision is itself an unrealistically distorted idealization. For example, vision is wrongly thought to be transparently available to consciousness, and innocent of any systematic distortions that would reduce its trustworthiness. And these characteristics are assumed to be just as true of the other modalities as they are of vision. A more sensitive treatment of vision might lead us to question the homogeneity of such assumptions across the modalities—it could be that the senses are not homogeneous with regard to either outward directedness (or "transparency") or trustworthiness. And, once we start thinking about interactions with other modalities, we might begin to think differently about how vision itself operates.

Howard Hughes, Robert Fendrich, and Sarah Streeter (Chapter 12) take up the question of how the traditional conception of vision misleads. There are cases of vision that are too ephemeral to count as reasons for knowledge; there are even cases of vision that are completely unconscious. Conversely, there are many cases where damage to parts of the brain result in an inability to identify objects of various kinds (such as faces or letters), even though visual acuity is maintained. Finally, there is the recruitment of visual areas of the brain for the processing of input from other senses, raising questions about the plasticity of visual processing.

Visual substitution technology helps problematize this last point, that is, the plasticity of visual processing. Starting with Paul Bach-y-Rita at the University of Wisconsin Medical School, a series of devices was developed that converted camera input into the stimulation of a tactile vibrator array or sound sequence. With vibro-tactile substitutes for the retina, subjects using these "sensory substitution devices" begin to be able to sense distal objects as projected to the tactile array and to report sensations of depth and perspective. Exploring the implications of sensory substitution, Ophelia Deroy and Malika Auvray (Chapter 13) wonder what kind of awareness is provided by these devices: is it like touch or like sight? Their answer is that it is like neither but is rather a third sort of thing, which has some characteristics of both. Mazviita Chirimuuta and Mark Paterson (Chapter 17) explore a different aspect of this question: to what degree does sensory substitution suggest that the spatial framework of the senses is transferable across the senses. On this point, their treatment should be set alongside Matthen's account of space (Chapter 2). Matthen argues that since active perception is multimodal, it requires cross-modal spatial location. This either requires that one of the modalities is privileged (which Stokes and Biggs assert—Chapter 14—and Chirimuuta and Paterson, in effect, deny), or that space is "pre-modal." The latter seems to have been Kant's view, which Matthen defends.

It is arguable that the philosophical way of thinking about vision is itself fundamentally mistaken. We think of colour—perhaps the most fundamental visual property—as a similarity structure. This kind of thinking harks back to Aristotle, who thought of the colours as arrayed between just two poles, black and white. It's difficult to see how Aristotle could have thought of (for example) brown and green as one "more white" and the other "more black", but this illustrates the unreliability of this kind of intuition. By now, of course, we think of colours as a *three*-dimensional similarity space, with all the colours arrayed between white and black, red and green, and blue and yellow. C. L. Hardin discusses the inadequacy of this schema. He recounts the experiments that create reddish-green experiences in (some) observers. He also discusses the possibility that colour vision treats the "unique hues" as distinguished points in colour-similarity space, not merely null points for one or other of the hue dimensions.

Erik Myin, Ed Cooke, and Karim Zahidi (Chapter 16) explore an issue central to cross-modal influences, asking how changing the functional properties of a sense would affect associated experiences. They ask, for example, whether the phenomenal character of auditory experience would become like the phenomenal character of olfactory experience if audition took on some of the functional roles actually played by olfaction. Rather than taking a firm stand on this question, however, they answer that even those who think that functional properties determine phenomenal character can accept that, say, vibro-tactile sensory substitution does not generate experiences with a visual phenomenal character—roughly, because the functional properties associated with touch that are essential to vibro-tactile sensory substitution may play the greatest role in determining the phenomenal character of vibro-tactile experiences. While all contributors agree that vision should not be taken as the paradigm sense, Dustin Stokes and Stephen Biggs (Chapter 14) consider what makes vision special. They argue that, alone among the sensory modalities, the visual possesses rich spatiality, and consequently, the visual dominates the spatial sense of the other senses. They suggest that this visual dominance makes vision especially important both psychologically and epistemically, which partly explains (but does not excuse) the traditional focus on vision.

A closely related shortcoming of traditional theorizing about the senses is its insufficient exploration of criteria for individuating the senses (see MacPherson 2011, Matthen forthcoming). A criterion for individuating the senses is a criterion for identifying the kinds of senses there are, and to which kind of sense any individual sensing belongs. Philosophers have proposed a number of candidates, many of which have been operative in relevant sciences. Several contributors suggest that these familiar criteria should be abandoned in favour of either a preferred alternative or a view on which the senses work seamlessly together—see, especially, chapters under the heading "Relating the Modalities". We now consider the most familiar four criteria, which distinguish senses by one of receptive organ, proper sensible, representational character, or phenomenal character (cf. Grice 1962).

Aristotle distinguished the eyes, ears, skin, nose, and tongue as the five sense organs. He also observed that each sense organ is sensitive to the world in virtue of a different medium through which information about the object of perception is transmitted. Influenced by these and other similar empirical observations, many have thought that the senses have fundamentally different modes of sensitivity and different objects of perception. This suggests two criteria for individuating the senses: the *receptive organ criterion* holds that for each receptive organ there is exactly one sense; the *proper sensible criterion*, which offers at least a necessary condition for being a sense, holds that each sense uniquely detects at least one property (e.g., colour for vision). These criteria seem to converge, yielding the familiar five: the eyes, which alone detect colour, are distinct from the ears, which alone detect sound, and so on. Accordingly, Aristotle's approach was thought to be undisputable until at least the middle of the 19th century. At this point, scientists came to realize that the senses do not end at the receptive organs. The input provided by these organs awaits further processing in the brain. And this processing need not be as distinct and separate as the sense organs themselves. The discovery of sensory data-processing thus weakens the case for modality-specificity.

Putting the point about sensory processing aside, a little reflection on our physiology problematizes each criterion. The sense organs that Aristotle recognizes rely on multiple kinds of receptors, each of which is sensitive to different properties: the eyes contain rods and (three kinds of) cones; touch relies on stretch, pain, and pressure receptors; olfaction relies on a variety of chemical receptors; and so on. The processing pathways associated with these receptors, moreover, are kept distinct for at least some short distance in early sensory processing in the brain. It is far from obvious, then, that Aristotle's criteria yield the familiar five senses—why vision, rather than a "rod-sense" and a "cone-sense"? More broadly, how to apply either criterion is far from obvious. Is the joint presence of rods and cones in the eye an adventitious by-product of the use of a lens to focus light? Or is there a deeper reason these cells should be thought of as contributing to a single modality? What about the many kinds of touch receptor?

An alternative proposal resembles the proper sensible criterion, holding that senses are distinguished by the properties they represent, which makes for clear distinctions since each sense uniquely represents at least one property. This *representational criterion* requires an account of the conditions in which a sense represents a property. The most common naturalistic accounts hold (in one way or another, and many qualifications aside) that a mental state represents just those properties that *cause* it. So, for example, vision represents colour, shape, and size since these cause visual representations.

Given any such causal account of representation, however, the representational criterion struggles to account for the McGurk effect and the rubber hand illusion. Recall that in the McGurk effect, subjects' *auditory* representations of speech result, to a significant extent, from the *visual* stimulus, while in the rubber hand illusion their *proprioceptive* and *tactile* representations result, to a significant extent, from the *visual* stimulus. Given any causal account of representation, this suggests that, contrary to the representational criterion, audition and touch can represent proper sensibles of vision.

An advocate of the representational criterion may respond with an alternative account of representation. One alternative holds that which properties are represented in any given experience is determined entirely by the phenomenal character of that experience. On this interpretation, the representational criterion collapses into the last of the four familiar criteria, the *phenomenal character* criterion, which holds that there is exactly one sense for each kind of sense experience. Vision is distinct from audition, then, because the phenomenal character of visual experience (i.e., what it's like to see) differs from the phenomenal character of auditory experience (i.e., what it's like to hear), and so on.

The phenomenal character criterion faces a few obvious challenges. First, the evidential value of phenomenological claims is disputed. Second, the criterion is no help in the attempt to individuate nonhuman senses. It is no help, for example, when determining whether bat echolocation is hearing, vision, or something else entirely, because we cannot know on the basis of phenomenology what it's like to echolocate the way bats do. This is a serious concern since an account of the kinds of senses there are should be a full-fledged account, not limited to the kinds of human senses there are—unless only humans have senses. Third, as we illustrate next, phenomenology provides little help in individuating human senses in controversial cases. This is a serious shortcoming because controversial cases are precisely where guidance is needed most.

Sensory substitution phenomena present further challenges to each traditional criterion. Take, for example, tactile visual sensory substitution (TVSS), in which subjects detect shape and perspective distally on the basis of tactile stimulation projected from a camera. The representational and proper sensible criteria imply that TVSS is a form of *colourless vision*. The receptive organ criterion implies that TVSS allows one to detect shape and perspective *distally* through *touch*. Both implications are problematic. The phenomenal character criterion provides little guidance, in part because those using such devices struggle to classify their experiences into any sensory kind, as Deroy and Auvray (Chapter 13) report. Thinking about sensory substitution systems even makes some wonder whether any single, suitable criterion could motivate an answer to the question, "Am I seeing or feeling?"

These kinds of concerns have inspired an intriguing suggestion: rather than treating the familiar individuation criteria as competing, one should treat them as dimensions of a single criterion, which identifies senses by their position in a multi-dimensional state space (Macpherson 2011). Senses may cluster in this space in ways suggestive of the traditional categories, but they may not. In any case, since this *multi-dimensional criterion* is not committed to just one feature that makes a sense a sense, it can flex with new theory and data.

Although the multi-dimensional criterion is interesting, it faces its own challenges. Developing the view requires overcoming technical problems with characterizing the state space—for example, specifying how the dimensions relate, quantifying them, and so on. Some implications of the view, moreover, may be unpalatable; for example, many may reject the implication that there is a distinct sense for each (occupied) position in the state space. The multi-dimensional criterion, moreover, may retain some of the problems from each traditional criterion; for example, taking each criterion on board does nothing to tell us whether rods and cones are distinct receptive organs or parts of a single receptive organ, and thus, whether they constitute multiple dimensions of the state space or only one. In Chapter 18, Fiona Macpherson takes these challenges on, thus giving further substance to her new start.

Of course, there are other ways to react to difficulties with individuating the senses.[3] The most radical reaction rejects individuation altogether. On the traditional view, "sensory images" would faithfully reflect information separately gathered by the eyes, ears, and other sense organs, each of which would have its own proper sensible(s). But it is questionable whether this model is ultimately

---

[3] Matthen (forthcoming) reacts by distinguishing sensory from perceptual modalities. The latter are individuated by the kinds of activities we undertake when we actively probe our surroundings by means of perception. Matthen's claim is that the traditional modalities are individuated by mutually reinforcing sets of perceptual activities.

defensible. More broadly, once one acknowledges that sense experiences are highly processed entities, the prime motivation for sharply distinguishing kinds of senses may be lost. There are, of course, various ways to counter this concern. The crucial question is whether counter-considerations are any better than ad hoc ways to save an outmoded distinction.

Still, distinctions between, say, visual and auditory stimuli, visual and auditory receptive organs, visual and auditory experience, and so on may be inescapable. Imagine trying to explain the McGurk effect without them! One might be tempted, therefore, to adopt a deflationary stance on individuation, taking the senses to be *pragmatic*, rather than *ontological*, categories. On this way of thinking, an individuation criterion that is appropriate in one context may be inappropriate in another; perhaps, for example, one criterion is appropriate for discussing cross-modal priming and another for discussing attention-cuing. The goal of individuation, then, would not be discovering or legislating which senses there are, but something else, perhaps finding an individuation criterion that achieves the best fit with other theoretical commitments in a given context.[4] Roberto Casati, Jérôme Dokic, and François Le Corre (Chapter 19) consider these issues while exploring relations between the project of individuating the senses on the basis of folk psychology and the project of individuating the senses on the basis of empirical science.

The difficulties of individuating the senses arise largely because theorists treat the senses as entirely distinct conduits of information. The critic resists this traditional view by maintaining that perception is essentially *multisensory*.[5] She notes, first, that the senses interact in ways that traditional theorizing would not predict, in ways that (arguably) they could not interact if they were largely discrete conduits of information. She explains this by observing that the senses inform us about a single reality beyond our minds. Given that the information garnered from different sense organs and different groups of receptors are about the same external world, one would expect these information channels sometimes to reinforce and sometimes to act as checks on one another. Thus, a well-designed perceptual system would allow cross-communication between processing streams.

Interactions within the complex flavour system illustrate the point. As noted earlier, flavour is the product of the taste receptors in the tongue, retronasal olfaction, and trigeminal stimulation—receptors that belong to distinct senses on most criteria. Although these sources can be activated independently of one another or in subgroups, in ordinary flavour perception each influences the others, which, as noted, leads Spence, Auvray, and Smith (Chapter 10) to treat them as a single

---

[4] See Nudds 2004 for similar suggestions, and Macpherson 2011 for further discussion.

[5] Those who agree that perception is multisensory can dispute both what grounds its being multisensory, and where its multisensory nature can be detected. Some might hold, for example, that while the phenomenal characters of sense experiences are discrete, the neural bases for "information pick-up" are continuous, or vice versa.

perceptual system. Other senses, moreover, can influence these sources themselves: the apparent taste of tasteless dyed water seems to depend on the colour
of the dye (except, of course, when subjects are blindfolded (see Clydesdale 1984).
Similar points can be made for the other senses. Just as ordinary flavour perception uses multiple kinds of inputs; vision uses rods and cones; touch uses stretch,
pain, and pressure receptors; and so on—at least touch, moreover, is strongly
influenced by the exploratory activity of the perceiver. Just as vision can influence
taste, moreover, it influences audition in the McGurk effect, proprioception in the
rubber hand illusion, and touch in a variety of cases—indeed, even visual *imagination* can influence nonvisual perception (see Stokes and Biggs, Chapter 14). This
all intimates that the perceptual system uses any available information, integrating
it at various stages of processing, with little concern for receptive organ or proper
sensible.[6]

One might wonder why perception integrates information across modalities so freely given that integration can mislead us, as vision "misleads" taste in
the dye-experiment, audition in the McGurk effect, and proprioception in the
rubber-hand illusion. The reason may be that integration, Stokes and Biggs suggest, is ordinarily beneficial. Subjects who see a briefly flashed picture (say, of a
dog) are much more likely to identify the depicted object correctly when also presented with a semantically congruent sound (say, barking) than when presented
with a semantically incongruent sound (say, whistling), or no sound at all (cf.,
Chen and Spence 2010). This may reflect a kind of "priming" that takes advantage
of environmental regularities: one dog-indicating stimulus (barking) readies the
perceptual system to identify other stimuli as emanating from a dog, and this aids
both in interpreting ambiguous stimuli and in locating the source of the barking.

Interactions among the senses also inform us of predicative relations. In the
ventriloquist effect, the ventriloquist produces sounds with minimal lip and
mouth action, but moves a dummy's mouth, with the effect that the sound is nar-
rowly and irresistibly located in the dummy. Why is this? Not because vision picks
up auditory information, but rather because it sometimes provides information

---

[6] Potential neural bases for these kinds of inter-sense interactions have been identified. For example, a series of studies find that when a *tactile task* concerns object identification (or shape, size, or
orientation discrimination), the *visual cortex* is regularly active. Further, this activation seems to be
functionally operative; when the visual cortex is disrupted with transcranial magnetic stimulation
(TMS), performance on the tactile discrimination tasks diminishes significantly. Remarkably, this
visual effect on touch is evident even when visual stimuli are removed. Researchers infer that visual
imagery is invoked (sometimes tacitly, sometimes strategically) to aid in the tactile task (Sathian et al.
1997; Zangaladze et al. 1999; Zhang et al. 2004; and see Djordjevic et al. 2004 for similar research on
visual-olfactory interaction). Similarly, although the lateral occipital complex (LOC) (a region in the
ventral visual pathway in the human brain) is traditionally considered to be responsible for processing
visual information, given substantial research suggestive of task-specific and performance-enhancing
activation of the LOC during various touch tasks, some researchers now suggest that this area is multisensory, responsible for processing object-level or macrospatial information, which can then be used
for either visual or touch tasks. See Amedi et al. 2002; Amedi et al. 2001; James et al. 2002; and Zhang
et al. 2004 for discussion of opposing interpretations of these data.

that helps resolve auditory information in conditions that are not conducive to accurate resolution. Thus, social interactions demand that we know *who* is speaking and, ideally, his or her *intentions* vis-à-vis conveying a message, and this task is improved with the influence of vision. Giving visual information a role in the interpretation of the voice stream improves perceivers' ability to gather semantic information. Indeed, a similar explanation might be given of the McGurk effect. A few contributors consider how multilevel interactions among the senses might be beneficial.

Whatever the value of the interactions, a multisensory view holds that each sense is influenced by others. Some go further down the path of integration, claiming that each sense can be influenced by learned states. Recent work in cognitive psychology may support this view. Studies find, for example, that pictured objects are perceived as being their typical colour even when the picture is adjusted to achromatic grey: subjects see an achromatic grey picture of a banana as yellow and an achromatic grey Smurf cartoon character as blue (Witzel et al. 2011). This suggests that one's culture may influence what one senses. Reinforcing this suggestion, German subjects see an achromatic grey UHU glue tube as being its typical colour (yellow), but do not see an achromatic grey Ferrari icon as being its typical colour (also yellow), presumably because the former is more familiar to them. (See Hansen et al. 2006; Olkkonen et al. 2008; Witzel et al. 2011 for these studies.)

Racial stereotypes may have a similar effect on visual perception. In online matching tasks, subjects tend to judge greyscale faces with typical Caucasian features as lighter, and greyscale faces with typical Afro-American features as darker, in spite of the target faces being identical in luminosity. This effect can even be produced for racially ambiguous faces simply by labelling them 'WHITE' or 'BLACK' (Levin and Banaji 2006). Culturally specific associations have even stronger effects on other senses. For example, a wealth of recent research suggests that beliefs regularly and powerfully influence flavour perception—for example, beliefs about the price of the wine, the brand of ketchup, and where one consumes a meal affect both the capacity for successful flavour distinctions and the pleasure reported.

These results suggest that beliefs and culturally acquired concepts directly affect visual experience. However, the mechanism of these influences is unclear. Is it really *belief* that influences perception (Farkas and Bitter 2012)? Suppose that subjects are *told* that they are about to be presented with achromatic banana images. Would the resultant belief modify their tendency to experience bananas as yellow, or would the bias to yellow persist despite a contrary belief? Might the effect be due to association and conditioning rather than belief? It is unclear, therefore, how much this discussion overlaps with the spirit of the New Look movement in psychology, led by Jerome Bruner and colleagues in the mid-20th century. The movement held that perception is continuous with cognition (beliefs, desires, values) in that how we perceive the world via the senses is always informed by one's "mental set". The New Look movement produced many results, similar to those discussed here. These results were interpreted as showing that cognition profoundly influences perception—that is, that cognition "penetrates" perception—but as indicated, the jury is still out on the extent of the phenomenon.[7]

One might worry that any influence of cognition on perception would be epistemically pernicious. How could the senses work quickly enough, deliver objective reports, or even update beliefs at all if they were influenced by background beliefs (cf. Fodor 1984), let alone desires? Although these concerns are serious, merely raising them does not decide the issue. In the first place, these kinds of influences need not be unconstrained: a dog's bark might predispose a perceiver to interpret visual stimuli as dog-like, but it does not follow that she will be perceptually disposed to interpret scientific observations in a way that favours her preferred theory. Perhaps the function by which we combine input from online stimuli with input from memory is faster, is more objective, and tracks truth better than a system that ignores input from memory or allows memory input only at the level of judgment. Perhaps, then, by integrating incoming and remembered information the perceptual-cognitive system generates a "report" that optimally guides action. Both Clark's discussion of predictive coding and Shea's discussion of top-down versus bottom-up effects are especially relevant here (Chapters 1 and 3, respectively).

The discussion thus far has touched on many questions. How are improvised stimuli built into rich perceptual experiences (see Chapters 1–3)? Is perception always modality specific or can it be multimodal (see Chapters 4–6)? What can we learn by investigating senses other than vision (see Chapters 7–12)? What can we learn through a careful reappraisal of vision (see Chapters 13–15)? How should we think about individuating the senses, and, more broadly, how do the senses interrelate (see Chapters 16–19)?

These questions, and the many others that are addressed in this volume, invite a foundational question that largely remains in the background: what makes something a sense modality? This question has received almost no attention, perhaps because it is taken to be uncontroversial that a sense is a faculty by means of which a subject monitors her immediate environment in "real time". This characterization, however plausible it may be, does not define the property *being a sense*, at least because it provides only a necessary condition. After all, the body monitors blood CO_2 levels and uses the information it gathers for homeostatic regulation in real time, for example, to regulate respiration and heartbeat, but surely *that* is not a sensory process. Brian Keeley (2002) made an important start to sorting out this question: he suggests that the senses convey information from the outside world into the central nervous system in order to guide specific responses to a certain

---

[7] For recent theorists who have argued that some of these data are best explained in terms of cognitive effects on perception (called 'cognitive penetration'), see Macpherson 2012; Siegel 2011; Stokes 2012; Stokes and Bergeron (unpublished manuscript); Wu 2013. See also Deroy 2013 for worries about whether the alleged effect is a genuine *cognitive* one. See Stokes 2013 for an overview of the debate.

kind of ambient energy. On the other hand, it is quite plausible that there is a pain sense. What is the difference? As Picciuto and Carruthers (Chapter 11) put it in their consideration of the "inner sense": "What constitutes a system as a sense modality?"

There are two approaches to this question. Picciuto and Carruthers look for essential differences between those systems that count as sense modalities and those that do not. There are at least two crucial differences between the senses and mechanisms such as the blood CO_2 monitor. They "issue in nonconceptual representations with mind-to-world direction of fit". And these representations "are used to guide the intentional behavior of the organism (perhaps issuing in phenomenally conscious sensations)".

A complementary approach, taken by Mohan Matthen (forthcoming), is to focus on the functions of the senses *as a group*. As noted earlier, the senses furnish us with *additive* complementary information: there is a barking (audition) dog (vision); here is a cool (touch), shiny (vision) ball. The blood CO_2 monitor does not complement other information-gathering faculties in this way; that is, the evidence does not contribute to a nexus. More notably, the evidence of the other senses does not affect its control of bodily processes. Second, the senses are used to *learn* about the environment and *anticipate* what will happen in ways that nonsensory mechanisms are not. Specifically, the senses feed into learning systems (such as association and conditioning) that initiate action on the basis of not only sensory input but also learned associations (which can be either intramodal or intermodal). Picciuto and Carruthers focus on the representational states that issue from the senses; Matthen emphasizes that these representations work together across the modalities. This cooperation is, in the end, the rationale for multimodality: the senses are designed to work as a group.

One should now have a sense not only of the shortcomings of traditional theorizing about the senses, not only of how much room there is for a new, better understanding, but also of how challenging achieving a better understanding will be. Despite the challenges, we are optimistic that an improved understanding is possible. The chapters commissioned for this volume are a testament to that optimism. We hope that they will pave the way to a new, better understanding of the senses, and in turn a new, better understanding of perception.

References

Amedi, A., Jacobson, G., Hendler, T., Malach, R., & Zohary, E. (2002) "Convergence of Visual and Tactile Shape Processing in the Human Lateral Occipital Complex." *Cerebral Cortex*, 12: 1202–1212.

Amedi, A., Malach, R., Hendler, T., Peled, S., & Zohary, E. (2001) "Visuo-Haptic Object-Related Activation in the Ventral Visual Pathway." *Nature Neuroscience*, 4: 324–330.

Auvray, Malika and Spence, Charles (2008) "The Multisensory Perception of Flavour." *Consciousness and Cognition* 17: 1016–1031.

Ayer, A. J. (1956) *The Problem of Knowledge*. London: Macmillan.

Bullot, Nicolas and Egré, Paul (2010) *Review of Philosophy and Psychology*, vol. 1, no. 1. New York: Springer.

Chen, Y.-C. and Spence, C. (2010) "When Hearing the Bark Helps to Identify the Dog: Semantically-Congruent Sounds Modulate the Identification of Masked Pictures." *Cognition* 114: 389–404.

Clydesdale, F. M. (1984) "The Influence of Colour on Sensory Perception and Food Choices." In J. Walford (Ed.), *Developments in Food Colours*. London: Elsevier Applied Science: 75–112.

Deroy, O. (2013) "Object-Sensitivity versus Cognitive Penetrability of Perception." *Philosophical Studies* 162 (1):87–107.

Djordjevic, J., Zatorre, R. J., Petrides, M., and Jones-Gotman, M. (2004) "The Mind's Nose Effects of Odor and Visual Imagery on Odor Detection." *Psychological Science* 15(3): 143–148.

Farkas, Katalin and Bitter, David (2012) "Perceptual Learning and the Cognitive Penetration of Perceptual Experience," unpublished paper presented at the Workshop on Perceptual Learning, University of York (England), 20 March 2012.

Fodor, J. (1984). "Observation Reconsidered." *Philosophy of Science* 51: 23–43.

Hansen, T., Olkkonen, M., Walter, S., & Gegenfurtner, K. R. (2006) "Memory Modulates Color Appearance." *Nature Neuroscience* 9: 1367–1368.

Held, R., Ostrovsky, Y., de Gelder, B., Gandhi, T., Ganesh, S., Mathur, U., & Sinha, P. (2011) "The Newly Sighted Fail to Match Seen with Felt." *Nature Neuroscience* 14: 551–553.

James, T. W., Humphrey, G. K., Gati, J. S., Servos, P., Menon, R. S., & Goodale, M. A. (2002). "Haptic Study of Three-Dimensional Objects Activates Extrastriate Visual Areas." *Neuropsychologia* 40: 1706–1714.

Keeley, Brian L. (2002) "Making Sense of the Senses: Individuating Modalities in Humans and Other Animals." *Journal of Philosophy* 99: 5–28.

Koffka, Kurt (1935) *Principles of Gestalt Psychology*. London: Paul, Trench, Trubner.

Kohler, Wolfgang (1929) *Gestalt Psychology*. New York: Liveright.

Levin, D. and Banaji, M. (2006) "Distortions in the Perceived Lightness of Faces: The Role of Race Categories." *Journal of Experimental Psychology: General* 135: 501–512.

Macpherson, Fiona (2011) Introduction, in Macpherson (Ed.), *The Senses: Classic and Contemporary Philosophical Perspectives: Classic and Contemporary Philosophical Perspectives*. New York: Oxford University Press.

Macpherson, Fiona (2012) "Cognitive Penetration of Colour Experience: Rethinking the Issue in Light of an Indirect Mechanism." *Philosophy and Phenomenological Research* 84(1): 24–62.

Matthen, Mohan (forthcoming) "Individuating the Senses," in M. Matthen (Ed.), *Oxford Handbook of the Philosophy of Perception*.

Morgan, Michael J. (1977) *Molyneux's Question: Vision, Touch, and the Philosophy of Perception*. Cambridge: Cambridge University Press.

Nudds, Matthew (2001) "Experiencing the Production of Sounds." *European Journal of Philosophy* 9: 210–229.

Nudds, M. and O'Callaghan, C. (2009) *Sounds and Perception: New Philosophical Essays.* Oxford: Oxford University Press.

O'Callaghan, Casey (2007) *Sounds: A Philosophical Theory.* Oxford: Oxford University Press.

Olkkonen, M., Hansen, T., & Gegenfurtner K. R. (2008) "Colour Appearance of Familiar Objects: Effects of Object Shape, Texture and Illumination Changes." *Journal of Vision* 8: 1–16.

Pasnau, Robert (1999) "What Is Sound?" *Philosophical Quarterly* 49: 309–324.

Sathian, K., Zangaladze, Andro, Hoffman, John, & Grafton, Scott (1997) "Feeling with the Mind's Eye." *Neuroreport* 8(18): 3877–3881.

Siegel, S. (2011) "Cognitive Penetrability and Perceptual Justification." *Nous* 46: 201–222.

Spence, Charles (2012) "Is It the Plate or is It the Food? Assessing the Influence of the Color (Black or White) and Shape of the Plate on the Perception of the Food Placed on It." *Food Quality and Preference* 24: 205–208.

Stokes, D. "Perceiving and Desiring: A New Look at the Cognitive Penetrability of Experience." (2012) *Philosophical Studies* 158: 479–492.

Stokes, D. (2013) "Cognitive Penetrability of Perception." *Philosophy Compass* 8: 646–663.

Stokes, D. and Bergeron, V. "Modular Architectures and Informational Encapsulation: A Dilemma," unpublished manuscript.

Witzel, C., Valkova, H., Hansen, T., & Gegenfurtner, K. "Object Knowledge Modulates Colour Appearance." *i-Perception* 2 (2011): 13–49.

Wu, W. (2013) "Visual Spatial Constancy and Modularity: Does Intention Penetrate Vision?" *Philosophical Studies* 165(2): 64, 69.

Zangaladze, A., Epstein, Charles, Grafton, Scott, & Sathian, Krish (1999) "Involvement of Visual Cortex in Tactile Discrimination of Orientation." *Nature* 401: 587–590.

Zhang, M., Weisser, V. D., Stilla, R., Prather, S. C., & Sathian, Krish (2004). "Multisensory Cortical Processing of Object Shape and Its Relation to Mental Imagery." *Cognitive Affective Behavioral Neuroscience* (4): 251–259.

PART I

New Models of Perception

Perceiving as Predicting

Andy Clark

1. Perceiving as Predicting

1.1. PREDICTIVE CODING

A familiar view depicts perception as essentially a process of 'bottom-up' feature detection. Thus, in the case of vision, detected colours, edges, and shapes might act as the building blocks for detected objects (cats, dogs) and states of affairs (dogs chasing a cat, perhaps). Scientific versions of the paradigm depict early perception as building towards a complex world model by a feedforward process of evidence accumulation. Visual cortex, to take the most-studied example, is thus "traditionally viewed as a hierarchy of neural feature detectors, with neural population responses being driven by bottom-up stimulus features" (Egner et al. 2010, p. 16601). This is a view of the perceiving brain as passive and stimulus-driven, taking energetic inputs from the senses and turning them into a coherent percept by a kind of stepwise buildup moving from the simplest features to the more complex. From pixel intensities up to lines and edges and on to complex meaningful shapes (like teacups), accumulating structure and complexity along the way in a kind of Lego-block fashion. In these models[1] then, "sensory processing was considered to consist mainly of the sequential extraction and recombination of features, leading to the veridical reconstruction of object properties" (Engel, Fries, and Singer 2001, p. 704).

"Predictive coding"—the main topic of the present treatment—works by a kind of reversal of such passive evidence accumulation schemes. In these models (see Rao and Ballard (1999), Lee and Mumford (2003), Friston (2005) (2010)), percepts emerge via a recurrent cascade of predictions that involve (mostly subpersonal) expectations, spanning multiple spatial and temporal scales, about the present nature and state of the world as presented via the driving sensory signal. That driving sensory signal is compared to the predictions, and mismatches send forward error signals that nuance or alter the prediction until a match is found and the

---

[1] Examples include Hubel and Wiesel (1965), Marr (1982), Biederman (1987).

sensory data are 'explained away'. This process runs concurrently and continuously (until it settles) across multiple levels of a processing hierarchy.

At first sight, this seems extremely implausible. How can perception, a process that surely puts us in contact with the world, be a matter of prediction? Doesn't this mistake perception for (something more like) imagination? And anyway, how can we issue a prediction unless we already know a good deal about what's out there?

To see how the predictive coding alternative works, it helps to start by noticing that the key predictions made by the brain concern not what is about to happen but what is already the case. Specifically, the predictions made by the brain concern the current states of some of its own neural populations. In perception, if these models are correct, each layer of neural processing is trying to predict the current input to the layer below (except for the bottom layer, such as the retina, which 'simply' transduces an energetic signal).[2] Each layer does this while simultaneously responding to predictions from the layer above. The key task of the brain (or at any rate, the cortex) is thus to learn a stack of models that capture regularities in how the sensory signal is most likely to vary in time and space. By deploying the right models at the right time, the brain can then issue correct predictions (so it is minimising its own prediction errors). This (as Hohwy (2007) also notes) induces a striking reversal in which the driving sensory signal is really providing corrective *feedback* on the top-down predictions. Friston expresses the point well:

> In this view, cortical hierarchies are trying to generate sensory data from high-level causes. This means the causal structure of the world is embodied in the backward connections. Forward connections simply provide feedback by conveying prediction error to higher levels. In short, forward connections are the feedback connections. This is why we have been careful not to ascribe a functional label like feedback to backward connections. Friston (2005, p. 825)

It is the forward flow of error that must now carry any new information coming from the world, allowing new predictive models to be selected and deployed in the top-down cascade. The upshot is that

> In predictive coding schemes, sensory data are replaced by prediction error, because that is the only sensory information that has yet to be explained. Feldman and Friston (2010, p. 2)

Each layer in these systems thus displays two functionally distinct properties. It encodes how it takes the world to be, and it registers mismatches between those 'takings' and predictions coming from the layer above. Mismatches flow forward as error signals to the level above, while its best guesses about the state of the world

---

[2] Actually, a variant form of predictive coding also characterizes the work of the retina (see Hosoya et al. (2005)). But this nicety need not concern us here.

flow downward as predictions to the layer below. Perception occurs when, across multiple layers of such processing that capture regularities at many spatial and temporal scales, the hugely interanimated set of predictions matches the evolving sensory inputs, explaining them away so that the forward flow of error ceases or settles.

Importantly, such models can be acquired by learning, and that learning can *itself* be driven by the ongoing attempt to minimise errors in the multilayer prediction of inputs. This is because the brain's predictions improve when it uses a good model of the structured signal source. Good predictions thus increase the posterior probability of the model. In this way the attempt to predict can be used to drive the learning itself, generating the very models that are then used to predict. In this pleasingly boot-strappy way ('empirical Bayes') a multilayer system can acquire its own priors (the expectations used in prediction) from the data, as it goes along.

Thus consider, as a simple early example, Rao and Ballard's (1999) model of predictive coding in the visual cortex. Rao and Ballard implemented a multilayer neural network whose input was samples (image patches) from pictures of natural scenes. These visual signals were processed via a hierarchical system in which each level tried (in the way just sketched) to predict the activity at the level below it using recurrent (feedback) connections. If the feedback successfully predicted the lower-level activity, no further action needed to ensue. Failures to predict enabled tuning and revision of the generative model (initially, just a random set of connection weights) being used to make the predictions, thus slowly delivering knowledge of the regularities governing the data. The forward connections between levels carried only the 'residual errors' (Rao and Ballard (1999), p. 79) between top-down predictions and actual lower-level activity, while the backward or recurrent connections carried the predictions themselves. Changing prediction thus corresponds to changing or tuning a hypothesis about the nature and temporal evolution of the lower-level activity. This kind of prediction error calculation, operating within a hierarchical organisation, allowed information pertaining to different spatial and temporal scales within the image to be played off one against the other such that

> prediction and error-correction cycles occur concurrently throughout the hierarchy, so top-down information influences lower-level estimates, and bottom-up information influences higher-level estimates of the input signal.
> Rao and Ballard (1999, p. 80)

After exposure to thousands of image patches, the system had learnt to use responses in the first-level network to extract features such as oriented edges and bars, while the second-level network captured combinations of such features corresponding to patterns involving larger spatial configurations. Using the predictive coding strategy, and given only the statistical properties of the signals derived from the natural images, the network was thus able to induce a simple multilayered model of the structure of the data source (images of natural scenes).

Notice that as processing in this network unfolds, all that is passed forward from level 1 to level 2 is error (the deviations from the predictions being sent downward from level 2), and all that is passed downward is prediction. When downward prediction fully accommodates ('cancels out') the incoming signal, no more error flows forward and we perceive the world. The simulation also neatly captured well-documented 'non-classical receptive field' effects such as 'end-stopping' (see also Rao and Sejnowski (2002)) where a neuron responds strongly to a short line falling within its classical receptive field but that response tails off as the line gets longer. The predictive coding explanation is that the response tails off as the line gets longer because longer lines and edges are the statistical norm in these natural scenes! So, after learning, longer lines are what is first predicted (and fed back, as a hypothesis) by the level two network. The strong firing of those level 1 'edge cells' when driven by shorter lines thus reflects error or mismatch: the unusually short segment was not initially predicted by the higher-level network. This means that end-stopped cells may be learnt and reflect the way the world is—they reflect the typical length of the lines and edges in natural scenes. In a different world, such cells would learn different responses.

1.2. GENERATIVE MODELS

An important feature of the internal models that power such 'predictive coding' approaches is that they are *generative* in nature. That is to say, the knowledge (model) encoded by the units and weights at an upper layer must be such that those units and weights are capable of predicting the response profile of the layer below. That means that the model at layer N+1 becomes capable of generating the sensory data (i.e., the input as it would there be represented) at layer N (the layer below) for itself. Since this story applies all the way down to layers that are attempting to predict the inputs at the lowest level (the level of sensory transduction), that means that such systems are fully capable of generating 'virtual' sensory data for themselves.

This is, in one sense, unsurprising. As Hinton (and for similar comments see Mumford (1992)) notes:

> Vivid visual imagery, dreaming, and the disambiguating effect of context on the interpretation of local image regions suggests that the visual system can perform top-down generation. Hinton (2007b, p. 428)

In another sense it is surprising. It means that perception (at least, as it occurs in creatures like us)[3] is co-emergent with (something quite like) imagination. And

---

[3] By 'perceive' I here mean 'perceive in a rich, full-blooded manner'. Obviously, a simple robot that locomotes to a light source need not, and probably should not, deploy a stack of generative models

it means too—or so I suggest—that no creature is truly able to perceive anything that, in principle, it cannot imagine. Otherwise put, any creature that can perceive some state of affairs X also has the resources endogenously to generate a kind of 'virtual' version of that percept via top-down means alone. Of course, this does not mean that it can, by some deliberate act of will, bring this about. Indeed, it seems very likely that for some creatures acts of deliberate imagining (which I suspect may require the use of self-cueing via language) are simply impossible. But if these models are correct, then any creature able to perceive some state of affairs X has the neural resources to generate the very same sensory states (where that means the ones that would occur were X to be veridically detected) in the absence of X.[4] Whether that generation induces a conscious experience of a quasi-sensory nature is a question I here leave open. But at the very least, there now emerges a deep duality between perception and the endogenous generation of 'virtual' sensory data.

The use of such 'generative models' for perception and recognition is increasingly dominant in both theoretical and applied work on machine learning. It is no accident that early explorations of these themes involved items with names such as the 'wake-sleep algorithm' (Hinton et al. (1995)) and talk of the network generating patterns for itself 'in fantasy'. In all these models, top-down connections are generative ones, capable of causing (generating) the very same kinds of patterns of lower-level activity that would ensue given apt sensory (bottom-up) input. A more recent example can be found in Hinton's 2007a treatment, aptly titled "To Recognize Shapes, First Learn to Generate Images". Here, instead of attempting to directly train a neural network to classify images, the network first learns to generate such images for itself. An important achievement of Hinton and colleagues (see Hinton et al. (2006), and the review papers Hinton (2007b), (2010), Bengio (2009)) is to show how to learn, using unlabelled (i.e., not pre-classified) data a deep multilayer version of such a generative model.[5] This was an important advance over previous 'connectionist' work (Rumelhart et al. (1986)) that struggled to show appropriate representations in a deep multilayer context, and that required large bodies of pre-classified data to power learning using the back-propagation of error.

---

to do so. The need for generative models emerges most clearly when systems must deal with noise, ambiguity, and uncertainty.

[4] The (theoretically mandated) duality of perception and generation means that a percept and a hallucination could (in principle at least) involve identical neural states. This may put pressure, it seems to me, on some (but not all) formulations of disjunctivism—the idea, roughly, that veridical percepts and hallucinations, illusions, and so on share no common kind. Much turns, of course, on how the somewhat obscure disjunctivist claim is to be unpacked. For a pretty comprehensive sampling of possible formulations, see essays in A. Haddock and F. Macpherson (eds.) (2008), and in A. Byrne and H. Logue (eds.) (2009).

[5] The crucial innovation was to learn one layer of representation at a time using what Hinton calls Restricted Boltzmann Machines, with a further tweak to fine-tune the resulting overall model—for an accessible summary, see Hinton (2007).

There are, however, important differences separating the recent work by Hinton and colleagues (using so-called Restricted Boltzmann Machines—see Hinton (2007)) and the predictive coding story (see the review by Huang (2011)). The differences mostly concern the kinds of message passing scheme that are, and are not, allowed, and the precise ways that top-down and bottom-up influences are used and combined during both learning and trained performance.[6] What they share, though, is this emerging (indeed, state-of-the-art) emphasis on the use of generative models in learning and in recognition.

1.3. ANALYSIS-BY-SYNTHESIS

Work that uses generative models to predict inputs implements the much older idea of 'analysis by synthesis' (Neisser (1967), Yuille and Kersten (2006)) where this names a processing strategy in which

> The mapping from low- to high-level representation (e.g. from acoustic to word-level) is computed using the *reverse* mapping, from high- to low-level representation. Chater and Manning (2006, p. 340)

In this paradigm the brain does not build its current model of worldly causes by accumulating, bottom-up, a mass of low-level cues. Instead, the brain—in learning, in perceiving, and (see Friston, Mattout, and Kilner (2011)) in acting—tries to predict the current suite of low-level cues from its best high-level models of possible causes (see Bar (2007), Hohwy (2007), Friston (2010)). In this way,

> Predictive, or more generally, generative models turn the inverse problem [here, the problem of converting sensory 'measurements' into information about external objects and sates of affairs] on its head. Instead of trying to find functions of the inputs that predict their causes, they find functions of estimated causes that predict the inputs. Friston (2002, p. 233)

1.4. HIERARCHIES OF HIDDEN CAUSES

Finally, it is worth stressing that the top-down generation of the sensory patterns that characterises these models or approaches always proceeds (after learning) via multiple layers of processing that involve intermediate levels of representation. Thus (to offer an admittedly simplistic example) a program capable of dealing with written text might learn layers that deal (respectively) in words, in letters, and in the various kinds of strokes that make up the letters. Each of these levels of structure has its own characteristic regularities. Certain strokes tend to go together,

---

[6] Compare, for example, the kinds of models described by Hinton (2007) with that of Jehee and Ballard (2009).

as they form distinct letters; certain letters tend to go together as they form real words; certain words tend to go together as they make grammatical sentences, and so on. Each level of the processing hierarchy thus deploys a probabilistic generative model whose target is the layer of the hierarchy immediately below.[7] The internal processing hierarchy thus tracks nested causal structure in the source (sentences). In these models each layer embodies knowledge (taking the form of probability density distributions) about the hidden regularities (for example grammars, causes, or any so-called latent variables) that are structuring the data as it is registered at the level below. An interesting implication is thus that the layered structure of the internal model will attempt to recapitulate actual (but hidden) structure in the world. In this way:

> The hierarchical structure of the real world literally comes to be 'reflected' by the hierarchical architectures trying to minimise prediction error, not just at the level of sensory input but at all levels of the hierarchy. Friston (2002, p. 238)

To perceive the world, on these accounts, is to attempt to unearth layer upon layer of the actual causal structures that generated the sensory signals impinging on the organism.

2. The Case for Predictive Coding

2.1. EVIDENCE

The predictive coding approach, by using a hierarchical generative model to do top-down sensory prediction in learning and recognition, makes good sense of— and very efficient use of—a complex neuro-anatomy in which recurrent connectivity is massive and apparently functionally asymmetric (see, e.g., Friston (2005), Bubic et al. (2010)). It also explains several superficially distinct phenomena via a single fundamental mechanism. These include priming, end-stopping (see section 1, this chapter), repetition suppression, and confirmation bias. In the case of priming, recent results show that an expected percept becomes consciously available about 100 ms faster than an unexpected one (see Melloni et al. (2011)). This, as the authors note, is easily explained if the process of stimulus recognition involves the activation of a top-down generative model that is attempting to match the incoming data stream with its own predictions. It is also well known that stimulus-evoked neural activity is reduced by stimulus repetition. Summerfield et al. (2008) manipulated the local likelihood of stimulus repetitions, showing that the repetition-suppression effect is itself reduced when the repetition is

---

[7] It will not in general, however, be easy to determine what individual units/neurons within a layer represent—see Hinton (2007), box 2, p. 433.

improbable/unexpected. This too is fluently explained by the predictive coding story: repetition normally reduces response because it reduces prediction error. Repetition-suppression may thus be a direct effect of predictive coding strategies at work in the brain and would hence vary according to our local perceptual expectations.

More generally, there is an emerging body of supportive fMRI (functional magnetic resonance imaging) and EEG (electroencephalographic) work dating back to a pioneering fMRI study by Murray et al. (2002) that reveals just the kinds of relationships posited by the predictive coding story. Here, as higher-level areas settled into an interpretation of visual shape, activity in V1 was dampened, consistent with the successful higher-level predictions being used to explain away (cancel out) the sensory data. Recent studies confirm this general profile (see, e.g., Alink et al. (2010)).

2.2. QUESTIONING PREDICTIVE CODING

Early examples of the predictive coding approach (such as the seminal 1997 work by Rao and Ballard described in section 1) were, however, met with some puzzlement, since they seemed radically different from the more standard picture of an (admittedly attention-modulated) feedforward cascade of simple to complex feature detection. This puzzlement is well captured by the comments from Koch and Poggio that accompanied the publication of this work. The passage is so perfectly expressive of some quite common worries that I hope the reader will forgive a long extract:

> In predictive coding, the common-place view of sensory neurons as detecting certain 'trigger' or 'preferred' features is turned upside down in favor of a *representation of objects by the absence of firing activity*. This appears to be at odds with [data indicating that neurons] extending from V1 to inferior temporal cortex, respond with *vigorous activity to ever more complex objects*, including individual faces or paperclips twisted in just the right way and seen from a particular viewpoint.
>
> In addition, what about all of the functional imaging data from humans revealing that particular cortical areas respond to specific image classes, such as faces or three-dimensional spatial layout? *Is it possible that this activity is dominated by the firing of … cells actively expressing an error signal, a discrepancy* between the input expected by this brain area and the actual image? Both quotes from Koch and Poggio (1999, p. 10), my emphasis.

There are two main worries being expressed here. First, a worry that the accounts are abandoning representation in favour of silence, since well-predicted elements of the signal are 'explained away'. Second, a worry that the accounts thus seem in tension with strong evidence of increasingly complex representations tokened by activity in higher areas. Neither worry is justified however. To see why not, recall the architectural story outlined earlier. Each layer, that story insists, must somehow support two functionally distinct kinds of processing. For simplicity, let's follow Friston (2005) and imagine this as each layer containing two functionally distinct kinds of cell or unit:[8]

- 'representation units', that encode that layer's current best hypothesis (pitched at its preferred level of description) and that feed that hypothesis down as prediction to the layer below.
- 'error units', that pass activation forward when local within-layer activity is not adequately accounted for by incoming top-down prediction from the layer above.

That means that more and more complex representations are indeed formed, and used in processing, as one moves up the hierarchy. It is just that the *flow* of representational information (the predictions), at least in the purest versions, is all downward. It is in this sense that, as we saw earlier, the role of feedback is inverted in these models. Moreover, the upward flow of prediction error is itself a sensitive instrument, bearing fine-grained information about very specific failures of match. That's why it is capable of inducing, in higher areas, complex hypotheses (consistent sets of representations) that can then be tested against the lower-level states.[9] As a result, neither of the two worries raised by Koch and Poggio gets a grip. There are representational populations all the way up, and their activity is determined by the flow of error signals and the hypotheses that they select.

2.3. AN EXAMPLE: THE FUSIFORM FACE AREA

Consider again the standard model of a stream of increasingly complex feature-detection, such that responses (at the highest levels) reflect the presence of such items as faces, houses, and so on. What the predictive coding story suggests is not that we abandon that model but that we enrich it, by adding within each layer cells specialised for the encoding and transmission of prediction error. Some cells at each level, if this is correct, are encoding features while others are registering errors relative to predictions about those features coming from the level above.

The right evidence here is only just appearing, but it actually seems to fit best with this more complex 'predictive coding' profile. Thus consider the well-established

---

[8] Possible alternative implementations are discussed in Spratling and Johnson (2006), and in Engel et al. (2001)).

[9] It is also worth noting that models that fit the rather more general profile described in section 1.2 (viz., using hierarchical generative models to predict the sensory signals) are not compelled to endorse the full 'explaining away' procedure. Instead, at each level, the full 'silencing' of representation units by (good) downward prediction is actually only one—neat, easy-to-grasp, but potentially quite extreme— option among many for how best to combine top-down predictions with bottom-up inputs (for some glimpses of the much larger computational spaces hereabouts, see Feng et al. (2002), Hinton (2007), Bengio and Lecun (2007), Heess et al. (2009), Hinton (2010)).

finding (Kanwisher et al. (1997)) of increased activity in the fusiform face area (FFA) when a person is shown a face rather than (say) a house. Surely, a critic might say, this is best explained by simply supposing that neurons in FFA have learnt to be active complex feature detectors for faces. It is immediately apparent that this is no longer straightforward, however, given that the predictive-coding story allows that FFA may indeed harbor units that specialise in the representation of faces, as well as ones that specialise in the detection of errors (mismatches between top-down predictions reaching FFA and the bottom-up signal). Thus, the difference is that if the predictive coding story is correct, FFA should *also* harbor error units that encode mismatches with predicted (face) activity. This provided a nice opportunity for some telling empirical tests.

Egner et al. (2010) compared simple feature detection (with and without attention) and predictive coding models of recorded responses in FFA. The simple Feature Detection Model predicts, just as Koch and Poggio suggested, that FFA response should simply scale with the presence of faces in the presented image. The Predictive Coding Model, however, predicts something rather more complex. It predicts that FFA response should "reflect a summation of activity related to prediction ("face expectation") and prediction error ("face surprise")" (Egner et al. 2010, p. 1601). That is to say, it predicts that the (temporally rather blunt) fMRI signal recorded from the fusiform face area should reflect the activity of both putative kinds of cell: those specialising in prediction ("face-expectation") and those specialising in detecting errors in prediction ("face-surprise"). This was then tested by researchers who collected fMRI data from area FFA while independently varying both the presented features (face vs. house) and—by means of a simple (though not explicitly revealed to the participants) preceding cue—manipulating the subjects' unconscious degree of face expectation (low, medium, high) and hence their proper degree of 'face surprise'. To do this, the experimenters probabilistically paired presentations of face/house with a 250 ms preceding color frame cue giving 25% (low), 50% (medium), or 75% (high) chance of the next image being a face.

The results were clear. FFA activity showed a strong interaction between stimulus and face-expectation. FFA response was maximally differentiated only under conditions of low face expectation. Indeed, and quite surprisingly, FFA activity given *either* stimulus (face *or* house) was indistinguishable under conditions of high face expectation! There is a very real sense then, in which FFA might (were it first investigated using these new paradigms) have been dubbed a 'face-expectation area'. The authors conclude that, contrary to any simple feature-detection model,

> [FFA] responses appear to be determined by feature expectation and surprise rather than by stimulus features per se. Egner et al. (2010, p. 16601)

The authors also controlled (by further model comparisons) for the possible role of attentional effects. But these could not, in any case, have made much contribution since it was face surprise, not face expectation, that accounted for the larger part of the BOLD (fMRI)[10] signal. In fact, the best-fit predictive coding model used a weighting in which face-surprise (error) units contributed about twice as much[11] to the BOLD signal as did face-expectation (representation) units, suggesting that much of the activity normally recorded using fMRI may be signalling prediction-error rather than detected features!

This is an important result. In the authors' own words:

> the current study is to our knowledge the first investigation to formally and explicitly demonstrate that population responses in visual cortex are in fact better characterized as a sum of feature expectation and surprise responses than by bottom-up feature detection (with or without attention). Egner et al. (2010, p. 16607)

3. A New Look at Sensory Processing

Among the guiding themes of this volume, we find the notion of the senses as "integrated information pickup systems" and various puzzles involving multimodal and crossmodal effects, plasticity, and the individuation of the senses. Hierarchical predictive processing offers insights into all these phenomena, rendering unsurprising much that was previously puzzling, and also rendering a little more puzzling some things that we might otherwise take for granted. In this final section I offer a few (tentative and preliminary) reflections on this altered landscape.

3.1. CAUSES AND OPERATORS

Reich et al. (2011) report some interesting new fMRI findings regarding the so-called Visual Word Form Area (VWFA). This is an area within the ventral stream that responds to proper letter strings: the kind that might reasonably form a word in a given language. Response in this area was already known to be independent of surface details such as case, font, and spatial location. The recent study shows that it is actually tracking something even more abstract than visual word form. It appears to be tracking word form regardless of the modality of the transducing stream. Thus the very same area is activated in congenitally blind subjects

---

[10] This is a measure of relative neural activity ('brain activation') as indexed by changes in blood flow and blood oxygen level. The assumption is that neural activity incurs a metabolic cost that this signal reflects. It is thus widely acknowledged (see, e.g., Heeger and Ross (2002)) to be a rather indirect, assumption-laden, and 'blunt' measure compared to, say, single cell recording. Nonetheless, new forms of multivariate pattern analysis are able to overcome some of the limitations of earlier work using this technique.

[11] This could, the authors note, be due to some fundamental metabolic difference in processing cost between representing and error-detection, or it may be that for other reasons the BOLD signal tracks top-down inputs to a region more than bottom-up ones (see Egner et al. (2010), p. 16607).

during Braille reading. The fact that the early input here is tactile rather than visual makes no difference to the recruitment of VWFA. This supports the idea (Pascual-Leone and Hamilton (2001)) of such brain areas as 'metamodal operators' that are "defined by a given computation that is applied regardless of the sensory input received".

All this fits neatly, as Reich et al. (2011, p. 365) themselves note, with the predictive coding account in which higher levels of the cortical hierarchy learn to track the 'hidden causes' that account for, and hence predict, the sensory consequences of distal states of affairs. In a deliberate echo of the Egner et al. work on the fusiform face area, Reich et al. speculate that much activity in VWFA might reflect modality-transcending predictions about the sensory consequences of words. Just as (as we saw in section 2.3) much of the activity in FFA is related to top-down face-prediction rather than the bottom-up detection of faces, so the VWFA might be generating top-down predictions using modality-transcending models of wordhood. The metamodality of VWFA would then "explain its ability to apply top-down predictions to both visual and tactile stimuli" (Reich et al. (2011), p. 365).

3.2. CROSSMODAL AND MULTIMODAL EFFECTS

The widespread existence of cross- and multimodal context effects on early 'unimodal' sensory processing constitutes one of the major findings of the last decade of sensory neuroscience (see, e.g., Hupé et al. (1998), Murray et al. (2002), Smith and Muckli (2010)). Thus Murrray et al. (2002) display the influence of high-level shape information on the responses of cells in early visual area V1, while Smith and Muckli (2010) show similar effects (using as input partially occluded natural scenes) even on wholly non-stimulated (that is to say, not directly stimulated via the driving sensory signal) visual areas. In addition, Murray et al. (2006) showed that activation in V1 is influenced by a top-down size illusion, while Muckli et al. (2005) and Muckli (2010) report activity relating to an apparent motion illusion in V1. Even apparently 'unimodal' early responses are influenced (Kriegstein and Giraud (2006)) by information derived from other modalities and hence will commonly reflect a variety of multimodal associations. Strikingly, even the expectation that a relevant input will turn out to be in one modality (e.g., auditory) rather than another (e.g., visual) turns out to improve performance, presumably by enhancing "the weight of bottom-up input for perceptual inference on a given sensory channel" (Langner et al. (2011), p. 10).

This whole smörgåsbord of context effects flows very naturally from the hierarchical predictive coding model. If the so-called visual, tactile, or auditory sensory cortex is actually operating using a cascade of feedback from higher levels to actively predict the unfolding sensory signals (the ones originally transduced using the various dedicated receptor banks of vision, sound, touch, etc.) then we should not be in the least surprised to find extensive multimodal and crossmodal effects (including these kinds of 'filling-in') even on 'early' sensory response.[12] One reason this will be so is that the notion of 'early' sensory response is in one sense now misleading, for expectation-induced context effects will simply propagate all the way down the system, priming, generating, and altering 'early' responses as far down as V1. Any statistically valid correlations, registered within the 'metamodal' (or at least, increasingly information-integrating) areas towards the top of the processing hierarchy, can inform the predictions that then cascade down, through what were previously thought of as much more unimodal areas, all the way to the areas closer to the sensory peripheries. Such effects are inconsistent with the idea of V1 as a site for simple, stimulus-driven, bottom-up feature-detection using cells with fixed (context-inflexible) receptive fields. But they are fully consistent with (indeed, mandated by) models that depict V1 activity as constantly negotiated on the basis of a flexible combination of top-down predictions and driving sensory signal.[13]

3.3. EXPECTATIONS AND CONSCIOUS PERCEPTION

All this has implications for the study of (the neural correlates of) sensory awareness. The key observation (Melloni et al. (2011)), and one that will surely add new layers of complexity to many familiar experimental paradigms, is that expectation speeds up conscious awareness.

We can creep up on this with some mundane reflections. It is intuitively obvious that, for example, a familiar song played using a poor radio receiver will sound

---

[12] This may also have implications for other familiar questions, such as whether context *really* alters the nature of a perceptual experience. Does the wine really taste better when tasted within sight of the sea? Or do we merely then judge it to taste better (do we, that is, merely judge the *same taste differently*, due to some contextual effect)? Or is this simply a non-question (recall Dennett's (1988) treatment of the coffee tasters Chase and Sanborn)? The proposed framework allows us to at least frame the issue better, though a proper resolution remains elusive. Thus suppose selection of some top-level amodal feature complex ('fresh, healthy') is caused by the need to account for (predict) visual sea-features impinging on the eyes. If that in turn affects which higher-level generative models are selected and applied to predict the unfolding taste and flavor of the wine, that might favour encodings of, for example, 'young and vital' over close rivals like 'acidic and immature'. Since this kind of multimodal give and take is just the norm for *any* perceptual unfolding on these models, I'd like to say that means the wine really *tastes* different. But unfortunately it is not yet clear that this is mandated. Someone could say (pursuing a more conservative option) that the wine really tastes different only if such contextual nuancing alters the suite of predictions that are being successfully applied far down the gustatory processing hierarchy, at levels that are intuitively encoding information about the low-level driving chemical signals themselves. If so, then were there no alteration in *those* predictions that would mean no alteration in the target experience. Alternatively, experience could be much more holistically determined so that alterations anywhere up the hierarchy would impact the percept, even if they make the very same predictions lower down. This is my own preferred (but admittedly unargued) option: conscious experience reflects the settling of the whole hierarchy into some temporarily stable state.

[13] Reflecting on this new vision of 'early' sensory processing, Lars Muckli writes, "It is conceivable that V1 is, first of all, the target region for cortical feedback and then, in a second instance, a region that compares cortical feedback to incoming information. Sensory stimulation might be the minor task of the cortex, whereas its major task is to…predict upcoming stimulation as precisely as possible" (Muckli (2010), p. 137).

much clearer than an unfamiliar one. But whereas we might have thought of this, within a simple feedforward feature-detection framework, as some kind of memory effect, it now seems just as reasonable to think of it as a genuinely perceptual one. The clear-sounding percept, after all, is constructed in just the same way as the fuzzy-sounding percept, albeit using a better set of top-down predictions (priors, in the Bayesian translation of the story). That is to say—or so I would suggest—the familiar song *really does* sound clearer. It is not that memory *later* does some filling-in that affects, in some backward-looking way, how we judge the song to have sounded. Rather, the top-down effects bite in the very earliest stages of processing, leaving us little[14] conceptual space (or so it seems to me) to depict the effects as anything other than enhanced-but-genuine perception.

We can illustrate this with a little thought experiment. Imagine we discover a creature whose auditory apparatus is highly tuned to the detection of some biologically relevant sound. Imagine too that that tuning consists largely in a strong set of priors for that sound, such that the creature can detect it despite considerable noise in the ambient signal (a kind of cocktail party effect). Surely we would simply describe this as a case of acute perception. Then we must say the same, it seems to me, of the music-lover hearing a familiar song from a low-quality radio.

In exactly this vein, Melloni et al. (2011) show that the onset time required to form a reportable conscious percept varies according to our expectations. Following a fairly complex series of experiments (due to the need to carefully control for effects that would be best attributed to nonperceptual 'advance guessing' rather than to genuine enhanced visibility for the better-predicted stimulus), the authors conclude that 'expectations alter the threshold of visibility' (Melloni et al. 2011, p. 1393). They explain this result by explicit appeal to a hierarchical predictive coding framework in which "conscious perception is the result of a hypothesis test that iterates until information is consistent across higher and lower areas" (p. 1394). Using electroencephalographic (EEG) signatures, it was calculated that conscious perception could occur as rapidly as 100ms faster for a well-predicted stimulus, and hence that "the signatures of visibility are not bound to processes with a strict latency but depend on the presence of expectations" (Melloni et al. (2011), p. 1395).

In addition, Muckli (2010) reports that predicted stimuli, although able to drive better and faster behavioural responses, showed reduced fMRI activation in V1. This is further evidence for the predictive coding story since "Finding reduced activity related to increased performance fits well with the framework of predictive coding... but is difficult to explain otherwise" (Muckli (2010), p. 135).

---

[14] There is doubtless some kind of slippery slope here, as we progressively degrade the driving signal and upregulate the expectations. Negotiating this complex terrain is, however, a task for another day.

3.4. SENSORIMOTOR CONTINGENCY THEORY

The notion that sensory experience is in some way bound up with predictions and expectations resonates to some degree with recent important and influential work in 'sensorimotor contingency theory' (O'Regan and Noë (2001), Noë (2004), Noë (2009)). There are, however, some notable differences. First, sensorimotor contingency theory (SMC) staunchly champions the view that the predictions that matter will mostly concern the ways the sensory signal will vary with bodily movement. That is to say, they are both prospective (they concern future variation in the incoming signal) and their contents are sensorimotor profiles. Such prospective sensorimotor predictions, though often extremely important, constitute merely one dimension of the very large space of features and properties that can figure in the downward-cascades posited by hierarchical predictive coding accounts. Moreover, the SMC model (at least as explicated and defended by Noë (2004) (2009)) looks committed to an implausibly shallow processing account (see Clark (2008), ch. 8) that omits any essential appeal to those multiple, stacked layers of internal representation—the crucial hierarchical generative model—that translate top-down predictions, via many intervening stages, into predictions concerning the actual ebb and flow of the driving sensory inputs. SMC models, though absolutely correct to highlight prediction and expectation in their account of perception, are thus neglecting the critical machinery (of prediction-induced hierarchical generative models) that enable brains like ours to infer complex hidden causal structures in the world.

3.5. DISTINGUISHING AND EXTENDING THE SENSES

The predictive coding framework offers, we saw, a powerful way of accommodating all manner of cross- and multimodal effects on perception. It depicts the senses as working together to provide feedback (recall the explanatory inversion highlighted in section 1.3) to a linked set of prediction devices that are attempting to track unfolding states of the world across multiple spatial and temporal scales. This delivers a very natural account of efficient multimodal cue integration (see Ernst and Banks (2002)), and allows top-down effects to penetrate even the lowest (earliest) elements of sensory processing. It also induces (section 1.2) a potent duality between sensing and top-down generation, so that to perceive some state of affairs requires the system to be capable (though not necessarily of its own volition) of endogenously generating the relevant sensory signature. Certain things that might otherwise be taken for granted then stand in need of explanation.

One is the existence of distinct modalities in experience. Why, given that the senses work together to provide ongoing feedback on predictions that aim to track causal structure in the world, do we experience sight as different from sound, touch as different from smell, and so on? Why, that is, do we not simply experience states of affairs without the sense of distinct modalities? I would speculate (and no more than speculate) that the answer may involve the different kinds of uncertainty that are associated with different sensory channels. In a thick fog, for example, vision is unreliable (delivering information with high uncertainty) while audition is less affected. The brain will need to mark these differences so as to weight and integrate the available cues (from multiple sense organs) in different ways on different occasions. Perhaps we experience sensory modalities as different from one another just to the extent that they are prone (in many contexts) to deliver information with very different degrees of uncertainty. Where the uncertainties more nearly match, we experience one modality (e.g., vision) with multiple sense organs (two eyes).

This would mean that the character of sensory experience has (at least) two components. One is the stacked set of generative models that capture the regularities in the world. The other is the signature forms of uncertainty associated with the sensory channel itself.

3.6. PERCEIVING AND IMAGINING

Another question the new framework raises is, Why is imagination not just like conscious perception? Given the role of generative models, and the deep duality between perception and the top-down generation of the sensory signal, one might expect imagination to share the full (rich, vivid) experiential signature of ordinary perception.[15] Yet (bracketing cases of hallucination, etc.) this does not seem to be the case. Here too, I will venture one last (mere) speculation.

Sensory processing, on these models, involves predicting (across a hierarchy of processing regions) the driving signal transduced from the world. That means that the flow of information from the environment really matters, as it delivers the evolving data stream that the top-down model has to try (using the linked stack of generative models) to match. An important feature of this process is that the weight that is given to the driving sensory signal (hence the value of prediction errors concerning that signal) can be varied according to its degree of certainty or uncertainty. This is achieved by altering the gain (the 'volume' to use the standard auditory analogy) on the error-units accordingly. The effect of this is to allow the brain to vary the balance between sensory inputs and prior expectations at different levels (see Friston (2009), p. 299). This means that the weighting of sensory prediction errors (hence the relative influence of sensory inputs and prior expectations) at any level of processing within the whole hierarchical cascade may itself be flexibly modulated. This is sometimes described as optimising "the relative precision of empirical (top-down) priors and (bottom-up) sensory evidence" (Friston (2009), p. 299). All this is suggestive, it seems to me, of a possible explanation for the experiential asymmetry between perception and (ordinary nonvivid) imagination.

---

[15] Thanks to Mark Sprevak (personal communication) for raising this issue.

Thus, suppose you are looking for an object on a crowded surface. You expect to see it somewhere, but you are not sure where. Your brain must temporarily increase the weighting on the fine spatial information carried by the driving signal. That way, you don't simply mistakenly see it *there* (at such and such a location) just because you are expecting to see it *somewhere*. To match the driving signal with a top-down prediction here demands accounting for the sensory signal in great detail, all the way down (as it were).

Nonvivid mental imagery, by contrast, may be calling only upon higher levels of the generative model. Thus, compare the case where you are asked to imagine your walk to work. Here, early (closer to retinotopic) stages of the processing hierarchy can be allowed substantial leeway and need not be forced to settle into one interpretation or another. It seems plausible (though this is, to repeat, currently no more than speculation) that under such conditions one might experience the self-generated imagery as fuzzier and less distinct than online perception, even though perception and imagination are simply different ways of deploying the very same circuits and fundamental capacities.[16]

4. Conclusions: Perceiving, Imagining. . . . Knowing?

The main purpose of this chapter has been to introduce the notion of sensory perception as a form of probabilistic prediction involving a hierarchy of generative models.[17] This broad vision brings together frontline research in machine learning and a growing body of neuroscientific conjecture and evidence. It provides a simple and elegant account of multimodal and crossmodal effects in perception and has implications for the study of (the neural correlates of) conscious experience. It also suggests, or so I have argued, a deep unity between perceiving and imagining. For to perceive the world (at least as we do) is to deploy internal resources capable of endogenously generating those same sensory effects: capable, that is, of generating those same activation patterns via a top-down sweep involving multiple intermediate layers of processing. That suggests a fundamental linkage between 'passive perception' and active imagining, with each capacity being continuously bootstrapped by the other. Perceiving and imagining (if these models are on the right track) are simultaneous effects of a single underlying neural strategy.

---

[16] Reddy et al. (2010) neatly demonstrate that imagery and perception are not simply activating overlapping neural areas but are actually deploying the very same fine-grained internal representations when they do so. In the cases they investigate, that overlap is restricted, as the present speculation suggests, to somewhat higher levels of the visual-processing hierarchy. The authors suggest, though, that were the task to have demanded it, lower-level areas such as V1 might have been reactivated in the same top-down manner.

[17] Technically, there is then a single (but hierarchical) generative model. Nothing in the present treatment turns on this detail.

In closing, I cannot resist sharing one further thought, even though it goes far beyond the conclusions warranted by the present treatment. It is that this unity of perceiving and imagining in turn suggests a deep continuity between perceiving (thus construed) and understanding.[18] For such systems are able to predict the way the sensory signal will evolve, on multiple temporal and spatial scales, and to generate those transformations in advance using endogenous resources alone. When such systems perceive the world, they know how the world is structured by hidden causes and they know how it is likely to evolve over time. This, surely, is to make deep inroads not just into the explanation of effective perception but also into the origins of meaning and semantics: the elusive realm of 'aboutness' itself.

Acknowledgments

This chapter owes much to discussions and exchanges at *The Senses Research Workshop* (Institut Jean-Nicod, Paris, 2009), at the workshop on *Predictive Coding and the Senses* (Institute of Philosophy, London, 2011), and during my stay as a Visiting Fellow at the SAGE Institute at UC Santa Barbara. Thanks to Dustin Stokes, Mohan Matthen, and Barry Smith for many useful discussions and for making the workshops possible. Thanks to Mike Gazzaniga and the audiences at UCSB, and especially Michael Rescorla. Thanks too to Karl Friston, Jakob Hohwy, and Chris Williams for helping me begin to negotiate the dizzying maze of work on predictive coding, active inference, and generative models. They are not to blame for any errors or speculative excesses. The chapter also benefitted greatly from helpful suggestions from Jon Bird, and from the editors of the present volume. This work was supported in part by an AHRC Speculative Research Grant (PI Y. Rogers, Open University) 'Extending the Senses and Self Through Novel Technologies'.

References

Alink, A., Schwiedrzik, C. M., Kohler, A., Singer, W., and Muckli, L. (2010). Stimulus predictability reduces responses in primary visual cortex. *Journal of Neuroscience* 30: 2960–2966.

Bar, M. (2007). The proactive brain: Using analogies and associations to generate predictions. *Trends in Cognitive Sciences* 11(7): 280–289.

Bengio, Y. (2009). Learning deep architectures for AI. *Foundations and Trends in Machine Learning* 2(1): 1–127.

---

[18] For a rather more conceptual route to what seems to me to be a similar conclusion, see Timothy Williamson's *New York Times* 'Opinionator' blog entry 'Reclaiming the Imagination' available at http://opinionator.blogs.nytimes.com/2010/08/15/reclaiming-the-imagination/.

Bengio, Y., and Le Cun, Y. (2007). Scaling learning algorithms towards AI, in *Large Scale Kernel Machines*. Cambridge, MA: MIT Press.

Biederman, I. (1987). Recognition-by-components: A theory of human image understanding. *Psychological Review 94*: 115–147.

Bubic, A., von Cramon, D. Y., and Schubotz, R. I. (2010). Prediction, cognition and the brain. *Frontiers in Human Neuroscience 4*(25): 1–15.

Byrne, A., and Logue, H. (eds.). (2009). *Disjunctivism: Contemporary Readings*. Cambridge, MA: MIT Press.

Chater, N., and Manning, C. (2006). Probabalistic models of language processing and acquisition. *Trends in Cognitive Sciences 10*(7): 335–344.

Clark, A. (2008). *Supersizing the Mind: Embodiment, Action, and Cognitive Extension*. New York: Oxford University Press.

Dennett, D. (1988). Quining qualia, in A. Marcel and E. Bisiach (eds.), *Consciousness in Modern Science*. New York: Oxford University Press. Reprinted in W. Lycan (ed.), *Mind and Cognition: A Reader*. Cambridge, MA: MIT Press, 1990; A. Goldman (ed.), *Readings in Philosophy and Cognitive Science*. Cambridge, MA: MIT Press, 1993.

Egner, T., Monti, J. M., and Summerfield, C. (2010). Expectation and surprise determine neural population responses in the ventral visual stream. *Journal of Neuroscience 30*(49): 16601–16608.

Engel, A., Fries, P., and Singer, W. (2001). Dynamic predictions: Oscillations and synchrony in top-down processing. *Nature Reviews: Neuroscience 2*: 704–716.

Ernst, M. O., and Banks, M. S. (2002). Humans integrate visual and haptic information in a statistically optimal fashion. *Nature 415*: 429–433.

Feldman, H., and Friston, K. (2010). Attention, uncertainty, and free energy. *Frontiers in Human Neuroscience 4*(215): 1–23.

Friston, K. (2002). "Beyond phrenology: What can neuroimaging tell us about distributed circuitry?" *Annual Review of Neuroscience 25*(1): 221–250.

Friston, K. (2005). A theory of cortical responses. *Philosophical Transactions of the Royal Society of London B: Biological Sciences 360*(1456): 815–836.

Friston, K. (2009). The free-energy principle: A rough guide to the brain? *Trends in Cognitive Science 13*: 293–301.

Friston, K. (2010). The free-energy principle: A unified brain theory? *Nature Reviews: Neuroscience 11*(2):127–138.

Friston, K., Mattout, J., and Kilner, J. (2011). Action understanding and active inference. *Biological Cybernetics 104*: 137–160.

Haddock, A., and Macpherson, F. (eds.). (2008). *Disjunctivism: Perception, Action, and Knowledge* (Oxford: Oxford University Press).

Heeger, D., and Ress, D. (2002). What does fMRI tell us about neuronal activity? *Nature Reviews/Neuroscience 3*:142–151.

Heess, N., Williams, C., and Hinton, G. (2009). Learning generative texture models with extended fields-of-experts. *Proceedings of the British Machine Vision Conference 2009*: 1–11

Hinton, G. (2007a). To recognize shapes, first learn to generate images. In P. Cisek, T. Drew, and J. Kalaska (eds.), *Computational Neuroscience: Theoretical Insights into Brain Function*. Amsterdam: Elsevier.

Hinton, G. E. (2007b). Learning multiple layers of representation. *Trends in Cognitive Sciences* 11: 428–434.

Hinton, G. E. (2010). Learning to represent visual input. *Philosophical Transactions of the Royal Society of London B: Biological Sciences* 365: 177–184.

Hinton, G., Dayan, P., Frey, B. J., and Neal, R. M. (1995). The wake sleep algorithm for unsupervised neural networks. *Science* 268: 1158–1161.

Hinton, G. E., Osindero, S., and Teh, Y. (2006). A fast learning algorithm for deep belief nets. *Neural Computation* 18: 1527–1554.

Hohwy, J. (2007). Functional integration and the mind. *Synthese* 159(3): 315–328.

Hosoya, T., Baccus, S. A., and Meister, M. (2005). Dynamic predictive coding by the retina. *Nature* 436(7): 71–77.

Huang, Y., and Rao, R. P. N. (2011). Predictive coding. *Wiley Interdisciplinary Reviews: Cognitive Science* 2: 580–593.

Hubel, D. H., and Wiesel, T. N. (1965). Receptive fields and functional architecture in two nonstriate visual areas (18 and 19) of the cat. *Journal of Neurophysiology* 28: 229–289.

Hupé, J. M., James, A. C., Payne, B. R., Lomber, S. G., Girard, P., and Bullier, J. (1998). Cortical feedback improves discrimination between figure and background by V1, V2 and V3 neurons. *Nature* 394: 784–787.

Jehee, J. F. M., and Ballard, D. H. (2009). Predictive feedback can account for biphasic responses in the lateral geniculate nucleus. *PLoS Computational Biology* 5(5): e1000373.

Kanwisher, N. G., McDermott, J., and Chun, M. M. (1997). The fusiform face area: A module in human extrastriate cortex specialized for face perception. *Journal of Neuroscience* 17: 4302–4311.

Koch, C., and Poggio, T. (1999). Predicting the visual world: Silence is golden. *Nature Neuroscience* 2(1): 9–10.

Kriegstein, K., and Giraud, A. (2006). Implicit multisensory associations influence voice recognition. *PLoS Computational Biology* 4(10): e326.

Langner, R., Kellermann, T., Boers, F., Sturm, W., Willmes, K., and Eickhoff, S. B. (2011). Modality-specific perceptual expectations selectively modulate baseline activity in auditory, somatosensory, and visual cortices. *Cerebral Cortex* (advance access e-publication doi: 10.1093/cercor/bhro83).

Lee, T. S., and Mumford, D. (2003). Hierarchical Bayesian inference in the visual cortex. *Journal of Optical Society of America* 20(7): 1434–1448.

Marr, D. (1982). *Vision*. San Francisco: Freeman.

Melloni, L., Schwiedrzik, C. M., Muller, N., Rodriguez, E., and Singer, W. (2011). Expectations change the signatures and timing of electrophysiological correlates of perceptual awareness. *Journal of Neuroscience* 31(4): p1386–p1396.

Muckli, L. (2010). What are we missing here? Brain imaging evidence for higher cognitive functions in primary visual cortex V1. *International Journal of Imaging Systems and Technology* 20: 131–139.

Muckli, L., Kohler, A., Kriegeskorte, N., and Singer, W. (2005). Primary visual cortex activity along the apparent-motion trace reflects illusory perception. *PLoS Computational Biology* l3: e265.

Mumford, D. (1992). On the computational architecture of the neocortex II: The role of cortico-cortical loop. *Biological Cybernetics* 66: 241–251.

Murray, S. O., Kersten, D., Olshausen, B. A., Schrater, P., and Woods, D. L. (2002). Shape perception reduces activity in human primary visual cortex. *Proceedings of the National Academy of Science U.S.A. 99*(23): 15164–15169.

Murray, S. O., Boyaci, H., and Kersten, D. (2006). The representation of perceived angular size in human primary visual cortex. *Nature Reviews: Neuroscience 9*: 429–434.

Neisser, U. (1967). *Cognitive Psychology*. New York: Appleton-Century-Crofts.

Noë, A. (2004). *Action in Perception*. Cambridge, MA: MIT Press.

Noë, A. (2009). *Out of Our Heads: Why You Are Not Your Brain, and Other Lessons from the Biology of Consciousness*. New York: Farrar, Straus and Giroux.

O'Regan, J. K., and Noë, A. (2001). A sensorimotor approach to vision and visual consciousness. *Behavioral and Brain Sciences 24*(5): 883–975.

Pascual-Leone, A., and Hamilton, R. (2001). The metamodal organization of the brain. *Progress in Brain Research.* 134: 427–445.

Rao, R., and Ballard, D. (1999). Predictive coding in the visual cortex: A functional interpretation of some extra-classical receptive-field effects. *Nature Neuroscience 2*(1): 79.

Rao, R., and Sejnowski, T. (2002). Predictive coding, cortical feedback, and spike-timing dependent cortical plasticity, in R.P.N. Rao, B.A. Olshausen, and M.S. Lewicki (eds.), *Probabilistic Models of the Brain*. Cambridge, MA: MIT Press.

Reddy, L., Tsuchiya, N., and Serre, T. 2010. Reading the mind's eye: Decoding category information during mental imagery. *NeuroImage 50*(2): 818–825.

Reich, L., Szwed, M., Cohen, L., and Amedi, A. (2011). A ventral stream reading center independent of visual experience. *Current Biology 21*: 363–368.

Rumelhart, D. E., Hinton, G. E., and Williams, R. J. (1986). Learning internal representations by error propagation. In D. E. Rumelhart, J. L. McClelland, and the PDP Research Group (eds.), *Parallel Distributed Processing. Explorations in the Microstructure of Cognition. Volume 1: Foundations*, pp. 318–362. Cambridge, MA: MIT Press.

Smith, F., and Muckli, L. (2010). Nonstimulated early visual areas carry information about surrounding context. *Proceedings of the National Academy of Science (PNAS)* early edition (in advance of print).

Spratling, M., and Johnson, M. (2006). A feedback model of perceptual learning and categorization. *Visual Cognition 13*(2): 129–165.

Yuille, A., and Kersten, D. (2006). Vision as Bayesian inference: Analysis by synthesis? *Trends in Cognitive Science 10*(7): 301–308.

2

Active Perception and the Representation of Space

Mohan Matthen

In the *Transcendental Aesthetic* of the *Critique of Pure Reason*, Kant famously asserts that (a) space is **the** form of outer appearance, and time **the** form of inner sense (B42, 49). Space is (b) 'a condition of the possibility of appearance' (B39), and (c) 'found in us prior to any perception of an object' (B41). It is (d) 'the subjective condition of sensibility, under which alone outer intuition is possible for us' (B42). Our representation of space is, moreover, (e) the source of our certainty regarding geometrical truths (B41).

Encapsulating the above in contemporary terms, we find in Kant the following:

Pre-Modality Thesis:

[*Commonality*] There is a single representation of space and of time common to all modalities. (a, c, d)

[*Apriority*] These representations are templates for the perceived spatiotemporal ordering of objects and are not derived from information that impinges on the senses. (b, c, e)

[*No Privileged Modality*] No single modality has priority with regard to these templates. The common representation of space is not simply projected from vision or touch to the other modalities. (b, c)

[*Outerness*] 'Appearances' purport to be about the world outside the mind by virtue of being arrayed in the metric denoted by the pre-modal representation of space. (a, d)

Kant's position about space was surely controversial at a time when Molyneux's question was thought to be deeply revealing about the epistemic significance of experiences provided by the sensory modalities (Sassen 2004). Suppose that every sensory impression belongs to some modality. Sense impressions of different modalities differ in (what we would now call) phenomenal character. At the time, it was assumed that if any two sense impressions were phenomenally different, then they must be different with respect to their cognitive significance. (It is safe to say that this assumption retains much of its intuitive appeal today.) It follows that when there are sense impressions of the same quality in different modalities—for example, the visual and tactile impressions of sphericity—they would, nevertheless, differ with regard to their cognitive significance. Thus, it would be possible to *doubt* that they were of the same quality. This was Locke's thought in response to Molyneux's question. Kant swam against this tide. According to him, the sensory representation of space does not belong to any modality. This undercuts Locke's approach because the representation of space would span the modalities. Kant's thesis continues to be controversial today.

The theses articulated above are, of course, only a part of Kant's theory of space. I shall not be concerned here with another closely associated position that he articulates in the *Transcendental Aesthetic*: the idea that because it is known *a priori*, space is a *mental* template, and does not characterize things in themselves. My general attitude is that this is a *non sequitur*. One could grant that the perceptual representations of space and time are *a priori* mental constructs, but still insist that space and time are objective entities represented by perception, whether veridically or not. (Evolution or God could have ensured a large degree of convergence between space and time and their representations.) In this chapter, I am interested primarily in what Kant had to say about the representations of space and time. I shall take a realist stance about space and time themselves, but offer no more than a cursory defence of this position.

My main aim here is to defend Kant's Pre-Modality thesis as summarized earlier. However, I will not devote much attention to Outerness. Though it forms an integral part of Kant's thinking about this subject, I don't think that he formulates the Outerness thesis in exactly the right way—see note 2. To me, it seems that Outerness has a good deal of merit and deserves further investigation, but it goes well beyond my aims here to try and construct a corrected version that would be worth defending.

1. Kant's Arguments

Kant's Pre-Modality thesis has fallen out of view in philosophical discussions of space, but it is important and original and, in my opinion, essentially correct. In the *Transcendental Aesthetic*, we find hints of two arguments in support of it. In this opening section, I present these arguments and argue that they are inadequate. My aim in the chapter is to offer a different argument in support of Pre-Modality—a Common Measure argument, as I shall call it. The Common Measure argument is an important supporting foundation for any view which holds that perception is multimodal.

1.1. OUTERNESS AND PRE-MODALITY

Kant seems to have thought, first, that the Outerness thesis implies the rest of the
Pre-Modality thesis. Before I attempt to reconstruct his argument, let me explain
what he means by Outerness.

Kant claims that things appear to be outside the perceiver's mind because the
senses locate them in space. In other words, he holds (in something of an echo of
Descartes's conception of matter as essentially extended) that the perception of things
as spatially ordered is constitutive of perceiving them as existing objectively.[1]

It is instructive to compare Kant's position here with that of Hume:

> ...tho' every impression and idea we remember be consider'd as existent, the
> idea of existence is not deriv'd from any particular impression. (*Treatise* I.II.vi)

According to Hume, the perceptual image, or idea, of something is the same
whether one thinks of it as existent or not. In other words, when I imagine a scene
as nonexistent, what I imagine is qualitatively the same as when I imagine the
same scene as existent. Since supposing things to be existent does not change how
they appear to the senses, existence must be an extra-sensory idea. Kant agrees
with this: he famously holds that existence is not a 'predicate'.

> When I think a thing, through whichever and however many predicates
> I like [even in its thoroughgoing determination], not the least bit gets added
> to the thing when I posit in addition that this thing is. (*Critique of Pure
> Reason*, B628)

Hume's position concerns *existence*. Kant introduces a new and different notion in
the *Transcendental Aesthetic*: the perceptual appearance of being 'outer' (i.e., outside the mind, or objective). Hume would presumably have held that the notion
of outerness too is not 'deriv'd from any impression': he would have held that for
any impression that a perceiving subject 'consider'd as' external, there could be an
exactly similar impression that the subject takes as possessing no external correlate. Thus, he would have held, no sensory quality differentiates things perceived as
outer and those perceived as inner. This is where Kant gets off the boat. He thinks
that when something looks to be located in space, it appears as if it exists outside
the mind. For Kant, in other words, the perceptual appearance of spatial location
is *constitutive of* the appearance of outerness.[2]

---

[1] *Pains* are felt to be spatially located in the body—and in a subject-perspective independent way,
to boot (Matthen 2014). Kant ought, therefore, to ascribe to them the same kind of felt objectivity that
he ascribes to visual stimuli: that is, he should hold that pains are bodily disturbances, not "feelings" or
inner experiences. By contrast, thoughts and emotions are not felt as located in the body (or anywhere
else). He should count them, therefore, as mental occurrences apprehensible only by outer intuition.

[2] Actually, he is not exactly right. Susanna Siegel (2006) has argued that in order to appear as if they
exist outside the mind, things must look as if their location does not depend on the subject's location
and perspective. Floaters and phosphenes are apparently spatial, and are spatially related to each other,
and so they satisfy Kant's requirement. However, they fail Siegel's test; they are always in the same place

Does this notion of space as the mark of the outer yield an argument for Pre-Modality? Perhaps Kant thought so, for he writes:

> one can represent only one space, and if one speaks of many spaces, one thereby understands only parts of one and the same unique space. These parts cannot precede the one all-embracing space as being, as it were, constituents out of which it can be composed, but can only be thought as *in it*. It is essentially one; the manifold in it, and therefore also the general concept of spaces, depends solely on limitations. *It follows from this that an a priori intuition (which is not empirical) underlies all concepts of space.* (B39; emphasis added)

This passage makes a bold and important claim that goes well beyond the Outerness thesis. This further claim is that 'one can represent only one space,' or, in other words, that one cannot sense two objects as outer without sensing that they are located in the same space.[3] He claims, in other words, that we represent sensory space as *unique*:

[1SS] To sense something as external is *eo ipso* to sense it as existing in the same space as everything else sensed as external.

1SS is, according to Kant, an *a priori* intuition. Clearly, his position is contestable. For one might think that the 'one all-embracing space' is given to us by reason and is not embedded in perceptual experience *a priori*. (I don't agree with this objection to Kant, as will emerge later.)

Let's grant Kant 1SS for the sake of argument. The question arises, Does 1SS imply that there is only one intuition of space common to all the modalities? Kant's line of thought seems to run as follows.

  i. Each of the modalities locates things in space, and thereby as existing objectively.
 ii. But 'one can represent only one space.'

---

relative to the subject, so their apparent location relative to things in objective space changes as she moves. And they are not seen as existing outside the subject's consciousness; they are seen as figments. But even the subject-independent location test doesn't quite do the trick. For though Siegel's thesis is plausible concerning vision, it is less so with regard to audition. Music heard through earphones has subject-dependent location—even when the subject moves it continues to sound as if it comes from her left or right—but it nonetheless appears to exist outside the subject's mind.

    [3] Fiona Macpherson (personal communication) raises the interesting question, What do two things look or sound like when they look or sound as if they are in one space? The answer must be that they appear to be spatially connected, i.e., to have space between them. Since this connecting space might not itself be seen or heard, it might be somewhat misleading to say that when the connecting space is occluded or otherwise obscured, the objects *look* or *sound* as if they inhabit a single space. Thus, the appearance of spatial connectedness would be amodal, much like the appearance of continuity of an object that is partially occluded behind an opaque picket fence—Albert Bregman (1990) discusses auditory analogues of occlusion—or the appearance of an object having a back that cannot be seen. Kant thinks that it is *impossible* to see two things as outer without them appearing amodally to be connected.

   iii. Therefore, there is a unique perceptual representation (or 'intuition') of space in which every modality locates things.[4]

   iv. [Aprioricity may be thought to follow from the thesis of a modality-independent representation of space: see the following subsection.]

Again, this is not a good argument. For though we might represent only one space, it does not follow that there is just one representation of it. (This is exactly the point made by the different-phenomenal-character argument outlined in the introductory section of this chapter.) Grant that our representation of things as existing objectively implies that they exist side by side in one and the same space. It may nonetheless be that each modality represents space in its own way, and it may not be evident to us how these diverse representations of space match up (Hopkins 2005). This, after all, is the problem posed by Molyneux.

To elaborate, consider touch and vision.

> I may see my finger, and feel a pin pressing down on it. The finger looks as if it is in front of the TV, but the pinprick does not feel as if it is in front of the TV. The TV, the pin, and the pinprick are all spatially located, one by vision, one by both vision and touch, and the last by touch. But perception does not appear to represent space in a way that makes the relationship of the three objects evident.
>
> Place your left and right index fingers on the wall in front of you. Now, close your eyes and try to touch your nose to the wall so that it lies on a straight line between the two fingers. It is very hard to do this. (I did it in the shower, so that my digits and nose left wet imprints on a glass divider. Usually, the nose came out higher, though it was possible to get it right by attending carefully.) Again, it seems as if touch does not immediately represent how parts of your body are related to one another relative to the visual representation.

These failures, or limitations, of spatial matching suggest, at the very least, that the perceptual matching of visual and haptic representations of space is imperfect.[5] On the other hand, it seems that the match between vision and audition is smooth: if you hear a sound coming from a particular place, you can spatially

---

[4] I am not entirely certain that the passage that I quote above is meant to apply to the Pre-Modality thesis. See, however, Gareth Evans (1985, esp. 369–370), who suggests that it is.

[5] See Millar and Al Attar (2005). Brigitte Sassen (2004) argues that Kant does not require this kind of cross-identification, and that this is why he fails to mention Molyneux's problem. All that he requires, according to her, is that each sense place objects "side by side." As an example, heard objects should appear to be spatially connected to seen objects. This seems right, as far as it goes. However, I think she underestimates the strength of Kant's demands on cross-modal identification. First, if it visually appears that X is to the left of Y, then it should also haptically and auditorily appear that X is to the left of Y. Secondly, there should be cross-modal "side-by-side" relations that add up to a shared Euclidean structure. These two conditions are strong enough to generate Molyneux's problem.

relate it to things you see. In short, there are cross-modal matches of spatial representation as well as limitations of cross-modal matching. My pre-modality view has to address these limitations. But at the very least, they show that one cannot argue for Pre-Modality *a priori*, as Kant seems to do.[6]

1.2. COGNITIVE NECESSITY AND PRE-MODALITY

A second argument appeals to cognitive necessity. We cannot conceive of *perceived* space as other than three-dimensional and Euclidean, Kant says;[7] these features of space are 'apodeictic'. But nothing that we learn through the senses is apodeictic: any empirical proposition can be conceived to be otherwise. It follows that the three-dimensional Euclidean character of space must be known *a priori*, not inferred from the data provided by sensation. (Actual measurements tend to show that haptic representations of space depart significantly from Euclidean structure: see, for example, Kappers and Koenderink 1999. So even if Kant is right about cognitive necessity, he is wrong about the content of these cognitive necessities, and in particular about perceived space being Euclidean.) He argues further that only those propositions that are known by the senses are confined to a single modality.

Kant rightly thought that this argument supports the idea that our perceptual representation of space is not arrived at discursively, that is, by induction, but is rather an '*a priori* intuition'. (It's an 'intuition' because space is apparently an object of the senses.) Of course, the argument does not show that there is no *a posteriori* component in spatial perceptions. Obviously, I can only know by looking (or by feeling by touch) that my pen is to the right of my keyboard, not to the left. Nevertheless, there are apodeictic aspects of my perceptions of spatial arrangement. For instance, I cannot perceive something as being external without perceiving it as being somewhere. Moreover, certain spatial relations are apodeictic despite being perceived: for example, that the straight path from my pen to my keyboard is shorter than the more circuitous route via the computer monitor. (This is the triangle inequality.) It is implicit in my perception of these three things that *in virtue of appearing straight*, a line appears to be the shortest distance between two points.[8] This kind of idea is constitutive of what Kant calls the *a priori* intuition of space.

---

[6] Millar (2008) contains detailed synoptic discussion of empirical evidence regarding cross-modal matching.

[7] It is unclear, but I think irrelevant, how Kant would have reacted to non-Euclidean geometry. I take his argument in the *Transcendental Aesthetic* to be about certain norms regulating the perceptual representation of space. It is not about "space itself"—which does not exist in Kant's way of thinking. I take it that faced with Einstein's theory that gravitation bends space, Kant *could* have conceded that physics requires a non-Euclidean space, and perhaps even that we could have a non-Euclidean *concept* of space, while denying that we can perceive space as non-Euclidean.

[8] Perhaps there could be Escher-like presentations to the contrary, but it must be remembered that these are two-dimensional renderings of three-dimensional impossibilities. This makes a difference: he

Thus understood, however, our ideas about spatiotemporal structure are not our only *a priori* intuitions. Consider the representation of colour. The visual awareness of colour also carries apodeictic awareness of certain relations among the colours. For example, one cannot experience anything as orange without experiencing it as containing a mixture of *yellowish* and *reddish* components. And analogously to the triangle inequality, it seems necessary that pure *yellow* is more similar to *orange* than it is similar to pure *red*.[9] Again, it is often suggested (by Wittgenstein, for example, in the *Remarks on Colour*) that the intuition that nothing could be reddish and greenish at the same time is not derived from colour experience *a posteriori*.[10] The reddishness that presents itself as a component of *orange* also presents itself as impossible to combine with a greenish hue. Awareness of this and other aspects of the 'similarity space' of colour is, as it were, 'the subjective condition of the possibility of visual appearance of colour.'[11]

Kant discovered an important phenomenon: that certain aspects of *individual* spatial perceptions are imbued by feelings of cognitive necessity, that is, by the 'intuition' that things *must* stand in certain spatial relations. But he did not appreciate that this is true of the perception of any quality. In the case of colour perception, this feeling is the product of a certain kind of formatting. This does not, as Kant mistakenly thought, imply that the *qualitative fields* in which these cognitive necessities are found must be mental constructs. One could, consistently with the formatting supposition, insist that what we perceive as colour is real: for example, that it is surface reflectance.[12] The colour vision system takes in particular instances of this real field and records them in a certain format: simply speaking, it *encodes and displays* every reflectance as a combination of three values on the orthogonal axes of blue-yellow, red-green, and dark-light. (This format is not dictated by the physical nature of colour.) The cognitive necessities of colour perception arise from the structure of this coding. For example, the impossibility of something being both reddish and greenish arises from the fact that these are opposite ends of a single coding axis. Similar things can be said of other perceptual qualities. Psychophysicists have constructed similarity spaces for pitch and flavour. Arguably, even primary qualities such as shape and motion present themselves in similarity relations that reflect more how they are perceptually coded than anything about the physical character of what is perceived.

---

did not present us with three-dimensional violations of three-dimensional Euclidean geometry; nor do his drawings violate two-dimensional geometry.

[9] See Izmailov and Sokolow (1991) for a recent geometrical formulation of colour similarity.

[10] Wittgenstein: "We may call lilac a reddish-whitish-blue or brown a blackish-reddish-yellow—but we *cannot* call a white a yellowish-reddish-greenish-blue. And *that* is something that experiments with the spectrum neither confirm nor refute. It would, however, also be wrong to say "Just look at the colours in nature and you will see that it is so." For looking does not teach us anything about the concepts of colours (*Remarks on Colour*, §72).

[11] For further discussion, see Matthen 2010a.

[12] The surface reflectance view is over-simplified—luminances and transmittances are colours too. But this does not matter for my present point.

In similar fashion, suppose that space is real. It may nevertheless be that our perceptual system encodes the spatial locations of things in a Euclidean framework. For example, it receives contingent locational data from my pen and my keyboard and represents these as points in a Euclidean frame. What we should take from Kant's argument is not that space itself is perceptually constructed, but that the *a priori* intuition of space arises from a perceptual encoding scheme.[13]

None of this helps with the Pre-Modality thesis, however. Why should Kant have thought that the perceptual representation of space is not specific to the sense modalities? Possibly, his thinking may have gone something like this:

(i)   The perceptual representation is *cognitively necessary*, so it is *a priori*.
(ii) *A priori* representations do not depend on sensory input.
(iii) Mental representations that do not depend on sensory input are not modality-specific.

Therefore:

(iv) The perceptual representation of space is not modality-specific. (Commonality)
(v)   [No Privileged Modality follows from (ii) and (iii); Aprioricity from (i) and (ii).]

This argument is defeated by the above diagnosis of cognitive necessity in perception. It lays cognitive necessity and aprioricity at the feet of perceptual coding. But, as the example of colour shows, perceptual coding can be modality-specific. Premise (iii) is the source of the error.

Kant's argument points to certain structural '*a priori* intuitions' of space. Plausibly, these arise from the manner in which spatial qualities are encoded by perceptual systems. One can see this as a limited defence of the Aprioricity thesis stated earlier. But the inference from the Aprioricity of such intuitions to their Pre-Modality is impermissible.

---

[13] Not all perceptual coding effects give rise to apodeictic appearances. Weber's Law states that the discriminability of perceptual magnitudes (such as brightness or volume) depends on the ratio of these magnitudes (not their absolute difference). (Thus, if a light of brightness 10 is just discriminable from one of brightness 11, then a light of brightness 20 will be just discriminable from one of brightness 22.) This is a coding effect. For as Stanislas Dehaene has written:

> "Ernst Weber discovered what we now know as Weber's Law: over a large dynamic range, and for many parameters, the threshold of discrimination between two stimuli increases linearly with stimulus intensity. Later, Gustav Fechner showed how Weber's law could be accounted for by postulating that the external stimulus is scaled into a logarithmic internal representation of sensation" (Dehaene 2003, 145). There is, however, no apodeictic perception that corresponds to Weber's Law, no feeling of certainty, no feeling of any sort, that the larger a stimulus, the more similar it appears to its close neighbours.

2. The Pre-Modality of Time Perception

Our sense of time is multimodal. Events sensed in one modality line up temporally both with one another and with events sensed in all other modalities. When one witnesses a musical song-and-dance act, the music one *hears* temporally lines up with the dancing one *sees*; when one sees a flash of light and is jabbed on the finger with a pin, the flash and the jab are sensed as standing in a particular temporal ordering. More generally:

> To be aware of an event E_1 in any modality and aware of event E_2 in any modality (including non-external modalities) is to be aware of an apparent temporal relationship between E_1 and E_2 (provided that E_1 and E_2 are close enough in time that their temporal relationship can be sensed, rather than calculated or inferred).[14]

All awareness is *inter alia* awareness of time. So it seems that time is a common measure of events sensed both within and across modalities. How does this work? And is the representation of space cross-modal in a similar way?

The temporal matching of objects of experience seems bound up with what Ian Phillips (forthcoming) has called a 'naïve view' (which he vigorously defends). In his words:

> When all goes well, your stream of consciousness simply inherits the temporal structure of the events which are its contents. . . . As a result the temporal structure of experience matches the temporal structure of its objects. In cases of illusion, it is as if this is so.

The idea is that the temporal structure of experience represents the temporal structure of experienced events. For example, you experience a song as taking a certain amount of time by your experience of the song taking that amount of time.

The naïve view can be summed up in the following principle:

Exportation of Temporal Operators (First Pass)

> A subject perceptually experiences events E_1 and E_2 as standing in temporal relation R if and only if her perceptual experiences of E_1 and E_2 stand in temporal relation R, subject to the proviso that she perceptually experiences E_1, E_2,[15] and the temporal relation R.[16]

---

[14] It has traditionally been supposed that since sensory experience is temporally punctate, duration cannot be sensed, and that somehow memory is involved in the experience of duration. I think that this is irrelevant: the iconic retention of experience in short-term memory and its temporal measurement is part and parcel of the perceptual process.

[15] One point to be noted here is that one can experience a process *without* experiencing every constituent event. For example, I can experience an object moving from A to B *without* experiencing it located at every point in between. However, if I experience O moving from A to B without experiencing it at intermediate points C and D, then (I would contend) I do not experience a temporal relation between O being located at C and its being located at D. Thus, the example does not contradict the Exportation Principle.

[16] There is a question about what admissible substituends for 'R' might be. There might be intuitive units of time, perhaps measured by internal clocks (Wittman 2009). If so, a person might experience an

For example, S experiences E_1 occurring *a little earlier* than E_2 if and only S's experience of E_1 occurs a little earlier than her experience of E_2.

At first sight, the Exportation Principle offers a very simple explanation of the temporal synchronization of the song and dance that one hears and sees, one that altogether bypasses the *representation* of time. The dance and the accompanying music seem simultaneous because the experiences take place at the same time. The organizing matrix that gives events their perceived temporal order is *time itself*. Since time is real, not merely a perceptual representation, the representation of temporal order is extra-sensory. (Of course, Kant would disagree with this last statement.)

Actually, things are more complicated than this. Temporal sequencing in perception is the result of a complex computational process. As an illustration of why such a process is needed, and why it is quite complex, consider first what happens when somebody touches your toe and your nose simultaneously. Normally, the tactile experiences are felt to be simultaneous; that is, you have the capacity to judge whether the two touches were simultaneous or not. Yet, the neural signal from the toe, having a much longer distance to travel, arrives at the brain later than the signal from the nose. The brain must, for this reason, tag signals by their point of origin, hold them in abeyance until signals from other parts of the body arrive (this buffer is around 80 milliseconds (ms) long, as it turns out), and then sort out temporal relations within the buffer according to point of origin (Eagleman 2010). Similarly, a time lag of less than 150 ms between a subject's finger movements and visual data regarding these movements is disregarded: when the lag is longer the seen movements are not perceived as the subject's own; when it is shorter, they are (Hoover and Harris 2012).

Temporal illusions are further evidence of this. David Eagleman (2009) writes:

> Imagine that every time you press a key, you cause a brief flash of light. Now imagine we sneakily inject a tiny delay (say, two hundred milliseconds) between your key-press and the subsequent flash. You may not even be aware of the small, extra delay. However, if we suddenly remove the delay, you will now believe that the flash occurred *before* your key-press.[17]

Illusions are a much used method of getting the brain to reveal its computational methods: this is a case of association being used to compute temporal sequence.

The extraction of temporal structure from the data stream holds for external events as well. The McGurk effect (see the Introduction to this volume) shows that

---

interval of time as thus-and-so long in this intuitive sense, and this interval of time might be the same as say 10s. Thus, to say that a person experienced two events as occurring 10s apart would mean that she experienced them as separated by an interval that happens to be the same as 10s, though the experience would not be sufficient to tell the subject that the interval was 10s. Another point to note here is that the time interval between E_1 and E_2 must be short enough if time for time perception to operate.

[17] See also Harrar and Harris (2008).

speech perception depends in part on vision: the visual perception of the speaker's mouth is relevant to what phoneme is heard. It is *also* true that the perceived time of the voice stream depends on vision. For even when the auditory stream lags the visual stream by as much as 170 ms, the two streams are perceived as synchronized (van Wassenhove, Grant, and Poeppel 2007).[18] (Note that there is also a difference of processing time for the different senses.)

Further, there is no *a priori* reason to believe that when a subject experiences two events as standing in temporal relation R, her experiences of these events actually stand in relation R. They may simply seem to do so. For it is natural to think that a subject's experience of two events standing in temporal relation R is separate from her experiences of the two events; it is a meta-experience, an experience of experiences. As William James (1890) wrote: 'The mental stream, feeling itself, must feel the time-relations of its own states' (628). And this is one natural interpretation of what happens in the temporal illusions: in Eagleman's example (earlier), it is natural (though not mandatory) to suppose that though the experiences of the flash (F) and of the key-press (K) are virtually simultaneous, there is a meta-experience of the experience of F being earlier than the experience of K. All that we are safe in saying is this:

> When two events are sensed as standing in a temporal relation, it is because the perceptual system has determined (rightly or wrongly) that they do.

To summarize: when it seems to the subject as if her experiences of the said events stand in relationship R, we may conclude that the system has determined that they stand in this relationship. However, nothing follows about when the system first received information about these events, or even about when these events were experienced. It may often be true that the temporal structure of experience mirrors the experience of temporal structure, but there is no reason to think that this *must* be so.

For these reasons, Phillips (2008) is surely wrong to say that 'we cannot make sense of the idea that experience systematically seems to one's rational introspective reflection to possess a certain temporal ordering, when it is not in fact genuinely so ordered' (183). The meta-experience notion makes it possible to make sense of this idea. For instance, there is no reason to think that when one experiences a touch on one's nose and on one's toe as simultaneous, the experiences of the two touch experiences must really be simultaneous. Again: an auditory voice stream may *systematically* be experienced as simultaneous with visually experienced mouth movements when the lag is anywhere between −30 ms and 170 ms.

---

[18] Charles Spence reports to me in correspondence that when his lab ran this experiment, a degree of confusion was observed with time lags of as much as half a second! (The experimenter kept halting the experiment because she or he thought that the asynchronized version had mistakenly not been played.)

It is unclear how 'rational introspective reflection' would affect these impressions of simultaneity.[19]

The Exportation Principle is thus not only inaccurate as stated previously, but also wrong about the causation of experience. It should be amended as follows:

Exportation of Temporal Operators (Amended)
    (i) A subject perceptually experiences events E_1 and E_2 as standing in temporal relation R if and only if her perceptual experiences of E_1 and E_2 **are sensed as** standing in temporal relation R (subject to the proviso that she perceptually experiences E_1, E_2, and the temporal relation R).
    (ii) They are so sensed because the perceptual system determines that they stand in this relation.

Experience of temporal order results from a process that bears at least some similarity to the one that Kant envisaged. The process is, as he urged, cognitively managed—I would prefer to say, 'managed by the perceptual system.' Further, our sense of time is not derived from information that impinges on the senses. Rather, it is the measure of perceived events. It is an *a priori* template for the ordering of perceived events.

Temporality is a common measure of perceived events. This is illustrated by the fact that all perceptual experience presents its objects as they are *now*, that is, as they are at the time of the experience. This constraint operates across modalities: when you hear the song and see the dance, both are sensed as happening now, and hence simultaneously. This matching is not explained by the *facts*; it does not happen simply because the song and the dance *are* simultaneous (for even if they are simultaneous, the system's determination 'screens off' simultaneity). And it cannot be specific to vision or audition. Therefore, the representation of time cannot be modality-specific.[20]

Obviously, all of the analogues of the *now* condition fail for experience of space. Not everything is presented as occurring *here*, that is, where the experience is, or in any other single place. One does not, for instance, experience two things X and Y as 10 feet apart by having an experience of X that is apparently 10 feet away from the experience of Y. (This would happen only if one were to move 10 feet every time one had such an experience.) There is, thus, a crucial disanalogy between

---

[19] On the other hand, Husserl (1905/1964, 31) seems to exaggerate when he writes: "Our ideas do not bear the slightest trace of temporal determinateness." Husserl's examples seem to counter the First Pass of the Exportation Principle: for example, "If, in the case of a succession of sounds, the earlier ones were to be preserved as they were while ever new ones were also to sound, we should have a number of sounds simultaneously in our imagination, but not succession" (32). Here it seems as if the sensations are simultaneous, and the notes are heard as simultaneous.

[20] Plato undertakes a similar line of thought in the *Theaetetus* (185). How do we know that a sound and a colour are different from each other, and like or unlike one another, as the case may be? Not by looking, since sounds cannot be seen. Similarly, not by listening. Plato suggests that all such cross-modal comparisons must be made by "the soul" (not the senses).

space and time: the perceived spatial relations of things are not projected from a modality-neutral proxy.

A different kind of argument is needed to support the Pre-Modality Thesis for space. This is what I shall now try to provide. As we shall see, Pre-Modality for the perceptual representation of space is somewhat analogous to the case of time: just as time is a common measure of events presented by different modalities, so space is a common measure as well. As we shall see, the most plausible account of the common measure entails Pre-Modality.

3. Active Multimodal Perception

Active perception is purposeful activity by which a subject investigates the perceptual properties of a thing by interacting with it.[21] For example, she might test the sharpness of a knife by gingerly running her thumb across it: this requires the coordination of touch and bodily motion and, for most of us, of vision as well. Or she might investigate the regularity of a shiny surface by feeling it while also looking for how light reflects off it as she manipulates it in her hands. Again, she might locate a squeak in her couch by bouncing on it in different places and listening for where the squeak seems to come from. In each of these cases, the subject investigates a thing by acting on it and observing the results; she knows what she does by monitoring her own activity; she uses the information that she gets from different modalities to determine exactly how the thing is. Clearly, this requires a coordination of spatial representations in various modalities, as well as those that guide action.

Consider audition. It receives two sonic images, one from each ear. Each of these images is a frequency-amplitude function: that is, the basilar membrane in each ear separates the incoming auditory signal into frequencies, and measures the amplitude of each frequency as it occurs in the signal. From these two images, the auditory system constructs an image of sound sources distributed in three-dimensional space. When you listen to a symphony orchestra and a new instrument enters—a bassoon, say—the auditory system manages to detect a coordinated group of notes with similar timbre and separates it out of the soundscape as a separate sound. This permits you to locate it accurately enough to enable you to pick the bassoonist out visually: perhaps his body is moving in synchrony with the bassoon melody you hear. Once you single out the bassoonist, the sound seems to be more precisely located. In this sort of case, the auditory and visual object-location systems seem to be acting together and reinforcing each other in a temporally extended process that involves bodily action such as visual scanning.

---

[21] The term "active perception" as well as my characterization of the activity derive from and generalize J. J. Gibson's (1962) notion of active touch. Earlier I used the term "sensory exploration" (Matthen 2014).

For the sake of discussion, here is an account of an elementary, yet fairly complex, piece of active multimodal perception:

> One day a while ago, I felt a tiny chafing somewhere between my shoulder blades. I couldn't tell what it was: it could have been an irritation of the skin, or perhaps something poking at me. What I did next is exactly what most would have done. I squirmed and wiggled my shoulders. At this point, it became obvious that there was something sharp poking and rubbing against my skin, for I felt it move across my skin as I wiggled my shoulders. Moreover, since the movement of the sharp point seemed to coordinate with the movement of my jacket across my back, it was clear that there was something sharp caught in the cloth. I took the jacket off, but could see nothing. But holding and bracing the cloth with my fingers and feeling around with my thumbs, I finally detected what was wrong. A stiff plastic thread had come loose from the padding of the jacket, and its sharp end was poking through the lining. Looking closely, I was finally able to see it. It was thin and more or less transparent. No wonder I had not been able to see it until then.
>
> Suppose I had looked at the outside of the jacket and seen a similar thread poking through. It would have been natural for me to wonder whether it was the same thread. What would I have done to find out? Perhaps I would have tried to feel along its length. Or I could have pulled the thread on one side to detect movement or tension on the other.

These ways of poking and pushing at the world are low-tech. We often see animals undertake actions like this. Suppose you glue your dog's toy to the ground. She goes to play with it, and finds that it doesn't move. Or suppose you put it into a fretted box with a concealed entrance. She can see the toy but doesn't quite know how to get it. Faced with these unusual situations, dogs will nose and poke and pull and play around with the toy in ways that are similar to the actions by which I got at what turned out to be a thread in my jacket. Much the same is true of cats and birds, and (of course) primates. Perceptual skills can be honed and refined; they can even be taught and learned. But they are available to anybody—indeed any higher organism—with normal sensory and motor capacities.[22]

4. Isotropic Perceptual Models from Egocentric Perceptual Information

When I investigated the thread in my jacket, I was able to construct a complex multisensory model, consisting of a spatial configuration of perceived things and their sensory properties. In the limit, this model is perspective-independent, or

---

[22] For further discussion of active perception, with particular reference to its epistemological force, see Matthen (forthcoming).

isotropic: even when I move my jacket, I can see and feel that the thread retains its location relative to other parts of the jacket. Very briefly, such a model is a three-dimensional configuration of the parts of the jacket. The locations of things are represented relative to one another, not relative to the perceiver. They are not represented differently from different perspectives. I always perceive the jacket from a particular point of view, but my perception can be informed and interpreted in light of an isotropic model that represents how its parts spatially relate to each other.

Formally, an isotropic perceptual model consists of at least the following:

    i. A set of perceivable things, P (e.g., parts of my jacket);
    ii. for each member, x, of P, a set of sensory qualities instantiated by x; and
    iii. for each pair $\{x, y\}$ of members of P, the distance between x and y.[23]

As one builds up one's store of perceptual information concerning an object like the jacket, one's image of it becomes progressively more complete and progressively more independent of perspective. But the information that one receives in any one view from any one point of observation will be largely egocentric. When I first began to be aware of it, the thread in my jacket manifested itself as merely an irritation of my skin. And even when I became aware of it as an external object, I still had no idea of how long it was, what colour it was, or where it was relative to the jacket. All that I knew at this point was that it was pointy and sharp, and where it was relative to the irritation of my skin. When I took the jacket off and manipulated it, I was able to place the thread relative to the shoulders and sleeves of the jacket in a way that enabled me to re-identify it even when the jacket is turned around. The isotropic model is built up from a collection of egocentrically specified information derived from one sense modality at a time. The question is how. What is the representational structure that enables active perception to construct an isotropic model?

Before we think more about this question, let us note that isotropy is ubiquitous in *retained* perceptual images. Consider iconic memory.[24] Think of a house in which you spent many childhood years. You recall how the front hallway looked from both ends, how conversation in the living room sounded when you were standing in the kitchen and how it grew louder and more distinct as you walked down the hall toward the living room, the tactile feel of the bannister and how your hand got hotter as you rubbed against it on the way down, and so on. You can, at will, generate the perceptual experience of skirting the house clockwise, or counter-clockwise; you know how it was to come in from the back, and from the front. Each of these memories is experienced from a perspective; it is a feature

---

[23] The pairwise distances determine the shape of a three-dimensional object up to Kant's incongruous counterparts.

[24] For more about scenes in iconic memory, see Matthen 2010b.

of the display that there must always be a point of view, and that each property displayed must be more or less determinate. Thus, the mental view of the house when you approach it from the front, is a view from the front. It is not, as it were, a 'view from nowhere.' But each can be generated at will, including some that you never actually experienced yourself. It's possible that you never climbed out on the roof above the porch, but you can easily imagine what the house looks like from there. (We will encounter similar considerations concerning isotropic scenes in the following section, when we consider the ideas of shape that a blind person entertains.)

In retained images, perspectival views are generated from an isotropic model. The alternative is to suppose that the mind stores a vast bank of perspective-dependent images, which it draws on in the right order to string together a mental pathway. This alternative is implausible for several reasons. Consider first the free alternation between 'field' and 'observer' perspectives in iconic memory. When you mentally recall walking to the front door of your house, you can generally do it in two modes. You can experience the event from your own perspective, that is, as if you were looking out of your own eyes, so to speak. This is the field perspective. Or you can experience it from outside your own body, viewing yourself as a part of the scene. This is the observer perspective. Since the observer perspective is (of course) not one that you could ever have experienced, it is clear that *this* perspectival view is generated from some underlying representation. And a similar thing happens when you generate images that you have never experienced, for instance, the view from the roof above the porch mentioned in the preceding paragraph. This shows that there is a mental process by which views from different perspectives are generated.[25]

A second point to consider is that isotropic perceptual models correspond quite closely to what Shepard and Metzler (1971) and Kosslyn (1980) call 'mental images' (though they were concerned exclusively with visual images). These psychologists showed that we are able mentally to manipulate mental images: we can rotate them, zoom in and out, change some aspects, and so on. For instance, imagine an unsymmetrical shape, such as a Swiss Army knife with several of its attachments extended—say, a scissors pointing leftward, a bottle opener extended upward, a knife blade downward. One can mentally recreate how this would look if rotated: where the three instruments would point, how the foreshortening would change, how the protrusions would recede and approach relative to one another, and so on. Like the alternation between field and observer perspectives, this indicates that the underlying mental images do not *themselves* encode observer

---

[25] For the observer-field perspective distinction in memory, see Georgia Nigro and Ulric Neisser (1983) and also Endel Tulving (1985). The idea was earlier noted by Freud (1899) and mentioned by Don Locke (1971, 88–89). Bernard Williams (1966/1973) makes a similar point about imagination, noticing that he is able to visualize "from the outside a figure who is myself" but also imagine things from his own point of view.

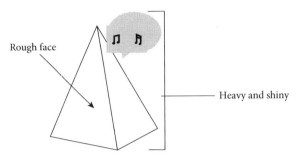

FIGURE 2.1. *Isotropic model with sample elements: The pyramid is an object; and so are its significant parts—including faces, edges, and so on. These objects have features: shape, colour, sound emission, and so on. Since the distances between the objects are constant, the whole scene is a rigid solid that remains the same under rotation, and as the perceiver approaches or recedes.*

perspectives. They are stored in memory; and perspective-dependent views are constructed from them on the fly. But they are always presented from a perspective when they are entertained. (The psychologists referred to above use the term 'image' to refer both to that of which we are consciously aware and the underlying mental representation. I find it more appropriate to refer to the object of conscious awareness as an image—this is always from a point of view—and the underlying mental representation as an isotropic model.)

There are two transformations that must be considered with regard to the construction of isotropic models. When we experience an object, certain of its aspects are presented egocentrically. It is, for example, presented as having a back that is out of view, even when the sensory characteristics of the back are out of view and unknown. Its side face might be foreshortened and it may therefore be impossible to figure out how deep it is. We may hear a sound coming from behind it, and we may not know what sort of object is emitting the sound. Isotropic models are created out of many such presentations. Their creation is a perceptual process of interaction, exploration, and collation. This process comes naturally to us; it is not an act of sophisticated cognition. With every movement and every shift of attention, we continually and always undertake a process that takes us some of the way to building this perspectival view into an isotropic model (see Figure 2.1).

On the other hand, when we already possess an isotropic perceptual model of something, we generate egocentric views of it in the mind's 'eye' (as well as in the mind's ear and the mind's skin). And when we perceive a familiar thing, we experience a scenario that is pregnant with the model (or model fragment) that we have already built up: for though we only glimpse the thing from one point of view, what we see is influenced by this. Generally, we cannot form a view of something without viewing it from a certain perspective. (This is not true of audition: I hear a band play a tune; later, I play the tune in my head, and it doesn't seem to come from any place in the auditory field.)

Summing this up, we have the

Isotropic Multimodality Thesis

There are retained perceptual representations that are (to varying degrees, dependent on how much information the perceiver has) independent of the subject's perspective or point of view. These representations are generated by 'active perception,' which involves interaction with the object in order to get multiple views of it. When a visual image is episodically entertained, it is always from a perspective. This perspective-dependent image is generated from the retained isotropic model. Both retained and episodically entertained images are multimodal.[26]

These are dogmatic claims, and I will not attempt to justify them any further here. My concern is with the role of the representation of space in active perception. Constructing an isotropic model—a model that retains its spatial encoding under rotation—requires that our perceptual systems collate features provided by different modalities in locations common to those modalities.

In short, it requires a cross-modal representation of space that specifies locations in an observer-independent coordinate system.

5. Three Grades of Multimodal Involvement

The fact that multiple senses can act together has not, of course, escaped the attention of philosophers and psychologists. In fact, thanks to William Molyneux, an Irish writer of the late 17th century, it became one of the central problems of early modern philosophy. How are the spatial perceptions, or sensations, of different modalities related to one another? Given the cognitive nonequivalence of ideas of different modalities, how can the modalities work together? What is the nature of the information that allows information specific to one modality to be collated with that specific to another? Approaches to this problem vary in their commitment to real integration, as I shall now recount.

5.1. THE PRIVILEGED MODALITY VIEW: CROSS-MODAL MATCHING

The traditionally most widely accepted idea about the multimodal representations of space is that there are none. Any given property, spatial or otherwise,

---

[26] Casey O'Callaghan (this volume) has an account of multimodal binding that is similar in intent, but somewhat different from this, inasmuch as it is event-based rather than object-based. Charles Spence and Tim Bayne (this volume) tentatively deny that there is simultaneous awareness of features in different modalities; they would not, however, deny the existence of isotropic multimodal models.

is represented in just one modality, and the other modalities do not represent it, though they may represent qualities associated with it.

Berkeley's treatment of the Moon Illusion is a good illustration of this. In the illusion, the 'confused' or shimmery-blurry character of the Moon on the horizon is associated with greater distance. In other words, the Moon appears farther away when it is on the horizon than at its zenith because it looks more confused. Because the same-sized retinal image indicates greater size given greater distance, it follows that the Moon appears larger when on the horizon. *Distance* is not, however, visually represented, according to Berkeley (*New Theory* §2–20); for the way a point is projected onto the retina is independent of its distance. Distance is represented by touch[27]—by the sensation of reaching for a thing, or travelling toward it, or by turning one's eyes inward when looking at it. Distance is a tactile idea that is simply associated with visual confusedness. Similarly, size is not visually represented: the size of the retinal image is co-determined by the size of the projecting object and its distance. Size too is a tactile quality inferred from distance, which in turn is inferred from the visual appearance of confusedness.[28]

One problem with the Privileged Modality view is that there are reasons to assign some spatial properties to one modality and some to another. As just mentioned, Berkeley thought that *distance* and *size* are represented tactually, not visually. However, when it comes to *shape*, some (including Diderot, discussed later) think that vision has an advantage.[29] (Stokes and Biggs, this volume, take a similar view, though on different grounds.) However, distance is a component of three-dimensional shape, and so it makes no sense to assign it to a different modality than shape.

Diderot offered one canonical argument to the effect that touch does not represent shape. According to him, there is no *simultaneous* tactual idea of shape.

> How does a man congenitally blind form ideas of shape? I believe that the notion of direction is given to him by the movements of his body, the successive existence of his hand in different places.... If he runs his fingers along a taut thread, he will get the idea of a straight line; if he follows the line of a sagging wire, he will get that of a curve.... For a blind man, unless he be a geometer, a straight line is nothing but the memory of a succession of sensations encountered along a taut string.... Whereas we combine coloured

---

[27] It would have been more appropriate to include proprioception, since both touch and proprioception are involved in estimating the distance one has walked or how far one is reaching toward an object. But Berkeley seems to adhere very much to the five-senses view.

[28] The distance illusion is no longer accepted as an explanation of the Moon illusion.

[29] Visual dominance is often cited in this context—the phenomenon that when vision conflicts with other modalities with regard to spatial information, the visual information is taken over by the other modalities at the expense of their own. Now, this does not show that the visual representation of space is privileged—that no other modality represents space. To the contrary, it shows that each modality has an estimate of spatial properties that can be compared with the visual estimate of the same; thus, it assumes a common, cross-comparable, and transferable spatial measure.

points, he combines only palpable ones, or, to speak more exactly, only his tactile memories. ('Letter on the Blind,' translated in Morgan 1977, 39)

A blind person takes in shape by a temporally extended process of feeling a thing, Diderot suggests, while a sighted one takes it in a single, temporally punctate, visual act. But *shape* is not a temporal succession. And in any case it is not any particular succession that a blind person might employ on a given occasion—feeling the broad end of an arrowhead first and the point later is a succession of sensations different from feeling the point first, but the shape is one and the same and hence not identical with either. The blind man's experience is thus not of *shape* as such. Diderot concluded that shape is a visual idea that the blind can only represent abstractly (provided that they have some knowledge of geometry). Let's call this Diderot's Thesis Notice that Diderot's Thesis is opposed to the Isotropic Multimodality Thesis of the preceding section: his claim is that the retained tactile representation of shape is a connected collection of perspectival images, rather than an isotropic model.

Now, it makes no sense to think that spatial properties can be distributed across modalities, such that some are specific to one, and others to another. The spatial properties, such as size, distance, and shape, are an inter-related group, and it makes little sense to split them up. The spatial properties are defined and measured by space. So the question arises, To what modality does the representation of space belong, and how can a modality-specific representation of space be applied across modalities, as well as to 'abstract' quantities? The Privileged Modality view is in trouble if it is unable to give a unified treatment of all spatial properties as belonging to the same modality.

Another—and, in my opinion, a decisive objection to the Privileged Modality view—is simple introspection. Berkeley holds that we have no visual idea of size. But this is simply false: things almost always *look* as if they are a certain size. (Admittedly, very distant things can often look indeterminately large, but this is irrelevant to my point.) It is simply obvious that size is represented visually as well tactually.

Gareth Evans (1985) appeals to something like this consideration in his treatment of Molyneux's question. He notes that it is absurd to think that direction is represented *indirectly* by some modalities:

No one hears a sound *as coming from the same side as the hand he writes with* in the sense that, having heard it thus, he has to say to himself 'Now I write with this hand' (wiggling his right hand) so the sound must be coming from there (pointing with his right hand). (384)

The same sort of thing can be said of size. One doesn't see something as large by first forming the idea that one can touch it by stretching out one's arm, and then noticing that when things project an image of *this* angular size when they are an arm's length away they are large. (This assumes that visual angle, which is a spatial property, is proprietary to vision, while size, another spatial property, belongs to touch—a questionable dichotomy, as mentioned earlier.) There is a simple visual impression of size. This is precisely what the Moon Illusion illustrates. The Moon *looks* large on the horizon. It does not simply look confused and of the same angular size as when it is at its zenith.

Associationism does not make things easier for Berkeley. His idea is that size is inferred from distance, which is in turn inferred from visual confusedness. But there is something in the phenomenology that this explanation passes over. To account for the phenomenology of visual appearance of size, Berkeley must account for how things come to *look* a certain size. But he cannot do this. *Seen* size does not exist for him; his theory simply denies that anything *looks* large or small. Whether cross-modal matches are made innately or by past association is not the central sticking point for his theory. It is the *look of size* that his Privileged Modality view cannot accommodate.

The driving idea behind the Privileged Modality view is that cross-modal correspondences are post-perceptual. Since perception is, on this view, a process that begins and ends within a single modality, the appearance of sameness between spatial relations as seen and spatial relations as felt cannot be ascribed to perception. Of course, there is no reason, as Evans remarked, that there should not be an appearance of similarity between a spatial relation or shape as seen and as felt:[30]

> There is nothing on the most radical empiricist view that precludes sensations produced by the stimulation of different sense modalities being sufficiently close together in the innate similarity space for responses conditioned to the one to generalize to the other. There is nothing particularly upsetting to an empiricist theory of concept formation in the suggestion that human subjects who are trained with the use of 'harmonious' in the case of sounds might generalize its use (without further training) to the case of certain combinations of colours. (376–377)

However, as Evans recognizes (by his talk of 'concept formation'), such an 'appearance' of similarity cannot (on this view) be perceptual in origin since perception does not reach into any conscious state in which cross-modal comparisons are made. The similarity of felt and seen shape is thus of a very different sort than that of red and pink, or any other two visual qualities.

---

[30] John Mackie (1976) takes a similar line with regard to Locke. Since both the visual and tactile ideas of a cube resemble a cube, the newly sighted man should be able to visually differentiate a cube and a globe by the fact that the visual idea of the first resembles a globe, and that of the second a cube. This constitutes a relevant similarity between the tactual and visual idea of a globe.

5.2. THE BEHAVIOURAL SPACE VIEW: MULTIMODAL CALIBRATION

Let us say that something looks to be over to the left of me. It cannot look this way *merely* in virtue of a certain visual sensation with modality-specific phenomenal character that marks things as over on the left—a certain 'visual leftishness,' if you will. For, as Evans forcefully argues (citing George Pitcher 1971 and Charles Taylor 1979), it would then be possible to sense a perceived thing visually leftish, but fail to know that one had to stretch out one's left arm to reach for it. Evans writes:

> We do not hear a sound as coming from a certain direction, and then have to *think* or *calculate* which way to turn our heads to look for the source of the sound.... Since this does not appear to make sense, we must say that having the perceptual information at least partly consists in being disposed to do certain things.... The subject...hears the sound *up*, or *down, to the right* or *to the left*.... It is clear that these terms are *egocentric* terms; they involve the specification of the position of the sound in relation to the observer's own body. (Evans 1985, 382–383)

Visual and auditory sensations of location are not contingently connected to location in behavioural space. Evans concludes that in all modalities, these locations are 'specified in the same, egocentric, terms' and are 'used to build up a unitary picture of the world.' 'There is only one behavioural space,' he says (390), meaning that in every modality, space is specified in behavioural terms. (The thought would have been clearer if Evans had written, "There is only one representation of space, and it is behavioural.")

This is an extremely important argument. Visual leftishness is necessarily connected to the feeling that one would have to stretch out one's left hand, or walk leftward, to reach for it. Equally, *auditory* leftishness is necessarily connected to the same behaviour. Spatial awareness is coordinated across all of the senses; otherwise, there could be no coordinated multisensory awareness. And this seems to hold up empirically. Pawan Sinha's investigation (with colleagues) of newly sighted individuals in India (Held et al. 2011) reveals that it takes these patients a few days, at the least, to correlate shapes across the modalities. But he and his colleagues do *not* report that these subjects experience any difficulty at all with visually guided reaching or navigation (as surely they would have if they had noticed any such difficulties). They do not, for example, report that newly sighted patients have a problem looking over to the left when they hear a sound from there, or that they have to learn how to point or turn toward a sudden bright flash of light.[31]

Evans's argument runs parallel to the argument about the representation of time in section 2 of this chapter. The argument of section 2 established that time

---

[31] Sinha confirms in correspondence with Alex Byrne that they did not notice any such deficiency in the newly sighted.

must be pre-modal because, across all modalities, experiences have a common temporal dimension. Evans's argument is a Common Measure argument of the same kind. The idea is that since one can deliberately move one's own body relative to anything that one experiences through the senses, so anything that is experienced through the senses must be experienced as located relative to one's own body. Perception, taken as a whole, offers us, as Evans says, a 'unitary picture' of things laid out in space.

As with time, it is important to recognize that the common measure is given through a *representation* of spatial properties. As with time, this placement of things in a common perceived space is not *automatic*: it is the result of perceptual data processing. And, as noted in section 1, bodily sensations may possess location in a scheme that does not smoothly coordinate with the scheme of the external modalities. On occasion, the perceptual system gets it wrong: this is illustrated by the 'ventriloquist illusion' in which the system locates the ventriloquist's voice in the moving mouth of the dummy. Again, there is the 'rubber hand illusion' in which a subject's hidden hand and a visible rubber hand are simultaneously stroked—subjects report that they feel the stroking where the rubber hand is (Botvinick and Cohen 1998, 756). As the experimenters observe, 'this illusion involves a constraint-satisfaction process operating between vision, touch, and proprioception—a process structured by correlation normally holding among these modalities.' In other words, the system's activity in placing modal stimuli in a common space results, in this case, in an illusion.

Common Measure arguments are, as I said earlier, extremely important. However, the Behavioural Space view suffers from some of the same difficulties as the Privileged Modality view. Suppose that, as Evans insists, the perceptual representation of space is 'in terms of the behavioural dispositions and propensities to which such information gives rise' (371). Consider first the idea that visual experience of location has a characteristic phenomenal character. Some things *look* as if they are over on the left. This phenomenal character that marks the look of being on the left is not the same as the phenomenal character that marks a sound as coming from the left. Yet, if visual and auditory space were simply behaviourally specified, these would both amount to awareness of the behaviourally specified location of such things—and thus be the same. But neither the look nor the sound is, as such, the awareness of where one would have to reach for it. For something to look or sound as if it were over on the left is not *the same* as for it to appear as if one would have to reach for it over on the left. The behavioural awareness *comes with* and is *integrated with* the look and with the sound, which are in turn integrated with one another in this respect. But they are not all the same act of awareness.

Putting this in another way, the Behavioural Space view is exactly the same as the Privileged Modality view, *except* insofar as it is coded in terms of an efferent rather than afferent representation. But this difference between *incoming* (that is, sensory) and *outgoing* (that is, motor) representation is irrelevant to the solution of Molyneux's problem. As discussed earlier, the problem arises from the fact that two representations are *cognitively* non-equivalent. The representation of where one should reach in order to touch something is different from the representation of where the source of the sound is; thus, it is unclear how newly sighted people know where to turn or reach when they see a flash of light.

Secondly, the Behavioural Space view cannot account for the formation of isotropic images. Behavioural space is the body's representation of space for the purposes of actions such as reaching or grasping. Such representations are egocentric. To reach for a dog's collar, for example, I must know where it is relative to my hand at the moment of reaching. Now suppose that this was the primary representation of the dog-collar's spatial position—that is, where it is relative to my hand. Then, it would not be possible *directly* to register that the dog and its collar had retained its position relative to my hand while both had moved, for any such perception of motion would have to track both the hand and the book against a space within which behaviour occurs. Yet this is exactly how isotropic images are formed. To form such an image of a large three-dimensional object such as a house, I have to walk around it, keeping track of how I move and how the house looks as I move.

Evans was well aware of isotropic representations. He quotes Pierre Villey, 'a blind Montaigne scholar who was evidently riled by the suggestion that the blind did not have genuine spatial concepts.' Villey wrote:

> If, an hour after feeling it, I search in my consciousness for the memory of the vanished chair...I do not reconstruct it by means of fragmentary and successive images. It appears immediately and as a whole in its essential parts.... There is no procession, even rapid, of representations....I couldn't tell in what order the parts were perceived by me. (Quoted by Evans, 369)

Yet images from any one point of view, including motor representations, are perspective dependent. If you remove the framework space in which both point of view and changes of point of view can be represented, it is hard to see how Villey's representation could be possible. It is ironic that Evans, who emphasizes so strongly the wrongness of Diderot's thesis, falls into exactly the same quandary.

5.3. THE PRE-MODAL SPACE VIEW: MULTIMODAL INTEGRATION

Active perception is an activity that involves the coordinated use of all the different senses. And it enables us, in an instinctive and largely untutored way, to arrive at increasingly isotropic models of the world outside the mind. The coordination of both process and product argue for a level of integration among modality-specific representations of space that the Privileged Modality view cannot accommodate. The Behavioural Space view attempts to fill this lacuna by making the representation of space extra-modal. The virtue of this view is that it embraces a common measure of space across modality-specific perceptions. However, it does so by adding one more representation of space into the mix. It is unclear how this is different from positing a new privileged modality. Moreover, the egocentricity of perceptual representations of space that this view implies results in a fragmentation and temporalization of perceptual models. The only way to accommodate isotropic multimodal images is to posit a pre-modal representation of space.

I conclude with a brief discussion of some main elements of a pre-modal view of the perceptual representation of space.

6. The Pre-Modal View

Think of an old car. You are looking at it as your friend starts it up. When the engine comes to life, you hear the rumbling noise; you can see and hear the hood vibrate; when you touch it, you can feel the vibration; as the engine warms up, you pick up the faint odour of motor oil. All of these events are sensed as localized in the same region: the sound is perceived as coming from the car, even the smell, if you move around and sniff. (Think of a garage full of cars: the enclosed space smells of oil, but you are told that only one of the cars is leaking oil. Can you find it by moving around and sniffing?)

In the pre-modal view, there is a representation of space that underlies the location of these sensory qualities: a three-dimensional matrix that is able to receive features regardless of modality. As each sense provides the active perception system with information, features are pasted onto locations in this matrix. To a static observer using only one sense, the locations are egocentrically identified. If, for example, you are looking at something from a stationary perspective, you will have information about how visual features are distributed in space, relative to your eyes. The use of the other senses, even from this fixed observation post, provides information that is somewhat more perspective-independent. Touch, for example, provides information relative to parts of the body other than the eyes. Haptic features such as warmth or vibration are felt by the hands, but are nevertheless referred to the thing that you see yourself touching. (Think of the rubber hand illusion: the feeling of being stroked by a brush is referred to the rubber hand that you see, not to your own hand, which is being stroked and is the origin of the sensation.) Movement increases the perspectival independence of the perceptual model. You discover previously hidden features, which are then incorporated into your mental image. In the limit, your perceptual model is of a rigid solid replete with sense-features. The underlying representation of space enables the construction of this model.

The pre-modal view of space can be likened to the representation of space in a touch screen device. You touch a visual icon on your smartphone and it reacts appropriately. It does not do this by cross-identifying the representation of space that governs its icon placement with the representation that locates your pressure on a part of the screen. Rather it has a single underlying representation of space relative to which the touch and the icon are both located. When it detects your touch, it looks up what icon occupies that same location. Multimodal scenes are constructed in a similarly pre-modal manner.

There are two sources for the construction of an isotropic scene: the features detected by each sense and the spatial matrix in which they are placed. By analogy with the smartphone touchscreen, the latter is not provided by the senses. Rather, as Kant realized, it is a pre-modal framework needed for the spatial coding of perceived models. Of course, the senses provide enough spatial information to determine, for example, whether one thing is to the left or the right of another. But the pre-existing model regiments such information. For instance, although auditory spatial information is much coarser in grain than visual information, sounds are precisely located in things that appear to be emitting them. (For instance, vaguely located voices are precisely located in a moving mouth, as in the Ventriloquist Illusion.) And where touch and vision give information about the same thing, the information is reconciled, giving due weight to the reliability of each in the situation being examined. (See, for example, Ernst and Banks 2002; Millar and Al Attar 2005). Perceived spatial relations will, therefore, have an *a posteriori* component. Kant's insight, however, was that every spatial relation has an *a priori* component that depends on the structure of the underlying matrix.

The pre-modal view faces a difficulty that we cannot fully resolve here—the apparent incongruity of spatial relations in bodily sense and the external senses. As mentioned earlier, I may feel a pinprick in my finger and observe visually that my finger is in front of the TV without feeling the pinprick in front of the TV. Two observations will, however, help to suggest a fruitful approach to this question. The first observation is that although the bodily sense locates feelings in a body scheme—that is, these feelings are felt to be located in parts of the body—it is nevertheless the case that subjects have a sense of how parts of the body are located relative to external things. The second observation is that there is a certain incoherence of spatiality within the body sense itself. For instance, as Ned Block (1983) has observed, I may feel a pain in my thumb and feel that my thumb is in my mouth without feeling the pain in my mouth. The second observation suggests that the body sense has a special and separate sense of space, one that is located *only* relative to body parts, and which does not carry information about the location of these body parts relative to other things (including other body parts). The first observation suggests that though the special spatial framework of the body sense is not fully integrated into the pre-modal representation of space, the bodily sense also participates in pre-modal sense. For instance, it is possible to sense whether the index fingertip of your raised right hand is higher or lower than your nose. Thus, it might be that feelings such as itches and pains are localized only relative to body parts, but that body parts themselves are localized relative to the external objects of vision, and so on. However this may be, the safest course here is to allow that the bodily spatial sense is somewhat anomalous and may at best partially and imperfectly participate in the pre-modal representation of space.

7. Conclusion

The traditional notion is that we perceive space through sensory information. It was, and still is, thought, for example, that spatial information is contained in the biretinal and the binaural images. This conception of spatial perception is unable to account for the construction of isotropic multimodal models in active perception. It is often said that active perception uses cognitive resources far in excess of the sensory process alone. And this is undoubtedly true, even on a very capacious view of the sensory process. Nevertheless, the system must coordinate the spatial images that each modality provides in order both to control action and to construct isotropic models—each modality-specific sensory image needs to be coded in a way that allows it to be collated with every other. The Privileged Modality view and the Behavioural Space view offer inadequate accounts of this process. What is needed is much more like the coding used in a touchscreen: a pre-existent spatial representation that provides a coordinate space for the placement of features from all of the modalities. Kant's view that space and time are *a priori* intuitions conceives of space and time in much this way—that is, as common measures of information received by the different modalities. The perceptual representation of space is not, as he clearly saw, proprietary to any one modality, and it is not behavioural space.

References

Block, Ned (1983) "Mental Pictures and Cognitive Science," *Philosophical Review* 92: 499–541.

Botvinick, Matthew and Cohen, Jonathan (1998) "Rubber Hands 'Feel' Touch That Eyes See," *Nature* 391: 756.

Eagleman, David M. (2009) "Brain Time," in M. Brockman (ed.), *What's Next? Dispatches on the Future of Science: Original Essays from a New Generation of Scientists.* New York: Vintage: 155–169.

Eagleman, David M. (2010) "How Does the Timing of Neural Signals Map onto the Timing of Perception?" in R. Nijhawan and B. Khurana (eds.), *Space and Time in Perception and Action.* Cambridge: Cambridge University Press: 216–230.

Ernst, Marc O. and Banks, Martin S. (2002) "Humans Integrate Visual and Haptic Shape Information in Statistically Optimal Fashion," *Nature* 415: 429–433.

Evans, Gareth (1985) "Molyneux's Question," in A. Phillips (ed.), Gareth Evans, *Collected Papers.* Oxford: Clarendon Press: 364–399.

Freud, S. (1899) Screen Memories. *Standard Edition,* 3: 301–322. London: Hogarth Press.

Gibson, J. J. (1962) "Observations on Active Touch," *Psychological Review* 69: 477–491.

Held, R., Ostrovsky, Y., deGelder, B., Gandhi, T., Ganesh, S., Mathur, U., and Sinha, P. (2011) "Newly Sighted Cannot Match Seen with Felt," *Nature Neuroscience* 14: 551–553.

Hopkins, Robert (2005) "Molyneux's Question," *Canadian Journal of Philosophy* 35: 441–464.

Hoover, Adria E. N. and Harris, Laurence R. (2012) "Detecting Delay in the Visual Feedback of an Action as a Monitor of Self-Recognition," *Experimental Brain Research* 222: 389–397.

Husserl, Edmund (1905/1964) *The Phenomenology of Internal Time-Consciousness*, M. Heidegger (ed.) and J. S. Churchill (trans.). Bloomington: Indiana University Press.

Harrar, Vanessa and Harris, Laurence R. (2008) "Effect of Exposure to Asynchronous Audio, Visual, and Tactile Stimulus Combinations on the Perception of Simultaneity," *Experimental Brain Research* 186: 517–524.

Izmailov, Ch. A and Sokolow, E. N. (1991) "Spherical Model of Color and Brightness Discrimination," *Psychological Science* 2: 249–259.

James, William (1890) *The Principles of Psychology.* New York: H. Holt.

Kappers, A. M. and Koenderink, J. J. (1999) "Haptic Perception of Spatial Relations," *Perception* 28: 781–796.

Kosslyn, S. M. (1980) *Image and Mind.* Cambridge, MA: Harvard University Press.

Locke, Don (1971) *Memory.* London: Macmillan.

Nigro, Georgia and Neisser, Ulric (1983) "Point of View in Personal Memories," *Cognitive Psychology* 15: 467–482.

Mackie, John (1976) *Problems from Locke.* Oxford: Clarendon Press.

Matthen, Mohan (2010a) "The Sensory Representation of Color," in J. Cohen and M. Matthen (eds.), *Color Science and Color Ontology.* Cambridge, MA: MIT Press, 2010: 67–90.

Matthen, Mohan (2010b) "Is Memory Preservation?" *Philosophical Studies* 148: 3–14.

Matthen, Mohan (2014) "How to Be Certain: Sensory Exploration and Empirical Certainty," *Philosophy and Phenomenological Research* 87: 38–69. DOI: 10.1111/j.1933-1592.2011.0054 8.x.

Millar, Susanna and Al Attar, Zainab (2005) "What Aspects of Vision Facilitate Haptic Processing?" *Brain and Cognition* 59: 258–268.

Millar, Susanna (2008) *Space and Sense.* Hove, England: Psychology Press.

Morgan, Michael J. (1977) *Molyneux's Question: Vision, Touch, and the Philosophy of Perception.* Cambridge: Cambridge University Press.

Peacocke, C. (1983) *Sense and Content: Experience, Thought and Their Relations.* New York: Oxford University Press.

Phillips, Ian B. (2008) "Perceiving Temporal Properties," *European Journal of Philosophy* 18: 176–202.

Phillips, Ian B. (forthcoming) "The Temporal Structure of Experience," in D. Lloyd and V. Arstila (eds.), *Subjective Time: the Philosophy, Psychology, and Neuroscience of Temporality.* Cambridge MA: MIT Press.

Pitcher, George (1971) *A Theory of Perception.* Princeton, NJ: Princeton University Press.

Sassen, Brigitte (2004) "Kant on Molyneux's Problem," *British Journal for the History of Philosophy* 12: 471–485.

Shepard, R. N. and Metzler, J. (1971) "Mental Rotation of Three-Dimensional Objects," *Science* 171: 701–703.

Siegel, Susanna (2006) "Subject and Object in the Contents of Visual Experience," *Philosophical Review* 115: 355–388.

Taylor, Charles (1979) "The Validity of Transcendental Arguments," 79: 151–165.

Tulving, E. (1985) "Memory and Consciousness," *Canadian Journal of Psychology* 26: 1–12.

van Wassenhove, V., Grant, K. W., and Poeppel, D. (2007) "Temporal Window of Integration in Auditory-Visual Speech Perception," *Neuropsychologia* 45: 598–607.

Villey, Pierre (1922) *The World of the Blind.* London: Simpkin, Marshall, Hamilton, Kent.

Williams, Bernard (1966/1973) "Imagination and the Self," British Academy Annual Philosophical Lecture, 1966, published (1973) in Williams, *Problems of the Self.* Cambridge: Cambridge University Press.

Wittman, Marc (2009) "The Inner Experience of Time," *Proceedings of the Royal Society B* 364: 1955–1967.

3

Distinguishing Top-Down from Bottom-Up Effects
Nicholas Shea

1. Introduction

The distinction between top-down and bottom-up effects plays a central role in experimental psychology. But there is a problem with the way it is standardly drawn. Even if there were a completely Fodorian perceptual module, fully encapsulated against the effects of any beliefs, desires, or other representational states found elsewhere in the psychological architecture, it would still rely on its own pre-existing store of information. After all, the idea of a Fodorian module, as opposed to a mere reflex, is of a genuine information processing system, one in which the transitions between representations within the module embody or encode information that is appropriate to the circumstances in which it operates. A visual module that uses a contrast map to calculate the edges of objects embodies the information that contrast boundaries are a reasonably reliable sign of edges. These inbuilt expectations, implicit in the operation of the module itself, are rightly not considered to be top-down effects. Yet they exemplify the impact of pre-existing information in the system on the operation of a perceptual process. If the question of the relative influence of top-down information is to be well posed, we need to show that the top-down influence of antecedent information can be distinguished from the proprietary information embodied in a module.

The purpose of this chapter is to say something constructive—although by no means conclusive—about how top-down effects on the operation of a psychological process should be distinguished from the influence of the information implicit in the operation of the process. So formulated, the distinction between top-down and bottom-up effects can be put to philosophical work. It allows us to ask, for any psychological mechanism, how much its operation is driven by current input and to what extent it is influenced by prior information. Answering that question will form an important part of spelling out how sensory information is processed. It also provides a basis for asking epistemological questions about the relations between sensory systems and the world, relations amongst sensory systems, and their relations to other psychological capacities. These issues also arise in the phil-osophical literature on the cognitive penetrability of perception by cognition. The top-down versus bottom-up distinction allows us to pose some of those questions more generally, not just about paradigmatically perceptual states. So the distinc-tion would allow some of the concerns in the cognitive penetrability debate to be preserved, even if a distinctive category of the perceptual turned out to be theo-retically unsustainable.

Section 2 introduces the top-down/bottom-up distinction and sets up the prob-lem. Section 3 uses the distinction between explicit and implicit representations to address the problem. Section 4 shows that, even if it is problematic to think that there is a distinctive category of the perceptual, the top-down/bottom up dis-tinction is suited to characterising some philosophical issues about the balance between current input and pre-existing information that arise in the cognitive penetrability literature.

2. Top-Down versus Bottom-Up

A central concern about the senses is to understand the extent to which a process that uses current input to track current and potentially changing features of the immediate environment is also influenced by antecedently represented informa-tion. In scientific psychology that question is approached by asking to what extent a psychological process is driven by top-down as opposed to bottom-up informa-tion. Here is how it is usually presented in standard psychology texts:

> Bottom-up processing is processing which depends directly on external stimuli, whereas top-down processing is processing which is influenced by expectations, stored knowledge, context and so on. (Eysenck, 1998, p. 152)
>
> In bottom-up processing (also called data-driven or stimulus-driven pro-cessing), the process starts with the features—the bits and pieces—of the stimulus, beginning with the image that falls on the retina. This information is processed hierarchically by successively higher levels of the visual system until the highest levels (the 'top' of the system) are reached, and the object is perceived. Top-down processing (also called knowledge-driven processing) involves the use of contextual information supplied from memory—the 'big picture'. (Carlson et al., 2010, p. 202)

The first quotation brings out the essential difference between information directly drawn from a stimulus and information that already exists in the system. The sec-ond quotation illuminates why the metaphors of 'bottom' and 'top' are used—they come from an assumed hierarchy of information processing. To the extent that antecedently stored information has an effect on processing, it is assumed to derive from higher levels in this hierarchy. That gloss is subsidiary. The core is the distinction between incoming and pre-existing information.

Two other connotations of the term should be set aside. First, especially in cognitive neuroscience, top-down is sometimes understood in neural terms. Top-down effects are those that proceed causally from 'higher' to 'lower' neural areas (Mechelli et al., 2003) where there is a pre-existing conception of which brain areas are higher and which lower in the hierarchy (very approximately: moving forward from the back of the brain, with the prefrontal cortex at the top of the hierarchy, but with the motor cortex somewhat anomalous in that it lies behind the prefrontal cortex but comes later in information processing and is more closely tied to the periphery than prefrontal, and most temporal and parietal areas).

The distinction is not at base a neural one. The difference between higher and lower neural areas itself derives from a rough model of where various areas fall in an information processing hierarchy. Visual information proceeds from the retina, through the lateral geniculate nucleus and is first processed cortically in the occipital lobe. Visual information then flows through a hierarchy of visual areas in the occipital cortex before spreading to the temporal lobe and the parietal lobe (usually thought to occur in parallel, in ventral and dorsal visual streams). It may then be used directly to drive the motor cortex and drive action (in a sensorimotor loop), but that process may be controlled or modulated by information processing in the prefrontal cortex at the top of the hierarchy. There are lots of places to object to this parody of the hierarchy of information processing in the brain, but something like this underlies the idea, to take one example, that connections from prefrontal or parietal cortex to the occipital lobe carry top-down information. The categorisation of a neural area as higher or lower derives from the information processing hierarchy in which it is located. So the neural distinctions are not constitutive of, but merely evidence of, the difference between top-down and bottom-up effects.

A second connotation is that top-down influences are voluntary, or derive from the self, the will, or the all-purpose homunculus that is sometimes hidden behind the label 'executive control'. That gloss is not important for our purposes here, so I will set it aside—top-down effects need not emanate from some special locus of endogenous or voluntary control, if indeed there is such an entity, which is doubtful.

The distinction we focus on here is drawn in terms of causal effects of prior representations, but not all causal effects are relevant: only those that occur within information processing. A prior belief might causally influence perceptual processing by causing a subject to move her eyes, thus changing the input. Then visual processing would have been 'influenced by stored knowledge', but not in the way psychologists were thinking of. Their concern is with cases where prior representations have a representational influence on the processing of input—with influences that occur computationally, that is to say, either directly, or via a chain of other representations.[1] Causal influences mediated by the world do not count.[2]

---

[1] That is to understand computation in a broad sense, not restricted to classical computation.
[2] Thanks to James Stazicker for pressing me to make this explicit.

The psychologists' distinction between top-down and bottom-up effects can be used to frame two philosophical questions about any psychological process. Firstly, in characterising a psychological process (for example here, a sensory process), we can ask how much the process is driven by incoming information from external stimuli, and how much it is affected by antecedent representations that were already in place before the stimulus was encountered. Secondly, there is an epistemological question. We can ask how the outcome of any piece of processing M1 is suitable for belief formation or any other piece of subsequent processing M2, if antecedent representations in M2 have affected the output of M1. It is not just the effect of cognition on perception that raises the risk that we may be illegitimately pulling ourselves up by our own epistemic bootstraps. Any kind of circular relations between earlier and later processing raises questions about the reliability of the process (Lyons, 2011). There are many other potential sources of unreliability, of course, including the effects of stored expectations on input as just noted, but top-down influences are a central and unified category to investigate. An appropriate account of the epistemic profile of a sensory process—its sensitivity, specificity, and positive and negative predictive value—will be heavily dependent upon the extent to which there are top-down as well as bottom-up influences on that process.

That is not to say that top-down influences are necessarily epistemically pernicious. On Karl Friston's comprehensive model of the brain, feedforward signals consist only of prediction errors (Friston, 2010; Friston & Stephan, 2007). It is the top-down signals that represent what is the case. In this way, top-down signals directly affect, or even constitute, what you represent, but without creating a self-reinforcing cycle, because it is not the result of these predictions that is fed forward as input to subsequent processing, but only the difference between prediction and current input.[3] Similarly, in the closely related Bayesian models of neural processing, priors (antecedent representations) strongly constrain the way incoming information is processed (and hence what is perceived), but because of Bayesian updating, the priors don't just end up confirming themselves in a cascade of illusory justification; they are gradually updated in the direction of the incoming evidence. Of course, false priors can compromise veridical perception, and if you start with very bad priors you can end up misperceiving for a very long time. But that is not enough to show that the influence of prior representations on what you perceive violates an epistemic norm. Indeed, Bayesians think that reaching hypotheses about what is the case by combining antecedent beliefs with incoming information via a Bayesian updating rule constitutes compliance with an epistemic norm.

It is not only on Friston's model that top-down influences are seen to be epistemically acceptable. In general, the question of how top-down influences affect

---

[3] Structurally the same point is true of the interplay between feedforward and feedback processing in Eliasmith and Anderson's control-theoretical model of the brain (Eliasmith & Anderson, 2003).

the reliability of a psychological process should be considered case-by-case, in the light of an assessment of what the top-down effects are and how they operate. Some top-down influences, including from background beliefs, may be helpful in narrowing the range of expected stimuli or changing the priors about what is likely to be encountered, in a way that increases detectability, discriminability, or processing speed. Others may reduce the reliability with which features of the world are represented, especially in novel contexts. The impact on reliability will also depend on the kinds of environments in which the psychological process operates. In short, although the influence of top-down effects on the online processing of current input need not in principle be epistemically pernicious, whether it is in fact remains an important question that can only be properly answered in the light of knowing how bottom-up and top-down information combine to drive the information processing involved. Furthermore, a normative account of the epistemic relations between various representational states should be informed by the way that top-down and bottom-up information are in fact balanced by the actual psychological systems in question.

So the psychologists' category of top-down effects is well-suited to formulating some central philosophical concerns about sensory and other psychological systems. There is a problem, however, with the psychological distinction. Top-down effects are defined as influences of an individual's expectations, goals, and stored knowledge (Eysenck, 1998, p. 152). On the face of it, that includes the expectations that are implicit in the operation of a psychological process—in its dispositions to transition from one representation to another. Perceptual learning, for instance, affects the way processing within a perceptual module is disposed to unfold (Fahle & Poggio, 2002). As a result of perceptual learning, the system will process input in a different way. The new transitions it is disposed to make will embody a different set of expectations. But the process does not do so by drawing on a separate source of information antecedently represented elsewhere. Indeed, the information implicit in the operation of a perceptual process, resulting from perceptual learning, is not explicitly represented anywhere.

For example, the ability to discriminate visual gratings with different luminance distributions improves with experience, but the effect does not transfer between vertical and horizontal gratings, suggesting that changes relatively early in visual processing are responsible for the improvement (Fiorentini & Berardi, 1980). Similar effects are found in many other domains such as visual acuity (Fahle, Edelman, & Poggio, 1995) and discriminating the direction of visual movement (Watanabe, Nanez, & Sasaki, 2001). Neuroimaging results suggest that the plasticity responsible for some of these changes occurs within the neural areas that carry out the early stages of processing (Maertens & Pollmann, 2005). Neurophysiology confirms that some of the changes in processing categorised as visual adaptation, on shorter timescales up to a few minutes, are due to changes within, rather than influences on, the processes constituting early sensory processing (Kohn, 2007). Information processing models show how such effects can be achieved by changes to the way a psychological process is disposed to transition between various representational states (Poggio, Fahle, & Edelman, 1992).

These kinds of changes in the online processing dispositions of a psychological process do not only occur within low level perceptual processes. Another large class of results concerns sensorimotor learning. Rather than asking subjects to make a perceptual discrimination that is reported in some unnatural manner, like pressing a button, sensorimotor experiments are more dynamic, requiring subjects to mediate between stimulus and action in a fluid way (like visually guided reaching for a potentially moving target). These sensorimotor loops also undergo rapid adaptation or tuning in the light of experience (Mazzoni & Krakauer, 2006), often mediated by primary sensory or motor cortices, or the cerebellum (D'Angelo & De Zeeuw, 2009). A sensorimotor loop, consisting of a set of dispositions to connect perceptual input with motor behaviour, can be tuned by experience through modifying those dispositions via synaptic plasticity, without that being mediated by the effect of some separate explicit representation on the system (De Zeeuw et al., 2011).

By contrast, in other cases there is evidence that relatively early cortical systems processing sensory input are affected by information antecedently represented beyond those systems (Di Lollo, Enns, & Rensink, 2000; Summerfield & Koechlin, 2008; Ulzen et al., 2008)—although the empirical evidence is still unfolding. Of course, it is by no means settled that all, or even any, of the effects described in the large literatures on perceptual learning and sensorimotor adaptation are definitely the result of changes to the dispositions embodied in a psychological process, rather than being mediated by influences from other parts of the system. But the important thing for our purposes is that these debates are coherent. The question asked in the perceptual learning literature is whether a piece of perceptual learning consists merely in a modification in the dispositions to respond bottom-up to stimuli, or whether instead it depends upon top-down influences. For that question to be well posed, the contrast must reflect a genuine distinction. The problem is that such cases fall within the letter of the psychological definition of top-down effects, while falling outside the spirit that the distinction is aiming to capture. That would spell trouble for placing reliance on the top-down/bottom-up distinction to formulate philosophical questions, unless the distinction can be clarified to exclude these cases in a principled way.

3. Explicit versus Implicit

To recap: to make it legitimate to appeal to the top-down/bottom-up distinction for our philosophical purposes, we need to show that the top-down influence of antecedent representations can be distinguished from the effect of information that is implicit in the set of inferential dispositions embodied in a psychological process.[4] There is an obvious way of drawing that distinction, which doesn't quite work, but can be turned into a tenable solution.

The obvious distinction is between the occurrent and dispositional senses of representation. When beliefs, desires, or other mental states affect the processing of sensory information, they are occurrent, and their being tokened is necessary for there to be an effect on sensory processing. By contrast, the information embodied within a perceptual module or other piece of psychological processing exists in virtue of dispositions—the disposition of the process to move from certain representational states to others (e.g., from such-and-such arrangement of visual contrast to representations of edges). Can't we just say that top-down effects occur only when *occurrently represented* pre-existing expectations, beliefs, memories, and so on influence the way incoming information is processed?

Not quite, because of a difficulty with construing the occurrent/dispositional contrast. A representation becomes occurrent when it is tokened—when there is a physical change such that an instance of that representation type is realised in such a way that it can have a causal influence on subsequent psychological processing. The difficulty arises because there is, of course, a causal basis for perceptual learning, sensorimotor adaptation, and so on. In general, the dispositions that a psychological process has, to transition between certain types of representational states, will have a physical basis. When those dispositions change, it is because the physical basis changes. Since it is legitimate to think of those dispositions as embodying expectations or containing information, the causal basis of the disposition is the causal basis of the storage of that information. That furnishes a sense in which the causal basis of this apparently dispositional information is actually being tokened all the while the agent possesses the disposition, and is causally efficacious when the disposition is manifested. That does not imply that there is a representation with that information as its content. But it does show that we need to do more than simply rely on the difference between tokened information and mere dispositions.

Fortunately, there is a relatively straightforward way to sidestep this difficulty. We can make use of one final distinction: between implicit and explicit representations. These labels are used to mark many different contrasts (e.g., conscious vs. unconscious, verbally reportable vs. not), but there is a rather tightly delineable sense that will serve our purposes. The expectations or information embodied in the dispositions of a psychological process to transition from one representation to another are implicit, in the sense that they can have no impact on subsequent processing except via the representations they connect. An explicit

---

[4] I use 'inference' here widely to include all transitions between representations (e.g., abductions, approximations) that broadly make sense in the light of their semantic content (cf. Pylyshyn, 1999, p. 365, note 3, who preserves 'inference' for truth preservation and uses 'rational' for the wider category). Such inferences can accordingly take place between nonconceptual representations without propositional structure or any other semantically significant constituent structure.

representation can potentially have an impact on many pieces of downstream processing. Consider, for example, a feedforward system that was disposed to make transitions from a light contrast map to representations of where the edges of objects lie. Those inferential dispositions implicitly encode, inter alia, the information that the edges of objects tend to occur at the spatial locations where discontinuities in contrast levels are found. That information has an effect on subsequent processing, but that influence is wholly in virtue of its effect in producing the representations of edges. By contrast, the representation of the location of edges is an explicit occurrent representation. It can act as input to many different systems: object discrimination, object categorisations, online guidance of reaching, and so on.

One clear illustration of this contrast is in the way information is stored and acted on by a connectionist network. A feedforward connectionist network has a set of dispositions to transition from patterns of distributed activation at its input layer, through patterns of activation at hidden layers, to a pattern of activation at its output layer. The complete set of its dispositions to make transitions between these occurrent representations is fixed by the network's weight matrix. As a result of training, the network can acquire dispositions to transition from input to output that encode information. For example, the network might have a disposition to respond to representations of letters at the input layer by transitioning to a phonetic space at the hidden layer (including a contrast between vowels and consonants), and then onwards to a classification of the input by phonetic features at the output layer (Rumelhart & McClelland, 1986). Those inferential dispositions embody information about relevant statistical patterns in the material on which the network was trained. In that sense, the weight matrix itself encodes information. But that information is not explicit in the weight matrix or in the set of dispositions to move between distributed patterns of activation. The weight matrix only has an effect on downstream processing via the occurrent representations, dispositions to transition between which it underpins. The pattern of activation at the output layer, or a hidden layer, could act as input to many different subsequent pieces of processing. The weight matrix itself is not available to guide processing in that way. The information contained in the weight matrix is effective only in the way that it underpins dispositions to transition between explicit representations, from input through hidden to output layer.

So there is no need to deny that there is a sense in which the information embodied in the disposition to transition between representations in a particular way is itself realised—or tokened—in the causal basis of those dispositions. Rather than trying to argue that these are not occurrent for some reason, we can simply rely on the fact that this information is not explicit. Only explicit representations can act as input to further computations. The information that is implicit in the dispositions embodied in a psychological process cannot act as input to further computations. Its only impact on information processing is through the dispositions it underpins to transition between occurrent representations.

When an early perceptual process learns to discriminate the signs of a luminance boundary more finely, or when a sensorimotor process re-learns a mapping between visual input and motor output, the dispositions to transition between representations at various stages of processing are altered, but without the new information embodied in the process being explicitly represented anywhere, either to drive learning, or as a result of learning. (At least, that is one of the positions that is being argued for in debates about perceptual learning.) So asking whether the influence on psychological processing is merely implicit, or whether it is caused by some explicit representation outside that process, is a good way of distinguishing modifications to a psychological process from top-down effects on the process. The implicit-explicit distinction we have drawn allows us to pick out a coherent category of top-down effects consisting of the influence on processing of pre-existing representations, distinguishing it from perceptual learning, sensorimotor adaptation, and the like.

To summarise, I would argue for using terms as follows:

Occurrent representation The tokening of a representation, that is, its realisation in such a way that it can have a causal impact on psychological processing.

Implicit representation A disposition to transition between two or more occurrent representations that can have no influence on subsequent processing except via the representations between which the disposition subsists.

Explicit representation Occurrent representation that is not implicit.

Top-down influence A representationally mediated effect of an explicit representation R on a psychological process, where R is not computed more directly than the representational influence of current sensory input on the process.

Bottom-up influence An effect on the outcome of a psychological process that is not a top-down influence.

This way of clarifying the use of terms does not clear up all difficulties, of course. In particular, I use a distinction between more and less direct computational routes, which could profitably be clarified further. But progress has been made: we have replaced the problematic distinction between the perceptual and the cognitive with a collection of better-understood psychological properties. Once we set aside representations that are merely implicit in dispositions to transition between various occurrent representations, the cash value of the distinction between top-down and bottom-up influences is a matter of directness of computational influence. For any psychological process whose output is relatively directly influenced by current sensory input we can ask whether the output is also affected by more indirect routes: either by antecedent representations whose tokening is not caused by the current stimulus, or by representations whose connection to current sensory input is more indirect than the influence of sensory input on the process itself. Relative extent of top-down and bottom-up influence will certainly be a matter of degree. Furthermore, whether an effect counts as top-down at all may also be a matter of degree, if the relative directness of the influence of sensory input on a psychological process is a matter of degree. But graded distinctions are tractable here, provided it is reasonably clear what the gradations depend upon.

The top-down/bottom-up distinction has other merits. It admits of top-down effects of one sensory process on another, as well as top-down effects of beliefs and desires on sensory processing. It also admits of top-down effects within a perceptual modality (e.g., the effects within vision endorsed by Pylyshyn, 1999). Epistemic questions arise whenever the processing of sensory input is constrained by pre-existing representations, even when those representations derive from processing of the same stimulus some milliseconds earlier. A related merit is that the distinction does not require a strict hierarchy of information processing (*pace* the metaphorical use of 'top' and 'bottom'). The relations between psychological processes may be overlapping, parallel and, intertwined in complex ways, but we can still in principle ask about the relative directness of two routes of influence on a given process. Furthermore, the distinction fits with the existence of 'vertical' sensorimotor loops that directly mediate between sensory input and motor output in a dynamic, continually adjusting way. The influence of beliefs, desires, or other antecedent representations in modulating the targets for or other properties of these sensorimotor loops fits within our framework—it would be counted as a top-down effect. In short, the top-down/bottom-up distinction can be drawn in an empirically tractable way that bypasses the objection we raised at the outset.

4. The Perception-Cognition Distinction

We have argued so far that the top-down/bottom-up distinction, when properly drawn, is a useful way to formulate important questions about the relative influence of incoming and pre-existing information on the operation of any psychological process. That is one of the issues at the heart of the philosophical literature on 'cognitive penetrability'—where it is formulated as the question of whether cognitive contents directly affect perceptual processes. Siegel defines the cognitive penetrability of visual perception as the nomological possibility that cognitive or affective states can cause a change in the visual contents that are or would be experienced while seeing and attending to the same distal stimuli under the same external conditions (Siegel, 2012, pp. 5–6; see also Pylyshyn, 1999).[5]

Two issues from the cognitive penetrability literature correspond to the questions we discussed earlier. First, it is thought to be central to an adequate characterisation

---

[5] For the case of desire rather than belief's (2012) *orectic penetration hypothesis* is the claim that desires or other desire-like cognitive states causally influence perceptual states via an internal mechanism.

of perceptual experience to identify the extent to which it is, or can be, penetrated by the contents of belief, desire, expectation, or other doxastic states. That is the correlate of our more general question as to how much any psychological process is influenced by pre-existing information explicitly represented in any other psychological process.[6] Within the literature on perception, this answers the question, How much is perceiving just a matter of receptivity to the outside world, and how much is it a constructive process based on what we antecedently represent?[7]

Secondly, the cognitive penetrability literature is interested in the epistemological question mentioned previously. If the operation of our senses is systematically affected by what we want or already believe, the epistemological project becomes more challenging. How then can perceptual contents justify beliefs? There is reasonable evidence that such cases occur, yet they make trouble for various accounts of the normative relations between perceptual contents and doxastic states (Siegel, 2012). There are, of course, sources of unreliability other than top-down effects on representational processing. Changing the input by moving the eyes is one example that could easily be epistemically pernicious. However, the psychological category of top-down effects forms a relatively unified collection to investigate and includes many of the results discussed in the literature on cognitive penetration (e.g., effects of beliefs, wishful thinking, fearful thinking, and arguably mood, fatigue, and changes in bodily state like wearing a backpack). Getting clear about these issues will be important for a full understanding of the senses.

Siegel's definition reflects a widely shared assumption in the literature on cognitive penetrability or cognitive penetration, in that it presupposes that there is a theoretically important distinction to be drawn between perception and cognition (Macpherson, 2012; Pylyshyn, 1999; Stokes, 2012). That assumption may be justified given the central role played by the idea of the perceptual in folk psychology. But it has come under pressure, so it would be useful if some of the concerns of those interested in cognitive penetrability could be raised without presupposing that the perceptual forms a distinctive category that differs in theoretically important ways from other forms of psychological processing.

This section sets out some problem cases suggesting that it may be more difficult to individuate the category of the perceptual than has been supposed. The point is not just that where to draw the line is currently unclear; nor just that there are borderline cases; nor that a representation's being perceptual is a matter of degree. Rather, the worry is that the important issues here, especially concerning the relative balance between input and pre-existing representations and the epistemological consequences thereof, arise in just the same way for a range of broadly

---

[6] Pylyshyn (1999) also defines his terms so that top-down effects form a broad category of which cognitive penetration is a proper subset, namely, where an organism's goals and beliefs have a top-down effect on the content of visual perception.

[7] Our formulation also allows us to ask that question about perceptual states that are not conscious or experienced, if there are any.

input-driven systems that are not paradigmatically perceptual. That suggests that there may be little merit in identifying a supposedly special class of perceptual representations and investigating their supposedly proprietary epistemic and processing properties.

It is now well established that cross-modal effects are common: the processing carried out by a single perceptual system is affected by information garnered by more than one sensory apparatus (Spence & Driver, 2004). For example, the perceived direction of motion of sounds is affected by information presented to the eyes (Soto-Faraco, Spence, & Kingstone, 2004). Less surprisingly, parsing a stream of speech sounds into phonemes is also multimodal, as demonstrated by the well-known McGurk effect (McGurk & MacDonald, 1976). These results put pressure on the idea that there is a parallel array of sensory systems, each with a dedicated sensory apparatus delivering a proprietary kind of information. They displace a naïve picture in which the information presented to the senses is only weighed up and integrated in the course of forming beliefs. However, the fact that some weighing and integration of information occurs at relatively early stages of processing does not on its own undermine the category of the perceptual. A single perceptual process, with apparent unity at the personal level, might take information from a number of different sensory modalities as input—it is a familiar point that the faculties of perception need not align precisely with the physical modalities that collect sensory input.

Other multimodally driven processes are less obviously taking place within a single perceptual modality, and are phenomenologically less like paradigmatic perceptual states. One set of examples is furnished by systems that detect properties that are more 'abstract' than low-level perceptual properties like colour and shape, pitch and timbre. We see an object as a dog, recognise a blob as a face, identify the presence of a particular friend by her voice, see a pattern of motion as biological, and so on. Many of these ways of detecting distal properties can be driven by several different sources of sensory input. These processes may not be entirely insulated against the influence of background information, but neither are they a matter of coming to considered judgements on the basis of everything we believe and perceive. The intense debates in philosophy about whether such properties are properly considered perceptual or cognitive (Hawley & Macpherson, 2011) are not enough to show that there is no fact of the matter about the question. Nor does the existence of borderline cases show that the category of the perceptual can do no useful work. But one possible diagnosis of the difficulty of drawing a line that corrals off the purely perceptual is that any putative way delineating the perceptual fails to capture a class that has sufficiently distinctive properties to play a special explanatory role. Questions that are typically asked about paradigmatically perceptual cases may be answered in similar ways when asked of other kinds of psychological processing.

An even greater challenge is presented by systems that are input-driven but have an amodal phenomenology. An example is the capacity to represent one's own spatial location. People and other animals represent the relative locations of various features of their environment and their own location within that map (Gallistel, 1990). That capacity probably depends in part on an evolutionarily ancient system that is shared at least with rodents, dependent in part on the firing of place cells in the hippocampus (O'Keefe & Burgess, 1996), which stores map-type information about the relative position of objects in the environment, in which the animal uses sensory cues to keep track of its current location (O'Keefe & Nadel, 1978). This system is genuinely amodal, in that it takes as input whichever kinds of sensory information are relevant in the current circumstances. Allocentric location can be updated on the basis of visual cues, olfactory cues, or, in the absence of these, by the animal integrating over its current speed and trajectory. But in other respects, representation of current location is like a perceptual process, in that its outputs are strongly constrained by sensory input and are by no means an all-things-considered judgement based on everything else the animal represents.

A case where we frequently experience the relative encapsulation of an amodal input system is the parsing of grammatical structure. I can hear a garden-path sentence as ungrammatical while at the same time knowing that it is grammatical, perhaps even while knowing how it ought to be parsed (Caplan & Waters, 1999). Granted, the online parsing of a sentence is affected by background knowledge: statistical expectations based on word frequency, anticipations about likely meaning based on semantic knowledge, and other kinds of expectation like scripts and thematic relations. Parsing can be driven by spoken language, sign language, or written language, or a combination of visual and aural cues, and is affected by other perceived aspects of the situation like the emotional context. So it is a process that relies on integrating a large array of different sources of information. Yet it has a fast and mandatory aspect that allows it to produce outputs at odds with our all-things-considered beliefs, which distinguishes it from paradigm cognitive states.

Susan Carey has emphasised another set of examples which she calls the systems of "core cognition" (Carey, 2009). These systems are intermediate between the paradigmatically perceptual and the paradigmatically cognitive. Two of her flagship cases concern numerosity. Carey (2009) marshals an impressive array of evidence for the existence of two different relatively low-level systems that are involved in representing quantities. The first is the object file system, which individuates small arrays of objects in parallel and keeps track of which is which as they move. While the numerosity of these sets is not represented explicitly, numerosity is implicit in the way the system operates: comparing arrays via 1-1 correspondence and keeping track of the addition or subtraction of small numbers of objects from the set. The second is the analogue magnitude system, which is capable of keeping track of the approximate number of items in a large set (Dehaene, 1997).

Carey argues that these processes deserve their own category in the psychological inventory. They are neither clearly perceptual nor clearly cognitive. They operate amodally, on a variety of modal inputs, but the calculations they perform are informationally encapsulated and relatively independent of what is going on in the rest of cognition. Carey argues that representations of agency are also part of "core cognition": when objects move in certain ways it just looks as if they are agents, driven not by external forces but by their own internal goals (think of cartoons of geometric figures moving in agentive ways (Abell, Happe, & Frith, 2000; Csibra et al., 1999)).

Another example on the borderline is in the perception of causation. In Michotte-style experiments (Michotte, 1963) the precise timing of the movement of two circles on a screen can make it appear as if the first hits the second and causes it to move ("launches" it). Introduce a slight delay, and it looks as if the second circle moves off on its own (Scholl & Tremoulet, 2000). The experienced difference between the two settings is input driven and partially encapsulated (e.g., against the knowledge that both are a matter of lights on a computer screen and neither is causal), but it is widely disputed whether a causal relation is something that can be perceived, as opposed to being contributed by cognition (Siegel, 2009).

Some might argue that detection of agency and causation are simply examples of 'high-level' perceptual experience. Other philosophers argue that the contents of genuinely perceptual experience are limited to more 'low-level' features, like colour and location, and pitch and timbre, in which case the agency and causation cases are nonperceptual. Either way, it is reasonably clear that these are not simply cases of belief. There is a contrast to be drawn between agency being represented by one of Carey's systems of core cognition (e.g., with the animated triangles) and having a personal level belief that something is an agent. So if these cases are to be counted as nonperceptual, then the perception-cognition distinction cannot cover all the cases. More seriously, these cases suggest that the range of input systems, on which belief formation eventually relies, is much broader than the paradigmatic examples of perceptual processing suggest. So in the project of characterising how beliefs are based on and justified by the processing of information from the senses, characterising these systems should be just as important. Furthermore, their borderline nature raises the possibility it may be impossible to distinguish them from perceptual states in such a way that the perception-cognition distinction does important explanatory work.

A final example is less familiar. There are many experimental paradigms in which subjects are able to solve a task without having any conscious awareness of how they do it (Dienes & Perner, 2003). Sometimes when subjects learn this kind of task they have no idea at all that they are getting it right; they report a phenomenology of guessing. In other situations subjects report a 'feeling of familiarity'. It turns out that, in those situations, the feeling of familiarity is a good guide as to whether they have learnt to perform the task accurately, but subjects still have no idea at all how they do it (Scott & Dienes, 2008). This feeling of familiarity is an amodal representation, triggered by external stimuli (the subject is familiar with some tasks but not others), and which feeds into downstream processing including verbal report and belief formation, but without itself being readily classifiable as either perceptual or cognitive.

These examples suggest that the range of input-driven psychological processes that produce representations of transitory features of the current environment extends far beyond the paradigmatically perceptual. Other ways of distinguishing the perceptual from the cognitive don't readily solve the problem, either. Perhaps perception is analogue, or obeys a 'picture principle' (that parts of the representation represent parts of the thing represented—Fodor, 2007). Another suggestion is that perceptual representations are iconic, in the sense that they represent in virtue of an isomorphism between representation and represented. Relatedly, it could be that perceptual representations are nonconceptual in the sense that they have no semantically significant constituent structure that represents individuals, properties, or anything else below the level of a complete 'saturated' proposition. A third possibility is that there is a phenomenological distinction between perceptual systems and other forms of processing of input—perhaps that the genuinely perceptual representations are more phenomenologically salient. However, each of these suggestions is highly controversial as being criterial of perceptual experience.[8] In respect of each, it looks to be a substantive rather than straightforwardly definitional question whether perception has that feature. More importantly, none covers all the borderline cases discussed. So if our focus is on explaining the set of input-driven psychological processes through which we gather new information about the world, none of these criteria will serve to count them all as perceptual.

The examples here put pressure on there being any clear personal level philosophical distinction between the perceptual and the cognitive that can do any deep explanatory work. Nor can we appeal to scientific psychology to vindicate the distinction. There it is not relied on as a theoretically important tool. Some psychological processes are indeed paradigmatically perceptual, but there is no clear dividing line between the perceptual and the cognitive, nor a clear continuum that plays any deep theoretical role in experimental psychology. Instead, the rough-and-ready distinction used in psychology is based on a loose assumption that the processing of incoming information takes place hierarchically, in a way that maps onto neural areas, with features that are readily extracted from incoming information being represented in primary sensory cortices, feeding forward to the processing of higher level features, and eventually arriving at the more

---

[8] A different tactic is to suggest that only certain kinds of property are perceptible and then to delineate top-down effects as being the effects of representations of 'higher level' properties that cannot be directly perceived. If that claim is based in the response-dependence of those properties or other features of our actual perceptual apparatus, then it presupposes a characterisation of which psychological processes are perceptual and so would not help for our purposes of drawing a perception-cognition distinction. On the other hand, if it is not a claim made relative to our actual perceptual apparatus, the claim that some physical properties are just not amenable to being perceived is hard to credit. Furthermore, defining top-down and bottom-up in a content-independent way allows us to formulate a substantial question about which kinds of contents have top-down influences.

mysterious central systems of personal-level thought. On no view can that hierarchy be strictly delineated.

It could turn out that the top-down/bottom-up distinction could be used to identify a distinctively 'perceptual' way of processing sensory input, if it should be that some input processes were immune from top-down influences entirely. That would be true, for example, if there were perceptual modules in the strict Fodorian sense. Then the collection of psychological processes that were immune from top-down influences might form a theoretically important class, one to which special epistemological principles apply, say. That result would be a vindication rather than a defeat for the view about the importance of the top-down/ bottom-up distinction advocated here. But it seems unlikely on the current state of the evidence. There are many putative examples of top-down effects even on relatively early processing of sensory input (Di Lollo et al., 2000; Summerfield & Koechlin, 2008; Ulzen et al., 2008). There appear to be many parallel processes at a level, connections across levels, and loops back from later to earlier processing. Even a strict hierarchy of information processing would only support a graded distinction between the more perceptual and more motoric, on the one hand, and the more cognitive, on the other. But when the interrelations between psychological processes are as richly intertwined as they have been found to be, we cannot appeal to psychology to substantiate any more than a rough-and-ready distinction based on how closely a process is tied to sensory inputs.

This rapid canter through the perception-cognition distinction is too brief to establish a positive argument against the distinction. Perhaps one of the ways of formulating it discussed previously will turn out to mark a deep, explanatory important divide. For the purposes of this chapter I just want to motivate the idea that the distinction may be more problematic than commonly supposed. Since the category of the perceptual does not derive strong support from psychology or neuroscience, and may turn out not to mark a theoretically important divide for philosophical purposes, there is merit in reformulating issues from the cognitive penetrability debate in a way that does not take for granted that the perceptual forms a theoretically important category. One merit of the distinction between top-down and bottom-up effects, as clarified in this chapter, is that it allows us to do so. We can simply ask, of any psychological process, To what extent and in which respects is it driven by bottom-up information, and in which by top-down information?

5. Conclusion

The distinction between top-down and bottom-up effects is relied upon widely in psychology and cognitive neuroscience. Its fruitful use in the science suggests that it corresponds to an empirically real distinction. A prima facie problem with the way standard psychological definitions capture the distinction can be overcome by appealing to some reasonably well-understood philosophical resources: the distinctions between occurrent and dispositional representation, implicit and explicit representation, and the contrast between more and less direct computational influences. So clarified, we can ask of any psychological process to what extent and in which ways it is driven by bottom-up information, and in which ways influenced by top-down information. The answer forms an important part of the story of how sensory input is used in psychological processing. It also forms the basis for an epistemological assessment of the output of the process. A further merit is that the top-down versus bottom-up distinction can be applied to any psychological process. Thus, if it turns out that the category of perceptual processes, presupposed by the literature on cognitive penetrability, cannot be individuated in a distinctive way that plays a theoretically important role, some of the issues in the cognitive penetrability debate can still be addressed in terms of the top-down/bottom-up distinction.

Acknowledgments

The author would like to thank Tim Bayne, Martin Davies, Zoltan Dienes, Eric Mandelbaum, Athanasios Raftopoulos, Susanna Siegel, and James Stazicker for discussion and comments on earlier drafts; the audience at 'At the Interface between Perception and Cognition' in Oxford for helpful discussion; and Dustin Stokes, Mohan Matthen, Stephen Biggs, and an anonymous reviewer for Oxford University Press (OUP) for helpful comments on a previous draft. This work was supported by the Wellcome Trust (grant number 086041), the Oxford Martin School, and the John Fell OUP Research Fund.

References

Abell, F., Happe, F., & Frith, U. (2000). Do triangles play tricks? Attribution of mental states to animated shapes in normal and abnormal development. *Cognitive Development, 15*, 1–15.

Caplan, D., & Waters, G. S. (1999). Verbal working memory capacity and language comprehension. *Behavioral and Brain Science, 22*, 114–126.

Carey, S. (2009). *The Origin of Concepts.* Oxford: Oxford University Press.

Carlson, N. R., Miller, H., Heth, C. D., Donahoe, J. W., & Martin, G. N. (2010). *Psychology: The Science of Behavior* (7th [International] ed.). Boston, MA: Allyn & Bacon (Pearson).

Csibra, G., Gergely, G., Bíró, S., Koós, O., & Brockbank, M. (1999). Goal attribution without agency cues: The perception of 'pure reason' in infancy. *Cognition, 72*(3), 237–267.

D'Angelo, E., & De Zeeuw, C. I. (2009). Timing and plasticity in the cerebellum: Focus on the granular layer. *Trends in Neurosciences, 32*(1), 30–40.

De Zeeuw, C. I., Hoebeek, F. E., Bosman, L. W. J., Schonewille, M., Witter, L., & Koekkoek, S. K. (2011). Spatiotemporal firing patterns in the cerebellum. *Nature Reviews Neuroscience, 12*, 327–344.

Dehaene, S. (1997). *The Number Sense.* Oxford: Oxford University Press.

Di Lollo, V., Enns, J. T., & Rensink, R. A. (2000). Competition for consciousness among visual events: The psychophysics of reentrant visual processes. *Journal of Experimental Psychology: General,* 129(4), 481–507.

Dienes, Z., & Perner, J. (2003). Unifying consciousness with explicit knowledge. In A. Cleeremans (Ed.), *The Unity of Consciousness: Binding, Integration, and Dissociation* (pp. 214–232). Oxford: Oxford University Press.

Eliasmith, C., & Anderson, C. H. (2003). *Neural Engineering: Computation, Representation, and Dynamics in Neurobiological Systems.* Cambridge, MA: MIT Press.

Eysenck, M. W. (1998). *Psychology: An Integrated Approach.* Harlow: Addison Wesley Longman.

Fahle, M., Edelman, S., & Poggio, T. (1995). Fast perceptual learning in hyperacuity. *Vision Research,* 35, 3003–3013.

Fahle, M., & Poggio, T. (2002). *Perceptual Learning.* Cambridge, MA: MIT Press.

Fiorentini, A., & Berardi, N. (1980). Perceptual learning specific for orientation and spatial frequency. *Nature,* 287, 43–44.

Fodor, J. (2007). The revenge of the given. In B. P. McLaughlin & J. Cohen (Eds.), *Contemporary Debates in Philosophy of Mind* (pp. 105–116). Oxford: Blackwell.

Friston, K. (2010). The free-energy principle: A unified brain theory? *Nature Reviews Neuroscience,* 11(2), 127–138.

Friston, K., & Stephan, K. E. (2007). Free-energy and the brain. *Synthese,* 159(3), 417–458.

Gallistel, C. R. (1990). *The Organization of Learning.* Cambridge MA: MIT Press.

Hawley, K., & Macpherson, F. (Eds.). (2011). *The Admissible Contents of Experience.* Oxford: Wiley-Blackwell.

Kohn, A. (2007). Visual adaptation: Physiology, mechanisms, and functional benefits. *Journal of Neurophysiology,* 97, 3155–3164.

Lyons, J. (2011). Circularity, reliability, and the cognitive penetrability of perception. *Philosophical Issues,* 21(1), 289–311.

Macpherson, F. (2012). Cognitive penetration of colour experience: Rethinking the issue in light of an indirect mechanism. *Philosophy and Phenomenological Research,* 84(1), 24–62.

Maertens, M., & Pollmann, S. (2005). fMRI reveals a common neural substrate of illusory and real contours in v1 after perceptual learning. *Journal of Cognitive Neuroscience,* 17(10), 1553–1564.

Mazzoni, P., & Krakauer, J. W. (2006). An implicit plan overrides an explicit strategy during visuomotor adaptation. *Journal of Neuroscience,* 26(14), 3642.

McGurk, H., & MacDonald, J. (1976). Hearing lips and seeing voices, *Nature,* 264, 746–748.

Mechelli, A., Price, C. J., Noppeney, U., & Friston, K. J. (2003). A dynamic causal modeling study on category effects: Bottom-up or top-down mediation? *Journal of Cognitive Neuroscience,* 15(7), 925–934.

Michotte, A. (1963). *The Perception of Causality.* Oxford: Basic Books.

O'Keefe, J., & Burgess, N. (1996). Geometric determinants of the place fields of hippocampal neurons. *Nature,* 381(6581), 425–428.

O'Keefe, J., & Nadel, L. (1978). *The Hippocampus as a Cognitive Map.* Oxford: Clarendon Press.

Poggio, T., Fahle, M., & Edelman, S. (1992). Fast perceptual learning in visual hyperacuity. *Science,* 256, 1018–1021.

Pylyshyn, Z. (1999). Is vision continuous with cognition? The case for cognitive impenetrability of visual perception. *Behavioural and Brain Sciences, 22*, 341–423.

Rumelhart, D., & McClelland, J. (1986). On learning the past tenses of English verbs. In J. McClelland (Ed.), *Parallel Distributed Processing: Explorations in the Microstructure of Cognition* (Vol. 2). Cambridge, MA: MIT Press.

Scholl, B. J., & Tremoulet, P. D. (2000). Perceptual causality and animacy. *Trends in Cognitive Sciences, 4*(8), 299–309.

Scott, R. B., & Dienes, Z. (2008). The conscious, the unconscious, and familiarity. *Journal of Experimental Psychology: Learning, Memory, and Cognition, 34*(5), 1264.

Siegel, S. (2009). The visual experience of causation. *Philosophical Quarterly, 59*(236), 519–540.

Siegel, S. (2012). Cognitive penetrability and perceptual justification. *Noûs, 46*(2), 201–222.

Soto-Faraco, S., Spence, C., & Kingstone, A. (2004). Cross-modal dynamic capture: Congruency effects in the perception of motion across sensory modalities. *Journal of Experimental Psychology: Human Perception and Performance, 30*(2), 330.

Spence, C., & Driver, J. (2004). *Crossmodal Space and Crossmodal Attention*. New York: Oxford University Press.

Stokes, D. (2012). Perceiving and desiring: A new look at the cognitive penetrability of experience. *Philosophical Studies 158*(3), 479–479.

Summerfield, C., & Koechlin, E. (2008). A neural representation of prior information during perceptual inference. *Neuron, 59*, 336–347.

Ulzen, N. R. van, Semin, G. R., Oudejans, R. R. D., & Beek, P. J. (2008). Affective stimulus properties influence size perception and the Ebbinghaus illusion. *Psychological Research, 72*, 304–310.

Watanabe, T., Nanez, J. E., & Sasaki, Y. (2001). Perceptual learning without perception. *Nature, 413*, 844–848.

PART II

Multimodal Perception

4

Is Consciousness Multisensory?

Charles Spence and Tim Bayne

Glossary

Crossmodal interaction: This term is used to refer to situations in which the presentation of a stimulus in one sensory modality influences the perception/performance of an individual responding to a stimulus presented in a different modality. (Note that we use the term modality as shorthand for sensory modality in the rest of this chapter.) Examples of multisensory integration (later in the chapter) can, then, be thought of as a subset of all crossmodal interactions. One example that may help to highlight this distinction concerns what happens when an alerting sound is presented that makes a person respond to a visual target more rapidly. This effect is crossmodal in the sense that the input from one modality (audition) affects an organism's responsiveness to a stimulus presented in a different modality (vision), but does not necessarily give rise to the integration of the component unisensory signals (hence, it does not qualify as an example of multisensory integration). Indeed, typically an 'alerting' sound should be presented some few hundreds of milliseconds before the visual target in order to obtain the largest behavioural effect. The term 'crossmodal' is also used to describe those attentional effects where the presentation of a stimulus in one modality leads to a shift of spatial attention that gives rise to a facilitation of performance when a target stimulus is subsequently presented in another modality (e.g., see Spence & Driver, 2004, for a review). Once again, these effects occur without positing the need for the multisensory integration of the constituent unisensory signals. That said, we are cognizant of the fact that there is a sense in which if the presentation of a stimulus in one modality impacts an organism's response to another stimulus presented in a different modality, then it might be said that the signals have been 'integrated' in at least some sense of the word.

Multisensory integration: The term, which originated in single-cell neurophysiological studies in the anaesthetised preparation, refers to the neural integration of signals from different sensory modalities (see Stein, Burr, Costantinides, Laurienti, Meredith, Perrault, et al., 2010).

Intersensory: Although this term is used much less frequently than it once was, we believe that preserving it is important to capture the sense of an emergent property, as in the case of intersensory Gestalten (e.g., see Gilbert, 1939), that do not reside in either of the component sensory modalities but only in (or as a result of) their combination (see Spence, Sanabria, & Soto-Faraco, 2007, for a review).

List of Abbreviations

AB Attentional blink
IDs Individual differences
MPO Multisensory perceptual object
MSV Multisensory view
TOJ Temporal order judgment
USV Unisensory view

> Five senses; an incurably abstract intellect; a haphazardly selective memory; a set of preconceptions and assumptions so numerous that I can never examine more than a minority of them—never become conscious of them all. How much of total reality can such an apparatus let through?
> —C. S. Lewis

1. Introduction

Is consciousness multisensory? Obviously it is multisensory in *certain* ways. Human beings typically possess the capacity to have experiences in at least the five familiar sensory modalities, and quite possibly in a number of other less commonly recognised modalities as well. But there are other respects in which it is far from obvious that consciousness is multisensory. This chapter is concerned with one such respect. Our concern here is with whether consciousness contains experiences associated with distinct modalities at the same time. We will describe those who endorse a positive answer to this question as endorsing a *multisensory* view (MSV) of the structure of consciousness, and those who endorse a negative answer to this question as having a *unisensory* view (USV) of the structure of consciousness.

We suspect that folk psychology is strongly committed to the MSV. We also find this commitment in many philosophical and scientific treatments of perceptual awareness. On the philosophical side, discussions of 'the unity of consciousness' typically assume the MSV, for it is often supposed that one of the main challenges facing any account of the unity of consciousness is to explain how contents drawn from *various* modalities are integrated, or bound together, into the subject's overall experiential perspective (e.g., Bayne, 2010; Bayne & Chalmers, 2003; Dainton, 2000; Searle, 2000; Tye, 2003).

On the scientific side, the ubiquity with which one finds references to inter-sensory, multisensory, intermodal, multimodal, polymodal, and/or crossmodal binding in the literature (e.g., Bushara et al., 2002; Pourtois et al., 2000) would also appear to suggest a fairly broad commitment to the MSV. According to Nelson Cowan, "if one is instructed to divide attention between visual and audi-tory channels, and one perceives the printed word 'dog' and the spoken word 'cat,' there should be no difficulty in determining that the two words are semantically related: stimuli that can be consciously perceived simultaneously can be compared to one another" (Cowan, 1995, p. 203). Finally, although discussions of 'the bind-ing problem' tend to focus on the binding of visual features (Crick & Koch, 1992; Revonsuo, 1999; Revonsuo & Newman, 1999), many theorists seem to have implic-itly assumed that features from various modalities can be bound together in con-scious perception.

That said, the multisensory conception of consciousness has not gone unchal-lenged. Writing more than 40 years ago, Ira Bernstein (1970) posed the following question in the title of one of his articles: "Can we see and hear at the same time?" Bernstein's (1970, p. 33) answer was that "we can and we can't". By this, we take him to have meant that although there are crossmodal interactions—for example, the fact that the simultaneous presentation of a sound will speed up a participant's behavioural response to a visual target—a person cannot direct his or her atten-tion to more than a single modality of input at any one time. Bernstein's view was a version of the single channel hypothesis, where each sense is assumed to consti-tute a separate channel (Bernstein, 1970; Regan, 1982). So, although many theorists have implicitly (and occasionally explicitly) endorsed the multisensory concep-tion of consciousness, there is widespread doubt in the psychophysical literature about its tenability, with many theorists apparently attracted to a unisensory con-ception of consciousness (e.g., Gladstones, Regan, & Lee, 1989; Kristofferson, 1967; Zimmerman, 1989). The aim of the present chapter is to take stock of the debate between these two views. In the next section we address the question of precisely how these two conceptions of consciousness might be understood. In the follow-ing sections, we provide a framework for evaluating the debate between these two views and offer some tentative steps toward exploring the relevant evidence.

2. Clarifying the Debate

The debate between the MSV and the USV is really a debate between two general conceptions of the structure of consciousness, and each position can be developed in a number of importantly different ways. In this section, we examine some of the central dimensions along which these two views can vary and we clarify those versions of each view on which we will focus our attention.

Our discussion focuses on four issues: the first concerns the assumption that every perceptual experience can be identified with a particular sensory modality; the second concerns the possibility of individual differences (IDs) in consciousness; the third concerns the relationship between consciousness and attention; and the fourth concerns the impact of the temporal structure of consciousness on how the debate about whether consciousness is multisensory is construed. We take these four issues in turn.

The senses. To determine whether consciousness is unisensory or multisensory, we need to have some way of associating experiences with particular sensory modalities. If it turns out that certain kinds of perceptual experiences cannot be associated with a particular modality, then the question of what it might mean to say that consciousness is—or, as the case may be, is not—multisensory will be obscure at best and indeterminate at worst.

One might think that associating experience with modalities is a straightforward matter, for isn't the experience that one has on looking at a cat a visual experience and the experience that one has on hearing the cat meow an auditory experience? In fact, it turns out that there are a number of reasons to think that associating experiences with particular modalities will often be problematic. For one thing, it may not be possible to associate experiences with sensory modalities without having an account of what distinguishes the various modalities from each other, and there is no such account—at least, none that is uncontroversial (see Macpherson, 2011). Particularly problematic here are questions concerning the individuation of the chemical senses (Auvray & Spence, 2008). Given the inter-relatedness between mechanisms that underpin the perception of taste, smell, oral-somatosensation, trigeminal sensation, and flavour, it is far from clear just how many chemical senses there are, or where exactly the borders between them might lie (e.g., Brillat-Savarin, 1835: McBurney, 1986; Stevenson, 2009; Stevenson & Tomiczek, 2007). Is there a distinct sense with which "flavour" experience might be associated, or are "flavor" experiences inherently multisensory? Here it is also perhaps worth noting that problems associated with the individuation of the senses may also have a developmental component, with some theorists arguing that the experience of neonates is 'monoaesthetic' rather than differentiated into distinct modalities (Bremner, Lewkowicz, & Spence, 2012; Marks & Odgaard, 2005).

Engaging with this issue in any depth would require a (lengthy) discussion of the kind that we simply do not have space to address here. Thus, we will dodge this issue by focusing exclusively on the relationship between the three main spatial senses—audition, vision, and touch. Note that we will treat touch and proprioception as constituting a single sense (see Fulkerson, this volume). Our question is whether neurologically normal adult humans can enjoy experiences associated with more than one of these three modalities at any one time. We will stipulate that advocates of the MSV answer this question in the affirmative whereas advocates of the USV answer it in the negative. Although a defense of this rather restricted version of the USV would clearly fall some way short of a defense of unrestricted versions of the USV, it would still constitute an important result. For one thing, the widespread assumption that multiple modalities can be simultaneously represented in consciousness does not make any special exceptions for the relationship between vision, audition, and touch. Moreover, it is not implausible to suppose that the truth of the restricted form of the USV might provide some—albeit, perhaps, rather limited—support for less restricted versions of the USV.

A second reason to worry that certain experiences cannot be associated with particular modalities derives from reflecting on crossmodal interactions. These interactions are characterised by the fact that the processing of stimuli presented in one modality is influenced by stimuli presented in another modality (see Glossary). For example, in the ventriloquism effect, the apparent source of a spatially discrepant sound source is mislocalised so that it more closely matches the seen source, be it the articulated lips of the ventriloquist's dummy, the sight of a loudspeaker cone, or some other temporally synchronised visual event (Bertelson & de Gelder, 2004). Now, there are two ways in which one might conceive of the experiences that subjects enjoy in the context of crossmodal interactions. According to what we might call the 'purely causal' view, such experiences can be fully identified with particular modalities. For example, in the ventriloquism effect, participants have a purely auditory experience of the sound source and a purely visual experience of the seen object (although these experiences need not be simultaneous). Another view—which we might dub the 'constitutive view'—holds that crossmodal interaction gives rise to experiences that are inherently multisensory (O'Callaghan, 2012). Applied to the ventriloquism case, this account might suggest that the experiences subjects have of the ventriloquised event are neither purely visual nor purely auditory but are in some sense 'audiovisual'.

Again, engaging with the respective merits of the purely causal and constitutive views goes beyond the ambitions of this chapter. We will simply note that although the truth of the constitutive view would entail that there is a sense in which consciousness is multisensory, it would not entail that consciousness is multisensory in the sense that is at issue in the debate between advocates of the MSV and advocates of the USV. When philosophers and psychologists suggest that consciousness is multisensory, what they typically appear to mean is that a subject's overall conscious state can, at a single point in time, include within itself experiences that can be fully identified with particular sensory modalities—i.e., that sense-specific experiences can be co-conscious. At any rate, this is what *we* mean by MSV. This claim is importantly different from the claim that there might be perceptual experiences that are not sense-specific.

Individual differences (IDs): One conception of the debate about whether consciousness is multisensory would associate both the multisensory and unisensory views with (near) absolute conceptions of human experience. In these terms, the advocate of the MSV should be understood to hold that humans—or at least those without significant neurological impairment—*always* have the capacity for multisensory experience, whereas the advocate of the USV should be understood to hold that humans—again, without significant neurological impairment—*never* have the capacity for multisensory experiences. (It is clearly *capacities* that matter here rather than the actual having of multisensory experiences, for a subject might possess the capacity to have multisensory experiences without actually having multisensory experiences, either because they have not been presented with stimuli in more than one modality or because the early sensory areas responsible for processing stimuli in certain modalities have been damaged.)

Although some theorists might accept the characterisation of the two views that has just been given, we think that the debate is best cast in terms of what conscious capacities the majority of neurologically normal individuals possess. We prefer this weaker characterisation of the debate because it takes into account the possibility that there might be IDs with respect to the capacity for multisensory experience. This possibility is not a purely theoretical one but ought to be taken seriously, for there is good evidence of significant IDs with respect to many features of consciousness. In addition to the well-known IDs associated with synaesthesia (Robertson & Sagiv, 2005; see also Rader & Tellegen, 1987), there are robust IDs associated with the capacity for mental imagery (Reisberg, Pearson, & Kosslyn, 2003; Spence & Deroy, 2013); the capacity to identify briefly presented visual stimuli (Cowan, 2000; Cowan et al. 1999; Luck & Vogel 1997); and the capacity to make reliable crossmodal temporal order judgments (TOJs) (Mollon & Perkins, 1996; Spence & Squire, 2003; Smith, 1933; Stone et al., 2001). In light of these findings, it would not be surprising to discover that there are significant IDs with respect to the question of whether consciousness is multisensory (Gilbert, 1939). By taking the debate between the multisensory and unisensory views as a debate about the structure of consciousness in the majority of neurologically normal adult humans, each side can accommodate the possibility of IDs. (Of course, even on this characterisation of the debate there might be no general answer to the question of whether consciousness is multisensory, for it might turn out that neither the MSV nor the USV does justice to the structure of consciousness in the majority of neurologically intact human beings.[1]

Consciousness and attention. The third of the issues on our agenda concerns the relationship between consciousness and attention. The fundamental problem that we face here is that although the debate between advocates of the MSV and advocates of the USV concerns the structure of consciousness, much of the evidence relevant to the debate comes from psychophysics, and the words 'consciousness',

---

[1] A further question is whether the structure of consciousness is invariant even with respect to a particular individual. One way in which intra-individual variation might occur concerns variation across the lifespan. For example, perhaps individuals have multisensory experience as neonates and only later develop unisensory experience (cf. Marks & Odgaard, 2005). A second way in which intra-individual variation might occur involves the transition between distinct 'background states' of consciousness. For example, it is possible that perceptual experience is unisensory in the context of normal waking consciousness but multisensory in the context of (say) delirium or rapid eye-movement (REM) dreaming. We leave the development of these speculations for another occasion.

'awareness', or 'experience' are rarely, if ever, seen in this literature (e.g., see Alais, Morrone, & Burr, 2006; Arrighi, Lunardi, & Burr, 2011). This issue is further clouded by the fact that in many psychophysical studies, the term 'attention' is used as a synonym for 'consciousness'. As Patrick Cavanagh (1998) has noted, scientists have often used the word 'attention', rather than 'consciousness' simply because (until recently, at least) 'consciousness' was not a publically acceptable term.

One way to deal with this problem would be to assume that all and only the contents of consciousness fall within the span of attention. Given this assumption, we could utilise the results of psychophysical studies that are couched in terms of attention without worrying about whether such studies are using 'attention' as a synonym for consciousness, or whether they mean to be picking out some other aspect of mental processing, for either way we could equate data about whether 'attention' is multisensory with data about whether 'consciousness' is multisensory.

Unfortunately, few theorists would be willing to grant us the assumption that the contents of attention are co-extensive with the contents of consciousness. Not only do some theorists argue that it is possible for the contents of perceptual experience to fall outside of the subject's attentional focus (e.g., Block, 2007; Lamme, 2003; Wyart & Tallon-Baudry, 2008), but some theorists also argue that it is possible to attend to an object or property without being conscious of it (Jiang, Costello, Fang, Huang, & He, 2006; Kentridge, 2011; Koch & Tsuchiya, 2007). Prudence recommends that we avoid embroiling ourselves in these debates if at all possible.

And perhaps it is possible. The central point is that the psychophysical studies that we will discuss study attention by means of measures that are regarded as *standard tests of consciousness*. That is, they attempt to determine what representational contents are directly available for guiding verbal report and the voluntary control of behaviour. So, we can use the results reported in the psychophysical literature just as long as we restrict ourselves to claims about consciousness insofar as it is tapped by the standard measures of consciousness. This is exactly what we propose to do.

The temporal framework. The final issue on our agenda concerns the temporal framework within which the debate about the multisensory structure of consciousness ought to be framed. Our awareness of the world is not temporally punctate. Consciousness does not take the form of a series of instantaneous snapshots, but instead has a dynamic and progressive structure. One series of events seems to follow on directly from a previous set of events and to lead, in turn, to a subsequent series of events. The experiential 'now'—the duration of time that seems to be immediately present to consciousness—is not an instant, but has a certain duration, known as the *specious present*.

With this point in mind, we can distinguish two ways in which the debate between the MSV and the USV can be framed. According to what we might call the 'thick' view, the debate concerns the possible contents of a single specious present. Thus understood, the advocate of the MSV holds that a specious present can contain contents associated with different modalities, whereas the advocate of the

USV denies that this is the case, and instead holds the view that the stream of consciousness takes the form of sense-specific specious presents that flow into one another. For example, a visual 'now' might flow into an auditory 'now', which, in turn, would flow into a tactile 'now' and so on.

A 'thin' conception conceives of the debate in terms of whether contents associated with different modalities can 'overlap' within consciousness: the advocate of the MSV allows overlapping experiences, whereas the advocate of the USV does not. On this way of setting up the debate, the advocate of the USV holds that experiences associated with distinct modalities can occur within a single specious present as long as the experiences in question are confined to distinct temporal parts of a single specious present.[2]

In this chapter, we focus on the 'thin' version of the debate between the USV and the MSV. In particular, we consider a version of the USV that holds that a subject's awareness of the world involves frequent and rapid alternations (or switches) between different modalities or 'channels' (Bernstein, 1970; Kristofferson, 1967; Tulving & Lindsey, 1967).[3] In principle, such switches could take place within the limits of the specious present. Whether this possibility could be realised in practice depends on the speed at which intermodality switches in consciousness can take place and the duration of the specious present.

Does this mean that the advocate of the MSV is committed to the thesis that subjects will also be aware of the contents of their experiences *as simultaneous*? We think not. For one thing, the MSV is strictly neutral on whether subjects might possess the capacity to become aware of the fact that they are, at any particular moment, simultaneously having conscious experiences of stimuli belonging to different modalities. Moreover, even if two perceptual experiences *do* represent their respective objects as occurring at the same time, it is a further question as to whether this feature of the subject's perceptual experience captures his or her attention in the form of some sort of multisensory 'pop-out' (that is, the automatic capture of a person's attention by the multisensory stimulus/event). In other words, the MSV makes no claims about what kind of meta-awareness subjects might have. So, although we think it plausible that subjects ought to have *some* sensitivity (not necessarily conscious) to the temporal relations between their conscious states (see Spence, 2010b), we do not take the MSV to entail that subjects

---

[2] This way of putting the contrast between the two views fudges the question of whether the contrast is to be understood in terms of the temporal framework of experiences themselves ('brain time', so to speak), or whether it is to be understood in terms of the contents of those experiences ('experiential time', so to speak). The contrast between these two conceptions might be important if, as some have argued, the temporal relations between experiences themselves can dissociate from the temporal relations of the objects of those experiences (see Dennett & Kinsbourne, 1992; although see Köhler 1947, p. 62; Vibell et al., 2007). However, we will move back and forth between talk of brain time and experiential time in the belief that doing so incurs no serious harm in this context.

[3] It is worth noting that in these early studies it is nearly always the case that when stimuli belong to different modalities they also refer to different objects, events, and/or streams of information. We return to this point in section 7.

are aware of those temporal relations. The upshot of all this is that although the existence of multisensory 'pop-out' might provide some motivation for the MSV, its absence should not necessarily be taken as providing evidence against it.

Let us take stock. Our aim in this section has been to examine the various ways in which the debate about whether consciousness is multisensory might be understood, and to clarify the versions of the USV and the MSV that we are interested in. We have made four central claims. Firstly, we are concerned here only with the relationship between experiences that are purely visual, auditory, or tactile, and will leave to one side questions both about the role that the chemical senses might play in these issues and about the possibility of 'inherently multisensory' experiences. Second, we noted that the possibility of significant IDs in consciousness 'problematises' the debate about whether consciousness is multisensory. With that point in mind, we suggested that the debate is best understood in terms of rival claims about the typical structure of consciousness in cognitively unimpaired individuals. Third, we drew attention to the fact that there is a gap between the psychophysical literature (that we will draw on later), which presents its results in terms of attention, and questions about the structure of consciousness. We suggested that this gap can at least partially be filled by focusing on the structure of consciousness only insofar as it is accessible by means of the standard measures of consciousness. Finally, we examined the bearing that debates about the temporal structure of consciousness might have on the question of whether it is multisensory, focusing on a 'thin' rather than a 'thick' conception of how the multisensory claim ought to be understood.

Even with these restrictions in hand, it is clear that the debate between the advocates of the USV and the MSV is both substantive and important. It is substantive, for it is by no means obvious whether the majority of cognitively unimpaired human beings have the capacity to be conscious of stimuli uniquely associated with distinct modalities at one and the same time. It is also important, for the upshot of this debate provides a much-needed constraint on accounts of the architecture of perceptual consciousness. The fact that experiences associated with distinct modalities can—or, as it may be, cannot—occur together within a single state of consciousness is something that an account of perceptual consciousness must respect and perhaps even explain.

3. The Appeal to Introspection

In adjudicating the debate between the advocates of the USV and the MSV, it is tempting to consider first the deliverances of introspection. When one does, it seems natural to think that introspection provides some support for the multisensory view. Consider what it is like to be at the cinema, listening to a sustained note whilst the camera tracks Tonto and the Lone Ranger riding across the desert. One might naturally take one's visual and auditory experiences to be simultaneously co-conscious, travelling companions much like Tonto and the Lone Ranger themselves. It is not implausible, then, to suppose that the multisensory view commands the widespread support that it does—at least among philosophers (e.g., Bermúdez, 1998, p. 141)[4]—because individuals find it introspectively plausible. Moreover, it might seem entirely *reasonable* to base one's views about whether consciousness is multisensory on introspective evidence. After all, the debate between the multisensory and unisensory accounts is a debate about the phenomenal contents of consciousness; and if introspection can tell us anything about the mind, it ought to be able to tell us about the contents of phenomenal consciousness.

However, matters are not as straightforward as they might first appear to be. First, introspective access is clearly limited to the structure of one's own consciousness. As such, it would be a further question as to whether the structure of one's own consciousness was representative of that of human beings in general, or whether the structure of one's own consciousness was anomalous. One could, of course, take the possibility of IDs into account by sampling a wide range of individuals and asking them to determine, on the basis of introspection, whether their own experience strikes them as unisensory or multisensory in nature. We have yet to conduct such a survey (or to come across anyone else who has), but our guess is that at least a significant minority of theorists would claim that their introspection does not support the MSV and might even support the USV.[5] Zimmerman (1989, p. 172), for example, appears to think that the USV has introspective support: "As we know from personal experience, our full conscious attention can be directed to only one sense organ at a time".[6]

Moreover, it is an open question as to whether introspection is able to deliver a justified verdict even with respect to the structure of one's own perceptual experience. According to the most plausible version of the USV, consciousness involves unisensory access to the results of multisensory information processing, with consciousness switching—often very rapidly—between the senses (e.g., Kristofferson, 1967; Spence, Nicholls, & Driver, 2001). Introspection is no doubt reasonably reliable when it comes to the question of whether consciousness draws on multiple modalities across extended periods of time, but it is far less obvious that it is to be trusted with respect to whether one's consciousness *simultaneously* draws on multiple modalities (cf. Yamamoto & Kitazawa, 2001). It is possible that the introspective feeling that some people have of being simultaneously conscious of (say) both visual and auditory stimuli is really an illusion, and their consciousness

---

[4] To the extent that the MSV is assumed in psychology and neuroscience—and it is unclear to us just how dominant it is in these disciplines—its influence might be best explained by appeal to the ubiquity of crossmodal/multisensory interactions (e.g., Bernstein, 1970; Bremner et al., 2012; Bushara et al., 2002; Calvert, Spence, & Stein, 2004; Stein, 2012). We examine the implications of crossmodal/multisensory interactions for this debate in §4.

[5] For what it's worth, this article itself arose out of the fact that one of the authors (TB) believes that the multisensory thesis receives introspective support, while the other (CS) does not!

[6] Of course, much hangs here on what exactly is meant by the qualifier 'full'.

in fact alternates (or switches) rapidly between visual and auditory inputs (see Kristofferson, 1967; Spence et al., 2001). In fact, the literature that deals with the effects of attention on our temporal awareness of events, shows that we are not particularly good at accurately judging the correct temporal order of environmental events in the sub-100 millisecond time range (cf. Spence & Parise, 2010, for a review). Given this fact, it is not implausible to suppose that subjects are also unreliable in judging whether certain of their own experiences are simultaneous or successive.[7]

Parallels can also be drawn between the considerations just outlined and those that will be familiar to anyone who has followed the literature on change blindness and/or inattentional blindness. Just as the introspectively based belief that one can see 'everything' before one's eyes at once has been severely undermined in recent years by the study of change blindness and scene perception (e.g., Gallace & Spence, 2010; Mack & Rock, 1998; O'Regan, 1992; Simons & Ambinder, 2005), so too one might also take this literature to undermine the belief that we are aware of content drawn from multiple modalities at any one time (e.g., Gallace et al., 2006; Mack & Rock, 1998; Pizzaghello & Bressan, 2008). Perhaps we mistake our ability to effortlessly and immediately bring (say) either tactile or auditory stimuli into consciousness for the fact that stimuli of both kinds are, in fact, simultaneously co-conscious. The 'effortless access' that one has to features of the world may give rise to the introspective 'illusion' that one is simultaneously aware in more than one modality at once, but—according to the proposal under consideration—this would be but another manifestation of the observation that we can be (very) wrong about certain aspects of our own experience (e.g., Bayne & Spener 2010; Schwitzgebel, 2008). So, even those who hold the view that introspection is *generally* reliable when it comes to questions concerning the structure and contents of consciousness might have reason to doubt whether introspection can be trusted with respect to the question of whether or not one's own perceptual experience is multisensory.

In light of these considerations we will leave appeals to introspection to one side here and focus instead on the question of what the data derived from experimental psychology and cognitive neuroscience might have to say about this debate.

---

[7] Indeed, if people are co-conscious of both auditory and visual inputs, say, as implicitly suggested by the multisensory view of consciousness, it is unclear why there should be any need for the 'personal equation'. This term, which has been in use for nearly two centuries, is used by psychologists to describe the amount of time that needs to be added to, or subtracted from, one observer's judgment of what counts as simultaneous in order for pairs of (as it happens) independent auditory and visual stimuli to bring his or her judgements into alignment with those of another observer (Spence, 2010b). In fact, it has been argued that it was the recognition of the need for the personal equation that launched the field of experimental psychology in the first place (see Mollon & Perkins, 1996; Spence, 2010b; Spence & Squire, 2003). To be absolutely clear, the personal equation refers to the temporal misalignment between individuals in terms of what counts as simultaneous (that is, the stimulus onset asynchrony) needed to elicit the maximum likelihood that a participant will judge the stimuli as synchronous.

4. Crossmodal Interactions

How do the findings of research in the field of experimental psychology bear on this debate between the unisensory and multisensory accounts of consciousness? Advocates of the multisensory view might well be tempted to appeal to the literature on crossmodal interactions. A large body of evidence drawn from the fields of experimental psychology and psychophysics over the last 70 years or so (Thomas, 1941; see London, 1954; Welch & Warren, 1986, for early reviews) has unequivocally demonstrated that perceptual modalities do not operate autonomously, but that processing in one modality is often influenced by stimuli presented (and processed) in other modalities. Indeed, the ubiquity of crossmodal interactions affecting brain activity in regions traditionally thought to be unisensory has even led some researchers to wonder whether it might not be better to think of the cerebral cortex as 'inherently multisensory' (Driver & Noesselt, 2008; Ghazanfar & Schroeder, 2006; Pascual-Leone & Hamilton, 2001).[8]

We have already mentioned one class of multisensory interactions in connection with the ventriloquism effect (see section 2), in which the spatial properties of stimuli presented in one modality can influence the spatial content of perception in another modality (e.g., Alais & Burr, 2004; Morein-Zamir Kingstone, & Soto-Faraco, 2003). Other multisensory effects concern the categorical content of perception. For example, in the McGurk effect, dubbing the phoneme /ba/ onto the lip movements for /ga/ normally produces an auditory percept of the phoneme /da/ (McGurk & McDonald, 1976). Other crossmodal interactions involve changes to the temporal contents of experience. So, for example, the perceived rate of visual flicker can be modulated by the rate at which a concurrent stream of auditory input is presented (see Spence et al., 2007, for a review). Crossmodal interactions can *even* modulate the number of events that a person experiences as having been presented. In the auditory-flash illusion, for example, subjects often misperceive a single flash of light as two flashes when it is paired with two beeps (Shams, Kamitani, & Shimojo, 2000). Surely, one might think, the results of such studies provide persuasive evidence against the unisensory claim.

Not necessarily! It is possible that crossmodal interactions occur outside of the perceiver's awareness. Although we are certainly aware of the *results* of crossmodal interactions, it is far from obvious that crossmodal interactions involve simultaneous conscious states in different modalities. We can explore this issue by considering the McGurk effect. This effect involves a visual percept (as) of someone uttering /ga/ and an auditory percept (as) of someone saying /ba/. However, the effect does not require that subjects are *conscious* of both stimuli (i.e., auditory and

---

[8] Note here that we refer to 'crossmodal' rather than 'multisensory' interactions in order to indicate that we are describing situations in which the stimulation presented in one modality exerts an influence on a person's awareness of stimuli presented in another modality (see the Glossary). Such interactions need not involve multisensory integration, although they might.

visual) contributing to the McGurk effect. Evidence relevant to this point comes from the finding that visually presented lip movements appearing in the ipsilesional hemifield of patients suffering from hemineglect can give rise to a McGurk effect when combined with auditory speech stimuli presented in the patient's (neglected contralesional) hemifield (Soroker, Calamaro, & Myslobodsky, 1995a, b; see also Leo et al., 2008).

Of course, it does seem highly plausible to suppose that the McGurk effect involves both visual and auditory awareness of the target individual. However, it is not obvious that this awareness must be simultaneous. Perhaps the McGurk effect involves perceptual awareness that alternates between vision and audition. Some reason to think that this possibility might not be a merely theoretical one derives from the fact that auditory and visual speech stimuli need not even be presented simultaneously in order to generate the McGurk effect. If the stimulus onsets are jittered slightly, a range of stimulus onset asynchronies can be found over which participants can both reliably judge which modality stream was presented first (thus implying an ability to judge temporal order correctly) and in which subjects still experience the integration of the auditory and visual inputs (see Soto-Faraco & Alsius, 2007, 2009).[9] The *result* of the multisensory interactions that give rise to the McGurk effect—that is, the representation of the target as uttering /da/—is, of course, conscious, but it is an open question as to whether the McGurk effect requires that subjects be simultaneously aware of the 'visual speech' and the 'auditory speech'.

More generally, the advocate of the USV might argue that although the senses can mutually and extensively influence one another, *all* such crossmodal interactions take place 'below' (or perhaps 'prior to') the level of awareness. In fact, the sceptic could argue that this is not merely possible but is actually *likely* to be the case. After all, many of the animals in which Stein and Meredith demonstrated multisensory integration were anaesthetised (see Stein & Meredith, 1993 for a review). Multisensory interactions most certainly did occur in these animals, but it is rather implausible to think that they involved interactions between conscious states within the animal. Similarly, when we turn to the case of human performance under conditions of simultaneous multisensory stimulation, there are situations in which a participant's performance demonstrates evidence of the integration of signals associated with distinct modalities, but in which the participant is only aware of stimuli associated with one modality (Leo et al., 2008).

One example of such an experimental phenomenon that has been demonstrated repeatedly in neurologically normal adult humans is the Colavita visual dominance effect (see Spence, Parise, & Chen, 2011, for a recent review). In a

---

[9] Soto-Faraco and Alsius (2007, 2009) presented an auditory /da/ together with a visual /ba/. This combination of auditory and visual stimuli normally gives rise to perception of /bda/, as in 'abduction'. The researchers investigated how far in advance the auditory /da/ had to be presented before the visual /da/ in order for the /bda/ percept to break down.

typical study, the participants are instructed to make one speeded response to visual targets, another speeded response to auditory targets, and either make both speeded responses or else make a third response (also speeded) when the auditory and visual targets happen (rarely) to be presented together (i.e., simultaneously). Although participants typically exhibit no difficulties when responding to the auditory or visual targets when presented individually, the oft-reported finding is that they sometimes fail to respond to the auditory component on the bimodal target trials (that is, when the auditory and visual targets are presented simultaneously). However, the fact that the 'visual' responses on such trials are typically faster than the visual responses seen on the unimodal visual target trials demonstrates that there has been some degree of *implicit* processing of the auditory stimulus despite the participant's failure to respond *explicitly* to the auditory stimulus. Thus, the Colavita effect indicates that representations of auditory and visual stimuli can be integrated (to at least some degree) 'outside' of consciousness.[10]

Of course, there may be forms of multisensory integration that do demand that the perceptual streams that contribute to the integration in question feature conscious states. Although we know of no reason to rule out the possibility of such forms of integration, as far as we can tell the forms of multisensory integration that have been studied most intensively do not conform to this description.

A rather different kind of multisensory interaction involves the dynamic structure and evolution of perceptual consciousness. In the case of visual experience, we are familiar with multistable (or metastable) stimuli such as the Necker cube, in which a stimulus appears to switch (or change) its orientation in a fairly predictable manner over time (that is, the timing/frequency of Necker cube reversals is predictable). Importantly, such stimuli are not restricted to the visual modality but can also be found in the auditory and tactile modalities as well (e.g., Carter et al., 2008; Gallace & Spence, 2011; see Spence et al., 2007, for a review). One question here is whether the principles that govern the temporal evolution of multistable percepts are modality-specific, or whether they are 'amodal' and apply to perceptual states independent of the modality to which they belong. One might argue that an amodal account of such principles would provide some support for the MSV of consciousness, whereas a modality-specific account of such principles might be taken to support the USV. So, do the principles in question differ from modality to modality, or is there a shared set of multisensory principles in action?

It is certainly true that there are crossmodal influences on the dynamic structure of perceptual experience (e.g., Bruno et al., 2007; Lunghi, Binda, & Morrone,

---

[10] There is also evidence that crossmodal *semantic* interactions can take place under conditions where participants fail to report on the occurrence of at least of one of the component unisensory stimuli (see Koppen, Alsius, & Spence, 2008).

2010; van Ee et al., 2009). For example, Bruno et al. have reported a study in which participants held a three-dimensional Necker cube and viewed it through one eye. Tactile exploration of this object modulated the frequency and duration of illusory reversals of the cube (and in this way increased the consistency between the felt and seen shape). However, other studies have reported that dynamic changes in one modality are independent of the information processing taking place in other modalities. So, for example, on the basis of their studies of simultaneous bi-stable perception in the auditory and visual modality, Hupé, Joffoa, and Pressnitzer (2008) have suggested that switches in visual awareness appear to be decoupled from switches in auditory awareness, and vice versa. This was true in their study even when the stimuli in question concerned a single audiovisual event. However, in general, we know rather little about the extent to which the principles that underlie the modulation of perceptual experience in one modality are related to those that govern the modulation of perceptual experience in other modalities.

Moreover, we would also need to be very careful in bringing such data to bear on the debate about the multisensory nature of human consciousness. Consider for a moment dynamic changes occurring solely within the structure of visual experience. While perceptual switches within vision sometime occur in parallel across the entire visual field (e.g., as when viewing multiple bi-stable apparent motion displays; Ramachandran & Anstis, 1983; see also Attneave, 1971), at other times they may occur more or less independently (as when simultaneously viewing multiple Necker cubes; see Long & Toppino, 1981). Bearing such results in mind, the advocate of the multisensory thesis could argue that consciousness could be multisensory even if (certain) changes within the dynamic structure of one modality were found to be independent of any changes taking place in the dynamic structure of perceptual experience in another modality, in just the same way that changes in the perception of one visually experienced Necker cube might be independent of the changes in the perceptual experience of another visually experienced Necker cube.

To summarise, in this section, we have addressed an intuitively plausible argument for the multisensory model that appeals to the widespread existence of multisensory interactions (described in terms of crossmodal interactions including those involving multisensory integration). In examining this argument, we have implicitly distinguished two forms that such interactions might take. *Exogenously driven* interactions occur when input in one modality (automatically) exerts an influence on a person's awareness of the stimuli presented in another modality; by contrast, *endogenously driven* interactions occur when the spontaneous (or voluntary) switches in the contents of experience in one modality (e.g., aspect switches) are coupled with the changes taking place in another modality. Contrary to what one might have assumed, it is not obvious that either form of multisensory interaction provides much, if any, evidence in support of the MSV.

5. Multisensory Emergence

In this section, we turn our attention to another line of evidence that the advocate of the MSV might appeal to—what we call the argument from multisensory emergence. The basic idea here is that one might be able to appeal to multisensory integration in the contents of perceptual experience to argue that experiences belonging to different perceptual modalities are unified in consciousness. This approach to the debate dates back at least as far as the 1930s and 1940s, when Gilbert and others were especially interested in the question of what kinds of 'intersensory Gestalten'—as the states produced by intersensory integration have traditionally been called—could be observed (e.g., see Gilbert, 1938, 1939).

Before we examine the argument from 'intersensory Gestalten' in detail, it will be instructive to consider an analogous debate in the unisensory sphere involving the split-brain phenomenon. It is commonly held that split-brain patients have a disunified consciousness, in that they simultaneously enjoy visual experiences associated with left and right hemisphere processing that are not integrated into a single overall visual experience. One of the central arguments for this claim appeals to the fact that patients cannot integrate the contents of left- and right-brain visual experiences in the ways that one would expect them to be able to were such experiences co-conscious (that is, unified). In a standard experimental paradigm, the split-brain patient is presented with two words at one and the same time (say, 'key' and 'ring'), where the two words are lateralised to different halves of the patient's visual field. The patient's behaviour (both verbal and nonverbal) indicates that she or he has visual experiences of each word but no conjoint or integrated experience of the two words together—that is, no experience of the word 'key-ring'. The fact that the contents of these two experiences are not integrated is widely taken as providing evidence that they are not co-conscious but instead occur within separate streams of experience (e.g., see Marks 1981; Sperry 1984). At the same time, the fact that neurologically normal human beings are able to integrate visual experiences of words presented in distinct visual hemifields is typically taken to provide evidence that the experiences in question are co-conscious (consider the quotation from Cowan, 1995, cited in section 1). The basic question behind the argument from multisensory emergence is whether neurologically normal adults can integrate the contents of experiences that belong to different modalities in the same way that they can integrate the contents of experiences that belong to the same modality. If they can, this would provide support for the MSV, but if they cannot, then this would provide some support for the USV.[11]

---

[11] In certain ways this argument resembles the argument regarding crossmodal interactions examined in the previous section. Both appeal to the alleged integration of the senses. However, it is important to note that the arguments are concerned with different forms of multisensory integration. The argument from crossmodal interactions appeals to various kinds of relations of counterfactual dependence between perceptual modalities whereas the argument from multisensory emergence concerns forms of integration that are directly reflected in the contents of perception itself.

In the literature, the term 'intersensory Gestalten' is often used in a very broad sense (see Spence et al., 2007, on this point), for example, as when referring to situations in which the perceptual stimulation taking place in one modality can be shown to be modulated by the stimulation presented in a different modality. Crossmodal interactions of this kind would not as such provide evidence for the MSV (see the following section). Rather, the kind of 'intersensory Gestalten' whose existence might support the MSV are Gestalten that possess a kind of multisensory organisation or structure—similar to what Allen and Kolers (1981, p. 1318) describe as a 'common or suprasensory organising principle'—that simply could not be obtained without perceptual representations in different modalities being (simultaneously) co-conscious.[12] Of course, the tricky issue here involves determining whether a certain perceptual experience really does have this preservative structure, or whether it has instead been produced by perceptual states that either lie outside of awareness or else are not simultaneous with the experience of interest (or both).

Leaving these issues to one side, let us turn to the question of what kinds of intersensory Gestalten one might hope to find if the MSV were to be true. Perhaps the most obvious Gestalten that one might expect would be an experience of simultaneity for stimuli detected by different modalities at approximately the same time. This might, in turn, give rise to a multisensory 'pop-out' effect for those stimuli that are represented as simultaneous—that is, they might be highlighted against the perceptual background of unisensory and/or asynchronous multisensory stimuli.

Does multisensory 'pop-out' occur? Although many researchers have looked for it, convincing evidence of multisensory pop-out has yet to be found. Some years ago, null results such as these led Piéron (1952, p. 295) to claim that whereas a 'rigorous impression' of simultaneity can occur for stimuli presented within a single modality, no clear sensation of simultaneity can be perceived for stimuli presented to different modalities (see also Fraisse, 1963; Guinzberg, 1928). More recently, Fujisaki and her colleagues also failed to find any evidence of the pop-out of multisensory temporal synchrony when viewing multiple visual and auditory stimuli (see Fujisaki et al., 2006; Fujisaki & Nishida, 2010; though see also Spence & Ngo, 2012; Spence, 2010c; Van der Burg et al., 2008, for evidence that audiovisual temporal coincidence, or synchrony, might capture spatial attention automatically, though presumably without an observer necessarily being conscious of the simultaneity of the auditory and visual stimuli).

A second kind of intersensory Gestalt that one might expect to find if the MSV were correct is apparent motion between stimuli that are perceived via different

---

[12] Paul Schiller (1935, p. 468) seems to have been getting at something like this when he argued that 'such configurational tendencies can come not only from the same but also from different heterosensorial fields. A perception is produced by sensations of different modalities, which often create intersensorial patterns'.

modalities. Just as the *intra*sensory perception of two events presented sequentially from different locations can generate an experience of motion between them, one might expect that two events will generate an experience of *inter*sensory motion when they are perceived in different modalities. One could think of this as a kind of multisensory Phi phenomenon (Gilbert, 1939). Note here, though, that one needs to distinguish *intersensory* apparent motion from *crossmodal* motion, where crossmodal motion occurs when apparent (or real) motion in one modality impacts the motion (either apparent or real) experienced in a different modality. By contrast, intersensory apparent motion would involve an experience of motion that could not be exclusively located within (or attributed to) either constituent modality.[13]

Does intersensory motion, either apparent or real, occur? Early research, based on unconstrained self-reports, was taken to suggest that it did (see Galli, 1932; Zapparoli & Reatto, 1969). For example, Zapparoli and Reatto (p. 262) describe the experience of intersensory apparent movement between auditory and visual stimuli as 'something that moves between the sound and the light or between the light and the sound, a light and sound tunnel which grows longer and shorter, or a light tunnel which grows longer and shorter while a sound passes through it.' More recently, Harrar, Winter, and Harris (2005) also described the perception of apparent motion that was observed following the presentation of a visual and a tactile stimulus from different spatial locations as feeling 'like an event at one location causing an event at another'. However, subsequent and more carefully controlled studies have failed to document any robust psychophysical evidence supporting the existence of intersensory apparent motion (e.g., Allen & Kolers, 1981; Huddlestone et al., 2008 Sanabria et al., 2005; see Gallace & Spence, 2011; Spence et al., 2007; Spence & Chen, 2012, for reviews). These latter studies have typically been based on psychophysical methods (rather than purely on anecdotal subjective report), in which the researchers concerned have attempted to rule out 'task demands' and experimenter expectancy effects as alternative accounts for the results obtained. Given the compelling evidence for intrasensory (unisensory) apparent motion within the visual, auditory, and tactile modalities (e.g., Lakatos & Shepherd, 1997), and given the clear evidence that stimuli in one modality can influence an observer's perception of motion experienced in another modality (see Soto-Faraco et al., 2004, for a review), the failure to find intersensory apparent motion provides significant evidence against the claim that consciousness is multisensory (in the sense identified here).

A third potential form of intersensory Gestalt involves the perception of rhythm. We have all experienced rhythm on the basis of unimodal visual, auditory, and tactile stimulus streams, but can we experience intermodal rhythm (see Fraisse, 1981; Guttman, Gilroy, & Blake, 2005)? Once again, the closest one

---

[13] See Churchland, Ramachandran, and Sejnowski (1994, pp. 30–32) for another intriguing, but once again anecdotal, example.

gets to evidence on this score comes from anecdotal subjective reports. So, for example, Guttman et al. (footnote 3, p. 234), point to a number of reports from participants claiming to have experienced complex rhythmic Gestalten that combined both auditory and visual inputs. However, Gebhard and Mowbray (1959, p. 523) also report—again albeit anecdotally—failing to observe any such phenomenon in their study of the auditory driving of visual flicker. Given this, all that can be said with any certainty at this point is that there is still *no* convincing evidence to support the existence of intersensory Gestalten involving the perception of rhythm.

In his 1963 book, *The Psychology of Time*, Fraisse wrote, 'A succession of sounds and lights will never allow perception of an organisation which integrates the two. There will be perception of a double series, one of sounds and one of lights' (p. 73). The evidence that has been surveyed in this section therefore suggests that Fraisse's intuition may well have been right. The literature on intersensory Gestalten casts doubt on the multisensory thesis, for firm evidence of such Gestalten has not been found despite the fact that researchers have been looking for them for many years now. However, it is difficult to say exactly how strong this evidence really is. The advocate of the MSV could argue either that such Gestalten are rather subtle and/ or that we simply haven't been looking for them in the right ways. They might also argue—with more plausibility from our perspective—that differences in representational format between the various modalities may simply prevent such intersensory Gestalten from arising, even though experiences in different modalities are co-conscious. For example, the advocate of the MSV could argue that there is no multisensory pop-out for synchronous multisensory events because the representational formats in which visual, auditory, and tactile experiences are encoded prevents the relevant kinds of information from being integrated in the way that such Gestalten would require. Of course, any response along these lines would need to reckon with the fact that there is extensive evidence of multisensory (and crossmodal) interactions that we have already documented, for the existence of such interactions demonstrates that the representational formats of vision, audition, and touch are capable of at least some forms of integration.

6. Attention and Capacity Limits

Let us now turn to whether the study of crossmodal attention and the capacity limits on consciousness might shed any light on the debate between the unisensory and multisensory conceptions of consciousness. One line of evidence that might be explored here concerns the ability of subjects to detect and/or discriminate targets (either objects or features) that have been presented simultaneously in multisensory displays. At first glance, the USV would appear to entail that this should not be possible, whereas the MSV would appear to entail the converse. What do the data say?

The answer here is somewhat mixed. A number of researchers have argued that people can simultaneously monitor, perceive, and possibly even respond to stimuli in two modalities when they happen to be presented at the same time. That said, robust dual-task costs have also been documented in many studies (e.g., Treisman & Davies, 1973; see Spence et al., 2001, Spence, 2010a, for reviews). A variety of methodological confounds have made the appropriate interpretation of many of these older results (on both sides of the debate) rather uncertain, but the last few years have seen some clarity brought to the area.[14] The general finding appears to be that people typically find it more difficult to respond to simultaneously presented targets (than to just a single target) if they *both* require a *speeded response* (see Jolicoeur, 1999; Spence et al., 2001) and/or if people are required to *discriminate* the identity, rather than merely to *detect* the presence, of the target events concerned (see Bonnel & Hafter, 1998; Spence, 2010a; Spence & Soto-Faraco, 2009). That said, several well-controlled laboratory studies have now convincingly demonstrated that people can sometimes make *unspeeded* discrimination responses to simultaneously presented auditory and visual targets with very little (or virtually no) performance cost (see Alais et al., 2006; Arrighi et al., 2011; Larsen et al., 2003). Interestingly, the auditory and visual stimuli in these studies involved distinct perceptual objects/events. We will return to this point in the next section.

Many of these empirical studies make absolutely no mention of awareness (or consciousness), and the authors normally refer to their results in terms of the limitations on the allocation of attention, using terms like 'perceptual capacity' and 'resources'. Such caution is perhaps justified given evidence that certain perceptual tasks can be performed perfectly well in the absence of awareness (e.g., see Mitroff & Scholl, 2005). Furthermore, given that there is absolutely nothing to stop an individual from shifting his or her attention back and forth between different modalities, what one concludes on the basis of the aforementioned results depends, at least to some degree, on one's view of the consequences for perception of relying on the information that is stored in some form of short-lasting iconic, echoic, or tactile memory. Clearly, sensory information must start to decay at some rate after it has initially been processed (Gallace & Spence, 2011; Harris et al., 2002; Lu, Williamson, & Kaufman, 1992; Uusitalo, Williamson, & Seppä, 1996; Zylberberg et al., 2009). So, if people can switch their attention between modalities sufficiently rapidly—that is, before the relevant stimulus representation has started to decay in iconic, echoic, or tactile memory—then switching might not give rise to any performance cost. Consequently, one might come away from a study of divided attention with the impression that participants must have

---

[14] We should also note that it is hard to discriminate between an individual who randomly directs his or her attention to one or other target modality on a trial-by-trial basis, say, and a person who can attend to both modalities simultaneously, but who suffers from a limited bandwidth of attention, such that they are incapable of taking in all of the perceptual content available to both vision and audition at the same time.

been simultaneously aware of both inputs/modalities whereas, in fact, they were simply rapidly switching their awareness from one modality to another. Those who know their cognitive psychology may well be reminded here of the much older debate about whether people can perform two tasks at once, or whether dual task performance always involves rapidly switching one's attention between each of the two tasks (e.g., Allport, Antonis, & Reynolds, 1972; Broadbent, 1958 Posner & Boies, 1971).

Another field of study that might be thought to have some bearing on this debate involves research on the phenomenon of the attentional blink (AB). The AB has traditionally been defined as a state of poor awareness concerning visual stimuli presented in a rapid serial visual presentation stream following a person's detection of a target stimulus presented earlier in the stream. The AB lasts for approximately half a second after the onset of the first target (Raymond, 2009). Given the tight connection between the AB and consciousness (Raymond, 2009; Shapiro Arnell, & Raymond, 1997), one might argue that the USV would predict the AB to be modality-specific, whereas the MSV might predict that the AB would be amodal. In other words, according to the USV, subjects would be temporarily 'blinded' only in the modality of the target to which they had just attended/detected, whereas the MSV would predict that subjects would be blind in all modalities following attention to the target stimulus (that is, they would predict that there should be a crossmodal AB).

So, is the AB modality-specific or is it multisensory? Again, the evidence here is rather mixed (see Spence, 2010a, for a review). First off, one needs to isolate the *perceptual* from any merely *decisional* (i.e., task-switching) component of any limitation of what an observer can report (i.e., is conscious of) at any given time. Hence, most informative here are the results of those studies in which participants had to make unspeeded judgements regarding the identity of target stimuli that were successively presented (at a relatively short stimulus onset asynchrony) in different modalities, and where (as far as possible) the same task is presented in the two modalities (e.g., Arnell & Larsson, 2002; Potter, Chun, Banks, & Muckenhoupt, 1998; Soto-Faraco & Spence, 2002). Although some researchers have failed to find evidence of a crossmodal AB under such conditions (Duncan et al., 1997; Hein, Parr, & Duncan, 2006; Soto-Faraco & Spence, 2002), other researchers have found evidence of a crossmodal audiovisual and a crossmodal visuotactile AB (see Arnell & Jolicoeur 1999; Soto-Faraco, Spence, Fairbank, Kingstone, Hillstrom, & Shapiro, 2002). Thus, at best, perhaps all one can say here with any confidence on the basis of the available literature is that for unspeeded tasks, the crossmodal audiovisual AB is weaker and much less stable than its within-modality counterpart (Hein et al., 2006).

We might also note that even if robust evidence of crossmodal AB were found, it is very much an open question whether it would in fact support the MSV of consciousness over the USV, for a crossmodal AB might occur simply because the mechanisms responsible for selecting the contents of perceptual experience refuse to engage with targets of a certain type while the current (unisensory) item of interest is being processed. The existence or otherwise of a crossmodal AB would seem to tell us more about the limits on rapidly switching attention between successively presented target stimuli that happen to have been presented in different modalities than it does about the limits on the number of modalities of stimulation that we can be aware of at any one time. So, even if reliable evidence of a crossmodal AB were to be found, it is far from clear that it would provide strong evidence for the MSV.

In sum, current research into the nature of crossmodal attention and capacity limits on consciousness fails to provide the kind of evidence needed to resolve the debate between the USV and the MSV of consciousness.[15] Ideally, here, it would seem as though the strongest evidence on which to address the question of whether awareness is unisensory or multisensory would come from those studies in which rapid streams of auditory and visual stimuli were presented simultaneously (as in many crossmodal AB studies) and where auditory and visual targets could be presented individually or at the same time. The rapid presentation of stimuli would ideally ensure that participants' performance could not be said to rely on the slowly (or rapidly) decaying iconic, echoic, or tactile memory trace (since that should presumably have been rapidly overwritten by the subsequent items in the respective stimulus streams), and the simultaneous presentations of the target stimuli would argue against participants failing to switch their attention/consciousness between rapidly, but sequentially, presented targets/stimuli.[16] Has anyone conducted such a study? Well, yes, one type of evidence comes from a series of studies of the Colavita visual dominance task reported by Sinnett, Spence, and Soto-Faraco (2007). The results of these experiments demonstrate that people can often report both of the simultaneously presented target stimuli. However, that said, the participants in these studies also sometimes failed to report the auditory target when it was presented at the same time as a visual target. What is more, the rate of stimulus presentation was sufficiently slow that participants could, once again, presumably have switched their attention rapidly from one modality to the other prior to the offset of the stimuli (and/or the occurrence of the next stimuli in the streams). Given this latter possibility, it is worth remembering that the limits of consciousness may be more severe than suggested even by the results of Sinnett et al.'s study.

---

[15] In addition to the experimental work discussed in this section, a few studies have also looked at the ability of individuals to count the number of stimuli simultaneously presented in unisensory and multisensory displays (see Gallace, Tan, & Spence, 2007). Although we lack the space to discuss this research here, we hope to engage with this literature on multisensory numerosity judgments in future work.

[16] Here it should be noted that the very phenomenon of temporal limits in the processing of rapidly, and more or less simultaneously, presented target stimuli would appear to be at least somewhat task-dependent (see Schumacher et al., 2001).

In sum, the literature documenting crossmodal limits on attention has either not (yet) provided empirical evidence that is of sufficient methodological rigour to support either side of the debate, or else turns out, on closer inspection, to be incapable of adjudicating between the two views. For this area of research to provide informative evidence, scientists will need to find a means of demonstrating that any apparent awareness of the stimuli presented in two modalities simultaneously could not instead be explained by participants simply shifting their attention rapidly from one modality to the other before the relevant short-term memory traces had decayed significantly.[17]

7. Multisensory Perceptual Objects

A final research domain that one might appeal to in attempting to adjudicate the debate between the USV and the MSV concerns the binding of features as referring to a common object or event. The idea here is that visual features are bound together to form visual objects. This is a familiar idea and one that does not seem all that controversial (e.g., Robertson, 2003; Treisman, 1996). At the same time, other researchers have argued that auditory features are also bound together in order to form auditory objects (e.g., Kubovy & Schutz, 2010; Kubovy & van Valkenburg, 2001; O'Callaghan, 2008). Similarly, there is no reason to think that the binding of tactile features should be any different, although it must be noted that this area has attracted far less research interest to date. But are features belonging to *different* modalities bound together in the form of multisensory perceptual objects (MPOs)?

This question would appear to be directly relevant to the question of whether consciousness is unisensory or multisensory. For, if the USV is correct, then one would not expect multisensory perceptual binding; instead, the expectation would be that the features belonging to various modalities would be bound together only in the form of modality-specific percepts. If, on the other hand, the MSV is correct, then we might expect that features from different modalities would be bound together to form MPOs. After all, since the MSV allows that features from different modalities can co-occur within consciousness, if the MSV were to be correct then there would be no obvious reason that features from different modalities should not be bound together to form MPOs. (Note, however, that the MSV does not require the existence of MPOs; as we have already noted, modality-specific

---

[17] It would likely also help in future research if a more formal/computationally specified account of switching could be provided. Note here also that it is possible to distinguish between two ways of thinking about switching: there might either be multiple different kinds of modality-specific attention with participants simply switching from one to another versus the alternative view that there is only a single pool of attentional resources that itself switches focus from one modality to another.

differences in format/encoding might limit the formation of such objects.) So, is there any evidence of MPOs?

Before examining the empirical evidence, let us first consider what might be meant by an MPO—or by intermodal (Pourtois et al., 2000) or crossmodal binding (Bushara et al., 2002; Cinel, Humphreys, & Poli, 2002; Kubovy & Schutz, 2010). First, it should be clear that the kind of MPOs in which we are interested here are those that are represented in *consciousness*. The existence of multisensory object files that contain information about an object's features where those features are not conscious (Kahneman, Treisman, & Gibbs, 1992; Mitroff, Scholl, & Wynn, 2005) obviously has no direct bearing on the question at hand. Nor would the existence of 'object files' that contain information from different modalities at different times be relevant to this debate, for the existence of such files (and their associated perceptual objects) would be consistent with both the USV and the MSV of consciousness. So, in other words, the kinds of multisensory objects that would provide support for the MSV must be both conscious and synchronously multisensory. So, from here on, we will restrict our discussion to those MPOs that meet this description.

A further distinction that it may be useful to hold in mind here is between broad and narrow senses of a multisensory 'object'. In the broad sense, a multisensory object is simply any entity that is experienced as having attributes or features belonging to distinct modalities. In this broad sense, certain events might qualify as MPOs. For example, one might argue that the shattering of a glass qualifies as an MPO insofar as one both sees and hears the impact of the glass, and the various visual and auditory features involved in that are bound together (causally related) in the form of the percept of a single multisensory event (Kubovy & Schutz, 2010). Researchers have been interested in the binding of features from different modalities into multisensory events for many years (e.g., Neisser, 1976, p. 29; see also Benjamins et al., 2008). This notion of an object should be contrasted with a narrower sense, according to which the only entities that can be represented as objects are concrete particulars that have reasonably stable properties through time, things such as cats, cups and coat hangers. As far as the debate about the multisensory nature of consciousness is concerned, it is the broad notion of an MPO that is relevant, and it is thus this notion on which we will focus here.

So, what does it mean for features to be bound together in the form of a single object? The literature suggests a number of radically different answers to this seemingly simple question. Some theorists appear to mean nothing more by this notion than that features drawn from different modalities are ascribed to the same spatiotemporal location (see Hupé et al., 2008; Logan, 1996; Pourtois & de Gelder, 2002; Turatto, Mazza, & Umiltà, 2005). It seems to us, however, that this is an unacceptably impoverished conception of what should be taken as the minimal requirements to constitute a multisensory object (see also Spence, 2012). After all, just imagine a dog barking from behind a verdant bush. You hear the dog's bark and look in the direction of its source. At that point, you see the green foliage and hear the yapping coming from the location where you happen to be looking. Even though the spatiotemporal constraints on multisensory objecthood have been met, it seems implausible to suppose that one's perceptual experience would be characterised by an MPO in any robust sense of that term. At any rate, the central point is that an MPO of this form would not provide any support for the multisensory view of consciousness.

Another conception of what it is for features to be bound together in the form of a common object appeals to the idea that objects occur as figures against a perceptual ground (see, e.g., Kubovy & van Valkenburg 2001). Visual objects stand out against a visual background, and auditory objects stand out against an auditory background. Do certain combinations of audiovisual (or, for that matter, audiotactile, or visuotactile) features ever stand out, as unified and integrated, against their respective perceptual backgrounds? Some authors seem to think so. In one recent paper, Kubovy and Schutz (2010, p. 54) write:

> To use phenomenological evidence [for audiovisual binding] we would need a clear criterion for saying when an acoustic event and a visual event were bound to form a single audio-visual object. Some cases are clear. The sound and sight of a glass shattering leave no doubt in our minds that what we heard and saw was caused by the same physical event. We cannot prevent the binding of the ventriloquist's voice with the movement of the dummy's lips, even though we know it's an illusion.

However, we think it is debatable whether the 'unity of the event' really is internal to one's experience in these cases, or whether it involves a certain amount of post-perceptual processing (or inference). In other words, it seems to us to be an open question whether, in these situations, one's experience is of an MPO or whether it is instead structured in terms of multiple instances of unimodal perceptual objects.[18]

In whatever way the notion of an MPO is spelled out, it seems highly plausible to suppose that such objects will play particular roles within the agent's cognitive economy. In other words, we should expect functional differences between a situation in which visual feature F and auditory feature G are bound to different perceptual objects and a situation in which they are instead both bound to a common perceptual object. To adopt the terminology common in the literature on 'object files' (Jordan, Clark, & Mitroff, 2010; Kahneman et al., 1992; Mitroff et al., 2005), we should expect functional differences between a situation in which F and G are associated with different object files, and a situation in which they are both associated with a common object file.

---

[18] Although it is beyond the scope of the present discussion, one might also want to integrate evidence here from those studies that have explicitly asked participants whether they perceive the various combinations of features placed before them as 'belonging together' or as 'appearing unified' (e.g., Laurienti et al., 2004; Lewald & Guski, 2003).

An example of the functional differences that object files might make is provided by the relative costs of switching attention between object features. Indeed, the notion of attention, and more particularly, the set of features that can be attended to at any one time plays a critical notion in many definitions of what an object (albeit an object possessing only unisensory features) is (e.g., Shinn-Cunningham, 2008). That is, it is taken as given that we can attend to *all* the features of an object simultaneously. Evidence in support of this claim comes from the many studies showing that people find it much easier to successively report on different visual features belonging to a single unimodal visual object than to report on the very same features when they happen to belong to distinct visual objects (e.g., Driver, 1999; Duncan, 1984). In the light of such findings, one might therefore think of using the differential costs of attention-switching as an indirect indicator that one is dealing with distinct perceptual objects in a multisensory context. In other words, one might assume that if the binding of features into a multisensory object representation occurs, then the costs of switching between those features should be significantly lower than the costs associated with switching one's attention between the sensory features or features belonging to different perceptual objects, even when those sensory features belong to different modalities.

To the best of our knowledge, the question of whether switching attention between features belonging to different objects incurs costs that are not incurred when switching between features belonging to the same object has not yet been systematically investigated in a crossmodal setting. Although a number of studies have compared the effects of dividing attention between (i.e., equivalent to report-ing on) two features presented in the same modality with those of dividing atten-tion between two features presented in different modalities, the stimuli in question (in the latter case) have always been linked to different objects (Gladstones et al., 1989; Martin, 1980; Rollins & Hendricks, 1980). Perhaps closest in this regard are a series of studies by Bonnel and her colleagues (Bonnel & Hafter, 1998; Bonnel & Prinzmetal, 1998; Bonnel, Stein, & Berlucci, 1992). In these studies, participants had to make judgments about two properties. Sometimes, the properties belonged to the same modality and to the same object (as when participants had to report on the colour and seen shape of a particular object). At other times, these prop-erties were from the same modality but belonged to different objects (as when the participant has to report on the colour of one object and the seen shape of a different object). The results showed that it was more costly for participants to discriminate two properties (rather than just one) when those features belonged to different objects than when the two features happened to belong to the same object. However, Bonnel et al. seem to have assumed that features presented from the same location would necessarily be represented as belonging to the same object (see also Pourtois & de Gelder, 2002; Turatto, Mazza, & Umiltà, 2005, for a similar position), and we have already noted that this assumption is highly problematic (see also Bedford, 2004; Spence, 2012). Clearly the notion of an MPO is in need of more investigation, both experimental and theoretical.

Before bringing this section to a close, let us briefly consider what implications the discovery of MPOs would have for the debate under discussion. If such binding involves the simultaneous experience of features belonging to different modalities then the USV would have been shown to be false, even in the restricted form in which we have considered it here (see section 2). However, proponents of the USV could perhaps accommodate the existence of multisensory binding by allowing that consciousness can admit stimuli from multiple modalities at once just as long as those stimuli concern a single intentional object.[19] Indeed, something like this position seems to have been present in the work of those theorists who, writing back in the 1970s and 1980s, argued for a single channel account of attention. Although they generally tended to identify channels with modalities, in places these theorists suggested that a new 'channel' might be formed around particular objects (e.g., Bernstein, 1970; Regan, 1982), thus allowing that a person might be able to attend simultaneously to auditory and visual information.[20] This version of the unisensory view of consciousness would involve a significant departure from the version with which we began in section 3, but it would nevertheless remain within the spirit of the approach insofar as it holds that there are severe limitations on the degree to which consciousness can straddle distinct sensory modalities.

Another possibility worth considering here is that consciousness is 'multisensory' but only insofar as 'amodal' information is concerned.[21] Suppose that one is holding an apple in one's hand while inspecting it visually. Over the course of this perceptual episode, vision will provide one with information about the apple's colour while the sense of touch will provide one with information about its texture. However, *both* vision and touch will provide one with information (albeit with different degrees of precision) about the apple's shape (Ernst & Banks, 2002). (In Aristotle's terms, shape is a *common* sensible rather than a *proper* sensible.) The suggestion, in other words, is that although *proper* sensibles from different modalities cannot jointly contribute to a subject's overall perceptual experience, common sensibles—or, in the language of psychologists, amodal stimulus attributes (such as size, shape, etc.)—can. Again, although this hypothesis might count as a version of the MSV strictly speaking, it is arguably more within the spirit of

---

[19] The advocate of this position might also allow that consciousness can include some multisensory information as long as this information is merely 'gisty' (e.g., Henderson & Hollingworth, 1999; Oliva, 2005)—that is, as long as it is restricted to information about the very general and coarse-grained features of the scene. So, for example, if the subject's experience is occupied with a visual object, then audition might represent only that there is a noise of some kind in the environment, without representing that noise with any precision.

[20] It is also worth noting that much of the evidence in favour of the USV comes from tasks in which the stimuli presented in different sensory modalities are linked to different objects. So, for example, crossmodal TOJs and simultaneity judgments are typically (in fact, nearly always; see Spence & Parise, 2010) made concerning pairs of stimuli that belong to *different* objects.

[21] Note that this use of the term 'amodal' needs to be distinguished from the notion of 'amodal completion' that is invoked in discussions of perceptual content.

the USV. At any rate, it seems to us to be a hypothesis worth taking seriously whatever label one applies to it.[22]

8. Conclusions

In this chapter, we have examined a number of broad lines of evidence that might be used to settle the debate between the USV and the MSV. Although the MSV is taken for granted in many discussions of consciousness, we hope to have convinced the reader that empirical evidence in favour of the view is actually surprisingly elusive. Having constrained the debate that we wished to address in section 2, we moved on in section 3 to examine attempts to defend the MSV by appeal to introspection. In our view, such appeals provide no convincing evidence for the MSV, for not only are these introspective reports not universally shared but there is also reason to think that introspection is not a particularly reliable tool when it comes to identifying the fine-grained structure of consciousness.

In section 4, we examined arguments for the MSV that appealed to the fact that perceptual processing in one modality is often very sensitive to perceptual processing in another modality (as a result of both crossmodal interactions and multisensory integration). In response to such arguments, we suggested that it might be possible to account for these crossmodal effects without supposing that consciousness itself is multisensory (or even that the organism exhibiting these interactions is necessarily conscious).

In section 5, we examined arguments for the MSV that appealed to the presence of intersensory Gestalten—that is, representational content that requires the simultaneous co-consciousness of experiences belonging to different modalities. We argued that the evidence in favour of such Gestalten is weak, as it nearly always takes the form of anecdotal report. Indeed, far from providing an argument for the MSV, the absence of such intersensory Gestalten may actually provide an argument against it. In section 6, we looked at what light the literature on attention and capacity limits might shed on the question of whether consciousness is multisensory, and suggested that the current evidence here is inconclusive. Finally, in section 7, we look at whether 'multisensory binding' might provide evidence against the USV, and tentatively suggested that it does not.

Where does this leave us? We suggest that the question of whether consciousness is unisensory or multisensory is still very much an open one. On the one hand, there would seem to be a certain presumption in favour of the MSV. As the ubiquity of crossmodal interactions demonstrates, perceptual processing is highly

---

[22] As an aside, it may also be worth pondering the just-mentioned question about the costs of shifting attention between features in different modalities when they happen to belong to the same versus different objects. Perhaps the answer to this question depends on whether the features concerned are common or proper sensibles. However, this is an issue that we leave for future discussion.

'multisensory', and given the behavioral advantages that would accrue from multisensory integration it is hard to see why evolution would not have allowed for multisensory experience. Moreover, given how little of the brain is unisensory (in the sense of being unaffected by inputs from more than one modality; Calvert et al., 2004; Driver & Noesselt, 2008; Ghazanfar & Schroeder, 2006; Pascual-Leone & Hamilton, 2001), it's not entirely clear how easy it might be for the human brain to realise a fully unisensory state of consciousness. On the other hand, however, our survey of the relevant experimental work failed to uncover any convincing evidence in favour of the MSV. Interestingly, even our limited discussion has highlighted the fact that one's answer to this question may hinge on whether those unimodal features belong to the same MPO, or, in a more restricted sense, refer to the same amodal feature.

Where do we go from here? One direction for future research is to explore in more depth the most promising experimental paradigms discussed in this review. For example, it would be interesting to know whether any form of intersensory Gestalten can be found. Can static auditory and static visual stimuli present at the appropriate spatiotemporal separation ever give rise to an impression of motion, either real or apparent (Spence & Chen, 2012)? Progress toward solving this debate might also require the development of new methods. Some of these methods might be behavioural; others might involve neuroimaging.[23] Indeed, some promising progress has already been made in this direction in both neurologically normal participants and in neuropsychologically compromised patients (e.g., see Hein et al., 2007; Johnson & Zatorre, 2005, 2006; Shomstein & Yantis, 2004; Smythies, 1997). That said, whatever their form, it will clearly require a great deal of ingenuity to determine whether consciousness is truly multisensory or merely involves rapid intersensory switching between unisensory states of consciousness. The answer to this question will, we hope, advance our understanding of consciousness, for it will shed light on whether the various forms of perceptual experience involve the activation of distinct and potentially autonomous mechanisms (Gallace & Spence, 2008; O'Brien & Opie, 1998), or whether instead they are merely distinct facets (or expressions) of a single underlying mechanism that integrates content drawn from different senses (Bayne, 2010; Searle, 2000; Tye, 2003).

Acknowledgment

This chapter has been written with the support of European Research Council grant 313552 *The Architecture of Consciousness*, for which we are very grateful.

---

[23] Consider the progress made by these techniques in resolving the mental imagery debates (Kosslyn, 1994; Kosslyn, Ganis, & Thompson, 2001) and in convincing skeptics of the reality of synaesthesia (Cytowic & Eagleman, 2009; Nunn et al., 2002).

References

Alais, D., & Burr, D. (2004). The ventriloquist effect results from near-optimal bimodal integration. *Current Biology*, **14**, 257–262.

Alais, D., Morrone, C., & Burr, D. (2006). Separate attentional resources for vision and audition. *Proceedings of the Royal Society B*, **273**, 1339–1345.

Allen, P. G., & Kolers, P. A. (1981). Sensory specificity of apparent motion. *Journal of Experimental Psychology: Human Perception and Performance*, **7**, 1318–1326.

Allport, D. A., Antonis, B., & Reynolds, P. (1972). On the division of attention: A disproof of the single channel hypothesis. *Quarterly Journal of Experimental Psychology*, **24**, 225–235.

Arnell, K. M., & Larson, J. M. (2002). Cross-modality attentional blink without preparatory task-set switching. *Psychonomic Bulletin & Review*, **9**, 497–506.

Arrighi, R., Lunardi, R., & Burr, D. (2011). Vision and audition do not share attentional resources in sustained tasks. *Frontiers in Psychology*, **2(56)**, 1–4.

Attneave, F. (1971). Multistability in perception. *Scientific American*, **225(6)**, 62–71.

Auvray, M., & Spence, C. (2008). The multisensory perception of flavor. *Consciousness and Cognition*, **17**, 1016–1031.

Bayne, T. (2010). *The unity of consciousness*. Oxford: Oxford University Press.

Bayne, T., & Chalmers, D. (2003). What is the unity of consciousness? In A. Cleeremans (Ed.), *The unity of consciousness* (pp. 23–58). Oxford: Oxford University Press.

Bayne, T., & Spener, M. (2010). Introspective humility. In E. Sosa & E. Villanueva (Eds.), *Philosophical Issues*, **20**, 1–22.

Bedford, F. L. (2004). Analysis of a constraint on perception, cognition, and development: One object, one place, one time. *Journal of Experimental Psychology: Human Perception and Performance*, **30**, 907–912.

Benjamins, J. S., van der Smagt, M. J., & Verstraten, F. A. J. (2008). Matching auditory and visual signals: Is modality just another feature? *Perception*, **37**, 848–858.

Bermúdez, J. L. (1998). *The paradox of self-consciousness*. Cambridge, MA: MIT Press.

Bernstein, I. H. (1970). Can we see and hear at the same time? Some recent studies of intersensory facilitation of reaction time. In A. F. Sanders (Ed.), *Attention and performance III, Acta Psychologica*, **33**, 21–35.

Bertelson, P., & de Gelder, B. (2004). The psychology of multimodal perception. In C. Spence & J. Driver (Eds.), *Crossmodal space and crossmodal attention* (pp. 141–177). Oxford: Oxford University Press.

Block, N. (2007). Consciousness, accessibility, and the mesh between psychology and neuroscience. *Behavioral and Brain Sciences*, **30**, 481–548.

Bonnel, A.-M., & Hafter, E. R. (1998). Divided attention between simultaneous auditory and visual signals. *Perception & Psychophysics*, **60**, 179–190.

Bonnel, A.-M., & Prinzmetal, W. (1998). Dividing attention between the color and the shape of objects. *Perception & Psychophysics*, **60**, 113–124.

Bonnel, A.-M., Stein, J.-F., & Bertucci, P. (1992). Does attention modulate the perception of luminance changes? *Quarterly Journal of Experimental Psychology*, **44A**, 601–626.

Bremner, A., Lewkowicz, D., & Spence, C. (Eds.). (2012). *Multisensory development*. Oxford: Oxford University Press.

Brillat-Savarin, J. A. (1835). *Physiologie du goût [The philosopher in the kitchen / The physiology of taste]*. J. P. Meline: Bruxelles. Translated by A. Lalauze (1884), *A handbook of gastronomy*. London: Nimmo & Bain.

Broadbent, D. E. (1958). *Perception and communication.* Elmsford, NY: Pergamon.

Bruno, N., Jacomuzzi, A., Bertamini, M., & Meyer, G. (2007). A visual-haptic Necker cube reveals temporal constraints on intersensory merging during perceptual exploration. *Neuropsychologia, 45,* 469–475.

Bushara, K. O., Hanakawa, T., Immisch, I., Toma, K., Kansaku, K., & Hallett, M. (2002). Neural correlates of cross-modal binding. *Nature Neuroscience, 6,* 190–195.

Calvert, G. A., Spence, C., & Stein, B. E. (Eds.). (2004). *The handbook of multisensory processes.* Cambridge, MA: MIT Press.

Carter, O., Konkle, T., Wang, Q., Hayward, V., & Moore, C. (2008). Tactile rivalry demonstrated with an ambiguous apparent-motion quartet. *Current Biology, 18,* 1050–1054.

Cavanagh, P. (1998). Attention: A peaceful haven for studies of conscious information processing. *Perception, 27,* 23.

Churchland, P. S., Ramachandran, V. S., & Sejnowski, T. J. (1994). A critique of pure vision. In C. Koch & J. L. Davis (Eds.), *Large-scale neuronal theories of the brain* (pp. 23–60). Cambridge, MA: MIT Press.

Cinel, C., Humphreys, G. W., & Poli, R. (2002). Cross-modal illusory conjunctions between vision and touch. *Journal of Experimental Psychology: Human Perception & Performance, 28,* 1243–1266.

Cowan, N. (1995). *Attention and memory: An integrated framework.* Oxford Psychology Series, No. 26. Oxford: Oxford University Press.

Cowan, N. (2000). The magical number 4 in short-term memory: A reconsideration of short-term mental storage capacity. *Behavioral and Brain Sciences, 24,* 87–185.

Cowan, N., Nugent, L. D., Elliot, E. M., Ponomarev, I., & Saults, J. S. (1999). The role of attention in the development of short-term memory: Age differences in the verbal span of apprehension. *Child Development, 70,* 1082–1097.

Crick, F., & Koch, C. (1992). The problem of consciousness. *Scientific American, 267*(3), 152–159.

Cytowic, R. E., & Eagleman, D. M. (2009). *Wednesday is indigo blue: Discovering the brain of synesthesia.* Cambridge, MA: MIT Press.

Dainton, B. (2000). *Stream of consciousness: Unity and continuity in conscious experience.* London: Routledge.

Dennett, D., & Kinsbourne, M. (1992). Time and the observer: The where and when of consciousness in the brain. *Behavioral and Brain Sciences, 15,* 183–247.

Driver, J. (1999). Egocentric and object-based visual neglect. In N. Burgess, K. J. Jeffrey, & J. O'Keefe (Eds.), *The hippocampal and parietal foundations of spatial cognition* (pp. 67–89). Oxford: Oxford University Press.

Driver, J., & Noesselt, T. (2008). Multisensory interplay reveals crossmodal influences on 'sensory-specific' brain regions, neural responses, and judgments. *Neuron, 57,* 11–23.

Duncan, J. (1984). Selective attention and the organization of visual information. *Journal of Experimental Psychology: General, 113,* 501–517.

Duncan, J., Martens, S., & Ward, R. (1997). Restricted attentional capacity within but not between modalities. *Nature, 387,* 808–810.

Ernst, M. O., & Banks, M. S. (2002). Humans integrate visual and haptic information in a statistically optimal fashion. *Nature, 415,* 429–433.

Fraisse, P. (1963). *The psychology of time.* London: Harper & Row.

Fraisse, P. (1981). Multisensory aspects of rhythm. In R. D. Walk & H. L. Pick, Jr. (Eds.), *Intersensory perception and sensory integration* (pp. 217–248). New York: Plenum.

Fujisaki, W., Koene, A., Arnold, D., Johnston, A., & Nishida., S. (2006). Visual search for a target changing in synchrony with an auditory signal. *Proceedings of the Royal Society (B)*, **273**, 865–874.

Fujisaki, W., & Nishida, S. (2010). A common perceptual temporal limit of binding synchronous inputs across different sensory attributes and modalities. *Proceedings of the Royal Society B*, **277**, 2281–2290.

Gallace, A., Auvray, M., Tan, H. Z., & Spence, C. (2006). When visual transients impair tactile change detection: A novel case of crossmodal change blindness? *Neuroscience Letters*, **398**, 280–285.

Gallace, A., & Spence, C. (2008). The cognitive and neural correlates of "tactile consciousness": A multisensory perspective. *Consciousness and Cognition*, **17**, 370–407.

Gallace, A., & Spence, C. (2010). Touch and the body: The role of the somatosensory cortex in tactile awareness. *Psyche*, **16**, 30–67. http://www.theassc.org/journal_psyche/archive/vol_16_no_1_2010.

Gallace, A., & Spence, C. (2011). To what extent do Gestalt grouping principles influence tactile perception? *Psychological Bulletin*, **137**, 538–561.

Gallace, A., Tan, H. Z., & Spence, C. (2007). Multisensory numerosity judgments for visual and tactile stimuli. *Perception & Psychophysics*, **69**, 487–501.

Galli, P. A. (1932). Über mittelst verschiedener Sinnesreize erweckte Wahrnehmung von Scheinbewegungen [On the perception of apparent motion elicited by different sensory stimuli]. *Archiv für die gesamte Psychologie*, **85**, 137–180.

Gebhard, J. W., & Mowbray, G. H. (1959). On discriminating the rate of visual flicker and auditory flutter. *American Journal of Psychology*, **72**, 521–528.

Ghazanfar, A. A., & Schroeder, C. E. (2006). Is neocortex essentially multisensory? *Trends in Cognitive Sciences*, **10**, 278–285.

Gilbert, G. M. (1938). A study in inter-sensory Gestalten. *Psychological Bulletin*, **35**, 698.

Gilbert, G. M. (1939). Dynamic psychophysics and the phi phenomenon. *Archives of Psychology*, **237**, 5–43.

Gladstones, W. H., Regan, M. A., & Lee, R. B. (1989). Division of attention: The single-channel hypothesis revisited. *Quarterly Journal of Experimental Psychology*, **41A**, 1–17.

Guinzberg, R. L. (1928). È possibile l'apprendimento di sensazioni eterogenee come perfettamente simultanee? [Is it possible to learn that heterogenous sensations are perfectly simultaneous?] *Archivi Italiani di Psicologia*, **6**, 103–114.

Guttman, S. E., Gilroy, L. A., & Blake, R. (2005). Hearing what the eyes see: Auditory encoding of visual temporal sequences. *Psychological Science*, **16**, 228–235.

Harrar, V., Winter, R., & Harris, L. (2005). *Multimodal apparent motion*. Poster presented at the 6th Annual Meeting of the International Multisensory Research Forum, Rovereto, Italy, 5–8 June.

Harris, J. A., Miniussi, C., Harris, I. M., & Diamond, M. E. (2002). Transient storage of a tactile memory trace in primary somatosensory cortex. *Journal of Neuroscience*, **22**, 8720–8725.

Hein, G., Alink, A., Kleinschmidt, A., & Müller, N. G. (2007). Competing neural responses for auditory and visual decisions. *PLoS ONE*, **3**, e320.

Hein, G., Parr, A., & Duncan, J. (2006). Within-modality and cross-modality attentional blinks in a simple discrimination task. *Perception & Psychophysics*, **68**, 54–61.

Henderson, J. M., & Hollingworth, A. (1999). High level scene perception. *Annual Review of Psychology*, **50**, 243–271.

Huddleston, W. E., Lewis, J. W., Phinney, R. E., & DeYoe, E. A. (2008). Auditory and visual attention-based apparent motion share functional parallels. *Perception & Psychophysics*, **70**, 1207–1216.

Hupé, J. M., Joffoa, L. M., & Pressnitzer, D. (2008). Bistability for audiovisual stimuli: Perceptual decision is modality specific. *Journal of Vision*, **8**(7),1, 1–15.

Jiang, Y., Costello, P. F., Fang, F. Huang, M., & He, S. (2006). A gender- and sexual orientation-dependent spatial attention effect of invisible images. *Proceedings of the National Academy of Sciences USA*, **103**, 17048–17052.

Johnson, J. A., & Zatorre, R. J. (2005). Attention to simultaneous unrelated auditory and visual events: Behavioral and neural correlates. *Cerebral Cortex*, **15**, 1609–1620.

Johnson, J. A., & Zatorre, R. J. (2006). Neural substrates for dividing and focusing attention between simultaneous auditory and visual events. *NeuroImage*, **31**, 1673–1681.

Jolicoeur, P. (1999). Restricted attentional capacity between modalities. *Psychonomic Bulletin & Review*, **6**, 87–92.

Jordan, K. E., Clark, K., & Mitroff, S. R. (2010). See an object, hear an object file: Object correspondence transcends sensory modality. *Visual Cognition*, **18**, 492–503.

Kahneman, D., Treisman, A., & Gibbs, B. J. (1992). The reviewing of object files: Object-specific integration of information. *Cognitive Psychology*, **24**, 175–219.

Kentridge, R. W. (in press). Attention without awareness: A brief review. In C. Mole, D. Smithies, & W. Wu (Eds.), *Attention: Philosophical and psychological essays* (pp. 228–247). Oxford: Oxford University Press.

Koch, C., & Tsuchiya. N. (2007). Attention and consciousness: Two distinct brain processes. *Trends in Cognitive Sciences*, **11**, 16–22.

Koppen, C., Alsius, A., & Spence, C. (2008). Semantic congruency and the Colavita visual dominance effect. *Experimental Brain Research*, **184**, 533–546.

Kosslyn, S. M. (1994). *Image and brain: The resolution of the imagery debate.* Cambridge, MA: MIT Press.

Kosslyn, S. M., Ganis, G., & Thompson, W. L. (2001). Neural foundations of imagery. *Nature Reviews Neuroscience*, **2**, 635–642.

Kristofferson, A. B. (1967). Attention and psychophysical time. In A. F. Saunders, *Attention and performance. Acta Psychologica*, **27**, 93–100.

Kubovy, M., & Schutz, M. (2010). Audio-visual objects. *Review of Philosophy & Psychology*, **1**, 41–61.

Kubovy, M., & van Valkenburg, D. (2001). Auditory and visual objects. *Cognition*, **80**, 97–126.

Lakatos, S., & Shepard, R. N. (1997). Constraints common to apparent motion in visual, tactile, and auditory space. *Journal of Experimental Psychology: Human Perception & Performance*, **23**, 1050–1060.

Lamme, V. A. F. (2003). Why visual attention and awareness and different. *Trends in Cognitive Sciences*, **7**, 12–18.

Larsen, A., McIlhagga, W., Baert, J., & Bundesen, C. (2003). Seeing or hearing? Perceptual independence, modality confusions, and crossmodal congruity effects with focused and divided attention. *Perception & Psychophysics*, **65**, 568–574.

Leo, F., Bolognini, N., Passamonti, C., Stein, B. E., & Làdavas, E. (2008). Cross-modal localization in hemianopia: New insights on multisensory integration. *Brain*, **131**, 855–865.

Logan, G. D. (1996). The CODE theory of visual attention: An integration of space-based and object-based attention. *Psychological Review*, **103**, 603–649.

London, I. D. (1954). Research on sensory interaction in the Soviet Union. *Psychological Bulletin*, **51**, 531–568.

Lu, Z.-L., Williamson, S. J., & Kaufman, L. (1992). Behavioral lifetime of human auditory sensory memory predicted by physiological measures. *Science*, **258**, 1669–1670.

Luck, S. J., & Vogel, E. K. (1997). The capacity of visual working memory for features and conjunctions. *Nature*, **390**, 279–281.

Lunghi, C., Binda, P., & Morrone, M. C. (2010). Touch disambiguates rivalrous perception at early stages of visual analysis. *Current Biology*, **20**, R143–R144.

Mack, A., & Rock, I. (1998). *Inattentional blindness*. Cambridge, MA: MIT Press.

Macpherson, F. (Ed.). (2011). *The senses: Classic and contemporary philosophical perspectives*. Oxford: Oxford University Press.

Marks, C. (1981). *Commissurotomy, consciousness and unity of mind*. Cambridge, MA: MIT Press.

Marks, L. E., & Odgaard, E. C. (2005). Developmental constraints on theories of synaesthesia. In L. Robertson & N. Sagiv (Eds.), *Synaesthesia: Perspectives from cognitive neuroscience* (pp. 214–236). New York: Oxford University Press.

Martin, M. (1980). Attention to words in different modalities: Four-channel presentation with physical and semantic selection. *Acta Psychologica*, **44**, 99–115.

McBurney, D. H. (1986). Taste, smell, and flavor terminology: Taking the confusion out of fusion. In H. L. Meiselman & R. S. Rivkin (Eds.), *Clinical measurement of taste and smell* (pp. 117–125). New York: Macmillan.

McGurk, H., & MacDonald, J. (1976). Hearing lips and seeing voices. *Nature*, **264**, 746–748.

Mitroff, S. R., & Scholl, B. J. (2005). Forming and updating object representations without awareness: Evidence from motion-induced blindness. *Vision Research*, **45**, 961–967.

Mitroff, S. R., Scholl, B. J., & Wynn, K. (2005). The relationship between object files and conscious perception. *Cognition*, **96**, 67–92.

Morein-Zamir, S., Soto-Faraco, S., & Kingstone, A. (2003). Auditory capture of vision: Examining temporal ventriloquism. *Cognitive Brain Research*, **17**, 154–163.

Neisser, U. (1976). *Cognition and reality: Principles and implications of cognitive psychology*. San Francisco: Freeman.

Nunn, J. A., Gregory, L. J., Brammer, M., Williams, S. C. R., Parslow, D. M., Morgan, M. J., Morris, R. G., Bullmore, E. T., Baron-Cohen, S., & Gray, J. A. (2002). Functional magnetic resonance imaging of synesthesia: Activation of V4/V8 by spoken words. *Nature Neuroscience*, **5**, 371–375.

O'Brien, G., & Opie, J. (1998). The disunity of consciousness. *Australasian Journal of Philosophy*, **76**, 378–395.

O'Callaghan, C. (2008). Object perception: Vision and audition. *Philosophy Compass*, **3**, 803–829.

O'Callaghan, C. (2012). Perception and multimodality. In E. Margolis, R. Samuels, & S. Stich (Eds.), *The Oxford handbook of philosophy and cognitive science* (pp. 92–117). Oxford: Oxford University Press.

Oliva, A. (2005). Gist of the scene. In L. Itti, G. Rees, & J. Tsotsos (Eds.), *Neurobiology of attention* (pp. 251–256). San Diego, CA: Elsevier.

O'Regan, J. K. (1992). Solving the "real" mysteries of visual perception: The world as an outside memory. *Canadian Journal of Psychology*, **46**, 461–488.

Pascual-Leone, A., & Hamilton, R. (2001). The metamodal organization of the brain. In C. Casanova & M. Ptito (Eds.), *Progress in Brain Research*, **134**, 427–445.

Piéron, H. (1952). *The sensations: Their functions, processes and mechanisms.* Translated by M. H. Pirenne & B. C. Abbott. London: Frederick Muller.

Pizzaghello, S., & Bressan, P. (2008). Auditory attention causes visual inattention blindness. *Perception,* 37, 859–866.

Posner, M. I., & Boies, S. J. (1971). Components of attention. *Psychological Review,* 78, 391–408.

Potter, M. C., Chun, M. M., Banks, B. S., & Muckenhoupt, M. (1998). Two attentional deficits in serial target search: The visual attentional blink and an amodal task-switch deficit. *Journal of Experimental Psychology: Learning, Memory, & Cognition,* 24, 979–992.

Pourtois, G., de Gelder, B., Vroomen, J., Rossion, B., & Crommelinck, M. (2000). The time-course of intermodal binding between seeing and hearing affective information. *Neuroreport,* 11, 1329–1333.

Pourtois, G., & de Gelder, B. (2002). Semantic factors influence multisensory pairing: A transcranial magnetic stimulation study. *Neuroreport,* 13, 1567–1573.

Rader, C. M., & Tellegen, A. (1987). An investigation of synesthesia. *Journal of Personality and Social Psychology,* 52, 981–987.

Ramachandran, V. S., & Anstis, S. M. (1983). Perceptual organization of moving patterns. *Nature,* 304, 529–531.

Raymond, J. (2009). Attentional blink. In T. Bayne, A. Cleeremans, & P. Wilken (Eds.), *The Oxford companion to consciousness* (pp. 66–68). Oxford: Oxford University Press.

Regan, D. (1982). Visual information channeling in normal and disordered vision. *Psychological Review,* 89, 407–444.

Reisberg, D., Pearson, D. G., & Kosslyn, S. M. (2003). Intuitions and introspections about imagery: The role of imagery experience in shaping an investigator's theoretical views. *Applied Cognitive Psychology,* 17, 147–160.

Revonsuo, A. (1999). Binding and the phenomenal unity of consciousness. *Consciousness and Cognition,* 8, 173–185.

Revonsuo, A., & Newman, J. (1999). Binding and consciousness. *Consciousness and Cognition,* 8, 123–127.

Robertson, L. C. (2003). Binding, spatial attention and perceptual awareness. *Nature Reviews Neuroscience,* 4, 93–102.

Robertson, L., & Sagiv, N. (Eds.). (2005). *Synaesthesia: Perspectives from cognitive neuroscience.* New York: Oxford University Press.

Rollins, R. A. Jr., & Hendricks, R. (1980). Processing of words presented simultaneously to eye and ear. *Journal of Experimental Psychology: Human Perception and Performance,* 6, 99–109.

Sanabria, D., Soto-Faraco, S., & Spence, C. (2005). Assessing the effect of visual and tactile distractors on the perception of auditory apparent motion. *Experimental Brain Research,* 166, 548–558.

Schiller, P. (1935). Interrelation of different senses in perception. *British Journal of Psychology,* 25, 465–469.

Schumacher, E. H., Seymour, T. L., Glass, J. M., Fencsik, D. E., Lauber, E. J., Kieras, D. E., & Meyer, D. E. (2001). Virtually perfect time sharing in dual-task performance: Uncorking the central cognitive bottleneck. *Psychological Science,* 12, 101–108.

Schwitzgebel, E. (2008). The unreliability of naïve introspection. *Philosophical Review,* 117, 245–273.

Searle, J. (2000). Consciousness. *Annual Review of Neuroscience,* 23, 557–578.

Shams, L., Kamitani, Y., & Shimojo, S. (2000). What you see is what you hear: Sound induced visual flashing. *Nature*, **408**, 788.

Shapiro, K. L., Arnell, K. M., & Raymond, J.E. (1997). The attentional blink. *Trends in Cognitive Sciences*, **1**, 291–296.

Shinn-Cunningham, B. G. (2008). Object-based auditory and visual attention. *Trends in Cognitive Sciences*, **12**, 182–186.

Shomstein, S., & Yantis, S. (2004). Control of attention shifts between vision and audition in human cortex. *Journal of Neuroscience*, **24**, 10702–10706.

Simons, D. J., & Ambinder, M. S. (2005). Change blindness: Theory and consequences. *Current Directions in Psychological Science*, **14**, 44–48.

Sinnett, S., Spence, C., & Soto-Faraco, S. (2007). Visual dominance and attention: The Colavita effect revisited. *Perception & Psychophysics*, **69**, 673–686.

Smith, W. F. (1933). The relative quickness of visual and auditory perception. *Journal of Experimental Psychology*, **16**, 239–257.

Smythies, J. (1997). The functional neuroanatomy of awareness: With a focus on the role of various anatomical systems in the control of intermodal attention. *Consciousness and Cognition*, **6**, 455–481.

Soroker, N., Calamaro, N., & Myslobodsky, M. (1995a). "McGurk illusion" to bilateral administration of sensory stimuli in patients with hemispatial neglect. *Neuropsychologia*, **33**, 461–470.

Soroker, N., Calamaro, N., & Myslobodsky, M. S. (1995b). Ventriloquism effect reinstates responsiveness to auditory stimuli in the 'ignored' space in patients with hemispatial neglect. *Journal of Clinical and Experimental Neuropsychology*, **17**, 243–255.

Soto-Faraco, S., & Alsius, A. (2007). Conscious access to the unisensory components of a cross-modal illusion. *Neuroreport*, **18**, 347–350.

Soto-Faraco, S., & Alsius, A. (2009). Deconstructing the McGurk-MacDonald illusion. *Journal of Experimental Psychology: Human Perception & Performance*, **35**, 580–587.

Soto-Faraco, S., & Spence, C. (2002). Modality-specific auditory and visual temporal processing deficits. *Quarterly Journal of Experimental Psychology A*, **55**, 23–40.

Soto-Faraco, S. Spence, C., Fairbank, K., Kingstone, A., Hillstrom, A. P., & Shapiro, K. (2002). A crossmodal attentional blink between vision and touch. *Psychonomic Bulletin & Review*, **9**, 731–738.

Soto-Faraco, S., Spence, C., Lloyd, D., & Kingstone, A. (2004). Moving multisensory research along: Motion perception across modalities. *Current Directions in Psychological Science*, **13**, 29–32.

Spence, C. (2010a). Crossmodal attention. *Scholarpedia*, **5**(5), 6309. doi: 10.4249/scholarpedia.6309.

Spence, C. (2010b). Prior entry: Attention and temporal perception. In A. C. Nobre & J. T. Coull (Eds.), *Attention and time* (pp. 89–104). Oxford: Oxford University Press.

Spence, C. (2010c). Crossmodal spatial attention. *Annals of the New York Academy of Science (The Year in Cognitive Neuroscience)*, **1191**, 182–200.

Spence, C. (2012). Multisensory perception, cognition, and behavior: Evaluating the factors modulating multisensory integration. In B. E. Stein (Ed.), *The new handbook of multisensory processing* (pp. 241–264). Cambridge, MA: MIT Press.

Spence, C., & Chen, Y.-C. (2012). Intramodal and crossmodal perceptual grouping. In B. E. Stein (Ed.), *The new handbook of multisensory processing* (pp. 265–282). Cambridge, MA: MIT Press.

Spence, C., & Deroy, O. (2013). Crossmodal mental imagery. In S. Lacey & R. Lawson (Eds.), *Multisensory imagery: Theory and applications* (pp. 157–183). Springer: New York.

Spence, C., & Driver, J. (Eds.). (2004). *Crossmodal space and crossmodal attention.* Oxford, UK: Oxford University Press.

Spence, C., & Ngo, M.-C. (2012). Does attention or multisensory integration explain the crossmodal facilitation of masked visual target identification? In B. E. Stein (Ed.), *The new handbook of multisensory processing* (pp. 345–358). Cambridge, MA: MIT Press.

Spence, C., Nicholls, M. E. R., & Driver, J. (2001). The cost of expecting events in the wrong modality. *Perception & Psychophysics*, **63**, 330–336.

Spence, C., & Parise, C. (2010). Prior entry. *Consciousness & Cognition*, **19**, 364–379.

Spence, C., Parise, C., & Chen, Y.-C. (2011). The Colavita visual dominance effect. In M. M. Murray & M. Wallace (Eds.), *Frontiers in the neural bases of multisensory processes* (pp. 523–550). Boca Raton, FL: CRC Press.

Spence, C., Sanabria, D., & Soto-Faraco, S. (2007). Intersensory Gestalten and crossmodal scene perception. In K. Noguchi (Ed.), *Psychology of beauty and Kansei: New horizons of Gestalt perception* (pp. 519–579). Tokyo: Fuzanbo International.

Spence, C., & Soto-Faraco, S. (2009). Auditory perception: Interactions with vision. In C. Plack (Ed.), *Auditory perception* (pp. 271–296). Oxford: Oxford University Press.

Spence, C., & Squire, S. B. (2003). Multisensory integration: Maintaining the perception of synchrony. *Current Biology*, **13**, R519–R521.

Sperry, R. W. (1984). Consciousness, personal identity, and the divided brain. *Neuropsychologia*, **22**, 661–673.

Stein, B. E. (Ed.). (2012). *The new handbook of multisensory processing.* Cambridge, MA: MIT Press.

Stein, B. E., Burr, D., Costantinides, C., Laurienti, P. J., Meredith, A. M., Perrault, T. J., et al. (2010). Semantic confusion regarding the development of multisensory integration: A practical solution. *European Journal of Neuroscience*, **31**, 1713–1720.

Stevenson, R. J. (2009). *The psychology of flavour.* Oxford: Oxford University Press.

Stevenson, R. J., & Tomiczek, C. (2007). Olfactory-induced synesthesias: A review and model. *Psychological Bulletin*, **133**, 294–309.

Stone, J. V., Hunkin, N. M., Porrill, J., Wood, R., Keeler, V., Beanland, M., Port, M., & Porter, N. R. (2001). When is now? Perception of simultaneity. *Proceedings of the Royal Society (B)*, **268**, 31–38.

Thomas, G. J. (1941). Experimental study of the influence of vision on sound localization. *Journal of Experimental Psychology*, **28**, 163–177.

Treisman, A. (1996). The binding problem. *Current Opinion in Neurobiology*, **6**, 171–178.

Treisman, A. M., & Davies, A. (1973). Divided attention to ear and eye. In S. Kornblum (Ed.), *Attention and performance* (Vol. 4, pp. 101–117). New York: Academic Press.

Tulving. E., & Lindsay, P. H. (1967). Identification of simultaneously presented simple visual and auditory stimuli. *Acta Psychologica*, **27**, 101–109.

Turatto, M., Mazza, V., & Umiltà, C. (2005). Crossmodal object-based attention: Auditory objects affect visual processing. *Cognition*, **96**, B55–B64.

Tye, M. (2003). *Consciousness and persons.* Cambridge, MA: MIT Press.

Uusitalo, M. A., Williamson, S. J., & Seppä, M. T. (1996). Dynamical organisation of the human visual system revealed by lifetimes of activation traces. *Neuroscience Letters*, **213**, 149–152.

Van der Burg, E., Olivers, C. N. L., Bronkhorst, A. W., & Theeuwes, J. (2008). Non-spatial auditory signals improve spatial visual search. *Journal of Experimental Psychology: Human Perception and Performance, 34,* 1053–1065.

van Ee, R., van Boxtel, J. J. A., Parker, A. L., & Alais, D. (2009). Multimodal congruency as a mechanism for willful control over perceptual awareness. *Journal of Neuroscience, 29,* 11641–11649.

Vibell, J., Klinge, C., Zampini, M., Spence, C., & Nobre, A. C. (2007). Temporal order is coded temporally in the brain: Early ERP latency shifts underlying prior entry in a cross-modal temporal order judgment task. *Journal of Cognitive Neuroscience, 19,* 109–120.

Welch, R. B., & Warren, D. H. (1986). Intersensory interactions. In K. R. Boff, L. Kaufman, & J. P. Thomas (Eds.), *Handbook of perception and performance: Vol. 1. Sensory processes and perception* (pp. 25, 1–25, 36). New York: Wiley.

Wyart, V., & Tallon-Baudry, C. (2008). Neural dissociation between visual awareness and spatial attention. *Journal of Neuroscience, 28,* 2667–2679.

Yamamoto, S., & Kitazawa, S. (2001). Reversal of subjective temporal order due to arm crossing. *Nature Neuroscience, 4,* 759–765.

Zapparoli, G. C., & Reatto, L. L. (1969). The apparent movement between visual and acoustic stimulus and the problem of intermodal relations. *Acta Psychologica, 29,* 256–267.

Zimmerman, M. (1989). The nervous system in the context of information theory. In R. F. Schmidt & G. Thews (Eds.), *Human physiology* (2nd Complete Ed., pp. 166–173). Berlin: Springer-Verlag.

Zylberberg, A., Dehaene, S., Mindlin, G. B., & Sigman, M. (2009). Neurophysiological bases of exponential sensory decay and top-down memory retrieval: A model. *Frontiers in Computational Neuroscience, 3:4,* 1–16.

5

Not All Perceptual Experience
Is Modality Specific

Casey O'Callaghan

1. Minimal Multimodality

Humans see, hear, touch, smell, and taste. Episodes of human sensory perceptual experience accordingly are associated with several ways or modes—modalities— of perceiving. Perceptual experiences may be visual, auditory, tactual, olfactory, or gustatory. If there are more or fewer modalities, name them and adjust accordingly.

Individual human subjects commonly see and hear at the same time; or hear and smell; or see, hear, and smell; and so on. Most times while you are awake, your perceptual experience is associated with more than one modality. Perceptual experience is, in this *minimal* respect, *multimodal.*[1]

Recent science demonstrates that the senses do not act merely in parallel or in isolation from each other. Different senses interact and influence each other, and this affects perceptual experience.[2] For instance, cross-modal perceptual illusions occur when stimulation to one sensory system impacts experience associated with another modality in a way that leads to misperception. The ventriloquist effect, for example, is an auditory spatial illusion generated by the visible location of an apparent sound source.

---

[1] If it were associated at most with one modality at a time, human perceptual experience at a time instead would be *unimodal.* See Spence and Bayne (this volume). I resist the unimodal experience view for the following reasons. The view is most plausible if (a) consciousness requires attention and if (b) attention is restricted to a single modality at a time. However, (a) is controversial, and it is possible that we do perceptually experience things that are outside the focus of attention. Even so, there are good arguments for rejecting (b) and holding that attention can range over more than one modality at a time. For instance, it is plausible that there can be multimodal objects of attention (see section 2.2; see also, for example, Karns and Knight 2009). Nevertheless, even rejecting all of this, it is plausible that the temporal grain of the experienced present is coarser than that of conscious shifts between modalities, and that there are no temporal gaps between experiences of distinct modalities, which implies that there are times during which experience is at least minimally multimodal.

[2] See O'Callaghan (2012) for extended discussion.

It does not follow that perceptual experience fails to remain *modality specific*. Sensory processes might interact causally while all perceptual experiences nevertheless belong to particular modalities. One sense might causally but not constitutively impact perceptual experience that is associated with another.

On phenomenological grounds, it is initially plausible that perceptual experience does remain modality specific. Visual, auditory, tactual, olfactory, and gustatory perceptual experiences have distinctive and recognizable phenomenal character that makes it tough to be fooled about when you are seeing, hearing, feeling, smelling, or tasting. This modality-specific character may seem uninfected by other senses. Visual experience, for instance, does not seem to incorporate auditory phenomenal character. Moreover, nothing stands out in exteroceptive perceptual experience beyond the visual, auditory, tactual, olfactory, and gustatory. Any perceptual experiences that coexist alongside seeing, hearing, feeling, smelling, and tasting generally have escaped philosophical attention. That overall perceptual experience just is the sum of proprietary visual, auditory, tactual, olfactory, and gustatory experiences thus may seem introspectively obvious. In virtue of its phenomenal character, therefore, perceptual experience may seem not more than minimally multimodal.

This chapter argues that perceptual experience is not merely minimally multimodal. It clarifies what it means to say that an aspect of perceptual experience is modality specific. And it presents forms of multimodal perceptual experience that undermine the claim that each aspect of perceptual experience is modality specific. It concludes that a multimodal perceptual episode may have phenomenal features beyond those that are associated with the specific modalities.

Some preliminary clarifications are needed.

First, this chapter concerns episodes of exteroceptive sensory perceptual experience rather than interoception, bodily awareness, or any wholly cognitive, intellectual form of perception. I'll just refer to perceptual experiences.

Second, a perceptual experience is a conscious episode with, among other attributes, phenomenal character. The phenomenal character of a perceptual experience is what it is like for its subject to undergo that episode. Phenomenal features are aspects of phenomenal character. This chapter concerns such phenomenal properties and their instantiations. It is about the respects in which they may be associated with a specific modality.

Third, my topic is not how to individuate or count modalities. Differing accounts specify how to individuate modalities of exteroceptive sensory perception. Such accounts appeal to distal objects; to what is represented; to proximal stimuli; to sense organs; to sensory systems; to phenomenal character; or to several of these.[3] Such accounts may be adapted to classify perceptual experiences according to modality. With exceptions I note, my discussion aims to be neutral

---

[3] See, e.g., Grice (1962); Macpherson (2011b, this volume); Casati et al. (this volume); Matthen (forthcoming).

among available accounts. I assume that some experiences are visual, some are auditory, some are tactual, some are olfactory, and some are gustatory, and that there could be a satisfactory account of what makes an episode of perceptual experience visual, auditory, tactual, olfactory, or gustatory. What distinguishes modalities and what makes an episode of perceptual experience visual, auditory, tactual, olfactory, or gustatory are questions related closely to this chapter's main topic, but they are not its primary target. This chapter begins where individuation and classification leave off.

Fourth, that perceptual experience is multimodal does not imply that a subject enjoys more than one token perceptual experience at a time. Tye (2003, 2007), for instance, denies that a subject's perceptual experience at a time comprises distinct token visual, auditory, tactual, olfactory, and gustatory episodes. Tye maintains that a subject's perceptual experience is a single, unified token event that may be characterized variously, as visual, auditory, tactual, olfactory, or gustatory. Without including multiple experiences, a conscious perceptual episode at a time thus may be both visual and auditory, for example. A single perceptual experience also may have phenomenal character associated with vision, audition, touch, smell, and taste.

The claim that all perceptual experience is modality specific in virtue of its phenomenal character thus can be reformulated to be more neutral, as the claim that all phenomenal character is modality specific. Thus, the thesis that perceptual experience is not more than minimally multimodal becomes the claim that the phenomenal character of any conscious perceptual episode is exhausted by that which is associated with vision, that which is associated with audition, that which is associated with touch, that which is associated with smell, and that which is associated with taste.

Finally, the unity of conscious perceptual experience poses a counterexample even to this revised thesis. Tye (2003, 2007), for example, argues that having an experience that is both visual and auditory—a visual experience co-conscious with an auditory experience—differs from having a visual experience and having an auditory experience at the same time. Thus, the unity among perceptual experiences associated with different modalities is a phenomenal property of multimodal perceptual experiences that is not associated with any specific modality, so not all phenomenal character is modality specific.[4]

If it succeeds, this argument from unity applies among all co-conscious experiences. It affects, for instance, bodily experiences, affective experiences, conscious thoughts, and visual experiences, not just perceptual experiences of different exteroceptive sensory modalities. The general unity of consciousness, however, is not my target. So I shall revise the thesis to reflect it. The thesis that perceptual experience is modality specific and thus not more than minimally multimodal

---

[4] See also Bayne (2010), and Macpherson (2011a) for helpful discussion.

becomes the claim that the phenomenal character of any conscious perceptual episode is exhausted by that which is associated with vision, that which is associated with audition, that which is associated with touch, that which is associated with smell, and that which is associated with taste, along with whatever phenomenal character accrues thanks *merely* to the co-conscious occurrence of visual, auditory, tactual, olfactory, and gustatory experiences.

2. Distinctiveness

Phenomenal character is commonly *associated with* a modality, such as vision, audition, touch, smell, or taste. There is what it's like to see red, what it's like to hear a squeak, what it's like to feel paste, what it's like to taste Vegemite, and what it's like to smell cinnamon. Some philosophers maintain that perceptual experiences of a given modality have a *distinctive* phenomenal character. Grice (1962, esp. 37, 53), for instance, emphasizes "the special introspectible character of the experiences of seeing and smelling," which differentiates them.[5] Suppose that phenomenal character *is associated with a given modality* just in case it is distinctive to that modality. If each experience of a given modality has a distinctive phenomenal character, this may enable us to determine readily, by introspecting, whether the phenomenal character of any conscious perceptual episode is exhausted by that which is associated with vision, audition, touch, smell, and taste.

Having distinctive phenomenal character could mean that all and only experiences of a given modality instantiate some common phenomenal feature, such as "the visual character." If so, all and only visual experiences resemble each other in virtue of possessing this unique phenomenal feature. This is one way to interpret Grice's remarks when he speaks of "a generic resemblance signalized by the use of the word 'look,' which differentiates visual from nonvisual sense-experience" (1962, 53).

Distinctiveness, however, does not require a specific, uniform qualitative feature shared by all experiences of a given modality. There might be a family or a class of distinct phenomenal characters whose instantiation is unique to a given modality. Suppose that for each modality, each experience of that modality has a phenomenal character that no experience not of that modality has. For instance, suppose every visual experience has some phenomenal character that all nonvisual experiences lack. For example, many but not all visual experiences instantiate *phenomenal redness*, and no nonvisual experience does.[6] Enough phenomenal

---

[5] Thus, Grice maintains that perceptual experiences belong to modalities in virtue of their phenomenal character.

[6] I'm taking no stance on the nature of *phenomenal redness*. I especially am not assuming it is an irreducibly qualitative or nonintentional quale. So this should be read as compatible with, for instance, strong intentionalism or naïve realism about phenomenal character.

character sharing of the right kind among visual experiences may generate Grice's "generic resemblance."

A perceptual experience of a given modality has a distinctive phenomenal character just in case its phenomenal character could not be instantiated by an experience that is not of that modality. If the phenomenal character of each perceptual experience of a given modality is distinctive, then the thesis that all phenomenal character is modality specific requires all phenomenal character to be distinctive to some modality. Alternatively, every phenomenal character is associated with a unique modality. This means that the phenomenal character of each perceptual experience is exhausted by that which is instantiated by an experience of some modality and could not be instantiated by an experience that is not of that modality.

2.1. LOCAL DISTINCTIVENESS

The thesis being considered is that all phenomenal character is modality specific. Thus, all phenomenal character is associated with a specific modality. I am now interpreting the thesis to imply that all phenomenal character is distinctive to some modality—is instantiated uniquely by perceptual experiences of that modality.

Difficulty for the thesis, so interpreted, surfaces if we consider phenomenal character associated with perceptual experiences of sensible features. I understand a feature to be a property or an individual.

Proper sensibles pose no trouble. These are features perceptible only through a single modality. Consider *redness*, for example. It is plausible that each visual experience as of redness has phenomenal character that is not instantiated by any perceptual experience that is not visual. Or consider sounds. It is plausible that each auditory experience as of a sound has phenomenal character that is not instantiated by any perceptual experience that is not auditory.

Common sensibles may pose trouble. These are features perceptible through more than one modality. Consider number, temporal features, or spatial features. Take, for example, *squareness*. You may visually or tactually perceptually experience squareness. (If you find this implausible, take another spatial feature, such as *angularity*.) It is not wholly obvious that the phenomenal character associated with a token *visual* perceptual experience as of *squareness*, considered as a phenomenal property that is distinct from, but coinstantiated with, the phenomenal character of one's visual perceptual experience as of other features, such as redness, must differ discernibly from the phenomenal character associated with a token *tactual* perceptual experience as of *squareness*, considered as a phenomenal property distinct from, but coinstantiated with, the phenomenal character associated with one's tactual perceptual experience as of other features, such as texture. Beyond the phenomenal properties that accrue thanks to the perceptual experience of other features, the phenomenal properties that accrue thanks to the perceptual experience of some common sensible need not differ between modalities.

The point is clearer if we suppose, temporarily, that token perceptual experiences are individuated finely. Suppose, for instance, that token experiences are distinct if they represent or involve awareness as of distinct token sensible features. So, if you see something red beside something green, you token an experience of redness that is numerically distinct from your token experience of greenness. If you see something red and round, you token an experience of redness that is numerically distinct from your token experience of roundness. (You also may have additional token experiences as of both features.) Supposing that experience tokens are so fine grained isolates the phenomenal character associated with experiencing a common sensible from the phenomenal character associated with experiencing other features. Each token visual experience of squareness per se need not differ in phenomenal character from every token tactual experience of squareness per se when the token perceptual experiences are, as it were, stripped of other sensible features.[7]

It is, however, equally plausible that any two token perceptual experiences of squareness per se may differ in phenomenal character when they belong to different modalities, even once we have controlled for differences in phenomenal character that stem from the perceptual experience of other sensible features. Perhaps differing modality-specific modes of presentation generate a phenomenal difference. Or perhaps phenomenal features depend holistically on other sensible features of which one is aware. Or, if perceptual modalities are akin to different intentional attitudes, like belief and desire, perhaps phenomenal character partially is a product of the modality.[8]

2.2. INTERMODAL BINDING

Another sort of case does undermine the claim that all phenomenal character is instantiated only by perceptual experiences of exactly one modality (again, making an allowance for mere co-consciousness). The case is a variety of multimodal perceptual experience. It involves perceptually experiencing the co-instantiation of attributes perceived through different modalities. For instance, you might perceptually experience something to be both loud and bright, or to be both red and rough. This is the experience of intermodal feature binding.[9, 10]

---

[7] This is especially clear on intentionalist accounts that identify phenomenal features with such properties as perceptually representing squareness.

[8] See, for example, Chalmers (2004) for discussion of modality-specific modes of presentation and modality-impure accounts of phenomenal character.

[9] Relevant empirical work on intermodal binding includes, for example, Pourtois et al. (2000); Bushara et al. (2003); Bertelson and de Gelder (2004); Spence and Driver (2004); Spence (2007); Kubovy and Schutz (2010).

[10] A note on my use of "cross-modal" and "intermodal": In this chapter, "cross-modal" means roughly "across modalities" in a way that implies directionality, such as in cases where one perceptual modality impacts or influences another. So, for instance, I talk about cross-modal illusions. "Intermodal" means roughly "between modalities" in a way that does not imply directionality, as in

To perceptually experience as of something loud and something bright differs from perceptually experiencing as of something loud and bright. You might hear a tuba blast while seeing the sun's reflection. But you might instead perceive a loud event also to be bright—you might perceptually experience the event that is loud to be that which is bright. Imagine, for example, an electrical transformer bursting ahead of you, perceptibly both flashing and popping. Or imagine a pair of hands clapping closely in front of you. Normally, you'll perceptually experience that event as a single happening with visible and audible attributes. Speech also is a nice example. When visually focused on a speaker's mouth, you perceptually experience it to be the sound source; you perceptually experience something common as having both visible and audible attributes.[11]

The phenomenology of intermodal feature binding sometimes breaks down. Imagine watching a poorly dubbed foreign movie or one whose soundtrack is not synchronized with the video. Outside a forgiving range, the experience stops being as of something that bears both visible and audible features, and it collapses into an experience merely as of something audible and something visible. This is disorienting when you anticipate a match. In cases that do not involve speech, the perceptual experience of intermodal feature binding can be more fragile. Whether the feature match is plausible matters more, and attention alone may affect the phenomenology of binding.[12] Certain disorders may impair intermodal integration for particular features. Autism, for instance, hinders combining cues about emotion from different senses.

The perceptual experience of intermodal binding may be illusory. No common event in the movie theater has both the visible and audible features you attribute to the speaking actors. (Likewise for computer demonstrations in the psychology lab.) And ventriloquism is not just an auditory spatial illusion but a carefully coordinated *illusion of identity* between something seen and something heard. A good

---

the experience of intermodal feature binding. "Intermodal" may refer to features or relations whose perception requires more than one modality.

[11] Cf., Tye (2003, 2007). Tye uses an argument with a similar structure to establish the conclusion that experiences of different modalities are co-consciously unified. But Tye's concern is the difference between having a visual experience and an auditory experience and having an experience that is auditory and visual. Some of Tye's examples involve objectual unity, but he does not draw the contrast I make in the text. This contrast holds between pairs of phenomenally unified audio-visual experiences. It is between a phenomenally unified audio-visual experience of hearing something F and seeing something G and a phenomenally unified audio-visual experience as of something F and G.

[12] See O'Callaghan (2012, esp. §4) for elaboration. Vatakis and Spence (2007), for instance, say:

When presented with two stimuli, one auditory and the other visual, an observer can perceive them either as referring to the same unitary audiovisual event or as referring to two separate unimodal events.. . . There appear to be specific mechanisms in the human perceptual system involved in the binding of spatially and temporally aligned sensory stimuli. At the same time, the perceptual system also appears to exhibit a high degree of selectivity in terms of its ability to separate highly concordant events from events that meet the spatial and temporal coincidence criteria, but which do not necessarily "belong together." (Vatakis and Spence 2007, 744, 754)

coincidence can prompt a perceptual experience with the phenomenal character of intermodal feature binding.

So, a perceptual experience as of something's being F and G may differ in phenomenal character from an otherwise equivalent perceptual experience as of something F and something G, where F and G are features perceptually experienced through different modalities (suppose, for clarity, that each is a proper sensible).

The perceptual experience as of co-instantiation of visible and tactual qualities by a single individual differs in phenomenal character from the mere co-conscious visual experience of color and tactual experience of texture. As I am about to argue, the former could not, however, bear only phenomenal character instantiated uniquely by visual or by tactual experiences. Therefore, the respects in which such contrasting multimodal perceptual experiences differ in phenomenal character cannot each be associated uniquely with a single modality. So, not all phenomenal character is distinctive to a specific modality.

The challenge is to account for the phenomenal character of episodes in which it perceptually appears that something—*the same thing*—bears features experienced with different modalities. Such phenomenologically evident *sameness* might be explained by *shared* phenomenal character. Perhaps two token experiences whose modality differs instantiate the same phenomenal feature, reflecting the impression that, for example, the same item is seen and felt. Or, perhaps, a single token experience of two modalities instantiates a phenomenal character that reflects the impression that a single item has both visible and tactual features.

Alternatively, the phenomenologically evident sameness could be explained by a novel phenomenal character instantiated by a variety of perceptual experience that does not belong to any of the familiar sensory modalities. For instance, one might perceptually experience the sameness or identity of what is seen with what is felt, where this experience is neither visual nor tactual. Instead, the perceptual experience as of the sameness of that which is colored and that which is textured occurs in addition to the visual experience as of something's being colored and the tactual experience as of something's being textured. The relevant phenomenal character then belongs to an extra-visual, extra-tactual, but nonetheless perceptual experience.

Each of these explanations for the phenomenologically apparent sameness evident in the perceptual experience of intermodal feature binding involves an aspect of phenomenal character that is not instantiated uniquely by perceptual experiences of a single modality and that does not accrue thanks merely to co-consciousness. Whether it involves shared phenomenal features or phenomenology of identification, the phenomenal character of a perceptual experience as of intermodal feature binding is not wholly modality specific, under the current interpretation. That is, not all such phenomenal character is instantiated uniquely by perceptual experiences of a given modality.

The argument from the perceptual experience of intermodal feature binding is not the same as the argument from common sensibles. The argument from intermodal feature binding requires that it is possible perceptually to experience visible and audible features to be co-instantiated, and the argument from common sensibles does not. Furthermore, it is not feasible to escape the argument from intermodal feature binding with help from modality-specific modes of presentation or modality-inflected phenomenal character. Each attempt leaves unaddressed the phenomenal character of perceptually experiencing that a single something has visible and audible features.

The phenomenally apparent sameness evident in a perceptual experience of intermodal binding requires phenomenal character that is instantiated either by perceptual experiences of more than one modality or by a perceptual experience that belongs to no particular modality. Therefore, if the thesis that all phenomenal character of perceptual experience is modality specific implies that all such phenomenal character is distinctive to some modality, the thesis fails. This is one respect in which perceptual experience is more than minimally multimodal.

2.3. GLOBAL DISTINCTIVENESS

Not every phenomenal character is such that every perceptual experience that instantiates it belongs to the same modality. This, however, need not undermine the claim that each perceptual experience that belongs to a modality has a distinctive modality-specific phenomenal character. It is plausible, for instance, that the phenomenal character of an episode of visual experience does not wholly match that of any possible auditory experience. In general, taken *overall*, or *globally*, the non-empty perceptual experience that belongs to a given modality during an interval has phenomenal character that could not be instantiated by an experiential episode that is not of that modality. This is because the perceptual experience as of proper sensibles and the perceptual experience of specific arrangements of sensible attributes both contribute distinctive modality-specific phenomenal character to the overall, or global, perceptual experience in a given modality. Even if not all local phenomenal character is distinctive to a modality, all global phenomenal character in a modality plausibly is.

This enables us to preserve the thesis that perceptual experience is modality specific and thus not more than minimally multimodal—the claim that the phenomenal character of any perceptual episode is exhausted by that which is associated with each modality, along with that which accrues thanks merely to co-consciousness. Suppose the phenomenal character of each perceptual experience of a given modality is distinctive in the global but not the local respect. If so, the thesis that all phenomenal character is modality specific now implies just that it is instantiated only by perceptual experiences that belong to a given modality and whose total phenomenal character is not instantiated by any perceptual experience not belonging to that modality. Specific phenomenal features thus could be instantiated by experiences of more than one modality, but the overall phenomenal character associated with each modality, under the current supposition, remains distinctive to that modality. The phenomenal character of any perceptual episode thereby may be exhausted by that which is distinctive to vision, audition, touch, smell, and taste.

This addresses the perceptual experience of intermodal feature binding. Suppose, for instance, that visual and auditory experiences involved in a multimodal perceptual episode instantiate a common phenomenal feature implicated in perceptually experiencing the very same thing to have both visible and audible features—without some such feature, the identity would not be experientially evident. That phenomenal feature, however, is unique neither to visual nor to auditory experience, so not every phenomenal feature is modality specific if that requires that it is distinctive to some modality. Nevertheless, the visual experience and the auditory experience bear other distinctive phenomenal features thanks to their respective proper sensibles and to the differing patterns of sensible attributes each reveals. Thus, the global phenomenal character of the visual experience could not be instantiated by a nonvisual experience, and that of the auditory experience could not be instantiated by a nonauditory experience. The phenomenal character of the visual experience and of the auditory experience is distinctive. It thus may be modality specific. Therefore, if the global phenomenal character associated with a modality is distinctive to experiences of that modality, intermodal binding experience is consistent with the thesis that the phenomenal character of perceptual experience is exhausted by that which is modality specific.

There is, however, an obstacle to asserting the thesis. The obstacle stems from the alternative explanation for the perceptual experience of intermodal feature binding described in section 2.2. Suppose the perceptual experience as of the sameness or identity of what is seen with what is heard, in which visible and audible features are presented as co-instantiated, is neither visual nor auditory. Suppose, instead, that it occurs in addition to the visual and auditory experiences. Such a supra-modal perceptual experience may have phenomenal character that is not associated with vision, audition, or any other familiar sensory modality. If so, even if we grant that visual and auditory phenomenal character are distinctive, not all perceptual experience is modality specific.

We cannot yet rule out this alternative. The trouble is that we are unable introspectively to discern whether the phenomenal character in question is associated with vision and audition or whether it belongs to some further, extra-visual, extra-auditory aspect of perceptual experience. Grant that the overall perceptual experience in a modality at a time has a distinctive phenomenal character—a phenomenal character that could not be instantiated by an experience not of that modality. Attention to distinctive phenomenal character nevertheless may deliver no clear verdict on whether or not some phenomenal feature is instantiated by an experience of a particular modality. Suppose I want to know, of a multimodal perceptual experience, whether or not an aspect of its phenomenal character is associated with a certain modality. Its modality cannot simply be read from a phenomenal feature instance. Unless the phenomenal feature itself is distinctive to that modality, it does not help to ask whether it is part of a complex phenomenal character that is distinctive. In a rich multimodal perceptual experience, many differing collections of its phenomenal features could be distinctive to a modality, so there may be many candidates for *the* distinctive overall phenomenal character associated with that modality. Some may include the phenomenal feature in question, and some may not. In multimodal contexts, it may be no help to ask which phenomenal features are co-instantiated since, for phenomenal features of perceptual experience, co-consciousness suffices for apparent co-instantiation.

So, alternative accounts disagree about whether the perceptual experience of intermodal feature binding involves only phenomenal character of experiences that belong to specific modalities. Granting that the overall perceptual experience in a given modality at a time has a distinctive phenomenal character does not resolve things. It leaves open whether or not a certain phenomenal feature belongs to the phenomenal character of the overall perceptual experience in that modality, since the overall phenomenal character may be distinctive with or without the phenomenal feature in question. Appealing to the fact that the phenomenal character of any perceptual experience that belongs to a given modality is globally distinctive does not settle which phenomenal features are associated with that modality on an occasion. Therefore, recognizing that perceptual experiences of a given modality have distinctive phenomenal character does not enable us to determine whether all phenomenal character is modality specific. It thus does not enable us to determine whether perceptual experience is more than minimally multimodal.

Talk of the distinctiveness of perceptual experiences of a modality such as vision suggests that in multimodal contexts we are able simply to recognize which determinate complex phenomenal character belongs to experiences of that modality. The presence of distinctive phenomenal features, such as those associated with the perceptual experience of proper sensibles, does mark when, for instance, a visual experience occurs. And it enables us to say of such phenomenal features that they belong to visual experience. This, however, is compatible with numerous ways to delimit the phenomenal character of the visual experience. Attention to globally distinctive phenomenal character cannot by itself determine the boundaries of visual experience. Introspection thus provides no secure way to settle whether all phenomenal character is modality specific.

3. Pure and Mere

The thesis being considered is that all phenomenal character is modality specific. The question now is whether the phenomenal character of any perceptual episode is exhausted by that which is instantiated by an experience of one of the modalities. Does each phenomenal feature of a perceptual experience belong to the distinctive phenomenal character associated with some modality? The previous section's lesson is that introspection cannot always settle whether or not a phenomenal feature is instantiated by a perceptual experience that belongs to a specific modality. We therefore need another way to address the question.

3.1. PURE EXPERIENCES OF A MODALITY

The way forward begins with two attractive ideas. The first is that perceptual experiences of different modalities may come apart. If it is possible to have a multimodal perceptual experience that involves visually experiencing and auditorily experiencing, then it should be possible to have a corresponding visual experience without any auditory experience, and it should be possible to have a corresponding auditory experience without any visual experience.

The second is that the notion of a perceptual experience that belongs *purely* to one modality—a purely visual experience or a purely auditory experience, for example—is coherent. Strawson, for instance, famously appealed, in *Individuals* (1959), to a purely auditory experience, and he claimed that it would be nonspatial. By a purely visual experience, for example, I mean a perceptual experience that is visual but not auditory, tactual, olfactory, or gustatory (and so on). Consider, to start, subtracting a human's perceptual modalities one at a time, as through deafness, failing receptors, or brain damage, until only vision remains. But this fails to avoid any tainting by experiences of the other modalities. So we might instead imagine a creature evolved only with human-like vision but no other senses. Or we might take a human born only with functioning vision. Or one subjected only to visual stimulation. For instance, try to conceive of a human visually stimulated but weightlessly immobilized and fed intravenously in a silent, odorless, temperature-controlled "vision room." In each case, perceptual experience presently and historically is exclusively visual, delivering at any time a *purely* visual experience. What matters is that it is possible that a creature could have a purely visual, purely auditory, purely tactual, purely olfactory, or purely gustatory experience. Call these *pure* experiences of a modality.

Now put these ideas together. For any multimodal perceptual experience that involves a given modality, we can talk about a *corresponding* perceptual experience purely of that modality. For instance, for a multimodal perceptual experience that is partly visual, we can talk about a *corresponding purely visual experience*. For any multimodal perceptual experience that involves a given modality, a corresponding pure perceptual experience of that modality is a perceptual experience purely of that modality under equivalent stimulation.

Now stipulate, of each perceptual experience that is visual, that the phenomenal character it instantiates that is *associated with vision* includes only that which a corresponding purely visual experience could have. In a multimodal perceptual experience, for example, the phenomenal character that is associated with vision includes only that which a corresponding purely visual experience could have. This allows that each visual experience has a distinctive phenomenal character associated with vision, but it does not require that each phenomenal feature associated with vision is distinctive.

Extend the stipulation to the other modalities. In general, for each perceptual experience of a given modality, say that the phenomenal character that is associated with that modality includes only that which a corresponding pure experience of that modality could have.

This provides a way to operationalize what is required *on an occasion* for phenomenal character to be *associated with a given modality* and, thus, what it takes on an occasion for phenomenal character to be *modality specific*. It does not require appealing to introspection, and it does not require appealing directly to an account of how to individuate sense modalities or of how to type experiences by modality. It applies in the first case to phenomenal feature instances, or to phenomenal features on an occasion, rather than to types or to repeatable phenomenal properties. (A distinctive complex global phenomenal character then can be said to be associated with a modality just in case on some occasion it is associated with that modality.)

We now may restate the thesis that all phenomenal character is modality specific. This is the claim that the phenomenal character of any perceptual episode is exhausted by that which is associated with each of its modalities on that occasion, which now implies that it is exhausted by that which, for each of its respective modalities, could be the phenomenal character of a corresponding pure experience of that modality. The phenomenal character of any perceptual episode includes only that which could be the phenomenal character of a corresponding purely visual, purely auditory, purely tactual, purely olfactory, or purely gustatory experience, plus that which accrues thanks to simple co-consciousness. If so, on any occasion, every aspect of phenomenal character is associated with one of the modalities, and in this respect perceptual experience is not more than minimally multimodal. It also follows that there are no aspects of a perceptual experience's phenomenal character that a pure experience of some modality could not instantiate.

3.2. COUNTEREXAMPLES

Some perceptual experiences that belong to a given modality may require prior perceptual experiences of another modality. Thus, for a typical human, even a perceptual experience that belongs to just one modality may have phenomenal character that a corresponding pure experience of that modality could not have. Therefore, it is not the case that the phenomenal character of each perceptual episode is exhausted by that which could be instantiated by a corresponding pure experience of each respective modality. The following two sections develop the counterexamples.

3.2.1. Cross-Modal Completion

Section 2.2 explained the perceptual experience of intermodal feature binding, in which it perceptually appears that something bears features that are perceived with different modalities. For instance, you might perceptually experience that something is both bright and loud. Good reasons suggest, in addition, that in a unimodal context it is possible with one modality to perceptually experience something as the sort of thing that bears or that could bear features perceptible only through another modality with which it is not presently perceived. For instance, in having an auditory but not visual experience, you might perceptually experience something heard as being the sort of thing that could be seen—as something with visible but unseen features. If so, such a perceptual experience has phenomenal character that no pure experience of any modality could have. The auditory perceptual experience as of something that has or that could have visible but unseen features thus has a phenomenal character that no purely auditory experience does.

So-called *amodal completion* occurs when you perceptually experience something to have perceptible but unperceived features. For instance, you may visually experience a region to continue behind an occluder; you may visually experience an expanse to be the facing surface of a solid object; or you may auditorily experience a tone to persist through a burst of masking noise. Without perceiving the hidden features, you perceptually experience as of something which bears them. This impacts the phenomenal character of perceptual experience. For instance, visually experiencing two bounded regions of space as parts of a single continuous surface differs phenomenologically from visually experiencing those same two bounded regions as disconnected, wholly distinct entities. Auditorily experiencing two tone bursts separated by an interval of time as temporal parts of a single persisting sound differs phenomenologically from auditorily experiencing those same two tone bursts as being discrete, wholly distinct sound events.[13] The claim is not that you perceptually experience the hidden features. Perceiving an individual does not require perceiving all of its parts or features. Nevertheless, you perceptually experience a thing that has such parts or features, and you perceptually experience it as such. Such completion effects, which shape the phenomenal character of perceptual experience, occur within particular modalities. Perceptually experiencing a surface to continue behind a barrier is a visual effect, and it impacts the phenomenal character of visual experience. So, "amodal completion" is not a perfect label. Such effects are an *intramodal* sort of amodal completion.

---

[13] See O'Callaghan (2008) for further discussion.

It is plausible by analogy that a *cross-modal* sort of amodal completion occurs when through one modality you perceptually experience as of something that has perceptible but unperceived features of another modality, or perceptually experience it to be the sort of thing that has or could have such features. For instance, you may perceptually experience an audible vocalization to have visible but unseen features; you may perceptually experience a visible surface to have tangible but unfelt attributes; or you may olfactorily experience some food to have gustatory but untasted qualities. In each case, a perceptual experience generated by stimulating only one sensory system presents an object as something that bears features of another modality without presenting those hidden features. And this affects the phenomenal character of perceptual experience. Perceptually experiencing a sound to belong to an event that has visible but unseen features differs phenomenologically from auditorily experiencing a pure sound as such, as isolated from any visible source.[14] Perceptually experiencing a visible surface to be impenetrable to touch may differ phenomenologically from visually experiencing it to be holographic and from visually experiencing it in a way that is indifferent about its tangibility. While only a perceptual experience of a single modality occurs (only features perceptible through that modality are perceived), it would be misleading to say that such completion effects involve only a single modality. Since their explanation implicates perceptible features and perceptual expectations of more than one modality, these are *cross-modal* cases of amodal completion.

If cross-modal amodal completion occurs, then there are perceptual experiences that belong to a modality whose phenomenal character no pure experience of that modality could have. For instance, a purely auditory experience could not have the phenomenal character of an auditory perceptual experience as of a sound source with visible but unseen features. A visual perceptual experience as of a solid surface may have phenomenal character that no purely visual experience could have. Thus, perceptual experiences that belong to a given modality may have phenomenal character that is not associated with that modality, according to the current stipulation concerning what it is for phenomenal character of a perceptual experience to be associated with a modality. It follows that there may be perceptual experiences whose phenomenal character is not exhausted by that which is associated with each of the specific modalities to which it belongs. If so, under the current interpretation, not all phenomenal character is modality specific. The phenomenal character of perceptual experience is not exhausted by that which could be instantiated by a pure experience of each of its respective modalities.

There are two potential objections. First, it is reasonable to oppose my characterization of intramodal and cross-modal amodal completion as affecting the phenomenal character of perceptual experience. Some may choose to explain away what I call a phenomenological difference by appealing to expectations or beliefs

---

[14] Scruton (1997) argues that such *acousmatic experience*, which involves hearing a sound independently from its source, is essential for musical listening.

that do not affect perceptual experience; some may say that the difference in phenomenal character belongs to imagination or to extra-perceptual cognition.

Second, it may be possible, after all, to capture the phenomenal character of a perceptual experience of cross-modal completion wholly through phenomenal character that corresponding pure experiences could have. Consider the phenomenal character of perceptually experiencing an audible event to be something that has visible but unseen features. While that perceptual experience has phenomenal character no purely auditory experience has, it may have only phenomenal features that a purely auditory or a purely visual experience could have. For instance, it could be that a perceptual experience of cross-modal completion instantiates phenomenal character associated with hearing a sound *and* with visual amodal completion. The former could be instantiated by a purely auditory experience, and the latter could be instantiated by a purely visual experience. Some thus may contend, against intuition, that each such case of cross-modal completion in fact is both an auditory and a visual experience, rather than just an auditory experience. The perceptual experience, therefore, may instantiate phenomenal character associated with audition and with vision. If every case of cross-modal completion belongs to more than one modality, the thesis may survive under the current interpretation.

3.2.2. Cross-Modal Parasitism

Strawson (1959) argues in *Individuals* that a purely auditory experience would be nonspatial. Strawson states, however, that ordinary perceivers perceptually experience direction and distance "on the strength of hearing alone," and he concedes the "full force" of that phrase (1959, 65–66). Hearing spatial features thus does not require making inferences, and it does not require that the correlations between auditory and visual experiences that make auditory spatial perception possible are accessible to cognition as reasons for auditory spatial beliefs. Instead, having nonauditory experiences simply is a necessary condition on hearing spatial features. Suppose, then, that the capacity auditorily to perceptually experience spatial features depends upon the capacity visually or tactually to perceptually experience spatial features. If so, auditory spatial awareness is *cross-modally parasitic* on visual or tactual spatial awareness.[15]

Strawson's case is not entirely unique. Berkeley (1975) says that perceiving spatial features visually depends on tactual acquaintance with spatial features. Another type of example is that it may be possible visually to perceptually experience materiality or tangibility. A sculpture or a painting may visibly appear to have certain features, such as being solid or being rough, only thanks to the capacity to feel those features. And it need not just be in respect of saturation or transparency

---

[15] I have argued elsewhere against Strawson's own strong claim that a purely auditory experience would be wholly nonspatial (O'Callaghan 2010). Nevertheless, it may be that some determinate forms of auditory spatial awareness depend upon vision.

that a brick looks different from a hologram. It also is not entirely implausible that one might visually experience an imbalance in the weight of a tilted column. Or imagine auditorily experiencing a sound as produced by or as generated by an extra-acoustic event. Without the capacity to perceptually experience a seen event to cause a heard sound, it might not be possible auditorily to experience a sound to have such a source. Finally, speech and language present a range of intriguing examples. Consider, for instance, the perceptual experience of spoken or written language. It may be possible, for instance, auditorily to perceptually experience motoric or gestural features, but only thanks to tactual or bodily awareness. It may even be possible visually to perceptually experience properties such as *shouting, vocalizing,* or *voice,* but only thanks to previous auditory experiences.[16]

Cross-modal parasitism thus occurs when a feature is perceptible through perceptual experiences that belong to one modality (the *parasite*) only thanks to, or in a way that depends upon, perceptual experiences of another modality (the *host*). To borrow Strawson's slogan, the feature becomes perceptible "on the strength of hearing alone"—or, solely on the strength of perceptual experiences that belong to the parasitic modality. The capacity to perceptually experience a feature by way of experiences that belong to one modality is cross-modally parasitic just in case it requires having exercised the capacity to perceptually experience that or some other feature by way of experiences of another modality.

Consider a perceptual experience that requires cross-modal parasitism. A Strawsonian candidate is an auditory perceptual experience as of distance that is not also a visual experience. Suppose that this auditory perceptual experience is cross-modally parasitic on the visual experience of space. This auditory perceptual experience as of distance differs phenomenologically from any purely auditory experience. It has phenomenal character that no purely auditory experience could have. It thus has phenomenal character that is not associated with audition.

In general, a parasitic perceptual experience as of some feature may differ phenomenologically from any pure perceptual experience of the parasitic modality. It thus may have phenomenal character that, in the current sense, is not associated with that modality. If cross-modal parasitism occurs, therefore, a perceptual experience may have phenomenal character beyond what is associated with each of the respective modalities to which it belongs. So not all phenomenal character is modality specific, according to the current understanding.

Someone might object that these examples of cross-modal parasitism are too controversial to ground a credible argument. Cross-modal parasitism, however, is just a vivid form of cross-modal dependence. Strawson's case and each example

---

[16] Alleged cases of cross-modal parasitism are familiar from the phenomenological tradition, which provides a number of curious examples. Merleau-Ponty (1948, 59–63), for instance, says that the perceptible stickiness particular to honey is inextricably bound both to the particular viscous texture and to the particular golden hue of honey. Thus, in visually experiencing honey and its color, one cannot help but experience its stickiness. Perhaps a more plausible example is visually experiencing the honey's viscousness. Merleau-Ponty also quotes Sartre talking about tasting the shape and color of a cake.

given involve a common feature that is perceptible through experiences of one modality only thanks to perceptual experiences of another modality. This draws attention to an underappreciated type of common sensible: those that require perceptual experiences of one modality in order to be perceptually experienced with another modality. But cross-modal parasitism need not involve a common perceptible feature. It could involve the capacity to perceptually experience some novel feature. Or it could simply involve a new sort of experience. The argument requires only that there are perceptual experiences of one modality that could not occur if not for perceptual experiences of another modality. A variety of reasons could explain the dependence. An indirect example involves cognitive influences upon perceptual experience. Suppose experiences of one modality are required to have certain thoughts. And suppose that such thoughts may alter experience in a second modality in a distinctive way. An experience of the dependent modality thus may differ in phenomenal character from any pure experience of that modality. What matters here is only that some such case of cross-modal dependence is possible. If so, then an ordinary perceptual experience that belongs to a given modality may have phenomenal character that could not be instantiated by a corresponding pure experience of that modality.[17,18]

3.3. MERE EXPERIENCES OF A MODALITY

There is a straightforward repair. The repair depends on an alternative way to understand what it is for phenomenal character to be *associated with* a given modality on an occasion. What it is for phenomenal character of a perceptual experience to be modality specific differs accordingly, as does the thesis that all phenomenal character is modality specific.

If the notion of a perceptual experience that belongs *purely* to one modality is coherent, then so is the notion of a perceptual experience that belongs *merely* to one modality. A *merely visual experience*, for example, is a perceptual experience that is visual but not auditory, tactual, olfactory, or gustatory (and so on). But a merely visual experience does not require that its subject never has had a perceptual experience of another modality; it allows that the subject is entirely normal, with a rich background of auditory, tactual, olfactory, and gustatory perceptual experiences. Suppose a well-traveled, typical human subject is admitted to the "vision room" and stimulated only visually. Or imagine getting a disease that leaves vision intact but eliminates your capacity to experience auditorily, tactually,

---

[17] One consequence is that impairments to one modality may, in some respects, impoverish perceptual experiences of another modality. Of course, such impairments may in other ways lead to enriched experiences in another modality.

[18] Even if no such cross-modal dependence occurs, the counterexamples of section 3.4 still refute the thesis that all phenomenal character is modality specific. If there is no cross-modal dependence, a perceptual experience's corresponding pure and mere (see section 3.3) experiences do not differ in phenomenal character.

olfactorily, and gustatorily. We need to be careful in imagining to control for spontaneous sensory activity and for the distinction between experiencing absences and failing to experience. An experience merely of one modality allows prior perceptual experiences of other modalities but requires while it occurs that its subject's overall perceptual experience remain wholly or solely of one modality. Call these *mere* experiences of a modality.

If the examples from section 3.2 succeed, then, under equivalent stimulation, the phenomenal character of a pure perceptual experience of some modality commonly differs from the phenomenal character of a mere perceptual experience of that modality. For instance, with equivalent retinal stimulation, the phenomenal character of a purely visual experience may differ from that of a merely visual experience. Having had perceptual episodes of other modalities makes a difference to visual experience.

For any multimodal perceptual experience that involves a given modality, we can talk about a *corresponding* perceptual experience *merely* of that modality. For instance, for a multimodal perceptual experience that is partly auditory, we can talk about a *corresponding merely auditory experience*. For any multimodal perceptual experience that involves a given modality, a corresponding mere perceptual experience of that modality is a perceptual experience merely of that modality under equivalent stimulation.

Now stipulate that for each perceptual experience of a given modality, the phenomenal character it instantiates that is *associated with that modality* on that occasion includes only that which a corresponding mere experience of that modality could have. For instance, of each multimodal perceptual experience that is partly visual, the phenomenal character it instantiates that is *associated with vision* on the occasion includes only that which a corresponding merely visual experience could have.[19]

This delivers a better account of what is required on an occasion for phenomenal character to be associated with a given modality and, thus, of what is required on an occasion for phenomenal character to be modality specific. We now may restate the thesis that all phenomenal character is modality specific, replacing talk of pure experiences of a modality with talk of mere experiences of a modality.

So, the claim that the phenomenal character of any perceptual episode is exhausted by that which is associated with each of its modalities now implies that it is exhausted by that which, for each of its respective modalities, could be the phenomenal character of a corresponding mere experience of that modality. The phenomenal character of any perceptual episode includes only that which could be the phenomenal character of a corresponding merely visual, merely auditory,

---

[19] To be clear, by "under equivalent stimulation," I mean *overall* stimulation, rather than just to the sense organs of the relevant modality. This is needed to accommodate causal cross-modal influences upon experience of a given modality. The overall *experience*, however, remains unimodal in a mere experience of a modality.

merely tactual, merely olfactory, or merely gustatory experience, plus that which accrues thanks to simple co-consciousness. If so, there are no aspects of phenomenal character that are not associated with one of the modalities, and perceptual experience is not more than minimally multimodal. It also follows that there are no aspects of a perceptual experience's phenomenal character that a mere experience of some modality could not instantiate.

Interpreted this way, the thesis accommodates cross-modal completion. A merely auditory experience, unlike a purely auditory experience, could have the phenomenal character of an auditory perceptual experience as of a sound source with visible but unseen features. A merely visual experience, unlike a purely visual experience, could instantiate the phenomenal character of a visual perceptual experience as of a solid surface. The thesis also is compatible with cross-modal parasitism. A merely auditory perceptual experience could have the phenomenal character of an auditory perceptual experience as of distance. Therefore, neither cross-modal completion nor cross-modal parasitism requires ascribing to a perceptual episode that belongs to a given modality phenomenal character that is not associated with that modality—that a corresponding mere experience of that modality could not have. In this respect, phenomenal character remains modality specific.

3.4. COUNTEREXAMPLES

Suppose some perceptible feature instances are accessible only multimodally. If so, it is possible multimodally to perceptually experience some feature instances that you could not perceptually experience through a corresponding mere experience of any modality. Suppose, moreover, that a multimodal perceptual experience of some such feature instance has phenomenal character that could not be instantiated by a corresponding mere experience of any modality. It thus has phenomenal character that is not exhausted by that which is associated with each of its respective modalities. The multimodal perceptual experience of such a novel feature instance would challenge the thesis that all phenomenal character is modality specific.

3.4.1. Intermodal Identity

The perceptual experience of intermodal feature binding provides one type of example. It involves perceptually experiencing visible and audible features (for instance) to be coinstantiated. In such cases, something common perceptually appears to bear both visible and audible features. But neither a corresponding merely visual experience nor a corresponding merely auditory perceptual experience could have the phenomenal character instantiated by a multimodal perceptual experience as of the *identity* of what is seen with what is heard. The phenomenal character of such a perceptual experience, therefore, is not exhausted by that which is associated with vision and that which is associated with audition. It is more than minimally multimodal.

Someone might object that an audible and visible individual may be auditorily and visually experienced in a manner that makes a further perceptual act of identification unnecessary. For instance, in a case of intermodal feature binding, suppose that rather than or in addition to distinct token auditory and visual experiences, each of which attributes features to an apparent individual, there is a single token multimodal perceptual experience as of an individual that bears both visible and audible features. That token multimodal perceptual experience, in which an individual is ascribed both visible and audible attributes, is an auditory and visual experience. Thus, it has phenomenal character associated with audition and phenomenal character associated with vision. This phenomenal character may overlap. That is, a single phenomenal feature instance may be associated on an occasion both with vision and with audition. Thus, no further identification is needed. Someone therefore might contend that the phenomenal character associated with audition, the phenomenal character associated with vision, and that which accrues thanks to mere co-consciousness suffices to capture the phenomenal character of a multimodal perceptual experience as of the relevant identity.[20]

My reply is that no collection of merely auditory and merely visual perceptual experiences captures the phenomenal character of a perceptual experience as of the identity of something audible with something visible. No two merely auditory experiences distinguish a case in which something is heard and possibly seen from a case in which something is heard and also seen. Likewise for merely visual experiences. And mere co-consciousness alone does not suffice to capture the difference. Thus, a perceptual experience whose phenomenal character is exhausted by that which could be instantiated by corresponding merely visual and merely auditory experiences must fail to distinguish auditorily experiencing something (which might be seen) and visually experiencing something (which might be heard) from auditorily and visually experiencing as of the same thing. So, according to the current understanding, not all phenomenal character is modality specific.

Nevertheless, it helps to have additional counterexamples.

3.4.2. Intermodal Relations

If it is possible to perceptually experience a relation that holds between items perceptually experienced through different modalities, then we have a case of a novel feature instance accessible only thanks to multimodal perceptual experiences.

Perceptible spatial relations provide examples. Consider, for instance, perceptually experiencing a sound to be in the same location as a visible source, or perceptually experiencing your visible hand to encircle the felt surface of a cold drinking glass. Simple perceptible temporal relations also provide examples. For

---

[20] The phenomenal character associated with audition and with vision on such an occasion thus should be distinguished from that of wholly distinct token auditory and visual perceptual experiences, which, even if co-conscious, involve distinct phenomenal feature instances. Further recognition of the identity thus is required.

instance, consider the contrast between perceptually experiencing a visible event to occur just a moment prior to an audible sound and perceptually experiencing a gap of a few seconds.

These cases, however, may just involve perceptually experiencing spatial or temporal locations through different modalities, along with simple co-consciousness, rather than genuinely perceptually experiencing intermodal spatial or temporal relations.

Further cases that involve temporal features are more compelling. Consider first a case of intermodal synchrony.[21] Imagine seeing a drumstick strike a snare drum at the precise moment you hear its sound, or seeing a performer jump just as you hear a cymbal. It is plausible that you perceptually experience the events as occurring at the same time. But take the stronger example of intermodal rhythm perception.[22] Consider, for example, perceptually experiencing an audiovisual rhythm pattern, such as that which holds between a flashing light and a banging sound. Try the following with a partner. Look at your partner's right hand while she uses it to "air drum" the rhythm *tap–tap [pause], tap–tap [pause].* Next, close your eyes while your partner taps on a table the simple beat *[pause] [pause] tap, [pause] [pause] tap.* Finally, open your eyes and have your partner combine these two steps. So, she air drums a couple of taps while holding her left hand out of your view and using it to drum a *tap* just when her right hand pauses. It is possible perceptually to attend to the rhythm of the visible hand movement and

---

[21] Intermodal synchrony perception is the subject of a rich empirical literature. Müller et al. (2008) report, "A great amount of recent research on multisensory integration deals with the experience of perceiving synchrony of events between different sensory modalities although the signals frequently arrive at different times" (309). Fujisaki et al. (2004) say:

> To perceive the auditory and visual aspects of a physical event as occurring simultaneously, the brain must adjust for differences between the two modalities in both physical transmission time and sensory processing time.. . . Our findings suggest that the brain attempts to adjust subjective simultaneity across different modalities by detecting and reducing the time lags between inputs that likely arise from the same physical events. (Fujisaki et al. 2004, 773)

Spence and Squire (2003) suggest that a "moveable window" for multisensory integration and a "temporal ventriloquism" effect help explain perceptually apparent synchrony. Stone et al. (2001) found that the optimal audio-visual *Point of Subjective Simultaneity* generally requires a visual stimulus to precede an auditory stimulus, on average (across subjects) by about 50 milliseconds (msec). See also, for example, Morein-Zamir et al. (2003); Zampini et al. (2005); Arrighi et al. (2006).

[22] The fascinating results of Huang et al. (2012) establish intermodal meter perception between audition and touch.

> We next show in the bimodal experiments that auditory and tactile cues are integrated to produce coherent meter percepts.. . . We believe that these results are the first demonstration of cross-modal sensory grouping between any two senses. (Huang et al. 2012, 1, abstract)

(For simplicity, I do not here distinguish rhythm from meter—feel free to substitute meter for rhythm in the text.) See also Guttman et al. (2005), which, in a discussion of "hearing visual rhythms" (compare the arguments of §3.2) notes in an aside, "Interestingly, several observers reported experiencing a complex rhythmic gestalt that combined the auditory and visual inputs. However, information from the two senses remained clearly distinguishable" (234, fn. 3).

the audible drumming.[23] It also is possible to attend just to the visible rhythm or just to the audible rhythm. Perceptually experiencing the intermodal rhythm differs phenomenologically from perceptually experiencing either of the unimodal rhythms in isolation and from perceptually experiencing two simultaneous but distinct rhythms.[24]

If human subjects are able multimodally to perceptually experience features such as audiovisual rhythm, then we have a counterexample to the thesis that on any occasion all phenomenal character is modality specific. Consider a multimodal perceptual experience as of an audiovisual intermodal rhythm. On such an occasion, the phenomenal character that is associated with vision includes only that which a corresponding merely visual experience could have, and the phenomenal character that is associated with audition includes only that which a corresponding merely auditory experience could have. Neither the corresponding merely auditory experience nor the corresponding merely visual experience could have the phenomenal character of perceptually experiencing the specific audiovisual rhythm pattern. And simple co-conscious unity does not have or guarantee the phenomenal character of perceptually experiencing a rhythm. So, the multimodal perceptual experience has phenomenal character that is not associated either with vision or with audition on that occasion. We thus have a perceptual episode whose phenomenal character is not exhausted by that which is associated with vision, that which associated with audition, that which is associated with

---

[23] If you are worried that the visible hand prompts auditory imagery, substitute a tactual tap on your arm for your partner's visible air drumming.

[24] A similar argument may be grounded in a case of intermodal motion perception, such as when you hear something moving toward you and then pick it up visually and continue to track its motion. A more compelling case would involve a novel determinate motion pattern that differed from both the audible and visible motion patterns—for instance, a zig-zag pattern of alternately audible and visible movements, or merely apparent intermodal motion. On visuo-tactile apparent motion, see Harrar et al. (2008), who say, "These experiments have confirmed that multimodal motion between lights and touches can occur" (816). Compare Huddleston et al. (2008), who say of the audiovisual case, "Although subjects were able to track a trajectory using cues from both modalities, no one spontaneously perceived 'multimodal [apparent] motion' across both visual and auditory cues" (1207); and "The results of Experiment 3 provide initial evidence that, although subjects could use information from both modalities to determine the trajectory of the stimulus, the stimulus used in this experiment was not sufficient to overcome the need for spatial and temporal congruence to integrate multimodal cues for the perception of motion across modalities and, therefore, did not lead to the perception of a unified 'audiovisual' stimulus" (1215). However, despite the latter authors' report of subjects' subjective impressions, their results demonstrate some facility with tracking audiovisual intermodal motion and suggest that lower "accuracy" in the multimodal condition stems from good cues that tell against identifying the auditory and visual stimuli over time as a common item moving through space. In their multimodal condition, subjects correctly determined the intermodal direction of motion at 90% when each stimulus was presented for at least 175 msec (vision reaches this accuracy at 100 msec) (Huddleston et al., 2008, 1214, Figure 6). Notably, this was better than in their audition-only condition (vertical display) using one type of sound, which never reached above 80% (Figure 6). Tellingly, subjects achieved the same accuracy in the multimodal condition as for an auditory-only stimulus in the horizontal plane that used qualitatively *different* sounds (1211, Figure 4).

touch, that which is associated with smell, and that which is associated with taste, along with simple co-consciousness.

One type of objection is that if you perceptually experience only events in time but not temporal properties and relations, then this example fails. While I have little sympathy for this objection, it helps to have other examples of intermodal relation perception.

The perceptual experience of intermodal causality provides one such example. According to a moderately liberal account, humans perceptually experience causal relations. Intermodal cases provide some good examples.[25] For instance, imagine hearing an audible sound a moment after seeing a visible flash. You may perceptually experience the visible event to cause or to produce the audible sound. Likewise, an audible sound may perceptibly appear to cause a visible flash. On an occasion of perceptually experiencing an audiovisual intermodal causal relation, the phenomenal character that is associated with vision is that which a corresponding merely visual experience could instantiate. The phenomenal character of the multimodal perceptual experience that is associated with vision thus does not include that of a perceptual experience of causation. The same holds for audition. The phenomenal character as of a perceptual experience of intermodal causality therefore is not exhausted by that which is associated with each of its respective modalities plus simple co-consciousness.

Each case in this section involves a multimodal perceptual experience of a relational feature that holds between things perceptually experienced through different modalities. The most plausible reasons to deny that such cases occur also support denying that it is possible to perceptually experience relational features—spatial, temporal, or causal—that hold among things perceptually experienced through a single modality, such as those that hold among parts of a visual scene, among sounds presented over time, or among parts of a thing in contact with different fingers. According to a moderately liberal account of perceptual experience in general, therefore, there is no compelling reason to deny that some such intermodal cases occur.

The phenomenal character of such a multimodal perceptual experience is not exhausted by that which is associated with each of its modalities along with simple co-conscious unity. Each case involves the instantiation by a multimodal perceptual experience of additional phenomenal features. For example, an audiovisual multimodal experience may have phenomenal features associated neither with vision nor with audition, since they could not be instantiated by a corresponding merely auditory or merely visual experience. According to the current understanding of what it is for phenomenal character of a perceptual experience to be modality specific, it follows that not all phenomenal character on every occasion is

---

[25] See, for example, Siegel (2009), on the visual perceptual experience of causation. See, e.g., Nudds (2001) on perceptually experiencing audio-visual causation. See also, for example, Sekuler et al. (1997); Guski and Troje (2003); Choi and Scholl (2006).

modality specific. Here is another way to put the lesson. It is temping to hold that the phenomenal character of any perceptual episode is equivalent to that of corresponding mere perceptual experiences of each modality along with that which accrues thanks to simple co-conscious unity. To accept this is mistaken.

3.4.3. Flavor

Another type of case deserves attention.

Each example in the previous section involves a perceptible relation whose relata are perceived with different modalities. The perceptual experience of the relation instance is multimodal. The phenomenal character of such a multimodal perceptual experience is not exhausted by that which is associated with each of its modalities. It involves phenomenal features that are not, in the sense of section 3.3, associated with any particular modality—features a mere perceptual experience could not, under equivalent stimulation, instantiate.

Each relation, however, also may have instances whose relata are perceptible with a single modality. The perceptual experience of the relation instance thus may belong to a single modality. For example, it is possible visually to perceptually experience causality and auditorily to perceptually experience rhythm. A mere visual experience therefore could have the phenomenal character of a visual perceptual experience of causality, and a mere auditory experience could have the phenomenal character of an auditory perceptual experience of rhythm. The phenomenal character of a perceptual experience of causation or rhythm thus may be exhausted by that which is associated with vision or with audition.

Accordingly, the phenomenal character of a multimodal perceptual experience of such a relation need not be entirely novel. It need not, for instance, involve perceptually experiencing a wholly unfamiliar type of feature. Thus, there is room to hold that every phenomenal feature instantiated by a human perceptual experience is, in some perceptual experience, associated with some specific modality. That is, no perceptual experience has phenomenal features of a type that could not be instantiated *under some conditions* by a mere experience of some modality. Therefore, it may be that the phenomenal features of multimodal perceptual experiences are exhausted by those which, in some circumstance or other, could be instantiated by a mere perceptual experience of some modality. This provides a dramatically weaker alternative way to understand the thesis that all phenomenal character is modality specific.[26]

---

[26] This, of course, raises the opportunity to discuss whether the instantiation of such phenomenal features by a multimodal experience depends on their instantiation by an experience that belongs to a modality. This would enable us to consider the stronger claim that all phenomenal character originates in an experience of some specific modality, which implies the weaker claim. I won't take up the question here.

But consider a type of feature whose instances are perceptible only multimodally. This might provide an example of a multimodal perceptual experience with phenomenal features possessed by no mere perceptual experience of any modality.

Flavor sometimes is cited as an example of such a feature.[27] To perceptually experience flavor requires stimulating both taste buds and smell receptors. That is why food seems bland when you're stuffed up with a cold. The tongue and taste system suffices to enable one to perceptually experience the basic tastes of salty, sweet, bitter, sour, and umami, but retronasal olfaction is required to perceptually experience flavors, such as that of butter, fried chicken, pineapple, or cardamom. Odors sensed after traveling up through passages at the back of your mouth (retropharynx) are "referred" to the mouth and contribute to apparent flavor.

Flavors are apparent perceptible features attributed to stuff in the mouth, such as a volume of fruit juice or a piece of fried chicken. Flavors are complex features. Tastes are one aspect of flavor. For instance, both sweetness and sourness are aspects of the flavor of pineapple. But tastes do not exhaust flavor. Olfactory attributes also are aspects of flavor. For instance, an important part of the distinctive flavor attributed to chocolate in the mouth is a quality that can be perceptually experienced through smell.[28] Somatosensory attributes also are a crucial aspect of flavors. Capsaicin gives chilis their pungent flavor by activating nociceptors; nicotine is bitter at low concentrations but burns at increasing concentrations; tannins give pomegranates and pecans their astringent flavor; even salt is an irritant at high concentrations.[29] Flavor involves the co-instantiation of such gustatory, olfactory, and somatosensory features.[30] To perceptually experience a flavor therefore may require a multimodal perceptual experience. Thus, no mere perceptual experience of any modality itself is a flavor experience. Flavor is a novel feature accessible only through multimodal perceptual experiences.

This does not yet show that any perceptual experience of flavor has phenomenal features that could not be instantiated by a mere experience of some modality. That claim requires the further assumption that apparent flavor is not identical with a conjunction of features each of which may be perceptually experienced through an individual modality. That is, there is more to apparent flavor than taste, smell, and touch. If so, tastes, smells, and tactual features are parts of complex flavors, but sense-specific features fail to exhaust flavor. In that case, perceptually experiencing a flavor may differ from perceptually experiencing the mere co-instantiation, even by a common sensible individual, of sensible attributes of taste, smell, and touch. It instead may involve perceptually experiencing the instantiation of a complex but unified flavor property, generally by a sensible individual that appears to be located

---

[27] See, for example, Smith (2007, 2011); Spence et al. (this volume); cf., Macpherson (2011a). My own understanding of flavor owes a great deal to Smith's work on tasting and flavor and to conversations with him about these topics.

[28] See Small et al. (2005).

[29] See Simon et al. (2008).

[30] The co-instantiation is perhaps only ever merely apparent.

in the mouth. This property has sense-specific attributes among its components, but the apparent flavor is not identical with the simple apparent coinstantiation of sense-specific aspects. It must involve something else, such as a particular structure or pattern of co-instantiation, or an "organic unity" among the sense-specific aspects. Perhaps flavor is like a multimodal gestalt.

If so, not only are some flavors perceptible only multimodally, but the multimodal perceptual experience of flavors provides an example of novel phenomenal features that could not be instantiated by any mere experience of any modality. No combination of phenomenal character that could be instantiated by mere perceptual experiences of different modalities captures what it is like to taste fried chicken. Thus, even the weakened thesis that all phenomenal character is modality specific fails.

This sketches how flavor perception might involve wholly novel phenomenal character that emerges only in multimodal perceptual experiences. If accurate, it refutes even a very weak interpretation of the thesis that all phenomenal character is modality specific, according to which each phenomenal feature instantiated by a perceptual experience is of a specific type that could be instantiated by a mere experience of some modality. At least three objections must be answered.

The first objection is that flavor perception is a distinct modality of exteroceptive sensory perception, in addition to sight, hearing, touch, taste, and smell. The claim is that while it shares organs and proximal stimuli with taste, smell, and touch, flavor perception is a distinct perceptual system. This system is supposed to ground perceptual episodes in which human subjects perceptually experience a novel range of flavors, which are sensible attributes distinct from tastes, smells, and tactual features. If so, the perceptual experience of flavor is compatible with an even stronger version of the claim that all phenomenal character is modality specific. Each perceptual experience of flavor may have only phenomenal character that could be instantiated by a corresponding mere perceptual experience of the flavor modality. Thus, the phenomenal character of a flavor experience is exhausted by that which is associated with each of its specific modalities.

This objection is unconvincing. First, each familiar exteroceptive sensory modality has a dedicated organ that transduces physical stimulation from the environment.[31] Flavor perception lacks a dedicated organ. Moreover, apparent flavors do seem constitutively to involve gustatory, olfactory, and somatosensory attributes. The apparent flavor of dark chocolate, for example, requires bitterness and certain olfactory qualities. Thus, you could not perceptually experience as of the flavor of dark chocolate without bitterness and certain olfactory qualities being perceptually accessible among its components. A mere perceptual experience of the flavor modality therefore could not instantiate the phenomenal character of a perceptual experience of the flavor of dark chocolate.

---

[31] Keeley (2002).

The second objection is that the perceptual experience of flavor belongs to taste.[32] Flavor experience perhaps requires a healthy olfactory system and past olfactory experiences, without which you could perceptually experience only simple tastes, such as bitterness, but no flavors. A purely gustatory experience thus could not be a flavor experience. We may even grant that episodes of flavor experience commonly are multimodal perceptual experiences involving both taste and smell. Even so, it may be that each flavor experience is an episode of tasting, while not every flavor experience is an episode of smelling. If so, the phenomenal character of a flavor experience could be instantiated by a corresponding merely gustatory experience. Its phenomenal character thus may be exhausted by that which is associated with each of its specific modalities.

This objection has force, but we should resist it. Suppose, with the evidence, that stimulating the tongue's taste receptors does not suffice for flavor experience and that flavor experience requires concurrent olfactory stimulation. But such olfactory stimulation also suffices for olfactory experience, so unless flavor perception blocks olfactory experience, it follows that there could be no merely gustatory perceptual experience as of flavor.

Moreover, apparent olfactory qualities plausibly do form a constitutive part and not merely a dissociable concomitant of flavor. This is especially clear in cases such as the flavor of coffee or of a spice such as cardamom. But the point is obscured by the fact that olfactory components of flavors are not perceptually experienced as being in the usual place—as taken in through the nose from the environment outside the nose—that we associate with the familiar class of olfactory objects and qualities that includes the odors and scents. Instead, the olfactory qualities that belong to flavors commonly are referred or localized to the mouth when they are smelled retronasally and when there is food in the mouth.[33] This is not an illusion or a mistake.[34] It is part of the normal, adaptive olfactory perceptual experience of food in the mouth, and it provides useful information about, for instance, whether or not to swallow. More to the point, it is a kind of smelling, facilitated by chewing and swallowing, that is part of what it is to perceptually experience flavors.[35] That such experiences are olfactory is supported by the fact that olfactory components to flavors can be smelled through retronasal olfaction in the absence of food in the mouth. A flavor experience *is* in part an olfactory experience of food in the mouth. This variety of olfaction differs in important respects from the more discussed sort of olfaction whose objects are in the outside environment. It nevertheless is a variety of olfaction—whose objects commonly are in the mouth. Such olfaction is critical to the perceptual experience of flavors in this way: the olfactory qualities

[32] See Macpherson (2011a).
[33] See, for example, Small et al. (2005).
[34] Cf. Smith (2011).
[35] Cf. Macpherson (2011a, 460–461).

it reveals are constitutive features of flavors. The perceptual experience of flavor, therefore, does not belong wholly to taste.

The issue turns on the third objection. Allow that flavor is a complex perceptible feature with qualitative components or aspects drawn from taste, smell, and touch (to simplify). Thus, to perceptually experience flavor requires a multimodal perceptual experience. No mere perceptual experience of any modality has the phenomenal character of a flavor experience. Nonetheless, it may be objected that no flavor experience has phenomenal features beyond those associated with each of its respective modalities. If apparent flavor just is a bunch of gustatory, olfactory, and tactual qualities, attributed to something in the mouth, then flavor experience instantiates no wholly novel phenomenal feature. The phenomenal character of a multimodal perceptual experience of flavor in fact may have phenomenal character exhausted by that which is associated with each of its respective modalities. The objection challenges the thought that apparent flavor involves either an organic unity or an additional qualitative component beyond its modality-specific features.

My judgment is that we should not rule out that flavor involves structured rather than merely compresent features of the several modalities. One reason is that it seems possible in principle to perceptually experience olfactory qualities, somatosensory features, or basic tastes alongside but as distinct from flavors. Another is that it seems possible that some human could perceptually experience specific olfactory, somatosensory, and taste qualities as co-instantiated but not as constituents of a unified flavor property. The arrangement of constituent features, especially in time, seems to matter for flavor. Nevertheless, defending the claim that flavor is structured raises questions that are well beyond this chapter's scope and that I cannot anyway hope to resolve here. So I'll point to the crux and leave unresolved the question of whether a multimodal perceptual experience may bear phenomenal features not instantiated by *any* mere perceptual experience of any modality.

For all I have said, therefore, it could be that no perceptual experience instantiates phenomenal features that are not also instantiated by some merely visual, merely auditory, merely tactual, merely olfactory, or merely gustatory experience. I want to emphasize that this much weaker claim does not imply that the phenomenal character of any perceptual episode is exhausted by that which could be instantiated by a corresponding merely visual, merely auditory, merely tactual, merely olfactory, or merely gustatory experience. It thus does not establish that all phenomenal character is modality specific.

4. Conclusion

This chapter argues against the idea that all perceptual experience is modality specific. In particular, it argues against the thesis that all phenomenal character is modality specific (even making an allowance for co-conscious unity). And it supports the claim that the phenomenal character of perceptual experience is more than minimally multimodal.

Section 2 argued that not every phenomenal feature is distinctive to some particular modality. That is, not every phenomenal feature is instantiated by a perceptual experience of a given modality and could be instantiated only by experiences of that modality. Thus, in that respect, not every determinate phenomenal feature type is associated with exactly one specific modality. The overall phenomenal character of a perceptual experience that belongs to a given modality nevertheless may be distinctive, since it is plausible that it is instantiated only by experiences of that modality. Such complex phenomenal character types thus are associated with a specific modality. But, among the determinate phenomenal features that are not themselves distinctive to a modality, introspecting a perceptual episode cannot settle decisively which such features belong to the complex phenomenal character associated with a given modality on an occasion. So, of a rich, multimodal perceptual episode, introspection cannot settle which token determinate phenomenal features are instantiated by an experience of a given modality and which are not. Even granting that the phenomenal character of any perceptual experience belonging to a given modality is distinctive to perceptual experiences of that modality does not enable us to determine introspectively whether or not on each occasion all phenomenal character is associated with some specific modality. Another methodology is required.

Section 3 argued that the phenomenal character of a perceptual experience is not always exhausted by that which is associated with each of the respective modalities. Suppose we assume that for a phenomenal feature to be associated with a given modality on an occasion requires that it could be instantiated by a perceptual experience purely of that modality under equivalent stimulation. This focuses attention on the phenomenal features that could be instantiated by experiences of a single, wholly isolated modality. However, under this supposition, cases of cross-modal completion and cross-modal dependence show that there are perceptual episodes whose phenomenal character is not exhausted by that which is associated with a specific modality on that occasion. Suppose instead we assume, more reasonably, that for a phenomenal feature to be associated with a given modality on an occasion requires only that it could be instantiated by a perceptual experience merely of that modality under equivalent stimulation. This allows for the richer experiences made possible by having a history of experience with more than one exteroceptive sensory modality. Nonetheless, under this assumption, perceptible intermodal identity and other relations show that there are multimodal perceptual episodes whose phenomenal character is not exhausted by that which is associated with a specific modality on that occasion. In addition, the case of flavor may show that there are novel phenomenal features that could not be instantiated by any mere experience of a given modality. Section 3 thus establishes that it is not the case that the phenomenal character of each perceptual episode is exhausted by that which on that occasion is associated with vision, that which is associated with audition, that which is associated with touch, that which is associated with smell, and that which is associated with taste, plus that which accrues thanks merely to co-consciousness. Thus, not all phenomenal character is, even in this relatively weak respect, modality specific. Perceptual experience thus is more than minimally multimodal.

Acknowledgments

I am grateful to Stephen Biggs, Mohan Matthen, and Dustin Stokes for their valuable feedback. Thanks also to David Chalmers, Charles Siewert, and Barry C. Smith for helpful exchanges. And many thanks to Jeff Speaks for incisive written comments.

References

Arrighi, R., Alais, D., and Burr, D. (2006). Perceptual synchrony of audiovisual streams for natural and artificial motion sequences. *Journal of Vision*, **6**(3):260–268.

Bayne, T. (2010). *The Unity of Consciousness*. Oxford University Press, Oxford.

Berkeley, G. (1709/1975). Essay towards a new theory of vision. In Ayers, M. R., editor, *Philosophical Works, including the Works on Vision*, pages 7–70. Dent, London.

Bertelson, P. and de Gelder, B. (2004). The psychology of multimodal perception. In Spence, C. and Driver, J., editors, *Crossmodal Space and Crossmodal Attention*, pages 141–177. Oxford University Press, Oxford.

Bushara, K. O., Hanakawa, T., Immisch, I., Toma, K., Kansaku, K., and Hallett, M. (2003). Neural correlates of cross-modal binding. *Nature Neuroscience*, **6**(2):190–195.

Chalmers, D. J. (2004). The representational character of experience. In Leiter, B., editor, *The Future for Philosophy*, pages 153–181. Oxford University Press, Oxford.

Choi, H. and Scholl, B. J. (2006). Measuring causal perception: Connections to representational momentum? *Acta Psychologica*, **123**(1):91–111.

Fujisaki, W., Shimojo, S., Kashino, M., and Nishida, S. (2004). Recalibration of audiovisual simultaneity. *Nature Neuroscience*, **7**(7):773–778.

Grice, H. P. (1962). Some remarks about the senses. In Butler, R. J., editor, *Analytical Philosophy, Series 1*, pages 133–153. Blackwell, Oxford.

Guski, R. and Troje, N. F. (2003). Audiovisual phenomenal causality. *Perception and Psychophysics*, **65**(5):789–800.

Guttman, S. E., Gilroy, L. A., and Blake, R. (2005). Hearing what the eyes see: Auditory encoding of visual temporal sequences. *Psychological Science*, **16**(3):228–235.

Harrar, V., Winter, R., and Harris, L. R. (2008). Visuotactile apparent motion. *Perception and Psychophysics*, **70**(5):807–817.

Huang, J., Gamble, D., Sarnlertsophon, K., Wang, X., and Hsiao, S. (2012). Feeling music: Integration of auditory and tactile inputs in musical meter. *PLoS ONE*, **7**(10):e48496.

Huddleston, W. E., Lewis, J. W., Phinney, R. E., and DeYoe, E. A. (2008). Auditory and visual attention-based apparent motion share functional parallels. *Perception and Psychophysics*, **70**(7):1207–1216.

Karns, C. M. and Knight, R. T. (2009). Intermodal auditory, visual, and tactile attention modulates early stages of neural processing. *Journal of Cognitive Neuroscience*, **21**(4):669–683.

Keeley, B. L. (2002). Making sense of the senses: Individuating modalities in humans and other animals. *Journal of Philosophy*, **99**(1):5–28.

Kubovy, M. and Schutz, M. (2010). Audio-visual objects. *Review of Philosophy and Psychology*, **1**(1):41–61.

Macpherson, F. (2011a). Cross-modal experiences. *Proceedings of the Aristotelian Society*, **111**(3):429–468.

Macpherson, F., editor (2011b). *The Senses: Classical and Contemporary Philosophical Perspectives*. Oxford University Press, Oxford.

Matthen, M. (forthcoming). The individuation of the senses. In Matthen, M., editor, *Oxford Handbook of Philosophy of Perception*. Oxford University Press, Oxford.

Merleau-Ponty, M. (2004/1948). *The World of Perception*. Routledge, New York.

Morein-Zamir, S., Soto-Faraco, S., and Kingstone, A. (2003). Auditory capture of vision: Examining temporal ventriloquism. *Cognitive Brain Research*, **17**(1):154–163.

Müller, K., Schmitz, G. A. F., Schnitzler, A., Freund, H.-J., and Prinz, W. (2008). Inter- versus intramodal integration in sensorimotor synchronization: A combined behavioral and magnetoencephalographic study. *Experimental Brain Research*, **185**(2):309–318.

Nudds, M. (2001). Experiencing the production of sounds. *European Journal of Philosophy*, **9**:210–229.

O'Callaghan, C. (2008). Object perception: Vision and audition. *Philosophy Compass*, **3**(4):803–829.

O'Callaghan, C. (2010). Perceiving the locations of sounds. *Review of Philosophy and Psychology*, **1**(1):123–140.

O'Callaghan, C. (2012). Perception and multimodality. In Margolis, E., Samuels, R., and Stich, S., editors, *Oxford Handbook of Philosophy of Cognitive Science*, pages 92–117. Oxford University Press, Oxford.

Pourtois, G., de Gelder, B., Vroomen, J., Rossion, B., and Crommelinck, M. (2000). The time-course of intermodal binding between seeing and hearing affective information. *Neuroreport*, **11**(6):1329–1333.

Scruton, R. (1997). *The Aesthetics of Music*. Oxford University Press, Oxford.

Sekuler, R., Sekuler, A. B., and Lau, R. (1997). Sound alters visual motion perception. *Nature*, **385**:308.

Siegel, S. (2009). The visual experience of causation. *Philosophical Quarterly*, **59**(236):519–540.

Simon, S. A., de Araujo, I. E., Stapleton, J. R., and Nicolelis, M. A. L. (2008). Multisensory processing of gustatory stimuli. *Chemosensory Perception*, **1**(2):95–102.

Small, D. M., Gerber, J. C., Mak, Y. E., and Hummel, T. (2005). Differential neural responses evoked by orthonasal versus retronasal odorant perception in humans. *Neuron*, **47**:593–605.

Smith, B. C. (2007). The objectivity of tastes and tasting. In Smith, B. C., editor, *Questions of Taste: The Philosophy of Wine*, pages 41–77. Oxford University Press, Oxford.

Smith, B. C. (2011). The true taste of a wine? In Chassagne, D., editor, *Wine Active Compounds 2011: Proceedings of the Second Edition of the International Conference Series on Wine Active Compounds*, 283–286. Oeno Plurimedia, Chaintré.

Spence, C. (2007). Audiovisual multisensory integration. *Acoustical Science and Technology*, **28**(2):61–70.

Spence, C. and Driver, J., editors (2004). *Crossmodal Space and Crossmodal Attention*. Oxford University Press, Oxford.

Spence, C. and Squire, S. (2003). Multisensory integration: Maintaining the perception of synchrony. *Current Biology*, **13**(13):519.

Stone, J. V., Hunkin, N. M., Porrill, J., Wood, R., Keeler, V., Beanland, M., Port, M., and Porter, N. R. (2001). When is now? Perception of simultaneity. *Proceedings of the Royal Society of London. Series B: Biological Sciences*, **268**(1462):31–38.

Strawson, P. F. (1959). *Individuals*. Routledge, New York.

Tye, M. (2003). *Consciousness and Persons: Unity and Identity*. MIT Press, Cambridge, MA.

Tye, M. (2007). The problem of common sensibles. *Erkenntnis*, **66**:287–303.

Vatakis, A. and Spence, C. (2007). Crossmodal binding: Evaluating the "unity assumption" using audiovisual speech stimuli. *Perception and Psychophysics*, **69**(5):744–756.

Zampini, M., Guest, S., Shore, D. I., and Spence, C. (2005). Audio-visual simultaneity judgments. *Perception and Psychophysics*, **67**(3):531–544.

6

Is Audio-Visual Perception 'Amodal' or 'Crossmodal'?

Matthew Nudds

The senses are modal in the following ways. The different senses—or, at least, the senses of vision, touch, and hearing[1]—each function to enable us to perceive objects and their features, and each can operate independently of the others. We can see something without hearing or touching it, hear something without seeing or touching it, and so on. Each sense modality is, therefore, (relatively) functionally independent of the others. In addition, each sense modality enables the perception of a range of modality-specific objects or features—objects or features that can be perceived only with that particular sense. We can only see colours, only hear sounds and their features, only feel heat, and so on.

Although the senses are (relatively) functionally independent of each other, they do not, for the most part, operate independently of each other. Our perceptual experience at any time is the result of the simultaneous operation of all our senses, and many of the things we perceive, we perceive with more than one sense simultaneously. We often perceive the same particular thing, and the same features of that particular thing, with more than one sense. If you look at a coin you hold in your hand, you both see and feel the coin, and you can both see and feel its shape. When you drop the coin to the floor, you can both see and hear it strike the floor, and both see and hear when and where it strikes the floor. So although the senses are modal, perception is often multisensory.

Multisensory perception[2] might be supposed to be simply the combined operation of each of the individual senses. That is, the multisensory perception

---

[1] The following is not obviously true of the senses of smell and taste. It is arguable that smell and taste enable us to perceive only smells and tastes rather than objects that have smells and tastes, and they may not be functionally independent of each other.

[2] I use the term 'multisensory perception' for any perception by an individual involving more than one sense modality, irrespective of whether there is any integration of information across senses; 'multimodal perception' is perception of something involving a multimodal sensory process that integrates or combines information across different sensory systems. We should allow for the possibility that not all multisensory perception is multimodal perception in this sense.

of something might be supposed to be the combination of what would be perceived by each sense operating independently of the others; and the awareness we have of something with features perceived with different senses to consist in the post-perceptual combination of what is perceived with each sense individually.

This picture of multisensory perception cannot be right. We can perceive the same properties of a particular object using more than one sense modality. So the different sensory processing streams that constitute these different sense modalities process information about the same features of the same things. For example, both hearing and vision process spatial information about the same events and objects. The fact that this information comes from the same source object does not guarantee that it will match across the different processing streams. A particular stream may be affected by noise, or by conditions that prevent its optimal operation, so that although the spatial information in the two streams derives from the same distal object it may be inconsistent across streams, or be much less accurate in one stream than in the other.

The function of perception is, at least in part, to guide action. For example, the spatial content of the perceptual experiences of an object determines the spatial properties of object-directed actions. In order for perception to perform its action-guiding function, whenever the same thing is perceived with more than one sense, some process is required to eliminate inconsistencies. Suppose that you can both hear and see some object that you want to reach. If the spatial information concerning the location of the object is different in vision and audition, then in order to determine the trajectory and end point of your reaching the inconsistency must be eliminated. Either spatial information from one sensory modality must be selected over the other, or information from both senses must be integrated. So, the fact that we act on particular things that we perceive with more than one sense, requires that there be processes to select or integrate information across senses. If the spatial information concerning the location of the object is more accurate in one stream than in the other, then these processes must either select the most accurate information or combine or integrate information in some way to enhance its accuracy. Only by doing this are we likely to be successful in reaching the object.

Multisensory perception cannot, therefore, simply consist in the combined operation of the individual senses: some multisensory perception involves multimodal perceptual processes. The fact that the same objects and the same features of those objects can be simultaneously perceived with more than one sense means that there must be inter-sensory connections between different sensory systems, and inter-sensory integration of information across senses. This argument appeals to the action-guiding function of perception, but a similar argument could be made by appeal to the fact that a function of perception is to produce accurate or veridical perceptual states. What is the nature of these inter-sensory connections and integration of information and what do they tell us about perception and the nature of the senses? In this chapter I try to shed light on these questions by focusing on audio-visual interactions.[3]

In auditory perception we hear things in virtue of hearing the sounds they produce. Sounds are individual things that can instantiate a range of different acoustic properties, such as loudness and pitch. These properties are modality-specific. It is possible for us to hear a number of distinct sounds at the same time—the sound of a bird outside, the buzzing sound made by the computer, and so on—each of which instantiates a range of acoustic properties.

Sounds are distinct from their sources—the things that produce them.[4] The source of a sound is often a material object, something that instantiates a range of non-acoustic properties such as shape, size, and colour. Since sounds and material objects are not indiscernible, sounds are not identical with material objects. A sound is produced only when something happens to a material object—when an event of some kind occurs—so sounds are produced by events. In most cases, our ordinary ways of individuating the events that produce sounds distinguish them from the sounds they produce: a particular sound may have been produced by the breaking of the glass,[5] but the breaking of the glass produces a number of distinct sounds, so the particular sound is not identical to the breaking of the glass. So sounds are not identical to the events that produce them, at least not as those events are ordinarily individuated.[6]

It would be a mistake to think that because we hear the sources of sounds in virtue of hearing the sounds that they produce, the content of auditory perception is restricted to sounds and their features. Berkeley held this kind of view: 'when I hear a coach driving along the streets, all I immediately perceive is the sound.... I am said to "hear the coach"... [but] *in truth and strictness nothing can be heard but the sound*'. His reasons for thinking this derive from his empiricism: it is not possible to explain how auditory perception could be the perception of anything other than sounds within that empiricist framework. If we accept Berkeley's restriction, crossmodal interactions involving auditory perception are inexplicable: those interactions involve the integration of information about the same objects and

---

[3] There are similar kinds of interactions to those I discuss involving vision and touch, and much of what I say generalises to them. (Interactions involving flavour, taste, and smell perception appear to be different. See Spence, Auvray, and Smith, this volume.)

[4] There are a number of different accounts of the nature of sounds. See, for example, Pasnau (1999), Casati and Dokic (2005), Kulvicki (this volume), O'Callaghan (2007), Matthen (2010), and the papers in O'Callaghan and Nudds (2010). My discussion in this chapter is, I think, neutral between these different accounts.

[5] An event that begins with my hitting the glass and ends with pieces of glass at rest on the floor.

[6] It might be suggested that we can think of the sound of the breaking of the glass as a single sound, but our doing so is a result of hearing a sequence of individual sounds as grouped or connected. It's always possible to specify a source event in terms of the sound it produces (a ringing in terms of a ringing sound, a scratching in terms of a scratching sound). The claim that we hear the sources of sounds is not simply the claim that we hear such 'sounding' events. An argument along these lines is defended in more detail by O'Callaghan (2007, 21ff).

features perceived with more than one sense. On a Berkeleian view of sounds, sounds are distinct from the material objects we see, so we never see and hear the same objects and features. Furthermore, the integration of information from vision and hearing would have to involve the integration of information from different objects and different features: information about the sounds we hear—sounds that are distinct from material objects—somehow being integrated with information about the features of material objects perceived with other senses.

We should reject Berkeley's restriction. Once we do so, we can allow that the purpose or function of auditory perception is the perception of the sources of sounds, and not simply the sounds they produce. If that's right, then auditory perception has the function of representing the sources of sounds. We perceive sound sources by perceiving the sounds they make, so we perceive sounds and their sources,[7] but we shouldn't think that sounds somehow get in the way of our perceiving their sources, or cut us off from them: quite the opposite—they put us in touch with their sources. A proper defence of these claims requires an account of auditory perception—of how we perceive sounds and their sources. I don't have space for such an account here.[8] In what follows I will assume that auditory perception represents both sounds and their sources, and hence that multimodal perception involving auditory perception involves the multimodal perception of the sources of sounds, not of sounds; and that inter-sensory integration involves the integration of information about the features of sound sources.

* * *

We can perceive the same particular thing with more than one sense. What is involved in perceiving particular things in vision and in audition?

In the case of vision, we see particular objects. We do so in virtue of our visual experience representing them as such. The visual process in virtue of which we see objects is relatively well understood. It begins with information extracted from the patterns of illumination detected by the retina. Early visual processing involves a number of distinct retinotopic feature maps that operate in parallel to analyse and extract information about different features of objects. Features from different maps that correspond to the same distal object must be grouped or 'bound' together into states that correspond to that object. The result of binding is that a conjunction of features that are likely to be features of the same distal object are grouped together. One influential account of binding hypothesises that features are bound together on the basis of their spatial location.[9]

This kind of feature binding is necessary for object representation, but to represent something as an object requires more than just representing a conjunction of features at a particular place. It requires representing those features as features of

---

[7] Brian Loar (1996, 144ff.) similarly argues that olfaction represents smells and their sources.
[8] See Nudds (forthcoming).
[9] Treisman (1998).

something that is cohesive, bounded, and spatio-temporally continuous.[10] To say that something is represented as cohesive, bounded, and spatio-temporally continuous is to say that it is represented as having parts that belong together as parts of the same object (the parts are all connected, and move together) and as distinct from other objects (so they won't merge with other objects they come into contact with), and as maintaining its identity over time and through changes in location. To be a representation as of an object, a group of features must have an identity that is not just that of the conjunction of features.

One way to think of representations of objects is in terms what Kahneman, Triesman, and Gibbs (1992) call 'object files'. Object files are representations that maintain the identity of an individual object through changes in its features. When an object is perceived, information about it is placed into a file. This information might include information about its features—its location, shape, colour, and so on. As more information about the object accumulates over time—information about, for example, the kind of object it is—is added to the file. If the object moves or changes, then the object file is updated to reflect this.

Evidence that visual information is grouped into object files comes from what is known as an *object specific preview benefit*.[11] This is demonstrated with an experiment in which two objects are presented on a screen. Letters are briefly displayed on each object, and the objects then move to a new position. When the objects stop, a letter is displayed on one of them. The subject's task is to name the letter. In 'same object' trials, the same letter is displayed on the object before and after it moves; in 'different object' trials, the letter that was displayed on the other object is displayed; and in a third set of trials a novel letter is displayed. Subjects are quicker at naming the letter in the same object trials than in the other trials. This can be explained on the assumption that information about objects is stored in a file.

In the case of audition, we hear particular sound sources, and we can hear a number of distinct sound sources simultaneously. The auditory process in virtue of which we hear sound sources is less well understood than the visual process in virtue of which we see objects. At any time the sound waves that reach the ear will have been produced by any number of distinct sound sources. To perceive individual sources, the auditory system must organise the different frequency components that make up the sound wave into groups (or streams) that normally correspond to distinct environmental sources,[12] with the result that grouped frequency components are experienced as a single sound. These frequency component groups or streams correspond to, and carry information about, the particular things in the environment that produced them. As well as organising frequency

---

[10] See Matthen (2005, ch.12) for a discussion of the idea that features are bound to particulars; see Burge (2010, ch.10) for a recent discussion of the necessary conditions for the visual representation of objects. Both contain further references to relevant empirical literature.

[11] See Palmer (1999, sec. 11.2.6) for a summary of the relevant experiments and of what they show, and further references.

[12] See Bregman (1994, ch.3) and Nudds (2010) for further discussion.

components into groups at a time, the auditory system groups sequences of frequency components over time in ways that correspond to their sources, with the result that sequences of sounds are experienced as belonging together. A sequence of sounds produced by a single source is normally experienced as having been produced by a single source; that is, a sound at one time is experienced as having been produced by the same source as sounds experienced earlier.[13] So in auditory processing there are states that correspond to and carry information about particular sound sources.

It is not clear what auditory experience represents the sources of sounds as: in particular, it is not clear whether it represents the sources of sounds as particular objects, or as events of certain kinds. In many cases the sources of sounds are particular objects, but sounds are normally only produced by something happening to a particular object. For example, sounds are only produced by a metal bar when it is struck or otherwise caused to vibrate. So does auditory perception represent the sources of sounds as the particular objects that produce sounds when something happens to them, or does it represent them as the sound-producing events that happen to particular objects?

I suggested that to represent something as an object requires that it be represented as having properties constitutive of being an object: as cohesive, bounded, and spatio-temporally continuous. If we think that auditory perception cannot represent those kinds of properties, then we might conclude that it does not represent the sources of sounds as objects, but merely as events happening to objects. For example, auditory perception doesn't represent the volumetric shape of sound sources, so if representing something as bounded and cohesive requires representing its volumetric shape, then auditory experience doesn't represent anything as bounded and cohesive. If that's right then we might doubt that auditory perception represents sound sources as objects.

We should be careful, however, not to rule out the possibility that auditory perception represents objects simply on the grounds that it lacks something that is distinctively visual. (Representing shape may only be required for representing something as an object when the input is a two-dimensional retinal array.) We can find auditory analogues of the properties that are constitutive of visual object representation. Particular sound sources are perceived as a consequence of the—in many cases, nonspatial[14]—way that auditory perception 'segments' the auditory scene; distinct sounds are grouped together in virtue of having the same source, so auditory perception is able to track sound sources over time and through changes; auditory perception is sensitive to whether a sound source maintains its

---

[13] See Bregman (1994, chs. 2 and 4).

[14] The role of spatial properties in auditory grouping is not straightforward. In vision, features are spatially 'indexed' and two features with the same spatial properties may be bound together. In audition, features are not spatially indexed, but acoustic features may be bound together because they share nonspatial cues that indicate that they were produced at the same location. Sharing such spatial cues is, however, not necessary for acoustic features to be grouped. See Nudds (2009, pp. 78–83).

cohesiveness over time—think of the difference between hearing a bottle drop to the floor and bounce, and hearing it break—and, since many sounds are such that their nature is partly determined by the structure—volume, shape, and material construction—of the object that produced them, many sounds are such that they could normally only have been produced by a single, cohesive, object. It would seem, then, that auditory perception can track the kinds of properties that are constitutive of being an object. So it's not implausible to suggest that auditory perception represents the sources of sounds as having properties that are constitutive of being an object. Furthermore, there is some evidence that information about sound sources is bound together into a representation—an 'auditory object' file—that functions in auditory perception in a way that is similar to the way object files function in visual perception.[15]

Both visual and auditory perception represent particular things and their features. Visual perception represents objects as such; auditory perception represents the sources of sounds, if not as objects, then as events.[16] In both cases, we can think of information about particular things as stored in 'object' files, allowing that auditory object files may have identity conditions similar to those of events rather than of objects (in what follows, I will call these 'visual-object' representations and 'auditory-object' representations). Given this, how should we understand multisensory perception and the inter-sensory integration of information?

* * *

I argued that integration of information across different senses is necessary given that the same particular things, and the same features of those things, can be perceived with more than one sense modality. What does it mean to say that information is integrated? On the face of it, the integration of information required by multisensory perception is consistent with two different models: the 'crossmodal' model, and the 'amodal' model.

According to the amodal model, there are a number of distinct low-level processing streams corresponding to each of the different sensory modalities, but these processing streams lose their distinctness at higher levels. At lower levels, information in each stream may be grouped together in ways that correspond to the distal object from which it comes—that is, into visual-object and auditory-object representations; but at higher levels, information from the distinct processing streams that corresponds to the same distal object is combined

---

[15] Zmigrod and Hommel (2009). This is not an area that has been much investigated. One reason for this is that in some discussions, auditory objects are supposed to be sounds, rather than the sources of sounds, and so evidence is sought that there are object files that represent sounds and their features. Given what I have been arguing about sounds in relation to their sources, what we want is evidence that there are object files that represent the *sources* of sounds and their features rather than sounds and their features.

[16] Although I think there is a case for saying that auditory perception represents sound sources as objects, the substance of the following discussion is not much affected if it turns out that auditory perception represents the sources of sounds as events.

into a single 'amodal' representation of that object. Since the distinct low-level visual- and auditory-object representations will contain information concerning some of the same properties of an object, there are mechanisms that combine or integrate this information in an optimal way that maximises accuracy and resolves any inconsistencies. According to this model, the perceptual system represents objects amodally: a number of initially distinct processing streams combine to produce a single amodal representation of an object that represents it as having features—such as spatial and temporal features—that may have been perceived with more than one sense modality, as well as features—such as colour—that are modality specific. A single amodal object representation may represent an object as shaped, coloured, and as the source of a sound. It follows that the same kind of amodal-object representation plays a role in explaining our perceptual awareness of particular things perceived with any of the sense modalities. Both our visual perception of an object and our auditory perception of a sound source is explained by appeal to the same kind of amodal object representation.

According to the crossmodal model, each sense modality that represents particular objects does so by means of modality-specific object representations. There are a number of distinct processing streams corresponding to the different sensory modalities. In each stream there are representations of particular objects and their features—visual-object representations, auditory-object representations, and so on. In addition, there are crossmodal connections that function to modulate the information within each of the processing streams in the light of information in the other streams in such a way as to maximise accuracy and consistency of these distinct object representations. The same distal object may be represented simultaneously by means of distinct object representations in two or more sensory modalities; when that happens the crossmodal mechanisms operate to ensure that the features an object is represented as having—in particular the spatial and temporal features—are consistent across representations in the different sensory modalities. The modality-specific object representations are modulated, but remain distinct. Distinct kinds of modality-specific object representation play a role in explaining our perceptual awareness of things perceived with each of the sensory modalities. Our visual perception of an object is explained in terms of a modality-specific visual-object representation of an object, our auditory perception of a sound source is explained in terms of a modality-specific auditory-object representation of an object, and so on.

The difference between these two models is not in the existence of inter-sensory connections or the inter-sensory integration of information. Both models involve inter-sensory integration. The difference is in the effects of this integration: whether it results in a single amodal object representation or instead modulates several distinct modality-specific object representations. In both cases, a single distal or environmental object will be represented, but in one case it will be represented by means of an amodal object representation and in the other by two or more modality-specific object representations.

According to the crossmodal model, each sense modality represents particular objects. The visual system represents particular objects, and the auditory system represents particular objects, and there are principles that ensure that when the same distal object is represented both visually and auditorily, information about the non-modality-specific properties of these objects is integrated. The result of the integration is that, with respect to features that can be perceived with more than one sense, the visual-object representation and the auditory-object representation represent the object as having the same features, for example, as being at the same location, occurring at the same time, and so on, but the visual-object representation of the object will also represent it as having features that are specific to vision, and the auditory-object representation of the object will also represent it as having features specific to audition. Perception is *crossmodal* in the sense that information from other senses contributes to and helps to determine what is represented in any particular sense modality. But it is not *amodal* because there are distinct object representations of the same distal or environmental object in each of the sense modalities, and these distinct sense-specific object representations explain our perceptual awareness of objects perceived with each of the senses.

According to the amodal model, rather than distinct sensory modalities each representing the same particular object, information from distinct sensory modalities is integrated into a single amodal representation of a particular object. The result is that there is a single amodal representation of an object that represents the object as having both features that can be perceived with more than one sense, and features that can only be perceived with one sense.

Of course, the existence of amodal object representations doesn't rule out the existence of modality-specific object representations, and a system that produces amodal object representations could do so by combining modally specific object representations.[17] So the difference between the two models is not in whether there are modality-specific object representations. The amodal model could accept that there are. Rather, the difference concerns the existence of amodal object representations and the explanation of our perceptual awareness of distal or environmental objects: according to the amodal model, both our visual and our auditory perception of particular objects is explained by appeal to the same kind of amodal object representation. According to the crossmodal model, our visual and our auditory perception of distal or environmental objects—even when it is the same object perceived simultaneously with two senses—is explained by appeal to distinct (modality-specific) object representations of the object.

Another way to think of the difference between the two models is in terms of the consequences inter-sensory interactions have for the way distal or environmental objects are perceptually represented. Do inter-sensory interactions result

---

[17] It wouldn't necessarily operate in this way. If there are amodal representations, then it's a further question what the mechanisms are that produce them: are there modal representations that are combined, or simply mechanisms that produce amodal representations?

in objects perceptually represented by means of different kinds of (coordinated) modality-specific object representations, or by means of a single type of amodal object representation? If the former, then our perceptual awareness of objects is explained in terms of modality-specific object representations; if the latter, then our perceptual awareness of objects is explained in terms of amodal object representations. These two different explanations have consequences for both the account we give of the veridicality conditions of experiences of objects and for the account we give of object representation more generally.

If the crossmodal model is correct, then senses can be said to be fundamentally functionally independent of each other.[18] According to this model, when an object is perceived with a single sense modality, our perception of it is explained in terms of a modality-specific object representation produced by a process whose operation is fundamentally independent of the operation of the other senses. We only need to consider other senses when an object is perceived with more than one sense, and then only in order to understand how what is perceived in one sense is modulated by what is perceived in the other. If the amodal model is correct, the senses are not fundamentally functionally independent of one another. The operation of one sense modality cannot be understood in isolation from the other sense modalities, and we need to consider the other senses even when an object is perceived with only one sense. Even when an object is perceived with a single sense modality, our perception of it is explained in terms of an amodal representation produced by a process that is in part common across sense modalities, and whose operation is not independent of them. So, for example, the explanation of our auditory awareness of the sources of sounds will appeal to the same representational capacity that we appeal to in order to explain our visual awareness of objects.

* * *

I have sketched these two models in a very general way; there are other, more complicated, possibilities that I am ignoring.[19] I am ignoring them because I am

---

[18] The very existence of inter-sensory interactions might be thought to undermine this claim. Fodor's original characterization of modularity (1983) views modules as encapsulated, with no exchange of information between them. Inter-sensory interactions might therefore be thought to show that the senses are not encapsulated, hence not modular. That conclusion, however, is too quick. The organization of the brain is such that there are significant connections between functionally specialized systems that we have good reason to think are functionally independent (see Shallice [1988, ch.11] for a discussion of this point). Two things follow. First, Fodor's characterization of a module needs to be amended—in particular to allow *some* exchange of information—if it is to be of use in neuropsychological explanation; second, the functional organization that the crossmodal model describes can be viewed as describing functionally specialized, independent, sense modalities. For more detailed discussion of these issues, see Nudds (2011).

[19] There could be modality-specific representations of objects and—in virtue of the operation of some supramodal perceptual or attentional mechanism—amodal representations of objects; or there could be modality-specific *perceptual* representations of objects, but amodal representations of objects for guiding *action*. I am ignoring these to focus on the possibility and consequences of amodal perceptual representations of objects.

interested in the explanation of our perceptual awareness of particular objects: is our perceptual awareness of objects explained in terms of amodal representations of objects, or only ever in terms of modality-specific representations of objects? The answer to this question has consequences for the veridicality conditions of perceptual experiences. If perceptual awareness of objects is explained in terms of amodal representations of objects, then when the same thing is both seen and heard it will be represented by means of a representation of it as having both visual and auditory features. For example, suppose you hear someone you can see speaking: you hear speaking and you see lip movements. Your perceptual experience will represent the person you see as the source of the sounds you hear. If the person you see is not the source of the sounds, then the representation, and hence your perceptual experience, is non-veridical. If, on the other hand, perceptual awareness of objects is explained in terms of modality-specific object representations then your experience does not represent the person you see as the source of the sounds: your perceptual experience does not represent a single object by means of a single representation of it as having visual features and as the source of the sounds; instead, it represents the object by means of one auditory representation that represents it as the source of the sound, and by another visual representation that represents the person, and each of these representations represents the (matching) spatio-temporal features of the object. These representations, and hence your perceptual experience, are veridical if the sounds come from the same place as the person you see, even if the person you see is not the source of the sounds.

Which account of the veridicality conditions is correct will have further consequences for our view of perception and the senses, some of which I'll mention later. But now, having sketched the two models, I want to turn to the question of how we determine which of them is correct. An obvious place to start is with empirical studies of inter-sensory interactions.

* * *

There are inter-sensory interactions that don't involve the kind of integration of information across object representations described by the two models. Some of the ways in which the senses influence each other can be explained in terms of one sense modality bringing about or causing a change in another sense modality, without appeal to representations of objects as such.

For example, there are processes that are responsible for calibrating spatial frames of reference across different sensory systems. In order to act on objects we can see, the bodily frame of reference that guides reaching must be aligned with the frame of reference relative to which the things we see are located. One kind of mechanism by which this calibration might occur uses optic flow—a pattern of change that can be specified at the level of the retina—to calibrate the direction of movement of the body within a visual frame of reference. This kind of calibration mechanism doesn't require recognising that something perceived with one sense (kinaesthesia) is the same as something perceived with another (vision), so doesn't require information about particular objects to be integrated. Instead, information about the alignment of the spatial frames of reference in different sensory systems is available and can be used to produce a general calibration across senses, without reference to particular objects.[20]

In some cases an interaction that appears prima facie to involve object representations of particular things in fact doesn't. A single brief visual flash accompanied by two auditory beeps can result in the illusion of two flashes having occurred.[21] Conversely, a double flash accompanied by a single beep may be misperceived as a single flash.[22] In both cases, the auditory experience alters the visual experience of the flash to produce an illusion. This illusion occurs as a result of low-level connections between the auditory and visual cortex that enable activity in the auditory cortex to modulate activity in the visual cortex. In this case the modulation is temporal, and the auditory input changes the temporal properties of visual features. That the activity in the visual cortex occurs at the same time as activity in the auditory cortex indicates that it is likely to have been produced by the same environmental event. Given that likelihood, and the fact that the auditory resolution of time is more accurate than the visual, this kind of modulation may function to enhance the accuracy of the visual perception of brief environmental events.[23]

Although this example involves an interaction between the processes that ultimately produce perceptions of particular objects, it can be explained in terms of a mechanism that doesn't involve the integration or combination of information concerning particular objects. Activity at a low level in one sensory system modulates the activity at a low level in another sensory system. This results in changes in the properties of low-level feature detectors in a way that generally enhances perceptual performance.[24] But this interaction doesn't require temporal information from vision and audition to be integrated or combined; and since these early stages of perceptual processing don't involve representations of particular things, it would be implausible to suppose that it involves the integration of features associated with distinct object representations.

Although these kinds of interactions help co-ordinate and improve the performance of different sensory systems when they operate together, they do not involve either crossmodal or amodal perception. They can be explained in terms

---

[20] Bruggeman, Zosh, and Warren (2007).

[21] The illusion can be produced by briefly displaying a white disk against a black background, accompanied by a series of auditory beeps. Subjects who are asked to report how many flashes they see incorrectly report seeing multiple flashes when a single flash is accompanied by more than one beep. See Shams, Kamitani, and Shimojo (2000).

[22] Watkins et al. (2007).

[23] Watkins et al. (2006).

[24] Although it's not clear why these low-level connections produce the illusions, it may be that the visual flashes are close to the temporal threshold of what is visually perceivable. Modulation of low-level visual attention mechanisms may resolve what is, in effect, an ambiguous visual stimulus in a way that normally improves the reliability of visual perception, without there being integration of information. See Macaluso (2006).

of the causal influence of modality-specific sensory processes: what happens in one sensory system causes changes in another sensory system. Not all multisensory perception can be explained in this way.

* * *

One of the most familiar kinds of inter-sensory interaction is the ventriloquism effect. When a ventriloquist speaks without moving her lips, her voice seems to come from the mouth of the dummy whose moving mouth visually appears to be the source of the sounds. The ventriloquism effect produces an apparent change in the location of the source of the sound towards what visually appears to be the source of the sound. The effect occurs even for simple stimuli such as light flashes and tones: perceivers generally misjudge the location of a sound source if they hear the sound at the same time as they see a flash of light at a different (but nearby) location.

A similar phenomenon occurs in the temporal domain. In one experiment, subjects had to judge the order in which two small lights, arranged one above the other, were illuminated. Brief sounds were played from a loudspeaker behind the lights. On some trials there were no sounds or the sounds occurred simultaneously with the lights; on others, one tone was played before the first light was illuminated and the second after the second light was illuminated. The sounds played before and after the lights led to an improvement in the subjects' performance. In another experiment, the first sound was played after the first light and before the second light, and the subjects' performance was worse than it was without the sounds. The sounds appear to have produced a temporal ventriloquism effect by 'pulling' the lights into temporal alignment with the sounds and so either increasing or reducing the apparent temporal separation between them, and therefore improving or reducing the subjects' ability to judge their temporal order.[25]

Something similar to the ventriloquism effect can occur for the auditory and visual perception of movement. This is demonstrated in the case of subjects who had to determine the apparent direction of the motion of a sound source, whilst ignoring the apparent motion of a light. The light could appear to move in a direction that was either congruent or incongruent with the apparent motion of the sound. The results 'demonstrate a strong crossmodal interaction in the domain of motion perception. . . [they] suggest the obligatory perceptual integration of dynamic information across sensory modalities, often producing an illusory reversal of the true direction of the auditory apparent motion'.[26]

---

[25] Morein-Zamir, Soto-Faraco, and Kingstone (2003). The temporal ventriloquism effect shows that there doesn't have to be precise temporal synchronisation across different senses for information to be integrated. Given data from a temporal order judgement task it is possible to determine how big the temporal interval between the stimuli can be for them to still be perceived as occurring at the same time (or the interval for which the subject is as likely to judge that the first stimulus came before the second as they are that the second came before the first).

[26] Soto-Faraco et al. (2002, p.145). Does the perception of motion in these cases involve a temporal mismatch (with the time of a flash incongruent with the time of a sound) or a spatial mismatch (with

Why do these different kinds of ventriloquism effect occur? In general, vision provides more accurate and more reliable spatial information than hearing, and hearing provides more accurate and more reliable temporal information than vision. When information about spatial and temporal features across different sense modalities conflicts, the perceptual system combines or integrates it in a way that favours the most accurate and reliable source of information. Greater weight is given to whichever source of information is most reliable in the circumstances. If visual information about spatial location is poor (as it might be in poor visibility), more weight is given to auditory spatial information; normally, however, (in good visibility) more weight is given to visual information. Integration involves the 'near optimal combination of visual and auditory space cues, where each one is weighted by an inverse estimate of the noisiness, rather than one modality capturing the other'.[27] The result is that the perception of spatial and temporal features of objects and events perceived with both vision and hearing is more accurate than it would have been if no integration occurred:[28] by integrating two or more sources of information, the variance inherent in each is reduced.[29] Multisensory perception is, therefore, more reliable and more accurate than perception with a single sense modality.

What does ventriloquism show about the nature of integration? Unlike the low-level interactions of the kind required to explain the flashing lights illusion, these effects can only be explained on the assumption that information concerning the same object, perceived with different senses, is integrated or combined. Why? Because the apparent location of an object—where the object perceptually appears to be—is the result of the optimal combination of information from different senses. The process of combining information must take as input the location of the object as represented in the auditory system and the location of the object as represented in the visual system, together with some estimation of the reliability of each, to produce an (optimal) representation of the location of the object. The consequences of spatial ventriloquism cannot be explained simply in terms of one sensory system causally modulating the operation of the other: it involves the combination of the spatial information about an object from two different senses. The same argument applies in the temporal case, and in the case of motion.

---

the location of flash incongruent with the location of a sound)? It could perhaps be either, or neither. The information integrated may be sense-specific information about direction of movement.

[27] Alais and Burr (2004, p. 260). This kind of optimal integration occurs across other senses too. Vision is more precise for discriminations along the horizontal, proprioception is a more reliable for discriminations in depth. There is evidence that the perceptual system takes this into account, giving extra weight to information from proprioception when the task requires depth discrimination, and extra weight to vision when it requires discrimination along the horizontal. It's not the case that vision always dominates touch; it does so only when it is the more reliable source of information. See Ernst and Bülthoff (2004). See also Stokes and Biggs (this volume) for a discussion of visual dominance, explained in terms of the unique, rich spatial nature of vision and visual imagery.

[28] See Alais and Burr (2004), and Battaglia, Jacobs, and Aslin (2003).

[29] Ernst and Bülthoff (2004).

Furthermore, in the temporal case it appears that there is a 'temporal window' within which audio-visual integration can occur. This window is asymmetrical and flexible:[30] its size changes according to the distance of a visually apparent sound source from the observer, and is wider for sounds from a more distant event. This suggests that the perceptual system is able to compensate for the fact that light from an object reaches the observer before the sound it makes, and that the gap between the two is greater for a sound from a more distant object. The properties of the temporal window can be explained in terms of the perceptual system compensating for this discrepancy in the perceived properties of particular objects; it can't be explained in terms of causal modulation.[31]

The very fact that inter-sensory integration involves the integration of a range of features associated with a distal or environmental object perceived with more than one sense might be taken to support the amodal model. Multisensory perception can be viewed as the parallel processing of information about features of objects detected by different sensory modalities. That means there is an inter-sensory binding problem analogous to the binding problem in visual perception. In visual perception, features in parallel processing streams that correspond to the same distal object must be grouped or 'bound' together into states that correspond to that object. In multisensory perception features in different sensory modalities that correspond to the same object must be treated as belonging to the same distal object. Inter-sensory integration occurs when features in different sensory modalities that correspond to the same object are treated as features of a single object. So, it might be suggested, inter-sensory integration produces states that represent groups of features as belonging to particular distal objects; that is, inter-sensory integration produces amodal representations of objects, and so rules out the crossmodal model. O'Callaghan, in a recent discussion, suggests that inter-sensory integration 'shows that there is a subpersonal grasp, at the level of sensory or perceptual processing, of sources of stimulation that must be understood in multimodal or modality-independent terms. If you are willing to attribute content to subpersonal perceptual states, the corresponding states possess multimodal content'.[32] If that's right, then inter-sensory integration implies the existence of amodal representations.

But that conclusion is drawn too quickly. We can explain the different kinds of ventriloquism effect in a way that doesn't involve amodal object representations. For inter-sensory integration to occur, features of the same object perceived with different senses must be identified so they can be integrated. The perceptual system makes use of a number of different cues to determine whether information

---

[30] Integration occurs when visual stimuli lead auditory stimuli by up to about 300ms, or lag by 80ms; subjects find it more difficult to detect asynchrony when the visual signal leads, than when the auditory signal leads.

[31] Though the process breaks down for distances of more than about ten metres (Sugita and Suzuki, 2003). For a survey of temporal ventriloquism, see Vatakis and Spence (2010).

[32] O'Callaghan (2007, 14).

across senses is likely to have come from the same object. Some of these cues are bottom-up and rely on correspondences between sensory features in different processing streams. For example, representations along early stages of visual processing may encode features such as changes in luminance and changes in motion; those along the early stages of auditory processing stages encode changes in intensity and changes in pitch and motion cues; these features correspond to the same properties of distal objects. If these features are correlated in time (and perhaps in space), they are likely to correspond to features of a single distal object. The perceptual system can exploit this and treat features that are correlated in this way as corresponding to a single distal object.

Other cues are top-down, and draw on the subject's semantic or associational knowledge—on whether the subject takes, or is likely to take, what is perceived with two different senses to be a single distal object, or to be features of a single distal object. This is often labelled 'the unity assumption': 'the assumption that a perceiver makes about whether he or she is observing a single multisensory event rather than multiple separate unisensory events'.[33] Making this assumption needn't involve explicitly judging that what is perceived with one sense is the same as what is perceived with another.[34] It might result from a past association in experience of features associated with a single object, or from knowledge that certain features are likely to go together, in the way that the visual appearance of a steam kettle goes together with the whistling sound it makes. The perceptual system is able to exploit this knowledge, and treats features that are 'assumed' to belong together as corresponding to a single object. (Conversely, when features are 'assumed' not to belong together—when the unity assumption is false—the perceptual system treats them as belonging to distinct objects.)[35] In most circumstances, both top-down and bottom-up cues are likely to operate at the same time, with the result that information in different senses is integrated if and only if it is likely to have a single distal source.[36]

Integration does not only occur on a feature-by-feature basis. The fact that a feature in one sense is treated as corresponding to the same object as a feature in another sense means that information about that feature is integrated across the senses; but it also makes it likely that information about other features associated with that distal object are integrated across the senses. For example, if there are cues to indicate that spatial features in two senses are likely to be features of a single object, then information about those spatial features is integrated; but that makes it likely that information about the temporal features associated with the object is integrated too. So when one feature is treated as belonging to the

---

[33] Vatakis and Spence (2007, 744).
[34] But what we judge or know does affect whether cross-modal integration occurs.
[35] See Vatakis and Spence (2007, 2008, 2010).
[36] Vatakis and Spence (2007, 753).

same single object across senses, then other features associated with that object are treated as belonging together across the senses.

This is nicely illustrated by the following demonstration of the ventriloquism effect. When a speech recording was played with a video recording of a talking head, inter-sensory effects were modulated by whether the gender of the voice matched that of the head in the video. 'Participants found it significantly easier to discriminate the temporal order of the auditory and visual speech stimuli when they were mismatched than when they were matched [i.e., when the gender of the voice didn't match rather than matched that of the video].' These results don't just provide 'psychophysical evidence that the "unity assumption" can modulate crossmodal binding of multisensory information at a perceptual level'[37]; they show that when one—in this case, high-level—feature is treated as belonging to the same object across senses, other features associated with that object are treated as belonging to the same object and so are integrated.

In some cases, then, the fact that a feature represented by two distinct object representations is likely to be a feature of the same distal object results in the integration of information about that feature across the representations; but it also leads to the integration of information about other features represented by the two object representations. The fact that one feature is integrated across senses as coming from the same distal object leads to the integration of other features of the same object. We cannot explain that in terms of the association of features across senses: the two object representations that represent those features must be associated. But that association of two object representations is consistent with the crossmodal model. An object representation in one sensory system can be associated with an object representation in another sensory system—on the basis of the kinds of cues that I have described—so that information about some of the features of the distal object that they represent can be integrated, without the two object representations being merged into a single object representation, and so without the formation of a single amodal object representation.

For example, in the ventriloquism effect we see the dummy's moving mouth and hear speech. We might suppose that the visual object representation of the moving mouth and the auditory object representation of the source of the speech are associated on the basis of shared temporal properties. As a consequence, information about spatial features represented by the auditory object representation is integrated with information about the spatial features represented by the visual object representation, so that we hear the speech as coming from the place that we see the mouth of the dummy to be. But this could happen without the spatial features losing their identity as features represented by two distinct object representations, and without the other features represented by the two object representations being merged into a single amodal object representation.

---

[37] Vatakis and Spence (2007, 752).

If that's right, then inter-sensory integration—at least of the kind involved in the ventriloquism effects—requires associating object representations of a single distal object across sensory modalities so that information about *some* features can be integrated, but it does not require that *all* the features associated with the two object representations are merged into a single object representation, and so does not require amodal object representations.

I argued that whilst there's a sense in which the senses are modal, multisensory perception could not simply consist in the combined operation of each of the individual senses. The kind of inter-sensory integration required to explain the ventriloquism effects substantiates that conclusion: when the same thing is perceived with two or more senses, the senses interact with each other in such a way that what is perceived with one sense can only be explained by appeal, in part, to what is perceived with the other senses. But this kind of integration does not undermine the idea that perceptual states are modality specific: that although the representational contents of the perceptual states of one modality are influenced by the contents of the perceptual states of another modality, our perceptual awareness of distal objects is explained in terms of modality-specific object representations.

* * *

If the kind of inter-sensory integration involved in the various kinds of ventriloquism effects doesn't give us any reason to reject the crossmodal model, then what would? That is, what would show that inter-sensory interactions involved amodal object representations? According to the amodal model, when a single distal object is perceived with two senses and inter-sensory integration occurs, all the information about that distal object is combined into a single object representation—into a single amodal 'object file'. This amodal object file will contain information about all the features associated with the distal object, features that are perceived with more than one sense modality. So it will contain information about both auditory and visual features. On the other hand, according to the crossmodal model there are distinct sense modality-specific object representations—sense-specific 'object files'—associated with each sense modality. Although information concerning some features—those perceived with both senses—is integrated across these representations, each representation contains information about features specific to that sensory modality. So the visual-object representation will represent visual features of the distal object that the auditory-object representation doesn't, and vice versa.

That suggests that we can test the claim that there are amodal object representations by testing whether information about sense-specific features from more than one sense is contained within a single object file. I described how the existence of an object-specific preview benefit provides evidence that visual information about different features is grouped into an object file. If information about features specific to more than one sense modality is contained within a single object file, then we would expect there to be crossmodal object-specific preview benefits.

I have not been able to find many attempts to test this suggestion, but in one experiment subjects saw two object targets that briefly displayed pictures (of a dog, whistle, train, hammer, piano, and phone); the objects then moved to a new position and a sound (of a dog bark, a whistle blow, a train horn, a hammer blow, a piano note, and a phone ring) was played from a position that corresponded to the position of one of the objects. In some trials the sound played was one that matched the picture previously displayed on the object, and in others the sound played was one that matched the picture previously displayed on the other object. Subjects had to report whether what they heard corresponded to what they had previously seen. An object-specific previous benefit was found.[38]

This result is just what we would expect if inter-sensory integration involves amodal object files. The subject produces a response on the basis of auditorily perceiving an object (hearing the sound); the fact that there is a preview benefit suggests that the auditory object file contains information contained in the visual object file associated with the object they saw moving; so there is a single file that contains both auditory and visual information as I suggested there would be if the amodal model is correct. Of course, this is only a single experiment, and it doesn't show that *all* the information associated with the object is contained within a single file. But I think it is difficult to explain these results on the assumption that there are sense modality-specific object representations.

A different kind of evidence comes from the fact that auditory experience can tell us about changes to, or events occurring in, objects that are not otherwise visible. To take a simple example, if a box on your desk is making a ticking sound, then you can perceive something is happening to it even though there is nothing visibly happening to it. The two models of inter-sensory integration give different accounts of what you perceive in this kind of case.

If there are amodal object representations, then auditory information about what is happening to a distal object will be combined with visual information into a single amodal object representation. Such a representation will not contain information just that an event occurred, but that an event occurred to a visible distal object. So you perceive something happening to the thing you can see. If there are distinct, sense-modality-specific object representations, then auditory information about what is happening to a distal object will be contained in an object representation that is distinct from the visual-object representation of the same object. There will be an auditory representation of an event, and a distinct visual representation of an object. These representations might represent some of the same features of the distal object—the same spatial features, for example—but the auditory features and visual features are not represented as features of a single object: there is not a single amodal representation of an object as having both auditory and visual features. So although you hear something happening at the same

---

[38] Jordan, Clark, and Mitroff (2010).

place as an object that you can see, you do not hear something happening to the object that you can see.

The occurrence of an illusion in which auditory information disambiguates a visually ambiguous display provides empirical evidence in favour of the amodal account of this kind of case.[39] The illusion involves two objects, each of which start out at the top corner of a screen and then move diagonally to the bottom corner, crossing in the centre. The display is ambiguous. It can be perceived either as the objects colliding with each other in the centre of the screen and rebounding (as if the objects had 'bounced' off each other), or as each object following a straight path to the opposite bottom corner and so 'streaming' past the other in the centre of the screen. If an auditory event—a tone or tap—coincides with the moment they meet, the objects are seen as bouncing. The auditory event disambiguates the display. The disambiguating effect of the sound (the auditory event) is reduced if it is flanked by other sounds. That seems to be because when it is flanked by other sounds, the sound is perceived as part of a distinct auditory object (the stronger the grouping of the sound with the flanking sounds, the less likely it is to have a disambiguating effect).[40]

The experiences of the display differ according to whether or not an event—a collision of the objects—is perceived to occur. A collision is perceived to occur when the meeting of the objects in the centre of the screen is perceived as the source of the sound—as a collision that produces the sound. Since the sound's source has the same spatio-temporal properties in all cases, but only disambiguates the display in some, it is not sufficient for the meeting of the objects to be perceived as the source of the sound that it is perceived to have the same spatio-temporal properties as the source of the sound. It is not possible to explain the disambiguation as a spatio-temporal effect.

When the source of the sound is perceived to be something that produces a sequence of sounds (that is, when the sound is perceived as part of a distinct auditory object)—and so to be unrelated to the meeting of the objects—no collision is perceived to occur. It seems, then, that the best explanation of the perception of a collision is that the source of the sound is represented as an event involving the meeting of the two objects; that is, an event is represented as both the meeting of the two objects and as the source of the sound. Such a representation would not just contain information that an event occurred, but that an event occurred to a visible object. It would be an amodal representation. Since the best explanation of this illusion is in terms of the amodal representation of an event, the occurrence of the illusion supports the amodal model of multimodal perception.

* * *

I have described two kinds of evidence that lend support to the suggestion that the multisensory perception involves the amodal representations of objects, but

---

[39] Sekuler, Sekuler, and Lau (1997).

[40] Watanabe and Shimojo (2001).

clearly more is needed. Representing something as an object involves representing it as cohesive, bounded, and spatio-temporally continuous, and that involves
being able to keep track of it over time and through changes. If objects are represented amodally, then capacities to track objects over time and through changes
will be amodal capacities. For example, an object might be tracked initially by
hearing it, and then by later by seeing it. In vision, the capacity to keep track of an
object visually consists, partly, in perceptual anticipation: what is perceived at one
time has consequences for what will be perceived at a later time. Does perceiving
an object with one sensory modality generate perceptual anticipations in other
senses? If the capacity is amodal, we might expect hearing an object to generate
visual expectations. The literature on child development contains many elegant
experiments that probe the properties of infants' visual representations of objects,
including their ability to visually track objects over time. It would be interesting to
discover whether their ability to track objects is amodal: for example, if an infant
hears something behind a barrier, would she be surprised, when the barrier is
removed, to *see* nothing there?[41]

* * *

I began by arguing that multisensory perception cannot simply be the combined
operation of each of the individual senses, but that some kind of integration of
information across the senses is required. I sketched two different models of what
that integration of information might involve. Many examples of multisensory
perception are consistent with both models, but I have described some evidence
that supports the suggestion that some multisensory perception involves the amodal representation of distal objects. Much of our theorising about perception takes
place within a modality-specific framework. We focus on vision, or on audition,
and consider it in isolation from the other senses. If perception is amodal, then
such theorising is likely to leave out something fundamental about the nature
of perception—that it involves capacities that are shared across different senses.
For example, considered in isolation from vision, auditory perception can appear
limited in what it can tell us about the world, perhaps limited to telling us about
sounds and their features. But considered in conjunction with vision, as a form of
perception that draws on the same capacities to perceive objects as vision does,
auditory perception appears far less limited—a form of perception that enables
us to perceive the same material objects that we see. Any account of auditory
perception must explain how vision and the other senses—and capacities shared
across the senses—contribute to what is auditorily perceived; and any account that
doesn't do so will leave out something central to auditory perception. If perception
draws on amodal representational capacities, then that argument applies generally: just as audition cannot be understood in isolation from vision, so vision cannot be understood in isolation from audition.

---

[41] Richardson and Kirkham (2004) used a multimodal object tracking experiment that may lend
support to the suggestion that they would, but is perhaps better explained as a semantic rather than a
perceptual effect.

Acknowledgments

I would like to thank the editors for many helpful suggestions.

References

Alais, David, and David Burr. "The ventriloquist effect results from near-optimal bimodal integration." *Current Biology: CB* 14, no. 3 (February 3, 2004): 257–262.

Battaglia, Peter W., Robert A. Jacobs, and Richard N. Aslin. "Bayesian integration of visual and auditory signals for spatial localization." *Journal of the Optical Society of America. A, Optics, Image Science, and Vision* 20, no. 7 (July 2003): 1391–1397.

Bregman, Albert. *Auditory Scene Analysis.* Cambridge, MA: MIT Press, 1994.

Bruggeman, Hugo, Wendy Zosh, and William H. Warren. "Optic flow drives human visuo-locomotor adaptation." *Current Biology* 17, no. 23 (2007): 2035–2040.

Burge, Tyler. *Origins of Objectivity.* Oxford: Oxford University Press, 2010.

Casati, Roberto, and Jerome Dokic. "Sounds." *Stanford Encyclopedia of Philosophy* (Fall Edition), ed. Edward N. Zalta (2005). http://plato.stanford.edu/archives/fall2005/entries/sounds/.

Ernst, Marc O., and Heinrich H. Bülthoff. "Merging the senses into a robust percept." *Trends in Cognitive Sciences* 8, no. 4 (April 2004): 162–169.

Fodor, Jerry A. *The Modularity of Mind.* Cambridge, MA: MIT Press, 1983.

Jordan, Kerry E., Kait Clark, and Stephen R. Mitroff. "See an object, hear an object file: Object correspondence transcends sensory modality." *Visual Cognition* 18, no. 4 (2010): 492.

Kahneman, Daniel, Treisman, Anne, and Gibbs, Brian. "The Reviewing of object files: Object-specific integration of information." *Cognitive Psychology* 24, (1992): 175–219.

Macaluso, Emiliano. "Multisensory processing in sensory-specific cortical areas." *Neuroscientist* 12, no. 4 (2006): 327–338.

Matthen, Mohan. *Seeing, Doing, and Knowing: A Philosophical Theory of Sense Perception.* Oxford: Oxford University Press, 2005.

Matthen, Mohan. "On the diversity of auditory objects." *Review of Philosophy and Psychology* 1 (2010): 63–89.

Morein-Zamir, Sharon, Salvador Soto-Faraco, and Alan Kingstone. "Auditory capture of vision: Examining temporal ventriloquism." *Cognitive Brain Research* 17, no. 1 (June 2003): 154–163.

Nudds, Matthew. Sounds and space. In Matthew Nudds and Casey O'Callaghan, eds., *Sounds and Perception: New Philosophical Essays.* Oxford: Oxford University Press, 2010.

Nudds, Matthew. "What are auditory objects?" *Review of Philosophy and Psychology* 1 (2010): 105–122.

Nudds, Matthew. "The senses as psychological kinds." In Fiona Macpherson, ed., *The Senses: Classical and Contemporary Readings.* Oxford: Oxford University Press, 2011: 311–40.

Nudds, Matthew. "Auditory Perception." In Mohan Mathen, ed., *Oxford Handbook of Perception.* Oxford: Oxford University Press (forthcoming).

Nudds, Matthew, and Casey O'Callaghan. *Sounds and Perception: New Philosophical Essays.* Oxford: Oxford University Press, 2010.

O'Callaghan, Casey. "Perception and multimodality." MS. http://www.oxfordhandbooks. com/view/10.1093/oxfordhb/9780195309799.001.0001/oxfordhb-9780195309799. DOI: 10.1093/oxfordhb/9780195309799.013.0005.

O'Callaghan, Casey. *Sounds: A Philosophical Theory.* Oxford: Oxford University Press, 2007.

Palmer, S. *Vision Science: From Photons to Phenomenology.* Cambridge, MA: MIT Press, 1999.

Pasnau, Robert. "What is sound?" *Philosophical Quarterly* 50 (1999): 309–324.

Richardson, Daniel C., and Natasha Z. Kirkham, "Multimodal events and moving locations: Eye movements of adults and 6-month-olds reveal dynamic spatial indexing." *Journal of Experimental Psychology, General* 133, no. 1 (March 2004): 46–62.

Sekuler, R., A. B. Sekuler, and R. Lau. "Sound alters visual motion perception." *Nature* 385, no. 6614 (January 23, 1997): 308.

Shallice, Tim. *From Neuropsychology to Mental Structure.* Cambridge: Cambridge University Press, 1988.

Shams, Ladan, Yukiyasu Kamitani, and Shinsuke Shimojo. "Illusions: What you see is what you hear." *Nature* 408, no. 6814 (December 14, 2000): 788.

Soto-Faraco, Salvador, et al. "The ventriloquist in motion: Illusory capture of dynamic information across sensory modalities." *Cognitive Brain Research* 14, no. 1 (June 2002): 139–146.

Sugita, Yoichi, and Yôiti Suzuki. "Audiovisual perception: Implicit estimation of sound-arrival time." *Nature* 421, no. 6926 (February 27, 2003): 911.

Treisman, A. "Feature binding, attention and object perception." *Philosophical Transactions of the Royal Society B: Biological Sciences* 353, no. 1373 (August 29, 1998): 1295–1306.

Vatakis, Argiro, and Charles Spence. "Crossmodal binding: Evaluating the 'unity assumption' using audiovisual speech stimuli." *Perception & Psychophysics* 69, no. 5 (July 2007): 744–756.

Vatakis, Argiro, and Charles Spence. "Evaluating the influence of the 'unity assumption' on the temporal perception of realistic audiovisual stimuli." *Acta Psychologica* 127, no. 1 (January 2008): 12–23.

Vatakis, Argiro, and Charles Spence. "Audiovisual temporal integration for complex speech, object-action, animal call, and musical stimuli." In Jochen Kaiser and Marcus Johannes Naumer, eds., *Multisensory Object Perception in the Primate Brain.* New York: Springer, 2010: 95–121.

Watanabe, K., and S. Shimojo. "When sound affects vision: Effects of auditory grouping on visual motion perception." *Psychological Science: A Journal of the American Psychological Society / APS* 12, no. 2 (March 2001): 109–116.

Watkins, S. et al. "Sound alters activity in human V1 in association with illusory visual perception." *NeuroImage* 31, no. 3 (July 1, 2006): 1247–1256.

Watkins, S. et al. "Activity in human V1 follows multisensory perception." *NeuroImage* 37, no. 2 (August 15, 2007): 572–578.

Zmigrod, S., and B. Hommel. "Auditory event files: Integrating auditory perception and action planning." *Attention, Perception & Psychophysics* 71, no. 2 (February 2009): 352–362.

PART III

The Nonvisual Senses

7

What Counts as Touch?
Matthew Fulkerson

In front of me sits a warm mug of coffee. I perceive the mug using a variety of senses. I see the mug, becoming aware of its particular shape, size, and color. I touch the mug, feeling its heft, warmth, and solidity. I also smell the aroma of the coffee in the mug, and taste its chocolate undertones. It seems obvious that we experience the world using distinct senses. This gives the appearance that individuating the senses should be a relatively straightforward affair.

The situation is more complicated. The philosophical project of individuating the senses faces numerous difficulties.[1] Proposals for individuating the senses must address a host of potential counterexamples. In addition, recent empirical work has increasingly focused on the deep interconnections between sensory systems. This suggests that our perceptual experience of the world is multisensory in ways that are sometimes not immediately apparent to the perceiver. These considerations seem to undermine the intuitive idea that the senses are easily distinguished from one another.

Despite these difficulties, I want to address the closely related but distinct question of what we mean by "the sense of touch." In particular, I am interested in whether we can ground the common practice of separating pains, itches, tingles, throbs, hunger pangs, and the like, from those qualities usually associated with touch, like pressure, texture, vibration, shape, and thermal properties. This question is one that raises a number of important issues about the relationship between seemingly distinct sensory subsystems and how they interact. It also plays an important role in understanding how some features become *externalized* (in a sense to be explained) whereas others seem to be mere sensations. This issue takes on special importance in light of our understanding of the senses as fundamentally connected. Even if the individual sensory modalities are not separate modular channels, they (or more accurately, their constituent subsystems) do hang together in a special way that ought to be emphasized even as we move to a more

---

[1] For an excellent introduction to the issues, see the essays in MacPherson (2011).

connected, multisensory view of perception. Using touch as an example, I want to suggest one way that the individual senses provide us with a kind of unique perceptual contact with the world. This contact is characterized by the way that the constituent systems group the perceived properties of objects, which I shall refer to as *sensory features*.[2]

The purpose of this chapter is to suggest a relatively straightforward way of determining which features belong to touch and which do not. My view is that the sensory systems that belong to touch are those that *group* or *associate* a specific set of sensory features, generating a unified representation of tangible objects. This grouping does not occur for the features (if there are any) found in typical pains, itches, tingles, throbs, and the like. This allows us to give a robust means of separating or distinguishing certain bodily sensations from perceptual touch, while providing independent motivation for accepting certain features as part of touch. This special grouping relation is not exotic or surprising in vision, where it is referred to as *sensory binding*. My claim is that touch also involves the grouping of features into coherent object representations. There is a special set of tangible features that enter into relations of sensory feature binding and the systems that code for these features are the ones that constitute the sense of touch. The systems that code for pains, itches, tingles, and other bodily sensations do not group their features into coherent assignments on external objects, which explains both their seemingly subjective nature and distinguishes them from genuine tangible properties.

1. Individuation

What are the necessary and sufficient conditions for something to count as touch rather than vision or hearing? Many philosophical proposals for answering this kind of question have been provided over the years. For example, Brian Keeley (2002) argues that the sense modalities can be defined this way:

> On my account, to possess a genuine sensory modality is to possess an appropriately wired-up sense organ that is historically dedicated to facilitating behavior with respect to an identifiable physical class of energy. (6)

Keeley uses this account to ground his criterion for sensory individuation. Any two putative sensory modalities that differ along these four criteria count as distinct senses. Vision, for instance, seems to possess a distinct sensory channel starting with the eyes and leading to the visual cortex, and it facilitates a unique set

---

[2] I use "sensory features" whereas Austen Clark (2008) refers to them as "phenomenal properties." Despite the different terminology, the phrases pick out the same thing, as in Clark's description: "In the first instance phenomenal properties characterize how the *world* seems: how the entities that one perceives in the world *appear* to the subject who perceives them" (407).

of behaviors relative to a unique class of physical energy (namely, visible light). Keeley's view provides a means of deciding how many senses a creature has and whether two sensory systems count as part of the same sense or not. Given its focus on measurable criteria and its explicit denial of a role for qualitative experience in individuating the senses, the view seems especially useful in assessing the sensory capacities of nonhuman animals. While there is some question about whether this view ultimately succeeds in general as a way to properly individuate the senses (especially given that the senses do not seem to involve wholly distinct informational channels), it immediately runs into difficulties with the sense of touch. The view seems to suggest that what we call the sense of touch is actually several separate sensory modalities. This is because touch does not have anything resembling a single, "appropriately wired-up sense organ." While the skin is a plausible candidate for such an organ, the skin itself is not a sensory transducer. Instead, a variety of distinct sensory channels are located in the skin. And these transducers are sensitive to distinct types of physical energy (thermal properties, solidity, elasticity, etc.). In addition, the skin includes receptor channels that code for pains, itches, tingles, and other bodily sensations. According to Keeley, it seems that each of these separate transducer populations would qualify as a distinct sense. What is missing from this view, I want to suggest, is a role for the grouping of distinct channels, for how distinct transducer populations work together, coordinating and blending their operations in a unified, coherent manner.

An alternative view, advocated by Matthew Nudds (2003), claims that the significance of sensory individuation is rooted in convention. Nudds argues that this significance is grounded in the unique set of properties a person can come to know about through a particular modality, and the conventional importance accorded to these sets of properties. On this view, touch is distinguished from the other senses because there is a unique set of properties that touch allows a person to know about. Learning that someone touched a vase, rather than learning that they saw it or heard it, tells us which properties of the vase that person experienced. While this is a plausible account of sensory significance (that is, why we conventionally divide the senses into the five that we do), and it seems correct in dividing the senses by the properties unique to each sense, it does not yet explain the particular constitution of features unique to each sense, especially those that belong to touch.

A similar concern arises for Fred Dretske (1992). He argues that the sensory modalities are distinct channels that represent certain classes of information. While it is plausible that each modality involves the representation of a unique set of sensory information, he does not yet provide an explanation for *why* the sense of touch consists of just the features that it does—that is, why include thermal properties but not pains?

While these views offer plausible accounts about what individuates or is significant about the distinct sensory modalities, they do not yet account for the one thing that should interest us the most: is there some principled explanation for the classification of certain features as belonging to the sense of touch? D. M. Armstrong (1962) asked a very similar question. He pointed out that bodily sensations could be divided into two kinds: the transitive and the intransitive. The transitive sensations could be described by transitive verbs typical of other perceptual experiences (he feels the warm table), but the intransitives can uniquely be described using intransitive verbs: my leg throbs; my arm itches; my head aches. For Armstrong, the transitive sensations belong to touch, the intransitive do not. For my purposes this is not yet an account of the distinction; it is rather a clear statement of the problem. What we need is an account of why bodily sensations divide up in this way. The goal of this chapter is to offer such an account.

2. The "Sense" of Touch

While touch is typically included among the major sensory modalities—along with sight, hearing, smell, and taste—there is reason to question whether touch is a single sense. The sense of touch involves a number of distinct sensory systems that could be considered separate (though interacting) senses. Consider thermal perception. Our experience of hot and cold surfaces through our skin is typically included as part of touch. While the receptors involved in thermal perception are located within our skin, this awareness is actually mediated by a distinct physiological channel largely separate from discriminative touch. Now consider many pains: most nociceptors are also located in the skin and bodily surfaces. In fact, they share many important physiological characteristics with thermal receptors. But pains are often taken to be distinct from the sense of touch proper.[3] The status of other bodily sensations—tingles, itches, tickles, hunger pangs, and others—is unclear. They too have distinct physiological channels, but they nevertheless seem closely associated with touch. The situation is more difficult for those properties clearly connected with touch, since features like vibration, surface solidity, and texture are coded by more or less distinct channels and in some cases can be clearly dissociated from one another. It is rather puzzling then that we count these specific components as belonging to touch given the many systems involved and the fact that we seem to have, at best, a vague intuition about which constituents belong to touch.

The question hardly arises for the other senses in exactly this way (though as we'll see, the issues to follow are not unique to touch). Perhaps one reason for the difficulty with touch is that it seems to possess a greater functional complexity than the other senses, a complexity that codes a large range of distinct phenomenal qualities through easily distinguished sensory channels. This point has been noted in several discussions on how we ought to individuate the senses, dating

---

[3] See, for instance Aydede (2009).

back to Aristotle. He held that there were five senses, each with their own "proper" defining feature, a feature that was unique to each sensory modality. Touch, however, unlike the other senses, did not seem to possess a single defining property. According to Aristotle, the class of tangible properties did not form a single genus (*De Anima*, bk 2, ch 11).

Summing up these reflections: there seems to be a legitimate and long-standing question about what sensible features (or the sensory subsystems that code for them)[4] properly belong to the sense of touch. On the one hand, there seem to be clear intuitive answers: thermal properties, solidity, vibration, and spatial properties are almost universally included as parts of touch. On the other hand, there is no systematic account of such intuitions that makes sense of why pains and itches are almost always excluded from touch, or that gives us direction in handling a wide range of intermediate cases: to which sense belong the tingles, twinges, throbs, and various proprioceptive properties of somatosensory experience? We turn now to providing such a systematic account.

3. The Positive Account

How can we determine which sensory features belong to the sense of touch? I start with the assumption that the sensory modalities assign features to objects in the world.[5] These assignments are *structured*; they occur in systematic ways that can be measured and explained. For instance, in vision science the strength of feature binding can be measured by its effect on error rates in selection tasks using bound and unbound sensory features (some of these studies are discussed in Ashby et al., 1996). Appealing to this structure offers a robust means of characterizing touch experiences: those constituent systems that co-assign tangible features count as touch; those that do not should be considered separate. According to this criterion, thermal perception counts as part of touch because we feel objects as hot and cold along with the other tangible properties. But pains, tingles, and itches are never co-assigned as features of external objects.[6] While pains might carry

---

[4] One can ask this question in two different ways: either about the features themselves or about the various systems that code for them. I do not think these two formulations can be easily teased apart. Therefore, for the purposes of this chapter, I shall hereafter drop the inelegant locution "sensible features (or the sensory systems that code for them)," and move as needed between talking about sensory systems and their associated sensory features.

[5] It is possible that sensory systems exist that do not assign sensory features. An example might be human vomeronasal perception. These are problematic cases, and in what follows I shall simply assume that being a genuine perceptual modality involves some assignment of features or qualities to the world (whether those assignments need to be consciously available is a separate and unexplored issue).

[6] What matters here isn't that the perceptual objects are external to the body but that they are external to the experience. On some accounts, pains don't assign features to anything external to the experience and therefore don't co-assign to any objects (Aydede 2009). On representational accounts

information about tissue damage, say, they do not typically group with other representations concerning external objects. Warmth, while also a simple signal, does combine with externalized properties like shape, weight, and texture, and so it too comes to represent features of items external to the experience itself.

My proposal is to classify those systems together that co-assign features to objects external to the experience.[7] The co-assignment or binding relation is empirically tractable, clear, and aligns nicely with our intuitive conception of what counts as the sense of touch. This notion does not provide necessary or sufficient conditions for the individuation of sensory modalities, for there may be more (perhaps much more) to a sensory modality than just co-assignment. The notion of sensory binding offers instead an explanatorily robust criterion of sensory classification. Such classification does not purport to individuate the senses into natural kinds or find the essential properties of each of the sensory modalities. Instead, it justifies the way in which certain sets of sensory systems are already classified by both folk and cognitive science. Such classification is relative to theoretical practice and explanatory needs, meaning there could be equally legitimate alternative classification schemes. Nevertheless, co-assignment tracks an important actual feature of sensory systems and justifies our current practice of grouping them. Sensory feature binding can account for our classificatory practices. While my focus here is on the sense of touch, I believe sensory binding allows for a robust means of explaining and justifying our classification of other sensory systems as well.

As I understand it, feature binding involves only *basic* sensory features.[8] Basic sensory features are those with maximally determinate qualitative values. While visual textures and colors are often bound together, higher-level properties like *being a police officer* or *being my childhood home* are not. This view is consistent with the general claim that feature binding is "the process of linking together the attributes of a perceptual object" (Ghose & Maunsell, 1999). Such binding is most often discussed in visual perception and refers to the way in which features or attributes are assigned to distinct particulars by a perceptual modality. In vision, for example, basic features like colors, shapes, textures, and motions are co-assigned to individual visual objects. To see a cup on the table is to see a particular object possessed of a range of features that belong to the cup. We see the cup as an object separate from its surroundings in part because we experience its various features as belonging to it and not the other objects around it. If we close our eyes and reach out to the table, feeling with our hands for the cup, we would also experience

---

of pains, pains do assign some (minimal) features to a state of the body, but there is no co-assignment (no other tangible features are assigned to the direct objects of pain experience).

[7] The phrase "external to the experience" leaves open the possibility that the body itself, despite not being "an external object," can be the bearer of grouped or bound properties.

[8] This is a further constraint on sensory binding not meant to track usage in the empirical literature, where "binding" is used in a wide variety of (sometimes inconsistent) ways.

its features—its heft, solidity, warmth, texture, size—as belonging to it and not to the other objects in the vicinity.[9]

The co-assignment of sensory features is discussed in other nonvisual sensory modalities. For example, in audition the assignment and grouping of features is well studied, where it is known as auditory scene analysis (Hall et al., 2000).[10] Similar grouping effects occur in olfaction and taste. In haptic processing, however, the notion of sensory binding is rarely discussed. Yet touch also involves the co-assignment of features to objects, and these assignments play a prominent role in object segmentation, grouping, and identification. Like the other senses, touch involves the co-assignment of various sensible features. When we feel an object as *squishy* or *slippery* or *metallic* we are feeling a blended combination of several distinct basic tangible features. Feeling something as metallic, for example, involves feeling a cool, smooth, solid surface. The unified, blended nature of these feelings indicates that these features have been co-assigned and bound to an object (Sullivan, 1923; Zigler, 1923).

While each of the senses, including touch, seems to involve the co-assignment of distinct sensory features to objects, they assign these features in unique ways, according to distinct principles of sensory grouping. For example, the binding of visual features seems largely subpersonal and automatic. No action in particular needs to be done (by us) in order to bind visual features. This means that visual binding is (largely) nonvolitional:

> **Nonvolitional binding**: Features X and Y are nonvolitionally bound to an object, o, if (1) o is sensed as having both basic features X and Y, and (2) (at that moment) sensing o as X without sensing it as Y (and vice versa) cannot be achieved by a simple volitional act (for example, blinking or closing one eye).

When one sees a painting with its various colors and shapes and textures, one cannot simply subtract out just the colors (or a particular color) by moving one's head just so or snapping one's fingers. The bound features are still seen as part of or essentially belonging to the objects, and they can't be easily separated. While touch also involves the co-assignment of features directly to objects, it differs from vision in requiring a volitional act in order to bind tangible features. In particular, features are bound in touch by the unifying and coordinating effects of specialized exploratory actions. By altering the exploratory actions we perform, we can change the set of features assigned to tangible objects. Touch thus seems to involve *exploratory binding*:

---

[9] The literature on sensory binding is enormous. The interested reader is encouraged to start with the highly influential work of Anne Treisman (e.g., her 1998 article).

[10] Similar effects have been studied in olfaction. See Wilson and Stevenson (2006).

Exploratory Binding: Features X and Y are exploratorily bound to an object, o, if (1) o is sensed as having both basic features X and Y, and (2) sensing o as X and Y (at that moment) is a result of a specific act of perceptual exploration.

Touch, unlike vision, requires that we reach out and explore the world with our sensory surfaces. And which features we experience is a result of which exploratory actions we deploy. Haptic exploration temporally and spatially unifies the signals coming from distinct receptor types, signaling that the information coming from these distinct channels concerns the same object. It is through such exploration that the distinct features involved in touch are properly assigned to the objects around us.

Touch involves a specialized class of exploratory actions that coordinate and unify the separate subsystems classified as touch. When we reach and pick up various objects in our environment, the reaching and grasping action unifies and co-activates the various processing streams, allowing for the experience of several distinct tangible features of an object all at the same time. Susan Lederman and Roberta Klatzky (1987) proposed that haptic touch involves a specialized set of actions they call "exploratory procedures." They suggest that haptic touch involves eight distinct exploratory procedures (Jones & Lederman (2006) later reduce the list to six). They demonstrated that there is a close relationship between the particular exploratory movements used to tactually perceive an object and the set of features that are assigned to it. The experience of some individual features—fine shape, for example—require the performance of specific exploratory acts. Other movements are "redundant"; they allow a range of object features to be experienced through a single exploratory act. Such actions ground tangible object recognition, which depends on the co-presence of certain sets of salient features. When we pick up a hammer and recognize it as such through touch, this recognition occurs very quickly and involves the pickup of several sets of diagnostic features at once (Klatzky & Lederman, 2008; Klatzky et al., 1993; James, Kim, & Fisher, 2007). For example, when we grasp and lift an object, the very motion of picking up the object allows us to feel at once its heft, shape, size, material constitution, texture, and thermal profile. Such motions bind distinct features to individual objects, allowing us to quickly and very accurately identify them through touch. This binding, while exploratory in nature, is analogous to the assignments of sensory features found in the other senses.

This concept of sensory binding can justify the classification of features to touch. The various functionally distinct systems that count as touch are those that assign basic sensory features to external objects in relations of exploratory sensory binding. What counts according to this criterion? This is ultimately an empirical question, to be determined by careful experimental investigation. Yet we can get a good sense of how things will play out by considering a typical tactual experience, like holding a pen. In holding a pen, one comes to experience a range of features that seem to belong to the pen. They are co-assigned or bound to the object, allowing us to recognize and make use of the object. The features assigned to the pen might include its temperature, heft, size, solidity, texture, and several others. These features all seem to be bound to or assigned to the pen in virtue of our holding it a particular way. A less technical way of putting this is to say that we feel a particular set of the pen's actual sensory features in virtue of picking it up. The basic features assigned to the pen in virtue of this exploratory action should, according to the criterion mentioned, be classified as part of the sense of touch. By considering the full range of tangible actions, we should be able to determine which features routinely enter into relations of exploratory binding. Importantly, this allows us to separate out other potential tangible features like pains, itches, and tingles. This is because the properties assigned by pains are never associated with external objects or bound along with other tangible features. When a sharp needle is inserted into one's arm, the pain it causes is never experienced as a property of the needle. While other features like sharpness, size, and temperature may be experienced as properties of the needle, stinging pain is never experienced as a property of the object. By applying this simple test of sensory binding, we should be able to say which systems belong to touch, and which belong to separate modalities.

While more speculative, we can expand this account of tactual classification to other sensory modalities. Sensory binding involves a set of basic sensory features that can enter into relations of binding with one another (they can be co-assigned to objects), and we can use this set to characterize a unitary mode of experience: it is one that involves members from a single set of basic sensory features, defined by their ability to bind with one another. Such relations between basic features can be described as *a binding set*:

> **Binding Set**: A binding set is a set of determinable features, all of whose determinates can enter into relations of feature binding. More formally, let β be a binding set such that for any two classes of sensory features q and q^*, if determinate values of q and q^* can be bound together in experience, then $q \in \beta$ and $q^* \in \beta$.

There is a consistent set of basic feature types that can be bound in visual experience. These features include motions, textures, colors, shapes, and several others. The binding between these features can be empirically measured and forms the basis for the most plausible accounts of visual object segmentation, grouping, and recognition. The totality of these feature types constitutes the set of determinable visual features. This set is not exhaustive of visual experience, for there could be other nonbasic features represented in visual experience that do not enter into relations of feature binding. For example, there is no reason to rule out a creature that can see only a single color. Similarly, there are many visual experiences that do not involve feature binding (a uniform color field or Ganzfeld would presumably not involve binding). Instead, the idea is that one of the primary functions of the sensory modalities is to provide robust coordinated information about certain basic classes of object properties, and this important function provides a strong motivation for classifying physiologically distinct sets of sensory systems as parts of a single mode of experience.

The individual sensory modalities, despite being composed of distinct functional subsystems and entering into multisensory interactions with each other, have their own unique set of basic features (the distinction between these relations and those involved in multisensory integration are discussed shortly). It is the coordinated assignments, what I'm calling sensory binding, that explain their membership in the set and give a robust way of distinguishing the features in one modality from those in another, even in cases where a single feature overlaps. In other words, part of what it means for a feature to be a *visual* feature is that it can bind together in appropriate ways with the other visual features to provide a unified visual representation of the object. Particular textures and odors never bind together in experience; textures and colors do. Similarly, we could perhaps distinguish visual texture from tactual texture because the former, but not the latter, is capable of binding to other visual features. That is, despite picking out the same physical feature of an object, the representations in each modality are members of different binding sets, and therefore enter into different qualitative relations with other basic sensory qualities.

4. Classifying Touch

The account sketched thus far serves two explanatory purposes. First, it offers a principled reason for classifying thermal, surface, and vibration features as parts of touch, while excluding pains, itches, and tingles. Second, it offers a way of distinguishing those components of touch from analogous systems in other modalities that code for the same features. For example, texture and shape are processed by both vision and touch. It is this second goal that is the focus of this section.

The binding view thus described offers of way of distinguishing the parts of touch from the analogous systems that belong to other senses, even when they code for the same physical features. Here is the difficulty: if binding involves *just* the assignment of sensory features to objects, then it now seems we will have difficulty separating touch from the other senses—especially vision—since both touch and vision seem to assign properties, often the very same properties, to the same external objects. This is a serious worry, but thankfully there are relatively easy ways to distinguish intermodal feature binding from multisensory integration (MSI).

For one thing, the overlapping features found in vision and touch are members of distinct binding sets. Tangible texture, for instance, is coded by a distinct system that binds its representations with thermal, texture, and other such properties. The system that codes for tangible texture does not bind its output to colors, sounds, or tastes. In addition, the systems that code for these features function in distinct ways, according to distinct principles of association. Visual binding occurs according to principles that differ from those operating in touch. Touch, as we've seen, involves the co-assignment of features that result from specific exploratory interactions with objects. These distinct interactions and principles of operation—all rooted in the general function of co-assigning properties to objects—allow us to classify tangible texture as belonging to a distinct modality from visual texture, and so on.

Again, to speculate somewhat, it makes sense that sensory systems perform their co-assignments individually. The senses often provide information about the same objects or events in the world. Sometimes this information is complementary or reinforcing, providing distinct but useful information about an object or event—seeing a dog while hearing it bark, for instance. Other times, the senses provide redundant information about objects. For instance, audition, touch, and vision can all provide information about an object's location; vision and touch can both provide information about an object's texture; and smell and taste can both provide information about an object's palatability. In these redundant cases, the information provided by the individual senses can sometimes disagree. These discrepancies need to be resolved by our perceptual systems in order to generate a coherent and unified percept of the world. This is done through integration of the information provided by each of the senses.[11]

While vision and the other senses also assign features to external objects, the features that they assign are not bound together with tangible features, and the processes and systems involved in cross-modal integration are functionally distinct from those involved in the binding of sensory features. There is a clear difference between the mechanisms of feature binding in the individual modalities and those involved in multisensory integration. Consider the different ways that touch and vision code for roughness. Klatzky and Lederman (2010) argue that vision encodes roughness in a manner that is distinct from touch, but that these distinct representations can be integrated at later stages of processing. As they summarize:

> Studies of visual texture perception suggest that roughness is judged from clues that signal the depth of and spatial distribution of the surface elements. People find it natural to judge visual textures, and few systematic differences are found between texture judgments based on vision vs touch. In a context where vision and touch are both used to explore a textured surface, vision appears to be biased towards encoding pattern or shape descriptions, and touch toward intensive roughness. The relative weights assigned to the senses appear to be controlled, to a large extent, by attentional processes. (222)

Sensory binding involves the co-assignment of features to objects, and these assignments are generated in each of the sensory modalities. While both touch

---

[11] See the discussion in Chirimuuta and Paterson (this volume) for a complementary discussion of sensory substitution and overlap.

and vision provide information about the texture of objects, they do so (at least initially) in isolation of one another, via distinct mechanisms and unique associations of sensory features. Usually these distinct representations are coherent and facilitate perceptual tasks like object recognition and grouping. Sometimes, however, they come into conflict with one another and various processes of integration serve to reconcile and coordinate these representations according to precise algorithms and attentional processes.

Looking at the individual modalities, including touch, we can see that there is a constrained set of basic features that enter into the unified, bound object representations. Multisensory integration then coordinates this already grouped information (see, e.g., Klatzky & Lederman, 2010; Calvert, 2004; Rock & Victor, 1964). Such reconciliation is not the only kind of multisensory interaction. There are many distinct processes, including facilitation, summation, suppression, vetoing, and dominance. These processes seem to involve already present streams of information from the individual sensory modalities that make some difference to the other sensory modalities. While similar in some respects, these various multisensory interactions involved in MSI do not function in the direct assignment of basic sensory features but rather operate to enhance or coordinate such assignments. The sensory assignments in the individual modalities are subject to a range of coordinated processing, allowing for a coherent, unified experience of the world.

The functional differences in the structure and processes of sensory binding provide a strong reason for separately classifying the features coded by touch and by vision. Each sensory modality assigns its features to objects, and these assignments are then corrected or brought into alignment at later stages of processing. So while both vision and touch assign features to the same sets of objects, they do so by binding their individual representations independently, prior to passing them along to multisensory areas of processing. As Klatzky and Lederman (2008) note, concerning object perception in vision and touch:

> Visual and haptic object recognition share basic mechanisms, such as a progression from sensory primitives to abstract representations and use of prior knowledge and context where possible. But these general similarities notwithstanding, the two channels turn out to be quite different, and the emergent model of haptic object identification is fundamentally different from its visual counterpart. (186)

The individual modalities assign basic features to objects in distinct ways, according to different rules. These independent assignments then feed into dedicated multisensory areas that reconcile and coordinate the information provided by the distinct sources of perceptual information. Individual modalities involve sensory feature binding, which in turn allows for object segmentation, grouping, and ultimately recognition. These bound bundles are compared and coordinated (and corrected if needed) by multisensory areas, resulting in coherent, unified representations of the world.

5. Conclusion

I have argued that there is a good reason for treating some sensory features (and the systems that code for them) as belonging to the sense of touch, and for excluding others. I began with the assumption that none of the extant accounts of sensory individuation are capable of providing a clear account of why we should count certain features—including solidity, temperature, and texture—as part of touch, while excluding pains, tingles, itches, tickles, and hunger pangs. Mere externalization is not enough, since it does not offer a means of separating tangible features from visual or auditory features, which are also externalized. My argument has been that touch, like the other senses, functions to produce unified, bound representations of objects, and that the structure and coordination among these features provide a principled means of classifying certain sensory systems as belonging to touch. When we explore the world through touch, we represent a range of objects and their features, and these representations involve the co-assignment or binding of certain sensory features. While thermal profiles and textures are assigned to objects in this manner, pains and tickles are not. Similarly, while touch and vision, for example, assign some basic features to the same objects, they do not bind or co-assign these features. Instead, features are assigned within each modality, and then reconciled or coordinated at later stages of multisensory processing. The binding of sensory features has been discussed almost entirely in the visual domain. It is my belief that such coordinated assignment of features occurs as well in touch, and that it occurs as distinct processing units are coordinated by coherent exploratory actions. Such an expansion of the concept to the realm of touch offers a promising starting point for understanding the processes and interactions that generate coordinated, unified experience of the world.

References

Aydede, M. (2009). Is feeling pain the perception of something? *Journal of Philosophy,* 106(10): 531–567.

Armstrong, D. M. (1962). *Bodily Sensations.* New York: Routledge & Kegan Paul.

Ashby, F. G. et al. (1996). A formal theory of feature binding in object perception. *Psychological Review,* 103: 165–192.

Calvert, G. (2004). Multisensory integration: Methodological approaches and emerging principles in the human brain. *Journal of Physiology-Paris,* 98(1–3): 191–205.

Clark, A. Phenomenal properties. *Philosophical Issues,* 18: 406–425.

Dretske, F. I. (1992). *Naturalizing the Mind.* Cambridge, MA: MIT Press.

Ghose, G., & Maunsell, J. (1999). Specialized representations review in visual cortex: A role for binding. *Neuron,* 24(1): 79–85.

Hall, M. D., Pastore, R. E., Acker, B. E., & Huang, W. (2000). Evidence for auditory feature integration with spatially distributed items. *Perception & Psychophysics,* 62(6): 1243–1257.

James, T. W., Kim, S., & Fisher, J. S. (2007). The neural basis of haptic object processing. *Canadian Journal of Experimental Psychology,* 61(3): 219–229.

Jones, L. A., & Lederman, S. J. (2006). *Human Hand Function.* New York: Oxford.

Keeley, B. (2002). Making sense of the senses: Individuating modalities in humans and other animals. *Journal of Philosophy,* 99(1): 5–28.

Klatzky, R., & Lederman, S. (2008). Object recognition by touch. In *Blindness and Brain Plasticity in Navigation and Object Recognition,* edited by J. J. Rieser, D. H. Ashmead, F. F. Ebner, & A. L. Corn (pp. 185–207). New York: Lawrence Erlbaum.

Klatzky, R., & Lederman, S. (2010). Multisensory texture perception. In *Multisensory Object Perception in the Primate Brain,* edited by M. J. Naumer & J. Kaiser (pp. 211–230). New York: Springer.

Klatzky, R., Loomis, J., Lederman, S. J., Wake, H., & Fujita, N. (1993). Haptic identification of objects and their depictions. *Perception & Psychophysics,* 54: 170–178.

MacPherson, F. (2011). *The Senses.* New York: Oxford University Press.

Nudds, M. (2003). The significance of the senses. In *Proceedings of the Aristotelian Society.* Presented at the Proceedings of the Aristotelian Society, University of London, Senate House, October 27.

Rock, I., & Victor, J. (1964). Vision and touch: An experimentally created conflict between the two senses. *Science,* 143: 594–596.

Sullivan, A. (1923). The perceptions of liquidity, semi-liquidity and solidity. *American Journal of Psychology,* 34: 531–541.

Treisman, Anne. (1998). Feature binding, attention, and object perception. *Transactions of the Royal Society,* 353: 1296–1306.

Wilson, D. A., & Stevenson, R. J. (2006). *Learning to Smell: Olfactory Perception from Neurobiology to Behavior.* Baltimore, MD: Johns Hopkins University Press.

Zigler, M. (1923). An experimental study of the perception of clamminess. *American Journal of Psychology,* 34(4): 550–561.

8

Sound Stimulants

DEFENDING THE STABLE DISPOSITION VIEW

John Kulvicki

1. Introduction

The physics and biology of sound perception are well understood. We know quite well how objects vibrate in response to being stimulated, how those vibrations create pressure waves in the ambient air, how those waves affect the eardrum, how the ear transduces mechanical input into neurological signals, and how those signals are processed from the inner hair cells into the cortex. Unknown details abound, of course, but they don't threaten the general scientific picture. Refinement, not revolution, will most likely characterize future work on sound and sound perception. Much the same can be said for our understanding of color and color perception.

Despite all of that, there is no obvious consensus on what sounds or colors are. Where, in the chain of events leading to a typical experience, should we locate the sound that causes it? Can we locate it anywhere at all? These are quite general questions unsettled by the scientific progress that, at a certain level of description, is more poised for refinement than revolution. The same, unsurprisingly, can be said for color.

This chapter builds support for the view that sounds can be understood as stable dispositions of objects to vibrate in response to being mechanically stimulated (Kulvicki 2008a), against the trend that suggests sounds are better conceived as events (Casati and Dokic 1994, 2010, O'Callaghan 2007, Pasnau 2009). Two apparently simple questions animate this discussion. First, do sounds have durations? And second, do sounds seem to have durations? If sounds have durations, then they are quite unlike qualities or dispositions, which might be instantiated for durations, here and there, but are in themselves durationless. One good piece of evidence for the claim that sounds have durations is that they seem to have durations. If so, then any account of sounds contrary to those seemings commits one to an unpalatable error theory of sound perception.

Section 2 presents the stable disposition theory of sounds, while section 3 raises the worry about sound duration and unpacks competing event accounts of sounds. Section 4 rejects the claim that sounds seem to have durations in a way that threatens the stable disposition view. Section 5 denies that the best explanation of uncontroversial claims about audition is that sounds have durations. Section 6 takes up a friendly suggestion by Jonathan Cohen (2010) that differences in spatiotemporal acuity between vision and audition explain away the intuition that sounds have durations. As stated, Cohen's proposal does not do the work required of it, but there is a way to fix the problem. Section 7 addresses an objection to the stable disposition view raised by Roberto Casati and Jérôme Dokic (2010). Throughout the chapter, the theme is that understanding the force of the stable disposition view depends upon recognizing the role that sound stimulants—the mechanical impulses that reveal the sounds of things—play in the view as a whole. The defensibility of this view raises general questions about how best to think about perception and its objects across modalities.

2. The Stable Disposition View

Some New England churches boast bells fashioned by Paul Revere. They count out the hours and call the faithful to services. Should you be within earshot of town, you will hear such a bell many times each day. The closer you are to the tower, the better your sense of the bell's sound. You can still hear it farther out, of course, but you can't hear it as well. In addition to being quieter, the sound is a bit washed out: low frequencies predominate, as the high frequencies are long since lost in the wind. Each bell is unique. Listen carefully and you can tell whether you are in Norwich, Vermont, or Woodstock, Vermont. Revere bells are prized partly because of their maker's role in the American Revolution and partly because the man made some good bells. They don't look terribly interesting—they look like bells—but their sounds are distinctive and pleasant. The bells in Norwich and Woodstock, for example, are more worth hearing than the bells in many nearby towns.

Talk about sounds is quite varied, and it's simply impossible to read an account of the natures of sounds from our talk about them. This talk about bells, however, is rather congenial to the stable disposition view. Bells *have* sounds, and these sounds can be heard many times throughout the day. We distinguish bells based on the sounds they have, and we can distinguish the sounds of bells under a number of circumstances: near or far, on a windless day, or in a spring rain. In each case, the auditory experience is distinct, but each experience is recognizable as being of that bell.

According to the stable disposition view, sounds are objects' dispositions to vibrate in response to mechanical stimulation. They are, in that sense, qualities of objects. We hear sounds when objects in fact vibrate, producing the pressure waves to which our ears are sensitive. Sounds are neither the pressure waves themselves nor the vibratory events that enable us to hear. They are the dispositions revealed by such events and waves (Kulvicki 2008a).

There are many advantages to identifying sounds with stable dispositions to vibrate. The proposal is theoretically simplifying and fertile. All accounts of sound agree that we perceive individuals and their qualities, though these accounts differ in how they identify those individuals and qualities. Visually, we take the individuals we perceive to be, for example, medium-sized ordinary objects. They are perceived to have colors, locations, and shapes, among other features. Colors, on such a view, are qualities of the individual objects we see. The stable disposition view of sounds aligns the individuals heard with those seen, and it identifies sounds, like colors, with qualities of those objects. Sounds are objects' dispositions to respond to mechanical stimulation while colors are objects' dispositions to respond to light. Views that identify sounds with events, or waves, put the audition of ordinary objects at one remove (at least) from the perception of sounds.

The architectural simplicity achieved by aligning the objects of hearing and sight, and setting up a tight analogy between color and sound, is motivated by reflection on auditory experience. As with color, there is a range of circumstances under which the bell's sound can be heard, but not anything goes. We can only hear the bell's sound when it is struck appropriately under the appropriate circumstances. Illuminate an object with a laser or very dim light and you cannot discern its color. Strike a bell with a pillow or tap it with your finger and you get at best a dim sense of its sonority. Try to strike a Revere bell with a sledgehammer and a phalanx of pitchforks will run you out of town. Attach a loudspeaker to the bell's surface, blast your favorite punk rock song, and you will be politely, but firmly, asked to leave. The locals will hear their bell amid the music, and they'll hear it most distinctly when the loudspeaker projects the drums, but they will find this neither interesting nor amusing. The drums are effective because as stimulants they satisfy the relevant norms: not too hard, not too soft, and broad spectrum, please. That's exactly what a bell's hammer does, and it's strictly analogous to the ideal stimulant for revealing things' colors. Light should be bright enough, not too bright, and broad spectrum.

Stimulate an object with broad-spectrum energy—energy across a range of frequencies—and you give it a chance to respond by vibrating in its characteristic manner, revealing its sound. Objects have stable dispositions to vibrate in response to stimulation—a point that has been clear since Helmholz (1877)—and these dispositions are good candidates for being sounds. We only hear sounds when objects are stimulated to vibrate and thus produce pressure waves in the ambient air. Without stimulation, or without air, you can't hear objects. Perceiving objects' qualities requires perceptual contact with them, after all. Light enables visual contact, while pressure waves enable auditory contact. Objects do not typically emit light or pressure waves unprompted: you need light sources and vibration sources. We are ideally suited to learning an object's color when appropriately bright broad-spectrum light shines upon it, just as we are ideally suited to learning an object's sound when it is struck by appropriately intense broad-spectrum impulses. In both cases, even stimuli that are far from ideal can reveal these qualities of objects. The reddish light at dusk does not undermine our ability to notice things' colors, and odd ways of thwacking the bell need not undermine our ability to identify its sound.

Constancies in perception favor the view that we latch on to stable features of objects amid a variety of situations in which they are perceived. In a similar fashion, constancies have been mobilized in support of stable disposition views of color. They suggest that what we do when perceiving is latch on to properties of objects that are stable across a range of viewing or hearing conditions. Two things that affect these conditions, both for colors and sounds, are the stimulants—light sources, mechanical inputs—and the ambient environment—hazy, windy, still, and so on. Constancies require a more elaborate treatment from accounts that identify sounds with vibration events (O'Callaghan 2007, Pasnau 2009, Casati and Dokic 1994), or with waves (Sorensen 2008, ch 14). This is because constancies are understood to abstract over features of the individual vibration events and waves that accompany any instance of hearing. For such views, the constancies are not so much about sound perception, but about sound source perception.[1]

While the stable disposition view simplifies things along one theoretical dimension, it is fertile because of how it complicates auditory experience. We see colors and shapes, but also discern features of the illuminant in virtue of which colors are seen. Similarly, we hear objects' sounds while noticing aspects of the mechanical stimulant that reveals those sounds (Kulvicki 2008a, 13–14). We see objects' colors through the haze in the reddish dawn light just as we hear their sounds through the rain and wind. We hear speech, as in hearing what is said, but we also hear the speaker and we can identify her across a wide range of things she can say (Kulvicki 2008a, 10; cf. Smith 2010).

Like colors, sounds seem arrayed in space. You can hear a solitary crow, left of the murder and right of the catfight. The spatial acuity of sound perception compares unfavorably to vision, as we will see in section 5. Nevertheless, we hear things located in space and in that sense we perceive the shape of the auditory landscape. These *shapes* are not stable vibratory dispositions, just as visible patterns are not colors. They are patterns of color, and auditory space presents patterns of sounds. Those patterns are not as central to identifying objects in the auditory case as they are in vision. It's rare to hear an object as being a specific shape, though audition

---

[1] Matthew Nudds suggested this formulation. Things are far from settled concerning how to deal with constancies in perception, especially vis-à-vis their consequences for how we should think of the qualities/objects we perceive. See, for example, Byrne and Hilbert (2003), Cohen (2009, 53–57), and Matthen (2009, 76–77) for discussion. It's beyond the scope of the chapter to address these issues in detail. Allan Hazlett (personal communication) made the nice suggestion that an event view of sounds, according to which sounds are events that reveal stable dispositions to vibrate, could handle some of the worries about constancies and would thus be harder to pry apart from the quality view on offer here.

does put us in touch with other features of things, like their hollowness and solidity. Despite the lack of spatial acuity, it's been important for most recent accounts of sounds, from Casati and Dokic's (1994) through Casey O'Callaghan's (2007) and Robert Pasnau's (2009), to show that they can accommodate sounds' apparent locations.

There is a lot one can say for and against the stable disposition view of sounds. For present purposes, a sketch of its virtues suffices, since the point of this chapter is not a full positive defense. Instead, the goal is to focus on examples that seem decisively to favor event views of sound. To many, it seems obvious that sounds have durations, while qualities do not. If they are right about this, there is little hope for the stable disposition view, regardless of its other virtues.[2]

3. A Problem: Sounds Seem to Have Durations

A preponderance of examples seems to run contrary to the stable disposition view. Examples don't vote, of course, but it's difficult to overcome the influence of so many cases in which sounds seem to have *durations*. "A sound has a beginning, a middle, and an end" (O'Callaghan 2007, 22). Even the bell is not immune to this claim. The bell rings, then it goes quiet. At the outset, the sound is bright and sharp in response to being struck. It then mellows out into a stable decay, slowly fading from hearing. Strike the bell hard and it makes a sound that lasts longer than if you strike it lightly. The *sound* lasts longer under certain circumstances than under others. When the bell strikes three, three sounds are made, indicating the hour. This way of talking is clearly contrary to the view that sounds are qualities. Qualities do not have durations, and while you can count instantiations of qualities, you can't count them as multiple qualities, absent a relatively controversial account of qualities.

Following straightforward English idiom, sounds can seem like particular individuals and are treated as such. Moreover, they are treated as particular individuals that take time. Events are good candidates for being sounds if one follows this line of thought. Casati and Dokic (1994, 2010) suggest that sounds are vibration events, for example. A sound exists when an object vibrates within a range of intensities at a certain range of frequencies. These events have the characteristics that much ordinary language suggests they do. They have pitch, timbre, and loudness, and they last limited amounts of time. When the bell vibrates in the vacuum, there is

---

[2] Kulvicki (2008a) offers a fuller defense and articulation of the stable disposition view. Also, it bears mention that I am not the only one supporting a view of sounds as qualities. Matthew Nudds suggests that sounds are qualities of pressure waves produced by vibrating objects. The account is somewhat surprising. Nudds thinks that the function of the auditory system is to inform us about qualities of vibrating objects (2010, 284), and he identifies pressure waves as analogous to light in vision (2010, 286), but he is unwilling to say sounds are qualities of those vibrating objects. It's worth looking into the different advantages and disadvantages of each account, but beyond the scope of this chapter to do so.

a sound, but the lack of air renders the sound inaudible. You can't hear a bell if it's stuck in the vacuum, but the bell does make a sound.

In a similar vein, O'Callaghan (2007) suggests that sounds are events in which an object disturbs the ambient medium in which it finds itself, typically the atmosphere, resulting in pressure waves that allow us to hear the sound. For O'Callaghan, the bell makes no sound in an evacuated chamber. It vibrates, but fails to disturb a medium because it is not ensconced in one. The differences between these views are interesting and worth reflection (see Kulvicki 2008b) but much less important for present purposes than what they have in common. Sounds are individuals—namely, events—that themselves have qualities like pitch, timbre, and loudness.

4. Do Sounds Really Seem to Have Durations?

The claim that sounds have durations and are thus more like individuals than qualities is supposedly based on a kind of perceptual seeming. Sounds seem to have durations, and this makes it plausible to believe they really do have durations. Such perceptual seeming must be unambiguous and rather compelling. It is not enough that experience is compatible with the claim that sounds have durations. Rather, the claim is that if an account of sounds denies they have durations, it conflicts enough with the way things seem to be an error theory of sound perception. If sounds are stable dispositions to vibrate, and are thus durationless, we misperceive sounds as having durations. Or so the intuition goes. In that sense, it is on a par with the claim that some greens are yellowish, while some green is neither yellowish nor bluish. Any account of color denying the latter claim is an error theory of color perception.

Let's try to build this strong claim about how things seem out of obviously uncontroversial claims about audition. First, experiences of sounds have durations, which are often brief. Second, we somehow hear events. Cars skid, doors slam, and trees fall in the woods. That's not to say we understand *how* we perceive events, whether such events are directly or mediately perceived, and so on. It's just to say that events are among the things we ordinarily take ourselves to learn about by using our ears. Third, and most important for what follows, the events we hear take time, which is often coincident with the duration of the related auditory experience. That is to say, the door's slamming or the car's skidding takes roughly the same amount of time as the experience through which we come to know about the event. None of these three claims is open to serious dispute, even though more than one could stand some refinement.

The conjunction of the three claims does not entail that sounds themselves seem to have durations, let alone that they do in fact have them. They are together neutral with respect to whether sounds, or merely the episodes in which sounds can be heard, have durations.[3]

---

[3] For more on this claim see Kulvicki 2008a, Cohen 2010, and Nudds 2010.

Perhaps the lack of entailment just mentioned is beside the point because we have an independent intuition to the effect that sounds have durations. Perhaps sounds just seem that way, and there is nothing more to be said about it than that. But that claim is not at all obvious, not in the way required by event view partisans. Surely there is a sense in which sounds might seem that way—an event view of sounds is not obviously incompatible with auditory phenomenology—but we are after a strong sense of perceptual seeming, according to which the stable disposition view renders phenomenology misleading. That intuition is lacking here, and even if some have it, it's difficult to see what weight we should place on it.

These three intuitively clear claims are on firm ground. We might not feel a need to defend them, given how intuitive they are, but defenses are not hard to find. For example, we have nonhearing access to events and can confirm that what people hear involves such events. Similarly, we have a good sense of what it means to say we only hear something for brief periods of time and can, though probably wouldn't, scientifically investigate whether such claims are true. By contrast, the intuition that sounds have durations is not as obviously open to investigation, independent of theorizing about sounds philosophically, especially in light of the claim that experiences of sounds are typically brief. So, if the three uncontroversial claims do not require sounds to have durations, supporters of event views cannot help themselves to that as a desideratum. That is, they cannot insist that the intuition is strong enough to convict a quality view of sounds of being an error theory.

5. Is Duration the Best Explanation?

Perhaps we should say that the three uncontroversial claims are *best explained* by the claim that sounds have durations. For example, because sounds have durations, we only perceive them for the periods of time in which they exist. No one, not even event theorists, has understood the dialectical situation in these terms, but it seems much more plausible than the approach sketched in the previous section. If the best explanation of the three bedrock intuitions is that sounds have durations, then the stable disposition view of sounds is in trouble. It's difficult to know what makes an explanation best, but the following offers what seems to be the strongest argument in favor of the event view of sounds being a better explanation of the three uncontroversial intuitions than the stable disposition view is.

One way to put pressure on the stable disposition view is to examine the visual analogs for the three intuitions about audition. The stable disposition view suggests a similarity between sounds and colors, for example, which leads one to ask whether the visual analogs of the three claims are plausible. If not, that lends support to the idea that audition is less analogous to vision than the stable disposition view claims.

Two of the three visual analogs of our auditory intuitions are fairly obvious. Visual experiences have durations; we sometimes see colors and other visible qualities for only brief periods of time. We close our eyes, the lights go out, or we turn our heads.

It's also hard to deny that we see events. Chameleons change from brown to green, and back. The lights flicker and change color. The philosopher crosses the room. As in the auditory case, it's unclear how we see events—directly, mediately, or otherwise—but uncontroversial that we learn about ordinary events by using our eyes.

The third auditory intuition, however, has no obvious visual analog. Is it really true that the events we see take time that is often coincident with the duration for which a color, or shape, is seen? In a certain sense, the claim seems true, but in another sense, it seems false. Let's consider a pair of examples that brings out this worry.

First, the chameleon changes color from brown to green and back again. The greenness goes away just as the event of changing to and from green terminates. In place of the green we see brown, which is just what we saw before the whole event got started. This seems quite similar to the auditory case: seeing the green corresponds in time to the event of the change to and fro, just as hearing the wheels corresponds in time to the car's skidding. So, in this sense, it seems as though visual experiences of events take time coincident with the time of the event perceived. It's interesting, too, that in this case one is not tempted to think of the green itself as an event (though see Pasnau 2009). The turning from brown to green and back is an event, and perhaps the chameleon's being green is an event, but the green seems like a quality, not an event, even though it is seen for only a limited time, identical to the time of an event in which it is involved.

But now let's consider a different example, one in which an event can be both seen and heard. In a quiet, well-lit room, drop a glass onto a stone floor. You don't hear much of anything until the glass hits the floor, and silence follows the event. The experience of the crash constitutes all of your auditory contact with the situation. You hear the glass, you might also hear the floor, and you hear the many shards as they break apart. The auditory experience lasts exactly as long as the crash, and informs you about it. It's fair to understand the sound itself as an event, by which other events like the breaking of the glass are revealed. Because this is a shattering event, the vibratory dispositions of the objects in question are changing quite quickly, but it's not obvious that the best way to characterize your experience is as of changing sounds. There is a big, complex sound that changes over time, which corresponds to and informs you about the shattering of the glass.[4]

By contrast, you see the colors and shapes of the glass and its shards throughout the event in question. The event is seen, extracted from a rich matrix of visual experience that doesn't in any interesting sense seem to end when the action is over. Sure, the visual experience *of the event* seems to last about as long as the event lasts, and in that sense we have a visual analog to the third auditory intuition. But

---

[4] There are other ways of characterizing what we hear. The editors suggested, for example, that we hear many sounds at once, and that these sounds each have qualities and change over time. This does not in and of itself suggest that the stable disposition view is correct. I agree. I focus here on the view that there is one big, changing sound because that is the characterization best suited to the event view's needs, and the one that most clearly makes this case fail to be analogous to the visual one.

the experience of the event happens against a backdrop of consistent awareness of things' colors and shapes. The colors and shapes don't seem like events. They seem like the qualities whose changes constitute the events that are seen. Visual event perception is typically the perception of changes in a fairly stable, *perceived* layout of qualities like colors and shapes. The things singled out as events involve alteration of objects' qualities over time. (Remember this is just a point about how we typically sort things seen into events and qualities. It's not a theory of events or qualities.) Colors, in part because of the way they are seen, are not regarded as events so much as event fodder: the things whose instantiation and change can constitute events. The individuals seen are ordinary objects that can have colors, which change. Sounds seem markedly different from colors and ordinary objects in this regard. They are individuals with their own qualities.

The sound exists for the duration of the crash, changing over its brief life, until things go quiet again. Pitch, timbre, and loudness are features of the sound much as color and shape are qualities of the glass. Both the sound and the glass are individuals, the kinds of things that can have qualities. Unlike the glass, sounds are events because they have durations: the room erupts in changing pitch, timbre, and loudness, only to go silent shortly thereafter. Audition is so closely tied to things that seem to take up time that it makes sense to identify sounds with events in a way that it does not make sense to identify the glass, or its shapes and colors, with events. Yes, colors and shapes change over time, but the felicitous unpacking of that remark is that objects change with respect to color and shape. In some displaced sense, we hear ordinary objects too: the glass is heard insofar as the sounds it makes are heard.

The foregoing seems like the best way to deploy phenomenology in the service of the event view of sounds. Seeing events is quite different from hearing events, along the dimensions indicated. Indeed, it's easy to understand why one would suggest that sounds themselves are events, rather than something like qualities. None of this gets anywhere near the claim that a stable disposition view of sounds commits one to an error theory of sound perception. But it might suggest that the event view of sounds is the better explanation of the difference between auditory and visual phenomenology. Even that is not obvious, however, for a few reasons.

First, there is a sense in which the third auditory intuition is on stable ground in the visual case. While experiences of color do not end with the glass's shattering, the experiences relevant to the perceived event stop once the action ends. The visible event involves movement, and changes in color and shape. Once those have stopped, the event is over, and in that sense, sight of the relevant qualities ends with the end of the event. We have to extract visible events from a backdrop of visible features, but that does not show that the third auditory intuition has no good visual analog.

Second, the stable disposition view offers an alternative explanation of the third auditory intuition. The theory suggests that stable vibratory dispositions are revealed by mechanical stimuli, which are focused and brief. They typically affect few of the objects within earshot and last mere moments. It's possible, but far from typical, to find a long-lasting, broad-spectrum mechanical stimulant. A simple thwack is ideal because at the proper magnitude it constitutes the perfect broad-spectrum stimulus (Kulvicki 2008a) and it allows the object to respond in its characteristic fashion. Audible events typically involve mechanical contact and so for the stable disposition theorist it is unsurprising that we hear events for about as long as we hear sounds. Both of these explanations work, so it's hard to see that one is clearly better than the other. Sunlight is quite different from mechanical stimulants, as it shines throughout the day, stimulating all objects to respond in such a way that they can be seen. Objects have colors and they have sounds, but the sounds can typically be heard only briefly. It's rare that one can hear all the objects in one's environment at once, and if they could be heard simultaneously, we would have a hard time sorting them all out, as we will see in the next section. Leaving out mechanical stimulants ignores an important part of the stable disposition view of sounds.[5]

Third, it's a bit misleading to say, even in the quiet room, that one has no auditory experience before and after the glass shatters. In a dark room with eyes open we notice that we cannot see anything, likely because it is so dark. Similarly, we notice that things are quiet when no objects are stimulated to vibrate at the right magnitudes and frequencies. In neither case do senses go offline. We notice the lack of visibility and audibility. The differences in stimuli account for the differences in perceptual episodes, as mentioned earlier. We could imagine a world in which things were consistently bathed in broad-spectrum mechanical energy and thus consistently hummed at their characteristic frequencies. In that world, the distinction between sounds and colors would seem less profound, but as the next section suggests, we might want differently structured auditory systems.[6]

In sum, the most compelling case for the event view, based on intuitions about sound's duration, is an inference to the best explanation. The best way to explain the three uncontroversial claims about hearing is that sounds have durations and are thus nicely modeled by events. But such an inference is most compelling when one ignores the role played by mechanical stimulants in revealing sounds, and how they differ from light. Sounds seem distinct from visible qualities because they are revealed by focused and brief stimulants. That explanation leaves room for sounds to be qualities, undermining the claim that the event view's explanation is best. The next section develops this thought by considering a sympathetic suggestion by Jonathan Cohen about how vision and audition relate.

---

[5] In addition, it pays to remember that event theorists do not obviously have an easier time accounting for the auditory perception of ordinary events than stable disposition theorists do. The events they identify as sounds are related but not identical to the events, like shattering glass, that we take ourselves to hear, so they too owe some explanation of how that all happens (see Kulvicki 2008a).

[6] Pasnau (1999, 322) proposes a variant of this example. J. O. Urmson (1969, 124) was careful to point out that the most obvious visual analogs to sounds were blips and blinks. They are, in the sense that they share temporal qualities with our experiences of sounds: a color is revealed for a brief period of time, only to wind up hidden once again. But that fact doesn't help with whether sounds are individuals or qualities. And we already know that hearings are events.

6. Spatial and Temporal Sensitivity

Cohen (2010) is skeptical of claims that sounds seem to have durations in the strong sense required to bolster the event view. He believes these intuitions are due to the fact that perceivers are more sensitive to differences in color across space, at a time, than they are to differences in color across time, while exactly the reverse is true of sounds. Observers are acutely sensitive to differences in color when surfaces are presented side by side, under good illumination, at a given time. If, however, these surfaces are presented over time, even under good conditions, observers have a harder time detecting the differences. This is intuitive enough: try to remember the shade of paint you pick while at the hardware store and whether it will work in the living room. Cohen's claim is that, as it happens, we are better at distinguishing distinct sounds across time than we are at doing so across space, at a given time. His example is "the discrepancy between our abilities to discriminate melodies on the one hand, and our abilities to discriminate chords on the other" (Cohen 2010, 310). The idea is supposed to be that melodic lines unfold in time while chords happen all at once. Chords are akin to simultaneously presented color patches while melodies are more like patches presented in sequence.

Upon reflection, however, it seems as though Cohen's example fails to capture the analogy of interest. First, Cohen articulates the example in terms of distinguishing melodies, or chords, from one another. Presumably the point is, however, distinguishing the notes in a melody from one another, and distinguishing the notes in a chord from one another. Also, the point is not identification of the notes—that's an A-sharp—so much as distinguishing them as the same or different from one another. We are more sensitive, as Cohen says to "spatial inhomogeneities" in the color case and "temporal inhomogeneities" (2010, 310) in the sound case. Because we are so sensitive to such temporal inhomogeneities, we are apt to take sounds to be creatures of time, akin to events, rather than qualities or anything else that lacks duration.

Once we have worked out the relevant points of analogy, Cohen's claim becomes that we are better able to distinguish distinct sounds when they are presented across time than we are when they are presented at once. Evidence for his original claim about distinguishing chords and melodies is anecdotal but it fails to carry over to the revised version of his example. We need to bracket those impressively trained or luckily endowed individuals with perfect pitch for the moment, especially if we stick to Cohen's musical example. In that case, however, one's ability to distinguish sounds presented in time depends on the amount of time between presentations. Sounds presented simultaneously, or quickly one after the other, are readily identified as alike or distinct. Those presented with large gaps between them—seconds or longer—are difficult to compare. The same holds for color. Cohen points out that it's easy to compare colors presented at once, just as it is easy to compare colors presented quickly, one after the other. Difficulty increases with greater spans of time.

It is difficult to disagree with the claim that there are differences between auditory and visual perception, and it's exactly right to look for theoretically interesting differences that might explain what Cohen sees as a potentially misguided metaphysical intuition to the effect that sounds have durations. The following suggests two helpful points closely related to Cohen's. They reveal that the dispositional view really comes into its own once we recognize the importance of stimulants to the perception of sounds.

First, visual spatial acuity is far superior to auditory spatial acuity. We can distinguish visual inhomogeneities on the order of an arc minute while we can only distinguish azimuthal auditory inhomogeneities to within a few degrees (Recanzone et al. 1998), and we are much worse than that at identifying auditory inhomogeneities in elevation. In both the visual and auditory cases, sensitivity depends in part upon characteristics of the stimulus, such as brightness, color, loudness, and spectral composition. Spatial acuity itself has little to do with the question of whether sounds seem to have durations but, as we will see, a closely related phenomenon does.

Second, insofar as vision is more spatially acute, it not only provides more information about the spatial location of a single thing but it can also provide information about more things arrayed in space than audition can. Foveal vision presents a spatially dense mosaic of features, much denser than that provided by hearing. In addition, while it is completely ordinary for the visual scene to present many visible features densely arrayed in space all at once, it is uncommon for hearing to do so, even at its more limited spatial resolution. The stimulant relevant to seeing things is ambient light, which tends to be diffuse and consistent over time. We have organs for sight well-suited to this. Foveal vision is much better than peripheral vision, and we can move our eyes over the visual scene in order to collect large amounts of information about it. Within the fovea, we are able to see much spatial detail. Eyes are designed to make abundant information available about densely packed features, all at once, within the foveal range.

In the auditory case, the stimulants are typically spread widely throughout the environment and they typically do not last long. Factory floors and crowded cafés, in which sounds are rendered audible consistently and at great spatial proximity to one another, can be impressively difficult scenes to organize and understand aurally. This seems to be the core insight behind Cohen's remark about sensitivity to spatial inhomogeneities. At a given time, we are better at taking in a lot of information about a dense visual scene than we are at taking in a lot of information about a dense auditory scene.

Complex spatial patterns of color are much easier to appreciate than complex spatial patterns of sound. We haven't evolved the ability to do this in audition in part because the stimuli that render things audible are neither diffuse nor consistent over time. They are typically focused and brief. Cohen's example doesn't quite capture this, for reasons articulated earlier, but it's reasonable to think that he had something like this in mind, especially if you expand his example of distinguishing one chord from another to distinguishing between two even more densely packed arrays of sounds. It's not that it would be easy to appreciate such an array if the parts were presented one after another, but just that at a given time the auditory system is not set up for spatially detailed work. The spatial acuity of the auditory system is not a good guide to the spatial potential of audition because of how poor the auditory system can be at handling sounds presented all at once.

Cohen did not approach the problem of distinguishing audition and vision with a positive account of sounds in mind. He was more interested in establishing an important negative point, namely, that auditory phenomenology does not unambiguously suggest that sounds have durations. The philosophical intuition that sounds seem to have durations, motivated by ordinary talk, is for Cohen more rooted in differences in how sounds and visible features are perceived than in metaphysical distinctions in what is perceived.

The current approach is a bit different, in two ways. First, it begins with a specific account of sounds, one that closely relates them to visible qualities like colors. And second, it suggests that minor differences between sounds and colors, particularly differences in the stimuli required to make them perceptible, can help account for intuitions to the effect that there are deep metaphysical distinctions between them. Indeed, if this is right, then the nature of sound stimuli might play a role in explaining why hearing works as it does: why we perceive sounds and colors differently. As with the earlier discussion, the stable disposition view is on the firmest ground when one recalls the nature of sound stimulants.

7. Casati and Dokic on Occurrent, Unheard Sounds

Casati and Dokic suggest that the stable disposition view of sounds misses an important phenomenon: occurrent, unheard sounds.

> What are those individuals that we hear when the object sounds? The main problem a dispositional account of sounds has to face is that even if we accept that sounds are sound dispositions, there appear prima facie to exist, on top of those dispositions, the individual, occurrent sounds—those that last when the disposition is realized. (2010, section 3.3.1)

They don't deny that objects have dispositions to vibrate in response to stimulation, and they don't deny that episodes in which sounds are heard last only moments. Their worry seems to be that there should be a theoretically interesting place for sounds as the things that last when objects realize dispositions to vibrate. And the stable disposition view fails to provide such space. They continue:

> Kulvicki denies that this [stable disposition] account entails an error theory because he thinks that intuitions are not particularly telling about the distinction between hearing as an individual event and hearing a sound. However, a threefold distinction should apply here. Grant the dispositional

sound. Grant hearing episodes. Now, the duration of a hearing episode is different from the duration of an occurrent sound. You set a tuning fork in motion. It vibrates for thirty seconds. But then, after ten seconds, you get bored and block your ears with your hand. The duration of your hearing is ten seconds. But the sound is still there, for another twenty seconds. Generally speaking, unheard sounds are accounted for in the dispositional theory only as unrealized dispositions. Occurrent unheard sounds are invisible to the dispositional account. (2010, section 3.3.1)

It pays to be careful about what it means to say that some phenomenon is "invisible" to an account. The phenomenon in question is completely consistent with, indeed required, for the stable disposition theory to work in the first place. The way we learn about objects' sounds is when they realize their dispositions to vibrate, creating waves in the ambient medium, picked up by the ears. These unheard occurrences are not a kind of sound, according to the view. Sounds are not occurrent anythings: they are qualities. There seems to be no strong pre-theoretic intuition to the effect that these phenomena are *sounds*. Trees falling in lonely forests have sounds and they make those sounds audible as they fall. Absent perceivers, those sounds are unheard, just as they are unheard absent stimulation or absent pressure waves in an appropriate medium.

Like the objection based on apparent duration considered in section 3, this worry is most plausible when one only considers part of the stable disposition view. Once the role of mechanical stimulation is clear, the phenomenon to which they point neatly fits within the account. In the case they describe, the hearing episode ends because you cover your ears, and, but for that, you could know the sound of the tuning fork. But there are many preconditions for hearing a thing, and the stable disposition view casts the vibration as a revelatory response to stimulation. The situation is not so much an occurrent, unheard sound as an occasion on which a sound is audible, absent obstructed ears.

The stable disposition view has perhaps the most elaborate set of preconditions for hearing, because it locates sounds at the greatest remove from perceivers. The object must be stimulated, it must vibrate, it must disturb the medium in which it sits, and that disturbance must result in pressure waves that manage to excite the ears. The account with the thinnest set of preconditions for hearing sounds is unsurprisingly the one that identifies sounds with experiences. It helps to remember that a stable disposition view of color is a model for the stable disposition view of sounds. We see colors, and doing so requires that the object be stimulated appropriately with light. Some perceptual encounters with colors are brief, because one closes one's eyes or because the lights go out. This doesn't suggest that such views are relevantly blind to occurrent, unseen colors.

Perhaps Casati and Dokic's objection is motivated by one of the more unpalatable consequences of the stable disposition view. Sounds are always there, everywhere around us, much as the visible qualities of objects are. They lurk in the quietest corridors. The silence many covet is usually understood as an absence of sound. We escape noisy environments, settling down where there are no occurrent sounds, as Casati and Dokic would have it. But there is no theoretical pressure to characterize silence in this way. Silence is plausibly a situation in which there are no audible sounds, where such inaudibility is not due to obstructed ears. We cover our ears in environments with many otherwise audible sounds. Just as a mask helps those who prefer the dark sleep, earplugs help those who prefer silence.

8. Conclusion

Because of the way vision has dominated philosophical thinking about perception since the early modern period, theories of sounds are unavoidably fashioned with explicit regard to how audition relates to vision. Yes, hearing is quite different from seeing, but in what respects, exactly? How much of the theoretical apparatus that helps understand vision can be deployed in the service of understanding hearing?

Though we certainly take ourselves to hear ordinary objects, most theoretical talk about sounds situates those ordinary objects at some remove from the sounds we hear. Sounds have lives of their own, less tethered to ordinary objects than colors and shapes are. On these views, sounds are the objects of audition, which serve as a window onto other objects and events of interest. We hear sounds, and thereby we hear doors, trees, and the events in which they figure.

The stable disposition view, by contrast, tethers sounds to ordinary objects. Sounds are qualities of what are often the very same objects we see. These qualities are revealed by impulses of mechanical energy and the nature of these stimulants accounts for much of what makes audition different from vision. We see objects and their qualities thanks to light, while we hear objects and their qualities thanks to mechanical impulses.

A number of the most pressing objections to this view focus on sounds' temporality. With these worries put on firm footing, the goal has been to show that they do not carry the day, in large measure because of how the stable disposition view understands sound stimulants. Sound stimulants are a complication for theories of sound required by the idea that sounds are dispositions to vibrate, but that complication enfranchises helpful responses to objections. Though it's beyond the scope of this chapter to go into the issue in detail, the stable disposition view suggests that auditory perception is rather more complicated (and in that sense more like vision) than other views suggest (Kulvicki 2008a, esp. 13–14). Others—for example, Mohan Matthen (2009), Matt Nudds (2010), and Barry Smith (2010)— also stress the need to complicate our picture of audition, though none of them endorses my way of complicating things.

Where do we go from here? Temporality objections to the stable disposition view suggest an important area for future research. The vast majority of work on visual perception, from philosophers at least, focuses on objects and qualities, not events. No one denies that we see events, somehow, and that doing so takes time, but we don't understand how we do so or how this relates to the visual perception of qualities like colors and shapes, and the objects that have them. The same questions apply to audition. We do hear events, but it is unclear how we do so. This is not merely a problem for the stable disposition view. Those who suggest that sounds are events typically suggest that they are not identical to the interesting events—clapping hands, skidding cars, and so on—that we take ourselves to hear. Event perception is perhaps more salient in the auditory case than it is in vision because audition more saliently takes place in time. Clues to event perception gleaned from audition can shed light on the complimentary phenomenon in vision.

Acknowledgments

Versions of this chapter were presented at the Institut Jean Nicod and the University of Edinburgh's PPIG seminar. Thanks to the organizers—Roberto Casati, Jérôme Dokic, and Mark Sprevak—and participants for their helpful feedback. Also, the editors and a referee for Oxford University Press provided helpful written comments for which I am most grateful.

References

Byrne, A. and D. Hilbert. 2003. Colors and reflectances. *Behavioral and Brain Sciences* 26(1): 3–21.

Casati, R. and J. Dokic. 1994. *La philosophie du Son*. Nimes: Chambon.

Casati, R. and J. Dokic. 2010. Sounds. *Stanford Encyclopedia of Philosophy*. E. Zalta, ed., http://plato.stanford.edu/entries/sounds/ (accessed June 23, 2011).

Cohen, J. 2009. *The Red and the Real*. New York: Oxford University Press.

Cohen, J. 2010. Sounds and temporality. *Oxford Studies in Metaphysics*, Vol. 5, D. Zimmerman, ed. Oxford: Oxford University Press, 303–320.

Helmholtz, H. 1877/1885. *On the Sensations of Tone*. Trans. A. J. Ellis. London: Longmans Green.

Kulvicki, J. 2008a. The nature of noise. *Philosophers' Imprint* 8(11): 1–16.

Kulvicki, J. 2008b. Review of Casey O'Callaghan's *Sounds: A Philosophical Theory*. *Mind* 117: 1112–1116.

Matthen, M. 2009. On the diversity of auditory objects. *Review of Philosophy and Psychology* 1(1): 63–89.

Nudds, M. 2010. What sounds are. *Oxford Studies in Metaphysics*, Vol. 5, D. Zimmerman, ed. Oxford: Oxford University Press, 279–302.

Pasnau, R. 1999. What is sound? *Philosophical Quarterly* 50(196): 309–324.

Pasnau, R. 2009. The event of color. *Philosophical Studies* 142(3): 353–369.

Recanzone, G. H., S. Makhamra, and D. Guard. 1998. Comparison of relative and absolute sound localization ability in humans. *Journal of the Acoustical Society of America* 103(2): 1085–1097.

Smith, B. 2010. Speech sounds and the direct meeting of minds. In *Sounds and Perception: New Philosophical Essays*, M. Nudds and C. O'Callaghan, eds. Oxford: Oxford University Press, 183–210.

Sorensen, R. 2008. *Seeing Dark Things*. New York: Oxford University Press.

Urmson, J. O. 1969. The objects of the five senses. *Proceedings of the British Academy* 54: 117–131.

9

Olfactory Objects

Clare Batty

1. Introduction

Consider the following visual situation:

(V)   There is a baseball cap lying on the driveway. You are looking at it.

Now consider how we might describe an olfactory analogue of (V). It would likely read something like this:

(O)   There is a dead rat in the living room. You sniff it.[1]

I take it that, in describing your experience to someone else, you could, and would, describe it in something like the following way:

(D_v)   I saw a baseball cap on the driveway.

(D_o)   I smelled a dead rat in the living room.[2]

In each case, you report that you perceived some object—in the first case, visually, and in the second case, olfactorily. And both (D_v) and (D_o) would be considered accurate. Still, the experiences that (D_v) and (D_o) refer to seem disanalogous in a crucial way. Olfactory experience does not seem overtly object-based. Unlike visual experience, olfactory experience doesn't seem to present individuals that correspond, in any obvious way, to ordinary material objects. We might even go so far as to say that olfactory experience seems disengaged from objects of any kind. It certainly seems to lack a kind of organization that its visual counterpart enjoys.[3] Why, then, do we accept that, not only (D_v) is accurate, but (D_o) as well?

---

[1] Unfortunately, I take this circumstance from my own personal repertoire.

[2] I take it that you could, and would, if you had the appropriate knowledge of the source of the smell—for instance, if you had already visually located the rat. Otherwise, you would likely describe yourself as having seen or smelled *something*—perhaps a pungent odor (qua emanation) or simply something pungent. These other descriptions work equally well for the contrast this example is meant to set up. I return to these important issues later in the chapter.

[3] Consider Chalmers's claim: "Smell has little in the way of apparent structure and often floats free of any apparent object, remaining a primitive presence in our sensory manifold" (1996, 8).

In this chapter, I consider this question in light of an emerging view of olfaction. Recently, some olfactory scientists have begun to question the traditional, feature-centric, way of characterizing olfactory perception. Championed by Wilson and Stevenson (2006, 2007) a new object-based approach to analyzing olfactory perception is emerging as its rival. I argue that this approach is distinctive because it suggests a way of understanding object perception that departs significantly from the reigning visual model. In particular, I argue that it makes available a view according to which object perception can involve something akin to object recognition without object individuation. In stressing that object recognition is, in some cases, more basic than object individuation, such a view forces us to think more deeply about what it means to say that perceptual experience represents objects.

2. Background

The best way to understand the novelty of Wilson and Stevenson's approach is to consider its origins and, in particular, the kind of approach to explaining olfactory perception it aims to replace. Driving their object-based approach is their dissatisfaction with what they call the traditional Stimulus-Response Model of olfactory processing (from hereon SRM). Olfactory processing begins when odor meets receptor sheet.[4] In humans there are two such patches of tissue, roughly the size of a dime, lying approximately 7cm. within each nostril. Each patch contains three types of cells—olfactory receptor neurons, sustenacular cells, and basal cells—and the olfactory glands that produce the olfactory mucosa. Sustenacular cells support those neurons while basal cells differentiate and divide to form new olfactory neurons.[5] Necessary for the generation of an olfactory experience in humans are the receptor neurons themselves.[6] It is now estimated that humans have roughly 300 different types of olfactory receptors, allowing for a remarkable amount of analysis of an odor at the receptor site (Wilson and Stevenson 2006, 2007).[7] According to the SRM, an analysis of olfactory experience involves uncovering how the particular features of a chemical stimulus are represented in experience. In particular, this

---

[4] By "odor" I mean a collection of volatile molecules, a gaseous emanation given off by a source object. Odors are not ordinary objects; but they are objects nonetheless. "Odor" is sometimes used in property-talk, to denote the distinctive properties presented to one in olfactory experience. I will only use "odor" in object-talk and reserve "smell," in its nominal form, to denote such a property.

[5] Olfactory neurons are distinctive in that they are the only neurons of the adult human that are able to regenerate.

[6] Here "necessary" refers to nomological necessity. I am not claiming that is a matter of logical necessity that the human olfactory system is functionally the way it is.

[7] This is due to the discovery by Buck and Axel (1991) of a large gene family that encodes olfactory G-protein receptors—a discovery for which they received the Nobel Prize in Physiology or Medicine in 2004. The family consists of 1,000 different genes that give rise to an equivalent number of olfactory receptor types. In humans, there are roughly 300 different types of functional genes.

approach assumes that olfactory experience is analytic—that the various features of a chemical stimulus (i.e., those that trigger receptor excitation) and/or receptor type will map onto features of the resulting experience. The SRM assumes that, in some important sense, olfactory experience can be "broken down" into, or will reflect, those initial features of the stimulus and/or receptor types sensitive to those features.

Wilson and Stevenson (2003, 2006) claim that the SRM, in some guise or another, has shaped much of the history of olfactory research. And, as they note, employing such a model has involved devising classification schemes for the range of olfactory experiences we undergo. That is to say, the approach involves attempting to understand the stimulus and receptor site by first classifying the various phenomenal properties of olfactory experience. In the discussion that follows, I assume, in accordance with the SRM, that these phenomenal properties are intentional insofar as they feature in a characterization of the representational content of olfactory experience. I will say nothing, however, about the nature of the properties represented by those experiences—for example, whether they are physical, dispositional, sui generis properties of the olfactory stimulus, properties of experience, or indeed properties of nothing at all. Given that I will be concerned primarily with the "experience side" of the SRM, what is important is not the nature of the properties represented but rather certain issues about those properties *as they appear to us*.[8]

The earliest classification schemes were what I call *categorical systems* in that they assigned a range of olfactory stimuli to basic categories that reflect the characteristic experiences caused by those stimuli. Put in philosophical terms, stimuli falling under a given category were thought to evoke experiences with common, or at least similar, phenomenal properties. As they stood, such systems were simply a means of grouping, but not ordering, "like with like." The earliest cited system of this kind is Linnaeus's (1756). His system consisted of seven categories used to classify botanical as well as other medicinal materials.[9] It was followed by Zwaardemaker's nine-category system (1895), which, unlike that of Linnaeus, was used to speculate about the physico-chemical basis of perceived quality. That is, Zwaardemaker intended his system as a means of asking, and ultimately answering, the question of what physical properties unite all stimuli of a given category.[10]

However, each system proved to be too simple—although, likely due to its more recent publication and its aim to move beyond the classification of specialist

---

[8] At one point, Wilson and Stevenson refer to these properties as "olfactory qualia" (2006, 11). Given that there is a philosophical use of "qualia" such that qualia are nonintentional properties of experience, I refrain from muddying the waters by taking on their usage.

[9] Linnaeus's seven categories were (1) aromatic, (2) fragrant, (3) ambrosial (musk-like), (4) alliaceous (garlic-like), (5) hircine (goat-like), (6) foul, and (7) nauseating. He also proposed a second, related classification scheme in which he grouped these seven categories according to their appeal—that is, pleasant and unpleasant. As Harper et al. (1968) note, this secondary scheme is often overlooked. I also overlook it in the present chapter, as it is unnecessary for understanding the transition from the SRM to Wilson and Stevenson's object-based approach.

[10] Zwaardemaker, a Dutch physiologist, altered Linnaeus's system slightly, adding two more categories: (8) ethereal (e.g., beeswax) and (9) empyreumatic (burnt-like as in, e.g., tobacco smoke or roasted coffee). The first was adopted from Lorry (1784–5) and the second from von Haller (1763).

materials, Zwaardemaker's system has received more critical attention. For example, Titchener (1912) argued that a significant number of stimuli could not be matched under any of Zwaardemaker's nine categories. Similarly, Titchener noted that some of the stimuli that Zwaardemaker had placed under different categories seemed to have more in common with one another than others that he had included under the same category. In general, neither system attempted to capture the similarity and difference relations between the various apparent properties evoked by the listed stimuli. Apart from locating stimuli under the same category and, in Zwaardemaker's case, dividing three categories into subgroups,[11] these systems had nothing to say about the relations between apparent olfactory properties. Stimuli were simply filed under single categories without representation of the degree to which they are similar to other stimuli in that category or, as the problems with Zwaardemaker's system show, stimuli in other categories.[12]

In the twentieth century, drawing on recent success in the color domain, categorical systems gave way to the idea of an olfactory *quality space*. The quality space for a given modality is an ordering of the phenomenal properties of that modality. In particular, that ordering forms a system of resemblance relations among those properties. A given phenomenal property for a sensory modality is a location within that modality's quality space. In the olfactory case, these models were anchored by a set of phenomenal primaries—those apparent properties that cannot be matched by a mixture of any other. Commonly referred to as the "odor primaries," these properties were thought of as the olfactory equivalents of the "unique hues."[13] That is to say, it was thought that all other apparent olfactory properties were mixtures of some subset of the odor primaries.[14] I call the systems of classification formed in such a way *primary systems*.[15]

---

[11] According to Zwaardemaker, aromatic stimuli could be divided further into those that are (i) camphoraceous, (ii) spicy, (iii) aniseed-like, (iv) citrous, or (v) almond-like. Floral stimuli could be divided into those that are (ii) lilaceous, (iii) vanilla-like, or have (iii) the scents of flowers. Finally, alliaceous stimuli could be divided into those that are (i) garlicky, (ii) cacodylic, or have (iii) the scent of bromine.

[12] As Harper, Bate-Smith, and Land (1968) note, Zwaardemaker himself expressed reservations about the categorical system of classification and, in particular, the method of assigning multiple stimuli to a single category.

[13] Here the use of "odor" diverges from my own. See fn. 4.

[14] As it stands, the systems to follow did not have anything analogous to saturation and brightness in the color domain. It might be thought that perceived intensity would be analogous to brightness. However, perceived intensity does not behave as nicely as brightness does in the case of color. In many cases, with changes in intensity of the stimulus come robust changes in perceived quality. So, although it might be an appropriate way of describing changes to the concentration of a stimulus, it is questionable whether intensity is an appropriate way of capturing any kind of continuum on which apparent properties might fall. As my primary interest is not in modeling olfactory quality space, I leave this question.

[15] It is important to note that the idea of a primary odor marks a significant assumption on the part of models of this kind. A model that mapped the relations between the phenomenal properties of a modality but lacked primaries would still count as an ordering of those properties and, in doing so, would count as a quality space for that modality.

The most famous of the primary systems are Henning's (1916) "odor prism,"[16] Crocker and Henderson's (1927) numerical similarity orderings, and Amoore's (1952; 1963; 1970) stereo-chemical theory of olfactory processing. The details of these various models are not important for present purposes. Rather, like Linnaeus's and Zwaardemaker's systems before them, what *is* important is what they have in common.[17] All of these systems aimed to capture the complexity of perceived quality that Zwaardemaker, as well as his critics, worried his system could not. In doing so, like Linnaeus and Zwaardemaker, they each proposed that olfactory experience was largely analytic. In turn, each proposed explicit connections between the "components" of perceived quality and features of the receptor site and/or stimulus. It is reasonable to say, then, that these three primary systems mark the SRM in its most developed form.

Although the SRM made olfactory processing seem neat and tidy, each of the three SRM-inspired systems had problems. For the most part, those problems came in the form of exceptions. In Henning's case, stimuli with a structure that ought to have fallen on a certain plane of the prism were found to fall elsewhere. Some stimuli were even found to fall within the prism; but, according to Henning, none fell within it. All could be classified by their position on the surface of the prism.[18] As Harper et al. (1968) note, Crocker and Henderson's model failed to get consistent results from untrained subjects and raised concerns over its attempt to quantify the contributions that each primary made to the perceived quality of a stimulus. Finally, many grew suspicious of Amoore's hypotheses regarding the relationship

---

[16] Again, the use of "odor" here diverges from my own. See fn. 4.

[17] I will, however, provide a few details. According to Henning, there were six olfactory primaries: (i) fragrant, (ii) ethereal or fruity, (iii) resinous, (iv) spicy, (v) putrid, and (vi) burned. Henning plotted these primaries on a geometrical form—the prism. With the primaries occupying the points of the prism, Henning took it that all apparent properties could be plotted on one of the three surface of the prism, at relative distances from the set of primaries that occupied the points of the relevant side. According to Henning, no apparent properties fell within the prism. Like Henning, Crocker and Henderson attempted to improve upon earlier "categorical" systems by mapping the relative similarities and differences between the apparent properties of olfactory stimuli. Their system, however, was unlike Henning's both in that it did not involve a geometrical form and the number of primaries was only four: fragrant, acid, burnt, and caprylic. According to Crocker and Henderson, the experience resulting from a given stimulus could be assigned a four-digit number, with each of the four numerals involved (between 1 and 8) representing, in ascending order, the degree to which each of the four primaries (in the order of fragrant, acid, burnt, and caprylic) was represented by that experience. Finally, Amoore hoped that, just as color-blindness had helped unlock the mystery of the receptors involved in color vision, certain relative inabilities to detect certain odorous compounds known as specific anosmias would do the same for olfaction. Although he was interested in uncovering primaries, and was interested in the quality space to this degree, his was not an attempt to model the entirety of olfactory quality space. For Amoore, uncovering primaries provided a potential way of uncovering the number of receptor types employed by the olfactory system. Compiling a list of common labels used to describe olfactory stimuli in the literature, the most common of these came to denote his seven primaries: (a) ethereal, (b) camphoraceous, (c) musky, (d) floral, (e) minty, (f) pungent, and (g) putrid. Amoore's hypothesis was that the specific anosmias and the seven primaries together suggested seven receptor types.

[18] For a good summary of the problems with Henning's model, see MacDonald (1922).

between features of the stimulus and receptor type.[19] Moreover, Amoore's contention that there was a mapping between types of anosmia ("smell-blindness," as it were), receptor types, and the odor primaries equally suffered. As the known anosmias grew in number, so did suspicion of modeling olfactory quality space, and indeed the mechanisms of the olfactory system, in accordance with a set of "odor primaries" thought by Amoore to be indicated by those anosmias. [20]

But, as Wilson and Stevenson (2006) argue, there are more general reasons to give up on primary systems and, in turn, the SRM. The SRM posits that olfactory experience is analytic, that it has various distinguishable components. But olfactory experience doesn't live up to that standard. Olfactory experience is largely synthetic—that is, the various properties of the stimulus produce a largely irreducible experience. Because of this, the various features of the stimulus are not distinguishable at the level of experience—as the SRM would have them. As a way of highlighting this point, Wilson and Stevenson (2006, 2007) draw attention to the fact that much of what we encounter and recognize with our noses is chemical mixtures. For example, the stimulus that gives rise to the "coffee" olfactory experience is such a mixture. Sniffing coffee provides a unique kind of olfactory experience; but it is not one where we are able to discriminate the over 600 volatile compounds that constitute the coffee odor.[21] As Wilson and Stevenson (2003, 2006) note, it is now commonly accepted that even experts are able to distinguish only two or three of the major components that constitute a given odor. Now, to demand that an olfactory experience discriminate every compound that constitutes an odor might be to overstate the success conditions for the SRM. Still, what is clear from Wilson and Stevenson is that while olfactory experience does not entirely fail to be analytic in some cases (i.e., it can be less-than-synthetic), it does not succeed in anything like the way we should expect it to if the SRM is true. As a result, the SRM doesn't succeed in characterizing the nature of olfactory experience. What kind of view would? That's where Wilson and Stevenson's Object Recognition Model comes in.

3. Olfactory Objects

The SRM is a feature-based model of olfactory experience. The views based on it claim that nothing more is needed to characterize a given experience than an inventory of the properties it represents. On the SRM, individual features of the stimulus are represented in olfactory experience in a one-one mapping. Such a

---

[19] These problems are well documented. See, for example, Moncrieff (1967).

[20] As Wilson and Stevenson (2006) note, at last count there were upward of seventy specific anosmias.

[21] Here I appeal to Wilson and Stevenson's cited source, Maarse 1991, who reports that number as 655. Others, however, have reported upwards of 1,000 volatile compounds.

mapping is enough, on the SRM, to account for the phenomenology of experience. In contrast to this, Wilson and Stevenson (2003, 2006, 2007) argue that the best way to characterize olfactory experience is not in these "feature-centric" terms, but in terms of the representation of objects. According to their object-based approach, olfactory experience represents not only the properties in the vicinity but also the objects to which those various properties belong. On what I call their Object-Recognition Model of olfactory processing (from hereon ORM), olfactory experience represents "olfactory objects" or, as they sometimes put it, "odor objects."[22]

There is much to learn from Wilson and Stevenson's account of olfactory processing. It offers up a wealth of detail regarding the formation of these odor objects. In what follows, I am concerned with the status of these olfactory objects—and, in particular, with the question of whether it is *objects* that the system represents. As Wilson and Stevenson state it, their main project is to answer the following question: "How does the olfactory system extract an odor object from a complex olfactory scene?" (2006, 22). Unlike Wilson and Stevenson, my primary concern is not with *how* the olfactory system extracts an odor object from a complex olfactory scene.

Still, in order to address *my* question, it is useful to say something more about how they go about answering *theirs*. Consider again what happens when you smell the coffee brewing. A remarkable amount of analysis occurs at the olfactory epithelia. Eight hundred different compounds are brought into the nose and 300 different types of olfactory receptors recognize relevant features of those compounds. But, in most circumstances outside of the lab, our noses are barraged with other molecules than those given off by the coffee. Yet, we are able to smell *coffee*. How does olfactory experience achieve this feat? According to Wilson and Stevenson (2003, 2006, 2007), *learning* and *memory* play a fundamental role in olfactory processing. They claim that, over time, the olfactory system builds up a store of templates in the olfactory cortex of patterns of receptor input. Once stored, these enable the system to recognize those patterns against variable arrays of receptor excitation. According to Wilson and Stevenson (2003, 2006, 2007), this kind of processing endows us with certain discriminatory abilities—for example, the ability to smell coffee even though there are other smelly things about.[23] I will return to

---

[22] Although Wilson and Stevenson (2006) suggest that the odorant analysis inherent to the SRM is reinforced by Buck and Axel's discovery of a large gene family that encodes olfactory receptors, they later suggest (2007) that Buck and Axel's focus on the combinatorial nature of receptor sensitivity supports a move to their ORM. See also fn. 7.

[23] It is important to note that this recognitional capacity does not entail the ability to name or otherwise identify a certain olfactory stimulus. "Successful recognition may or may not be followed by successful identification, in which the name associated with the object is retrieved" (2001, 1). In other words, discrimination (which recognition allows for) must be distinguished from naming and identification. To be sure, out of the ORM falls a natural explanation for why we are able to name and identify certain stimuli much more easily than others (because the templates associated with them are more entrenched). But naming or identification is not necessary for recognition.

these abilities shortly. For now it is enough to note that when we do smell the coffee in these complex circumstances, rather than being presented with an "array" of discriminable apparent properties each of which can be traced back to features of the coffee stimulus and/or receptor site, as the SRM would have it, we are presented with a "wholistic, unitary percept" (2007, 1821), incapable of being broken down into more than two or three identifiable component features—if at all.[24] According to Wilson and Stevenson (2006, 2007), these unitary percepts are not simply conjunctions of those component features; rather, they are olfactory objects to which olfactory experience attributes certain features. Given that Wilson and Stevenson also refer to these objects as "odor objects," it is safe to assume that they take these perceptual objects to correspond to odors—collections of volatile, airborne molecules. In the coffee case, we are presented with what I call a "coffee object."

The ORM moves beyond thinking of olfactory perception as feature based and posits the representation of objects in it. That is to say, olfactory perception is a form of object perception and, according to Wilson and Stevenson, "substantial conceptual, if not mechanistic, similarities exist between visual object perception and olfactory perception" (2006, 29). They recognize that, in the case of vision, "perceiving objects . . . involves the recognition of complex sets of features—objects" (2007, 1821) and that, on the ORM, olfactory perception involves something very similar, namely, "the formation of statistically reliable patterns—objects" (2007, 1821). In other places, they describe these odor objects similarly as "meaningful combination[s] of chemical[s]" (2006, 18), "odor combinations" (2006, 20), "'patterns of stimulation" (2006, 20), and, in more straightforwardly phenomenological terms, "unitary olfactory percepts" (2006, 33) or "synthetic odor objects" (2006, 6). I return to these definitions later and, in particular, how there seem to be two distinct uses of "object" here.

Now: *does* olfactory experience represent objects? In philosophical terms, the claim that olfactory experience involves the representation of olfactory objects amounts to a claim about the structure of olfactory experience. In particular, it amounts to the view that olfactory experience has a subject-predicate structure—that is, in experience, properties are attributed to individuals.[25] Following Cohen (2004), I refer to those individuals as "sensory individuals." In these terms, on the ORM, when you sniff the coffee brewing, your olfactory experience has a subject-predicate structure. In this case, it involves the attribution of a property, or set of properties to an odor individual—the "coffee-object."[26]

---

[24] These latter cases of "wholly synthetic" olfactory experiences might be thought of as those that present *one* identifiable feature. I turn to this proposal, and the questions it raises about the ORM, shortly.

[25] Given that visual experience has such a structure in the case of illusory as well as hallucinatory experience, read "properties" and "individuals" as "apparent properties" and "apparent individuals," respectively.

[26] Sensory individuals need not correspond to objects. For example, Clark (2000) holds that visual individuals correspond to *places*. In the auditory domain, O'Callaghan (2007, 2008, 2010) argues that its individuals correspond to *events*.

Drawing on empirical theories of vision, philosophers of perception have distinguished two kinds of perceptual phenomenon, each of which deserves the label "object perception." They are *object individuation* and *object recognition*. Using vision as a case study, consider each phenomenon in more detail.[27] Central to object individuation is the *grouping* of perceptual features. It is easiest to understand what grouping is by considering a problem that it enables vision to solve—namely, the Many Properties Problem. The Many Properties Problem is the problem of distinguishing between scenes in which the same properties are instantiated but in different arrangements. It is clear that there is a difference between (1) seeing a red cube to the left of a blue sphere and (2) seeing a blue cube to the left of a red sphere. In each case, the same properties are instantiated. But your visual experience reports on the different arrangements of those properties, and does so by grouping them together to form sensory individuals. In the visual case, these individuals correspond, more or less, with ordinary material objects.[28] In (1), one individual is red and cubical, while another is blue and spherical; in (2) one individual is blue and cubical, while another is red and spherical. Conceiving of the visual system as one that only extracts features from the scene could not account for the difference between (1) and (2). The properties instantiated in each case are the same; the difference lies with the individuals to which these properties are attributed. In the visual case, those individuals typically correspond to ordinary material objects. In representing those objects, visual experience provides information about their *edges* or *boundaries*. It also allows for *figure-ground segregation*, or the ability of a perceiver to discriminate objects from one another as well as a background.

Now object recognition. As it is typically characterized, object recognition draws on object individuation in achieving further object-involving tasks. Again in the visual case, those sensory achievements that fall under the heading "object recognition" are *tracking, persistence,* and *amodal completion*. Objects can be tracked across space and time. For example, you can track a ball as it moves through the air toward the goal. If that ball gets a bit muddy over the course of a match, it doesn't appear to you as though a new round object—one with brown patches—has come onto the scene. Rather it appears to you as though the very same object has undergone a change in its properties. That is to say, you perceive the ball to persist through changes in its apparent properties. Finally, if your dog scampers behind a picket fence, you do not see an array of individual objects in between the fence posts. What you see is your dog (or at least an object) behind the posts. That is to say, your dog appears to continue uninterrupted—"complete"—behind other occluding objects.

---

[27] Recently, O'Callaghan has argued that audition achieves both object individuation and object recognition, although it does so temporally rather than spatially. Because the puzzle I started with contrasts olfactory experience with visual experience, I focus on vision.

[28] Examples of exceptions are those sensory individuals that correspond to portions of liquids, individual clouds, and patches of light.

Far from being isolated phenomena, it would appear that visual object recognition depends on object individuation in a significant way. That is, it would seem that if there is no object individuation, there is no object recognition. What we track are objects. What we visually perceive to survive changes in apparent properties are, again, objects. And what we perceive to continue uninterrupted behind other occluding objects (oops!) are just those—objects! On the visual model, then, object individuation and object recognition can be seen as two *levels* of object perception—with the former the more basic. There might be object individuation without object recognition, as in the case where we are unable to track an object that goes in and out of view at random places. But object recognition without object individuation remains in doubt—at least on initial phenomenological grounds. And that phenomenological benchmark is the main thing to keep in mind when exploring the olfactory case.

Object individuation and object recognition in the visual case form the core of what philosophers of perception have considered object perception. Assume, for the sake of the present argument, that object perception in general can be modeled to some degree or another on the visual case.[29] This assumption is in keeping with Wilson and Stevenson's claim that "substantial conceptual, if not mechanistic, similarities exist between visual object perception and olfactory perception" (2006, 29).[30] If this is right, then olfaction ought to exhibit something like the object individuation and object recognition of vision. Moreover, it should be expected that object individuation forms the basis of object perception.

Drawing on the visual case, and what it is safe to assume about it prima facie, I turn now to the claim that olfactory perception is a form of object perception. In particular, consider the ORM and the view of olfactory experience it espouses. Wilson and Stevenson hold that it is wrong to think of olfactory experience as feature based, as the SRM would have it. And, in general, their reasons for rejecting the SRM are the same as the reasons for thinking that visual experience is not feature based. In the case of vision, a feature-based view does not account for perceptual grouping (and, thereby, cannot solve the Many Properties Problem). Now, Wilson and Stevenson do not stress perceptual grouping in their criticism of the SRM. As they stress, olfactory experience is largely synthetic. Still, their criticism

---

[29] It might seem suspect to use vision as the model, especially given that philosophers are becoming increasingly wary of doing so—at least as a general rule. But there are some success stories. Drawing on recent work in auditory scene analysis, O'Callaghan (2008), for example, argues that there are auditory analogues of object individuation and object recognition. As will become clear, I make this assumption only as a means of exploring the similarities and differences between the visual case and that prescribed to olfaction by the ORM. As I will argue, the places where the ORM fails to match the visual case—or where one could question that it succeeds in doing so—provide unique insight into the nature of olfactory experience.

[30] Wilson and Stevenson (2006) also claim that olfactory object perception bears similarities to that of the auditory and somatosensory systems. In keeping with the comparison between vision and olfaction that I opened with, and because drawing attention to similarities with vision is Wilson and Stevenson's main concern, I set aside these similarities with other sensory systems.

of the SRM draws on the fact that, like a feature-based view in the case of vision, it does not capture what experience is like. In the case of olfaction, the SRM posits an "analytic" structure to olfactory representation when in fact, for the most part, it is largely synthetic. Individual features simply aren't represented in the way the SRM posits. What they suggest instead is that, like visual experience, olfactory experience involves objects or, as the philosopher might put it, has a subject-predicate structure. The "subject" of that relation is, according to Wilson and Stevenson, a "synthetic odor object" (2006, 6).

But it is not simply because olfactory experience is largely synthetic that Wilson and Stevenson claim it represents objects. It is, rather, what it can allegedly achieve as a result of being synthetic that lends favor to the view. According to Wilson and Stevenson, the "defining feature for [perceptual] objecthood" (2007, 1823) is "figure-ground separation" (2007, 1821).[31] Remember that figure-ground segregation is characteristic of the object individuation of vision. And in the visual case, it is achieved spatially. An object is visually perceived to occupy a position in space distinct from other objects as well as a common background. Although Wilson and Stevenson (2006) claim that olfactory experience is aspatial,[32] they claim that it still achieves figure-ground segregation. I hinted at their reasons earlier. We are not creatures of the laboratory; odors are not presented to us in isolation. Day-to-day, at every instant, we are presented with collections of volatile molecules originating from the many objects around us. It is not simply the coffee that is sloughing off such molecules; it is the freshly baked bread, the sour milk, the rubbish in the bin, the cedar of the chopping block, and so on. Just think of how many things around you at any given time are the kinds of things that smell. Your olfactory environment consists of a grand mixture of molecules from a variety of sources. Yet, somehow, when we take in an olfactory scene—literally, through our noses—elements of that scene appear to us as separated from one another. There is coffee and freshly baked bread. There is also sour milk and cedar. Moreover, often certain elements of that scene appear more pronounced than others. It might not even appear as though some present in the scene are, indeed, present at all. So, for example, when you sit at breakfast, the "coffee element" (to remain neutral for a moment between coffee qua object and coffee qua property) might appear more pronounced than the "freshly baked bread" element and the "sour milk" element may not appear to you at all (even though the milk on the table has gone off). Wilson and Stevenson characterize this phenomenon of "experiential prominence" as the experience of figure-ground segregation. In the visual case, we know that the apparent figures correspond, for the most part, with ordinary material objects. In the olfactory case, Wilson and Stevenson refer to the apparent figures as

---

[31] According to Wilson and Stevenson (2007), they adopt this definition from Kubovy and Van Valkenburg (2001).

[32] For example, they claim that "odors, unlike visual stimuli, do not intrinsically contain a spatial component, though they may vary in intensity over space as they diffuse from their source" (2006, 44).

odor objects and, as I noted earlier, it is fair to assume that they take them to correspond to certain odors—that is, certain collections of volatile molecules in the environment. In terms of the example case, then, they claim that the coffee odor is experienced as distinct from a "noisy" background—one that includes collections of molecules given off by freshly baked bread, sour milk, various bits and pieces in the rubbish, and so on.

Wilson and Stevenson (2003, 2006, 2007) argue that underlying this achievement is their template model of olfactory perception. Olfactory experience isolates target objects in virtue of a "match" between incoming information about the stimulus at the receptor site and stored patterns of receptor input in the olfactory cortex. What this allows for is a kind of filtering of the information generated at the receptor site. On this picture, stable, or "repeated," stimuli are adapted out of the scene, whereas novel, or "newly arrived," stimuli are matched to existing templates and given experiential prominence. (This explains why a person, although initially overpowered by the smell of a bath and body shop, after a moment or two is able to walk around and detect the smells of individual products.)[33] Their being given such prominence amounts to the representation of an odor object as distinct from a background. Of course, if such a picture is correct, it is likely that a perceiver will have matching templates for more than one odor in the vicinity (the freshly baked bread template, for example), and yet only one odor object (the coffee object, for example) might appear prominent. Wilson and Stevenson (2006) argue that in many cases, it is not the mere comparison between receptor excitation and stored templates that determines what will appear prominent in a given scene. The story is typically much more complex than that. In addition to stressing the importance of memory and learning in olfactory discrimination, the ORM takes into consideration the effects of other influences such as expectation, attention, and cross-modal interaction. For example, past experience might constrain a perceiver's expectations with respect to whether a certain odor is present and underlie the template associated with that odor assuming experiential precedence. Similarly, one's current needs, desires, or emotions might inform experience. When I get up in the morning, I want coffee. Food, even if freshly baked bread, comes second. As a result, when I wake up, I smell coffee.[34]

At this point, it is helpful to stress a further difference between the SRM and the ORM. Unlike the ORM, the SRM pays little or no attention to the separation of odors in a scene. Of course, the SRM assumes that the coffee odor will result in a distinctive pattern of receptor activation—and that this is discoverable when we consider the inhalation of that odor in isolation. But in anything but exceptional circumstances, we encounter a mix of odors in our environment. And this creates

---

[33] Again, I use "smell" in its nominal position to denote an olfactory property.

[34] There is a growing philosophical literature on the issues of cognitive penetrability and cross-modal interaction. For examples of the former, see Lyons (2011), Macpherson (forthcoming), Siegel (forthcoming-a, forthcoming-b) and Stokes (forthcoming). For examples of the latter, see Macpherson (forthcoming), and O'Callaghan (forthcoming).

trouble for the SRM. When I smell coffee and newly baked bread in the kitchen, my total receptoral activation is different from when I smell either in isolation. Yet I still smell coffee and I still smell baked bread—not some amalgam of the two. On the SRM, there is no good reason to think that my experience should present my surroundings as such. On the SRM, what I perceive ought to correspond to the total receptor activation at any given moment. To be sure, it ought also to be largely analytic—which, as Wilson and Stevenson note, it is not. But, even so, there is nothing about the SRM which suggests that my experience of coffee and baked bread should be separated, albeit minimally, as it is. The SRM seems caught between the proverbial rock and a hard place. Because it posits that olfactory experience is largely analytic, our olfactory experiences should present arrays of olfactory features—those belonging to the coffee and baked bread stimuli. But they do not. Because they do not, we might ask, Why is it that there is any separation at all? It is not clear that the SRM has the resources with which to answer this question.

Of course, as I said earlier, the ORM's mechanism of template matching provides it a way of answering the question. Indeed, as I noted previously, it is this very question that motivates the ORM. Of course, my explanation of that mechanism has simplified and it is important to note that Wilson and Stevenson (2006, 2007) offer up more detail regarding the range of our discriminatory abilities as well as the further top-down mechanisms in place to allow for them. Again, my concern is with the status of their odor objects and less so with how they are generated. For the purposes of the present discussion, it is enough to note that we have these discriminatory abilities in the face of such overwhelmingly diverse mixtures of molecules at the nose, and that Wilson and Stevenson claim those discriminations play a definitive role in olfactory object perception by providing for figure-ground segregation.

Before moving on to consider whether they do play this definitive role, it is necessary to consider further accomplishments of the olfactory system that Wilson and Stevenson claim count in favor of the ORM. According to the ORM, the olfactory system can achieve an analogue of visual amodal completion. They argue that degraded or partial input at the receptor site and/or olfactory bulb can be completed at the level of experience.[35] Just as one does not receive visual information about some parts of a dog sitting behind a picket fence, one does not receive olfactory information about all of the components of an odor stimulus. And, in turn, like one sees that there is a dog (or at least an object) behind the fence, as opposed to an array of individual objects located between the fence posts, one smells that there is certain odor object present as opposed to, or in addition to, some other. As

---

[35] Among the evidence that Wilson and Stevenson (2003) cite is a series of experiments conducted by Slotnick et al. (1997). In these experiments, rats with parts of the olfactory bulb removed are nevertheless able to perform a series of detection and discriminatory tasks as well as, or nearly as well as, normal rats. What Wilson and Stevenson take this ability to show is that olfactory perception is not wholly determined by the excitation at the receptor site or the output of the olfactory bulb. Further top-down influences play a significant, if not central, role in olfactory discrimination. The template model of the ORM, they argue, is the most plausible way of accounting for these further influences.

Wilson and Stevenson stress, this is common given that there are typically many odors present in the environment at any given time—"overlapped" in space, as we might think of them—and this inevitably leads to partial, or degraded, input at the receptor site. This situation is further compounded because, given the kinds of objects they are, odors are dispersed through the atmosphere and may be more concentrated in some locations (such as at the source) than others. To be sure, sometimes a change in the intensity of an odor stimulus makes for a wholesale change in perceived quality. For example, at lower concentrations, methyl heptinoate smells like violets while, at high concentration, it smells foul.[36] Of course, with the knowledge of this variation, one may be able to recognize methyl heptinoate as being the same thing, from lower to higher concentrations. At other times, however, there is no such stark difference with changes in intensity. We simply perceive it to be the same thing.[37] In terms of the ORM, these achievements of discrimination and perceptual constancy allow for the perceived persistence of an olfactory object as well as, it would seem, for the ability to track an object through space (in this case an odor), as when we search for its source. Wilson and Stevenson argue that underlying these achievements of completion and constancy in the face of fluctuations in concentration and/or other odorant "noise" is the template model of the ORM. To return to a previous example, if the pattern of excitation associated with the "coffee" template is incomplete, or degraded, at the receptor and/or olfactory bulb levels (as it will be in many cases), the "coffee" template is nevertheless able to "lock onto" the existing pattern of excitation, generating the kind of experience one has when the input is complete—namely, the "coffee" kind of experience.

In total, the phenomena that Wilson and Stevenson cite that bear resemblance to aspects of visual object perception are *figure-ground segregation, amodal completion,* and arguably, *tracking,* and *persistence.* Figure-ground segregation falls within the domain of object individuation. Amodal completion, tracking, and persistence fall within the domain of object recognition. The next step is to consider whether they are similar enough to do the same kind of theoretical work as their visual counterparts and, if they are not, whether this matters for object perception.

4. Olfactory Objects?

When assessing the ORM, it is important to distinguish two questions:

(i) *Does olfactory experience achieve object individuation?*
(ii) *Does olfactory experience represent objects?*

I begin with (i).

---

[36] See Gross-Isseroff and Lancet (1988).

[37] Here I intend to remain vague regarding the question of whether, on the ORM, you smell the same *kind* of thing or the same *particular* of a certain kind. I revisit these issues in my conclusion—although I do not, in this chapter, intend to settle the issue.

Up until now, I have been assuming what I have called the visual model of perception. On that model, object individuation and object recognition form the core of object perception, with object individuation forming the basis of object recognition. There might be object individuation without object recognition. But object recognition without object individuation remains doubtful. Vision achieves figure-ground segregation at the level of object individuation.[38] Figure-ground segregation is an effect of what is characteristic of object individuation in the visual case—namely, the perceptual grouping of visual properties—and that grouping is done spatially. Due to the perceptual grouping of visual properties, visual experience provides information about the edges and boundaries of sensory individuals and allows for figure-ground segregation. The fact that vision achieves such grouping and, in turn, makes these further accomplishments rules out the view that visual experience is feature based.

Now compare the olfactory case to the visual one. Recall that Wilson and Stevenson claim that olfactory experience is aspatial. Despite this, they also claim that, like the visual case, olfaction achieves figure-ground segregation and that, unlike what I have suggested in the visual case, this achievement is their "defining feature [of perceptual] objecthood" (2007, 1823). As I suggested, the traditional visual model takes perceptual grouping as the central feature of object individuation—the basic level of object perception. Wilson and Stevenson do not say anything about perceptual grouping—a point I return to shortly. Still, it achieves aspatial figure-ground segregation and that it does so forms the basis of their claim that olfactory experience represents objects. In terms of the visual model, then, object perception, for Wilson and Stevenson, is achieved at the level of object individuation and their answer to (i), "*Does olfactory experience achieve object individuation?*" is "yes." In particular, the answer to the following question is "yes":

(i′) *Does olfactory experience achieve figure-ground segregation?*

The trouble is, the answer to (i′) is underdetermined by the data.

This is because what Wilson and Stevenson say about figure-ground segregation at this level does not rule out a feature-based view. But if segregation constitutes the "defining feature [of perceptual] objecthood," then such a view should be rendered a nonoption. In order to see that this is so, consider again the coffee case. Wilson and Stevenson do not deny that, in being presented with the coffee object, we are presented with a distinctive property or, in the case of those less-than-synthetic experiences, a distinctive set of properties. For the sake of simplicity, assume the coffee experience is wholly synthetic; I will return to less-than-synthetic experiences in moment. When we sniff around the coffee, we are presented with what we can call the "coffee smell." Now suppose that the right view of such an experience

---

[38] As O'Callaghan (2008) notes, figure-ground segregation needn't be achieved spatially. He argues that, in the auditory domain, it is achieved temporally.

is one according to which your experience attributes a property to an object. If that is true, then there must be a way of rejecting the view according to which your olfactory experience simply registers the instantiation of a property (i.e., the coffee smell) in the vicinity. Given its reliance on analytic processing, it is doubtful that the SRM can provide such a view; as Wilson and Stevenson stress, it must project that there is no presentation of *a* coffee smell per se. But consider the following version of a feature-based view: in the coffee case, your olfactory experience reports "it is coffee-smelling here" where, just as we do not attribute heat to the referent of "it" in the sentence "it is hot in here," your experience does not attribute the coffee smell to anything at all.[39] Is it possible to rule out *this* view?

It isn't clear that we have the materials with which to adjudicate. Both the ORM and this feature-based view will grant that a distinctive property (the coffee smell) is presented to you in experience. Each can also grant that the property appears to stand out from the other properties instantiated in a scene. Of course, each will tell a different story about how that experiential prominence comes about. I have rehearsed ORM's story, in terms of template matching, earlier. And it would seem that feature-based views are no less equipped for telling their own story—at least prima facie. A feature-based view might claim that it is a matter of attention and/ or expectation. Or, as the ORM does, a feature-based view might appeal to mechanisms of learning and memory. For example, a certain olfactory property in one's environment might be "novel" to the system and so appear more prominently in the scene. Or the story might appeal to both types of influence. In any case, there are options. In sum, it would seem that a feature-based view could grant all of the perceptual phenomena that the ORM cites in favor of an object-based view—and yet remain a feature-based view.

As a result, something more needs to be said about how to rule out feature-based views like this. Earlier, I hinted that there seem to be two uses of "object" at work in Wilson and Stevenson. I will now say something more about this. At certain points of their discussion, Wilson and Stevenson speak of olfactory objects as the patterns of receptoral activity that are encoded as templates and stored in long-term memory. For example, they speak of olfactory objects as "statistically reliable patterns" and "patterns of stimulation." At other points of their discussion, they speak of such objects as the experiential output of template matching, as "unitary olfactory percepts" (2006, 33) or "synthetic odor objects" (2006, 6). It is important to note that responding to present worries about ruling out feature-based views requires more that simply drawing attention to the fact that there exist such patterns of excitation at the receptoral level, nor to the fact that such patterns are stored in long-term memory to expedite later olfactory discrimination. What is at issue is

---

[39] I must thank Austen Clark for raising this point to me in a Symposium on Non-Visual Perception at the 2010 Pacific APA. In the published version of his comments, Clark (2011) gives other examples, some arguably feature based, some individual based, but not object based. For the sake of space I consider only this of his examples.

whether these patterns and combinations show up, at the level of experience, as perceptual objects. The question is whether the experiential output of template matching—the "unitary olfactory percepts" or "synthetic odor objects"—ought to be characterized in object-based terms. And, again, it isn't clear that there are the materials to adjudicate between that kind of view and one that characterizes olfactory experience merely in terms of apparent properties—at least if we are relying on observations of experiential prominence to decide it.

A clearer answer might be in the offing if "object individuation" of the original (i) is taken to refer to something more central to visual object individuation— namely, perceptual grouping. Earlier I argued that central to object individuation in vision is perceptual grouping. Because visual experience groups properties, it represents edges and boundaries and achieves figure-ground segregation. Following the visual case closely, it is plausible to think that if olfactory experience achieves perceptual grouping, it will do so in such a way that it provides a distinction between figure and ground—something that Wilson and Stevenson claim is central to olfactory object perception. A natural next question, then, is this:

(i″) *Does olfactory experience achieve perceptual grouping?*

But, even in the case of (i″), the answer is uncertain.

I do not doubt that Wilson and Stevenson would have what they need to rule out a feature-based view if olfactory experience achieved something akin to the perceptual grouping that occurs in vision. But it remains unclear that they *do* have it. Remember that olfactory experience is largely synthetic. As a result, olfactory experience doesn't have the wealth of perceptual ingredients that visual experience has to work with. And this fact about the nature of olfactory experience raises initial questions about the claim that olfactory experience achieves anything like the perceptual grouping that vision achieves.

But it is not as if olfactory experience has *no* ingredients to work with. After all, as Wilson and Stevenson claim, olfactory experience is "*largely* synthetic" (my emphasis), allowing, in some cases, for us to distinguish two or three features of an odorant stimulus. Perhaps olfactory experience achieves "minimal grouping." Unfortunately, as I noted earlier, Wilson and Stevenson do not say much about these cases and I have no particular example to draw on. Still, it is possible to project what would go some way toward settling the issue. Suppose that a certain odor, O_1, has the discriminable features, f_1 and f_2 and that another odor, $O_2{}'$, has the discriminable features, f_3 and f_4. In each case, a combination of features is instantiated: $(f_1 + f_2)$, in the case of O_1, and $(f_3 + f_4)$, in the case of $O_2{}'$. If further combinations of these features were possible—namely, one or more of $(f_1 + f_3)$, $(f_1 + f_4)$, $(f_2 + f_3)$, and $(f_2 + f_4)$—then the idea that olfactory experience can achieve perceptual grouping (and, indeed, solve the Many Properties Problem in certain cases) would make sense. Unlike vision, this grouping would not be achieved along spatial lines—something that would fit nicely with Wilson and Stevenson's claim that olfactory experience is aspatial. Still, it would seem to be perceptual grouping nonetheless.[40]

Still, even if such cases were actual, they would likely form only a small subset of our stock of olfactory experiences. Again, as Wilson and Stevenson stress, olfactory experience is "largely synthetic" and their focus is on arguing that those experiences that *are* synthetic are also object based. If it turned out that some, less-than-synthetic olfactory experiences achieve perceptual grouping, then so much the better for the view that, in general, olfactory experience is object based. But it remains that the experiences that do not achieve that much are their chief concern. And it is those experiences that Wilson and Stevenson claim are also object based.

So far I have argued that it is unclear whether olfactory experience achieves object individuation in the way that Wilson and Stevenson claim is definitive of perceptual objecthood—namely, with aspatial figure-ground segregation. In response to (i'), what they say about segregation does not distinguish their object-based view from a feature-based one (and I gave an example of just such a view). The answer to (i'), then, is underdetermined. Then, with (i″), I drew attention to the possibility that individuation might be achieved with perceptual grouping. Again it is unclear how to answer the question. At best we do not yet know whether olfactory experience achieves grouping; at worst, it does not. What is the next step?

There is at least one more version of (i) to consider:

(i‴)   *Does olfactory experience report on the edges and boundaries of objects?*

Arguably it does when we put the appropriate amount of work into it. Consider what you typically do when you experience a bad smell in your home and do not have an idea of what it might be (as it is typical to say). You walk around and notice fluctuations in the intensity of the smell. In the hope of cornering its source, you determine where the smell is instantiated in the area around you and where it is not. You also use your other senses (typically your eyes) to latch onto that source. Arguably in such a case, your olfactory experience reports on the edges and boundaries of the odor that the source gives off. You know, for example, not to investigate the bedroom any further when you are no longer greeted with the stench when you enter. Of course, once you have found the source, you typically give up your attempts to trace the boundaries of the odor it gives off and get down to the task at hand—getting rid of that source. But, the point is that you *could* trace those boundaries further and, in doing so, get an idea of the layout of the odor's expanse. And, when you do, arguably your experience, extended through time as events are, presents not a part of a particular odor but the entirety of one. And it does so *in space*.

---

[40] I must thank Fiona Macpherson for helping me see these points about perceptual grouping.

What this example suggests is that we can have object individuation in olfactory experience. We track odors and, as a result, are able to experience them as extended through space. As Wilson and Stevenson stress, sometimes performing such investigative tasks will be complicated, given the mix of odors in our environment and differences in their intensities relative to one another and to the location of their parts. As I pointed out at the end of the previous section, familiarity with certain of the odors in our environment would seem to ease our navigation of the olfactory scene, allowing for tracking and persistence. This achievement of navigation, Wilson and Stevenson would presumably argue, can be explained by their template model of olfactory processing. Remember that, according to Wilson and Stevenson, the olfactory system is able to recognize patterns of receptor input allowing the system to lend experiential prominence to matched patterns. It does so by enacting stored templates of previous receptor input. A subject is able to smell the coffee odor despite the fact that her environment consists of a variety of such odors. She is also able to smell the coffee odor despite degradation of the stimulus or receptor input, or despite fluctuations in the concentration of that odor. Given the complexity—the confusion, it might be said—of our olfactory environment, these are particularly notable achievements.

Let me stress now that what aids us in these complex circumstances and, in turn, allows for the kind of object individuation I drew attention to earlier is not simply a type of discrimination but a type of *recognition*. But what does this recognition amount to? The recognition of properties, as a feature-based view would have it? Or the recognition of objects?

Clearly Wilson and Stevenson would claim that it is the latter and, as they see it, this recognition is necessarily informed by figure-ground segregation—a phenomenon in the province of object individuation. Remember that, for Wilson and Stevenson, figure-ground segregation is the defining feature of perceptual objecthood. For Wilson and Stevenson, then, object recognition involves object individuation. This is in keeping with the visual model, a model of object perception that grants object individuation a defining role. But there is another way to understand the ORM—a "remodeled" ORM. The remodeled ORM places less emphasis on figure-ground segregation—indeed on object individuation. In doing so, it allows for object recognition to play a driving role in object perception. That it can do so, the remodeled ORM argues, is especially evident in cases in which object individuation is arguably absent. Unlike what the visual model supposes, the remodeled ORM allows that, in the olfactory case, instances of object recognition need not involve object individuation. Moreover, in circumstances of tracking and tracing boundaries, object recognition might drive object individuation. And I take it that it is this kind of role for object recognition that, at root, Wilson and Stevenson want to stress with the ORM—a role that allows us, in certain common circumstances, to rule out feature-based views at the level of object recognition alone. In terms of my previous two questions, then, a remodeled ORM shows that we might have, in certain circumstances, an answer of "no" to all of the variations of (i), *Does olfactory experience achieve object individuation?* and an answer of "yes" to (ii), *Does olfactory experience represent objects?* Despite loosening the ties of what has been the prevailing model of object perception in philosophy—namely, the visual model—it is a position that comes naturally to us. Let me say more.

At least two things are natural to think about olfactory perception. First, as I highlighted in the introduction, the natural position is that we smell *things*—not simply properties. As I stated it then, it is natural to think that we smell ordinary material objects (source objects); but, despite the fact that we typically appeal to material objects in reporting what we smell, I hold that it is equally natural—perhaps more natural—to think that we smell odors. Odors are objects—just not ordinary ones, we might say. And we think of ourselves as smelling material objects by smelling the odors they give off. This indirectness makes olfactory perception unlike visual perception. But we do hold them to be alike insofar as each involves the perception of objects—ordinary ones and unordinary ones, in the case of olfaction. Second, we do not think of olfaction as acting in isolation. When we take it that we smell a certain kind of thing, we do so because we have had previous experience with those kinds of things—as the sources of smells or as the emanations given off by those source things. Sometimes we may have located those sources using our olfactory tracking skills in conjunction with (in most cases, I take it) our eyes. At other times we may have simply been told that a certain object (or kind of object) is the source of an odor (or kind of odor). In any case, we are armed with a robust network of background beliefs about our olfactory environment and the kinds of objects that feature in them. Given this network of beliefs, we come to think of our olfactory experiences as those in which we smell objects (odors and ordinary objects), and not simply properties distinctive of their kind. The natural view of olfactory perception—one according to which we smell objects—has it as importantly experience-based.

A story about how beliefs about objects manifest in particular cases likely has the following form. When you are first presented with a particular smell, you gather beliefs about its source. To see how you might do so, it is easiest to think of that smell as a novel one and as appearing to you in a relatively uncomplex scene—that is, one that is not comprised of a variety of odors. What do you do in such a circumstance? As I said, you look for its source, likely by gathering information about the instantiation of the smell. At the source, the smell will be more concentrated, allowing the filtering out of any other olfactory stimuli. In this way, a distinctive olfactory property becomes, at the level of belief, locked onto a specific source object. Armed with this information about that property, you may also track its odor, gathering beliefs about the spatial presentation of the odor it gives off. In any case, as a result of gathering beliefs about its source, you also gather beliefs about the kind of odor it puts forth into the atmosphere. "Dead rats give off an odor like *this*," you might say, where "this" refers to that odor's distinctive smell (i.e., some property or combination of properties).

When you next run into that distinctive smell, those beliefs about the kind of odor it belongs to and that odor's source are put into use. Indeed, in many cases, it is as though previous experiences help us discriminate—latch onto—a certain smell at a later date. But, most crucially, you are not merely poised to believe on the basis of your current experience that there are certain properties instantiated in your environment; rather, you are poised to believe that there are objects in your environment with that property. Faced with the dead rat smell in the living room again, I wouldn't simply come to believe that there is a distinctively distasteful property around, even if I had not located the source or traced the boundaries of the odor to which it belongs—that is, even if my experience arguably doesn't achieve object individuation.[41] Rather, I would come to believe that there is a smelly object (odor and/or ordinary object) of a certain kind (the dead rat kind) in my environment. In these circumstances, the natural view is that the content of my experience reflects these beliefs. On the natural view, that content is not simply, as the feature-based view I considered earlier might have it, "it smells pungent." Rather, we think of it as something like "the odor in this room is pungent" or "there is a rat around and it smells pungent." And it is fair to say that we would do so even if such an experience was not informed by the contribution of any current investigation—that is, moving about, tracing the boundaries of the odor, or finding its source. It is the recognition of what was formerly experienced, together with what presently is, that determines the content of my experience.

On the natural view, then, the content of olfactory experience is shaped by influences other than those strictly olfactory and, despite any failure to accomplish object individuation in a given case, it is still able to represent objects. The content of an experience is often characterized as the way the world appears to a subject when she has that experience. Now, the notion of "the way the world appears" is often one that is used intuitively. But one way to characterize "that way"—and indeed a characterization that is suggested by the olfactory case itself—is to ask what the subject is justified in believing on the basis of that experience. If that characterization is adopted, it is natural to say that, given earlier experiences, I am not only presently justified in believing that there are certain properties instantiated before me, but also that those properties belong to objects. If we never moved about, never used any other modality than olfaction, never gained beliefs on the basis of doing so, then perhaps we would be unable to rule out a feature-based view. But we do. And we gain beliefs about objects on the basis of doing so.

How does the ORM fit into to this story? According to what I have been calling the natural view of olfactory perception, olfactory experience represents objects and can do so despite, in certain circumstances, failing to achieve anything like object individuation. The ORM can explain how it is able to do so. For reasons I gave earlier, I take it that it is best to deemphasize Wilson and Stevenson's emphasis

---

[41] Luckily it has not happened again.

on figure-ground segregation for the olfactory case and focus instead on what is truly unique about the ORM—namely, its emphasis on the importance of object recognition as forming the basis, in many cases, of olfactory object perception. It is this that makes the ORM truly distinctive—and important for theorizing about olfaction and sensory perception in general. On the remodeled ORM it is in virtue of olfactory object recognition that we are able to latch onto relevant odors in our environments and enjoy much more complex representations of objects—of odors and, in virtue of those, of ordinary objects. Driving this ability to latch onto certain odors in our environment is learning and memory—in particular, the matching of stored templates. The experiential prominence that results from such a match can be seen, as the natural view would have it, as the representation of an object—just not one in which object individuation need play a fundamental role. As I argued, if the emphasis is placed on figure-ground segregation, then it is difficult to see how experiential prominence provides the basis for a rejection of a feature-based view. If we restrict Wilson and Stevenson's emphasis on figure-ground segregation and place even greater emphasis on top-down influences on olfactory content (what they refer to throughout as learning and memory), it becomes easier to see how the ORM can go about rejecting those views. As a consideration of the natural view has shown us, it is just those kinds of influences that allow, in many cases, for our ability to describe ourselves as smelling objects. If our descriptions of our experiences are correct, then the ORM provides a framework with which to account for their correctness. This is because the ORM makes available a way of ruling out feature-based views not merely at the level of individuation, as when we trace the boundaries of an odor in a relatively uncomplex scene, but also, in more complex scenes, at the level of object recognition alone. It is *this*—more than the ability to meet any parameters of the visual model—that should be stressed when we praise the novelty of this emerging approach to theorizing about olfaction.

5. Hats and Rats

Let me now say something more about the examples I began with. Recall that in the introduction I described two perceptual situations. In (V), there is a baseball cap lying on the driveway. You are looking at it. In (O), there is a dead rat in the living room. You sniff it. I claimed that, in each case, a certain description of the circumstances would be considered accurate. In (V), the following description of your situation would be considered accurate:

(D$_v$) I saw a baseball cap on the driveway.

And, in (O), the following description of your situation would be considered accurate:

(D$_o$) I smelled a dead rat in the living room.

Now, it might be argued that the way that I described (O) implies that you have located the rat, even that you see it. After all, I claimed, "you sniff *it*." This characterization, together with the visual situation it is drawn from, naturally brings with it the suggestion that you, the perceiver, have located the rat. In this case, it is easy to see why we regard (D_o) as true. But I do not want to focus on that kind of circumstance. The variant of the case that I want to focus on is the one in which the rat smell is not novel (you have experienced it before) and you have not located any rat or indeed traced its odor. You are simply standing there, struck with the smell. Arguably these are the kinds of experiences that Wilson and Stevenson are appealing to when they describe olfactory experience as aspatial. In such a case, (D_o) also seems accurate. But, as I indicated at the outset, it does so even though the experience it describes seems disanalogous to the visual experience that (D_v) describes. I then asked, How can that be explained?

The ORM, as I have formulated it, provides a particularly nice explanation. For the remainder of the chapter, let (O) be a case in which you have not located the rat or traced its odor, but its smell is not a novel one. As I claimed, the description (D_o) seems to accurately describe the experience you have in (O). But (O) is also a situation in which olfactory experience achieves none of the things that vision does at the level of individuation. It is for this reason, I take it, that we are apt to regard the experiences that (D_v) and (D_o) describe as importantly disanalogous. In (V), your experience achieves object individuation; in (O), it does not. And it is because it does not that we regard the experience involved in (O) as failing to be overtly object-based. "Overtly object-based," I maintain, refers to the kind of perceptual organization achieved at the level of object individuation. If we think of object perception as requiring object individuation, as I think philosophers are prone to do when we take the visual model seriously, then we are bound to think that cases in which there is no such individuation are cases where there is no object perception.

But, as consideration of the ORM has shown us, this assumption does not capture all cases of olfactory experience. And what this suggests is that what it is about visual experience that makes it the case that (D_v) is true might be different from what it is about olfactory experience that makes (D_o) true. In the case of (D_v), what explains its truth is arguably the fact that your visual experience achieves object individuation and, in virtue of that, is capable of object recognition. The case of (D_o) is different. As I have described it, (O) is not a situation in which anything like object individuation is achieved. Yet, it is one in which you recognize the smell of rat given your previous (unfortunate) experience with such a smell. Because you are disposed to believe that there is a rat around or that the odor you smell is the rat odor—that is, you are disposed to believe certain things about objects in your vicinity—your experience in such a situation arguably represents objects. After all, if we take seriously the view that the content of an experience is just the way that things appear to you when having an experience, and that "way" can in turned be cashed out in terms of what you are disposed to believe on the basis of that experience, then the content of your experience in (O) must appeal to rat odors, rats, or both.

Now, clearly there is more to be said about the view of object representation that the remodeled ORM espouses. One question I did not deal with is whether, in those olfactory experiences in which it claims there is object recognition without individuation, a subject's experience represents particular objects as opposed to, or perhaps in addition to, kinds of objects. What I have said on behalf of Wilson and Stevenson suggests that it can at least do the latter; but what about the former? As I have presented the ORM, the answer to this question remains open. And answering it is a natural next step. But in general, in making available a view according to which object perception can involve recognition without individuation, the ORM highlights interesting issues about the nature of object perception in general—issues that are much more difficult to isolate if we let the visual congest us.

Acknowledgments

I must thank the editors of this volume for a wealth of helpful comments along the way. In addition, I must thank an audience at the University of Glasgow for their comments on and help with some of the issues presented in this chapter as well as Tim Sundell for reading earlier drafts of it. All helped me improve it greatly.

References

Amoore, J. E. 1952. "The Stereochemical Specificities of Human Olfactory Receptors." *Perfume and Essential Oil Record* 43: 321–330.

Amoore, J. E. 1963. "The Stereochemical Theory of Olfaction." *Nature* 198: 271–272.

Amoore, J. E. 1970. *Molecular Basis of Odor*. Springfield, IL: Thomas.

Buck, L. and R. Axel. 1991. "A Novel Multigene Family May Encode Odorant Receptors: A Molecular Basis for Odor Recognition." *Cell* 85: 175–187.

Chalmers, D. J. 1996. *The Conscious Mind*. New York: Oxford University Press.

Clark, A. 2000. *A Theory of Sentience*. New York: Oxford University Press.

Clark, A. 2011. "Vicissitudes of Non-Visual Objects: Comments on Macpherson, O'Callaghan, and Batty." *Philosophical Studies* 153: 175–181.

Cohen, J. 2004. "Objects, Places, and Perception." *Philosophical Psychology* 17: 471–495.

Crocker, E. C. and L. F. Henderson. 1927. "Analysis and Classification of Odours." *American Perfumery and Essential Oil Review* 22: 325–356.

Gross-Isseroff, R. and D. Lancet. 1988. "Concentration-Dependent Changes of Perceived Odor." *Chemical Senses* 13: 191–204.

Harper, R., E. C. Bate-Smith, and D. G. Land. 1968. *Odour Description and Odour Classification*. New York: American Elsevier.

Henning, H. 1916. *Der Geruch*. Leipzig: Barth.

Kubovy, M. and D. Van Valkenburg. 2001. "Auditory and Visual Objects." *Cognition* 80: 97–126.

Linnaeus, C. 1756. "Odores Medicamentorum." *Amoenitates Academicae* 3: 183–201.

Lyons, J. 2011. "Circularity, Reliability, and the Cognitive Penetrability of Perception." *Philsophical Issues* 21: 289–311.

Maarse, H. 1991. *Volatile Compounds in Foods and Beverages.* New York: Marcel Dekker.

MacDonald, M. K. 1922. "An Experimental Study of Henning's System of Olfactory Qualities." *American Journal of Psychology* 33: 535–553.

Macpherson, F. 2011. "Cross-Modal Experiences." *Proceedings of the Aristotelian Society* 111: 429–468.

Macpherson, F. 2012. "Cognitive Penetration of Colour Experience: Rethinking the Issue in Light of an Indirect Mechanism." *Philosophy and Phenomenological Research* 84: 24–62.

Moncrieff, J. W. 1967. *The Chemical Senses,* 2nd edition. London: Leonard Hill Books.

O'Callaghan, C. 2007. *Sounds: A Philosophical Theory.* New York: Oxford University Press.

O'Callaghan, C. 2008. "Object Perception: Vision and Audition." *Philosophy Compass* 3: 803–829.

O'Callaghan, C. 2010. "Sounds and Events." In C. O' Callaghan and M. Nudds (Eds.), *Sounds and Perception: New Philosophical Essays*, 26–49. New York: Oxford University Press.

O'Callaghan, C. 2012. "Perception and Multimodality." In E. Margolis, R. Samuels & S. Stich (Eds.), *Oxford Handbook of Philosophy of Cognitive Science*, 73–91. New York: Oxford University Press.

Siegel, S. 2012. "Cognitive Penetrability and Perceptual Justification." *Noûs* 46: 201–222.

Siegel, S. 2013. "The Epistemic Impact of the Etiology of Experience." *Philosophical Studies* 162: 697–722.

Slotnick, B. M., G. A. Bell, H. Panhuber, and D. G. Laing. 1997. "Detection and Discrimination of Propionic Acid after Removal of Its 2-DG Identified Major Focus in the Olfactory Bulb: A Psychophysical Analysis." *Brain Research* 762: 89–96.

Stokes, D. 2012. "Perceiving and Desiring: A New Look at the Cognitive Penetrability of Experience." *Philosophical Studies* 158: 479–492.

Titchener, E. B. 1912. *A Textbook of Psychology.* New York: MacMillan.

Wilson, D. A. and R. J. Stevenson. 2003. "Olfactory Perceptual Learning: The Critical Role of Memory in Odor Discrimination." *Neuroscience and Biobehavioral Reviews* 27: 307–328.

Wilson, D. A. and R. J. Stevenson. 2006. *Learning to Smell: Olfactory Perception from Neurobiology to Behavior.* Baltimore: Johns Hopkins University Press.

Wilson, D. A. and R. J. Stevenson. 2007. "Odour Perception: An Object-Recognition Approach." *Perception* 36: 1821–1833.

Zwaardemaker, H. 1895. *Die Physiologie Des Geruchs.* Leipzig: Engelmann.

10

Confusing Tastes with Flavours

Charles Spence, Malika Auvray, and Barry Smith

1. Introduction

The uses of the terms 'taste' and 'flavour' are far from clear in either our everyday language or in scientific journals. To many, these terms are interchangeable (or at least they are used in that way); to others they are definitely not. But even among those who distinguish the two terms, their use of them is seldom consistent. Many researchers who recognise a distinction seem to use the term 'taste' when what they appear to mean is 'flavour'. We will use as our definition of flavour perception the following from the International Standards Organization (ISO 5492, 1992, 2008): 'Complex combination of the olfactory, gustatory and trigeminal sensations perceived during tasting. The flavour may be influenced by tactile, thermal, painful and/or kinaesthetic effects' (see Delwiche, 2004, p. 137; see also Green, 2004; Lundström et al., 2011; Spence, 2012b; Tournier et al., 2007). Taste is defined as those sensations that result from the direct stimulation of the gustatory receptors localised on tongue and occurring elsewhere in the oral cavity.

Although these definitions are broadly accepted, several core questions remain open: Can tastes be elicited by the stimulation of some receptor surface other than those found on the tongue and in the rest of the oral cavity (Nilsson, 1977; Trivedi, 2012)? Does flavour perception involve the stimulation of receptors other than those classically thought to be involved in taste, smell, and trigeminal sensation (Murphy et al., 1977; Spence et al., 2010)? In this chapter we show how the incautious use of the terms 'taste' and 'flavour' can lead to erroneous and confusing claims, which, in turn, may well slow progress when researchers attempt to provide a correct epistemology of flavour perception. Here, note that research on flavour is no longer the obscure topic (at least for psychologists, philosophers, and cognitive neuroscientists) that it once was. The increased interest in this field of investigation stems both from the broad consequences involved for the food and beverage industries (e.g., Simons & Noble, 2003), and from a growing belief amongst many cognitive neuroscientists that a better understanding of the multisensory processes at stake in the perception of the flavours of foods and beverages might well shed light on theories of multisensory integration more generally (see also Murray & Wallace, 2011; Spence, 2012a; Stevenson, 2009). The rapid growth of interdisciplinary research on the topic of flavour that has been seen in recent years[1] makes it all the more timely to try to get our terms straight (cf. McBurney, 1986, for an earlier attempt to take the confusion out of the fusion of the chemical senses).

Below, we review the evidence on flavour, taste, smell, somatosensory, and trigeminal sensations. We start by outlining some of the confusions that symptomatically occur at the linguistic level, before going on to discuss the perceptual and cognitive factors underlying these confusions. Finally, we end by proposing what we hope to be a satisfactory resolution to the confusing use of the terms 'taste' and 'flavour', namely, we claim that when we are talking about our perceptual experience, there is no taste that isn't a flavour.

2. Linguistic Issues and Explanations

This section aims to resolve some of the semantic issues in this area. After discussing the complexity of the use of the terms 'taste' and 'flavour', we provide basic characterisations of the terms used in the field of flavour research.

2.1. THE COMPLEXITY OF THE TERMS 'TASTE' AND 'FLAVOUR'

Starting with the term 'taste' and to what it refers in a food context, there are several possibilities: (1) taste (or tastes) as qualities of the foods or liquids we consume; (2) taste as the sense we use to discover these qualities; (3) taste (or tastes) as the characteristic experiences generated by that sense when we eat or drink. Note here that people often run together these different uses of the term, and the consequences of doing so are, we argue, far from trivial. Indeed, some have argued that the failure to resolve a number of important scientific debates, such as the nature-nurture debate, boils down, at least in part, to the way in which different groups of scientists have, over the years, understood and interpreted a few key terms (Angier, 2009; Lehrman, 1970; see also Reed & Knaapila, 2010). As Stein et al. (2010, p. 1713) put it:

> Whatever phenomenon we choose to study, first and foremost, we must define it. To do so we must deal with the issue of semantics because different definitions lead to different kinds of research questions. These, in turn,

---

[1] As, for example, evidenced by the launch of several new journals in this area, including a journal entitled *Flavour*, along with special issues and supplements appearing in many of the leading science journals, involving *Nature* (in 2012; see http://www.nature.com/nature/journal/v486/n7403_supp/index.html#out) and *Current Biology* (2013).

determine how we construct conceptual frameworks that help us to understand those phenomena.

As an illustration of this point, consider the term 'sense modality' as it is ordinarily used to speak about the five senses, and as it is used in the psychology and
neuroscience literature to talk about physiological mechanisms. Simply because
the same words are used in common sense and sensory science it doesn't follow
that they necessarily mean the same thing in both usages. It certainly doesn't follow from the fact that science distinguishes more than five senses that common
sense is mistaken (a point that has been cogently made by Nudds, 2011): that will
depend on how the common sense and scientific understandings of the notion of
sense relate to one another.

In the last few years a revival of interest has occurred in how exactly we should
distinguish between sensory modalities, and this question stands at the core of
several theoretical research areas (see Macpherson, 2011, for a recent volume
gathering both contemporary and classic articles on the topic). It is therefore all
the more critical in the growing field of research on flavour perception, where
definitions often vary across the different disciplines, to answer the question of
what exactly distinguishes taste from flavour since this has broader implications
for the debate concerning how we should distinguish between sense modalities.
It is not just a matter of what distinctions we can make between different perceptual experiences, but rather, a question of which distinctions matter in terms
of advancing our knowledge and understanding of the phenomena in question
(McBurney, 1986).

Not taking into account the question of definitions runs a risk of serious confusion. As an example, take the following quote from the introduction to philosopher Carolyn Korsmeyer's (2005, pp. 3–5) edited volume *The Taste-Culture
Reader: Experiencing Food and Drink*. There she states:

> Except where otherwise specified, the word "taste" in this book serves as a
> shorthand for the experience of flavour in all its dimensions, including those
> supplied by the other senses.

So far, so good. But then, shortly thereafter, she says:

> Not all flavours can be classified according to the four "basic" types, and
> some of the most sought-after tastes are spices. . .

Presumably the four 'basic flavour types' that Korsmeyer (2005) is referring to here
are actually the four basic tastes: bitter, salt, sweet, and sour (see a discussion of
additional basic tastes such as umami and metallic later in the chapter). It is easy
to see, then, how a reader might quickly become confused.

Similar problems also arise when it comes to our understanding and our use
of the term 'flavour'. In its everyday use, as well as when following the ISO definition, it is simply meant to pick out the combination of taste, smell, and trigeminal

irritation (should it occur). However, other influential researchers in the field use the term to talk about a separate psychological construct (e.g., see Prescott, 1999; see also Abdi, 2002; Petit et al., 2007; Stillman, 2002). For instance, according to John Prescott (1999, p. 350), flavour is a *functionally* distinct sense, although it is *cognitively* constructed from the integration of two sensory systems that are physiologically distinct: olfaction and gustation.

Here it is perhaps also important to bear in mind that others working in the food industry often refer to the odour/aroma of orange, say, as a flavour; they do so on the understanding that the majority, some say as much as 80%, of what we think of as flavour comes from the nose (e.g., Martin, 2004; Murphy et al., 1977; Rosenblum, 2010; Shankar et al., 2010).

Given these difficulties in disentangling what belongs to taste and what belongs to flavour, it is easy to see how a naive reader can become confused. Correspondingly, in the academic field, both food critics (e.g., Davidson, 1988, p. 13) and food scientists (e.g., McBurney, 1986, p. 123) have been known to express their frustration at their inability to define the relevant terms meaningfully when it comes to talking about the chemical senses and flavour.[2]

> We should resist the categorizing imperative. The senses did not evolve to satisfy our desire for tidiness. (McBurney, 1986, p. 123)

> If tastes are married to aromas, as they are to produce flavours, the whole problem of the description becomes even more difficult. And here I stop. (Davidson, 1988, p. 13)

The problem of providing a characterisation of taste and flavour goes far beyond merely idle terminology: whether one considers sweetness, for example, to be a taste or a flavour attribute, hinges fundamentally on what one thinks a taste or a flavour actually is. If human flavour perception is thought of as cutting across receptor types and defined as what provides basic information about the nutritional qualities of the foods and beverages we eat and drink (Auvray & Spence, 2008), then sweetness should certainly be considered a flavour. On the other hand, if one considers that the senses should be characterised by a strict correspondence to receptor types, the term 'sweetness' should only ever be correctly used to describe a taste; that is, a gustatory quality. This way of capturing the difference between sensory systems and human perception is in line with Matthen's means of distinguishing between sensory modalities and perceptual modalities (see Matthen forthcoming). Put in his terms, a basic taste such as sweetness is a taste as detected by a sensory modality but it is a flavour as detected by a perceptual modality.

---

[2] At a conference of leading food scientists held at the Ingestive Behavior Research Centre in Purdue, Indiana, in 2011, no consensus could be reached amongst the many international delegates present with respect to the question of how exactly to define flavour—or rather which senses contribute to our flavour experiences.

In addition, we argue that people are simply not able to isolate in experience the unique consequence of the stimulation of their gustatory receptors. And given that we deploy terms for tastes, such as 'sweetness', on the basis of our experience, we cannot be talking about tastes proper in this sense, by our (folk) use of the term 'sweetness'. Furthermore, given that the terms 'taste' and 'flavour' are often interchangeable in their everyday usage (see Rozin, 1982), our aim in this article is to argue that it does not make sense to treat taste attributes, such as, for example, sweetness, as belonging to a distinct category from flavour attributes, such as, for example, fruitiness or meatiness, which we recognise in our experience of eating and drinking.

2.2. BASIC CHARACTERISATIONS: TASTES, ODOURS, TRIGEMINAL SENSATIONS, AND FLAVOURS

With respect to scientific terminology, the basic *tastes* that we can detect are widely agreed to consist of bitter, sour, sweet, salty, and umami (e.g., Bartoshuk, 1978; Lawless, 2001; Schiffman, 2000; see Kawamura & Kare, 1987, on umami). The one other basic taste that has, on occasion, been added to this list is metallic (e.g., as in the taste of blood, and as an undesirable aftereffect of taking certain pharmaceutical drugs; see Lawless et al., 2005; Lindemann, 1996; Schiffman, 2000; though see Stevens et al., 2006).[3] However, it is important to bear in mind that there is still some debate here as to whether something's tasting metallic should count as a taste, physiologically speaking, since it sometimes appears to be modulated by the stimulation of the olfactory receptors in the nasal mucosa; that is, the experience can differ as a function of whether a participant pinches his or her nose (e.g., see Hettinger et al., 1990), and this is not usually thought to be the case for tastants. Hence, one might think, this qualifies it as a flavour rather than a taste (see Lawless et al., 2004; though see further discussion of this point later in the chapter).

It actually turns out to be very difficult to find a pure tastant (that is, one that can only be detected by gustatory receptors, and whose perception is not influenced by the stimulation of the olfactory receptors). As Mojet et al. (2005, p. 9) put it: 'We suggest that most tastants can be smelled and that this smell contributes to taste intensity ratings.' If we take such evidence seriously, and there seems to be no reason we should not, then the fact that a nasal contribution is involved in the experience of certain metallic-tasting compounds would not in and of itself provide a strong argument against metallic being a basic taste after all. Rather, we can turn this argument on its head and use it to argue that—contrary to popular

---

[3] Here we do not cover the topic of electrical tastes, that is, taste experiences elicited by the electrical stimulation of the tongue (see Bujas, 1971; Bujas et al., 1974; Keeley, 2002). Notice that electrical stimulation of the tongue can also give rise to the experience of metallic tastes (Cardello, 1981; Lawless et al., 2005).

scientific belief—most tastants actually give rise to flavour experiences (albeit flavours with only a very weak olfactory contribution).

Odour perception is particularly interesting given its dual status. The olfactory receptors located in the olfactory epithelium can be stimulated either via the nose when sniffing (this is known as orthonasal olfaction), or via the mouth, during eating and drinking, as volatile chemicals rise up through the nasopharynx (this is known as retronasal olfaction).[4] Thus, as Rozin (1982) noted some years back, olfaction appears to constitute a 'dual modality'. First, it provides information about objects in the environment: dangers such as predators and fire, food sources (Stevenson, 2009), and potentially appropriate mates (e.g., Rikowski & Grammer, 1999; Wedekind et al., 1995). Second, the (retronasal) olfactory system also provides information regarding something that an organism is soon to ingest and which is currently being masticated (i.e., chewed) in the oral cavity (note here that some food odours are only released following mastication, as in the case of cashew nuts; see Crocker, 1950). In people's everyday usage of the term, then, 'to smell' seems to mean detecting a substance whose source is localised outside the body (i.e., ordinary uses would appear to refer selectively to orthonasal olfaction or 'sniffing').

The trigeminal system provides information (conveyed by the fifth cranial nerve; Abdi, 2002; Lundström et al., 2011) concerning chemical irritation and nociception. In parallel with their anatomical separation from the taste nerves in the oral cavity, the trigeminal receptors in the nose (not to mention those found in the mouth, eyes, and, in fact, over the whole of the rest of the body surface; Lawless, 2001) are distinct and separate from the olfactory receptors (Lawless, 1989, p. 57). The influence of trigeminal inputs on flavour perception has, for many years, been underestimated—so much so that some researchers have described it as 'the forgotten flavour sense' (see Lawless, 1989). That said, it is now widely acknowledged that the trigeminal system often contributes to flavour perception (e.g., see Abdi, 2002; Green, 1996, 2004; Viana, 2011). Activation of the trigeminal system occurs, for example, when we eat hot chillies or mustard. It is what gives rise to a feeling of heat in the mouth and, on occasion, a pinching, painful sensation at the bridge of the nose (Lawless et al., 1985). The trigeminal system is also responsible for the pungency of certain foods (see Govindarajan, 1979; Green, 1996, 2004) while also mediating the cool sensation we experience when eating peppermint (Crocker, 1950; Nagata et al., 2005).

Capsaicin and piperine are amongst the purest of trigeminal stimulants: capsaicin gives rise to chemical heat (a warm or burning type of irritation) with little or no apparent taste, smell, or additional flavour elements present (Lawless, 1984). By contrast, many spices trigger a variety of irritative flavour experiences (Lawless, 2001, p. 627). It turns out that numerous ingredients are capable of activating

---

[4] Avery Gilbert (2008, p. 100) has suggested that we may be the only creatures to have two senses of smell. However, recent research suggests that rats have retronasal olfaction.

the trigeminal system: *The Handbook of Flavor Ingredients* lists about two dozen common spices and more than 40 flavour compounds that have irritant and/or astringent properties (see also Viana, 2011). Carbon dioxide is another of the 'pure' trigeminal stimulants, one that gives rise to an odourless sensation in the nose (Lundström et al., 2011; Wajid & Halpern, 2012). It is also what gives rise to the experience of carbonation (i.e., of fizziness) when one drinks sparkling water or champagne (see Chandrashekar et al., 2009; Dessirier et al., 2000).[5]

Oral-somatosensory cues also provide an important contribution to our experience of food and drink. The somatosensory system provides information about the texture and consistency of a food. The stimulation of the somatosensory receptors on the tongue appears to be crucial when it comes to complex food experiences such as the perception of creaminess/fattiness (Bult et al., 2007; though see also Chale-Rush et al., 2007; Mattes, 2009; Sundqvist et al., 2006 Wajid & Halpern, 2012). Our perception of the chewiness of a food results from the activation of the mechanoreceptors in the jaw (e.g., Delwiche, 2004; Lundström et al., 2011). Of course, it is the *active* mastication (not to mention the formation of the rounded food mass known as the bolus that occurs during swallowing) rather than merely the *passive* stimulation of the oral-somatosensory receptors that is key to delivering such experiences (see also Shepherd, 2012, chapter 17). This latter observation highlights the importance of proprioceptive/kinaesthetic inputs to our experience of foods. It is necessary for, but not a constitutive part of, flavour.

Thermal temperature cues constitute another important influence on our taste and flavour perception. As Crocker (1950, p. 7) put it more than sixty years ago: 'Hot beverages and soups depend upon temperature as an important part of their flavour.' Temperature and texture cues modulate, or else should be thought of as a part of, the multisensory perception of flavour. So, for example, when liquids (such as coffee) are cooled, their perceived bitterness is often accentuated. Similarly, chilling a wine enhances our perception of both its acidity and bitterness. Perceived sweetness, meanwhile, typically declines as the temperature at which a food or beverage is served falls. Thus, temperature is one of the attributes of a food or beverage that can influence not only our perception of complex flavours but also our perception of what are commonly considered the basic tastes. In recent years, technological developments have allowed researchers to demonstrate that the effects of temperature and texture change on flavour perception cannot simply be attributed to any physical change in the release of volatile compounds from the surface of the food or beverage (e.g., see Bult et al., 2007).

Thermal tastes refer to the 'illusory' tastes that many people experience when a tasteless thermal probe is placed on their tongue. These tastes are illusory in the sense that the entire experience derives from the temperature cue, whereas in

---

[5] Chandrashekar et al. (2009) actually title their paper "The Taste of Carbonation", creating yet another source of confusion in attempts to try to define, not to mention distinguish between, the sensory modalities involved in flavour perception.

the cases described previously, changes in the temperature of a foodstuff merely modulated the experience of a tastant that was already perceptible. It has been reported that roughly one-third to one-half of the population experiences such a 'thermal-taste' illusion (see Cruz & Green, 2000; Green & George, 2004). Barry Green and his colleagues found that by raising or lowering the temperature at various points on people's tongues they were able to elicit sensations of sweet, sour, salty, and bitter. Intriguingly, those individuals who experience the thermal-taste illusion also tend to experience other 'tastes', that is, flavours, as being more intense as well (Bajec & Pickering, 2008). As yet, little is known, about how thermal stimulation activates taste receptors. It may be akin to the electrical stimulation of the taste buds.

Flavour perception is the next issue for discussion. Where does it fit in? First, notice that when people describe the *flavour* of a foodstuff, they *often* use descriptors such as fruity, meaty, spicy, musty, stale, creamy, and so on. Are flavour descriptors used to cover everything else that we want to say about foods and beverages over and above the so-called basic tastes, and their respective combinations (Rozin, 1982)? Note first that it is rare to have such experiences in the absence of any contribution whatsoever from oral-somatosensation (Green, 2002), not to mention the proprioception/kinesthesis that comes with crunching, chewing, and oral-mastication (Shepherd, 2012, chapter 17). In this sense, flavour would normally involve the integration of more-or-less simultaneous inputs from gustation, retronasal olfaction, oral-somatosensation, and proprioception/kinesthesis (Lundström et al., 2011). While opinions vary, trigeminal sensations are readily incorporated into flavour perception as we see from the everyday use of food descriptors such as 'spicy', 'pungent', 'hot', and 'fizzy'.

However, we have argued earlier in this chapter that it seems reasonable to include 'sweet' among the flavour descriptors even though it is considered by some to be a descriptor for tastes proper. Perhaps the ordinary (and confusing) use of the word 'taste' has application here, but notice that when people talk about the 'taste of a banana' they are not really talking about a basic taste or even about a combination of basic tastes. Rather they are talking about the banana's flavour as experienced by means of the *act* of tasting (Halpern, 1983; Piggott, 1990). Note here that blocking the nose removes the fruit character of banana from experience (Finck, 1886; Shepherd, 2012, pp. 28–30; see also Smith, 2012).[6] As is the case with many other experiences in flavour, we do not experience taste alone: it is accompanied by odours, somatosensations, and/or trigeminal sensations. In other words, flavour experiences are always defined in a multisensory space. Although the contribution of one sensory modality can be missing, there is always more than a single sensory modality (or dimension of experience) involved.

---

[6] If this is done while eating, and there is still sweetness present in the mouth, then the likelihood is that the experience of flavour may persist (see Spence, 2012). Blocking the nose before eating/tasting commences, however, will prevent the establishment of any fruit character whatsoever.

2.3. CONFUSIONS ASSOCIATED WITH THE TERMS 'TASTE', 'TASTING', 'ODOUR', AND 'FLAVOUR'

The scientific characterisation of the terms taste, tasting, odour, and flavour given previously seem to be reasonably clear, and so one might be led to believe that confusions only occur in everyday language:

> In informal conversation, the sensory outcomes of eating or drinking are usually labelled 'taste'. Scientifically, however, taste is strictly the sensation experienced by means of the taste buds, and comprises but a part of what is more correctly labelled 'flavour'. (Stillman, 2002, p. 1491)

However, there are many confusions associated with these terms both in everyday language and in the setting of the laboratory/journal. Next we review some of the typical confusions in order to subsequently discuss their possible underlying causes.

In a study by Paul Rozin (1982), the author highlighted the extent to which taste and flavour are associated linguistically. He gave questionnaires to native English speakers. They had to judge whether 'taste' or 'flavour' was the most appropriate term to use in a series of 16 sentences given with a blank space to replace the relevant term. When items involved the four basic tastes (note that umami was not used in this study), taste was judged the most appropriate term; for 12 others involving olfactory components (e.g., banana), the two terms (taste and flavour) were used seemingly interchangeably.

In everyday language, people do not appear to make any principled distinction between the sweetness of a substance (according to the previous quote, a taste) and its fruitiness (according to the quote, a flavour), at least when consuming a sweet-tasting fruit. Both sweetness and fruitiness, we would like to argue here, are evaluated in similar ways by the 'act of tasting' (see Auvray & Spence, 2008; Gibson, 1966; Halpern, 1983; McBurney, 1986; Smith 2007) and count as flavours—albeit distinct ones. Most people have no idea of the physiological origins of the sensations they have when tasting. A fortiori, they have no idea that sweetness actually happens to be different from fruitiness in that the former results principally—though not exclusively, as has now been shown—from the stimulation of gustatory receptors, located on the tongue, among many other places,[7] while fruitiness is an attribute that requires the stimulation of both the nose (olfactory receptors) and mouth (gustatory receptors). They are both experienced as a result of acts of tasting and can thus be treated as belonging to the same category: that of flavours, which people often call 'tastes'.

---

[7] Note that taste receptors are also found in the nose, the stomach, the intestines, and in the pancreas where they influence appetite and help to regulate the release of insulin. They are also found in the airways and even in sperm (Trivedi, 2012).

People's failure to distinguish between what we think of here as two flavour attributes can certainly cause confusion in laboratory settings, if what is being investigated is taste proper. For instance, one cannot always be sure that what participants are reporting on (or are asked to rate) in psychophysical studies of flavour perception is only the sweetness of a fruity beverage, treated as purely the upshot of gustatory stimulation. When it has been claimed that the odours of a flavour influence what participants report about taste (Stevenson & Boakes, 2004)[8] this would constitute a confusion, according to us, between mere tastes which they don't experience and the odour enhanced flavour of sweetness, which they do.

Notice that what others would count exclusively as a taste term is often used for other things. Westerners, for example, are more than happy to describe odours as sweet, when smelling vanilla, caramel, or strawberry, say (Spence, 2008; Stevenson, 2012a; Stevenson & Boakes, 2004; see also Blank & Mattes, 1990). Here it is perhaps worth looking in rather more detail at what happens, for example, when people who smell ripe strawberries describe them as smelling sweet. In such situations, it would appear that people are applying the term 'sweet', a term they normally apply to what they are tasting, to something they are merely smelling. In addition, it may seem as though the transfer of a word for a taste onto a smell is due to a direct association between the taste and the smell. However, it is much more likely that the association is driven by the closeness of the aroma of ripe strawberries, sensed orthonasally, to the odour of ripe strawberries processed retronasally, and the fact that the latter is inseparably paired in our experience with the tastant sweet. It's that pairing that provides us with our experience of the flavour of strawberry. So the association is not between a taste and an orthonasal smell but between a flavour (a taste-smell interaction) and a orthonasal smell, mediated by the retronasal component of ripe strawberry flavour and the way that olfactory component is inextricably bound up with sweetness in our experience.

The transfer of the attribute sweet from what we taste to what we smell is easier to understand when we remember that much of what we taste is due to smell. It's just that the retronasal olfactory component of tasting something sweet, like ripe strawberries, goes missing in our experience. The attribute 'sweet' does not itself describe an aroma; rather, it is associated with aromas, like vanilla, that are normally paired with sweetness (at least for Westerners) in certain flavour compounds that we experience. There are several things to note here. First, we don't notice that we are applying a flavour attribute we taste to something we smell; at the outset, sweetness just seems to be an attribute of particular odours. Second,

---

[8] It should be mentioned that the phenomenon of 'halo dumping' makes this all the more difficult (Abdi, 2002; Clark & Lawless, 1994; Kappes et al., 2006): "Halo dumping occurs when subjects are provided with only one intensity scale (sweetness) to rate a mixture of two sensations (sugar and strawberry). Forced to use one scale for two sensations, the subjects "dump" the second sensation onto the only available scale. This dumping effect disappears as soon as subjects are provided with a scale for each sensation" (Abdi, 2002, p. 448).

when it is pointed out to us that sweet is something we taste, not something that we smell, we most likely think that we are associating the sweet taste of the strawberry directly with how it smells (orthonasally). Though, in fact, the association of sweetness with what we smell goes via the former's inseparability from retronasally detected strawberry odour and its closeness to what we recognisably smell as the aroma of strawberries.

The connection that people make between tastes and flavours is also illustrated in another way. When asked, many people will tell you that taste is the sense that gives rise to the perception of flavour (Nudds, 2004). People typically report that they have lost their sense of taste when they are suffering from a heavy cold or have otherwise lost their ability to smell. All they have actually lost (temporarily in the case of a cold) is their sense of smell. More generally, very often we think we're experiencing tastes when, in fact, we are using more than just the sense of taste in order to do so. This is another way in which taste and flavour are confused.

According to a popular way of seeing things, whenever people rate the *sweetness* of a food or beverage, what they are *trying* to do is refer to its *taste*—although according to the argument outlined here they are normally actually referring to its flavour. By contrast, whenever a participant refers to the fruitiness of a drink, the spiciness or pungency of a food (Viana, 2011), or the mustiness of a wine, they must either be referring to its *flavour*, or perhaps to its *aroma* (detected by orthonasal olfaction, as with sniffing).[9] One reason for the dual possibility in the latter case is that the vast majority of what we think of as the components of flavour actually result from the retronasal stimulation of the olfactory receptors in the nose and very (or relatively) little from the stimulation of the gustatory receptors on the tongue (e.g., Crocker, 1950; Martin, 2004; Murphy et al., 1977; Shepherd, 2012). Since most flavour descriptors can also be used as odour descriptors (see Figure 10.1), if a person merely sniffs a wine, say, it is clear that her description can only be of the odour (i.e., of the volatile compounds arising from the wine and detected via orthonasal olfaction) rather than of the flavour (since she hasn't tasted anything yet). But note here that what that person might be responding to is actually her expectancy of the wine's likely flavour given a particular orthonasal odour profile (see Stevenson, 2009) as in the case of a 'sweet-smelling' wine. By contrast, if someone actually tastes a wine and then says 'it's fruity', one might be tempted to think that what she is referring to is the flavour, drawing on the contribution from both aromas and tastes.

---

[9] Remember here also that many of those working in the flavour industry often use the term 'flavour' to describe orthonasal olfaction/aroma (see Shankar et al., 2010). We have also seen that people regularly transfer a term that they use for a taste, like 'sweet', to odours. This is an association of a smell with what can normally be tasted. Alternatively, however, it is because 'sweet' is a flavour term and so equally applicable to a flavour or an aroma (the argument forwarded here).

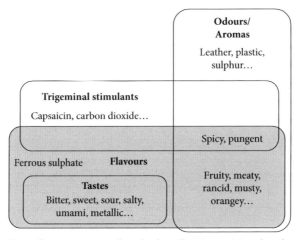

FIGURE 10.1. *Taste, flavour, trigeminal, and odour descriptors. Note that the only flavour that cannot also be smelled orthonasally is, apparently, ferrous sulphate (see Lawless et al., 2004).*

3. Physiological and Psychological Reasons for the Confusion

Apart from linguistic reasons, it is important to note that there are also other reasons that might help to explain why people confuse taste and flavour:

> To understand flavour completely, we must consider not only its chemistry and physics but also the physiology and psychology of its perception and our reactions to it. (Crocker, 1950, p. 7)

After emphasising the importance of smell/taste confusions both for clinical cases and for psychophysical research, and the frequent confusions between these latter two and trigeminal sensations, we will highlight the crucial role that *oral referral* and *attention* both play in terms of driving the confusion between the different components of flavour.

3.1. CONFUSING TASTES, FLAVOURS, AND TRIGEMINAL SENSATIONS

As already noted, the loss of smell is often identified by those affected as a loss of taste (Bull, 1965). For instance, blocking the nose (as when one has a heavy cold) dramatically reduces what one believes one can taste. In fact, however, we can all still taste salt, sweet, sour, bitter, umami, and presumably also metallic. This confusion has been taken to illustrate the fact that people simply do not recognise the crucial contribution that retronasal olfaction makes to what they think they are merely tasting. However, food appears to 'lose its taste' when one's nose is blocked, and this can (and frequently has) been taken to show that the sense of smell contributes to the perception of flavour in food and drink (e.g., Rozin, 1982). Confusions not only occur between tastes and flavours but also between tastes, flavours, and trigeminal sensations. Take, for example, the following:

> the sensory reaction to pepper compounds is not really a thermal sensation, even though we use the term "heat." It is more accurately classified as a chemically induced irritation that is different from both the sense of taste and the sense of touch. To physiologists, taste is defined as sensations derived from the taste buds on the tongue and soft palate which mediate our experiences of sweet, sour, salty, and bitter. Pepper heat is a chemical sensation from stimulation of the nerve endings of the trigeminal nerve, which is distinct from the nerves that make contact with taste buds and are involved in taste sensations. Although the trigeminal nerve is also responsible for touch, heat, cold, and pain sensations in the mouth, the pepper sensations cannot be classified as touch, either, since they involve no physical deformation of touch receptors. (Lawless, 1989, p. 57)

For the next example, let us return to the case of so-called *metallic tastes*. These can be elicited either chemically, when the taste buds on the tongue come into contact with solutions containing metal salts, or by direct stimulation by the metals themselves (Laughlin et al., 2011; Piqueras-Fiszman et al., 2012). Furthermore, it has also been reported that applying an electric current to the tongue can give rise to metallic tastes as well (just try sticking a 9-volt battery on your tongue). Here it can be seen how terms for tastes may actually refer to trigeminally, chemically, or even electrically induced sensations. However, it turns out that what people mostly refer to as a metallic 'taste' is often actually a metallic flavour (according to the traditional definition that flavours are only experienced when a perceiver's gustatory and olfactory receptors are stimulated at more or less the same time), since nasal occlusion tends to reduce the intensity of the percept for at least certain solutions such as, for example, in the case of ferrous sulphate ($FeSO_4$). In other words, what people refer to as a metallic taste sometimes involves a component of olfactory referral to the mouth (Murphy & Cain, 1980; Murphy et al., 1977).

However, the picture is even more complicated than this since the metallic taste elicited by copper metal, bimetallic stimuli (e.g., zinc-copper, lead-silver) or small batteries is apparently unaffected by nasal occlusion (see Lawless et al., 2005). The example of so-called metallic *tastes*, then, nicely illustrates how people's everyday experience does not allow them to discriminate between tastes and flavours, and as a result these are all called experiences of tastes; whereas some experiences of metallic are really experiences of metallic tastes, others are experiences of metallic flavours (according to the traditional view of flavours). This problem would disappear according to our way of resolving the confusions between tastes and flavours, since what surfaces in experience is a metallic flavour—even though different possibilities involving different compounds (stimulating one or more different kinds of receptors)—account for the way such experiences arise.

One of the only ways to distinguish between tastes and flavours might be to block a participant's nose to determine what remains in experience (see also Burdach et al., 1984; Nagata et al., 2005; Stevenson & Halpern, 2009). Such a procedure would likely help an individual who wants to distinguish between the various other components contributing to his or her experience in an act of tasting. It would not, however, be guaranteed to isolate tastes since, with the nose blocked, one may be experiencing a taste, a trigeminal, or thermal (or possibly even an electrical) sensation (see Wajid & Halpern, 2012). Note here that the test of a tastant as something that doesn't change when the nose is blocked or unblocked would show that 'sweetness', 'sourness', and others were not necessarily tastants. As already mentioned, Mojet et al. (2005) have shown that there is often a change in our perception of intensity of our experience of sweet, salty, sour, and bitter substances when olfaction is involved. Nagata et al. (2005, p. 193) have captured the very same problem that is often faced by participants when presented with stimuli at close to threshold. To them, in the case of absolute detection, that is, when there is a lack of qualitative information, it becomes very difficult to know which sense modality is responsible for the detection of the stimulus or object, especially when qualitative information is lacking, as it often is at the absolute detection threshold. The fact that tastants are not experienced alone has been nicely expressed by the eminent food scientist, Harry Lawless, in a quote that we fully endorse:

> Almost every chemical placed in the mouth has multiple sensory effects. The notion of a monogustatory tastant is illusory. (Lawless et al., 2005, p. 193)

These examples demonstrate that the experience of flavour is an intrinsically multisensory experience. Tastes are seldom if ever *experienced* on their own and their experience is modified by the presence of odours and trigeminal sensations.

3.2. ORAL REFERRAL

As Bartoshuk and Duffy (2005, p. 27) put it:

> 'Taste' is often used as a synonym for 'flavour'. This usage of 'taste' probably arose because the blend of true taste and retronasal olfaction is perceptually localised to the mouth via touch.

It is still a point of discussion as to quite how important (if at all) oral-somatosensation really is to the phenomenon of oral referral. Certain researchers currently working in the area believe that one also needs the presence of a tastant in the mouth for oral referral to take place (see Lim & Johnson, 2011, 2012). For example, Lim and Johnson (2012) have demonstrated that oral referral to the mouth is significantly stronger when the tastant is congruent with the olfactant. This perception of something as appearing to come from the mouth has been called the location illusion. This is where sensations occurring, or originating, in the nose are 'referred to' or experienced as if they were being transduced by the receptors in the mouth.

An example that should help to illuminate one of the principal reasons for this frequent confusion between the various components of flavour was documented some years ago by Murphy et al. (1977).

Murphy et al. (1977) demonstrated that when a tasteless aqueous olfactory stimulus was placed into a participant's mouth, he or she would usually label the resulting experience a taste, rather than a retronasal odour. The experience is also localised to the oral cavity, even though the sensory percept is itself principally mediated via the activation of the olfactory system. This example would certainly appear to suggest that the presence of a tastant isn't needed for oral referral to occur. However, before coming to any firm conclusion on this score it is worth seeing Stevenson's (2012) discussion on attention described later in this chapter (see also Murphy & Cain 1980; Rozin, 1982).

When speaking of what may be an illusion, it is important to pause for a moment to consider the cross-modal phenomenon of *sweetness enhancement*. This refers to the perceived increase of taste intensities when particular odours are added to sucrose solutions (e.g., see Stevenson & Boakes, 2004). For example, when a vanilla odorant (that does not give rise to any taste sensation) is added to a sucrose solution, the resulting mixture is rated as tasting sweeter than the pure sucrose solution when presented by itself in solution (see Stevenson et al., 1998). By contrast, adding a strawberry odour suppresses the sourness of solutions containing citric acid (see Stevenson et al., 1999), thus showing that odour-induced tastes can be functionally equivalent to sweetness. Note here also that sweetness isn't the only taste/flavour attribute that can be enhanced by means of the delivery of an associated olfactory stimulus. There is now also good evidence in support of the existence of saltiness, bitterness, and sourness enhancement by means of olfactory stimulation (e.g., see Lawrence et al., 2009; Seo et al., 2013; Stevenson et al., 1995; Yeomans et al., 2006). However, the discussion that follows focuses on the case of sweetness enhancement as that has been studied most extensively to date.

The next question that one can ask here is whether the phenomenon of sweetness enhancement is cognitively penetrable; that is, can the effect be cancelled as soon as we believe or know that it is (orthonasal) smell that is influencing our perception of sweetness? Or is it a robust, belief-independent effect in experience—like, for instance, the Muller-Lyer illusion? Can the sweetness enhancement effect be modified as a function of the particular tasting strategy that is adopted by participants during their exposure to odour-taste mixtures (for instance, by an analytic versus synthetic approach to the perception of flavor; see Bingham et al., 1990; Prescott et al., 2004)? If this is the case, then there should be an effect of prior training on such a phenomenon. However, Stevenson (2001) reported that training individuals to identify the separate components of an odour-taste mixture actually had no effect on the sweetness enhancement effects of suprathreshold odorants on sweetness ratings, or on their ability to identify the component parts of the odour-taste mixture. Indeed, it was findings such as these that led Stevenson and Tomiczeck (2007) to suggest that the failure to affect odour-taste by attentional manipulations requires a biological and not a psychological explanation:

> It is not that participants normally do not attend to flavors but rather that their capacity to do so is limited by biological constraints. These biological constraints are apparent when participants are expressly asked to discriminate the components of flavors (odors and tastes) or of taste mixtures alone or of odor mixtures alone. In all of these cases, participants—even with substantial training—are typically unable to do so. (Stevenson & Tomiczeck, 2007, p. 302)

Of course, olfactory-gustatory interactions such as the sweetness enhancement effect can occur when either one or both of the component stimuli are presented at a level that is individually subthreshold (see Dalton et al., 2000; Labbe et al., 2007; Shepherd, 2012, p. 122), and this is going to make it that much harder for an individual to unequivocally determine the correct physical source for a given flavour experience.

3.3. THE QUESTION OF ATTENTION

Finally, the question of attention and expertise proves crucial to understanding what exactly underlies most people's inability to discriminate the different components of flavour. Stevenson (2012a, b), for instance, has put forward an attentional account for why people do not recognise the olfactory component in flavour, and hence label as taste the perceptual experience of flavour. Here, though, one needs to be careful, since Stevenson's research is based primarily on the use of *orthonasally* presented odours, whereas what we are really interested in when it comes to the role of attention in the deconstruction of flavour is *retronasal* olfaction. Titchener (1909, p. 135) anticipated the link between attention and flavour when a little over a century ago he said:

> Think, for instance, of the flavour of a ripe peach. The ethereal odor may be ruled out by holding the nose. The taste components—sweet, bitter, sour— may be identified by special direction of the attention upon them. The touch components—the softness and stringiness of the pulp, the pucker feel of the sour—may be singled out in the same way. Nevertheless, all these factors blend together so intimately that it is hard to give up one's belief in a peculiar and unanalysable peach flavour. Indeed, some psychologists assert that this resultant flavour exists.

As we have just seen, however, there is evidence to suggest that people do not find it all that easy to direct their attention to the separable components of flavour even when directed to do so (Ashkenazi & Marks, 2004; Marks, 2002). Perhaps people do not recognise the olfactory component in flavour because with retronasal olfaction, different from orthonasal olfaction, they do not recognise that they can have voluntary control, as they do with sniffing (see Stevenson, 2009). The swallowing response pumps odours from the oral cavity via the nasopharynx, up into the olfactory epithelium. This can subsequently generate a flavour experience. Intriguingly, Ashkenazi and Marks (2004) reported that while participants could endogenously direct their attention to better detect a weak tastant (sucrose) when it was presented in isolation, they were unable to direct their attention to enhance the detection of vanillin (delivered in solution as a retronasal odorant), nor were they able to direct their attention to sucrose or vanillin when these were presented together (i.e., when presented as a traditional flavour stimulus).

The question of attention is closely linked to the question of expertise: if the confusion between smell and taste merely reflects a problem associated with the appropriate allocation of attention, then panellists trained to focus their attention on each component should be better able to report on only one of them. In other words, while the naïve participant might not make any meaningful distinction between taste and smell, perhaps the trained panellist can just report on the sweetness of a solution, or, having tasted it, report selectively on its retronasal odour (and not accidentally report on, or be influenced by, its flavour; see Bingham et al., 1990). But are they really able to do so?

According to Stevenson (2009, p. 155), there is indeed an expertise effect. In his book, *The Psychology of Flavour*, Stephenson suggests that in the case of retronasal odours, the identification of a particular element is much harder when other odours, tastes, and/or textures are present. That said, experts may be somewhat better at this than novices, at least for those odours that they happen to be familiar with. However, as we have just seen, being directed to attend to the olfactory element in a flavour does not appear to help naïve participants detect that element (Ashkenazi & Marks, 2004).

So, while the view that experts are better at distinguishing the retronasal component of a flavour from other components may be prevalent amongst some sensory scientists, it is important to note that people hardly ever report solely on the gustatory stimulation while at the same time successfully ignoring any contribution from olfaction. So it is not so clear that people, even experts, can selectively report on sweetness, say, and entirely ignore the contribution of olfactory cues (see Stevenson, 2001). For instance, in one descriptive analysis of the characteristics of a wide range of odours, 65% of assessors gave 'sweetness' as an appropriate descriptor for the odour of vanillin, while 33% described the odour of hexanoic acid as being sour (Dravnieks, 1985). 110 of 140 assessors reported strawberry odour as sweet and only 60 that it smelled of strawberries and 99 that it was fruitlike.

In addition, a number of studies have noted that expertise can certainly help at the conceptual level, but it does not necessarily help at the perceptual level (Stevenson, 2009). In other words, it can help an individual to categorise certain (familiar) flavour components more easily but it does not necessarily enhance perceptual capacities. This has been nicely illustrated in the case of wine expertise: while the perceptual abilities are similar for experts and regular wine drinkers, conceptual abilities are enhanced in experts and it has been argued that this allows them both to organise and use their perceptual knowledge more efficiently (e.g., Ballester et al., 2008; Berg et al., 1955; Hughson & Boakes, 2001; Parr et al., 2002; Solomon, 1997; see also Stevenson, 2009).

3.4. THE QUESTION OF SEPARABILITY

At this point, we can ask whether the various components of flavour are really separable? Brillat-Savarin (1835, p. 41) was 'tempted to believe that smell & taste are in fact but a single sense, whose laboratory is in the mouth & whose chimney is the nose'. Indeed, if experts and non-experts both have difficulties in distinguishing between taste and (retronasal) smell, the question arises of their very separability in experience. Thus, one additional reason for not wanting to make too sharp a distinction between taste and flavour is due to the fact that there isn't a simple one-to-one correspondence between taste perception and taste receptors, or even between smell perception and the stimulation of olfactory receptors in the nasal epithelium, given the possibility of pure trigeminal stimulants being experienced as if they were odours. Instead, it turns out that individual chemicals can activate multiple sensory systems, while multiple classes of sensory receptors can give rise to specific experiences (e.g., tastes/smells). So, for example, Nagata et al. (2005) have demonstrated that stimuli such as 1-menthol (the principal flavour in mint) actually stimulate several sensory systems simultaneously. In particular, 1-menthol leads to the stimulation of tactile (including thermal, in this case, cold), olfactory, gustatory (in this case, bitter), and nociceptive (i.e., pain), receptors (and hence sensations).

What is more, certain bitter-tasting compounds, including astringent compounds such as aluminium potassium sulphate (otherwise known as alum; Breslin et al., 1993), activate somatosensory neurons (e.g., see Finger et al., 2003; Liu & Simon, 1998). The polyphenols in wine skins and pips produce the tactile experience of astringency. These tannins, which one finds in strong tea, red wines, nuts, and some fruits, give rise to the experience of the 'drying or puckering' of the mouth by coagulating the proteins on the tongue, thus making the saliva less slippery. Some polyphenols are also thermal stimuli (Cruz & Green, 2000) and were thought of, in the past, as gustatory qualities (see Bartoshuk, 1978). Similarly, many olfactory stimuli give rise to irritation in the nose (Cometto-Muñiz & Cain, 1995), thus appearing to be trigeminal sensations. In fact, most olfactants will also stimulate the trigeminal system when presented at a suitably high concentration (Lundström et al., 2011; Wajid & Halpern, 2012). Some chemesthetic compounds also possess aroma and/or taste qualities (Green, 2004). Moreover, some taste compounds (such as salts and acids) elicit oral chemesthetic responses that give rise to oral irritation or pain (Dessirier et al., 2001). Thus, it can be seen once again that the origins of an individual's perceptual experience may be quite unknown, or hidden, to them. In fact, the idea that people do not know how their senses combine to give rise to flavour experiences crops up repeatedly in the literature (e.g., Lundström et al., 2011; Sundqvist et al., 2006). People nevertheless tend to classify their experiences as smells, tastes, or mouth-feels. But how do they arrive at these classifications when the experiences do not carry information about their origins? On what basis do people classify an experience as a taste, why does it seem so compelling to do so, and what does it mean to do so? Whatever the answer is here, a further question is how *ought* we to classify such experiences in order to gain insight theoretically into what is going on.

One might wonder whether there are flavours that are not also orthonasal odours. The only example that we have come across involves solutions of ferrous sulphate that Lawless et al. (2004) argue have little or no odour of their own out-side the mouth. As Lawless et al. (2005, p. 193) put it, 'they are not effective ortho-nasal stimuli at the concentrations which evoke a strong retronasal smell'. The idea here, then, is that odour is released in the mouth following some kind of catalytic reaction.

4. Taste and Flavour: Unravelling the Confusion

As we hope this review has made clear, many of the seeming taste sensations that we experience can be induced in a variety of different ways: for example, by ther-mally stimulating the tongue (Bajec & Pickering, 2008; Cruz & Green, 2000), by electrically stimulating the tongue (Bujas, 1971; Bujas et al., 1974; Cardello, 1981; Lawless et al., 2005), by the delivery of retronasal odours together with tasteless oral-somatosensory stimulation (Murphy et al., 1977), by the transduction of tas-tants in the mouth, and/or by some combination of all these (see Figure 10.2). All these routes to 'tastes' count as perfectly normal for many tasters. Should all of these experiences be called experiences of tastes, and should they be distinguished from flavours? They are not all taste (gustatory) sensations but they all get classi-fied by people as tastes in perception.

> Sensory pathways are known to overlap widely in the periphery, with so-called "gustatory nerves" responding to taste, tactile and thermal stimulation, all of which occur simultaneously during ingestion. (Delwiche, 2004, p. 142)

Of course, our perceptual experience of a taste doesn't necessarily have to illumi-nate the origins of the percept: it may be subliminal, as in certain cases of sweetness enhancement (Dalton et al., 2000; Stevenson & Boakes, 2004; see also Sundqvist et al., 2006). Even if the sensation, or percept, of a sweet taste is accompanied by, for instance, heat, it doesn't necessarily prevent us from having the feeling that we are tasting sweetness. Thus, if we want to restrict pure taste to what results solely from the firing of gustatory receptors on the tongue (not to mention in the rest of the oral cavity), then we cannot unequivocally relegate the perceived quality of sweetness to taste.

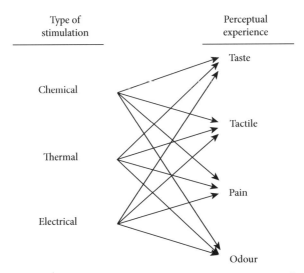

FIGURE 10.2. *Schematic illustration showing the many-to-many correspondence between sensory inputs and perceptual experiences (see also Iannilli et al., 2008; Nagata et al., 2005).*

Having an experience of tasting sweetness does not necessarily indicate that the taste receptors that code for sweetness are firing. It is better, then, to treat sweetness as a component of flavour, an ingredient in the perception of complex flavours or mixtures, however it may arise. If we can have experiences of sweetness when olfaction is knocked out and all other sensory effects, such as thermal sensations, are neutralised, this would be a case of pure taste, but it happens only under highly controlled laboratory conditions, or in cases of clinical pathology. Thus, we would argue that there is no bar to calling sweetness a flavour, and hence there are good reasons to reject the commonly held view in the food sciences that tastes and flavours can, and should, be distinguished in perceptual experience. Given the difficulties of experiencing a pure taste (under most conditions), we should not treat attributes, such as sweetness, as belonging exclusively to a category of taste attributes distinct from flavour descriptors, such as, for example, fruitiness, meatiness, or as in the above quote, 'oranginess' (at least when talking about our everyday experience).[10]

Does it really matter that 'pure' tastants are seldom experienced in isolation, and that even when they are experienced in clinical or laboratory conditions they are not recognised as such? It may well be reasonably common knowledge that acetic acid is a tastant that at suitably high concentrations can be smelled. However, the work of Mojet et al. (2005) suggests that basic tastants (such as sodium chloride,

---

[10] It should be noted that a radical implication of this claim would be to assume that, at least in the case of conscious perception, there is no such thing as a pure taste. Assuming such a position, however, does not require one to deny that correctly establishing the class of sensory receptors responsible for transducing specific stimuli isn't a worthwhile endeavour in its own right (Wajid & Halpern, 2012).

sucrose, caffeine, citric acid) when dissolved in a variety of substrates are rated as more intense (at least by younger participants) when their nose is open than when it is blocked with a nose clip. What is more, the presence of many of these tastants in a solution can also be detected at above-chance levels merely by orthonasal olfaction (sniffing). As Mojet et al. (2005, p. 20) put it:

> In conclusion, it can be said that, contrary to what is commonly assumed, all so-called 'pure tastants' used here—and in many experiments in the same or even less pure grades by others—are also olfactory stimuli.

It is worth dwelling here on the fact that responding to pure tastants in solution is a rather strange experience for most people. So, for example, in one recent experiment, the participants were unable to consciously name the tastants used as sweet, sour, bitter, and salty (Simner et al., 2010, p. 566). Instead, when descriptors were provided by the participants, they tended to be flavours and not tastes (e.g., orangey, lemony, metallic, and fishy, respectively).

Typically, people tend not to separate the unisensory elements that give rise to multisensory flavour percepts. The sweet taste of vanilla cream or almond paste leaves us assuming that the sweetness is in—or is part of—the vanilla or the almond. Undoubtedly, this is most likely a learned association (see Spence et al., 2010; Stevenson & Boakes, 2004; see also Shepherd, 2012, p. 122, 138)—hence, the culturally conditioned sweetness enhancement effect (see Spence, 2008) of some odours like vanilla for Westerners but not necessarily for native Japanese. In our everyday discourse, we do not separate out the taste of sweetness from the flavour we describe as fruity or having a vanilla 'taste' or from attributes such as stale or fatty, which, who knows, may have more to do with texture, touch, and/or gustation (Mattes, 2009; Mela, 1988; though see also Sundqvist et al., 2006).

A lot has been said about the nature of tastes, physiologically speaking, and the nature of the experiences that we take to be tastes. But where does that leave flavours and flavour perception? Our suggestion is that what we experience by acts of tasting are flavours. These are often labelled 'tastes' in everyday language, because people assume that tastes are what we experience through acts of tasting. There are far more flavour terms than proper taste terms and the category that people think of as tastes tend to extend to incorporate all the terms that are properly flavour terms. So the confusion of taste and flavour terms is somewhat understandable. However, it is to go further still to think that the experiences of the 'tastes' or flavours we enjoy in an act of tasting are generated by the single physiological sense of taste. Acts of tasting, unless specially contrived, or as the result of some clinical condition or other, *always* involve far more senses than merely gustation, as we have repeatedly seen. Thus, the phenomenology involved in eating and drinking is not that of separate sensations but a complex compound experience. Perceiving a sweet flavour is far easier, and more common, than perceiving the proper taste of sweetness (again as we have seen). Consequently, we would argue that sweetness should count among the flavour terms just as much as the other flavour attributes, such as fruity, and meaty, their being just as readily experienced (see Figure 10.1).

However, we are left with the following conundrum of flavour perception and of multisensory perception more generally. Is the single unified experience of a flavour—as we are told—the joint result of sensory information from taste, touch, and smell? In addition, we are told that this case illustrates that many of the experiences we think of as unimodal are, in fact, the product of multisensory integration; if so, how unimodal are the components we point to? Are the experiences of taste, touch, and smell that contribute to our experience of flavour themselves the result of inputs from more than one sensory modality? If so, we face a foundational problem. What are the building blocks that feature in multisensory perception and of what are they composed? If they are sensory modalities that require no input and no crossmodal influence from other modalities they may be very remote from conscious perceptual experience and so not the sorts of things that can be thought of as the senses we rely on in perceptual experience. On the other hand, our ordinary way of thinking about the senses has been shown to be at best confused and at worst inadequate when it comes to characterising experiences such as those that result from acts of tasting. Answering these questions is a task still to be completed and it is also crucial to many current research programs. Nevertheless, the right way to think about flavours and flavour perception will most likely benefit from avoiding unnecessary confusions between tastes and flavours.

References

Abdi, H. (2002). What can cognitive psychology and sensory evaluation learn from each other? *Food Quality and Preference*, **13**, 445–451.

Angier, N. (2009). When 'What animals do' doesn't seem to cover it. *New York Times*, July 21, D1. Downloaded from http://www.nytimes.com/2009/07/21/science/21angier.html?_r=1&ref=natalieangier.

Ashkenazi, A., & Marks, L. E. (2004). Effect of endogenous attention on detection of weak gustatory and olfactory flavors. *Perception & Psychophysics*, **66**, 596–608.

Auvray, M., & Spence, C. (2008). The multisensory perception of flavor. *Consciousness and Cognition*, **17**, 1016–1031.

Bajec, M. R., & Pickering, G. J. (2008). Thermal taste, PROP responsiveness, and perception of oral sensations. *Physiology & Behavior*, **95**, 581–590.

Ballester, J., Patris, B., Symoneaux, R., & Valentin, D. (2008). Conceptual vs. perceptual wine spaces: Does expertise matter? *Food Quality and Preference*, **19**, 267–276.

Bartoshuk, L. M. (1978). History of taste research. In E. C. Carterette & M. P. Friedman (Eds.), *Handbook of perception. IVA, tasting and smelling* (pp. 2–18). New York: Academic Press.

Bartoshuk, L. M., & Duffy, V. B. (2005). Chemical senses: Taste and smell. In C. Korsmeyer (Ed.), *The taste culture reader: Experiencing food and drink* (pp. 25–33). Oxford: Berg.

Berg, H. W., Filipello, F., Hinreiner, E., & Webb, A. D. (1955). Evaluation of thresholds and minimum difference concentrations for various constituents of wines. *Food Technology*, **9**, 23–26.

Bingham, A. F., Birch, G. G., de Graaf, C., Behan, J. M., & Perring, K. D. (1990). Sensory studies with sucrose-maltol mixtures. *Chemical Senses*, **15**, 447–456.

Blank, D. M., & Mattes, R. D. (1990). Sugar and spice: Similarities and sensory attributes. *Nursing Research*, **39**, 290–293.

Breslin, P. A. S., Gilmore, M. M., Beauchamp, G. K., & Green, B. G. (1993). Psychophysical evidence that oral astringency is a tactile sensation. *Chemical Senses*, **18**, 405–417.

Brillat-Savarin, J. A. (1835). *Physiologie du goût [The philosopher in the kitchen / The physiology of taste]*. J. P. Meline: Bruxelles. Translated by A. Lalauze (1884), *A handbook of gastronomy*. Nimmo & Bain: London.

Bujas, Z. (1971). Electrical taste. In L. Beidler (Ed.), *Handbook of sensory physiology. Vol. 4. Chemical senses. Part 2: Taste* (pp. 180–199). Berlin: Springer-Verlag.

Bujas, Z., Szabo, S., Kovacic, M., & Rohacek, A. (1974). Adaptation effects on evoked electrical taste. *Perception & Psychophysics*, **15**, 210–214.

Bull, T. R. (1965). Taste and the chorda tympani. *Journal of Laryngology and Otolaryngology*, **79**, 479–493.

Bult, J. H. F., de Wijk, R. A., & Hummel, T. (2007). Investigations on multimodal sensory integration: Texture, taste, and ortho- and retronasal olfactory stimuli in concert. *Neuroscience Letters*, **411**, 6–10.

Burdach, K. J., Kroeze, J. H. A., & Koster, E. P. (1984). Nasal, retronasal, and gustatory perception: An experimental comparison. *Perception & Psychophysics*, **36**, 205–208.

Cardello, A. V. (1981). Comparison of taste qualities elicited by tactile, electrical and chemical stimulation of single human taste papillae. *Perception & Psychophysics*, **29**, 163–169.

Chale-Rush, A., Burgess, J. R., & Mattes, R. D. (2007). Multiple routes of chemosensitivity to free fatty acids in humans. *American Journal of Physiology—Gastrointestinal and Liver Physiology*, **292**, G1206–G1212.

Chandrashekar, J., Yarmolinsky, D., von Buchholtz, L., Oka, Y., Sly, W., Ryba, N. J. P., & Zuker, C. S. (2009). The taste of carbonation. *Science*, **326**, 443–445.

Clark, C. C., & Lawless, H. T. (1994). Limiting response alternatives in time-intensity scaling: An examination of the halo dumping effect. *Chemical Senses*, **19**, 583–594.

Cometto-Muñiz, J. E., & Cain, W. S. (1995). Relative sensitivity of the ocular trigeminal, nasal trigeminal and olfactory systems to airborne chemicals. *Chemical Senses*, **20**, 191–198.

Crocker, E. C. (1950). The technology of flavors and odors. *Confectioner*, **34** (January), 7–10.

Cruz, A., & Green, B. G. (2000). Thermal stimulation of taste. *Nature*, **403**, 889–892.

Dalton, P., Doolittle, N., Nagata, H., & Breslin, P. A. S. (2000). The merging of the senses: Integration of subthreshold taste and smell. *Nature Neuroscience*, **3**, 431–432.

Davidson, A. (1988). Tastes, aromas, flavours. In T. Jaine (Ed.), *Oxford symposium on food and cookery—Taste (Proceedings)* (pp. 9–14). London: Prospect Books.

Delwiche, J. (2004). The impact of perceptual interactions on perceived flavor. *Food Quality and Preference*, **15**, 137–146.

Dessirier, J.-M., O'Mahony, M., & Iodi-Carstens, M., Yao, E., & Carstens, E. (2001). Oral irritation by sodium chloride: Sensitization, self-desensitization, and cross-sensitization to capsaicin. *Physiology & Behavior*, **72**, 317–324.

Dessirier, J.-M., Simons, C. T., Iodi Carstens, M., O'Mahony, M., & Carstens, E. (2000). Psychophysical and neurobiological evidence that the oral sensation elicited by carbonated water is of chemogenic origin. *Chemical Senses*, **25**, 277–284.

Dravnieks, A. (1985). *Atlas of odor character profiles*. Philadelphia, PA: American Society for Testing and Materials (Data series DS61).

Finck, H. T. (1886). The gastronomic value of odours. *Contemporary Review*, **50**, 680–695.

Finger, T. E., Bottger, B., Hansen, A., Anderson, K. T., Alimohammadi, H., & Silver, W. L. (2003). Solitary chemoreceptor cells in the nasal cavity serve as sentinels of respiration. *Proceedings of the National Academy of Sciences, USA*, **100**, 8981–8986.

Gibson, J. J. (1966). Tasting and smelling as a perceptual system. In *The senses considered as perceptual systems* (pp. 136–152). Boston: Houghton Mifflin.

Gilbert, A. (2008). *What the nose knows: The science of scent in everyday life*. New York: Crown.

Govindarajan, V. S. (1979). Pungency: The stimuli and their evaluation. In J. C. Boudreau (Ed.), *Food taste chemistry* (p. 53). Washington, DC: American Chemical Society.

Green, B. G. (1996). Chemesthesis: Pungency as a component of flavor. *Trends in Food Science & Technology*, 7, 415–424.

Green, B. G. (2002). Studying taste as a cutaneous sense. *Food Quality and Preference*, **14**, 99–109.

Green, B. G. (2004). Oral chemesthesis: An integral component of flavour. In A. J. Taylor & D. D. Roberts (Eds.), *Flavour perception* (pp. 151–171). Oxford: Blackwell.

Green, B. G., & George, P. (2004). 'Thermal taste' predicts higher responsiveness to chemical taste and flavor. *Chemical Senses*, **29**, 617–628.

Halpern, B. P. (1983). Tasting and smelling as active, exploratory sensory processes. *American Journal of Otolaryngology*, **4**, 246–249.

Hettinger, T. P., Myers, W. E., & Frank, M. E. (1990). Role of olfaction in perception of non-traditional 'taste' stimuli. *Chemical Senses*, **15**, 755–760.

Hughson, A. L., & Boakes, R. A. (2001). Perceptual and cognitive aspects of wine expertise. *Australian Journal of Psychology*, **53**, 103–108.

Iannilli, E., DelGratta, C., Gerber, J. C., Romani, G. L., & Hummel, T. (2008). Trigeminal activation using chemical, electrical, and mechanical stimuli. *Pain*, **139**, 376–388.

ISO (1992). *Standard 5492: Terms relating to sensory analysis*. International Organization for Standardization. Geneva, Switzerland.

ISO (2008). *Standard 5492: Terms relating to sensory analysis*. International Organization for Standardization. Geneva, Switzerland.

Kappes, S. M., Schmidt, S. J., & Lee, S.-Y. (2006). Color halo/horns and halo-attribute dumping effects within descriptive analysis of carbonated beverages. *Journal of Food Science*, **71**, S590–S595.

Kawamura, Y., & Kare, M. R. (1987). *Umami: A basic taste: Physiology, biochemistry, nutrition, food science*. New York: Marcel Dekker.

Keeley, B. L. (2002). Making sense of the senses: Individuating modalities in humans and other animals. *Journal of Philosophy*, **99**, 5–28.

Korsmeyer, C. (Ed.). (2005). *The taste culture reader: Experiencing food and drink*. Oxford: Berg.

Labbe, D., Rytz, A., Morgenegg, C., Ali, C., & Martin, N. (2007). Subthreshold olfactory stimulation can enhance sweetness. *Chemical Senses*, **32**, 205–214.

Laughlin, Z., Conreen, M., Witchel, H. J., & Miodownik, M. A. (2011). The use of standard electrode potentials to predict the taste of solid metals. *Food Quality & Preference*, **22**, 628–637.

Lawless, H. T. (1984). Oral chemical irritation: Psychophysical properties. *Chemical Senses*, **9**, 143–155.

Lawless, H. (1989). Pepper potency and the forgotten flavor sense. *Food Technology*, **11**, 52, 57–58.

Lawless, H. T. (2001). Taste. In B. E. Goldstein (Ed.), *Blackwell handbook of perception* (pp. 601–635). Malden, MA: Blackwell.

Lawless, H., Rozin, P., & Shenker, J. (1985). Effects of oral capsaicin on gustatory, olfactory and irritant sensations and flavor identification in humans who regularly or rarely consume chilli pepper. *Chemical Senses*, **10**, 579–589.

Lawless, H. T., Schlake, S., Smythe, J., Lim, J., Yang, H., Chapman, K., & Bolton, B. (2004). Metallic taste and retronasal smell. *Chemical Senses*, **29**, 25–33.

Lawless, H. T., Stevens, D. A., Chapman, K. W., & Kurtz, A. (2005). Metallic taste from electrical and chemical stimulation. *Chemical Senses*, **30**, 185–194.

Lawrence, G., Salles, C., Septier, C., Busch, J., & Thomas-Danguin, T. (2009). Odour–taste interactions: A way to enhance saltiness in low-salt content solutions. *Food Quality and Preference*, **20**, 241–248.

Lehrman, D. S. (1970). Semantic and conceptual issues in the nature-nurture problem. In L. R. Aronson, D. S. Lehrman, E. Tobach, & J. S. Rosenblatt (Eds.), *Development and evolution of behavior* (pp. 17–52). San Francisco: W. H. Freeman.

Lim, J., & Johnson, M. B. (2011). Potential mechanisms of retronasal odor referral to the mouth. *Chemical Senses*, **36**, 283–289.

Lim, J., & Johnson, M. (2012). The role of congruency in retronasal odor referral to the mouth. *Chemical Senses*, **37**, 515–521.

Lindemann, B. (1996). Taste reception. *Physiology Review*, **76**, 719–766.

Liu, L., & Simon, S. A. (1998). Responses of cultured rat trigeminal ganglion neurons to bitter tastants. *Chemical Senses*, **23**, 125–130.

Lundström, J. N., Boesveldt, S., & Albrecht, J. (2011). Central processing of the chemical senses: An overview. *ACS Chemical Neuroscience*, **2**, 5–16.

Macpherson, F. (Ed.). (2011). *The senses: Classic and contemporary philosophical perspectives*. Oxford: Oxford University Press.

Marks, L. E. (2002). The role of attention in chemosensation. *Food Quality and Preference*, **14**, 147–155.

Martin, G. N. (2004). A neuroanatomy of flavour. *Petits Propos Culinaires*, **76**, 58–82.

Mattes, R. D. (2009). Is there a fatty acid taste? *Annual Review of Nutrition*, **29**, 305–327.

Matthen, M. (forthcoming). The individuation of the senses. In M. Matthen (Ed.), *Oxford handbook of the philosophy of perception*. Oxford: Oxford University Press.

McBurney, D. H. (1986). Taste, smell, and flavor terminology: Taking the confusion out of fusion. In H. L. Meiselman & R. S. Rivkin (Eds.), *Clinical measurement of taste and smell* (pp. 117–125). New York: Macmillan.

Mela, D. J. (1988). Sensory assessment of fat content in fluid dairy products. *Appetite*, **10**, 37–44.

Mojet, J., Köster, E. P., & Prinz, J. F. (2005). Do tastants have a smell? *Chemical Senses*, **30**, 9–21.

Murphy, C., & Cain, W. S. (1980). Taste and olfaction: Independence vs. interaction. *Physiology and Behavior*, **24**, 601–605.

Murphy, C., Cain, W. S., & Bartoshuk, L. M. (1977). Mutual action of taste and olfaction. *Sensory Processes*, **1**, 204–211.

Murray, M. M., & Wallace, M. (Eds.). (2011). *Frontiers in the neural bases of multisensory processes*. Boca Raton, FL: CRC Press.

Nagata, H., Dalton, P., Doolittle, N., & Breslin, P. A. S. (2005). Psychophysical isolation of the modality responsible for detecting multimodal stimuli: A chemosensory example. *Journal of Experimental Psychology: Human Perception & Performance, 31*, 101–109.

Nilsson, B. (1977). Taste acuity of the human palate. *Acta Odontologica Scandinavica, 53*, 51–62.

Nudds, M. (2004). The significance of the senses. *Proceedings of the Aristotelian Society, 104*, 31–51.

Nudds, M. (2011). The senses as psychological kinds. In F. MacPherson (Ed.), *The senses: Classic and contemporary philosophical perspectives* (pp. 311–340). Oxford: Oxford University Press.

Parr, W. V., Heatherbell, D., & White, K. G. (2002). Demystifying wine expertise: Olfactory threshold, perceptual skill and semantic memory in expert and novice wine judges. *Chemical Senses, 27*, 747–755.

Petit, C. E. F., Hollowood, T. A., Wulfert, F., & Hort, J. (2007). Colour–coolant–aroma interactions and the impact of congruency and exposure on flavour perception. *Food Quality and Preference, 18*, 880–889.

Piggott, J. R. (1990). Relating sensory and chemical data to understand flavor. *Journal of Sensory Studies, 4*, 261–272.

Piqueras-Fiszman, B., Laughlin, Z., Miodownik, M., & Spence, C. (2012). Tasting spoons: Assessing how the material of a spoon affects the taste of the food. *Food Quality and Preference, 24*, 24–29.

Prescott, J. (1999). Flavour as a psychological construct: Implications for perceiving and measuring the sensory qualities of foods. *Food Quality and Preference, 10*, 349–356.

Reed, D. R., & Knaapila, A. (2010). Genetics of taste and smell: Poisons and pleasures. *Progress in Molecular Biology Translational Science, 94*, 213–240.

Rikowski, A., & Grammer, K. (1999). Human body odour, symmetry and attractiveness. *Proceedings of the Royal Society London B: Biological Sciences, 266*, 869–874.

Rosenblum, L. D. (2010). *See what I am saying: The extraordinary powers of our five senses*. New York: W. W. Norton.

Rozin, P. (1982). "Taste-smell confusions" and the duality of the olfactory sense. *Perception & Psychophysics, 31*, 397–401.

Schiffman, S. S. (2000). Taste quality and neural coding: Implications from psychophysics and neurophysiology. *Physiology and Behavior, 69*, 147–159.

Seo, H.-S., Iannilli, E., Hummel, C., Okazaki, Y., Buschhüter, D., Gerber, J., Krammer, G. E., van Lengerich, B., & Hummel, T. (2013). A salty-congruent odor enhances saltiness: Functional magnetic resonance imaging study. *Human Brain Mapping, 34*, 62–76.

Shankar, M., Simons, C., Shiv, B., McClure, S., & Spence, C. (2010). An expectation-based approach to explaining the crossmodal influence of color on odor identification: The influence of expertise. *Chemosensory Perception, 3*, 167–173.

Shepherd, G. M. (2012). *Neurogastronomy: How the brain creates flavor and why it matters*. New York: Columbia University Press.

Simner, J., Cuskley, C., & Kirby, S. (2010). What sound does that taste? Cross-modal mapping across gustation and audition. *Perception, 39*, 553–569.

Simons, C. T., & Noble, A. C. (2003). Challenges for the sensory sciences from the food and wine industries. *Nature Reviews Neuroscience*, **4**, 599–605.

Smith, B. (2012). Perspective: Complexities of flavour. *Nature*, **486**, S6.

Solomon, G. (1997). Conceptual change and wine expertise. *Journal of the Learning Sciences*, **6**, 41–60.

Spence, C. (2008). Multisensory perception. In H. Blumenthal, *The big Fat Duck cook book* (pp. 484–485). London: Bloomsbury.

Spence, C. (2012a). Multi-sensory integration & the psychophysics of flavour perception. In J. Chen & L. Engelen (Eds.), *Food oral processing—Fundamentals of eating and sensory perception* (pp. 203–219). Oxford: Blackwell.

Spence, C. (2012b). Auditory contributions to flavour perception and feeding behaviour. *Physiology & Behaviour*, **107**, 505–515.

Spence, C., Levitan, C., Shankar, M. U., & Zampini, M. (2010). Does food color influence taste and flavor perception in humans? *Chemosensory Perception*, **3**, 68–84.

Stein, B. E., Burr, D., Costantinides, C., Laurienti, P. J., Meredith, A. M., Perrault, T. J., et al. (2010). Semantic confusion regarding the development of multisensory integration: A practical solution. *European Journal of Neuroscience*, **31**, 1713–1720.

Stevens, D. A., Smith, R. F., & Lawless, H. T. (2006). Multidimensional scaling of ferrous sulphate and basic tastes. *Physiology & Behavior*, **87**, 272–279.

Stevenson, D., & Halpern, B. P. (2009). No oral-cavity-only discrimination of purely olfactory odorants. *Chemical Senses*, **34**, 121–126.

Stevenson, R. J. (2001). Is sweetness taste enhancement cognitively impenetrable? Effects of exposure, training and knowledge. *Appetite*, **36**, 241–242.

Stevenson, R. J. (2009). *The psychology of flavour*. Oxford: Oxford University Press.

Stevenson, R. J. (2012a). Multisensory interactions in flavor perception. In B. E. Stein (Ed.), *The new handbook of multisensory processes* (pp. 283–299). Cambridge, MA: MIT Press.

Stevenson, R. J. (2012b). The role of attention in flavour perception. *Flavour*, **1**, 7.

Stevenson, R. J., & Boakes, R. A. (2004). Sweet and sour smells: Learned synaesthesia between the senses of taste and smell. In G. A. Calvert, C. Spence, & B. E. Stein (Eds.), *The handbook of multisensory processing* (pp. 69–83). Cambridge, MA: MIT Press.

Stevenson, R. J., Boakes, R. A., & Prescott, J. (1998). Changes in odor sweetness resulting from implicit learning of a simultaneous odor-sweetness association: An example of learned synaesthesia. *Learning and Motivation*, **29**, 113–132.

Stevenson, R. J., Prescott, J., & Boakes, R. A. (1995). The acquisition of taste properties by odors. *Learning and Motivation*, **26**, 433–455.

Stevenson, R. J., Prescott, J., & Boakes, R. A. (1999). Confusing tastes and smells: How odours can influence the perception of sweet and sour tastes. *Chemical Senses*, **24**, 627–635.

Stevenson, R. J., & Tomiczek, C. (2007). Olfactory-induced synesthesias: A review and model. *Psychological Bulletin*, **133**, 294–309.

Stillman, J. A. (2002). Gustation: Intersensory experience par excellence. *Perception*, **31**, 1491–1500.

Sundqvist, N. C., Stevenson, R. J., & Bishop, I. R. J. (2006). Can odours acquire fat-like properties? *Appetite*, **47**, 91–99.

Titchener, E. B. (1909). *A textbook of psychology*. New York: Macmillan.

Tournier, C., Sulmont-Rossé, C., & Guichard, E. (2007). Flavour perception: Aroma, taste and texture interactions. *Food*, **1**, 246–257.

Trivedi, B. (2012). Hardwired for taste: Research into human taste receptors extends beyond the tongue to some unexpected places. *Nature*, **486**, S7.

Viana, F. (2011). Chemosensory properties of the trigeminal system. *ACS Chemical Neuroscience*, **2**, 38–50.

Wajid, N. A., & Halpern, B. P. (2012). Oral cavity discrimination of vapour-phase long-chain 18-carbon fatty acids. *Chemical Senses*, **37**, 595–602.

Wedekind, D., Seebeck, T., Bettens, F., & Paepke, A. J. (1995). MHC-dependent mate preference in humans. *Proceedings of the Royal Society of London B*, **260**, 245–249.

Yeomans, M. R., Mobini, S., Elliman, T. D., Walker, H. C., & Stevenson, R. J. (2006). Hedonic and sensory characteristics of odors conditioned by pairing with tastants in humans. *Journal of Experimental Psychology: Animal Behavior Processes*, **32**, 215–228.

PART IV

Sensing Ourselves

11

Inner Sense

Vincent Picciuto and Peter Carruthers

1. Introduction

A number of theorists have proposed the existence of an *inner*-sense modality. According to some of them, the faculty of inner sense both represents certain mental states and explains how they are phenomenally conscious (Armstrong, 1968; 1984; Lycan, 1996). These forms of theory purport to explain how it is that perceptual states acquire a dimension of phenomenology or "feel." It is held that they acquire such properties by being detected and represented through the operations of an inner sense. Other proponents of inner sense, in contrast, are somewhat less ambitious, and make no attempt to solve the "hard problem" of consciousness. Rather, they appeal to a faculty of inner sense to explain how it is that we have privileged and authoritative access to certain of our mental states, including both perceptual states and propositional attitudes (Nichols and Stich, 2003; Goldman, 2006).[1] Here inner sense is deployed to explain how we have a certain sort of knowledge of ourselves, not to explain what makes mental states phenomenally conscious. It is widely believed among philosophers that people have access to their own experiences and thoughts that is both privileged (not available to others) and authoritative (unable to be challenged by others). Inner-sense theories provide one candidate explanation of these supposed facts.[2]

All of the mentioned authors appeal to an internal faculty or mechanism that is receptive to one's own mental states—perceptual states, or attitudinal states, or both. Moreover, the internal faculty is generally regarded as an inner-*sense* modality. The notion of "sense" here is not metaphorical. For example, Goldman (2006)

---

[1] Although Nichols and Stich (2003) defend the existence of at least two introspective monitoring mechanisms (for identifying perceptions and attitudes, respectively), they do not themselves use the language of "inner sense" to describe their view. However, since the mechanisms they describe are functionally equivalent to what might plausibly be taken to be forms of inner sense, we propose to consider their views alongside inner-sense accounts that are explicitly formulated as such.

[2] See Carruthers (2011) for a view that denies that we have privileged and authoritative access to our own thoughts, while allowing that we have such access to some of our own perceptual experiences.

presents a perception-like account of inner sense, including an internal receptor–transducer system that is sensitive to neurophysiological properties; and Lycan (1996), too, regards inner sense as a genuine sense modality. The main goal of this chapter is to examine the extent to which faculties of inner sense of the sort proposed by such authors can legitimately be described as *sensory* in character.

There is one initial point of clarification. "Inner-sense theory" should, more precisely, be called "higher-order-sense theory." This is because we already have senses that operate within the body, such as interoception and proprioception, that are not intended to fall under the scope of inner sense. On the contrary, these are first-order senses on a par with vision and hearing, differing only in that their purpose is to detect properties of the body rather than properties of the external world (Hill, 2004). According to the sort of inner-sense theory that is the topic of this chapter, these internally directed senses, too, will need to have their outputs scanned and represented to produce *higher-order* contents so that those outputs can become phenomenally conscious or be attributed to oneself. In contrast, inner sense is supposed to detect and represent some of the subject's own *mental* states, not mere internal states of the body. If we were picking our terminology afresh, we would use the term "higher-order sense." But since the use of "inner sense" is now firmly established in the literature, we reluctantly employ it.

There are roughly four standard proposals for how to individuate the various sense modalities. To be clear, these proposals are aimed at answering the individuation question: "What is it about each individual sense modality that makes it a *distinct* sense from the others?" The four standard views are direct descendants of four criteria set forth by Grice (1962). There are, though, several other significant questions about the senses. The question we take up is this: "What is it about any given mental mechanism that constitutes it as a *sense* modality at all, and distinguishes it from non-sensory modes of cognition such as inference?"[3]

Our primary focus is on this second question as it pertains to the faculty of inner sense. Our topic is whether inner sense is really a sense. While the four standard proposals are accounts of sense *individuation*, we think they each suggest a corollary answer to the second question, about what constitutes a system as a sense modality at all. In section 2 we begin by reviewing these proposals with the aim of extracting a set of properties or general constraints that can constitute a prototypical sense modality. Our overall goal in this section is to articulate a theory of what it is that distinguishes sensory systems from other mental mechanisms, rather than merely to analyze our concept of a sense. We present this theory in prototype-format to facilitate judgments of degree when we come to consider whether inner sense is really a sense. Then in section 3 we discuss a range of inner-sense accounts, considering to what extent they conform to or deviate from the prototype. In section 4 we conclude.

---

[3] Few authors have taken up this question. Some notable exceptions are Heil (1983), Shoemaker (1994), and Keeley (2002). Grice (1962) acknowledges the question but swiftly proceeds to focus on the individuation issue.

Note: our aim is not to issue a categorical judgment that any of the proposed characterizations of inner sense do or do not qualify it as a sense. We do not offer the proposed criteria as necessary and sufficient conditions, but as a general model to help guide the reader's thinking about inner sense (or any new candidate sense, for that matter). Nor do we think the senses must individuate sharply. Rather, we think the more interesting project is to examine the ways in which inner sense is like a prototypical sense and the ways in which it is not. Our answers are all expressed in terms of *degree*.[4]

We should also stress that we will not be claiming that any of the candidate mechanisms of inner sense actually exist.[5] Our question is hypothetical: if the mechanisms that have been proposed by inner-sense accounts of self-awareness exist, then to what extent are they properly characterized as *sense* modalities?

2. The Properties of a Prototypical Sense

As many have argued, each of the four standard views on its own fails to provide necessary and sufficient conditions for individuating the senses. Similarly, each of the corollaries of the four standard views fails to provide necessary and sufficient conditions for a mental mechanism to count as a sense modality. However, we think that each standard view suggests a relevant property that forms at least part of the characterization of a prototypical sense.

Proponents of the four standard views attempt to individuate among the different senses by appeal to the relevant *sense organs, proximal stimulus, proper objects/ representational features*, or *phenomenal character*.[6] Keeley (2002) and Gray (2005) argue that roughly these criteria must be combined to form jointly necessary and sufficient conditions. We discuss each criterion separately before combining some with others to provide a model of a prototypical sensory system.

2.1. SENSE ORGANS

According to the sense-organ criterion, the senses should be individuated on the basis of the parts of the body that constitute the receptor systems for each putative sense, together with the brain regions that process information emanating from

---

[4] In fact, our view is a hybrid that combines several of the criteria endorsed by the standard four views, in the manner of Keeley (2002) and Gray (2005), but with additional constraints. However, since we are not attempting to propose necessary and sufficient conditions and since we do not think there is always a sharp answer to the question of whether some mental mechanism constitutes a sense, our view is more in line with the views of Heil (1983) and Macpherson (2011).

[5] One of us denies that they do (Carruthers, 2011), while the other is neutral on the question.

[6] Different authors use different terminology to label these criteria. Our chosen labels have been gleaned from existing literature. It is unclear that anyone defends the sense-organ criterion as such. But many discuss it before moving on to integrate it with other factors.

those receptor systems. For example, the cochlea and relevant parts of the brain that are used to hear are distinct from the eyes/retina and relevant parts of the brain that are used to see.

That specific sense organs play a crucial role in each of the senses is intuitive. Presented as an individuating condition, though, the sense-organ view encounters a fundamental difficulty, for there is no one physiological mechanism that seems necessary for a sense organ to constitute any given kind of sense modality. Bee eyes are very different from typical human eyes, consisting of multiple lenses each of which is directed at a distinct region of the bee's visual field. Yet it is surely clear that bees can see. If so, then the organ is insufficient to individuate the visual sense modality. In concluding that a creature has anatomical features that qualify as eyes, we must plainly be relying on some further criterion. In particular, we need some way of isolating the function of the relevant anatomical features.

While the sense-organ criterion fails as an individuation condition for the senses, it does form a very plausible component in our idea of a prototypical sense modality, and one might think that some or other organ is a necessary condition for a mental mechanism to qualify as a sense. But one plainly needs to build more into the idea of a sense organ than mere physical mechanism. For *all* cognitive systems are presumably realized in physical mechanisms of some sort. We need to know more about the function of the putative sense organ's relevant anatomical features. What seems crucial is that a sense organ should be charged with receiving, transposing, and generating representations from some set of physical stimuli. One possible way of spelling out the function of a candidate sense organ's relevant anatomical features is to appeal to the kind of energy (or range of a kind energy) to which they are sensitive. This leads us to consider the proximal stimulus criterion.

2.2. PROXIMAL STIMULUS

Proximal-stimulus accounts claim that what distinguishes one sense from another is the specific kind of physical stimulus or energy to which the putative sense organ is receptive (Heil, 1983, 2011). That is, to be an eye is to be receptive to light waves. To be an ear is to be receptive to pressure waves. The proximal stimulus criterion is a useful addition to the sense-organ criterion. However, proximal stimuli cannot always be so neatly carved up. The eyes of bees detect electromagnetic radiation, but they detect a different range than do human eyes (the ultraviolet range as well as portions of the "visible" range). Moreover, pit vipers have organs just below their regular eyes that are capable of detecting heat (electromagnetic radiation in the infra-red range; Gray, 2005). As a result, we can set the proximal-stimulus criterion a dilemma. On the one hand, it can be claimed that what individuates the sense of sight is a mechanism that is sensitive to a specific range of electromagnetic radiation (the "visible" range). But in that case we will be compelled to deny that bees have a sense of sight, since they can detect forms of radiation that we cannot.

Yet if it is claimed, on the other hand, that what individuates sight is sensitivity to *some* (unspecified) range of electromagnetic radiation, then we will have no option but to claim that pit vipers see heat. Indeed, we will be forced to conclude that they possess, not one, but two visual systems.

Our task is to delineate the properties of a prototypical sense, however, not to provide individuating conditions for the senses. And for this purpose a combination of the sense-organ criterion with the proximal-stimulus criterion provides a very plausible component of the prototype. One factor that inclines us to judge that pigeons and trout possess a magnetic sense, for example, enabling them to navigate via the Earth's magnetic field, is the discovery that they possess distinctive magnetism-sensitive structures in their heads that serve as the organ of magnetic sense (Wallcott et al., 1979; Walker et al., 1997). Likewise, it is partly the discovery of heat-sensitive pits underneath the pit vipers' eyes that inclines us to think that it has a heat-based sense modality.

It is plain that the mere presence of a physical mechanism sensitive to some range of physical energy or set of physical properties does not constitute a prototypical sense, however, for there are a great many detection systems in the body that we might hesitate to categorize as sense modalities. Many of them play a role in bodily homeostasis but never give rise to beliefs, nor do they guide behavior (except indirectly). For example, there are physical structures that detect blood pressure and others that measure heart rate, as well as numerous other receptors in the internal organs of the body (Vaitl, 1996). But people are generally at chance in attempting to judge the rate of their own heartbeat (Brener and Jones, 1974; Pennebaker, 1982). An important component of our idea of a sensory system is that the structures in question should deliver representations that guide the animal's intentional behavior, as we now discuss.

2.3. PROPER OBJECTS/REPRESENTATIONAL CONTENT

According to this account, the senses are individuated by appeal to the kinds of objects and/or properties to which each putative sense is receptive and which its outputs represent (such as color in the case of vision or pitch in the case of sound). Some have objected, however, that there are far too many types of object that can be perceived by a given sense (Sorabji, 1971). Others have argued that the proper objects criterion fails because a *conjunction* of properties is generally given in experience, which will include properties supposedly distinctive of more than one sense (Grice, 1962). Similarly, Nudds (2004) claims that the trouble with the proper objects criterion is that it allows us to individuate a sense only when it functions in isolation. We will not pause to evaluate these criticisms here. When our task is not to individuate the different senses, but rather to describe a prototypical sense modality, then we no longer need to be concerned with specific kinds of representational feature.

It is surely plausible, however, that any full-blown sense modality would produce representations of properties of the environment (or of the subject's own body), and that these should have a role in guiding the subject's behavior. (As we noted in section 2.2, this will mean that many detector-mechanisms within the body fail to qualify as senses to the fullest extent.) While these representations might (or might not) be distinctive enough for the individuation project, it will be necessary to include other components in a description of a prototypical sense, as we will see shortly. It will also be important to ask whether there are further restrictions on the kinds of representation in question. This issue is taken up in section 2.6.

Some theorists attempting to provide individuation conditions for the senses have claimed that representational content itself does not adequately characterize *what it is like* to undergo an experience produced by a given putative sense modality. This motivates some to appeal to the phenomenal character criterion.[7]

2.4. PHENOMENAL CHARACTER

According to this criterion, each sense has its own distinctive kind of phenomenal character, and it is these that individuate the senses (Grice, 1962; Leon, 1988; Martin, 1992; Lopes, 2000). It is like one thing to see a cube, but it is like quite another thing to feel a cube in one's hand. While there are current defenders of the phenomenal character account, it begs an important question when made part of a theory of what it is to have a sense *at all*. This is because higher-order theorists of consciousness will want to distinguish the senses themselves from what gives their output phenomenal character (Lycan, 1996; Carruthers, 2000; Rosenthal, 2005). Moreover, if such higher-order theories are correct, then it is far from clear that phenomenally conscious experience will be widespread in the animal kingdom. Indeed, it may be that the relevant forms of higher-order representation are unique to humans, or perhaps restricted to primates (Carruthers, 2000). If so, then possession of phenomenal character will fail to be a prototypical property of sense modalities in general for these are arguably possessed by almost all forms of creature (Carruthers, 2006).

It is an open question, then, whether phenomenal consciousness is a prototypical property of a sense modality. The answer will depend on the correct form for an account of consciousness (whether first-order or higher-order), together with facts about the cognitive powers of nonhuman animals. Since for present purposes

---

[7] Grice (1962) called this feature the "special introspectible character" of experiences. We take Grice here to be referring to what many philosophers now call phenomenal consciousness or, for better or worse, "what it's likeness." Since we wish to remain neutral about whether all introspected states are states with phenomenal character (states that *must* be phenomenally conscious), we call this criterion the phenomenal character criterion. Nudds (2004) refers to the criterion as the "experience" criterion. However, this is too general and ignores the crucial distinction between conscious and unconscious experiences.

we do not wish to rely on the truth of a higher-order account, we will include possession of phenomenal character in the discussions to come, noting that its inclusion is controversial.

2.5. A COMBINED PROPERTIES ACCOUNT

Our examination of the four standard views of sense-individuation has led us to an initial sketch of a prototypical sense modality. The latter should consist of a physical organ that is sensitive to some range of proximal stimuli, producing representations (perhaps phenomenally conscious representations) that serve to guide the organism's intentional behavior. In the present section we examine the account provided by Keeley (2002), who is one of the few theorists to focus on the question of the conditions under which a mental mechanism counts as sensory. This will enable us not only to confirm but also to elaborate and extend our account of the prototypical sense. Keeley's goal, however, is to provide a set of individually necessary and jointly sufficient conditions for a system to count as a sense. Our own goal is weaker. It is to describe the components of a prototypical sense. Our view is that there are likely to be numerous systems in the natural world that count as senses to some degree (of which mechanisms of inner sense might constitute good examples), and that the interesting question is *the extent to which* these systems approximate a prototypically sensory one.

Keeley's account combines some of the criteria discussed previously with others. He eliminates phenomenal character as a necessary condition for a sense modality. But he does so for different reasons than those discussed in section 2.4. (He is concerned with troubles posed by "qualia," whereas we think that these can be explained naturalistically; Carruthers, 2000; Picciuto, 2011.) But in positive mode, he presents the following four conditions: (i) physics, (ii) neurobiology, (iii) behavior, and (iv) dedication. We discuss them in turn.

Keeley's physics condition is roughly the proximal stimulus criterion considered in section 2.2. It specifies the external physical stimulus to which a putative sense is sensitive, thereby fixing the "space of possible modalities."[8] Gray (2005) points out a problem for the physics condition, however. This is that, as the pit viper case shows, there might be good reason to suppose that some distinct senses will be sensitive, not to a distinctive kind of energy (e.g., electromagnetic radiation), but to a distinct *range* within a kind of energy (e.g., infrared radiation). Gray therefore argues for a modification to the physics condition. We agree, and will thus assume that this condition should be stated in terms of *ranges* of physical energy of a distinctive kind, or *sets* of related physical properties (think of taste or smell).

---

[8] "External" should be taken to mean external to the sense in question, not external to the body or brain.

The neurobiology condition is a more detailed account of the sense-organ criterion. According to Keeley, a legitimate sensory organ must have three characteristics. It must physiologically respond to a naturally occurring range of physical stimulation; it must be wired up properly to the central nervous system; and it must include an "end organ," from which the informational signals to the central nervous system initiate (2002, 14). So, while the organ itself is not sufficient to constitute the existence of a sense, some kind of organ of this general sort is at least necessary.

Keeley's third criterion is "behavior." An organ that detects a specific kind of proximal stimulus must enable the organism to discriminate behaviorially between stimuli that differ only in terms of a particular physical energy type. The third criterion is supposed to address a problem that arises when considering only the first two criteria. This is the problem of vestigial sense organs. Roughly, the problem is that a sense organ sensitive to a range of physical stimuli might meet conditions (i) and (ii) but still not suffice to constitute a sense, because one may have such an organ but never make use of the information it processes. An implicit condition on a sense, then, is that the organism actually makes use of the information it generates. We agree; for as we noted in section 2.2, there are numerous detector mechanisms within the body that one might be reluctant to characterize as senses. This is because, while the information they deliver gets used by some system or other, that information is not available to guide the intentional behavior of the organism. A prototypical sense, then, should involve an action-guiding component.

We need yet another condition, according to Keeley (2002), because a sensory organ can fulfill the first three conditions without enabling the organism to *perceive* those stimuli. The last condition, "dedication," is supposed to provide the final component. Dedication is "the evolutionary or developmental importance of the putative sense to an organism. For example, we ought not attribute an electrical modality to an individual unless electrical properties of the world are part of the normal environment of that individual and to which the organism is attuned" (17). An eye might "detect" mechanical energy in that it will respond to pressure, say, but it is "receptive" only to electromagnetic stimulation, because it has evolved specifically to enable the organism to discriminate that sort of information.

We are happy to accept the dedication condition as providing one component of a prototypical sense modality. However, Keeley's four conditions are not complete. A prototypical sense should also issue in fine-grained (or nonconceptual) representations with mind-to-world direction of fit, as we explain in section 2.6.[9]

---

[9] While we use the language of nonconceptual content throughout, this is for convenience only; everyone allows that sensory representations are distinctively different from those employed in thought. Even McDowell (1994), for example, who denies the existence of nonconceptual content, allows that perception deals in a special class of fine-grained indexical concepts. If necessary, our discussion could be couched in such terms.

2.6. NONCONCEPTUAL WORLD-DIRECTED REPRESENTATIONS

While we noted in section 2.4 that it is highly controversial to include the phenomenal character criterion in an account of a prototypical sense, there is a related, less contentious, suggestion. One distinctive property of phenomenally conscious states is that they have a special sort of fine-grained, nonconceptual content. But presumably, the perceptual states of nonhuman animals possess such content, even if they aren't phenomenally conscious. Moreover, these contents have mind-to-world direction of fit. (If there is a mismatch, it is the perceptions that are in error, not the world.) One might wonder, then, whether a prototypical sense modality would produce not just *any* sort of representation that can guide the subject's behavior, but specifically *nonconceptual* forms of representation with mind-to-world direction of fit.

Suppose that by the year 2050 the "science" of parapsychology has advanced to the point that prescience is recognized to be a real phenomenon. There are some individuals, it is by then discovered, who can foretell the future in quite reliable ways. And suppose that there is some structure that is discovered in the heads of these individuals that proves sensitive to future-occurring events (perhaps as a result of quantum entanglement or some such). But the outputs of the system are just beliefs. A prescient individual will just find herself believing that there will be a train crash in Baltimore the next day, for example. She doesn't in any respect "see" the train crash, or experience any kind of nonconceptual representation of it (whether consciously or unconsciously). She just forms a belief. The lack of nonconceptual content in such a case would make us less inclined, at least, to describe the prescience-mechanism as a sense modality. Paradigmatic examples of existing sense modalities suggest that a prototypical sense should produce nonconceptual representations among its outputs. Perhaps the prescience-mechanism is like a prototypical sense in many other ways, but in this one important way it is not.

As for mind-to-world direction of fit, consider the structures in the nasal cavity that detect and respond to pheromones. It is presently unclear exactly what role these play in human cognition, but in other animals they modulate sexual attraction and other forms of affective behavior (Dulac, 2000). Suppose it is discovered, then, that the role of the pheromone-detection system is to make any opposite-gendered person to whom one is attending at the time seem to some degree sexually attractive or repulsive. In short, suppose that pheromones issue directly in feelings of desire. This, too, would surely disincline us to regard the pheromone system as a sense modality, despite the fact that it contains an organ that is sensitive to a specific sort of physical stimulus, and despite the fact that it produces nonconceptual representations of attractiveness as output. For even though, at the input level, there are representations with mind-to-world direction of fit, the representations that the system produces as output have the wrong direction of fit. They don't represent the world as being a certain way. Rather, they issue in feelings of desire or repulsion. Prototypical sensory systems are for representing the world, not for changing it (or not directly, anyway).

2.7. THE PROTOTYPICAL SENSORY SYSTEM

Pulling together all of the ideas discussed, we suggest that a prototypical sense modality (1) will be sensitive to some range of physical energy or set of related physical properties, (2) will include a detector mechanism that transduces that energy or those properties into informational signals sent to the central nervous system where (3) they are used to guide the intentional behavior of the organism (perhaps issuing in phenomenally conscious sensations). In addition, a prototypical sense (4) will have as its evolutionary function the detection and representation of the physical energy or properties in question, and (5) will issue in nonconceptual representations with mind-to-world direction of fit. While a full account of a prototypical sensory system would no doubt need to include some specification of the comparative importance of each component, a simple listing of the components will be sufficient for our purposes here.

3. To What Extent Is Inner Sense a Sense?

In the present section we consider the extent to which different models of the inner-sense faculty match the account of the prototypical sense modality outlined in section 2.

Inner-sense theory was first proposed by Locke (1690), but the view has been defended more recently as a theory of phenomenal consciousness by Armstrong (1968, 1984) and Lycan (1996), and as a theory of self-knowledge by Nichols and Stich (2003) and Goldman (2006). Recall that while both types of theory are inner-sense theories, they have quite different explanatory goals. Armstrong and Lycan use it to construct a theory of phenomenal consciousness, whereas Nichols and Stich and Goldman use it to construct accounts of self-knowledge. This difference is not relevant to our aims in this chapter (except insofar as it impacts the shape of the theories in question). For we are concerned with the ways in which inner sense resembles a prototypical sense modality (and the extent to which it does so), irrespective of distinct theoretical applications.

Each of the three most recent accounts has somewhat different implications for our question. We will discuss Lycan in section 3.1, Nichols and Stich in section 3.2, and Goldman in section 3.3.

3.1. SCANNED SENSORY-OUTPUT MODELS (LYCAN)

According to Lycan (1996), humans (and perhaps some nonhuman animals) not only have sense organs that scan the environment or body to produce fine-grained representations that can serve to ground thoughts and action planning, but they also have *inner* senses, charged with scanning the outputs of the first-order senses to produce equally fine-grained but higher-order representations of those outputs (allegedly rendering the latter phenomenally conscious).

On this account, inner sense is a perception-like faculty and is presumed to include a receptor-transducer system of some sort. Plainly, too, its outputs can guide intentional behavior (enabling people to make reports about their conscious experiences, for example). Moreover, those outputs have fine-grained nonconceptual contents with mind-to-world direction of fit (although in this case "the world" comprises the outputs of the first-order senses that are targeted by inner sense). In addition, since inner sense is presumed to have the *function* of representing the outputs of our first-order senses, it appears that on this account inner sense resembles a prototypical sensory system to some quite high degree.

Note, however, that on this account the mechanism of inner sense does not issue in outputs that are themselves phenomenally conscious. According to Lycan (1996), it is the outputs of our first-order senses that become phenomenally conscious when represented by inner sense, whereas the latter representations (the *outputs* of inner sense) are *not* phenomenally conscious. For this would require that they, in turn, were detected and represented by some sort of third-order inner-sense mechanism. If the account were intended merely as a theory of self-knowledge, however, rather than an account of phenomenal consciousness, then there would be nothing to prevent one from claiming that the outputs of the sensory monitoring mechanisms are themselves phenomenally conscious (except that there seems little introspective support for such a view).

One might worry, moreover, that the proposed receptor-transducer system would be too fragmentary and distributed to qualify as a sensory organ, for the various first-order sensory systems are realized in quite different areas of the brain. So it might seem that multiple receptor systems rather than just one would need to be involved. But it is a mistake to think that this would constitute any sort of problem for the view that inner sense is genuinely a sense, for our tactile sense, too, comprises a great many receptors of a number of different kinds distributed over the surface of the body. So it can't be a requirement of a sensory organ that it should comprise a unitary localized structure. Moreover, although neither Armstrong nor Lycan develop their views in this way, it might be said that the receptor mechanism of inner sense has to wait on the "global broadcast" of attended sensory representations (Baars, 1988, 1997). Since global broadcasting results in sensory representations being made widely available to other systems within the brain irrespective of sensory modality, this would mean that the inner-sense receptor mechanism could be a single local structure after all.

More significantly, one might worry that there is nothing physically distinctive about the properties that an inner-sense organ would be designed to detect. For one might question whether the neural properties of our perceptual states differ from those that the realizing mechanisms for *any* cognitive process would need to be sensitive to (where we wouldn't be tempted to talk of a sense). Ultimately all cognitive processes need to be realized in neural ones, and so all cognitive mechanisms will need to be sensitive to relevant properties of other such processes when taken as input. And one might expect that the mechanism involved in inner sense would pick up on the very same set of properties.

Consider, for example, the mechanism in humans and other animals that estimates the numerosity of a set from a perceptual representation of it. Since this mechanism is physically realized in the brain, it must at some level of description be responding to physical properties of the neural signals that code for the presence of the set in question. If these are the same kinds of properties that the inner-sense mechanism is sensitive to, then we face a dilemma. Either the inner-sense mechanism lacks a sensory organ (because there is nothing distinctive about the physical properties detected), or sensory organs will turn out to be rampant in the brain, existing at every physical interface between one cognitive system and another.

It might be possible to reply to this difficulty, in part by utilizing the idea of global broadcasting once again. Suppose this turns out to have a distinctive physical signature in the brain (perhaps involving synchronized neural oscillations in the high-frequency range 40–150 Hz; Rees et al., 2002). And suppose, too, that each kind of neural process that realizes the outputs of the various first-order sense modalities includes some modality-distinctive physical signature. Then one might envisage an inner-sense mechanism with a complex component structure. One component would be sensitive to those physical properties of a perceptual experience that realize its representational content. (This would be no different, in this respect, from any other cognitive mechanism.) But the others would be sensitive to more widespread neural oscillation frequencies in the brain, as well as to the physical properties distinctive of each sense. On the assumption that the latter are not detected as such by other mental mechanisms, then this would serve to distinguish the organ of inner sense from other cognitive systems after all.

It might also be possible to reply to the difficulty more directly; perhaps one can draw distinctions among cognitive systems regarding the level at which it is appropriate to describe their inputs. While all mental mechanisms must be sensitive to neural properties at *some* level of description, in many cases it might be more appropriate to describe them as sensitive to contentful or computational-syntactic properties instead. If this is so for the vast majority of cognitive systems, but *not* for inner-sense mechanisms, then this would vindicate the idea that the latter (and only the latter) contain physical transducers that respond to physical properties of mental states as such. However, it is unclear to us whether and how such a distinction might be justified. In any case, deep questions are raised about how one should select the appropriate level of explanation in cognitive science.

We conclude that the model of inner sense proposed by Lycan (1996) resembles a prototypical sensory system to some quite high degree. It is an evolved system, it generates nonconceptual representations with mind-to-world direction of fit, and these can guide the subject's intentional behavior. It is possible, too (albeit much more problematic), that the receptor component of the mechanism might count as a sensory organ that detects a distinctive range of physical properties.

3.2. BELIEF-OUTPUT MODELS (NICHOLS AND STICH)

Nichols and Stich (2003) argue that a number of distinct monitoring mechanisms are at work in the human mind-brain. There is at least one such mechanism for monitoring one's own perceptual experiences, issuing in knowledge that one is seeing or hearing something, for example. And there are other such mechanisms for monitoring one's propositional attitude states, especially beliefs and desires. They think that the mechanisms for monitoring perceptual states will need to be quite differently structured from those that monitor propositional attitudes. We discuss their account of perceptual self-knowledge first, before turning to the case of belief.

Nichols and Stich suggest that the perceptual monitoring mechanism would need to possess a complex internal structure, for it needs to receive nonconceptual representations of aspects of the environment or body as input while delivering fully conceptual beliefs as output, such as, "I am seeing the color gray," or, "That looks like a rock." In our view they overstate the need for internal complexity as many of the accounts of perception constructed by cognitive scientists suggest that the output of perceptual systems is already partly conceptual. While vision, for instance, involves fine-grained nonconceptual representations of colors, textures, and shapes, conceptual representations of categories are also bound into our visual percepts as a result of visual processing (Kosslyn, 1994). Hence one sees something *as* a rock or *as* one's mother's face, for example. So the mechanism that constructs higher-order awareness that one is seeing a rock would just need to redeploy one of the concepts embedded in the perceptual state that it receives as input, while also determining that *seeing* is the appropriate modality (perhaps on the basis of cues like color).

Whether Nichols and Stich's perceptual monitoring mechanism is simple or complex, however, it is plain that it has few of the properties of a prototypical sense modality. On the plus side, it does produce representations with mind-to-world direction of fit that can guide the subject's behavior, and it might well have been designed to do so. But the representations in question are higher-order beliefs, not nonconceptual perception-like states. Moreover (as we will see in connection with Nichols and Stich's postulated belief-monitoring mechanism), there is no suggestion that the perceptual monitoring mechanisms contain anything like an *organ* designed to detect some form of physical energy or set of physical properties. On the contrary, the mechanisms are thought to be syntactic in nature (or quasi-syntactic, in the case of perceptual monitoring). Like other inferential mechanisms in the human mind-brain, they are held to respond to syntax-like properties rather than to brain states as such.

Nevertheless, despite the fact that the outputs of the mechanism are mere beliefs (and hence are in this respect not perception-like), they might on some views be phenomenally conscious. (Nichols and Stich themselves are silent on this issue.) This is one respect in which it matters that the account is designed just to explain our knowledge of our own perceptual states and not to explain phenomenal consciousness, as this leaves a defender of inner sense free to endorse the views of Strawson (1994), Siewert (1998), Pitt (2004), and others, claiming that thoughts as well as experiences can be phenomenally conscious.[10] In particular, it can be claimed that the thoughts about one's own experiences that are a product of the inner-sense mechanism are sometimes phenomenally conscious.

Turning now to the postulated monitoring mechanisms for beliefs and desires, these are thought by Nichols and Stich (2003) to be simpler than the monitoring mechanism for perceptual states. Thus the belief-monitoring mechanism is designed to take any of one's current beliefs as input and to embed that representation into the content of a belief attribution. For example, taking as input the judgment that global warming is real, it embeds whatever syntax-like structure carries the content, *global warming is real,* into a higher-order representation with the content, *I believe that global warming is real.* The desire-monitoring mechanism operates similarly. But in both cases it is plain that the mechanisms in question would have few of the properties of a prototypical sense modality.

While these mechanisms have the function of delivering representations with mind-to-world direction of fit that can guide one's intentional behavior, the representations are not at all perception-like (although they might, on some views, be phenomenally conscious), and the mechanism that generates these representations is not much like a sensory organ. While these inner-sense systems might have a complex internal structure, with attitude-detector components located in the varied regions of the mind-brain where beliefs and desires are produced, they are sensitive to syntactic properties of the input, not neural properties as such. Hence what is detected by these monitoring mechanisms won't be physically distinctive but will be the same as the properties that are detected and deployed by any other inference mechanism. So inner sense, on this account, will only resemble a prototypical sensory system to some smallish degree.

3.3. MIXED MODELS (GOLDMAN)

Goldman's is perhaps the best-developed account of inner sense. On this view, introspection is a meta-representational process involving "recognition, redeployment, and translation" (2006, 254). Like first-order sensory systems, Goldman claims that inner sense involves a "transduction" process, taking neural properties of mental states as input. In response to those inputs, the transducer produces a representation in a proprietary code. Goldman calls this the introspective code, or the "I-code." The I-code operates in the language of thought and encodes certain

---

[10] For arguments to the contrary, see Tye and Wright (2011) and Veillet and Carruthers (2011).

properties of a given mental state that correspond to various aspects of stored concepts. Goldman isn't fully confident of exactly which properties are encoded in any given I-code representation. However, he speculates that an I-code representation of the attitude-type *hope*, say, will include its general type (that it is an attitude as opposed to a perception), a doxastic parameter with degrees of doubt or uncertainty as its values, together with a valence parameter with degrees of desire or aversion as its values. According to Goldman, these properties are then matched to the stored concept, *hope*, and thus the attitude is recognized.

Simultaneously with typing the kind of mental state in question, the inner-sense faculty also proceeds to self-attribute the content of the state, according to Goldman. It does this either by redeploying the content of the detected state into a meta-representation (in cases where the state in question is an attitude), or by "translating" it into conceptual form (where the state in question is a perceptual one). For example, it redeploys the content of a state of hoping that it will be sunny (namely, the content, *It will be sunny*) into the content of a higher-order belief with the content, *I hope that it will be sunny*. In connection with a visual perception of a sunny day, in contrast, the nonconceptual content in question first needs to be translated into conceptual form with the content, *It is sunny*, before being embedded into a higher-order belief state with the content, *I see that it is sunny*. (Note that Goldman accepts the need for translation in addition to redeployment on the same grounds as Nichols and Stich, and hence this aspect of his view is open to a similar criticism.)

To what extent does inner sense, thus conceived, resemble the prototype of a sense modality? Consider Goldman's account of self-knowledge of attitude states first. One important point to stress (which distinguishes the account from that of Nichols and Stich) is that the output of the mechanism is a mixed conceptual-nonconceptual representation. For example, while the output in a given case conceptually represents the content of a detected belief state (while also conceptually representing that it is a belief that is detected), the output of the mechanism will additionally represent the degree of certainty with which the belief is held, as well as the degree of positive or negative valence that attaches to it. In this respect, at least, the inner-sense mechanism seems very much like a prototypical sensory system—for the latter, too, generates mixed conceptual-nonconceptual representations, as we noted in section 3.2. And in both cases the representations produced have a mind-to-world direction of fit, and in both cases the output can be phenomenally conscious.

While Goldman does not say so explicitly, he can presumably maintain that the inner-sense mechanism has the evolutionary function of detecting and self-ascribing mental states. Moreover, he tries hard to make it seem that the mechanism in question would qualify as a sense *organ* of some sort, transducing neural properties into I-code representations. At this point, however, Goldman (2006) confronts essentially the same difficulty as Lycan (1996), for at some level of description *all* mental mechanisms need to be sensitive to neural properties, since all cognitive processes are realized in neural ones. Much may depend, then, on the detailed structure of the inner-sense mechanism, or on whether a distinction between cognitive mechanisms that detect syntactic properties and those that detect neural ones can be cashed out, as we noted in section 3.1.

Goldman's account of self-knowledge of perceptual states, in contrast, is in one way more like that of Nichols and Stich than it is like Lycan's; there seems to be no scope for nonconceptual representations of doxastic strength in a higher-order representation of what one sees or hears. Rather, the inner-sense mechanism will produce a conceptual representation with the content, *I see that it is sunny* (say). However, if valence representations as well as conceptual representations can be embedded into the content of perceptual states, as many think, then the valence-parameter in the higher-order I-code representation will generally be assigned some value. In that case there will at least be a *dimension* of nonconceptual content in the output of the inner-sense mechanism as it operates on perceptual states. And so to this extent the output can be phenomenally conscious, even without needing to rely on the views of those who think that thoughts per se can be phenomenally conscious (Strawson, 1994; Siewert, 1998; Pitt, 2004).

It seems, then, that on Goldman's (2006) account the mechanism that monitors perceptual states resembles a prototypical sensory system less closely than does the mechanism postulated by Lycan (1996). In contrast, Goldman's account of the mechanism that monitors attitude states resembles a prototypical sense *more* closely than do the mechanisms postulated by Nichols and Stich (2003).

4. Conclusion

If the account of a prototypical sense modality outlined in section 2 is correct, then there is likely to be a range of possible inner-sense mechanisms that conform more or less closely to the prototype. In section 3 we have found that existing theories of inner sense are distributed along just such a spectrum. Each of these theories is somewhat underspecified. This makes it difficult to judge, in some cases, whether the prototypical properties are present. But we can confidently conclude the following.

All of these postulated mechanisms are perception-like in the minimal respect of having as their function the creation of representations of a certain sort (higher-order representations), which have mind-to-world direction of fit, and which can guide one's intentional behavior.

Moreover, the mechanisms postulated by Lycan (1996) and Goldman (2006) are also perception-like in that their outputs are either nonconceptual or (like other forms of perception) mixed conceptual-nonconceptual representations. In addition, if these mechanisms aren't intended to account for the phenomenally consciousness status of the states that they target, then it can be claimed that their outputs are phenomenally conscious. They therefore conform to the prototype of a sense modality to some significant degree—indeed, to the extent that it would not be misleading, at least, to describe inner sense as a sense.

It also remains possible that the internal structure of the systems postulated by Lycan and Goldman might include components that differ from those employed in other sorts of cognitive system, in such a way that they detect, as such, the neural properties that realize our mental states. If so, then these would qualify as fully fledged sensory systems (or almost so, since on some views phenomenal qualities might be lacking in the output), and inner sense would turn out to be a genuine sense modality.

The mechanisms postulated by Nichols and Stich (2003), in contrast, fare much less well as putative sense modalities. While they produce representations with mind-to-world direction of fit that can guide one's intentional behavior, they only create conceptual representations, not nonconceptual ones. Moreover, because they respond to syntactic properties rather than neural ones, they fail to include anything resembling a sensory organ or transducer mechanism. So these mechanisms, if they exist, only remotely resemble a prototypical sensory system.

References

Armstrong, D. (1968). *A Materialist Theory of the Mind*. London: Routledge.

Armstrong, D. (1984). Consciousness and causality. In D. Armstrong and N. Malcolm (eds.), *Consciousness and Causality*, 103–192. Oxford: Blackwell.

Baars, B. (1988). *A Cognitive Theory of Consciousness*. Cambridge: Cambridge University Press.

Baars, B. (1997). *In the Theatre of Consciousness*. Oxford: Oxford University Press.

Brener, J. and Jones, J. (1974). Interoceptive discrimination in intact humans: Detection of cardiac activity. *Physiology and Behavior*, 13, 763–767.

Carruthers, P. (2000). *Phenomenal Consciousness*. Cambridge: Cambridge University Press.

Carruthers, P. (2006). *The Architecture of the Mind*. Oxford: Oxford University Press.

Carruthers, P. (2011). *The Opacity of Mind*. Oxford: Oxford University Press.

Dulac, C. (2000). Sensory coding of pheromone signals in mammals. *Current Opinion in Neurobiology*, 10, 511–518.

Goldman, A. (2006). *Simulating Minds*. Oxford: Oxford University Press.

Gray, R. (2005). On the concept of a sense. *Synthese*, 147, 461–475.

Grice, H. P. (1962). Some remarks about the senses. In R. J. Butler (ed.), *Analytical Philosophy*. Oxford: Blackwell.

Heil, J. (1983). *Perception and Cognition*. Berkeley: University of California Press.

Heil, J. (2011). The senses. In F. Macpherson (ed.), *The Senses*, 284–296. Oxford: Oxford University Press.

Hill, C. (2004). Ouch! An essay on pain. In R. Gennaro (ed.), *Higher-Order Theories of Consciousness*, 339–362. Philadelphia: John Benjamins.

Keeley, B. (2002). Making sense of the senses: Individuating modalities in humans and other animals. *Journal of Philosophy*, 94, 5–28.

Kosslyn, S. (1994). *Image and Brain*. Cambridge, MA: MIT Press.

Leon, M. (1988). Characterising the senses. *Mind and Language*, 4, 243–270.

Locke, J. (1690). *An Essay Concerning Human Understanding*. (Many editions now available.)

Lopes, D. (2000). What is it like to see with your ears? The representational theory of mind. *Philosophy and Phenomenological Research*, 60, 439–453.

Lycan, W. (1996). *Consciousness and Experience*. Cambridge, MA: MIT Press.

Martin, M. (1992). Sight and touch. In T. Crane (ed.), *The Contents of Experience*, 199–201. Cambridge: Cambridge University Press.

McDowell, J. (1994). *Mind and World*. Cambridge, MA: MIT Press.

Macpherson, F. (ed.). (2011). *The Senses*. Oxford: Oxford University Press.

Nichols, S. and Stich, S. (2003). *Mindreading*. Oxford: Clarendon.

Nudds, M. (2004). The significance of the senses. *Proceedings of the Aristotelian Society*, 102, 31–51.

Pennebaker, J. (1982). *The Psychology of Physical Symptoms*. Düsseldorf: Springer-Verlag.

Picciuto, V. (2011). Addressing higher-order misrepresentation with quotational thought. *Journal of Consicousness Studies*, 18, 3–4, 109–136.

Pitt, D. (2004). The phenomenology of cognition. *Philosophy and Phenomenological Research*, 59, 1–36.

Rees, G., Kreiman, G., and Koch, C. (2002). Neural correlates of consciousness in humans. *Nature Reviews Neuroscience*, 3, 261–270.

Rosenthal, D. (2005). *Consciousness and Mind*. Oxford: Oxford University Press.

Siewert, C. (1998). *The Significance of Consciousness*. Princeton, NJ: Princeton University Press.

Shoemaker, S. (1994). Self-knowledge and "Inner Sense." *Philosophy and Phenomenological Research*, 54, 249–314.

Sorabji, R. (1971). Aristotle on demarcating the five senses. *Philosophical Review*, 80, 55–79.

Strawson, G. (1994). *Mental Reality*. Cambridge, MA: MIT Press.

Tye, M. and Wright, B. (2011). Is there a phenomenology of thought? In T. Bayne and M. Montague (eds.), *Cognitive Phenomenology*, 326–344. Oxford: Oxford University Press.

Vaitl, D. (1996). Interoception. *Biological Psychology*, 42, 1–27.

Veillet, B. and Carruthers, P. (2011). The case against cognitive phenomenology. In T. Bayne and M. Montague (eds.), *Cognitive Phenomenology*, 35–56. Oxford: Oxford University Press.

Walker, M., Diebel, C., Haugh, C., Pankhurst, P., Montgomery, J., and Green, C. (1997). Structure and function of the vertebrate magnetic sense. *Nature*, 390, 371–376.

Wallcott, C., Gould, J., and Kirschvink, J. (1979). Pigeons have magnets. *Science*, 205, 1027–1028.

PART V

New Issues Concerning Vision

12

The Diversity of Human Visual Experience

Howard C. Hughes, Robert Fendrich, and Sarah E. Streeter

Webster's *7th Collegiate Dictionary* offers the following for the first three definitions of the verb *to see*: 1a) to perceive by the eye, 1b) to perceive or detect as if
by sight, and 2a) to have experience of vision. These seem perfectly reasonable
definitions, and the *Dictionary* goes on to provide many more definitions based
on the visual metaphor of understanding. These metaphors reflect the fact that
seeing involves much more than an analysis of the patterns of light entering the
eyes: it also entails an understanding of the physical environment that produced
those patterns (i.e., perception). Typically this understanding is coupled with an
experiential component, which we call a conscious visual experience. However,
scientific enquiries into the nature of vision have revealed modes of visual processing that are not captured by our common usage of the verb "seeing" as a "visual
experience conveyed by the eyes." This chapter is intended to explore some of the
often-surprising variations in the nature of seeing, especially with regard to variations in the correspondences (or lack thereof) between retinal images and the
experiences they evoke.

With a mass of approximately 1,400 grams (3 pounds), the human brain may be
the most complex physical system that has been the subject of scientific inquiry.
One indication of the importance of vision is that as much as half of the cerebral cortex is in some manner devoted to seeing. Every normally sighted human
routinely demonstrates great visual expertise, but this expertise is implicit, and
that can obscure the fact that our understanding of the process of seeing remains
quite elusive. It has been established, however, that the visual system is composed
of many subsystems that are mediated by diverse brain structures. Usually these
subsystems operate in a fluid and highly interactive manner to produce the unified
experience most of us think of as "vision," but this is not always the case. When
the functions of some of these subsystems are impaired, or they interact in an
abnormal manner, anomalous visual states can occur that exhibit many paradoxes
and dissociations. We begin by trying to provide a sense of the scope of human
visual experience by first describing some of the remarkable capabilities of the

normal human visual system and then describe some of the seemingly paradoxical limitations of human vision. We then turn to consider a variety of often surprising atypical states of human visual perception.

1. Counting Photons: The Absolute Threshold of Human Vision

In 1942, Selig Hecht, Simon Schlaer, and Maurice Henri Pirenne performed a remarkable experiment. Their goal was to determine the dimmest light that a human observer could detect. Although the question seems simple enough to pose, the experiment itself was actually quite elaborate. Hecht et al. (1942) found that under optimal conditions human observers reported seeing a small flash of light that contained an average of only 90 photons on 60% of the trials. They also concluded that a great deal of the variability in detection performance originated in the stimulus—quantum mechanics tells us that you cannot produce a light that contains a constant number of photons in each flash. That of course is true, but now we also know that a good deal of the variability in detecting very weak signals is attributable to sources of noise that are internal to the observer (e.g., Green and Swets, 1966).

Continuing with our description of the Hecht et al. (1942) experiment, the investigators further refined their estimate of the absolute threshold for vision. They recognized that 3% of the incident photons are reflected off the cornea and never even enter the eye. Moreover, the ocular media absorb 50% of the photons that do enter the eye, so those quanta never reach the retina. Hecht et al. (1942) reported that under optimal conditions, an average of 44 photons raining on a patch of the retina that contains approximately 500 rods (the photoreceptors that mediate night vision) has a probability of 0.6 of being seen. But one more step is required before we arrive at the remarkable conclusion of this famous experiment. Hecht et al. (1942) realized that only 20% of the photons reaching the retina are actually absorbed by the photoreceptors. Moreover, the probability that those 9–10 photons are each absorbed by *different* rods is 0.93. Thus, Hecht et al. (1942) arrived at the remarkable conclusion that human rods can signal the absorption of a *single* photon, and that the absorption of 10 photons by 10 different rods in a little patch of retina containing about 500 rods (a patch 50 microns in diameter) will more likely than not produce the faintest possible visual sensation.

This is an astonishing finding—rods can operate at the physical limit of visual sensitivity. They can signal the absorption of the smallest possible packet of electromagnetic energy: a single photon. However, sometimes rods produce tiny responses that are not the result of the absorption of light. This is because the pigment molecules within the rods (rhodopsin) are subject to thermodynamic noise. There is no way to distinguish whether a given quantal response resulted from the absorption of a photon or from a spontaneous isomerization of a rhodopsin molecule, which is probably why detection requires 9 or 10 simultaneous responses within a certain area—it serves as a hedge against photoreceptor noise.

The subjective experience at the absolute threshold for vision is really not at all like everyday visual experience. In a typical signal detection experiment there are two types of trials: trials in which a signal is presented and trials in which no signal is presented. The observers must report whether they thought a signal was presented or not. The observers are never really certain whether a signal was presented, and they often mistake the internal noise of their visual nervous system as a signal.

An understanding that visual processes are superimposed on a background of internal noise is the major insight gained by signal detection theory. The primary measure of detection performance comes from two readily observed quantities. The first is the probability of reporting a signal on trials in which a signal was actually presented. This is called the "hit rate." The second quantity is the probability of reporting a signal on trials in which no signal was presented. These are called "false alarms." If the hit rate is greater than the false alarm rate, then the observer has an ability to detect the signal. The magnitude of the difference between the hit and false alarm rates provides a measure of the observer's *sensitivity* to the signal. For our purposes, the main point to be made about visual detection is that when the signal intensity is very low it is impossible for an observer to always respond correctly: there are trials when a signal is presented but the observer reports no visual experience, and there are trials in which they do report a visual experience when no signal was presented. Under these admittedly atypical conditions, we therefore can have visual experiences that seem to be "by eye" but are not, and also have situations in which a real signal is simply mistaken as noise. In what follows, we will consider many additional examples of dissociations between what people "see" and what is "conveyed by their eyes."

Near-threshold vision is an unfamiliar experience for most of us. Indeed, we now know the concept of a discrete detection threshold is incorrect. The theory of signal detectability tells us that the detection process is analogous to statistical hypothesis testing: we estimate the likelihood that the internal state of our visual system was more likely to have been produced by a signal than by noise alone. We don't think of our daily visual experiences as being probabilistic and filled with uncertainty. More typically, we view environments that are illuminated by a flood of photons reflected off all manner of physical objects. The optical apparatus of our eyes forms an image of those objects on the retina, but the resulting retinal image does not bear a unique relationship with the object that produced it. Because of the distortions produced by geometrical perspective, a given object can produce an infinite set of retinal images (a square object rotated in depth produces a series of trapezoidal retinal images). The fact that there is not a unique relationship between the objects we see and the retinal images produced by those objects poses no particular problem for our visual systems, however. Any scene contains a bewildering array of edges, shading, and colored surfaces, but we are able to

segment which edges belong to which objects and recognize the physical properties of all those objects (i.e., their reflectance and overall shape) despite the ambi-
guities inherent in the patterns of light they reflect into our eyes. Indeed, we do
this with an alacrity that is nothing short of astonishing. Consider as an example
some experiments that examined the efficiency of visual recognition performed by
Mary Potter, from the Massachusetts Institute of Technology.

2. Seeing the Gist of a Scene

In 1969, Potter and Ellen Levy presented a group of college students with a series
of 128 color photos of different scenes, at rates ranging from one photo every two
seconds to eight photos every second (125 ms./photo). The investigators wanted
to determine the minimum exposure duration needed to encode a novel scene
in memory. To test for recognition of the rapidly presented photos, they subsequently showed their subjects a second series of pictures that was a mixture of
some of those previously presented and some new photos. The subjects were asked
to identify which photos they had seen in the original rapid serial visual presentation (RSVP). When photos in the memory set were presented at RSVP rates of
1–2 secs./photo, the subjects could easily identify previously seen pictures in the
recognition test. However, as the RSVP rate increased, recognition performance
became much worse. The rate of recall for a 2-second exposure was 93%, but it
fell to 16% when the exposure was 125 msecs. (Potter and Levy, 1969). Images that
are "seen clearly" are usually remembered. Conversely, images that were never
seen can't possibly be recalled (at least not accurately). What should we make of
the high rate of recognition failures at these short exposure durations? Potter and
Levy's results suggest that the visual processes needed to encode a novel scene to
a degree that supports later recognition take at least 1 second to complete. Does
this mean that at shorter exposure durations people are unable to "clearly see"
the individual scenes in an RSVP sequence? This could occur, for example, if at
shorter exposure durations the next scene in the RSVP stream "interrupts" the
processing of its predecessor.

However, the failure to remember pictures seen at high RSVP rates does not
appear to be attributable to simply not seeing them clearly. The situation is somewhat more nuanced than that. The information that can be gleaned from a brief
presentation appears to depend on the method used to evaluate an observer's
recognition. Thus, in a second experiment (Potter, 1975), Potter again presented
subjects with a series of RSVP photos, but this time asked them to look for one
specific object category, which was described to them prior to presentation with
either a brief title (i.e., "a boat" or "a child") or by showing them the target picture
itself. Subjects were able to perform this task fairly easily even when the scenes
were presented very rapidly. When each picture was presented for only 125 ms.,
subjects were able to detect whether the RSVP stream contained a member of the

target category more than 70% of the time (Potter 1975). The median exposure time required for the identification of a target described in advance was only 125 ms., whereas the median time required for the recognition task was greater than 300 msec. (Potter 1975). What information is gleaned from a briefly viewed scene apparently depends heavily on the goals of the observer. Whereas passive viewing of a rapid stream of unrelated images results in very poor memory of any of them, actively searching for members of a specific but abstract category is highly efficient. This highlights the importance of visual attention, which many believe is the key to visual memory: things that are attended are remembered, while things that are unattended fade from our consciousness in about a third of a second.

Perhaps not coincidentally, our perception of the visual world comes as a series of momentary fixations with each lasting about one-third of a second. The retinal image does indeed change approximately once every 300 msec. Potter's experiments provide some insight into how we are able to reliably understand what objects produced those retinal images from such brief glimpses. If the scene has content that is particularly significant, that content has increased salience, which in turn attracts our attention, and attention enables entry into visual working memory. Entry into visual working memory is in turn associated with conscious awareness. Attention and visual working memory allow us to "construct" a meaningful representation of a scene over several changes in fixation, and that can be accomplished in 1 to 2 seconds. But attention can also allow the visual system to pre-specify salience settings such that a particular class of objects is selectively processed (i.e., has high priority and can be processed first).

Computer scientists have used mathematical techniques in their attempts to explicitly mimic these abilities in machines. Interestingly, object detection has proven to be one of the most difficult areas of computer vision. Computers are not able to search for and detect objects with the efficiency and accuracy easily demonstrated by a small child. They have particular difficulty searching for a class of objects (Szeliski, 2011). While humans are remarkably good at recognizing that a new item belongs in a particular class of objects (e.g., chairs), as demonstrated in Potter's second experiment, computers are frequently poor at this task because they cannot readily match an unfamiliar target item (a novel image of chair) with a stored exemplar or prototype. Nevertheless, computer object detection technologies have recently become available. For example, new digital cameras can automatically detect faces in the picture being taken, and there is now photo organization software (iPhoto, Picasa, etc.) that can identify the same face in multiple photos.

Current research in computer vision continues to attempt enhanced scene recognition by mimicking the way the human visual system operates. One approach that might be useful is to first perform a rapid low-resolution scan and do a preliminary image analysis based on this low-resolution information (Torralba, 2001, 2003; Oliva and Torralba, 2006). It has been argued that the micro-genesis of human recognition proceeds in a similar manner, from a fast low-resolution system to a slower, high-resolution analysis (e.g., Hughes, Nozawa, and Kitterle, 1996).

3. "Hyperacuity" and Anorthoscopic Percepts

We briefly note two additional phenomena that illustrate the remarkable processing power of the human visual system. The first relates to the ability of the system to resolve small differences in the spatial alignment of objects (*vernier acuity*). Envision two vertical bars with one placed just above the other. The two bars may be perfectly aligned, or one may be slightly to the left or right of the other. What is the smallest offset between the two bars that can be detected? The answer is that under optimal viewing conditions observers can detect misalignments as small as 5 *arcseconds* of visual angle (Westheimer and McKee, 1977). For readers unfamiliar with visual angle measure, this would represent an offset of about.02 mm. if the bars were being viewed at a distance of 1 meter (or less than 1 thousandth of an inch at 1 yard). What makes this very high resolving power especially remarkable is that in the fovea, where visual resolution is the greatest, the individual cones subtend 30 arcseconds. Thus, as we illustrate schematically in Figure 12.1, vernier thresholds are 6 times smaller than the receptor mosaic. For this reason, vernier acuity in the range of 5 seconds of arc is often referred to as

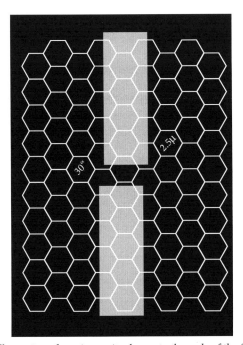

FIGURE 12.1. *An illustration of vernier acuity drawn to the scale of the foveal cone mosaic.*

"hyperacuity" (Westheimer and McKee, 1977). At first glance, hyperacuity scarcely seems possible. Intuitively, one would think that detection of misalignment would require that the terminations of the misaligned bars reliably fall on different cones. It has been shown however, that acuities substantially greater than the scale of the cone mosaic can be achieved by means of an interpolation process if information from a sufficient number of receptors is sampled (Fahle and Poggio, 1981). It has been suggested that the densely packed granule cells in layer IVc of the primary visual cortex could perform such an interpolation of the spatio-temporal pattern of activity on their inputs from the lateral geniculate nucleus (Crick, Marr, and Poggio, 1981). In the current context, the point to be noted is that the visual system employs sophisticated processing mechanisms to achieve spatial resolutions that are extraordinary.

The second phenomenon we briefly note has been termed "anorthoscopic" perception (Zöllner, 1862). Imagine viewing an object through a very narrow slit, so that only a small slice of the object can be seen at one time. If the slit is made narrow enough, it is impossible to identify the object no matter where the slit is placed: all that can be seen is a narrow strip of patterned light. Now if we sweep the object behind the slit in a smooth back and forth motion, a spatially extended percept of the complete object remarkably appears in the vicinity of the slit (although there may be spatial distortions, such as a compression along the axis of motion so that a circle is seen as an ellipse). The impression that most if not the entire figure is simultaneously visible can be so compelling that some investigators interpreted the phenomenon as an artifact produced by eye motions (Helmholtz, 1867; Anstis and Atkinson, 1967). These investigators argued that as the object sweeps behind the slit, the eye tends to move along with it, causing an extended image of the entire object to be "painted" onto the retina. Eye motions of this kind can be observed, and it has been pointed out that if the motion of the eye is slower than the motion of the object, compressions of the image (and therefore of the seen object) can also be explained. However, by using a "retinal stabilization" method that fixes the image of the slit onto the retina irrespective of an observer's eye movements, Fendrich, Reiger, and Heinze (2005) have conclusively demonstrated that retinal painting is not necessary for the formation of anorthoscopic percepts. Apparently, the visual system is able to use sequential information presented through the slit to construct a (albeit, sometimes altered) representation of what the object must have been and use that representation to generate a visual percept. Anorthoscopic percepts are therefore percepts of real objects in the world that are synthesized despite the absence of an actual retinal image of those objects. This phenomenon highlights the fact that visual percepts are not just passive renditions of the images formed on the retina—they are active constructions produced by the visual system (Figure 12.2).

In stark contrast to these demonstrations of the efficiency and power of the human visual system, human observers can have surprising difficulty detecting changes in a scene when the context and global structure remain constant. Thus, we now turn to a phenomenon known as "change blindness."

(a)   Image motion behind   (b)   What is visible to   (c)   What is perceived
      stationary rectangular   observer at one
      aperture   moment in time

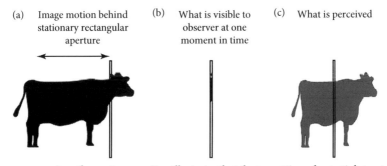

FIGURE 12.2. *Anorthoscopic perception illustrates that the perception of a spatial structure can be created over time.*

4. Looking without Seeing: The Paradox of Change Blindness

Change blindness is a phenomenon in which an obvious alteration in a scene (such as the addition, deletion, or a change in the color of an object) can go unnoticed, even after prolonged periods of careful scrutiny. The phenomenon has been extensively investigated by Rensink and colleagues (e.g., Rensink, 2002; Rensink, O'Regan, and Clark, 1997; Simons and Rensink, 2005), and demonstrations are readily available on the Internet. One way to produce change blindness is to introduce the change very gradually. If a movie contains an automobile that slowly changes color, the color change is likely to go unnoticed. This corresponds with the well-established fact that a pathway containing neurons tuned to spatio-temporal transients is formed within the retina and provides an important source of control over visual attention (Tolhurst, 1975). The ganglion cells that comprise the beginning of this pathway have large cell bodies with extensive dendritic arborizations. They were first identified by the great 19th-century neuroanatomist Ramon y Cajal. These cells are tuned to high temporal frequencies but have poor spatial resolution. They represent the beginning of what today is known as the Magnocellular pathway (e.g., Livingstone and Hubel, 1988; Shapley, 1990). Since our visual mechanisms are generally insensitive to gradual changes in luminance (i.e., we are insensitive to low temporal frequencies; Kelly, 1961), slow changes in a scene can be difficult to detect. Slow *color* changes can be especially difficult to detect because the magnocellular pathway, which is the subsystem most clearly tuned to temporal change, is not very sensitive to chromatic contours.

Abrupt changes can also go unnoticed however. One effective method for producing blindness to abrupt change is called the "flicker paradigm." This method is illustrated in Figure 12.3. The two images in Figure 12.3 are identical except for one conspicuous difference. The images are presented successively, with a blank interval between each presentation. Observers simply view the alternating images until they can identify the difference in the two scenes. Often it takes many cycles of these alternating presentations before the change can be identified. Why are scene

FIGURE 12.3. *A static illustration of a scene change that is likely to result in change blindness. If these two scenes are presented successively (with the intervening blank intervals), the appearance and disappearance of the jet engine is unlikely to be noticed. If the blank intervals are eliminated, then the change is readily apparent.*

changes so difficult to detect when the flicker technique is employed? The answer appears to lie in the way that spatio-temporal transients capture visual attention. Change blindness is entirely dependent on the insertion of the blank interval between each scene presentation. If that interval is removed and the scenes are presented in immediate succession, the change is quite conspicuous and is detected immediately. Current thinking attributes the difficulty to the fact that the blank screen produces a transient at *every* location, so the critical transient produced by the change fails to capture attention. While isolated transients capture attention quickly and automatically, the multiple transients produced by the blank interval overwhelm the mechanisms that guide attention. Because attention is not immediately directed to the critical part of the scene, the change goes unnoticed. Multiple transients produced by other means, such as the appearance of irregular dark patches that look like mud-splotches across a scene, can also be effective in producing change blindness when they are presented during the scene transitions (O'Regan, Rensink, and Clark, 1999). The blindness to change can be so profound that the scene changes often go unnoticed even when an observer actively searching for a change happens to look directly at the critical location (e.g., Caplovitz, Fendrich, and Hughes, 2008).

The limitations of visual processing revealed by change blindness stand in sharp contrast to the sensitivity and efficiency of other visual system processes. What can account for this difference? One possibility relates to visual short-term memory (VSTM). Consider the difference between change detection and object classification processes. Searching for a visual object that is a member of a specific object category does not require VSTM. The task of identifying whether a person was present in any one of a rapid sequence of images consists of segmenting the objects in each scene and deciding if any of those objects is a person. This process requires visual analysis, but not an explicit comparison between two successive visual representations. In contrast, detecting a change between two otherwise identical scenes requires an exhaustive comparison between image segments in scene 1 with stored representations of the corresponding segments in scene 2. The change is detected only if the contents of VSTM do not match the contents of the currently viewed scene. As the capacity of VSTM is quite limited (Sperling, 1960; Averbach and Coriell, 1961; Luck and Vogel, 1997) and the number of potential differences between the two scenes is very high, the likelihood that the critical segment of the scene will be stored in visual working memory is very low, so that an extensive (and often repetitive) search to acquire new samples is required. Thus, the difference between these cases may lie in the fact that in the case of change blindness a comparison between two current (and highly similar) visual inputs is required, whereas rapid object identification only requires comparison of the current (and probably fairly coarse) visual representation with a (nonvisual) representation of the target category.

5. Vision without Seeing: The Case of "Blindsight"

In 1856, Albrecht von Graefe described a patient who had suffered an injury to his occipital lobe. After extensive examination of the patient's vision, von Graefe was able to provide the first case study of *homonymous hemianopia*, blindness in one half of the visual field. Subsequent work during the later part of the 19th century showed that a smaller lesion in the visual cortex could produce a more restricted region of blindness called a scotoma, and careful study of the relationship between the area of the damage and the corresponding area of blindness led to the discovery of the retinotopic organization of the visual cortex. The blindness resulting from damage to what is now known as the primary visual cortex was considered to be as profound as that produced by damage to the retina or optic nerve, although it was understood that the pupillary light reflex was preserved in cortical blindness but not in blindness resulting from ocular or optic nerve damage or disease.

That view of cortical blindness changed little over the next 120 years. However, some data did not fit comfortably with this conventional wisdom. Although the visual system of Rhesus monkeys is quite similar to that of humans, it was found that monkeys without a striate cortex retained some primitive visual abilities (Kluver, 1942; Pasik, Pasik, and Krieger, 1959). These animals also displayed an intact pupillary light reflex, and Kluver (1942) proposed that monkeys deprived of primary visual cortex had a preserved capacity to discriminate different levels of luminous intensity. Then, in the 1960s, it was discovered that the visual abilities of monkeys without primary visual cortex could be substantially greater than had been previously realized (Weiskrantz, 1963; Humphrey and Weiskrantz, 1967). It was found that destriate monkeys could reach in the general direction of objects in motion, and distinguish stimuli with long contours from "salt and pepper" patterns even when these were equated for luminous flux. Moreover, these monkeys exhibited a substantial recovery of function with time and post-operative training. Initially, they lost their ability to perform simple visual discriminations they had learned pre-operatively, and could not navigate without bumping into obstacles in their path. Eventually however, they were able to relearn some of these discriminations and navigate under visual guidance. In addition, it was observed that human patients with striate cortical damage were sometimes able to detect the presence of moving objects in regions that seemed to be otherwise blind (the "Riddoch effect"; Riddoch, 1917). In 1972, observations such as these led Pöppel, Held, and Frost (1973) to perform an experiment designed to investigate the idea that visual responses in humans might also be found in regions of "cortical blindness" if their vision was accessed in a suitable manner. Rather than asking patients to simply report the presence or absence of stimuli, they asked those patients to try to shift their gaze to the locations of visual stimuli they claimed they could not see. The results indicated that there was a small but significant correlation between the position of the "unseen" targets and the shifts in eye position.

Weiskrantz and his colleagues (Weiskrantz, Warrington, Sanders, and Marshall, 1974; Weiskrantz, 1986) pursued this finding with a series of studies using two-alternative forced choice (2AFC) procedures. These procedures require that subjects select one of two alternative responses rather than simply verbally reporting whether or not they have seen a target. For example, instead of simply saying "yes" or "no" with regard to whether they perceived a flash, a subject may be required to say whether a flashed bar of light was horizontally or vertically oriented, or in the first or second of two time intervals (demarcated by tones). Such reports are made irrespective of whether the subject has subjectively experienced the flash and can reveal surprising visual capabilities that the patients do not believe they possess. Similar methods are used to evaluate visual abilities in monkeys. If, for example, you want to evaluate whether monkeys can discriminate a horizontal from a vertical grating, you reward the monkeys for choosing one of these gratings—say, the horizontal. Then you determine whether they can learn to consistently choose the horizontal grating (by touching it) and avoid choosing the vertical grating. You could then try to estimate the animal's visual acuity by testing them with progressively finer gratings until they fail to select the horizontal grating consistently. Weiskrantz and colleagues adopted the 2AFC method in cases of human cortical blindness.

Weiskrantz et al. (1974) initially described the results of testing carried out with patient DB. DB had an arteriovenous malformation (AVM) in his right occipital lobe. Because there was a danger it would hemorrhage, surgeons removed the AVM in a surgical procedure that required an extensive resection of the right primary visual cortex. As expected, the surgery left DB with a large scotoma in his left visual field. Within this scotoma, DB reported he had absolutely no experience of vision except for a slight Riddoch effect (explained earlier). However, using the 2AFC approach, Weiskrantz et al. (1974) found that DB was nonetheless capable of processing considerable visual information. He could localize stimuli presented within his scotoma with eye movements and with manual pointing responses. Moreover, he could distinguish between horizontal and vertical gratings, and report whether an "X" or "O" had been presented. These results have made DB of one of neurology's most celebrated cases (some other famous cases are HM, who suffered from anterograde amnesia following bilateral ablation of the hippocampus to relieve intractable epilepsy, and Paul Broca's patient Tan, who had a profound case of expressive aphasia which upon autopsy led to the discovery of the human frontal lobe language area now known as Broca's area). Weiskrantz et al. (1974) adopted the term "blindsight" to refer to DB's residual visual abilities. As can occur when normal observers are presented with near-threshold stimuli, we have a clear case of information that is "conveyed by eye" but the perceiver has no corresponding "visual Why is this carriage return here? experience." Blindsight has subsequently been demonstrated in a number of additional patients, and the range of reported abilities has expanded to include the discrimination of attributes such as color (wavelength) and the speed and direction of motion (see Stoerig and Cowey, 1997, for a review).

The neural substrate of blindsight has been the subject of substantial controversy. Pöppel, Held, and Frost (1973) proposed that the abilities of their patients might be attributable to a "secondary" visual pathway that allows retinal information to bypass the striate cortex. Weiskrantz and several other investigators have adopted this interpretation. Recently Schmid et al. (2010) have provided a convincing demonstration that the residual vision that follows resection of the striate cortex *in monkeys* is mediated by extra-striate projections of the lateral geniculate nucleus. It has also been proposed (Campion, Latto, and Smith, 1983) that blindsight could reflect the use of information conveyed by intra-ocular scattering of light that stimulates retinal areas at the edge of the scotoma, but subsequent work casts doubt on this explanation. For instance, the hypothesized scattered light does not enable patients to perform above chance when images are projected onto the optic disk, the natural blind spot. Interestingly, a recent proposal attributes blindsight to an especially strict sensory decision criterion, which is a central construct from the theory of signal detectability (see Green and Swets, 1966). This proposal, offered by Ko and Lau (2012), suggests that cortical blindness results from a failure to update the changes in the signal-to-noise ratio that result from damage to the primary visual cortex. As a result, patients do not realize their vision is constantly "near-threshold," and since none of their visual experiences are clear and confident, they believe they are blind. It has also been proposed that blindsight might actually reflect severely degraded levels of visual function within the primary visual cortex (Campion et al., 1983). Supporting the last of these hypotheses, there is evidence of isolated "islands of vision" within the scotoma of some blindsight patients (Fendrich, Wessinger, and Gazzaniga, 1992). Such islands might reflect the presence of corresponding islands of surviving tissue in the primary visual cortex.

To at least a first approximation, it seems that perceptual awareness depends upon activity in the primary visual cortex, although specific types of visual information (e.g., motion, form, color, contour orientation, and location) may be processed in the absence of the primary visual cortex. The notion that primary sensory cortex is necessary for perceptual awareness is consistent with the classic observations of Libet (1979), who identified specific late components of the evoked potentials in the primary somatosensory cortex (S1) that are associated with awareness of a somatosensory stimulus. Libet (1979) also showed that earlier components of these potentials recorded in S1 were not sufficient to produce awareness. These observations indicate that activity in the primary sensory cortex is necessary, but not necessarily sufficient, for perceptual awareness. The phenomenon of blindsight appears consistent with this view.

This leads us to consider the importance of perceptual awareness in general, and in visual function specifically. Suppose that in cases of blindsight some visual functions (e.g., the ability to discriminate colors, shapes, orientation, and spatial location) are preserved, but awareness of those visual functions is lost. A reasonable question might then be, "so what"? Visual functioning in the absence of awareness is striking to us because normal visual functions are so highly correlated with awareness of our visual experiences. As a result, we are easily seduced into assuming that awareness is a *necessary* component of those functions, but we all know that correlation does not imply causation. This raises the question of the degree to which the utility of vision actually depends on awareness. If visual functions are intact and awareness is abolished, what is the state of our sense of vision? We propose a pragmatic answer: it would depend on whether those preserved visual functions are (or can become) available during our daily activities.

One way to evaluate the practical consequences of having preserved visual functions in the absence of awareness is to see whether we can learn to use those functions more efficiently through training. In many situations, normal human observers can substantially improve their sensory abilities through practice (see Fine and Jacobs, 2002, for a review). We are therefore led to ask whether blindsight patients can learn to increase the utility of their residual abilities by practicing visual discrimination tasks and receiving accurate feedback concerning their performance. If the answer is yes, then the importance of awareness seems diminished from what we might at first presume. If the answer is no, then perhaps awareness is a necessary aspect of intact visual functioning.

Attempts to remediate cortical blindness have taken three basic approaches (see review by Schofield and Leff, 2009). The first is to use optical prisms to project images originating from areas within the scotoma into the good part of the visual field. The second involves training new oculomotor strategies—essentially attempting to train people to actively scan the areas within the visual field defect using intact areas of their visual field. The third remedial therapy attempts to improve visual performance within the field defect itself. The possibility that usable visual functions can be to some extent restored in the blind field by practice is most relevant to our present concerns.

At present, the answer to this question remains controversial. An early paper by Zihl (1980) reported improvements in three patients with large visual field defects. The patients were asked to make visually guided saccadic eye movements to eccentric visual targets that they claimed they could not see. Because of this lack of awareness, each visual stimulus had to be accompanied by an auditory click, so the patient would know when to initiate the saccade. There were two control conditions. In the first, performance on the same task was measured when the targets were presented in an intact portion of the visual field. The second consisted of "catch trials" (clicks with no corresponding visual stimulus) that were presented during testing within the scotoma. The reported results were very clear-cut. Saccade accuracy (the correspondence between target position and post-saccadic eye position) was high within the good portion of the visual fields of all three patients. When no visual targets were presented, the patients tended to make saccades of constant amplitude. When targets were presented within a patient's scotoma, saccades also initially tended to have constant amplitude, so accuracy was essentially at chance. However, after 10 or more training sessions, a high correlation developed between the eccentricity of the (unseen) targets and the magnitude of the saccades to them, although saccades to targets within the scotoma remained less accurate than those to targets presented outside the scotoma. Interestingly, the improvement in the accuracy of saccades to "unseen" visual targets did not depend on any type of feedback concerning their trial-by-trial accuracy. Perhaps even more interestingly, after 100 training trials, two patients reported having "feelings" about the accuracy of their saccades and were able to report whether their errors undershot or overshot the target location (Zihl, 1980).

Unfortunately, subsequent work using feedback training for a variety of visual functions (localization, shape or color discriminations) have not been nearly so successful, and the status of facilitated recovery of visual functions in cases of cortical blindness has become somewhat controversial (see review by Schofield and Leff, 2009). There are several reports indicating some restoration of conscious vision at the margins of the scotoma (e.g., Marshall et al., 2010), but some shrinking of scotomas without any special training is not an uncommon clinical finding. Moreover, many early studies did not include rigorous controls for small eye movements, which would allow patients to scan a larger region of space using their intact visual field and thereby produce an apparent decrease in the size of their visual field defect. Reinhard et al. (2005) provided a particularly convincing failure to demonstrate visual restoration by using a scanning laser ophthalmoscope to permit very accurate positioning of the stimuli on the retina. The failure to find a recovery of vision under these circumstances suggests that the earlier successes may be attributable to eye movements that were not noticed but allowed test stimuli to fall in the seeing portion of the patient's visual field. A recent study by Marshall et al. (2010) that also used rigorous controls to compensate for unwanted eye movements reported modest improvements in detection rates (average = 12.5%), but those improvements were restricted to the very margins of the field defects. Given the limited degree and spatial extent of these improvements, it is unlikely that these therapeutic regimens produced meaningful increases in the visual abilities of these patients. Thus, many clinicians continue to question the practical efficacy of visual restitution training programs. Blindsight may therefore have no real functional significance for patients, implying that awareness is an essential component to most of the pragmatic functions of vision.

The visual control of movements (i.e., grasping and navigation) may, however, constitute an important exception to this rule. In some cases, brain damage can leave an individual incapable of consciously discriminating specific visual attributes such as size, shape, and orientation, but these attributes can nonetheless guide motor responses (Goodale and Milner, 1992). Cases such as this have led to the suggestion that a visual subsystem that specializes in visually guided action operates outside of phenomenological experience (Goodale and Milner, 1992). B. de Gelder and colleagues (2008) provide a particularly dramatic demonstration of visually guided navigation in a patient who had bilateral destruction of the primary visual cortex and, as far as conscious detection is concerned, is completely blind. Despite his phenomenological blindness, this patient is able to successfully navigate a long corridor filled with a variety of obstacles (http://www.youtube.com/watch?v=GwGmWqXoMnM). But it should be recognized that blindsight patients with such remarkable abilities are rare.

6. Seeing without Vision: Anton-Babinski and Charles Bonnet Syndromes

Does everything have an opposite? "Ceiling" may be the opposite of "floor," but what might we consider the opposite of "rug"? Perhaps not everything has an opposite, but blindsight does. The opposite of blindsight is a mysterious disorder known as Anton's syndrome. At the very end of the 19th century, a German neurologist named Gabriel Anton published a paper describing a collection of patients with marked disorders of the central nervous system (including one blind and two deaf patients) who were seemingly unaware of any impairment in their perception (Anton 1899; translation in Forde and Wallesch, 2003). Anton's patients do not simply display a lack of awareness of any perceptual impairment; they insist that their perceptions are entirely intact. These experiences are either delusions or entirely internal fabrications, but do they classify as "perceptual" experiences? It seems entirely rational to conclude that a patient who claims she is blind can "see" in the sense that her forced-choice "guesses" are well above chance. But what should we make of a person who claims to "see" things when his or her verbal reports are completely inaccurate? While a few cases of patients unaware of their evident blindness had been described earlier (Forde and Wallesch, 2003), Anton's case published in 1899 remains the best-known early instance of this strange disorder.

In his paper, Anton described Ursula Mercz, a 56-year-old seamstress who was cortically blind—completely unable to see objects or movement of any kind, or to distinguish between light and dark. However, if asked to name an object presented to her, Ursula would provide an incorrect answer, either by randomly guessing or by palpating an object if it was within her reach (Forde and Wallesch, 2003). She would name objects even if none was actually shown to her, and persistently claimed she was able to see the presented objects, denying any blindness. Interestingly, Ursula also had difficulty speaking, specifically in accessing words (an "expressive aphasia"), but she was acutely aware of this deficit. She often became angry and frustrated when she was unable to come up with the name of an object and never denied her speaking disability. She was therefore *selectively unaware* of her visual impairment, suggesting that her inability to detect her own blindness was not the result of some pervasive cognitive impairment.

Unfortunately, Ursula Mercz died in a hospital after living with Anton's syndrome for only a few months. However, her death did allow Anton to examine her brain post-mortem, and he included a description of his initial pathological findings in his 1899 report. Among his many findings, he noted diffuse lesions evidenced by the shrunken appearance of isolated regions on both the left and right occipital lobes, which were considered the likely cause of what Anton considered total cortical blindness (Forde and Wallesch 2003). He also noted the destruction of multiple pathways that would have served to connect the occipital lobes to other brain areas important for normal vision. To Anton, these findings seemed to suggest that the damaged visual areas responsible for Ursula's cortical blindness were effectively disconnected from other functional brain areas, and this disconnection somehow resulted in Ursula's inability to detect her own visual deficit (see also Heilman, 1991).

Only 15 years after Anton's description of the intriguing case of Ursula Mercz, Joseph Babinski, a prominent late 19th-century French neurologist, published the first of a series of studies discussing patients with similar disorders. Babinski described patients who were unaware of their own paralysis. In this famous 1914 publication, Babinski introduced the term "anosognosia" as a general condition in which patients were unaware of their own deficits (Langer, 2009, 388). Today, the case of Anton's syndrome (or Anton-Babinski syndrome), characterized by the inability of patients to recognize their own blindness, is considered one of several forms of anosognosias, including conditions in which patients are unaware of serious deficits such as deafness, aphasia, and memory loss. In many cases these disorders are distinct from generalized dementia, as the patients' lack of awareness is specific to their particular deficit (Forde and Wallesch, 2003).

Advanced neuroimaging techniques have furthered our understanding of Anton's syndrome (e.g., Maddula, Lutton, and Keegan, 2009), although the neuropsychological mechanisms underlying the disorder remain the subject of scientific debate. Multiple hypotheses have been proposed, but sufficient studies have not been conducted to conclusively correlate the incidence of Anton's with any specific cortical area or neuropathology. This is largely due to the rarity of the syndrome (Prigatano, 1991). Ever since Babinski's first discussion of anosognosias, some physicians, scientists, and psychologists have suggested that these disorders may actually be some extreme form of psychological coping mechanism and not due to any specific neurological abnormality (Langer, 2009). However, a general consensus remains among those who have studied anosognosias that the disorders are a manifestation of organic disease (Langer, 2009; Prigatano, 2009). A recent hypothesis has suggested that Anton's is the result of intellectual impairments that prevent patients from performing the self-observation necessary to detect their own deficits (Levine, 1990). However, Anton's patients may be aware of other impairments—Ursula Mercz, for example, was aware that she had language difficulties.

The hypothesis that the syndrome results from a disconnection between damaged visual areas and intact areas involved in high-level visual cognition, which was first proposed by Anton himself, remains viable. Abutalebi et al. (2007) have reported a case in which they propose the occurrence of Anton's might be attributable to the involvement of their patient's corpus callosum following a severe stroke. Lesions affecting the splenium are related to another curious condition called "pure alexia" (or "alexia without agraphia") in which individuals lose their ability to read while their ability to write is preserved. Pure alexia is typically the result of lesions of the left occipital lobe (often with involvement of lingual and fusiform gyrus) that also involve the splenium of the corpus callosum. According to Geschwind's classic treatment of cortical disconnection syndromes (Geschwind, 1965a,b), pure alexia results from a disconnection between a functional right occipital lobe with the angular gyrus of the left hemisphere. In an analogous argument, Abutalebi et al. (2007) suggest that their patient's denial of blindness was mediated by a disconnection between the blinded left hemisphere and the right hemisphere, which (as proposed by Heilman et al., 1998) mediates "awareness of illness." There are several puzzling aspects of this case however. First, although most of the neuroradiological evidence indicated that the damage was confined to the left hemisphere and the splenium of the corpus callosum, and should therefore have produced only a right field hemianopia, the patient demonstrated cortical blindness in *both* hemifields. Second, despite the left hemisphere lesion, visual evoked potentials were normal *bilaterally* after 2 months. Thus, a coherent explanation of this particular case remains problematic. In fact, although the idea may seem somewhat far-fetched, it is possible that the visual defects in the left visual field represent a case of hysterical blindness (blindness in the absence of any detectable pathology, described in greater detail later in the chapter). If this were the case, the patient would simultaneously be demonstrating Anton's syndrome (a denial of blindness) in one hemifield and hysterical blindness (a denial of vision) in the other hemifield!

Finally, it has been suggested that Anton's syndrome occurs when patients are cortically blind due to a failure of the primary geniculostriate visual pathway, but still have some subcortical visual activity (Forde and Wallesch, 2003). To the extent that visual experience depends in some way on the activation of the visual association cortex, the putative subcortical activity would have to be conveyed to extra-striate visual cortical areas by some secondary pathway (Heilman, 1991). Therefore, whereas in blindsight it is argued that secondary pathways provide accurate information in the absence of phenomenal awareness, in Anton's syndrome those same visual pathways may be producing inaccurate visual experiences.

Anton's syndrome appears to reveal a "layer" or aspect regarding the neural substrates of perceptual awareness complementing that revealed by blindsight. Here, rather than a demonstration of residual visual function in the absence of awareness, we observe instead cortical blindness without an awareness of the blindness—that is, a failure to recognize the loss of a function. If we take the syndrome at face value and grant that the patient honestly believes he or she can see, it implies that brain regions beyond the boundaries of a lesion can produce the subjective impression that one is seeing when that is apparently not the case. But one need not turn to neurological conditions to find evidence that vivid visual percepts can be generated in the absence of ocular inputs: ordinary dreams produce a subjective experience of seeing that is certainly not conveyed by the eyes. In fact, research on brain function during REM (rapid eye motion) sleep (the stage of sleep where dreams are likely to occur) has indicated that during dreaming there is a suppression of activity in the primary visual cortex (Braun et al., 1998). Is it possible that this suppression of activity releases higher visual centers from processing "real" visual inputs, and this permits the internal generation of complex visual perceptions?

Although blindsight and Anton's syndrome seem to be polar opposites, it also seems logically possible that they could co-occur. A patient with Anton's syndrome would insist that his or her vision was intact but have no ability to describe visual stimuli presented to them. When shown a red balloon, the patient would be no more likely to describe a red balloon than a bunch of bananas. However, when asked to "guess" whether he or she was being shown a red or blue balloon in a 2AFC discrimination task, the patient could respond correctly more often than one would expect by chance. This would be an indication of co-existing blindsight in an Anton's patient.

We cannot consider Anton's syndrome without also considering another anomalous condition that results from pathologies within the visual pathways known as Charles Bonnet syndrome (see review by Menon et al., 2003). Bonnet syndrome is another condition in which an individual with severely degraded vision experiences vivid visual percepts that are not conveyed by the eyes (i.e., hallucinations). The essential characteristics of these hallucinatory experiences are that they (1) refer to the external environment, (2) are very vivid in detail, 3) are complex (as opposed to simple sensory experiences such as flashing lights, pinwheels, or geometric shapes), 4) are involuntary with regard to either their onset or termination, and 5) are recognized as being illusory. Thus, the main feature that distinguishes the Bonnet and Anton syndromes appears to be that Bonnet patients recognize their visual experiences as hallucinatory. In contrast, Anton's patients believe their experiences are real, regardless of whether they are best characterized as hallucinatory or delusional. Some have suggested that Bonnet syndrome hallucinations should be called pseudo-hallucinations, to emphasize their recognition that the percepts are not real. These internally generated experiences typically consist of isolated faces, human figures (sometimes in costume), animals, buildings, or other complex, well-formed inanimate objects (e.g., trees). They can be seen in miniature or much greater than "life-size." They are typically rigid and stationary, but in some cases they can drift in space or are even animated. An intriguing recent functional magnetic resonance imaging (fMRI) finding indicates that particular categories of visions are associated with cortical activations in brain regions associated with mediating visual percepts of that category (i.e., fusiform gyrus with visions of faces; see Ffytche, Howard, Brammer, Woodruf, and Williams, 1998), which accords with patient reports that their pseudo-hallucinations have a truly percept-like character. Importantly, Bonnet "faces" need not be familiar to the person experiencing them, so they do not necessarily reflect any previous visual experiences. Bonnet hallucinations typically are not emotionally disturbing or distressing to the individual who experiences them, and in fact are often described as pleasant or even humorous. This property distinguishes them from the hallucinatory experiences of psychotic patients. The eyes do not convey the vivid hallucinations of Bonnet patients. They appear quite simply to constitute yet another category of visual experiences that are independent of afferent activity in the optic nerve.

Charles Bonnet syndrome occurs both in cases of cortical and noncortical blindness (e.g., blindness due to optic nerve injury, retinitis pigmentosa, macular degeneration, glaucoma, or cataracts). It seems to be more prevalent in elderly patients, but an obvious explanation is that the antecedent causes of blindness are more likely in the elderly. It may be more common than is generally realized, since patients are hesitant to report that they are "having visions" because they do not want family members and care givers to think they are "losing their minds." It seems possible that Charles Bonnet patients and Anton's syndrome patients have similar phenomenological experiences. Both describe vivid hallucinations, and the major difference appears to be that Bonnet patients recognize the unreality of their visions whereas Anton's patients do not. However, even Bonnet patients can sometimes be deceived by their hallucinations, especially in the early stages of their condition, and most especially if their hallucinatory experience is appropriate to the context in which it occurs (Teunisse, 1997). In contrast with Bonnet patients, Anton's syndrome apparently occurs only when there is cortical damage, which suggests that the complete lack of insight regarding the hallucinatory nature of the visions is a deficit that is specific to cortical damage.

7. Hysterical Blindness

Dissociations between what we *can* see and what we *think we can see* do not necessarily depend on brain damage or the types of reorganized functions that might accompany brain damage. We now turn to cases in which apparently honest individuals report partial or complete blindness in the absence of any detectable medical impairment. The historical diagnostic term for this syndrome has been "hysterical blindness," although the influence of Freudian theory led to the adoption of the modern diagnosis of "visual conversion disorder." We employ the historical label, however, since the history of this condition has a fascinating and somewhat onerous history in medical science, and we wish to convey some of that history to those who might not be familiar with it.

The ancients made the first known diagnoses of "hysteria." It was described in Egyptian writings and was also recognized in the medical literature of Ancient Greece. The name derives from the Greek word for uterus (ὑστέρα, *hystera*), as the condition was attributed to some abnormality of the uterus, which Plato regarded as virtually a separate entity within the female body. The diagnosis was reserved exclusively for women, and the symptoms were so many and varied that almost any malady or physical complaint (from a female patient) could be considered symptomatic of hysteria. The great Roman physician Galen thought that hysteria was caused by sexual deprivation. From medieval times until the early part of the 20th century the prescribed treatment was either sexual intercourse (if the patient was married), marriage (followed by intercourse) if the patient was single, or, as a last resort, "pelvic massage." So frequent was the diagnosis and the accepted therapy required that demand led to the invention of the vibrator, which was widely advertised in such otherwise mundane publications as the Sears and Roebuck catalogue. This story forms the backdrop for the 2011 British romantic comedy film *Hysteria*.

Hysteria played a prominent role in much of the literature of the 19th and early 20th centuries, including the works of Dostoyevsky, who some scholars consider the greatest novelist of all time. Many consider its role in medical history proof of male dominance and chauvinism, an opinion that seems to have considerable merit. The expression "conversion disorder" derives from an explanation of the disorder that was first formulated by Breuer and Freud (1895), who proposed that the symptoms arose through attempts to repress unconscious sexual desires. In modern medicine, a diagnosis of conversion disorder requires a symptomatic somatic deficit (such as blindness or paralysis) without demonstrable pathology but with a closely antecedent psychological trauma (*Diagnostic and Statistical Manual of Mental Disorders; DSM*-IV). Here we concern ourselves mainly with cases of hysterical blindness or severe visual impairment.

A small but growing literature describes attempts to determine the neurological correlates of hysterical blindness. The fundamental question concerns whether objective evidence of a visual impairment is demonstrable. We know from blindsight that subjective reports do not necessarily reflect visual abilities. Are patients with this syndrome truly unable to process visual inputs, or do visual stimuli generate neural responses that somehow fail to generate visual percepts? One thing seems clear, the clinicians who have treated these people and written case studies about them are convinced that there is no malingering involved in visual conversion disorder—these people honestly believe they are blind.

Cortical activity can be recorded noninvasively via electrodes placed on the scalp. This is, for instance, the way the electroencephalograph (EEG) is obtained. If a stimulus is presented many times and the segment of the EEG that follows each stimulus presentation is averaged over the series of presentations, the background EEG, which is uncorrelated with any neural response to the stimulus, averages to zero volts. This trick of signal processing can reveal very small neural responses that are time-locked to the stimulus. Such time-locked responses to visual stimuli are called visual evoked potentials (VEPs). The primary visual cortex is typically considered to represent the first stage in the cortical processing of visual information. Traditionally, VEPs recorded from the striate cortex have been the "gold standard" for determining the functional integrity of the early visual pathways in the brain. For instance, visual and auditory evoked potentials are used to evaluate the integrity of vision and hearing in infants (e.g., Sherman, 1979; also see National Institute of Neurological Disorders and Stroke website). Several studies have reported normal VEPs in hysterically blind patients (e.g., Schoenfeld et al., 2011), suggesting that any visual impairments are the result of a suppression of visual processing that occurs at higher levels of processing than the primary visual cortex. However, some noteworthy studies have challenged this conclusion.

Wering et al. (2004) used fMRI to investigate cortical activity in five patients with a visual loss that had no detectable physical cause, and in fact demonstrated what were regarded as normal visual pattern-evoked potentials. All of these patients had developed their symptoms following a stressful life situation, and each met the American Psychiatric Association criteria for a conversion disorder. The patients were compared to a control group with normal vision and no history of neurological illness. Despite the fact that all of the patients produced normal VEPs, functional magnetic resonance imaging revealed that the patients generated significantly reduced bold signals in their primary and secondary visual cortices relative to the control subjects. Moreover, the patients showed *greater* activations than controls in diverse other brain regions including the inferior frontal cortex. These observations raise the possibility that hysterical blindness is at least in part mediated by active inhibition of visual cortical areas (including V1) by a diverse set of brain areas that may include portions of the frontal lobes, the basal ganglia, and the thalamus. This notion that cognitive functions mediated by the frontal lobes might be of fundamental import to perception is similar to the perceptual decision bias that Ko and Lau (2012) have suggested is at the heart of the blindsight phenomenon.

A recent case study (Waldvogel, Ullrich, and Strasburger, 2007) provides support for this idea. This report describes the case of patient BT, who became completely blind at the age of 20 after falling off a carousel and striking her head. Although no radiological evidence of brain damage could be found, the patient was diagnosed as suffering from cortical blindness due to a "craniocerebral trauma." Importantly, electrophysiological testing revealed a complete absence of VEPs. The diagnosis was complete cortical blindness. The patient learned Braille, used a Seeing Eye dog, and lived her life as a blind person. Thirteen years after her accident, however, BT was diagnosed with dissociative identity disorder, a condition popularly known as "multiple personality disorder." After two years of psychiatric therapy, a new personality emerged in BP, and incredibly, this new personality could see. Moreover, the patient could be prompted to switch between her new seeing personality and her previous main personality, which remained totally blind. When VEPs were recorded, they appeared normal when she adopted her new seeing personality, but completely vanished when she switched back to her blind state. The data from this patient suggest that the visual system has the ability not just to inhibit but to completely block the processing of visual inputs at the earliest level in the cortical visual hierarchy. How this might occur is uncertain, but one potential mechanism might be a profound inhibition of projection neurons within the lateral geniculate nucleus, the primary thalamic nucleus that relays information from the retina to the visual cortex (Guillery and Sherman, 2002; Sherman, 2009) and has already been implicated in cases of hysterical blindness (Werring et al., 2004). The extent to which such a gating process plays a role in other instances of hysterical blindness remains to be determined, but if the process is found to have some degree of generality, then the occurrence of even more selective gating—for example, the selective gating of information about color or facial features—becomes an intriguing possibility.

8. Modality Plasticity: A Modern Perspective on Vicariation?

The preceding discussion has considered a variety of curious disturbances of vision, where all are anomalies *of vision*. Johannes Müller was the first to propose that visual experiences are always the result of patterns of activity within the central *visual* pathways. This position is fully ingrained in the history of neuroscience as Müller's Doctrine of Specific Nerve Energies. Müller's doctrine is the basis for prosthetic devices like cochlear implants. Electrical stimulation of the auditory nerve produces auditory sensations, just as stimulation of the visual cortex produces visual sensations. If we could re-route the auditory nerve to innervate the lateral geniculate nucleus, then we presume that acoustic energy would produce visual experiences.

The fact that the organization of our sensory systems is so consistent across individuals seduces us into thinking of these systems as fixed and immutable. But evidence of functional plasticity and reorganization in the cerebral cortex has been available since the landmark work of Glees and Cole (1950), who demonstrated plastic changes in the mapping of the homunculus in the primary motor cortex following small lesions. More recent work has shown that experience-induced plastic changes can also occur in the sensory cortex (Kilgard et al., 2001). This evidence suggesting that cortical maps are dynamically adaptive raises many questions. For example, if training on the discrimination of a particular frequency increases the size of the cortical representation for that frequency, do the representations of other frequencies shrink as a result? What are the limits to this sort of plasticity? In general, the plastic changes appear on a relatively local level; sites that used to control the thumb can be modified to move the index finger if the original representation of the index finger is damaged. However, is it possible for cortical functions to change even more dramatically, so that, for example, what was once (or should have been) visual cortex comes to perform nonvisual functions? This idea has a history, one that dates back to the work of Karl Lashley (1943).

"Vicariation" is the term classical neurologists used to refer to a hypothetical capacity of neural tissue to perform a new function (e.g., Finger, 2010). Vicariation was regarded as one mechanism responsible for recovery of function following brain damage. According to the principle of vicariation, functions are localized within specific brain structures, but a function lost as a result of brain damage to that structure could recover because intact tissue could eventually reorganize itself to perform the lost function. One would think that there would be severe limits to this sort of functional reorganization, and perhaps the most important is anatomical. Over what distances do we suppose the re-routing of neural connections can occur?

Consider, for instance, vicariation of cortical functions. Certain aspects of the anatomical organization of cerebral cortex seem to lend itself to functional plasticity. One of these aspects is that in many ways, different areas within the neocortex share a similar anatomical organization. They all have six layers, and each layer is populated by similar cell types throughout the cortex mantle. Stellate cells are found in layer IV. Pyramidal cells are found in layers III, V, and VI. In addition, the input-output connections are similar in different cortical fields: cortico-cortical connections originate with layer III pyramidal cells, layer V pyramids provide the subcortical projections to the brainstem and spinal cord, and layer VI pyramids provide feedback connections to the thalamus. One might reasonably suggest that the main factor that distinguishes the functions of different cortical fields is their inputs: auditory cortex receives auditory inputs from the medial geniculate nucleus and visual cortex receives visual input from the lateral geniculate nucleus. The computations that occur within different cortical areas might be similar, and it has been suggested that cortical specializations arise by performing similar computations on different inputs (e.g., Douglas and Martin, 2004; Ebdon, 1993). Since the eyes provide the major source of sensory input to the primary visual cortex, we might expect very little vicariation in V1. However, some recent evidence suggests this expectation may need some revision.

There is a long-held and widespread belief that blind people develop enhanced capabilities in their remaining sensory modalities (e.g., Ashmead et al., 1998; Bull et al., 1983; Gougoux et al., 2004; Lessard et al., 1998; Niemeyer and Starlinger, 1981; Roder et al., 1999). Not all blind people demonstrate enhanced audition, but those who do generally became blind at an early age. Enhanced accuracy in localizing sound sources appears to be the most consistently observed improvement (Gougoux et al., 2005). Unlike vision, where location is specified to a large extent by retinal position, the location of sound sources must be computed—primarily by comparing subtle differences in the acoustic signals arriving at each ear. These comparisons take place at a number of processing stages within the auditory pathways, beginning with the third-order auditory neurons in the superior olive and extending into the auditory cortex. Subtle changes in the tuning characteristics of the neurons within these ascending pathways could account for enhanced sound localization accuracy. Another possibility is that blind people become especially efficient in utilizing subtle cues that are available to all of us. Thus, reports of enhanced hearing in the blind pose no particular problem for our present understanding of auditory psychophysics or physiology.

There are, however, observations that do pose a considerable conceptual challenge. A very provocative and puzzling observation is that blind individuals performing auditory (or tactile) tasks frequently display stimulus-evoked activity in their visual cortex, activity that is not observed when sighted individuals perform the same tasks (Gougoux et al., 2005; Merabet et al., 2008). Does this nonvisual activity reflect auditory (or tactile) processing in the visual cortex, and if so, how does the nonvisual information get there?

In the case of congenital blindness, or even early-onset blindness that results from neurological trauma, a reorganization of anatomical pathways could provide new sources of input to a visual cortex that no longer receives appropriate visual afferents. Because there is a great deal of post-natal neurogenesis and synaptic plasticity, early blindness could have a substantial impact on the trajectory of post-natal neural developments. We also know that there are many multimodal cortical areas that tend to be located in *higher* association areas that surround the *primary* sensory cortices (see Kandel et al., 2000). These multimodal areas receive converging inputs from the unimodal cortex, but could provide reciprocal feedback connections to the unimodal cortex. Perhaps those pathways are either amplified, reinforced, or do not undergo synaptic "pruning" in cases of early onset blindness. It is also possible that these activations in the visual cortex do not reflect auditory processing per se, but some higher-order cognitive operation that accompanies (for instance) sound localization processing in blind but not sighted individuals. Given the poor temporal resolution of the bold signal in fMRI, it is difficult to estimate the temporal dynamics between the activations observed in the auditory cortex and the mysterious nonvisual "sensory" activity in the visual cortex. The relationships between fMRI activations and behavior are correlations, so we cannot assume the activity is functionally related to the enhanced performance—the activations might be epiphenomenal.

The results provided by Pascual-Leone and colleagues (Merabet et al., 2008) are especially noteworthy, as they have observed vicariation of tactile and auditory functions in the visual cortex that occur with an astonishingly rapid time course (in blindfolded volunteers), *and* they have further shown that the activity in the visual cortex contributes to the ability of these volunteers to read Braille, since their reading was disrupted by transcranial magnetic stimulation applied to the occipital lobes.

9. Summary and Conclusions

We have considered many conundrums and paradoxes in the domain of human visual experience. On the one hand, the visual system displays remarkable sensitivity—9 or 10 quantal absorptions can initiate a cascade of neural activity that leads to a visual experience. On the other hand, various forms of neural pathology can result in (1) people who think they are blind but can produce objective evidence of vision, or (2) people who appear blind but do not realize (and may even vehemently deny) their disability, or (3) people who recognize their blindness but nevertheless consciously experience visual phantoms that are notably vivid although they are recognized as unreal. We have also seen how blindness can occur in the absence of any detectable pathology—a blindness that appears to be of psychological origin, but can nonetheless have objectively measurable neural correlates. This bewildering array of conditions presents a puzzle of considerable magnitude. The ad hoc nature of the extant explanations seems frustratingly incomplete, but that is entirely understandable.

One observation we would offer relates to the fact that from the first scientific inquiries into the nature of perception, theorists have recognized that perception involves an intricate interplay between the sensory signals originating from the retinal image and endogenous processes whose origins are largely unknown. The consequences of these endogenous processes include such robust effects as the voluntary deployment of attention (e.g., Posner et al., 1980) and observer expectancies (e.g., Hughes et al., 2001). Strange phenomena such as Anton's syndrome, Bonnet's syndrome, and hysterical blindness may be considered the most extreme cases of endogenously mediated percepts that we know of—they come entirely from within the brain. One can only hope that continued exploration of these strange phenomena will one day provide unique insights into one of the deepest mysteries in biology—the fundamental relationship between mind and brain.

References

Abutalebi, J., Arcari, C., Rocca, M. A., Rossi, P., Comola, M., Comi, G. C., Rovaris, M., and Filippi, M. (2007). Anton's syndrome following callosal disconnection. *Behavioural Neurology*, 18, 183–186.

Anstis, S. M., & Atkinson, J. (1967). Distortions of moving figures viewed through a stationary slit. *American Journal of Psychology*, 80, 572–585.

Anton, G. (1899). Ueber die Selbstwahrnehmung der Herderkrankungen des Gehirns durch den Kranken bei Rindenblindheit und Rindentaubheit. *Archiv für Psychiatrie*, 32, 86–127.

Ashmead, D. H., Wall, R. S., Ebinger, K. A., Eaton, S. B., Snook-Hill, M. M., et al. (1998). Spatial hearing in blind children with visual disabilities. *Perception*, 27, 105–122.

Averbach, E. and Coriell, A. S. (1961). Short-term memory in vision. *Bell System Technical Journal*, 40, 309–328.

Babinski, J. (1914). Contribution à l'étude des troubles mentaux dans hémiplégia organique cérébral (anosognosie). *Revue Neurologique* (Paris), 22, 845–884.

Braun, A. R. et al. (1998). Dissociated pattern of activity in visual cortices and their projections during human rapid eye features and conjunctions. *Nature*, 390, 279–281.

Breuer, J. and Freud, S. (1957/1895). *Studies on Hysteria*. Translated by J. Strachey. New York: Basic Books.

Bull, R., Rathborn, H., and Clifford, B. R. (1983). The voice recognition accuracy of blind listeners. *Perception*, 12, 223–226.

Campion, J., Latto, R., and Smith, Y. M. (1983). Is blindsight an effect of scattered light, spared cortex and near-threshold vision? *Behavioral and Brain Sciences*, 6, 423–486.

Caplovitz, G. P., Fendrich, R., and Hughes, H. C. (2008). Failures to see: Attentive blank stares revealed by change blindness. *Consciousness and Cognition*, 17, 877–886.

Crick, F. H. C., Marr, D. C., and Poggio, T. (1981). An information-processing approach to understanding the visual cortex. In *The Organization of the Cerebral Cortex*, edited by F. O. Schmitt, pp. 505–533. Cambridge, MA: MIT Press.

De Gelder, B., Tamietto, M., van Boxten, G., Goebel, R., Sahraie, A., van den Stock, J., Stienen, B. M. C., Weiskrantz, L., and Pegna, A. (2008). Intact navigation skills after bilateral loss of striate cortex. *Current Biology*, 18(24), R1128–R1129.

Douglas, R. J., and Martin, K. A. C. (2004). Neuronal circuits of the neocortex. *Annual Review of Neuroscience*, 27, 419–451.

Ebdon, M. (1993). Is the cerebral neocortex a uniform cognitive architecture? *Mind and Language*, 8(3), 368–403.

Fahle, M. and Poggio, T. (1981). 'Visual hyperacuity: spatiotemporal interpolation in human vision. *Proceedings of the Royal Society of London. Series B, Biological Sciences*, 213(1193), 451–477.

Fendrich, R., Rieger, J. W., and Heinze, H.-J. (2005). The effect of retinal stabilization on anorthoscopic percepts under free-viewing conditions. *Vision Research*, 45, 567–582.

Fendrich, R., Wessinger, C. M., and Gazzaniga, M. S. (1992). Residual vision in a scotoma: Implications for blindsight. *Science*, 258(5087), 1489–1491.

Ffytche, D. H., Howard, R. J., Brammer, M. J., David, A., Woodruff, P., and Williams, S. (1998). The anatomy of conscious vision: An fMRI study of visual hallucinations. *Nature Neuroscience*, 1(8), 738–742.

Fine, I. and Jacobs, R. A. (2002). Comparing perceptual learning across tasks: A review. *Journal of Vision*, 2, 190–203.

Finger, S. (2010). Recovery of function: Redundancy and vicariation theories. In *The Handbook of Clinical Neurology*, Vol. 95: *The History of Neurology*, edited by S. Finger, F. Boller, and K. L. Tyler, chapter 51, pp. 833–841. New York: Elsevier.

Forde, E. and Wallesch, C. (2003). "Mind-blind for blindness": A psychological review of Anton's syndrome. In *Classic Cases in Neuropsychology*, edited by C. Code, C. Wallesch, Y. Joanette, and A. R. Lecours, Vol. II, pp. 199–221. New York: Psychology Press.

Geschwind N. (1965a). Disconnexion syndromes in animals and man. I. *Brain*, 88, 237–294.

Geschwind N. (1965b). Disconnexion syndromes in animals and man. II. *Brain*, 88, 585–644.

Glees, P. and Cole, J. (1950). Recovery of skilled motor functions after small repeated lesions in the motor cortex in macaque. *Journal of Neurophysiology*, 13, 137–148.

Goodale, M. A. and Milner, A. D. (1992). Separate visual pathways for perception and action. *Trends in Neuroscience*, 15, 20–25.

Gougoux, F., Zatorre, R. J., Lassonde, M., Voss, P., and Lepore, F. (2005). A functional neuroimaging study of sound localization: Visual cortex activity predicts performance in early-blind individuals. *PLoS Biology*, 3(2), e27.

Gougoux F., Lepore F., Lassonde M., Voss P., Zatorre R. J., et al. (2004). Neuropsychology: Pitch discrimination in the early blind. *Nature*, 430, 309.

Green, D. M. and Swets, J. A. (1966). *Signal Detection Theory and Psychophysics*. New York: John Wiley.

Guillery, R. W. and Sherman, S. M. (2002). Thalamic relay functions and their role in corticocortical communication: generalizations from the visual system. *Neuron*, 33(2), 163–175.

Hecht, S., Shlaer, S., and Pirenne, M. H. (1942). Energy, quanta and vision. *Journal of General Physiology*, 25(6), 819–840.

Heilman, K. M. (1991). Anosognosia: Possible neuropsychological mechanisms. In *Awareness of Deficit after Brain Injury*, edited by G. Prigatano and D. Schacter, pp. 53–62. New York: Oxford University Press.

Heilman, K. M., Barrett, A. M., and Adair, J. C. (1998). Possible mechanisms of anosognosia: A defect in self-awareness. *Philosophical Transactions of the Royal Society B: Biological Sciences,* 353, 1903–1909.

Helmholtz H. von. (1962/1867). *Handbook of Physiological Optics.* Translated by J. S. Southhall. New York: Dover.

Hughes, H. C., Darcey, T. M., Barkan, H. I., Williamson, P. D., Roberts, D. W. and Aslin, C. H. (2001). Responses of human auditory association cortex to the omission of an expected acoustic event. *NeuroImage,* 13, 1073–1089.

Hughes, Howard C., Nozawa, George, and Kitterle, Frederick. (1996). Global precedence, spatial frequency channels, and the statistics of natural images. *Journal of Cognitive Neuroscience,* 8, 197–230.

Humphrey, N. K. and Weiskrantz, L. (1967). Vision in monkeys after removal of the striate cortex. *Nature,* 215, 595–597.

Kandel, E. R., Schwartz, J. H., and Jessell, T. M. (2000). *Principles of Neural Science,* 4th ed., chs. 18 and 19. New York: McGraw-Hill.

Kelly. D. H. (1961). Visual responses to time dependent stimuli. I. Amplitude sensitivity measurements. *Journal of the Optical Society of America,* 51, 422–429.

Kilgard, M. P., Pandya, P. K., Vazquez, K., Gehi, A., Schreiner, C. E., and Merzenich, M. M. (2001). Sensory input directs spatial and temporal plasticity in primary auditory cortex. *Journal of Neurophysiology,* 86, 326–338.

Kluver, H. (1942). Functional significance of the geniculostriate system. *Cold Spring Harbor Symposia on Quantitative Biology,* 7, 253–299.

Ko, Y. and Lau, H. (2012). A detection theoretic explanation of blindsight suggests a link between conscious perception and metacognition. *Philosophical Transactions of the Royal Society B: Biological Sciences,* 367(1594), 1401–1411.

Langer, K. (2009). Babinski's anosognosia for hemiplegia in early twentieth-century French neurology. *Journal of the History of the Neurosciences,* 18(4), 387–405.

Lashley, K. S. (1943). Studies of cerebral function in learning XII. Loss of the maze habit after occipital lesion in blind rats. *Journal of Comparative Neurology,* 79(3), 431–462.

Lessard, N., Paré, M., Lassonde, M., and Lepore, F. (1998). Early-blind human subjects localize sound sources better than sighted subjects. *Nature,* 395, 278–280.

Levine, D. (1990). Unawareness of visual and sensorimotor deficits: A hypothesis. *Brain and Cognition,* 13, 233–281.

Libet, B. (1979). Subjective referral of the timing for a conscious sensory experience. *Brain,* 102, 193–224.

Livingstone, M. S. and Hubel, D. H. (1988). Segregation of form, color, movement and depth: Anatomy, physiology and perception. *Science,* 240, 740–749.

Luck, S. J., and Vogel, E. K. (1997). The capacity of visual working memory for features and conjunctions. *Nature,* 390, 279–281.

Maddula, M., Lutton, S., and Keegan, B. (2009). Anton's syndrome due to cerebrovascular disease: A case report. *Journal of Medical Case Reports,* 3, 9028.

Marshall, R. S., Chmayssani, M., O'Brien, K. A., Handy, C., and Greenstein, V. C. (2010). Visual field expansion after visual restoration therapy. *Clinical Rehabilitation,* 24, 1027–1035.

Menon, G. J., Rahman, I., Menon, S. J., and Dutton, G. N. (2003). Complex visual hallucinations in the visually impaired: The Charles Bonnet syndrome. *Survey of Ophthalmology,* 48, 58–72.

Merabet, L. B., Hamilton, R., Schlaug, G., Swisher, J. D., Kiriakopoulos, E., Pitskel, N. B., Kauffman, T., and Pascual-Leone, A. (2008). Rapid and reversible recruitment of early visual cortex for touch. *PLoS ONE*, 3(8), e3046. Doi:10.1371/journal.pone.0003046.

National Institute of Neurological Disorders and Stroke. Neurological Diagnostic Tests and Procedures, http://www.ninds.nih.gov/disorders/misc/diagnostic_tests.htm.

Niemeyer W. and Starlinger, I. (1981). Do the blind hear better? II Investigations of auditory processing in congenital and early acquired blindness. *Audiology* 20, 510–515.

Oliva, A. and Torralba, A. (2006). Building the gist of a scene: The role of global image features in recognition. *Progress in Brain Research*, 155, 23–36.

O'Regan, J. K., Rensink, R. A., and Clark, J. J. (1999). Change-blindness as a result of "mud-splashes." *Nature,* 398, 34.

Pasik, P., Pasik, T., and Krieger, H. P. (1959). Effect of cerebral lesions upon optokinetic nystagmus in monkeys. *Journal of Neurophysiology*, 22, 297–304.

Pöppel, E., Held, R., and Frost, D. (1973). Residual visual function after brain wounds involving the central visual pathways in man. *Nature,* 243, 295–296.

Posner, M. I., Snyder, C. R., and Davidson, B. J. (1980). Attention and the detection of signals. *Journal of Experimental Psychology, General*, 109(2), 160–174.

Potter, M. C. (1975). Meaning in visual search. *Science*, 187, 965–966.

Potter, M. C. and Levy, E. I. (1969). Recognition memory for a rapid sequence of pictures. *Journal of Experimental Psychology*, 81(1), 10–15.

Prigatano, G. P. (1991). Disturbances of self-awareness of deficit after traumatic brain injury. In *Awareness of Deficit after Brain Injury,* edited by G. Prigatano and D. Schacter, pp. 111–126. New York: Oxford University Press.

Prigatano, G. P. (2009). Anosognosia: clinical and ethical considerations. *Current Opinion in Neurology*, 22, 606–611.

Reinhard, J., Schreiber, A., Scheifer, U., Kasten, E., Sabel, B. A., Kenkel, S., Vonthein, R., and Trauzettel-Klosinski, S. (2005). Does visual restitution training change absolute homonymous visual field? A fundus controlled study. *British Journal of Ophthalmology*, 89, 30–35.

Rensink R. A. (2002). Change detection. *Annual Review of Psychology*, 53, 245–277.

Rensink, R. A., O'Regan, J. K., and Clark, J. J. (1997). To see or not see: The need for attention to perceive changes in scene. *Psychological Science*, 8, 368–373.

Riddoch, G. (1917). Dissociation of visual perceptions due to occipital injuries, with especial reference to appreciation of movement. *Brain: A Journal of Neurology*, 40, 15–57.

Roder, B., Teder-Salejarvi, W., Sterr, A., Rosler, F., Hillyard, S. A., and Neville, H. J. (1999). Improved auditory spatial tuning in blind humans. *Nature,* 400, 162–166.

Schmid, M. C., Mrouka, S. W., Turchi, J., Saunders, R. C., Wilke, M., Peters, A. J., Ye, F. Q., and Leopold, D. A. (2010). Blindsight depends on the lateral geniculate nucleus. *Nature,* 466(7304), 373–377.

Schoenfeld, M. A., Hassa, T., Hopf, J-M., Eulitz, C., and Schmidt, R. (2011). Neural correlates of hysterical blindness. *Cerebral Cortex*, 21(10), 2394–2398.

Schofield, T. M. and Leff, A. P. (2009). Rehabilitation of hemianopia. *Current Opinion in Neurology*, 22, 36–40.

Shapley, R. (1990). Visual sensitivity and parallel retinocortical channels. *Annual Review of Psychology*, 41, 635–658.

Sherman, J. (1979). Visual evoked potential (VEP): Basic concepts and clinical applications. *Journal of the American Optometric Association*, 50, 19–30.

Sherman, S. M. (2009). Thalamic mechanisms in vision. *Encyclopedia of Neuroscience*, 929–944.

Simons, D. J., and Rensink, R. A. (2005). Change blindness: Past, present, and future. *Trends in Cognitive Science*, 9(1), 16–20.

Sperling, G. (1960). The information available in brief visual presentations. *Psychological Monographs: General and Applied*, 74, 1–30.

Stoerig, P., and Cowey, A. (1997). Blindsight in man and monkey. *Brain*, 120, 120–145.

Szeliski, R. (2011). *Computer Vision: Algorithms and Applications*. New York: Springer.

Teunisse, R. J. (1997). Charles Bonnet syndrome, insight and cognitive impairment. *Journal of the American Geriatric Society*, 45, 892–893.

Tolhurst, D. J. (1975). Reaction times in the detection of gratings by human observers: A probabilistic mechanism. *Vision Research*, 15(10), 1143–1149.

Torralba, A. (2003). Contextual priming for object detection. *International Journal of Computer Vision*, 63, 169–191.

Torralba, A. and Sinha, P. (2001). Recognizing indoor scenes. *MIT Artificial Intelligence Laboratory Memo 2001-015, CBCL Memo 202*.

Waldvogel, B., Ullrich, A., and Strasburger, H. (2007). Blind und sehend in einer Person. Schlußfolgerungen zur Psychoneurobiologie des Sehens. *Der Nervenarzt*, 78, 1303–1309.

Weiskrantz, L. (1963). Contour discrimination in a young monkey with striate cortex ablation. *Neuropsychologia*, 3, 145–164.

Weiskrantz, L. (1986). *Blindsight: A Case Study and Implications*. Oxford: Oxford University Press.

Weiskrantz, L., Warrington, E. K., Sanders, M. D., and Marshall, J. (1974). Visual capacity in the hemianopic field following a restricted occipital ablation. *Brain*, 97, 709–728.

Werring D. J., Weston, L. E. T., Bullmore, E. T., Plant, G.T., and Ron, M. A. (2004). Functional magnetic resonance imaging of the cerebral response to visual stimulation in medically unexplained visual loss. *Psychological Medicine*, 34, 583–589.

Westheimer, G. and McKee, S. P. (1977). Spatial configurations for visual hyperacuity. *Vision Research*, 17, 941–948.

Zihl, J. (1980). Blindsight: Improvement of visually guided eye movements by systematic practice in patients with cerebral blindness. *Neuropsychologica*, 18, 71–77.

Zöllner F. (1862). Über eine neue art anorthoskopischer zerrbilder. *Annalen der Physik und Chemie*, 117, 477–484.

13

A Crossmodal Perspective on Sensory Substitution

Ophelia Deroy and Malika Auvray

1. Introduction

Blind people's ability to navigate through unfamiliar environments forces us to wonder how they achieve this. It also leads to philosophical questions, which Descartes already captured:

> No doubt you have had the experience of walking over rough ground without a light, and finding it necessary to use a stick in order to guide yourself. You may then have been able to notice that by means of this stick, you could feel the various objects situated around you, and that you could even tell whether there were trees or rocks, or sand, or water, or grass, or mud, or any other such thing. It is true that this kind of sensation is somewhat confused and obscure in those who do not have long practice with it. But consider it in those born blind, who have made use of it all their lives: with them, you will find it is so perfect and so exact, that one might almost say that they see with their hands, or that their stick is the organ of some sixth sense given to them in place of sight (Descartes, 1637/1985, p. 153).

The development of refined conversion devices designed to compensate for blindness certainly makes Descartes's puzzle all the more relevant and difficult to solve. These substitution systems, which convert visual stimuli into tactile or auditory stimuli, give access to distant objects in a way that was not possible with white sticks. Can these devices offer a genuine substitute for vision or do they compensate its loss through other means? The name chosen for these systems—sensory substitution devices (SSDs)—seems to have embraced the most ambitious solution considered by Descartes in his quote, that is, that technical devices could enable blind people to see with some intact part of their anatomy. At first glance, sensory substitution devices certainly offer a striking functional equivalence with vision: they respond to electromagnetic stimuli, they enable blind people to navigate in new environments, to detect and identify remote objects and to judge their approximate distance. By bypassing the constraints of the mechanical trans-fer at stake in the white cane, SSDs convey information about the surrounding objects that is *richer* than the information previously accessed through the intact sense. What's more, they can do so at a *distance*, independent of an actual contact between the device and the object. Blind people now have access to the shape of out-of-reach objects, a privilege reserved so far to the sighted. Although training remains necessary and performance uneven, Descartes's first hypothesis seems to have been willingly embraced by most specialists in the field: SSD-users are said to 'see with their skin' (White et al., 1970) or with their ears (see Deroy & Auvray, 2012, for a critical review).

Expressions such as 'seeing with the skin' show how intuitive the assimilation of SSD-use to vision is. They also reveal an underlying tension: how could blind people ever see? If the definition of seeing involves proper visual processing, it is almost tautological to say that blind people, whose visual system is irreversibly damaged, cannot see. As the initial idea after all is that they 'almost see' (Descartes, 1637/1985, p. 153) thanks to sensory aids, the verb 'seeing' might then have to be taken less literally: is it not more appropriate to say that they have gained or recov-ered something *like* vision, or close to it? But what do people want to capture by this 'quasi-vision'? Once one agrees to talk about sensory substitution being quasi-visual, some difficulties arise: to what extent should we grant quasi-vision to trained users of SSDs? And more important: should we accept the idea that there is something like quasi-vision, and use it in our best philosophical accounts of sensory substitution?

1.1. TWO UNDERSTANDINGS OF QUASI-VISION

As SSDs superficially resemble vision, there is no doubt that they lead to the intui-tive idea that they are, if not visual, at least quasi-visual. This intuition, in turn, seems to have led to two distinct philosophical interpretations. On a first reading, quasi-vision has been taken to mean 'same but less than vision'. The claim, shared by what is known as the 'deference thesis' (e.g., Hurley and Noë, 2003), is that SSDs give a sense of vision, but to a lesser degree than regular vision. On a second reading, quasi-visual only means pseudo-visual (or deceptively visual). Theorists, defending the 'dominance thesis', want to stress that SSDs remain in the substitut-ing modality, for example, touch or audition depending on the device used (e.g., Humphrey, 1992; Block, 2003; Prinz, 2006). What has led authors to arrive at such strongly opposing views on the basis of what seems to be the same intuition? Each alternative needs to be considered and described in more detail.

The deference theory, according to which SSDs provide their users with a lower form of vision, is perhaps best expressed in Heil's comment that 'a person mak-ing intelligent use of a TVSS (tactile vision sensory substitution) may be said to be seeing (though perhaps only dimly) features of his environment' (Heil, 1983, p. 16). Heil implies here that SSD-use differs from traditional, non-augmented sight in that it provides a diminished form of vision: In other words, this mean that SSD-users have a less exact or less powerful sense of vision. Although the claim is not always clear, it seems to concern the capacity itself, not just the performance: SSD-users are not compared to, say, short-sighted individuals who are granted the same kind of sensory capacity or competence as others, but with a less good performance. They are considered as having a diminished competence altogether. The perceptual acuity of blind persons perceiving information through a visual-to-tactile SSD has been quantified using a standard ophthalmological test, and their 'visual' acuity averaged 40/860 (Sampaio, Maris & Bach-y-Rita, 2001)—which would be enough for anyone refusing to even consider these users as seeing. The idea then is not to put them on the same scale as sighted people but to accept another standard altogether. One thing that can be used to distinguish the standard used for traditional vision from that of SSD-use is the kind of objects at stake: trained users can indeed negotiate their way in simplified environments, with widely separated, very high-contrast objects (Collins, 1985; Jansson, 1983), but they cannot navigate successfully in real-world situations, such as environments cluttered with small and low-contrast objects. They are better at recognising simplified drawings than ordinary objects, not to mention whole scenes (Kim & Zatorre, 2008). The issue discussed here is known as a bandwidth problem when visual information is converted into touch (see Loomis, Klatzky, & Giudice, 2012, for a review). However, it is sometimes forgotten when discussing the status of SSDs. In addition, the bandwidth problem has not prevented optimists from claiming that SSD-users would in the future be on an equal footing with sighted people. This straightforward assimilation of SSD-use to classic or full-blown vision is nonetheless unwarranted, and the defenders of the deference thesis should follow Heil's moderate formulation when he notes that 'it is, to an extent, misleading to describe a TVSS-user as seeing in an unqualified sense' (Heil, 1983, p. 145).

Even once it is nuanced and takes into account the bandwidth problem, the deference thesis remains hard to pin down. What is the 'qualified' sense in which blind SSD-users are supposed to see? In this instance some theorists seem prone to defend the idea that visual perception comes in degrees; in other words, that it is not an all-or-none state, but a scale of skills that progressively develop as mastery improves (Hurley & Noë, 2003; Noë, 2004; O'Regan, 2011). According to these theorists, individuals are not just more or less good at seeing; they also have more primitive or complex seeing skills. An appropriate analogy here might be to that of improving in karate and updating the colour of the karate belt with each level of skill: going from a white belt to a black one does not just correspond to getting better at the same moves; it also involves expanding your move repertoire and being capable of new moves. In this way, it is possible to say that SSD-users, like holders of a karate white belt generally have poorer seeing (or karate) skills than sighted individuals, while participating nonetheless in the same general practice. The analogy comes from the way we individuate actions, by reference to their goals and independently of variations in means. We count performing a simple or complex karate move as the same kind of practice, but we also count cutting with a knife or cutting with an ax as the same kind of action; as a consequence, the case should be the same for seeing with one's eyes or through an SSD.

Such interpretation of SSDs comes with compromises, because it abandons the classical definition of vision as a single skill and as a non-graded term. Is there a less compromising option? According to a second, more conservative interpretation, the superficial similarity between SSD-use and vision must not be taken seriously and SSD-use is only deceptively visual. Our first intuitions simply suggest that using an SSD can be *mistaken for* vision; that it looks like vision when it is not. 'Seeing with the skin' or with the hand, as Descartes suggested, is considered to be only a confused way of speaking. As Leon wrote, saying that TVSS enables sight is not persuasive:

> It is not more persuasive than the suggestion that we would hear sounds and various properties by means of the eyes, simply because we observe an optical transformation of an aural input by using, say, an oscilloscope (Leon, 1988, p. 252).

This second interpretation is more often favoured by supporters of an all-or-none approach to sensory perception, especially those who think that acquiring specific qualitative states is constitutive of vision. Using an SSD or a white cane is allegedly not like having a visual experience: it does not give characteristically visual sensations, like colours, the feeling of empty spaces or other modes of phenomenal presence of objects (see Auvray & Farina, forthcoming, for discussion).

There are different ways to extend the interpretation that SSDs are only deceptively visual, yet the most common one is to claim that SSD-users still exert their intact sense of touch or audition, albeit in a more expert way. Audition or touch is recruited to achieve new tasks, usually performed through vision, but they do not become visual for this reason.

1.2. A PHILOSOPHICAL DISPUTE

The initial intuitions about the similarity between SSD-use and vision turn out to be rather confused. This partly explains why they have led to such opposite philosophical interpretations. The representatives of the enactive tradition (e.g., Hurley & Noë, 2003; O'Regan, 2011; O'Regan & Noë, 2001; Noë, 2004), along with remote sympathisers of the Gibsonian view of perception as a pick-up of information (such as Heil, 1983) claim that visually impaired users of SSDs gain a primitive sense of sight through learning. This can be maintained, according to them, even if what is obtained in terms of compensation falls short of being perfectly similar to vision as we commonly understand it. By contrast, the pseudo-visual interpretation attracts most of the representationalists and those who put emphasis on the qualitative characters of experience. People like Block (2003) or Leon (1988), for instance, claim that the intact modality, where sensations are obtained, remains dominant in sensory substitution. It is clear that the main source of disagreement between these two interpretations comes down to the definition given to seeing. Is it sufficient to have an access to the same kind of information or to respond to the same kind of stimuli for an ability to be defined as being visual? Is it possible to see without using one's eyes, or without enjoying any of the classic visual phenomenology of sighted people? These questions converge toward the more general problem of the individuation of the senses which has recently benefited from a resurgence of interest (see Keeley, 2002, 2013; Macpherson, 2011, for an overview). However, this renewed interest has not yet spread to the field of sensory substitution, or at least it has not led to an interest in updating their philosophical and empirical understanding. On the contrary, it has rather led to the idea that SSDs are 'not paradigmatic' (Gray, 2011) enough to constitute proper tests to assess the distinction between the senses. As a result, they have shifted out of the scope of recent discussions. At best, following Nudds (2004), they seem to encourage the negative conclusion that SSDs mostly raise terminology problems. As suggested by Gray (2011, p. 255), 'the presence of disagreement can itself be regarded as providing some support for the anti-realist view that there is no mind-independent fact of the matter about the case' (e.g., whether TVSS-users see or not).

The aim of our present chapter is to challenge this conclusion. SSDs, we claim, can contribute to the debates about the nature of the senses. To do so, the first thing to achieve is to bring the recent work about SSDs into the philosophical arena: thinking of SSDs as more advanced white canes, as they were in the 1970s, has been responsible, we believe, for the imperfect grasp of their quasi-visual status. Recent empirical studies, detailed in section 2, show how complex and deeply integrated the use of SSDs is. This makes it harder, but also more crucial, to determine whether they allow a form of genuine vision. The next step is to find better ways to address this difficulty. SSDs certainly provide good reasons to reject the dominant method of distinguishing the senses (e.g., Grice, 1962), that is, through an ecumenical combination of personal and sub-personal criteria (sections 3 and 4); they also challenge single-criterion distinctions between the senses that have been attempted more recently (section 5). This is, however, not a reason to think of SSDs as undecided cases, or to embrace a form of anti-realism about the senses. A way out of the dilemma comes with a third way of understanding SSDs that does not try to reduce their use to any of the existing modalities. We suggest that SSD-use leads to some novel ability, which does not, however, constitute a new sense properly speaking but a form of artificial crossmodal rewiring resting on pre-existing sensory capacities. The idea that SSDs are therefore not to be aligned with canonical senses is detailed in section 6.

2. The Integration of SSDs

SSDs were first developed in the late 1960s to improve blind people's ability to navigate in their environment and to identify objects (e.g., Bach-y-Rita et al., 1969).

The principle they rest on differs from the mechanical transfer at play in white canes: they start with a series of sensors, most often a camera, which respond to certain electromagnetic signals. These stimuli usually accessed through vision are converted into sensory cues that are detectable through an intact modality. Devices such as the TVSS (tactile vision sensory substitution), the TDU (tongue display unit), or the Optacon (optical to tactile converter) convert these light signals into tactile stimuli, that is, electromechanical or vibratory stimulation of different intensities and spatial distribution applied to the skin of a part of the body surface. In this case, the conversion from visual to tactile information is analogous. Other types of devices like the vOICe (Meijer, 1992) or the Vibe (Hanneton et al., 2010) capture the shapes of objects and their locations through a camera and convert this information into auditory signals. The conversion code translates several dimensions of the original signal into auditory dimensions, such as visual brightness into auditory loudness.

At first, and as was noted by Leon (1988) and Ross (2001), this conversion aspect of SSD-use seems to entail a form of indirect perception, analogous to the case where one has learned that heated metal becomes red and indirectly sees the temperature of the stove through directly seeing its redness:

> It may seem that use of a TVSS is a kind of vision without color. But while use of TVSS detects properties usually detected by vision—namely, spatial properties at a distance—and while its use can provide such information without reflective inference after a period of training, still its use is not a kind of vision because it is not a kind of direct perception. Rather, tactual properties are used as a basis to infer spatial properties (Ross, 2001, p. 501).

The same indirect interpretation could be applied to users of the vOICe *indirectly* accessing information about shapes through *directly* hearing certain sounds. However, this understanding of SSD proves to be questionable. First, many things have been encompassed under the heading of indirect perception. For the present purposes, and in line with what Ross means by the term 'indirect perception', it is defined as a two-step form of perception. It is supposed to be distinct from an inferential process where a first perceptual stage leads to a judgment. If one first *sees* the redness of the stove and then infers that the stove is hot, this does not qualify as indirect perception. One has to (indirectly) see the hotness of the stove *in* its colour. Both the directly and indirectly accessed information is somewhat concurrently present in experience: one can see both colour and warmth. For SSDs then to be interpreted as indirect perception, users would have to be able to perceive both the sounds and the shapes in the sounds. However, there is no scientific evidence to corroborate that both sounds and shapes are perceived at the same time. Before training, individuals using a visual-to-auditory device like the vOICe merely indicate perceiving noises through headphones. They then become able, through practice, to perceive shapes through the device and, when they do so, they are no longer paying attention to the sounds they first heard. By contrast, people who indirectly see the temperature of the stove in its colour are still paying attention to the colour—and perceiving it as such—independently of perceiving its temperature.

Similarly, with visual-to-tactile conversion systems, trained users no longer feel the tactile stimuli on their skin. In a much quoted report, Guarniero, a trained user of the TVSS (who was also a graduate in philosophy), explains:

> Very soon after I had learned how to scan, the sensations no longer felt as if they were on my back, and I became *less and less* aware that vibrating pins were making contact with my skin. By this time objects had come to have a top and a bottom; a right side and a left; but no depth—they existed in an ordered two dimensional space (Guarniero, 1974, p. 104–quoted by Leon, 2011, p. 165; Heil, 1983; 2003, p. 228, 2011, p. 288; Peacocke, 1983, p. 15).

The main problem now comes from capturing the exact way in which training allows users to move beyond the experience of stimulation to the location where it is transmitted (such as the tongue or the ears) and enables them to directly gain relevant information about the object-source.

Recent studies have illuminated this transition toward the direct pick-up of new information, and documented it under the label of an 'integration'. Although we have no objection in using the same expression, we think it is necessary to distinguish carefully different aspects of integration often associated in the literature on sensory substitution. Unlike cochlear implants, for instance, SSDs are worn intermittently and are not therefore fully anatomically integrated. The term 'integration' is rather meant to capture the effects of familiarisation with the device. It encompasses three different aspects that subsequently are described in more detail: distal attribution, direct acquaintance, and generalisation.

2.1. DISTAL ATTRIBUTION

First, training with SSDs has been reported to result in what is called 'distal attribution': the received information is taken to be *about* an object that appears to be independent of the perceiver.[1] The expression, as much as the correlated philosophical notion, has to be handled carefully. Distal attribution is often considered to be synonymous with *spatial projection*. It is thought to occur when the sensations felt on the skin or in the ears are projected onto a distant perceived object, which should correspond to the one captured by the camera. Being perceived as distant in space is nonetheless not necessarily conceptually equivalent to being perceived as mind-independent (e.g., objective; see the debates around Strawson, 1959, for instance, in Evans, 1980, and Burge, 2010). First, for certain SSDs, the sensor needs to be in contact with the object to be perceived, so that

---

[1] Note, however, that there are currently no unproblematic experiments that provide evidence of distal attribution with SSDs with methods other than explicit inference (see Hartcher O'Brien & Auvray, submitted, for a review).

distant objects cannot be accessed. The Optacon, for instance, and its predecessor, the Optophone, functions more like a scan, as pages of written text need to be put in close contact with the sensors before being converted into tactile Braille stimuli. Second, SSDs could be designed to compensate for the loss of a contact sense. This has actually been the case for instance with SSDs compensating for the loss of touch (e.g., see Bach-y-Rita et al., 2003) or pain (Brand & Yancey, 1993), which do not give access to remote objects.

Leaving the variety of current and possible devices aside, finally, what seems to be crucial for the best-known visual-to-tactile and visual-to-auditory SSDs is not so much the projection in distant space, but the transition to an allocentric representation of space. In other words locations are not just represented with respect to users' perspective, as it is classically assumed to be the case for touch, but within an external frame of reference which is independent of their actual position (see also Arnold et al., forthcoming for a discussion). As Guarniero (1974) reported, the objects seem to the user to have 'a left and a right', and not just to be felt relative to her own left and right. What distal attribution brings is first and foremost the perception of objects as being independent from the observer.

2.2. DIRECT ACCESS AND TRANSPARENCY

Integration also involves a second transition: users become 'directly aware of the distal object' (Siegle & Warren, 2010, p. 209). What this means is that the information about the independent objects appears to be delivered immediately, for example, literally not through the mediation of a sensational episode. This aspect is mainly documented in subjective reports and remains hard to interpret further at this stage. Most often, sensations in the intact sensory modality are said to somehow be merged into a new percept, from which they become inseparable. People perceive the shapes of objects, not mere sounds, when they use the vOICe.

The integrated use of SSDs may then count as a form of *transparent* access: perceiving the object is no longer dissociable from what it is like to use the device, in the same way as perceiving blue is not dissociable from what it is like to see blue (Tye, 2002). There is however an alternative interpretation, underestimated in our sense, according to which sensations remain present, but are less attended to (see, for instance, Noë, 2004).

In summary, immediacy, directness, and transparency are hard to define (see Smith, 2002, for a discussion). They are also difficult to separate and assess empirically (Auvray et al., 2005, 2007-b; Siegle & Warren, 2010).

2.3. GENERALISATION TO NEW OBJECTS

The third aspect of integration comes from what is called 'generalisation'. With training, users are able to recognise objects or to navigate in environments that differ from the ones they have been trained with. This crucially demonstrates that their learning can be transferred to unfamiliar situations and therefore does not just reduce to memorised routines about familiar cases (Auvray et al., 2007-a; Kim & Zatorre, 2008). For instance, having learnt to recognise a plant during their training, users of the vOICe are subsequently quite fast in learning to identify another plant. In addition, with tactile devices, once trained with the tactile matrix on a body surface, performance transfers to another body surface when the matrix is displaced (Arnold & Auvray, in press). Although generalisation to new objects remains limited and deserves further study, it rules out the hypothesis that SSD-users proceed only on the basis of associative memory: users learn to associate a specific pattern of sensory stimuli (a certain sound, a certain pattern of tactile vibrations) not only to a specific object or kind of object. Identification goes beyond the memorised associations and, as we just said, users are able to identify another pattern of sensory stimuli as being a new object of the same kind.

Here the data need to be very carefully interpreted: background knowledge certainly plays a role in SSD-use, as it does in everyday navigation or identification. A study by Siegel and Warren (2008) showed that, when using a minimalist visual-to-tactile device, people who are told to attend to proximal stimulation have worse performance than people who are told to directly attend to the distal source of stimulation. Having active training noticeably helps with the generalisation of learning. But, as the evidence stands, nothing rules out that conceptual knowledge and explicit rules do not provide users with other advantages, or good-enough substitutes. How much knowledge *that* and how much knowledge *how*—or practical mastery—enter in the integration of SSDs is certainly a hot topic for discussion; and above all, investigation. Anyhow, there is a form of spontaneous generalisation and there is a transfer of learning, and these can be taken as similar to perceptual learning, where, for instance, people do not need training to recognise new textures or new shades of colour.

As we can see, the evidence gained from the integrated use of SSDs encourages the intuitions that SSD-use is quasi-visual: gaining information in an immediate way, about new independent and possibly distant objects is almost like seeing. But is the status of SSDs thereby clarified?

3. In Which Sensory Modality Do SSDs Get Integrated?

The contention remains between the 'same but less than vision' theories (also known as deference thesis) and the 'not-vision' theories (usually associated to a dominance thesis). Overcoming this ambiguity requires explaining how and where to draw the line between seeing, touching, and hearing. As Nudds (2011) rightly wrote, the individuation of the senses is itself an intuitive matter, calling for further clarification:

> The distinction we make between the five senses is universal. Instead of saying in a generic way that we perceive something, we're talking about

a perception in one of these well defined five modes: we see, hear, touch, smell and taste things. But what exactly is our distinction, when we identify these specific ways of perceiving things? What is, in other words, a sensory modality? (Nudds, 2011, p. 311).

The vagaries surrounding the status of SSDs may reflect the vagaries of our concept of a sense. Instead of discouragement, this brings some hope that clarifying our theorising about SSDs will shed some light on the distinction between the senses.

3.1. FOUR CRITERIA TO DISTINGUISH THE SENSES

Among the various attempts to analyse our intuitive distinction between the senses, the most famous one came from Grice. In his 1962 paper, he proposed a list of the main criteria along which this distinction could be drawn. They can synthetically be specified as ranging over characteristic phenomenology, intentional objects, kinds of stimuli, and dedicated processing.

The most immediate distinction between our senses comes from phenomenology. Seeing usually does not feel like hearing or touching. Each sense corresponds to a specific kind or family of feelings; what Grice called 'special introspectible characters'.

> (Phenomenological criterion). Two senses, S1 and S2, are different as far as they give rise to experiences with different kinds of subjective feelings or conscious qualitative characters.

This criterion is reminiscent of Descartes's (1637/1985) remarks: what makes us think that blind people have a form of vision when using their canes results from an analogy with our own phenomenology or experience. *What it is like* for us to be moving in a room with a stick could be confused for *what it feels like to see,*[2] and therefore, the same might be true of blind persons.

The first comparison needs of course to be made with caution: what does it mean to say that touching a stone with a stick is subjectively similar to seeing the stone? Here though, it might only mean that one recognises the object explored with the cane, and when identifying it as a stone through her background knowledge, recalls how a stone looks. The phenomenological criterion is not supposed to apply to this form of mental imagery: if the experience in a sensory modality, S1, is accompanied by a vivid form of mental imagery pertaining to another modality, S2, this should not lead to say that S1 is the same as S2.[3] The criterion is supposed to apply to the initial or proper phenomenal modes of presentations, or kinds of experiences.

---

[2] Certainly, in our case, because of the strategic or automatic recruitment of visual imagery (see Spence & Deroy, 2013, for discussion).

[3] See, for instance, what happens with synaesthesia (Auvray & Deroy, in press; Keeley, in press).

The difficulty of applying this criterion is illustrated here by the difficulty of distinguishing between 'feeling like seeing' and 'feeling like one is acquainted with an object (strongly) associated to a visual image'.

This first criterion is strongly tied up with a second one, spelled out in terms of the objects or properties that are perceived.

> (Object criterion). Two senses, S1 and S2, are different as far as they give access to different characteristic kinds of objects or properties.

This second criterion is very largely reminiscent of the old Aristotelian way of drawing the distinction between the senses in terms of 'proper objects'. For instance, vision gives access to colours whereas audition gives access to sounds. It is important to note here that the distinction remains a psychological distinction: proper objects are intentional objects that are not necessarily identical to physical entities. Saying that vision's proper objects are, for instance, colours and visual shapes, does not presume of what colours and shapes are, metaphysically or physically speaking. This said, it is obvious that this criterion considers sensory modalities to be a way of accessing information: the question is what kind of information is *presented* to us, and how.

This way of conceptualising the senses leaves aside the fact that senses are also organs and physiological circuits; for example, they correspond to ways in which this information is *delivered*.

Two additional criteria are needed to capture this aspect. The first one appeals to a difference in terms of range of responses. Different senses are sensitive to different changes in the environment:

> (Stimulation criterion) Two senses, S1 and S2, are different as far as they respond to different kinds of physical stimuli.

Furthermore, the different stimuli serve as inputs to different and independent kinds of processing, which can be specified in computational and neurological terms. This criterion is sometimes also put in terms of sense-organs or kinds of receptors.

> (Processing criterion) Two senses, S1 and S2, are different, as far as they correspond to independent processing and neurological channels, or to different sense-organs.

A perceptual episode, for example, is visual if it is initiated by the stimulation of the retina by light waves, which results in the activation of the optic nerve and brain areas V1 to V5 in the occipital lobe. Another episode is auditory if it begins with the vibration of the eardrum, generated by acoustic waves, and extends through the activation of the auditory nerve and another part of the cortex, the temporal lobe.

3.2. ADAPTING GRICE'S DISTINCTION

Our definitions of the four criteria depart from Grice's in two important aspects. First, the definitions are all formulated in 'as far as' conditions. This is crucial to enable a graded application, needed to account for 'quasi' cases like SSDs. Absolute criteria, such as those used by Grice, mean that each condition needs to be perfectly met before categorising something as a certain sense. In other words, the phenomenology, object, kinds of stimulation, and/or kinds processing in SSDs must be *perfectly* identical to what they are in sighted people, for them to count as seeing. However, this requirement can be criticised as being too 'anthropocentric', the objection being that other animals might be granted a sense of vision in the absence of such perfect identity. Dogs have a sense of vision, although their experiences and neurological wiring might only be partially like ours. Likewise, we argue, it is also detrimental to the various realisations of vision (and other modalities) in human perceivers.

A second difference with Grice's view comes from the relation between the criteria. Grice's agenda was to show that the four criteria are all closely connected, although some have more importance than others (i.e., intentional objects and characteristic experiences). Here, we want to remain neutral about their connection or independence. Our concern is indeed to see whether they help clarify the status of SSDs, be it in combination or in isolation.

4. Why SSDs Challenge the Ecumenical Conception of the Senses

As was stressed by Grice, the common-sense distinction between the five senses mixes all four criteria. It encompasses broad ideas about access as well as delivery. Vision, for instance, is taken to involve a certain kind of experience, to be about a certain range of objects and properties, to be obtained through the visual system, and to start with specific stimuli. Problems arise when one wants to make a more precise articulation of these different criteria.

A precise combination of the four criteria creates immediate problems for SSDs, as they do for other cases (for instance, in animal perception, see Matthen, 2007). For example, a device like the vOICe comes out being both visual and non-visual depending on which criterion is applied. *Phenomenologically* speaking, the experiences are not canonically auditory, but they are not canonically visual either. Yet the *objects* that are perceived definitively resemble visual objects. In terms of *stimuli*, both auditory and visual ones seem to be involved in the functioning of the headphones and the camera respectively. Yet the sense-organ (i.e., *processing* criterion) which is used is certainly not visual. This at least explains that the ambivalent intuitions about the visual status of SSDs come from the contradictory results of these criteria. In terms of access (e.g., how it feels to access such and such proper object), a device like the vOICe can be characterised as neither visual nor auditory, but might still emerge as strongly visual if one considers the object as a visual one. In terms of delivery (e.g., what kind of stimuli and processing are involved), the vOICe counts both as visual and auditory.

If one wants to maintain that four criteria are needed to identify a sensory modality, it seems necessary to at least accept that not all of them are equally important. But which one of the four should prevail in the definition of a sense? Several factors might encourage philosophers to privilege the criteria of intentional objects and stimuli. These two criteria are the safer ones because they do not rely on subjective reports (like the phenomenological criterion) or on what can seem still to be unsettled or at least fast-changing neurophysiological accounts (like the processing criterion). Moreover, widespread representationalist tendencies support the criterion of intentional objects over the other criteria, whereas the externalist sympathies (also frequent) tend to stress the criterion of environmental stimuli. Now, these two criteria will make SSD-use come out as visual; which is often what is defended in the literature. Accordingly, a way to acknowledge that the other criteria do not go in the same direction, and to put them further down the list, is to add some nuance to the philosophical assimilation of SSD-use to vision, and talk about almost seeing or other quasi-visual cases as we discussed earlier (e.g., Heil, 1983).

The privilege given to the criteria of intentional objects and environmental stimuli is not appropriate when dealing with SSDs. In systems such as the vOICe or the TVSS, the human-machine interface is designed to provide access to 'visual objects' (e.g., objects and properties that are equivalent to objects and properties normally accessed by the sighted). The interface is also designed to start from inputs that are traditionally visual. Prioritising the criteria of intentional objects and stimuli offers a trivial reformulation of the initial goal: SSDs are designed to function as vision; therefore, they are visual. This reformulation does not make a distinctive contribution in defending the real visual status of SSDs. The problem is not 'what are SSDs used *for*?' but rather '*how* are they used?' It is a descriptive, and not a design or functional, question. The former question remains unanswered.

5. SSD Challenges to Single Criterion Approaches

If the combination of criteria raises problems, adopting a single criterion could lead to better results. Each of the four Gricean criteria has been thought, in turn, to be sufficient to draw the line between the senses; be it phenomenology (Leon, 1988; Lopes, 2000; O'Dea, 2011), stimulation (Gibson, 1966; see also Heil, 1983, 2011), objects (Roxbee Cox, 1970; Everson, 1999), or processing (see, for instance, Milner & Goodale, 2008, for a discussion in the domain of vision). Do single criteria perform better in clarifying the quasi-visual status of SSDs?

5.1. THE PHENOMENOLOGY CRITERION

The application of the first criterion introduces a methodological problem: this criterion cannot be investigated from a third person perspective. It is impossible to specify what the experience of trained blind people is really like—for instance, what a user of the vOICe really feels. We can only apprehend the associated phenomenology by using the device ourselves. However, even if we do so, there is no certainty that our experiences would be qualitatively similar, or even comparable, to those of other users, and especially to those of blind users. Taken at face value, the most recent studies tend to stress the inter- and intra-individual variations in the experiences enjoyed by trained users of SSDs.

One standard way of investigating others' conscious experiences is to ask them what these experiences resemble. This methodology was adopted in a series of interviews in which two blind users of the vOICe surprisingly reported visual experiences, involving colours, but this phenomenology was limited to certain kinds of objects (Ward & Meijer, 2010). One of them, for instance, reported:

> One day I was washing dishes and without thinking I grabbed the towel, washed my hands, and looked down into the sink to make sure that the water had got out and I realised Oh! I can see down. I can see depth.

Later on, she claimed:

> Over time my brain seems to have developed, and pulled out everything it can from the soundscape and then used my memory to color everything.
> JW: But if you look at someone's sweater or pants you wouldn't necessarily know the color? It could be blue or red.
> PF: My brain would probably take a guess at that time. It would be grayish black. Something I know such as grass, tree bark, leaves, my mind just colors it in (from Ward & Meijer, 2010, p. 496).

It is very difficult to know what to infer from these reports. The origin of the visual, colour imagery is crucial for the application of the phenomenological criterion. It is important to know whether or not the visual phenomenology is truly perceptual, or just given by imagination or memory, and then simply added to a more confused set of non-visual qualities obtained when using the SSD (see Auvray & Farina, forthcoming, for a discussion). Another related thing to be checked is what kind of visual imagery exactly is at stake. Blind people may not be the best ones qualified to report on this point, and mere reminiscence of crossmodal imagery might be at stake (e.g., Spence & Deroy, 2013). In a similar vein, recent studies have found a correlation between activation of the occipital cortex and the occurrence of new phenomenological experiences of phosphene in trained (late-blind) users of visual-to-tactile SSDs (Ortiz et al., 2011). Such novel phosphene experiences are not documented in congenitally blind individuals.

In their study, Auvray et al. (2007-a) asked sighted participants what it felt like to perceive with the vOICe. The replies varied importantly. While some of the participants claimed that their experience was close to visual experiences, others claimed it was closer to auditory ones. The hypothesis that the phenomenology does not come with a clear modal signature and is neither exactly visual nor exactly auditory can be confirmed by the responses of some who thought that their experience was best described as tactile or olfactory. Some even reported that their experiences felt more like a sonar sense, suggesting that they were trying to make sense of something quite new. Furthermore, the phenomenology differed depending on the task that was performed: most of the participants gave different descriptions of their qualitative experience for localisation tasks and recognition tasks. One of the participants for instance felt that her experience was visual when she was locating an object in space, but auditory when she was recognising the shape of the object.

The lesson of this survey is twofold: from a methodological point of view, it questions users' ability to establish classes of similarities between their experiences and thus to apply the phenomenological criterion in a rigorous or consistent way. For the present purpose, it shows that the phenomenological criterion is not sufficient to determine whether SSD-users see or not. The phenomenological criterion is by itself not stable or accurate enough to go beyond the intuition that using an SSD is quasi-visual.

5.2. THE OBJECT CRITERION

The object criterion proves easier to assess. Trained SSD-users are able to navigate in new environments and to make coarse but still accurate judgments about shapes and distances of remote objects. They rely on something that audition or touch cannot usually provide, and they have acquired something closer to vision. But the distinction in terms of kinds of objects does not prove more helpful when it comes to moving beyond this general characterisation.

There are indeed limits to the application of the object criterion in isolation. Distance is accessed both by sight, audition, and other distal senses. At best, therefore, if SSD-users are able to make distal attribution, they can be said to exercise a distal sense; whether it is visual or not remains open. Shape is not the *proper object* of sight either, as it can be accessed through touch as well. None of the mentioned aspects of the object criterion is therefore sufficient to declare SSD-use as being characteristically visual. A more promising suggestion comes from combining the two kinds of information, given that the joint access to distance and shapes seems unique to vision. Audition provides information about object distances but gives only limited and approximate information about an object's size (and even less information about shape); touch provides information about shapes, but not at a distance. But in SSDs, the question remains open as to whether the two kinds of information can be accessed jointly or, as suggested by previous experiments (Auvray et al., 2007-a), they are distributed in two distinct perceptual tasks (localisation and identification).

A second limit is that certain key visual properties are lacking in SSD-users' experiences. Their perception is limited to a smaller number of dimensions. Colours, for example, are recognised as being specific to vision, yet they are not accessed through the vOICe or the TVSS. Levels of grey are not even present in the TVSS. There is no reason to see this objection as decisive. The absence of colour is an actual technological limit and should not be taken for a principled impossibility. Current systems could be made to code for colour: the relevant sensors are available and the conversion can be performed. SSDs could theoretically give access to all the contents that are specific to vision. The main problem comes from the fact that the device blurs object dimensions. Each dimension in the lacking modality needs to be translated into another dimension in the intact modality, and in this instance it appears a real impossibility to map all visual dimensions simultaneously in modalities that have less dimensions such as touch (see Loomis, Klatzky & Giudice, 2012, for a review).

The object criterion remains compatible with the two-pronged nature of this dilemma. It is true that SSDs give access to a lesser number of properties than regular vision. This may mean that they are on a continuum with vision, or that they remain in the intact modalities, which share access to these properties. Taken in isolation, the object criterion is finally no more conclusive than the phenomenological one.

5.3. THE STIMULATION CRITERION: STARTING WITH ELECTROMAGNETIC WAVES

The criterion of stimuli provides a clear answer, if one agrees to consider the user and the device as a single system: the stimulus to which the overall system responds is the same as vision, since the sensors detect electromagnetic differences. The difficulty in applying this criterion comes from the way to accommodate the non-visual, intermediate step. What counts as 'stimuli' could be either the light waves received by the sensor or the auditory or tactile stimuli that get converted to by the device.

Note here that the stimulation criterion is distinct from the phenomenological one, about whether users feel auditory *sensations* when using the vOICe. The question concerns the role of the auditory *stimuli*, which undeniably occur. On the one hand, these auditory stimuli only exist because they are based on visual stimuli: both their existence and their nature depend on electromagnetic waves. This strict dependence on visual stimuli makes them somehow dispensable in the understanding of the input-output process. To take an extreme analogy, one does not count the chemical transduction of information through sensory channels as a sign that chemical stimuli are relevant for the functioning of every sense. On the other hand, auditory stimuli are certainly *necessary* for the proper functioning of the device. That is, they are constitutive of the way in which these SSDs have been designed. Switching from visual-to-auditory devices to visual-to-tactile devices, for instance, requires a completely new design, a unique translation code from vision to touch and a different training. The distinction between the senses in terms of stimuli does not deliver a single answer to the dilemma.

5.4. THE PROCESSING CRITERION

The answer given by the strict application of the neurophysiological criterion is no less problematic. The distinction between the senses has sometimes been thought to be only a matter of sense organs. Following this line of argument, Morgan (1977) pointed out the similarity between the visual system and the TVSS: in both cases, an image is formed on a bi-dimensional surface (the retina in the case of vision, the lens of the camera for the TVSS); this surface contains discrete elements (rods and cones in the eye, vibrators for the TVSS); these elements are connected to certain regions of the surface (receptive fields) that send electrical signals to the brain, the device (eye or camera). The sensor (eye or camera) can be moved, and its movements introduce changes in the image. Moreover, these two systems are similar in that the source of stimulation is remote and sensing is subject to the effects of occlusion, when an obstacle comes between the source object and the detection system. But are these structural similarities sufficient to conclude that the two are one and the same sense? The animal kingdom provides a perfect illustration of the difficulty: it is commonly said that dogs 'see'. These creatures are equipped with detection systems that share some similarities with human vision. It is more parsimonious to say that perceiving through these organs, or devices, is distal and discrete. Human vision, hearing, and many other animal senses can be grouped into this category, thereby denying the possibility to decide over the visual status of SSDs on such a criterion.

Can further neurological investigations help? Studies have shown increased activation in visual areas in trained users of visual-to-auditory (De Volder et al., 1999; Renier et al., 2005) and visual-to-tactile conversion devices (Ptito et al., 2005). There is thus a recruitment of visual areas through brain plasticity (see Poirier et al., 2007, for a review). Applying the processing criterion suggests that blind users acquire a form of vision: if perception recruits a channel identified as visual, it counts as visual.

We must, however, be cautious with this sort of inference: the studies that motivate the claim that the occipital lobe is visual have been performed on sighted, and not blind, people. Interestingly, Ptito et al.'s (2005) study revealed increased activation in the visual cortex only in trained congenitally blind people,—not in sighted ones reaching the same level of performance or in untrained people from both groups. We must also not forget that calling this area visual results from a functional mapping and that a common area may not be functionally similar in two groups of people, noticeably blind and visually impaired people.

Increased activity in a given brain area is not sufficient to deduce the presence of a normally associated function. In accordance with this conclusion, Kupers et al. (2006) used transcranial magnetic stimulation (TMS) in both blindfolded sighted and blind participants' visual cortex before and after training with a visual-to-tactile conversion system (the tongue display unit). When TMS was applied over the visual cortex before training, none of the participants reported any subjective tactile sensation. However, after training, when TMS was applied over the same brain area, some of the blind participants (3 out of 8 early blind and 1 out of 5 late blind) reported somatopically organised tactile sensations that were referred to the tongue, whereas no such sensations were reported by sighted participants. The authors concluded from their data that the subjective experience associated with increased activity in the visual cortex after practice is tactile and not visual (see also Ptito et al., 2008, for similar results with Braille reading).

The application of the sole processing criterion does not deliver a definite answer. At best what can be concluded is that using an SSD is distal (when users move in their environment), which we knew already from the study of SSD-integration; and that it requires some further perceptual processing, which can recruit unsolicited areas like V1 in blind people. Should we conclude that calling SSD information visual or not is just arbitrary? Or, as suggested by Nudds (2004), shall we call it a matter of pragmatic decision that offers no fact of the matter? These two lines, we suggest, can be resisted.

6. Shifting the Problem

It is impossible to clearly answer the question of whether blind people 'see' when using the vOICe through any of the usual accounts, whether they rely on a combination of criteria or a single privileged one. As we reviewed these criteria, it nonetheless became clear that the integration of such devices has noticeable effects on users.

The mistake comes, we claim, from not acknowledging this difference and trying to square SSD-use with one of the existing sensory modalities. The application of the criteria should thus lead to a more qualified re-description of the effects of SSD integration:

(Phenomenological criterion). Using an SSD leads to subjective impressions that cannot easily be compared with experiences in existing modalities.

(Object criterion). An SSD can give access to a variety of objects, constrained by the initial design and the number of dimensions in the stimulated modality.

(Stimulation criterion). An SSD uses a series of inter-dependent stimuli.

(Processing criterion). Integrating an SSD requires some supplementary neurological processing.

Altogether, these criteria lead to the conclusion that SSDs introduce something *new*, which, albeit intimately connected to the intact modality, does not reduce to it. It also strongly *depends on* the missing modality—which governs the design, for example, the selection of stimuli and kinds of conversion. What appears is an experience significantly different from both, while it can also be reminiscent of each modality, at times. Several recent accounts point toward the 'novelty thesis' and help climb above the dilemma and pragmatic renunciations discussed earlier. As detailed in Auvray and Myin (2009), SSDs are better compared to mind-enhancing tools than to perception. Following Clark's (2003) lines, such tools provide means to carry out cognitive functions in ways that would have been impossible without them, given the intrinsic or initial properties of the system. Accordingly, SSDs provide cognitive extensions to the existing senses, which might then be integrated to these senses.

Starting from a different perspective, Nagel et al. (2005) designed an SSD for entirely new intentional objects. They equipped participants with a magnetic belt that gave them some brand new information about changes in the magnetic field. With training, users were able to track their orientation relative to the cardinal points. The authors' main point was to establish that trained users had acquired a new 'modality', for example, a new sensorimotor skill. They nonetheless suggested that their results form a transformation of the existing spatial perception:

> Strictly speaking, the changes in perception indicate not a genuinely new modality, but modification of the meta-modality of spatial perception. The term 'metamodality' is used to reflect the fact that normal spatial perception is fueled by visual, auditory and somatosensory information. The ability to infer spatial information from these pooled 'primary' modalities may have thwarted our objective to create a completely new sensory modality. Instead, the acquired sensorimotor contingencies lead to a transformation of this already existing meta-modality (Nagel et al., 2005, p. 23).

The most noticeable aspects of SSDs, according to this account, come from their non-reducibility to the existing senses, and their dependence on them. As suggested by Nagel et al. (2005), the successful use of an SSD would not have been possible without the existing resources—in this case, in terms of intentional objects (spatial orientation) and stimuli (tactile vibration). Their non-reducibility and dependence on existing senses are constitutive features of SSDs.

This leads us to refine the idea of a novel ability. The best way to capture this novelty is to think about the integrated use of an SSD being something closer to a new set of automatic recognition abilities arising from a trained rewiring between other sensory modalities, and eventually other pre-existing capacities. Unlike other senses, whose developments occur in a parallel way, SSDs are modes of access and delivery that fundamentally arise—technologically and cognitively—and get crafted on the existing senses.

This novel perspective radically changes the way integration should be understood, that is, with SSDs fitting, so to say, among the existing senses. What we want to suggest is that there is no reason to think about sensory substitution as being comparable to exercising a single sense in the first place. SSDs are an augmentation and depend on the pre-existing senses, similar to the way that reading capacities depend both on audition and vision (see Deroy & Auvray, 2012, for a full account). That is, reading brings a new capacity in the form of a single modality (vision) but actually depends on the existence of a first modality (auditory speech perception). SSDs do not introduce new kinds of objects or rules in a modality that already exists, but bring a new capacity that must be analyzed as depending on two modalities, such as crossmodal capacities.

7. Conclusions

The common-sense intuition that SSD-use is somehow visual leads to a dead end given that SSD-use requires processing capacities from two senses (the substituted and substituting). As we have demonstrated, without both it is not possible to qualify the novel skills. Furthermore, trying to fit SSD-use into a single sense results in a philosophical dilemma that proves, in itself, impossible to overcome: are trained users of the vOICe or the TDU exercising a form of vision, or some capacity that is only deceptively visual and remains in the intact modality?

Although many hope that clarification could come from an agreement on the individuation of the senses, we have argued that the problem is actually independent of the way one chooses to define vision or the other senses. The problem of classifying SSDs, in other words, arises however one chooses to individuate the senses. Contrary to Gray (2011)—we don't think that the impossibility to fit SSDs into the existing classification of the senses should lead us to abandon the hope to fit them into our typologies of the mind. What needs to be abandoned is only the project of fitting them among the canonical sensory modalities.

As the new capacities brought by SSDs do not and cannot figure on the same list as one of the natural or existing senses, SSDs need to be understood at the intersection of two senses: for example, as analogous to the acquisition of reading. This alternate view avoids philosophical confusions and offers better ways to understand and push forward and higher the philosophical and empirical investigation of sensory substitution.

Acknowledgments

We would like to thank Dustin Stokes, Mohan Matthen, Stephen Biggs, and Jess Hartcher-O'Brien for their careful reading and comments on earlier drafts of this chapter.

Ophelia Deroy is funded by an AHRC grant in the Science and Culture Scheme, 'Rethinking the Senses'. Malika Auvray is funded by a grant from the Agence Nationale de la Recherche (ANR-11-JSH2-003-1). The Institut Jean Nicod laboratory finds support in ANR-10-LABX-0087 IEC and ANR-10-IDEX-0001-02 PSL.

References

Arnold, G., & Auvray, M. (in press). Perceptual learning: Tactile letter recognition transfers across body surfaces. *Multisensory Research*.

Auvray, M., & Deroy, O. (in press). How do synaesthetes experience the world? In M. Matthen (ed.), *Oxford handbook of philosophy of perception*. Oxford: Oxford University Press.

Auvray, M., & Farina, M. (forthcoming). Patrolling the boundaries of synaesthesia: A critical appraisal of transient and artificially-induced forms of synaesthetic experiences. In O. Deroy (ed.), *Sensory blending: New essays on synaesthesia*. Oxford: Oxford University Press.

Auvray, M., Hanneton, S., Lenay, C., & O'Regan, J. K. (2005). There is something out there: Distal attribution in sensory substitution, twenty years later. *Journal of Integrative Neuroscience*, 4, 505–521.

Auvray, M., Hanneton, S., & O'Regan, J. K. (2007-a). Learning to perceive with a visuo-auditory substitution system: Localization and object recognition with The Voice. *Perception*, 36, 416–430.

Auvray, M., & Myin, E. (2009). Perception with compensatory devices: From sensory substitution to sensorimotor extension. *Cognitive Science*, 33, 1036–1058.

Auvray, M., Philipona, D., O'Regan, J. K., & Spence, C. (2007-b). The perception of space and form recognition in a simulated environment: The case of minimalist sensory-substitution devices. *Perception*, 36, 1736–1751.

Bach-y-Rita, P., Collins, C. C., Saunders, F. A., White, B., & Scadden, L. (1969). Vision substitution by tactile image projection. *Nature*, 221, 963–964.

Bach-y-Rita, P., Tyler, M. E., & Kaczmarek, K. A. (2003). Seeing with the brain. *International Journal of Human-Computer Interaction*, 2, 285–295.

Block, N. (2003). Tactile sensation via spatial perception. *Trends in Cognitive Sciences*, 7, 285–286.

Brand, P., & Yancey, P. (1993). *Pain: The gift nobody wants*. New York: Harper Collins.

Burge, T. (2010). *Origins of objectivity*. Oxford: Oxford University Press.

Clark, A. (2003). *Natural-born cyborgs: Minds, technologies, and the future of human intelligence*. New York: Oxford University Press.

Collins, C. C. (1985). On mobility aids for the blind. In D. H. Warren and E. R. Strelow (eds.), *Electronic spatial sensing for the blind*. Boston: Martinus Nijhoff, 107–120.

Deroy, O., & Auvray, M. (2012). Reading the world through the skin and ears: A new perspective on sensory substitution. *Frontiers in Psychology*, 3, 457, doi: 10.3389/fpsyg.2012.00457.

De Volder, A. G., Catalan Ahumada, M., Robert, A., Bol, A., Labar, D., Coppens, A., Michel, C., & Veraart, C. (1999). Changes in occipital cortex activity in early blind humans using a sensory substitution device. *Brain Research*, 826, 128–134.

Descartes, Rene. (1637/1985). *Philosophical writings*, trans. J. Cottingham, R. Stoothoff & D. Murdoch. Cambridge: Cambridge University Press.

Evans, G. (1980). Things without the mind: A commentary upon chapter two of Strawson's Individuals. In Z. Van Straaten (ed.), *Philosophical subjects: Essays presented to P. F. Strawson*. Oxford: Clarendon Press, 76–116.

Everson, S. (1999). *Aristotle on perception*. Oxford: Oxford University Press.

Gibson, J. J. (1966). *The senses considered as perceptual systems*. Boston: Houghton Mifflin.

Gray, R. (2011). *On the nature of the senses.* In F. MacPherson (ed.), *The senses.* Oxford: Oxford University Press, 243–260.

Grice, H. P. (1962). Some remarks about the senses. In R. J. Butler (ed.), *Analytical philosophy (First series).* Oxford: Basil Blackwell, 248–268. Rept. in F. MacPherson (2011), *The senses.* Oxford: Oxford University Press, 83–101.

Guarniero, G. (1974). Experience of tactile vision. *Perception,* 3, 101–104.

Hanneton, S., Auvray, M., & Durette, B. (2010). Vibe: A versatile vision-to-audition sensory substitution device. *Applied Bionics and Biomechanics,* 7, 269–276.

Hartcher O'Brien, J., & Auvray, M. (submitted). A novel perspective on distal attribution through the prism of sensory substitution studies. *Multisensory Research.*

Heil, J. (1983). *Perception and cognition.* Berkeley: University of California Press.

Heil, J. (2003). *From an ontological point of view.* Oxford: Oxford University Press.

Heil, J. (2011). The senses. In F. MacPherson (ed.), *The senses.* Oxford: Oxford University Press, 284–296.

Hurley, S., & Noë, A. (2003). Neural plasticity and consciousness. *Biology and Philosophy,* 18, 131–168.

Humphrey, N. (1992). *A history of the mind.* New York: Simon & Schuster.

Jansson, G. (1983). Tactile guidance of movement. *International Journal of Neuroscience,* 19, 37–46.

Keeley, B. L. (2002). Making sense of the senses: Individuating modalities in human and other animals. *Journal of Philosophy,* 99, 5–28.

Keeley, B. L. (2013). What's exactly in a sense? In J. Simner (ed.), *Oxford handbook of synaesthesia.* Oxford: Oxford University Press, 941–958.

Kim, J.-K., & Zatorre, R. J. (2008). Generalized learning of visual-to-auditory substitution in sighted individuals. *Brain Research,* 1242, 263–275.

Kupers, R., Fumal, A., Maertens de Noordhout, A., Gjedde, A., Schoenen, J., & Ptito, M. (2006). Transcranial magnetic stimulation of the visual cortex induces somatotopically organized qualia in blind subjects. *Proceedings of the National Academy of Sciences,* 35, 13256–13260.

Leon, M. (1988). Characterizing the senses. *Mind and Language,* 3, 243–270.

Loomis, J. M., Klatzky, R. L., & Giudice, N. A. (2012). Sensory substitution of vision: Importance of perceptual and cognitive processing. In R. Manduchi & S. Kurniawan (eds.), *Assistive technology for blindness and low vision.* Boca Raton: FL: CRC Press, 162–191.

Lopes, D.M. (2000). What is it like to see with your ears? The representational theory of mind. *Philosophy and Phenomenological Research,* 60, 439–453.

Matthen, M. (2007). Defining vision: What homology thinking contributes. *Biology and Philosophy,* 22, 675–689.

MacPherson, F. (ed.). (2011). *The senses: Classic and contemporary philosophical perspectives.* Oxford: Oxford University Press.

Meijer, P. B. L. (1992). An experimental system for auditory image representations. *IEEE Transactions on Biomedical Engineering,* 39, 112–121.

Milner, A. D., & Goodale, M.A. (2008). Two visual systems re-viewed. *Neuropsychologia,* 46, 774–785.

Morgan, M. J. (1977). *Molyneux's question. Vision, touch and the philosophy of perception.* Cambridge: Cambridge University Press.

Nagel, S. K., Carl C., Kringe T., Märtin R., & König, P. (2005). Beyond sensory substitution—learning the sixth sense. *Journal of Neural Engineering*, 2, 13–26.

Noë, A. (2004). *Action in perception*. Cambridge, MA: MIT Press.

Nudds, M. (2004). The significance of the senses. *Proceedings of the Aristotelian Society*, 104, 31–51.

Nudds, M. (2011). The senses as psychological kinds. In F. MacPherson (ed.), *The senses*. Oxford: Oxford University Press, 311–340.

O'Dea. J. (2011). A proprioceptive account of the sensory modalities. In F. MacPherson (ed.), *The senses*. Oxford: Oxford University Press, 297–310.

O'Regan, J. K. (2011). *Why red doesn't sound like a bell: Understanding the feel of consciousness*. Oxford: Oxford University Press.

O'Regan, J. K., & Noë, A. (2001). A sensorimotor account of vision and visual consciousness. *Behavioral and Brain Sciences*, 24, 939–973.

Ortiz T., Poch J., Santos J. M., Requena C., Martínez A. M., Ortiz-Terán L., et al. (2011). Recruitment of occipital cortex during sensory substitution training linked to subjective experience of seeing in people with blindness. *PLoS ONE*, 66, e23264.

Peacocke, C. (1983). *Sense and content: Experience, thought and their relation*. Oxford: Oxford University Press.

Poirier C., De Volder, A. G., & Scheiber C. (2007). What neuroimaging tells us about sensory substitution. *Neuroscience and Biobehavioral Review*, 31, 1064–1070.

Prinz, J. (2006). Putting the brakes on enactive perception. *Psyche*, 12, 1–19.

Ptito, M., Fumal, A., de Noordhout, A. M., Schoenen, J., Gjedde, A., & Kupers, R. (2008). TMS of the occipital cortex induces tactile sensations in the fingers of blind Braille readers. *Experimental Brain Research*, 184, 193–200.

Ptito, M., Moesgaard, S. M., Gjedde, A., & Kupers, R. (2005). Cross-modal plasticity revealed by electrotactile stimulation of the tongue in the congenitally blind. *Brain*, 128, 606–614.

Renier, L., Collignon, O., Poirier, C., Tranduy, D., Vanlierde, A., Bol, A., Veraart, C., & De Volder, A. G. (2005). Cross-modal activation of visual cortex during depth perception using auditory substitution of vision. *NeuroImage*, 26, 573–580.

Ross. P.W. (2001). Qualia and the senses. *Philosophical Quarterly*, 51, 495–511.

Roxbee Cox, J. M. (1970). Distinguishing the senses. *Mind*, 79, 530–550.

Sampaio, E., Maris, S., & Bach-y-Rita, P. (2001). Brain plasticity: 'Visual' acuity of blind persons via the tongue. *Brain Research*, 908, 204–207.

Siegle J. H., & Warren W. H. (2010). Distal attribution and distance perception in sensory substitution. *Perception*, 39, 208–223.

Smith, A. D. (2002). *The problem of perception*. Cambridge, MA: Harvard University Press.

Spence, C., & Deroy, O. (2013). Crossmodal mental imagery. In S. Lacey and R. Lawson (eds.), *Multisensory imagery: Theory and applications*. Philadelphia: Springer, 157–183.

Strawson, P. F. (1959). *Individuals: An essay in descriptive metaphysics*. London: Methuen.

Ward, J., & Meijer, P. (2010). Visual experiences in the blind induced by an auditory sensory substitution device. *Consciousness and Cognition*, 19, 492–500.

White, B. W., Saunders, F. A., Scadden, L., Bach-y-Rita, P., & Collins, C.C. (1970). Seeing with the skin. *Perception & Psychophysics*, 7, 23–27.

14

The Dominance of the Visual

Dustin Stokes and Stephen Biggs

1. Introduction

Perception-studies has long been vision-centric in at least two ways. First, vision has been studied far more often than other sense modalities. Second, ignoring other senses has been excused partly on the ground that one can learn everything that can be learned about perception in general by studying vision. Thus, vision is taken to be the paradigmatic perceptual sense, and its structure is then imputed to the other sense modalities in a way that is insensitive to differences among modalities.

Recent theorists reject this vision-centrism. O'Callaghan (2011), for example, argues that studying audition reveals, among other things, both a diversity of perceptual objects and a banality of multimodal experiences that "an exclusively visual perspective" wouldn't admit. He also suggests that these diverse perceptual objects are unified in an interesting way, which implies that studying only vision leads to a false account of the property *being a perceptual object*. In a similar spirit Batty suggests:

> It is commonplace to hold that visual experience represents objects. After all, visual experience displays a rich form of perceptual organization that allows us to think and speak of individual apples and oranges, particular cats and dogs. Olfactory experience lacks such organization. If we take this organization as necessary for the representation of objects, we are led to the conclusion that olfactory experience does not represent objects. But we need not, and ought not, accept this conclusion. Olfactory experience does indeed represent objects—just not in a way that is easily read off the dominant visual case (Batty 2011: 162).

Others suggest that vision-centrism biases theorizing toward direct realism with regard to material objects. Lycan (2000), for example, suggests that direct realism would seem far less plausible if theorizing focused first on smell, since smells strike us, phenomenologically, as providing only mediated access to the ordinary material objects that emit them; McLaughlin (1989) claims the same for audition.

We sympathize with these concerns, broadly construed: theorizing about perception *should* be based on extensive studies of each sense, not exclusively, or even primarily, on studies of vision. We wonder, nonetheless, why such theorizing has been vision-centric. Is vision special? Even those who appeal for diversity often answer "yes." O'Callaghan calls the focus on vision "understandable" since we "undeniably are visual creatures" (p. 143). Batty agrees that "we are visual creatures," suggesting that a focus on vision "should come as no real surprise" since it "reflects human preferences in general" (p. 162). But what does it mean to say that we are visual creatures, or that we prefer vision? What makes vision special?

This question can be approached in many ways. One might imagine losing senses, or investigate actual losses, considering which loss would be, or is, most destructive—although people may say they care most about vision, losing proprioception would surely be more destructive. One might imagine building a creature from the ground up, asking which sense would be needed first in order for the others to develop as senses—Martin (1992) uses this strategy to argue that touch is especially important. One might consider whether vision has intrinsic properties that no other sense has, and whether any such properties are significant—Strawson (1959) uses this strategy to argue that vision is special because it alone is intrinsically spatial.[1]

We pursue a different, complementary path, starting from an extrinsic property of *the visual*: its *dominance* of other senses.[2] Quite roughly, the visual dominates another sense *S*, say audition, with respect to property *P* if the visual asymmetrically affects how auditory stimuli that are relevant to identifying *P* are processed, where the effect is asymmetric in that the auditory has no comparable effect on how visual stimuli that are relevant to identifying *P* are processed. We find that the visual dominates with respect to a wide range of properties in psychologically and epistemically significant ways, such that the dominance of the visual partly explains why we can rightly say that vision is special.

We first identify three levels at which a sense can be dominant, the levels of *experience*, *experience-based judgment*, and *all-things-considered judgment* (section 2). Then, taking touch as our test case, we argue that vision exercises two kinds of dominance, *perception-perception* dominance, in which visual perception affects how we interpret nonvisual stimuli (section 3), and *imagery-perception* dominance, in which visual

---

[1] More specifically, Strawson claims that because only vision is intrinsically spatial, only vision allows one to think of particular objects as distinct from oneself (making vision psychologically significant), and thus, only vision allows one to know about the world apart from oneself (making vision epistemically significant). That said, Strawson suggests that touch coupled with kinesthesia might give rise to spatial concepts, and ultimately, knowledge of objective particulars. See Strawson (1959), especially pp. 64–66 and subsequent discussion.

[2] For reasons that will become clear, we use "the visual" as a general term to denote both visual perceptual experience and visual imagery.

imagery affects how we interpret nonvisual stimuli (section 4). We then consider why vision exercises these kinds of dominance over touch (section 5), and how this makes vision both psychologically and epistemically special (section 6). This allows speculation about the conditions in which vision dominates touch (section 7). We close with a rough generalization to the relation between vision and other senses (section 8).

To be clear, we don't aim to legitimize vision-centrism in perception-studies. We aim, instead, to identify (some) relations among the senses that partly explain extant vision-centrism. In fact, our line of thought has the implication that modalities should be analyzed differently, given important phenomenological and informational aspects of vision by contrast with nonvisual modalities. By this same token, a methodological prescription of our analysis is that we should avoid an overcorrection in which perception studies would treat vision as just another sense.

2. Dominance at Different Levels

The McGurk effect (McGurk and MacDonald 1976) is perhaps the most familiar example of vision influencing another sense. In one version of the effect (Rosenblum et al. 1997), subjects see a video of a person saying "va," and hear an audio track of a person saying "ba." Saying "ba" requires compressing the lips together but saying "va" doesn't. So, the video and audio track are in conflict.[3] Subjects report *hearing* "va."

Exploring this effect unearths a few levels of dominance. Subjects encountering McGurk stimuli report hearing "va" *even after* learning that the audio track plays "ba," which implies that the phenomenal character of their auditory experience is as of "va," not as of "ba."[4] In the McGurk effect, then, subjects receive a visual stimulus appropriate to one phoneme, an auditory stimulus appropriate to another phoneme altogether, and have an *auditory* experience appropriate to the *visual* stimulus, not the auditory stimulus—presumably because the stimulus received by the eyes changes the phenomenal character of the auditory experience in a way

---

[3] How does the video conflict with the audio? The stimulus received by the eyes suggests that the face has the property *looks-like-produces-"va,"* the stimulus received by the ears suggests that the face has the property *sounds-like-produces-"ba,"* and the probability that the face has both properties simultaneously nears 0, but the product of the probability that the face has each separately doesn't near 0. The former nears 0 because, Michael Winslow aside, people rarely mouth one phoneme and produce another. Of course, mismatch is more likely between video and audio tracks, but a mismatch in which the visual and auditory stimuli are so temporally similar still nears 0.

[4] Here and throughout we presume that subjects' reports about the phenomenal character of their experiences are typically reliable such that if subjects report that their auditory experience is as of "va," then typically it is. If this presumption is false, our claims about experience can be rephrased as claims about *judgments about experience*. Given this rephrasing, inferring that vision dominates audition at the level of experience from subjects' reports that they hear, say, "va" only requires presuming that subjects are reporting their experiences *honestly*, not that they are reporting them *accurately*.

that the stimulus received by the ears doesn't change the phenomenal character of the visual experience. So, presuming that audition has no comparable effect on vision, vision dominates audition with respect to the phoneme *at the level of the phenomenal character of experience.*[5] (Henceforth, unless context suggests otherwise, "experience" is short for "the phenomenal character of experience," and, if it is clear which property is at issue, "with respect to . . ." is presumed.)

Dominance at the level of experience implies a further kind of dominance. Perceptual experience often guides judgment: Ethan has a visual experience as of a pine tree and judges that there is a pine tree. Sometimes, however, one judges against perceptual experience: Lindsay has a visual experience as of a ghost, but judges that there isn't a ghost, perhaps because of her background beliefs that she's exhausted and ghosts don't exist. Even when one judges against perceptual experience, we can talk about the judgment *one would make if one were judging on the basis of perceptual experience alone*, as Lindsay would judge that there *is* a ghost if not for her background beliefs. These are *experience-based judgments.*

Experience-based judgments come in two kinds. First, for any subject S and sense modality M, *narrow* experience-based judgments are those S would make on the basis of experience in M alone, independent of evidence from background beliefs, other senses, and so on. Second, for any subject S and sense modalities $M_1 \ldots M_n$, *broad* experience-based judgments are those S would make on the basis of experiences in $M_1 \ldots M_n$ alone, independent of evidence from background beliefs, other senses, and so on. To illustrate the difference, consider an unusual subject, Cathy, who has a visual experience as of a speaker mouthing "va" and an auditory experience as of the speaker uttering "ba" in response to McGurk stimuli. Cathy's narrow experience-based judgment for vision is "va", and for audition is "ba". Her broad experience-based judgment for the pair <vision, audition> could be "va," "ba," or neither, if she withholds judgment, depending on various factors (e.g., whether she's more inclined to trust vision, audition, or neither). We can speak of broad experience-based judgments *simpliciter* when $M_1 \ldots M_n$ includes all sense modalities.

When one sense dominates at the level of experience, it also dominates at the level of narrow experience-based judgment, and, if the modalities at issue are restricted to just these two modalities, at the level of broad experience-based judgment. For ordinary subjects encountering McGurk stimuli, for example, since vision dominates audition at the level of experience, it also dominates audition at the level of narrow experience-based judgment, and, if only vision and audition

---

[5] Does audition ever have a comparable effect on vision? One might think that it does, noting that subjects report hearing "da" when the auditory stimulus is "da" and the visual stimulus is "va," and often report hearing the fusion "da" when the auditory stimulus is "ba" and the visual stimulus is "ga." These results, however, don't provide evidence that audition has a comparable effect on vision because they don't show that subjects have *visual* experiences that are appropriate to the auditory stimuli. At any rate, we use the McGurk effect primarily to illustrate different levels at which one sense might dominate another, not to argue that the McGurk effect is a case of visual dominance—though, we think it is.

are at issue, at the level of broad experience-based judgment. (Since dominance at the level of narrow experience-based judgment implies dominance at the level of broad experience-based judgment when the sensory modalities are appropriately restricted, we often presume appropriate restrictions, and speak simply of dominance at the level of experience-based judgment.)

Of course, one might fight one's disposition to trust one or another sense in cases of conflict, or to trust the senses taken together when they converge; a subject encountering McGurk stimuli for the first time who has been told that the audio track plays "ba" might report that it plays "ba," whatever her senses say. Experience-based judgments ignore such background beliefs. Since these *all-things-considered judgments* often stem from factors that are independent of online perception, they are relevant to the present project just in case those independent factors aren't especially salient, in which case all-things-considered judgments follow broad experience-based judgment.

3. Perception-Perception Dominance

We now explore vision's perception-perception dominance over other senses by focusing on visual perception's asymmetric effect on tactile perception.[6] After running through several experiments, we sketch a picture of visual dominance over touch. To prefigure, the picture implies neither that the visual invariably controls judgment when it conflicts with the tactile, nor that the tactile never controls judgment when it conflicts with the visual, but does imply that the visual affects how tactile stimuli are processed in cases of conflict in a way that the tactile doesn't affect how visual stimuli are processed.

Rock and Victor (1964) placed a small plastic square (25 mm x 25 mm; 1 mm thick) in a box. Some subjects saw the square through an eyepiece that used a transparent optical element to distort the image along its horizontal axis such that the square's apparent width was roughly halved. Other subjects touched the square by reaching around to the back of the box, and then through a black, silk cloth. Still other subjects (those in the experimental group) did both simultaneously. (The cloth prevented subjects in the experimental group from seeing a distorted image of their own hand, which otherwise would have allowed them to infer that the viewer distorted what they saw.) After five seconds of exposure to the square, all subjects were asked to draw what they sensed. Subjects who touched-but-didn't-see the square drew squares. Subjects who saw-but-didn't-touch the square drew rectangles that were about twice as tall as wide. Subjects who touched-and-saw the square *also* drew rectangles that were about twice as long as wide, behaving just like subjects who saw-but-didn't-touch the square.

---

[6] Though haptic and passive touch (i.e., touching and being touched) may be distinct senses, we simply use "touch." See Fulkerson (this volume).

Rock and Victor repeated the experiment with a different measure of perceived shape: rather than drawing the target object, subjects chose from an array of candidate "matches." Even when the matches were selected by touch alone, subjects in the vision-only and vision-plus-touch conditions picked roughly the same *rectangular* "matches" for the original square. Subjects in the touch-only condition, unsurprisingly, picked squares. (See Miller, 1972, and Welch and Warren, 1980, for similar results.)

In these experiments, subjects' eyes received a stimulus appropriate to a particular rectangle, their skin received a stimulus appropriate to a particular square, and their judgments followed vision. These results suggest, then, that vision affects how we interpret tactile stimuli with respect to shape in a way that touch doesn't affect how we interpret visual stimuli—that is, with respect to shape, vision exercises *perception-perception* dominance over touch.

At what levels does this effect occur? Since subjects' choice of shape reflects their online perceiving, not background considerations, the effect occurs at least at the level of broad experience-based judgment. Does the effect extend to the levels of narrow experience-based judgment, and ultimately, experience? It would be bizarre if subjects who experienced tactile sensations as of a square drew/selected-as-matches the very same rectangles as subjects who merely saw the object—and did so without protesting (e.g., reporting a conflict between their senses). Plausibly, then, the effect originates at the level of experience, with the visual affecting the phenomenal character of tactile experience. A supplementary experiment supports this claim (Rock and Victor 1964). The experiment used a viewing apparatus that made objects appear smaller than they were. Subjects in the see-and-touch condition were asked to open and close their eyes, reporting whether the object felt different with their eyes closed. This is akin to asking subjects to open and shut their eyes during a McGurk-presentation to test whether what they hear changes. Most subjects (23 of 38) reported that the object felt larger when they closed their eyes, then smaller when they opened them. This suggests both that the effect occurs at the level of experience and that the effect is at least partly isolated, since subjects presumably didn't believe that the object was changing size as their eyes opened and shut. Subjects' surprise also reinforces the (antecedently plausible) claim that the effect extends to all-things-considered judgments—subjects would not be surprised by the conflict if they already believed that vision was misleading. Since the effect occurs at the levels of experience, experience-based judgment, and all-things-considered judgment, we can say that vision dominates touch at these levels.[7]

---

[7] Vision dominates touch at the level of all-things-considered judgment in only 80% of subjects. Of the remaining 20%, some discovered a conflict between their senses when they (failing to follow instructions) looked away from the viewing apparatus, thereby encountering a tactile-only stimulus of the square; others spontaneously reported that they were suspicious of the viewing apparatus. Such subjects were more likely to resolve the tension "more in the direction of touch" than were naive

This effect is amazingly resilient. Using a Rock-Victor-style task, Power and Graham found that the effect persists even when subjects are told to "really *feel* the object very thoroughly" (1976, p. 164). They also found that it holds even for those who have special facility with touch (expert potters). Others have found that repeated exposure doesn't undermine naivety: without receiving feedback pointing to inconsistency, subjects don't notice it spontaneously, even after repeated trials (see, respectively, Over 1966 and Power 1980). Still others have found that the effect persists even when the visual field is dimmed or objects are blurred (respectively, Warren 1979; Fishkin et al. 1975), suggesting that even degraded visual information (known to be degraded) often dominates at the level of experience.

Power (1980) explored the limits of our tolerance for inconsistency. In two Rock-Victor-style tasks, he varied the visually apparent length and then angles of a square. The apparent length varied such that the square appeared to be a rectangle with two sides being 50% or 80% longer than the others. The apparent angles varied such that the square appeared to be either a diamond (with acute angles of 75 degrees) or a parallelogram (with acute angles of 70 degrees). Even in the cases of most extreme distortion, subjects' judgments followed vision.[8]

These results suggest that when visual and tactile stimuli conflict, vision *often* dominates touch with respect to size and shape at the levels of experience, experience-based judgment, and all-things-considered judgment. But vision doesn't *always* dominate. One wonders, then, what modulates this dominance.

Heller (1983) identifies one factor. He presented subjects with clear acrylic, three-dimensional shapes, inscribing conflicting two-dimensional colored shapes (e.g., an octagonal clear piece of acrylic might inscribe a blue square). Subjects felt the shapes with their hands while viewing the shapes through stained glass, which prevented them from seeing the acrylic but allowed them to see the inscribed two-dimensional colored shape, although it was noticeably blurred. Most subjects (11 of 12) chose matches for the target object that were consistent with the *tactile* stimulus, not the visual stimulus. Heller concludes that vision doesn't dominate if two conditions are met: first, visual stimuli are sufficiently blurry; second, the discrepancy between visual and tactile stimuli is extreme.

---

subjects (Rock and Victor, 1964, p. 596). Since Rock and Victor say little about this result, it's not clear whether all such subjects drew/selected-as-matches squares, all such subjects drew/selected-as-matches rectangles that were closer to square than those drawn/selected by naive subjects, or only some such subjects did one of these.

[8] These subjects wore a thin glove to prevent them from seeing their distorted hand. When subjects wore no glove, their judgments typically compromised between the stimulus to their eyes and hands. This suggests that either the tactile stimulus played an increased role in determining judgment, or subjects relied on inference from their belief about the distorting effect of the lens (acquired from seeing their distorted hand). All subjects (gloved or not) judged the square to be a diamond or parallelogram, suggesting that even if one knows that vision is quite distorted, it is not fully dominated by un-distorted touch at any level.

Here, touch affects how subjects interpret visual stimuli at the level of all-things-considered judgment. Does it therefore affect vision in just the way that vision affects touch in the earlier experiments? Many subjects in Heller's experiment claimed they couldn't see adequately, some asking whether they should choose what they saw or what they touched. This contrasts sharply with results from Rock and Victor, in which subjects claim to feel, say, a rectangle even while touching a square, even though vision and touch are both *clear*—vision is clear in that, subjectively, the visual experience seems entirely clear, rather than blurry or otherwise misleading. Faced with conflicting clear vision and degraded touch, one surely would follow vision. So, although Heller identifies a limit on vision's dominance, he hasn't found a case in which touch affects vision in a way that challenges visual dominance.

Over (1966) identifies another factor that modulates visual dominance of touch. He found that when visual and tactile stimuli are wildly discrepant, subjects judge that an angle is the *mean* of the visually and tactically presented angles. Whether these judgments reflect compromise at the level of experience or conflict resolution at the level of broad experience-based judgment is unclear.

Lederman and Abbot (1981) and Heller (1982) identify yet another factor that modulates visual dominance. Each found that judgment might follow touch more closely than vision when assessing *texture*. Perhaps, then, touch dominates vision with respect to texture, at least at the level of all-things-considered judgment. At the very least, this result suggests that vision is less likely to dominate touch when touch's proper sensible is at issue than when a common sensible is. One might be tempted to infer that vision doesn't dominate other senses when the other senses' proper sensible is at issue, but the McGurk effect blocks this inference.

This begins to suggest a picture of visual *perception-perception* dominance of touch: given conflicting stimuli that are not wildly discrepant, and an appropriate target property P (e.g., shape, size), vision is likely to dominate touch with respect to P at each of the three levels, unless visual experience is much more degraded than tactile experience. This speculative picture relies on the vague properties *being an appropriate target property, being wildly discrepant*, and *being much more degraded than*. An ideal account would specify these properties—which some of our subsequent discussion does (see sections 5–7). Even as it stands, nonetheless, this picture strikes us as plausible, informative, and well suited to the data.[9]

---

[9] To be clear, this picture doesn't imply that visual dominance is "all or none," such that the visual dominates *completely* when certain conditions are met, but otherwise doesn't dominate at all. The conditions can be taken, accordingly, to mark the limit of a continuum ranging from the visual completely controlling judgment to the tactile completely controlling judgment. What the picture requires is that, given where this point lies, the visual dominates touch. An example illustrates the broader point. Suppose that in a Rock-and-Victor-style experiment subjects are asked to judge the shape of a four-inch by four-inch square. Suppose that the viewing apparatus initially presents a clear image of a two-inch by eight-inch rectangle. Suppose that subjects in this condition judge that the shape is a rectangle with its long sides four times longer than its short sides. Suppose that, as the viewing apparatus

4. Imagery-Perception Dominance

In the previous section, we found that vision exercises perception-perception dominance over touch, at least with respect to size and shape. In this section, we shift
to a more surprising discovery: vision exercises *imagery-perception* dominance over
touch. After explicating *mental imagery*, we consider evidence that visual imagery
asymmetrically affects how we interpret certain tactile stimuli.

4.1. MENTAL IMAGERY

Mental imagery is often described as *quasi-perceptual experience*, a characterization
that traces back at least to Hume (1739/2000). What makes mental imagery *perceptual*? Imagery experiences resemble perceptual experiences in some significant,
modality specific way, that is, the *phenomenal character of visual imagery* resembles
the *phenomenal character of visual perceptual experiences* in a significant way, and so
on for each modality for which there can be mental imagery. What makes mental
imagery merely *quasi*-perceptual? First, imagery and perceptual experiences have
different kinds of causes: ordinarily, only the latter are caused by confrontation with
the stimuli they represent. Second, imagery lacks the assertoric force of perceptual
experiences: ordinarily, only perceptual experience, absent any additional input or
belief-forming basis, leads one to judge that the world is as the experience represents
it to be.[10]

This last point requires elaboration. If encountering a tree causes one to have a
visual experience with a phenomenal character as of a tree, one is strongly inclined to
all-things-considered judge that there is a tree. By contrast, if visually imaging a tree
causes one to have an experience with a phenomenal character (at least roughly) as
of a tree, one is far less inclined to all-things-considered judge that there is a tree. The
spatiotemporal nature of the assertoric force is also important. When encountering
a tree leads one to judge (on the basis of visual experience) that there is a tree, one
typically judges that there is a tree *here* and *now*. By contrast, even if visually imaging
a tree leads one to make an all-things-considered judgment about a tree (e.g., that it
exists, has green leaves, etc.), the judgment is far less likely to be about what is here
and now.[11]

---

becomes increasingly blurry subjects judge that the shape is a rectangle with its long sides three times
longer than its short sides, and so on, until, with enough blurring of vision, subjects judge that the
object is square. The proposed picture of visual dominance is compatible with this possibility.

[10] For ease of presentation, we often talk as if perceptual experiences are representational. Nothing
turns on this way of speaking.

[11] This point also can be used to distinguish ordinary visual experience from iconic memory. Unlike
ordinary visual experience, iconic memory is assertive about the past, not the present, and the assertoric force has no special tie to the immediate environment. Thanks to Mohan Matthen for pointing
out the importance of these spatiotemporal differences.

Why these differences? Perhaps the phenomenal characters of perceptual and imagery experiences differ such that only the former produce relevant, narrow experience-based judgments, as if imagery experiences come stamped with a phenomenal marker that defeats their potential assertoric force, right at the level of experience. Perhaps, instead, the process that produces imagery produces beliefs that the experiences aren't perceptual, as if mental images get stamped with a doxastic marker that can defeat their assertoric force, right when they otherwise would affect all-things-considered judgment. While these models differ (and there may be others), they agree that *mental images come marked as non-perceptual* such that they lack the default assertoric force of perceptual experiences.

Imagery, then, differs importantly from illusory and hallucinatory experiences. One might have a defeater for illusory experiences, as when one sees the Muller-Lyer illusion and is informed of its illusory nature. One might have a defeater for hallucinatory experiences, as when one remembers ingesting hallucinogens. As a general matter, however, neither illusory nor hallucinatory experiences *come marked as non-perceptual*: when the uninformed see the Muller-Lyer illusion, they judge that the lines have different lengths; when the forgetful ingest hallucinogens, they judge that the pink elephants are parading. Even if this difference isn't metaphysically or cognitively necessary, it's certainly characteristic of typical imagery, illusory, and hallucinatory experiences. This yields the following characterization:

> *Mental imagery:* A mental image *i* is a perceptual-experience-like mental state/process that is not caused by the appropriate external stimuli (at least not in the ordinary way) and lacks assertoric force about the here and now (at least typically)—where *i* is *perceptual-experience-like* partly in that its phenomenal character resembles that of whichever modality (or modalities) it mimics.

In sum, although imagery experiences resemble perceptual experiences in some significant, modality-specific way, the two have different kinds of causes and different default assertoric forces. This characterization isn't offered as an ultimate definition. It ignores some features that have been thought of, perhaps rightly, as definitive of mental imagery.[12] It also leaves open, inter alia, how imagery experiences resemble perceptual experiences, and what makes their resemblance significant. We treat this characterization, then, as a "working definition," adequate for our purposes, even if incomplete.

---

[12] To name two: first, empiricists can hold that imagery relies upon information acquired through previous perception in a way that perception doesn't; second, imagery is arguably under immediate voluntary control in a way that perception isn't—I can't help but see the mountain if it's in front of me, my eyes are open, and my visual system is functioning properly, I can't "get myself to see" a mountain if none is present, and I can visually image a mountain, no matter my surroundings (Reid 1764/1997; Wittgenstein 1967; McGinn 2004; Thomas 2010).

4.2. EVIDENCE OF IMAGERY-PERCEPTION DOMINANCE

With this discussion of mental imagery in place, we consider the surprising discovery that visual *imagery* strongly affects how we interpret tactile stimuli during ordinary tactile *perception*.

Sathian et al. (1997) immobilized the right-hand index fingers of strongly right-handed subjects. They then ran small plastic domes across the immobilized index finger. The domes had gratings of varying widths cut into their faces. For some subjects, the gratings were run parallel to the immobilized finger. For others, the gratings were run perpendicular to the immobilized finger. The domes were hidden from sight for all subjects. In the control condition, subjects were asked to identify the width of the gratings as either small or large. In the experimental condition, subjects were asked to identify the orientation of the gratings as either horizontal or vertical (relative to the finger). In each condition, subjects succeeded 75% to 80% of the time.

Subjects in the experimental condition reported using visual imagery to perform the task. Subjects in the control condition didn't. Positron emission tomography (PET) scans corroborated these reports, finding brain activity appropriate to visual imagery only during the experimental condition. Specifically, PET scans found increased cerebral blood flow in subjects' left parieto-occipital cortex, an area of visual cortex that activates when subjects generate visual images in response to various stimuli, for example, verbal cues (Mellet et al. 1996; Kosslyn et al. 1995). This activated region also overlaps with a large region of visual association cortex in the parietal lobe, which is active during deliberate recall of visual patterns (Roland et al. 1990). These results suggest that visual imagery helps subjects perform the orientation task, even though the stimuli are only tactile.

Results from Zangaladze et al. (1999) further support this suggestion. They conducted an experiment like that described earlier, with one exception: they used transcranial magnetic stimulation (TMS) to disrupt activity in subjects' left parieto-occipital cortex. Success on the orientation task worsened significantly with the disruption, but success on the spacing task didn't. This further supports the claim that visual imagery plays a causal role in producing subjects' judgments about the orientation of the gratings—a role that is, moreover, beneficial, as we argue later. Self-reports fit this finding: robbed of visual imagery, many subjects said that they could feel the stimulus, but not identify its orientation. Zangaladze et al. conclude, therefore, that "visual cortical processing is *necessary* for normal tactile perception" (our italics, 1999, p. 588). Notice that since subjects don't see the plastic domes, this conclusion is about the role of the neural correlate of visual *imagery* in online tactile *perception*.

Is the effect symmetric? Is haptic imagery often invoked for relevantly similar visual tasks? Zhang et al. (2004) explored this question (see also Klatzky et al. 1987). In a visual task, participants saw images with a distinctive shape (e.g., a garlic) or texture (e.g., tree bark). In a haptic task, they touched (without seeing) three-dimensional shapes (e.g., a heart) and heavily textured objects (e.g., sandpaper). The participants were asked to think of (but not report) descriptors that characterize the stimuli. They lay in a functional magnetic resonance imaging (fMRI) scanner throughout. They regularly reported (after the task set and fMRI scan) using visual imagery for the haptic perceptual tasks, but didn't report using haptic imagery for the visual perceptual tasks. fMRI results corroborated these reports, finding strong activation of the visual cortex during haptic tasks, but no significant activation of brain areas that process haptic information during visual tasks. Furthermore, the vividness of the reported imagery strongly correlated with the strength of activity in the ventral visual pathway, specifically, the lateral occipital complex, which is responsible for identifying objects by shape and high-level kind, for example "egg" or "dog" (Kourtzi and Kanwisher 2001). Since the ventral visual pathway is associated with conscious visual experience, this also suggests that the phenomenal character of visual imagery experiences resembles the phenomenal character of visual perceptual experiences. This result supports the already plausible claim that the effect is asymmetric.

While we recognize that self-reports, neuroimaging, and TMS results can be problematic, we find the confluence among this evidence to be quite compelling: subjects' reports *predict* their performance in tasks, neuroimaging results, and TMS results.[13] Together, then, these experiments suggest that we often invoke visual imagery to learn about certain tactile stimuli, but we rarely if ever invoke tactile imagery to learn about visual stimuli. Recall that vision dominates another sense with respect to a certain property when the visual asymmetrically affects other senses in just this way. So, once again, vision dominates touch, now in virtue of visual *imagery* asymmetrically affecting tactile *perception*. So, the visual exercises *imagery-perception* dominance over touch.

At what level does this imagery-perception dominance occur? The visual exercises this dominance at least at the levels of all-things-considered judgment, and experience-based judgment. Whether it also exercises this dominance at the level of experience is unclear. Perhaps visual imagery tweaks tactile experience such that subjects in Sathian et al.'s experiment tactilely feel the gratings as oriented in the way that visual imagery suggests they are. Perhaps touch remains forever silent about the orientations. Future research should explore this issue. We conclude,

---

[13] Consider just a few problems with neuroimaging studies. First, since PET and fMRI measurements are rather coarse-grained, treating large groups of neurons as a single unit, they can find that different tasks produce the same exact activation even though not a single neuron is activated for both tasks. Second, since one judges that an area is activated for a task by contrasting activity during that task with activity during a control task, choice of control is crucial, but there are no clear methods for choice. Third, in order to identify a neural correlate of a conscious event, such as the neural correlate of visually imaging, one must have an independent measure to identify the presence of consciousness, but any such measure is controversial (cf. Chalmers 1998). Fourth, there is clear evidence that common methods for analyzing neuroimaging results can mislead us badly (cf. Bennett et al. 2010).

then, only that vision exercises imagery-perception dominance of touch *at least* at the levels of all things-considered and experience-based judgment.

Clearly, we don't always use visual imagery to interpret tactile stimuli. One wonders, then, what modulates visual imagery-perception dominance over touch. Some factors should be clear: we're unlikely to invoke visual imagery if visual perception is available, and we're more likely to invoke visual imagery for some tasks than for others (for example, detecting shape versus texture). That said, since relatively little research aims to explore this issue, we are left to speculate. For now, we speculate that the modulating factors here loosely resemble those for visual perception-perception dominance of touch. We return to this issue later.

5. Why the Visual Dominates Touch

Why does the visual dominate touch with respect to size and shape? What difference between vision and touch grounds visual dominance? The answer lies in the nature of *visual experience*. Some have claimed that visual experience is *uniquely spatial*. O'Shaughnessy, for example, says that "perception at a distance is uniquely visual in type," and "other varieties of perception encounter their object *without* spatial mediation" (2009. p. 114).[14] This claim should be rejected; after all, audition alone can place sounds at least in egocentric space, and touch alone lets us navigate in ways that require spatial information. Nonetheless, the claim gets something right: visual experience is uniquely *richly* spatial.

A kind of experience is richly spatial if and only if it allows one to identify multiple *macrospatial* properties and *allocentric* properties *all at once*. *Macrospatial properties* are "large-scale elements like shape, size and orientation" that contrast with "microspatial properties," which "are small-scale surface elements like texture or irregularities" (Stoesz et al. 2003, p. 41).[15] *Allocentric properties* are spatial relations among external objects that hold irrespective of any given perceiver, which contrast with egocentric properties, which are spatial relations between external objects and perceivers. Properties are identified *all at once* if and only if they are identified more or less immediately and more or less simultaneously.

Does visual experience allow one to identify multiple macrospatial properties and allocentric properties all at once? Yes. V*isual experience* presents the size, shape, and orientation of objects, as well as their relative locations, all at once. By contrast, unaided tactile experience, presents macrospatial properties and allocentric properties at best through a *series of experiences* that are generated by

---

[14] Others, for example, Strawson (1959), endorse similar claims, which are rooted in Berkeley's theory of vision (1713). See Evans (1980) for related discussion, and O'Callaghan (2011) for resistance to the aspatiality of audition.

[15] Although Stoesz et al., like most who use these labels, apply this distinction only to "tactile features," macrospatial properties are common sensibles, and some microspatial properties are too.

FIGURE14.1. *Tadashi Kawamata. Chairs for Abu Dhabi, 2012. Chairs, armchairs, sofas, benches, stools and metallic structure. 6 × 7 × 6 m. View of the installation, Abu Dhabi Art, Beyond, 2012 © Tadashi Kawamata. Photo: Daniel Suarez. Courtesy of the artist and kamel mennour, Paris, 9780199832811.*

extensive, slow exploration, such that tactile experience doesn't present multiple macrospatial or allocentric properties all at once. At the very least, visual experience allows one to identify multiple macrospatial and allocentric properties *so quickly* and *in such rapid succession* that it's natural to describe their presentation as more or less immediate and simultaneous, in a way that would be strikingly unnatural for tactile experiences.

An example reinforces this view. Suppose you enter the space that houses Kawamata's chair installation (see Figure 14.1). Your visual experience is immediately rich with macrospatial and allocentric information. You see the shape of the sculpture, its meandering curves, its massiveness, the chairs, their shapes, sizes, and orientations—some vertical, some horizontal. You see the chairs as tightly stacked, one on top of another, and the cavernous space surrounding the sculpture. You see all this, moreover, *all at once.* Plausibly, touch provides nothing like this wealth of information. That said, we only need the contrastive point that even if tactile experiences can provide the same information, it can do so only through a *series* of experiences that result from *extensive, slow* exploration, that is, "feeling around," which precludes the immediacy and simultaneity that visual experience ordinarily enjoys.[16]

---

[16] Although we talk as if visual experience represents high-level properties, such as *being a chair* and *being vertical*, we aren't wedded to that view. Even if visual experience presents only color and shape properties, visual-experience-based judgments that there are chairs oriented in various ways are immediate and simultaneous in a way that touch-experience-based judgments aren't.

Visual experience, then, is richly spatial in a way that touch isn't. This difference, we contend, provides the basis for the visual's perception-perception dominance. Can it also provide a basis for the visual's imagery-perception dominance?[17] Yes, because visual *imagery* experience significantly resembles visual *perceptual* experience (cf. section 4.1). One might object that the resemblance, however significant, doesn't extend so far that visual imagery experience inherits *being richly spatial*. Perhaps one is tempted to ground this objection by observing that visual imagery doesn't seem, phenomenologically, to be richly spatial. This concern merits two quick responses. First, the results from section 4.2 suggest that visual imagery experiences present the very macrospatial properties that ordinary visual experiences do, which suggests that imagery experiences are richly spatial *enough* to ground vision's imagery-perception dominance of touch. Second, when we (the authors) close our eyes and visually image Kawamata's sculpture, our imagery experiences seem to us to present many of the same macrospatial and allocentric properties that the original perceptual experiences presented, and we suspect that the same holds for most people, even if visual imagery experiences are, in some sense, mere shadows of their perceptual counterparts.[18]

We think, moreover, that the visual is *uniquely* richly spatial: it is richly spatial while the auditory, olfactory, and other senses are not. Brief reflection should reveal that audition is the only other relevant sense. And although audition provides some spatial information—a sound may be heard as coming from one's right, or as being "bigger" than a second sound—it is relatively impoverished in this regard, typically providing egocentric spatial information, and little if anything by way of macrospatial property representation. To see the point, contrast the information one can gather by listening to, say, a basketball game with the information one can gather by seeing it. We expect, then, that this case for the dominance of the visual over touch extends to other senses; the visual dominates other senses no less than it dominates touch. We revisit this claim, offering some preliminary evidence, in the final section.

6. Significance of Dominance

With this discussion of visual dominance in place, we now consider why this dominance makes vision special. We first note that this dominance is, rather trivially,

---

[17] To be clear, this is a claim about the *basis* for visual dominance, not about what *constitutes* its dominance. That is, we are not claiming that the visual dominates touch in that it gives us richly spatial properties but touch doesn't. We are claiming, instead, that the visual dominates touch with respect to properties P that can be detected (at least in part) by either sense (e.g., shape, size), and that this dominance with respect to P occurs because the visual gives us richly spatial properties Q but touch doesn't.

[18] Imagine a contest to quickly identify macrospatial and allocentric properties of the sculpture between two people who have seen it previously. One is free to touch, but not to see or visually image. The other is free to visually image, but not to see nor touch.

psychologically significant. We then argue that it is also *epistemically* significant in a surprising way: visual dominance of touch is *epistemically good*. Epistemically speaking, the visual *should* dominate touch.

Vision exercises perception-perception dominance over touch with respect to macrospatial and allocentric properties. The dominance is at the levels of experience, experience-based judgment, and all-things-considered judgment. Touch doesn't dominate vision for a comparably significant range of properties. So, because vision dominates touch, it contributes disproportionally to what we experience and think. This is enough to make vision significant *psychologically*. This point extends to visual imagery-perception dominance of touch, though whether visual imagery dominates at the level of experience is less clear.

Of more interest to philosophers, visual dominance over touch makes vision significant *epistemically*. Consider first visual perception-perception dominance. We, joining most philosophers, take perceptual experiences to provide (at least) prima facie justification for perceptual beliefs: if one has a perpetual experience as of a leafy green tree, one is prima facie justified in believing that there is a leafy green tree. So, since vision exercises perception-perception dominance over touch at the level of experience, and this dominance leads to dominance in judgment, vision contributes more to justification for perceptual beliefs (in cases of conflict, and plausibly ordinary cases) than touch does.

Although this shows that visual dominance of touch is epistemically *significant*, it doesn't show that this dominance is epistemically *good*. To support the latter claim, we consider, in broad outline, epistemic externalist and epistemic internalist views, presuming that readers can extend our discussion to their preferred versions.

Externalism about justification holds, roughly, that factors that are inaccessible to a believer can affect whether her beliefs are justified. The most prominent version of externalism is process reliabilism, which holds, roughly, that a belief is justified just in case it is produced by a reliable process (see, e.g., Goldman 1967). Accordingly, a process reliabilist will hold that beliefs produced by visual perception-perception dominance of touch are justified just in case the process by which vision exercises this dominance is reliable. We contend that it is. So, we conclude, given reliablism, visual perception-perception dominance of touch is epistemically good.

Why think that the process by which vision exercises perception-perception dominance over touch is reliable? Since visual experience is richly spatial but touch isn't, vision is better situated than touch is to inform us about various properties (e.g., size, shape, location), and thus, one's best bet for acquiring information about these properties from tactile stimuli is to use vision, until it becomes significantly degraded. This point extends to visual imagery-perception dominance: as per the results discussed in section 4, visual imagery is better situated to inform us about various properties (e.g., orientation) than touch is, and thus, absent visual experience, one's best bet for acquiring relevant information from tactile stimuli is to use visual imagery—hence, the success of subjects who use visual imagery to identify the orientation of felt gratings. So, the process that produces each kind of dominance is reliable. (This model can be buttressed with an evolutionary claim: use of the visual to form beliefs about macrospatial and allocentric properties, at least for creatures like us, affords clear adaptive advantages.)

One might object that this account of the reliability of visual dominance faces a dilemma that goes as follows. First horn: for any property P, if touch can provide any information about P that vision can, then the visual isn't better situated to provide information about (and so does not dominate with respect to) P. Second horn: if vision can provide information about P that touch can't, then tactile stimuli aren't relevant to detecting P and so the visual doesn't dominate with respect to P—since dominance would require the visual affecting how tactile stimuli that are relevant to identifying P are processed. We reject each horn.

Regarding the first horn: even if touch can provide any information about macrospatial and allocentric properties that vision can, there are many ways in which the visual is better situated to provide information about those very properties. For example, since touch requires extensive exploration to identify, say, the shape of a complex object, we should expect such identification to rely heavily on memory, which, we should expect, decreases its reliability—imagine what would be required of memory to use touch to identify the shape of Kawamata's chair installation. A second point concerns speed. Even if the tactile provides comparable information, it does so, again, only through extensive, time-consuming exploration. Vision, by contrast, provides this information in a way that affords smooth and rapid interaction with the environment. This is an epistemic advantage of vision over touch. Although these points could be developed and complemented further, the basic problem with the first horn should be clear: the potential to provide information about a property is not the only relevant epistemic good.

Regarding the second horn: even if vision can provide information about P that touch can't, tactile stimuli can be relevant to detecting P. In the aforementioned Sathian et al. experiment, for example, tactile stimuli are required to identify the orientation of the gratings even though one can't identify the orientation through touch alone. Relatedly, there may be a property P such that one can't identify P through touch alone even though one can identify P on the basis of tactile stimuli.[19] This objection, therefore, fails.

One might be tempted to object, instead, along the following lines. "Since vision can mislead us when exercising perception-perception dominance, as in the Rock and Victor experiments, the process by which vision exercises perception-perception dominance is unreliable. So, experiences produced by that dominance don't provide even prima facie justification. So, visual perception-perception dominance is

---

[19] Sometimes, moreover, properties other than P may not be identifiable without identifying P, as one might not be able to identify the shapes of overlapping objects without identifying various facts about orientation.

not epistemically good." This objection has the surprising result that beliefs produced by visual *perception*-perception dominance of touch are unjustified, even though beliefs produced by visual *imagery*-perception dominance are, presumably, justified. That should already make one suspicious. The objection, nonetheless, merits two replies.

First, if one individuates cognitive processes rather coarsely, such that the process that produces perceptual experiences in which vision exercises perception-perception dominance over touch *just is* the process that produces perceptual experiences in general, then the objector faces a dilemma. The objector must accept either that tactile experiences that result from dominance provide prima facie justification, even when they mislead us, or that visual experiences *never* provide justification because the process that produces them is *sometimes* unreliable, as when it leads to visual perception-perception dominance of touch in Rock-Victor-style experiments. The former horn undermines the objection; the latter horn should not be embraced.

Second, and more important, suppose that one individuates cognitive processes more finely. Does it follow that the process by which vision dominates is unreliable? No. Ernst and Banks (2002) argue rather effectively that visual perception-perception dominance of touch is "optimal." Their conclusion is based on several findings.

- First, in ideal conditions, vision alone allows subjects to accurately judge which of two sequentially presented bars is taller: even with only a small difference in height, subjects judge the taller bar as taller. So, in effect, the range of different bars that vision judges to be the same is very small. In ideal conditions, then, vision exhibits relatively *low variance*.
- Second, in ideal conditions, subjects using touch alone to judge the relative heights of the bars are much less accurate: the difference in height must be relatively large before subjects judge accurately. So, in effect, the range of different bars that touch judges to be the same is comparatively large. In ideal conditions, then, touch exhibits relatively *high variance*.
- Third, as viewing conditions are degraded for vision, pairs of bars that would have been judged accurately in ideal conditions are judged inaccurately, suggesting that the range of different bars that vision judges to be the same has increased. So, as viewing conditions are degraded, vision's *variance increases*.
- Fourth, given the first three findings, by systematically degrading viewing conditions for subjects using vision alone, one can identify how degraded vision must be before the variance for vision becomes as great as the variance for ideal touch: before one reaches what Ernst and Banks call the *point of subjective equality*. As it turns out, vision must be quite degraded before this point is reached, before vision is as poor at discriminating

heights as ideal touch always is. To emphasize the epistemic significance of this point, we call it the point of subjective *epistemic* equality.[20]

- Fifth, when subjects see and touch the bars simultaneously, vision has a greater influence on judgment than touch does (at least at the level of all-things-considered judgment, and presumably at the level of experience) right up to the point of subjective epistemic equality, the point at which (degraded) vision alone exhibits as much variance as ideal touch alone.

Visual dominance of touch, then, is optimal: *vision stops influencing judgment more than touch does exactly when vision ceases to be more accurate and touch tends to become more accurate*, which, as it turns out, isn't until vision is quite degraded while touch is still ideal. So, even if visual perception-perception dominance of touch occasionally misleads us, the process by which vision exercises this dominance is generally reliable.

This discussion easily extends to virtue-epistemology-inspired interpretations of reliabilism. According to virtue epistemology, agents themselves, not their doxastic commitments, are the primary targets for epistemic evaluation. Agents are virtuous, the theory goes, if and to the degree that they exhibit intellectual virtues. The potential virtue at issue here is the disposition to perceive the world in a certain way—a way that leads to visual dominance of touch. For the *virtue reliabilist*, this disposition is an intellectual virtue just in case it is truth conducive (Goldman 1993; Greco 1999, 2009, 2010; Sosa 1980, 2007). As per Ernst and Banks, this disposition *is* truth-conducive, since one is disposed to follow vision right up to the point of subjective epistemic equality, which is exactly when following vision would begin to lead one astray. More broadly, this disposition is reliable, and hence an intellectual virtue, because the visual (including imagery) is better situated than touch to teach us about macrospatial and allocentric properties, which are the very properties for which we are disposed to follow vision.

Now, consider internalism about justification, which holds that justification depends exclusively on "internal" factors.[21] While this broad claim can be specified in many ways, suppose the following rough characterization of internalism: for any proposition p and subject s, s is justified in believing p if and only if s can access the basis for her belief in p, and that basis is good. Even this rough characterization, which leaves a lot open (e.g., what counts as "good"), is controversial. Some internalists hold, for example, that a belief is justified only if its basis is actually

---

[20] Roughly, the point of subjective epistemic equality for two senses and some property P is the point at which, in ordinary circumstances, experiences in each modality provide equally reliable information about P. So, since rather seriously degraded visual experience is more reliable than touch at its best for many properties (e.g., shape), the point of subjective epistemic equality between vision and touch for those properties is not reached until visual experience is quite degraded.

[21] Epistemic internalism can be traced back at least to Plato and is clearly articulated by Descartes. Contemporary sources include Prichard (1950) and Chisholm (1977). See Alston (1989) for general discussion of theories of epistemic justification.

accessed. We ignore such controversy here, supposing that our discussion could be adjusted to suit any plausible version of internalism.

Do beliefs that result from visual dominance over touch typically satisfy these conditions? Yes. Beliefs formed on the basis of visual dominance are a subset of beliefs formed on the basis of perception. A standard, internalist picture of perception includes these: that perceptual experiences provide the basis for perceptual beliefs, perceptual experiences and their contents are accessible to their subjects (at least in principle), and perceptual experiences are a good basis for belief (at least ceteris paribus). So, given internalism, beliefs formed on the basis of visual dominance are prima facie justified.

Rejecting this argument requires showing that beliefs formed on the basis of visual dominance are relevantly different from ordinary perceptual beliefs. An objector might attempt to show this in either of two ways. First, the objector can deny that beliefs formed on the basis of visual dominance are even prima facie justified. Second, the objector can insist that such beliefs are invariably defeated in a way that ordinary perceptual beliefs are not. Consider these objections in turn.

Given any internalist account of the goodness of a basis for belief, if experiences that result from visual dominance are more problematic as a basis for belief than are dominance-free experiences, then (1) the former differ subjectively from the latter, and (2) that difference undermines the goodness of the former. Contrary to (1), we suspect that experiences that result from visual dominance are subjectively indistinguishable from relevant dominance-free experiences, at least ordinarily. So, for example, one who touches a rectangle while seeing a rectangle and consequently has a tactile experience as of a rectangle, and one who touches a square while seeing a rectangle and consequently has a tactile experience as of a rectangle (as in the Rock and Victor experiment) typically have subjectively indistinguishable tactile experiences. (Since the McGurk effect is more familiar, perhaps one should compare the auditory experience of "va" that results from visual dominance to an ordinary auditory experience of "va.")[22] Contrary to (2), we see no reason to think that subjective differences between dominance and dominance-free perceptual experiences (if, contrary to our suspicion, there are differences) undermine the epistemic goodness of dominated experiences. After all, subjects typically use experiences that result from dominance in the same ways epistemically that they use experiences that are dominance-free (e.g., to guide reasoning and behavior), which suggests there is no accessed epistemically relevant difference between them, which further suggests that there is no accessible epistemically relevant difference. And this, finally, suggests that there is no relevant difference that internalists can acknowledge.

---

[22] Even if dominance and dominance-free experiences are subjectively distinguishable in principle, it is quite likely that one rarely distinguishes them, which is relevant under formulations of internalism that require actual accessing where we require accessibility.

Next, an objector might grant that beliefs that result from visual dominance have prima facie justification but insist that they will be defeated quickly because, somewhere along the processing pathway, they get marked as epistemically pernicious. The objector will struggle to accommodate the fact that naïve subjects' judgments follow their dominated experience, which they would not if such experiences were invariably marked as epistemically pernicious in a way that subjects can access. Even the weaker claim that beliefs resulting from visual dominance get marked as *unusual* is not especially plausible given how surprised subjects are when the effects of dominance are revealed.

Given internalism, then, perceptual beliefs that result from visual dominance are prima facie justified. We now turn to one final way that visual dominance is epistemically important for an internalist. Consider an old, familiar story about vision: visual experience provides *direct awareness* of material objects in that, when having (veridical) visual experiences, one is immediately acquainted with material objects. This story is called *direct realism*. *Intentionalism* counters that visual experience requires a representational intermediary, present in both veridical and non-veridical experiences, that stands between those seeing and seen material objects. Disagreements between advocates of direct realism and intentionalism run deep.

The old familiar story can be qualified in a way that avoids commitment to either theory but acknowledges important insights that motivate each. Specifically, rather than holding that visual experience provides direct awareness of material objects, one can hold that visual experience *seems to the perceiver* (from the first-person perspective) to provide direct awareness of material objects.[23] Since this is a *phenomenological* claim, not a claim about the structure of vision, it is neutral between direct realism and intentionalism. It captures, nonetheless, part of the motivation for direct realism—while remaining acceptable to advocates of intentionalism.[24] We can express this claim by saying that visual experience provides *phenomenologically direct awareness* of material objects, which is to say it seems to those seeing as if vision provides direct acquaintance with chairs, tables, cars, people, dogs, and so on.

This phenomenological feature of the visual, we contend, is a consequence of vision's being richly spatial. As noted, both perceptual visual experience and visual imagery provide allocentric and macrospatial information all at once. It is because of this informational feature of the visual that it strikes one, phenomenologically, that visual experience provides direct awareness of material objects, as if

---

[23] Others have made this point, more or less explicitly. Two clear statements are Sturgeon (2000) and O'Callaghan (2011).

[24] Arguably, the intentionalist (or representationalist) notion of the *transparency of experience* is introduced to accommodate this very phenomenological fact (Harman 1990). So the disagreement between direct and indirect realists does not concern this *phenomenological directness*, but instead what one might call *structural directness*: whether, in perceptual (visual) experience, there is some intermediary between perceiver and world.

the objects are right there before one. Since the visual is richly spatial but the tactile is not, moreover, one should expect that the tactile is not phenomenologically direct. More broadly, since, as we suggest shortly, the visual is uniquely richly spatial, one should expect that *only* the visual can provide phenomenologically direct awareness of material objects, which, loosely following many advocates of direct realism, is plausible. This alone makes visual dominance epistemically important.

This kind of dominance is important for an internalist, moreover, since internalism requires that reasons for belief be cognitively accessible. Visual perception and visual imagery provide phenomenologically direct awareness of material individuals. Accordingly, one can be aware of, can access, the appearance properties of visual experience, thereby acknowledging the reason-conferring spatial content of what one sees. So, at least in the case where the visual exercises dominance over touch just at the levels of judgment, one's visual experience provides prima facie justification for beliefs formed.

A story about learning might buttress this internalist account. Early in human development, we learn that visual experience represents macrospatial and allocentric properties quite well. Presumably somewhat later, we learn that visual imagery also represents such properties quite well. We come to implicitly understand, then, that vision's being richly spatial makes relying on the visual to detect such properties a good idea. In this way, an internalist might provide an account of both knowledge and metaknowledge acquired through the visual.[25]

Both broad views on epistemic justification, then, suggest that visual dominance of touch is epistemically good. Visual dominance, then, makes vision special in a way that should interest philosophers.

7. The Picture Revisited

Given this discussion, we can specify the picture of visual dominance over touch as introduced at the close of section 3. That picture appeals to the vague properties *being an appropriate target property* and *being much more degraded than*. The discussion in section 5 suggests that appropriate target properties include at least the macrospatial and allocentric. The discussion in section 6 qualifies the relevant notion of degradation: visual experience is "much more degraded than" tactile experience if and only if the visual becomes more degraded than it is at the point of subjective epistemic equality, which is quantitatively defined by Ernst

---

[25] Of course, this understanding needn't be of any technical sophistication and might not itself be explicit in the agent's awareness. For many or most of us, it might instead be a procedural or skillful understanding. Instead, the idea here is just the following. If one knows a bit about vision or visual imagery (namely, that it tells one about spatial features of the environment), then one can know that one knows that P, since one can access one's acquired beliefs about the nature of the visual vis-à-vis rich spatial nature, and identify the fact that one is forming one's belief that P on the basis of that visual faculty.

and Banks. So, we get the following conditions for perception-perception and imagery-perception dominance, respectively:

- Given conflicting stimuli that aren't wildly discrepant, and a macrospatial or allocentric target property P, visual experience is likely to dominate touch with respect to P at each of the three levels, unless visual experience is so degraded that one passes the point of subjective epistemic equality for visual and tactile experience.
- Given that an object with a macrospatial or an allocentric target property P stimulates the skin but not the eyes, visual imagery is likely to dominate touch with respect to P at least at the level of all-things-considered judgment and experience-based judgment, unless visual imagery is so degraded that one passes the point of subjective epistemic equality for visual and tactile experience.

Each kind of dominance is significant psychologically and epistemically, and there is no reason to believe that other senses dominate the visual with respect to comparably significant properties, or a comparably wide range of properties.

8. A Conclusion: Other Senses, Other Properties

Does this picture generalize to other senses? Consider the standard Aristotelian senses. Even if olfactory and taste experiences present macrospatial and allocentric properties, neither presents multiple properties all at once. While it is more plausible that auditory experience presents macrospatial and allocentric properties, it doesn't present them all at once either: try to imagine learning all at once from auditory experience alone, the size, shape, and orientation of Kawamata's sculpture, or how various chairs are related to one another in space. This brief consideration already shows that visual experience is *uniquely* richly spatial, which implies that the picture generalizes: the visual dominates *all* other senses in similar ways. Further considerations support this conclusion.[26]

Does vision often dominate given target properties other than the macrospatial and allocentric? A number of results suggest that the answer is "yes": since the McGurk effect doesn't involve a macrospatial or allocentric target property, it suggests that vision can dominate for other kinds of properties; Royet et al. (1999) found that vision dominates smell when judging whether an odor comes from a comestible object, which is not obviously a judgment about a macrospatial or

---

[26] Two notes. First, if there are multimodal experiences, we conjecture that these can be richly spatial only if and to the extent that they have visual experiences as constituents. Second, a generalization would be given conflicting stimuli to the eyes and the organ for any nonvisual sense S, and a macrospatial or allocentric target property, vision is likely to exercise perception-perception dominance over S at each level, unless visual experiences are degraded *beyond the point of subjective epistemic equality* with experiences in S; likewise, mutatis mutandis for imagery-perception dominance.

allocentric property either.[27] We suspect that our picture can be extended to these cases, at least in broad outline, although working out the details requires an independent project.[28]

We close by suggesting another broad class of property for which we expect the visual to dominate other senses, although empirical evidence here is scant. Recall that Zhang et al. (2004) found that visual imagery affects judgments based on tactile-stimuli when we identify objects by high-level kind, such as egg or dog. We predict that this holds more broadly: that the visual is likely to dominate other senses when one aims to identify the source of a stimulus by such "medium-sized-dry-good" kind. We suspect that this dominance is as pervasive and significant as it is for macrospatial and allocentric properties. In order to support this speculation, we close by asking that you *imagine*:

> You're lying in your warm bed, early on a cold morning. Your partner prepares for work, somewhat noisily. For some sounds, the source is easy to identify: he's running a hair dryer, spraying hair spray, opening the fridge, running the clothes dryer. For other sounds, the source is mysterious: something in the dryer makes sustained metallic, clanging noises, but you can't tell what; some of the items being moved in the kitchen are identifiable, others aren't.

Suppose you want to identify the sources of the more elusive sounds? What would you do? Pause, and consider this question before reading on.

We suspect that, if it really mattered, if something important depended on getting the answer right, you would go look, however comfortable bed may be. But suppose that you can't or won't go look; you are too tired, lazy, injured, or whatever. What would you do then? Again, pause and consider this question before reading on.

---

[27] They exposed subjects to a wide variety of odorants. In the control condition, subjects were asked to identify each odor as familiar. In the experimental condition, subjects were asked to report whether the odor was one from a comestible object. In the experimental condition only, PET scans found increased cerebral blood flow to the visual cortex, suggesting that subjects invoke visual imagery when trying to identify important facts about an object. For more research on vision and olfaction, see Djordjevic et al. (2004) and Sakai et al. (2005). For research on visual imagery and audition, see Intons-Peterson (1992), De Volder et al. (2001), von Kriegstein et al. (2005), Amedi et al. (2005), and Hubbard (2010). For research on vision, visual imagery, and taste/flavor, see Clydesdale (1984) and Kobayashi et al. (2004).

[28] Of course, the claim that vision dominates other senses with respect to a wide range of properties is consistent with the claim that other senses dominate vision for some significant properties. O'Callaghan (2012), for example, reviews evidence that audition dominates vision with respect to at least some temporal properties—more broadly, though developed independently, O'Callaghan's account of dominance and our own are (largely) complementary. For empirical results relevant to auditory dominance of vision, see, for example, work by Shams and various colleagues (e.g., Shams et al. 2000), as well as Vroomen and de Gelder (2000).

We suspect that you would begin to image, *visually image*, candidate sources of the elusive sounds. You might run through candidate sources for the clanging in the dryer, for example, by visually imaging, in order,

(i)   trousers and tops (concluding that their buttons wouldn't clang so loudly),

(ii) coins (concluding that their clanging wouldn't be so sustained), and

(iii) a pair of jeans with a belt attached (concluding that these would make just the noise you hear, and would be in the dryer, given your partner's early morning absent-mindedness).

Here, visual imagery helps you generate and assess hypotheses: running through images of candidate sound-sources generates hypotheses; "cross-referencing" images against incoming auditory information tests them. Without visual imagery, you might never identify the source of the initially elusive sound—or, worse, you might need to get out of bed. At the very least, imagery is central to what you actually do.

Perhaps you did not spontaneously think to identify the source of the clanging through visual imagery. Even if you did, moreover, others won't. The use of visual imagery surely differs from person to person, and case to case: one who is bad at visually imaging might not be disposed to use visual imagery; one who has heard the clanging every morning for years won't need to. Our suggestion that you would invoke visual imagery, nonetheless, probably did not sound bizarre. But suppose we had suggested that you would invoke smell, taste, or touch imagery, perhaps *tactilely* imaging shirts, coins, and belts. This would have seemed immediately implausible. It is not too surprising, then, that many people spontaneously say they would appeal to visual imagery when we present the belt-in-dryer case, but none say they would appeal to other kinds of sense imagery. Similarly, it would have sounded bizarre if we had described a scenario in which you see something clearly, and then suggested that you might invoke auditory imagery to identify its source.[29]

We suspect that many properties, including "medium-sized-dry-good-kind," could be added to the list of target properties with respect to which the visual dominates other senses. We also suspect, that there are fewer properties with respect to which other senses exercise similar dominance over the visual; at the very least, there is no evidence that other senses dominate vision with respect to comparably significant properties, or a comparably wide range of

---

[29] This illustration depends itself on imagining the very scenario in which you purportedly invoke imagery, and this kind of imagining may invite you to use visual imagery when you otherwise wouldn't. So, the illustration is less than ideal. For audio recordings that may, depending upon the listener, trigger the phenomenon we have in mind, please see http://stokes.mentalpaint.net/Dominance-sound_samples.html.

properties.[30] And, as we have argued, the dominance of the visual is psychologically and epistemically significant. This dominance, then, goes a long way toward explaining the sense in which we prefer vision, in which we are visual creatures, and in which vision is special.

Acknowledgments

This work was thoroughly collaborative and the chapter thoroughly co-authored; the order of authors was chosen randomly. This chapter benefited from criticism from audiences at the *Knowledge through Imagination Conference*, Claremont McKenna College, 2012; Weber State University, 2012; and the University of Utah, 2013 (as the plenary colloquium at the Intermountain West Graduate Student Philosophy Conference). In particular, we thank Steve Downes, Lisa Downing, Amy Kind, Stacie Friend, Bob Fudge, Richard Greene, Magdalena Balcarek Jackson, Peter Kung, Peter Langland-Hassan, Sam Liao, Fiona Macpherson, Heidi Maibom, Kathleen Stock, Jim Tabery, Neil van Leeuwen, Blake Vernon, Mary Beth Willard, Tim Williamson, and Chris Zarpentine. (Sincere apologies for anyone we inadvertently failed to mention.) We also benefited from correspondence with Matt Fulkerson and Casey O'Callaghan while writing the chapter. Additional thanks to Mohan Matthen, Mariam Thalos, and an anonymous referee for Oxford University Press for feedback on the written version.

References

Amir Amedi, Katharina von Kriegstein, N. M. van Atteveldt, M. S. Beauchamp, & M. J. Naumer. (2005). Functional imaging of human crossmodal identification and object recognition. *Experimental Brain Research* 166: 559–571.

Clare Batty. (2011). Smelling lessons. *Philosophical Studies* 153 (Mar.): 161–174.

Craig M. Bennett, Abigail A. Baird, Michael B. Miller, & George L. Wolford (2010). Nueral correlates of interspecies perspective taking in the post-mortem Atlantic salmon: An argument for proper multiple comparisons correction. *Journal of Serendipitous and Unexpected Results* 1(1): 1–5.

G. Berkeley. (1713/1975). Three dialogues between Hylas and Philonous. In M. R. Ayers (ed.), *Philosophical Works, including the Works on Vision*. London: Dent.

David J. Chalmers. (1998). On the search for the neural correlate of consciousness. In Stuart R. Hameroff, Alfred W. Kaszniak, & A. C. Scott (eds.), *Toward a Science of Consciousness II*. Cambridge, MA: MIT Press.

---

[30] Although we only consider the dominance of the visual, one nonvisual sense sometimes dominates another; for example, audition sometimes dominates touch (cf. De Gelder and Bertelson 2003).

Clydesdale, F. M. (1984). The influence of colour on sensory perception and food choices. In J. Walford (ed.), *Developments in Food Colours* (pp. 75–112). London: Elsevier Applied Science.

Beatrice De Gelder & Paul Bertelson. (2003). Multisensory integration, perception, and ecological validity. *Trends in Cognitive Science* 7(10): 460–467.

Anne De Volder, H. Toyama, Y. Kimura, Kiyosawa, H. Nakano, A. Vanlierde, M. C. Wanet-Defalque, M. Mishina, K. Oda, K. Ishiwata, & M. Senda. (2001). Auditory triggered mental imagery of shape involves visual association areas in early blind humans. *Neuroimage* 14(1): 129–139.

J. Djordjevic, R. J. Zatorre, M. Petrides, & M. Jones-Gotman. (2004). The mind's nose effects of odor and visual imagery on odor detection. *Psychological Science* 15(3): 143–148.

Marc O. Ernst & Martin S. Banks. (2002). humans integrate visual and haptic information in a statistically optimal fashion. *Nature* 415: 429–433.

Gareth Evans. (1980). *Varieties of Reference*. Oxford: Oxford University Press.

S. M. Fishkin, V. Pishkin, & M. L. Stahl. (1975). Factors involved in visual capture. *Perceptual Motor Skills* 40(2): 427–434.

Alvin I. Goldman. (1967). A causal theory of knowing. *Journal of Philosophy* 64 (12): 357–372.

Alvin I. Goldman. (1993). Epistemic folkways and scientific epistemology. *Philosophical Issues* 3: 271–285.

John Greco. (1999). Agent reliabilism. In J. Tomberlin (ed.), *Philosophical Perspectives 13: Epistemology*. Atascadero: Ridgeview.

John Greco. (2009). *Epistemic Value*. Oxford: Oxford University Press.

John Greco. (2010). *Achieving Knowledge*. Cambridge: Cambridge University Press.

Gilbert Harman. (1990). The intrinsic quality of experience. *Philosophical Perspectives* 4:31–52.

Morton Heller. (1982). Visual and tactual perception: Intersensory cooperation. *Perception and Psychophysics* 31: 339–344.

Morton Heller. (1983). Haptic dominance in form perception with blurred vision. *Perception* 12: 607–613.

Timothy Hubbard. (2010). Auditory imagery: Empirical findings. *Psychological Bulletin* 136(2): 302–329.

David Hume. (1739/2000). *A Treatise of Human Nature*. Oxford: Oxford University Press.

Margaret Jena Intons-Peterson, Wendi Russell, & Sandra Dressel. (1992). The role of pitch in auditory imagery. *Journal of Experimental Psychology. Human Perception & Performance* 18(1): 233–240.

R. L. Klatzky, S. Lederman, & C. J. Reed. (1987). There's more to touch than meets the eye: The salience of object attributes for haptics with and without vision. *Journal of Experimental Psychology: General* 116: 356–369.

M. Kobayashi, M. Takeda, N. Hattori, M. Fukunaga, T. Sasabe, N. Inoue, Y. Nagai, T. Sawada, N. Sadato, & Y. Watanabe. (2004). Functional imaging of gustatory perception and imagery: "Top-down" processing of gustatory signals. *Neuroimage*: 23(4): 1271–1282.

Stephen Kosslyn, W. L. Thompson, I. J. Kim, & N. M. Alpert. (1995). Topographical representations of mental images in primary visual cortex. *Nature* 378: 496–498.

Zoe Kourtzi & Nancy Kanwisher. (2001). Representation of perceived object shape by the human lateral occipital complex. *Science* 293: 1506–1509.

Katharina von Kriegstein, A. Kleinschmidt, P. Sterzer, & A. L. Giraud. (2005). Interaction of face and voice areas during speaker recognition. *Journal of Cognitive Neuroscience* 17: 367–376.

S. J. Lederman & S. G. Abbott. (1981). Texture perception: Studies of intersensory organization using a discrepancy paradigm, and visual versus tactual psychophysics. *Journal of Experimental Psychology: Human Perception and Performance* 7: 902–915.

William Lycan. (2000). The slighting of smell. In N. Bhushan & S. Rosenfeld (eds.), *Of Minds and Molecules: New Philosophical Perspectives on Chemistry*. Oxford: Oxford University Press.

D. L. C. Maclachlan. (1989). *Philosophy of Perception*. Englewood Cliffs, NJ: Prentice-Hall.

Michael Martin. (1992). Sight and touch. In Tim Crane (ed.), *The Contents of Experience*. New York: Cambridge University Press.

Colin McGinn. (2004). *Mindsight*. Cambridge, MA: Harvard University Press.

Harry McGurk & John MacDonald. (1976). Hearing lips and seeing voices. *Nature*, 264: 746–748.

Emmanuel Mellet, Nathalie Tzourio, Fabrice Crivello, Marc Joliot, Michel Denis, & Bernard Mazoyer. (1996). Functional anatomy of spatial mental imagery generated from verbal instructions. *Journal of Neuroscience* 16(20): 6504–6512.

E. A. Miller. (1972). Interaction of vision and touch in conflict and non-conflict from perception tasks. *Journal of Experimental Psychology* 96: 114–123.

Casey O'Callaghan. (2011). Lessons from beyond vision (sounds and audition). *Philosophical Studies* 153(1): 143–160.

Casey O'Callaghan. (2012). Multisensory perception. In E. Margolis, R. Samuels, & S. Stich (eds.), *The Oxford Handbook of Philosophy of Cognitive Science*. Oxford: Oxford University Press.

Brian O'Shaughnessy. (2009). The location of a perceived sound. In M. Nudds & C. O'Callaghan (eds.), *Sounds and Perception: New Philosophical Essays*. Oxford: Oxford University Press.

Mark R. Stoesz, Minming Zhang, Valerie D. Weisser, S. C. Prather, Hui Mao, & Krish Sathian. (2003). Neural networks active during tactile form perception: Common and differential activity during macrospatial and microspatial tasks. *International Journal of Psychophysiology* 50: 41–49.

Ray Over. (1966). An experimentally induced conflict between vision and proprioception. *British Journal of Psychology* 57: 335–341.

Roderick Power. (1980). The dominance of touch by vision: Sometimes incomplete. *Perception* 9: 457–466.

Roderick Power & Anne Graham. (1976). Dominance of touch by vision: Generalization of the hypothesis to a tactually experienced population. *Perception* 5: 161–166.

Thomas Reid. (1764/1997). *An Inquiry into the Human Mind on the Principles of Common Sense*. Derek R. Brookes (ed.). University Park: Pennsylvania State University Press.

P. E. Roland, B. Gulyas, R. J. Seitz, C. Bohm, & S. Stone-Elander. (1990). Functional anatomy of storage, recall, and recognition of a visual pattern in man. *NeuroReport* 1, 53–56.

Irvin Rock & Jack Victor. (1964). An experimentally created conflict between the two senses. *Science* 143: 594–596.

Lawrence Rosenblum, Mark Schmuckler, & Jennifer Johnson. (1997). The McGurk effect in infants. *Perception and Psychophysics* 59(3): 347–357.

Nobuyuki Sakai, Sumio Imada, Sachiko Saito, Tatsu Kobayakawa, & Yuichi Deguchi. (2005). The effect of visual images on perception of odors. *Chemical Senses* 30: i244–i245.

Krish Sathian, Andro Zangaladze, John Hoffman, & Scott Grafton (1997). Feeling with the mind's eye. *Neuroreport* 8(18): 3877–3881.

Ladan Shams, Yukiyasu Kamitani, & Shinsuke Shimojo. (2000). What you see is what you hear. *Nature* 408: 788.

Ernest Sosa. (1980). The raft and the pyramid: Coherence versus foundations in the theory of knowledge. *Midwest Studies in Philosophy* 5: 3–25.

Ernest Sosa. (2007). *Apt Belief and Reflective Knowledge, Volume 1: A Virtue Epistemology.* Oxford: Oxford University Press.

Peter F. Strawson. (1959). *Individuals: An Essay in Descriptive Metaphysics.* London: Methuen.

Nigel Thomas. (2010). Mental imagery. In E. N. Zalta (ed.), *The Stanford Encyclopedia of Philosophy.* Stanford, CA: Center for the Study of Language and Information.

Jean Vroomen & Beatrice de Gelder. (2000). Sound enhances visual perception: Cross-modal effects of auditory organization on vision. *Journal of Experimental Psychology: Human Perception and Performance* 26: 1583–1590.

David Warren. (1979). Spatial localization under conflict conditions: Is there a single explanation? *Perception* 8(3): 323–337.

Robert Welch & David Warren. (1980). Immediate perceptual response to intersensory discrepancy. *Psychological Bulletin* 88: 638–667.

Ludwig Wittgenstein. (1967). *Zettel.* G. E. M. Anscombe & G. H. von Wright (eds.); G. E. M. Anscombe (trans.). Oxford: Blackwell.

Andro Zangaladze, Charles Epstein, Scott Grafton, & Krish Sathian. (1999). Involvement of visual cortex in tactile discrimination of orientation. *Nature* 401: 587–590.

Minming Zhang, V. D. Weisser, R. Stilla, S.C. Prather, & Krish Sathian. (2004). Multisensory cortical processing of object shape and its relation to mental imagery. *Cognitive Affective Behavioral Neuroscience* (4): 251–259.

15

More Color Science for Philosophers
C. L. Hardin

It has been twenty-five years since *Color for Philosophers* was first published.[1] Even in the relatively small color-vision science community, a great deal has happened during that period. It is time to look at a few of the scientific developments that bear on topics that I wrote about back then.

In general, I must say that at the present day, the science is somewhat clearer, but also significantly more complicated than I had once supposed. Anyone reading the book now should regard what was laid out in the first chapter to be a cartoon presentation of the opponent processing mechanisms. It is not drastically wrong, but it needs to be qualified in many points of detail. For instance, the opponent processes are not linear functions of cone excitations. Furthermore, most retinal ganglion and lateral geniculate nucleus (LGN) cells that bear spectral information do not have the unique hues at their null points. This has suggested to visual scientists that the phenomenology that Hering describes must have its neural correlates deeper within the visual areas of the brain.

1. Unique Hues and Brain Mechanisms

In the early 1990s after Derrington, Kraukopf, and Lennie[2] had established that the ganglion and LGN cells were not the sites of the Hering processes, I asked Peter Lennie when he expected the locus of the unique hues to be discovered. He then believed that it would be in the next five years. It has taken twenty years, but the end appears to be in sight. Recently Tailby, Solomon, and Lennie[3] have shown that although in general the opponent LGN cells carrying spectral information do not have the proper alignment of opponent hue axes, there is a small subpopulation

---

[1] Hardin (1988, 1993).
[2] Derrington et al. (1984).
[3] Tailby et al. (2008).

of LGN cells that indeed *does* have the proper hue signature. Recently, Stoughton and Conway[4] claimed to have found a brain locus for the unique hues. That claim has been contested by John Mollon[5] but Stoughton-Conway and other work seems promising. The situation is in flux. Stay tuned!

Unique hues are one part of the Hering scheme. The other is opponency. We now have reason to believe that the mechanisms supporting these two features are separable, albeit not in normal perception. Crane and Piantanida[6] had used a stabilized image technique to produce "filled-in" perceptions of reddish green and yellowish blue in some subjects. Images stabilized on the retina fade from view. If a stabilized region is surrounded by an unstabilized colored image, the stabilized region will be filled in with the surrounding color. Now what if the subject is presented with a bipartite image, one side red and the other side green, and the boundary region is retinally stabilized. What will the fill-in color be? Crane and Piantanida found that some of their subjects saw a color they could only describe as "reddish green" or "greenish red." This result was met with considerable skepticism among visual scientists. In 2001, Billock, Gleason, and Tsou[7] replicated the Crane-Piantanida experiment with improved techniques. Their seven subjects were professional psychophysicists. What, exactly, did they see? It is worth quoting the Billock paper at some length:

> We used a dual Purkinje image eye tracker to retinally stabilize bipartite color fields whose hues and achromatic border contrast were controlled.... If the colors were made equiluminant, no segmentation occurred and mixture colors were obtained from the filling-in process. If equiluminous red/green or blue/yellow bipartite fields were used, then subjects reported reddish greens or bluish yellows, in violation of Hering's laws. The quality of the experience varied between observers and over time. Some subjects (4 out of 7) described transparency phenomena—as though the opponent colors originated in two depth planes and could be seen, one through the other. Other times, the border would disappear and the subjects (5 out of 7) reported a gradient of color that ran from, say, red on the left to green on the right with a large region in between that seemed both red and green. Our subjects (like those in the Crane-Piantanida experiment) were tongue-tied in their descriptions of those colors, using terms like "green with a red sheen" or "red with green highlights." Typically the perception of these phenomena would last a few seconds before the entire field would switch abruptly to blackness or nothingness. Then the red/green bipartite field would regenerate, either spontaneously, or in response to a blink. On occasion (4 out of 7 subjects)

---

[4] Stoughton et al. (2008).
[5] Mollon (2009).
[6] Crane et al. (1983).
[7] Billock et al. (2001).

the percept was a homogeneous mixture color whose red and green components were as clear and compelling as the red and blue components of a purple. This percept tended to last longer than the gradient phenomenon. Experience may be a factor in what is seen; many subjects did not report non-Hering mixtures until after several trials, and in general, transparency and gradient effects preceded perception of homogeneous mixture colors. This bears on arguments that novel color percepts may be precluded by lack of early experience during perceptual development. Clearly the strongest form of this argument is not supported, but the effects of experience suggest that a gradual sensory reorganization may be taking place. Interestingly, after our experiments, two subjects noted independently that reddish- green or yellowish-blue colors could now be imagined.[8]

More recently, Livitz et al. (2011) showed that red-green binaries could be perceived under more normal circumstances, using induction displays rather than an eye tracker.

What conclusions can we draw from such experiments? First, although the Hering elementary hues are coupled to opponency in normal perception, under special circumstances they may be decoupled. This tells us that there are functionally distinct brain mechanisms for the perceptions of red, yellow, green, and blue. Earlier research had already suggested distinct mechanisms for the perceptions of black and white.

Second, there really are experiences of red-green binaries, attested to by expert observers. Whether this speaks against the supposed a priori status of the proposition that nothing can be red and green all over depends upon how that proposition is construed. If it is supposed to be on the same footing as the proposition that nothing is both red and yellow all over, that is, 100% red and 100% yellow, then the existence of red-green binaries is of no more consequence than the existence of red-yellow binaries, for example, the existence of orange. If the issue is whether something can *be* both reddish and greenish rather than just *looking* reddish and greenish, the present findings are of limited significance. But if one's reason for supposing that nothing could be both reddish and greenish is that such a situation is *unimaginable*, the experiment by Billock et al. should be of the first importance. What was unimaginable proved to be perceivable and what was then perceived came to be imaginable. Unimaginability once again proved to be a very shaky ground for inferring impossibility.

Third, the details of the experiments of Billock et al. underscore a commonplace among visual scientists: there is substantial individual variation in the perception of color. The philosophical importance of this fact is clear. If observers who are tested under the same set of conditions don't see the same colors, the

---

[8] Billock et al (2001), pp. 2398–2399.

obvious question is which, if any of them sees the colors as they are and which, if any of them, misperceives those colors?

This question has received much attention among philosophers. My own way of dealing with it is pretty well known,[9] and I shall largely leave it to others to discuss the matter further, although I shall touch on it at the end of this chapter. Here I would like to draw your attention to what is known (and not known) about the types of variation, how extensive they are, and what might cause some of them.

2. Variation among Color-Normal Observers: Metamerism

Everyone is aware that some people are color deficient. Much less appreciated are the significant differences that exist among "color normals," that is, people who pass the standard tests for color deficiencies. A "normal" or "average" observer is assumed for all color-order systems, but of course this is a statistical concept. It is interesting to see how wide the distribution is. Sixty-two years ago, Ralph Evans remarked,

> A rough estimate indicates that a perfect match by a perfect "average" observer would probably be unsatisfactory for something like 90 percent of all observers because variation between observers is very much greater than the smallest color differences which they can distinguish. Any observer whose variation from the standard was much greater than his ability to distinguish differences would be dissatisfied with the match.

It is possible to determine the extent of matching differences among normal observers and to gain some insight into the causes of the variation. The anomaloscope is a standard instrument for diagnosing color deficiencies. It consists of an eyepiece through which an observer sees a luminous split disk. One hemifield is a fixed yellow. The other hemifield is an adjustable mixture of red and green primaries. The observer turns a knob so as to set the red/green ratio to match the fixed yellow. The criterion for achieving the match is that the boundary between the two fields disappears and the circle appears to the observer to be a homogeneous yellow. Neitz and Neitz[10] found that for men, the distribution of ratios is bimodal, falling into two distinct groups, with 60% of the observers in one group and 40% in the other. The distribution of ratios for women is unimodal, and broader than that for men. In the last decade it was found that these distributions are correlated with genetically based polymorphisms of L (longwave) and M (middlewave) cone photopigments. More about this later.

---

[9] See, for example, Hardin (1988, 1993) and Hardin (2008) For a comprehensive survey of current philosophical controversies about color, see Maund (2006).

[10] Neitz and Neitz (1998).

The match that an observer makes between the two hemifields of an anomaloscope is a metameric match. The two sides have different spectra, but when the match is made, they look identical. Although metameric matches are not common in nature, they are very common in the modern world; the images of color photography and color television are metameric or approximately metameric matches to the color appearances of the objects that they represent, as are most colorant matches. Because of inevitable variations in viewing conditions and in observers, such matches are to one degree or another problematic and rely on the large reservoir of forgiveness that the human brain has for color variation when the samples are not put side by side.

3. Variation among Color-Normal Observers: Unique Hue Loci

Observers differ from each other in their color-matching and metameric classes, so it should come as no surprise that their opponent responses are different. In fact, the differences are large enough to be shocking, as we shall now see. The stimulus locus for a perception of unique hue has been studied with a variety of techniques for many years. Every study with a reasonably large number of observers has found a wide distribution of unique hue loci among normal perceivers. Because the studies have used different experimental protocols and different perceiver groups, the mean results do not agree well across experiments, but substantial variability among observers within any given study is a constant. It is often supposed that more "naturalistic" experiments using surface colors will reduce the amount of variance from one observer to another, so here are the results of a recent hue experiment with colored Munsell papers.[11] A forty-step hue set of constant lightness and chroma was used. The Munsell chips are approximately perceptually equispaced, so each chip is 1/40 of the hue circle. Observers adapted to a standard illuminant and viewed the chips against a light gray background. The figure shows the range of mean unique hue choices (Figure 15.1). Each observer performed the experiment three times. This enabled a comparison of variability within and between observers.

Only about 15% of the variability is intraobserver. The sum of the ranges in the diagram showing individual unique hue sample choices is 57.5% of the total. Observers can vary significantly in their individual "signatures" of unique hue choices. That is to say, there is no systematic relationship between the observer's locus of unique red, for instance, and her choice of locus for any other unique hue. This suggests that there may not be a simple mechanism that guides unique hue stimulus choices.

---

[11] Hinks et al. (2007)

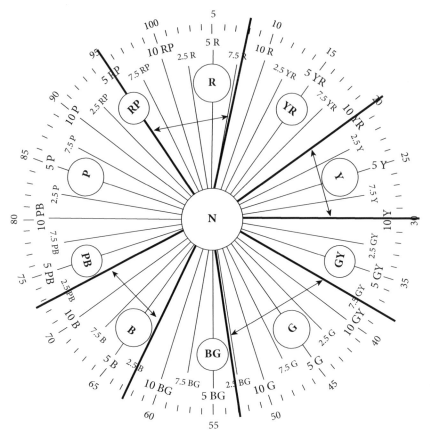

FIGURE 15.1. *The range of mean unique hue choices. See text. Figure courtesy of Rolf Kuehni.*

If the test is conducted with full-color chips, and thus not controlled for light-ness and chroma, the sum of the unique hue-choice ranges is reduced to 33% of the total. This is still a very substantial variation. One might seek to minimize the importance of the variation by suggesting that the problem only arises for "fine-grained" color determinations. In color science, the fine grain occurs when trained observers interpolate between single Munsell hue steps, all the way down to a tenth of a Munsell step. The samples in the forty-chip array are spaced at intervals of 2.5 hue steps. The range of determinations of any particular unique hue can thus extend across twenty-five Munsell steps. In this instance, the "fine grain" seems very coarse indeed!

It is worth mentioning that other studies have shown some variation in the average unique-hue choices from the speakers of different languages, but in every case the variation between observers speaking the same language was substantially larger than the variation across languages.[12] Unlike the anomaloscopic matching variability, there is so far no satisfactory explanation for the variability in unique hue choices.[13] It seems that the deeper in the brain we go, the more mysterious things become.

4. Color Variability and Retinal Genetics

On the other hand, recent studies of the retina using new techniques have yielded surprising results. We now know that the proportion of L to M cones varies by a factor of as much as four from one person's retina to another, and up to thirty if heterozygous females are included. The more extreme cone ratios manifest themselves as differences in color-matching tests. It has also been discovered that the distribution of L and M cones across the fovea is essentially random. Despite this, the cones manage to wire themselves into the more regimented functional center-surround configurations that are essential to both chromatic and achromatic contrast detection. Self-wiring has been found throughout the nervous system. For example, in people who have been blind since childhood, areas of visual cortex are recruited to enhance hearing performance.

A striking example of self-wiring occurred in a genetic "knock in" experiment with mice, which normally have just S and M pigments and are thus dichromats. Jacobs and his associates[14] inserted a human L pigment gene into a mouse genome, replacing one copy of the mouse M pigment gene. The result was a mouse that could be trained to discriminate a red light from a yellow light when the intensities of the lights were adjusted so that they stimulated the mouse M pigment equally. Unaltered mice could not perform this discrimination task. Mice have no trichromatic ancestors, so the neural machinery for putting an L cone to work did not exist prior to the gene insertion, even in residual form. The experimenters inserted the new photopigment and the mouse's visual system did the rewiring on its own. The Jacobs group thus produced a one-generation version of trichromacy that primates acquired through evolution.

Here is how the evolution of primate trichromacy took place:[15] the gene that is responsible for M pigments is linked to the X chromosome. Amino acid dimorphisms produced variations in the wavelength sensitivities of the resultant photopigments. This gave rise to polymorphic M cones. At some point in the past, the M gene was duplicated on the same X chromosome. Successive variations in this duplicated gene produced a photopigment whose peak sensitivity was shifted

[12] Webster et al. (2002).

[13] Added in proof: This situation may have changed. According to Schmidt, Neitz and Neitz (2014), "we show that color appearance, including individual differences never explained before, are predicted by a model in which S-cone signals are combined with L versus M signals in the outer retina."

[14] Jacobs et al. (2007).

[15] Osorio et al. (2008).

11nm toward the longwave end of the spectrum. This became the L cone, which self-wired, giving rise to a postreceptoral (L vs. M) opponent system. Over time, further variations produced the modern L cone with a peak sensitivity 30 nm from that of the modern M cone.

Polymorphisms of M and L photopigments have continued to appear until the present day. There have been two outcomes. There are deuteranomalous males with two slightly different L pigment genes and an unexpressed M pigment gene, and there are protanomalous males with two slightly different M pigment genes instead of an L and an M pigment gene. About 12% of the female population consists of mothers or daughters of these anomalous trichromats. They have the genes for normal L and M photopigments on one X chromosome, but on the other chromosome they might have the gene for the normal M pigment and the shifted hybrid L pigment, which has been called the L' pigment. This will give a woman who is a member of this sub-population a retina with four classes of cones. She will be a *retinal* tetrachromat. The interesting question is this: will her visual system wire itself in such a way as to take advantage of the extra cone type? Will she be a *functional* tetrachromat?

In a thorough study of twenty-four female carriers of anomalous trichromacy, Jordan and associates[16] found one participant—referred to by the experimenters as cDa20—who exhibited tetrachromatic behavior on all of their tests. For example, unlike all trichromats, she could not match an orange (590nm) spectral stimulus with any combination of red (670nm) and green (546nm) lights. Is cDa20 the tetrachromatic visual superwoman imagined in *Color for Philosophers* as the bearer of three opponent channels and novel hues? Probably not, although the tests she underwent were designed to be strictly hard-nosed forced-choice stuff so as to admit of quantitative comparison and analysis. Nobody asked the woman about the *quality* of her experience. Perhaps cDa20 could be persuaded to give a little interview to philosophers in exchange for a nicer name like "Mary."

We should not be surprised to find such a wide range of individual differences in color perception. Along with its enabler, natural selection, variation is a hallmark of living things. A perceptual system need only be good enough to guide its owner to perform tasks that will sustain its species in its ecological niche. The advantages that primates gained by developing chromatic vision involved such activities as identifying predators and prey in dappled forest environments, distinguishing more nutritious from less nutritious leaves, and spotting ripe fruit among the leaves, performing these tasks in various phases of daylight and in changing shadows.[17] There is no special premium that attaches to accomplishing these perceptual tasks with a high degree of precision or close agreement among perceivers. Biological mechanisms are typically a pastiche of earlier evolutionary endeavors. They are inherently rough, ready, and variable. Color experiences can be understood as *natural signs* of the filtered patterns of spectral power distributions in our environment. They should not be regarded as *simulacra* of the physical world that

---

[16] Jordan et al. (2010).
[17] Rowe (2002).

they represent. If we had all been born spectrally inverted, would this have made much difference in our ability to find our way around?

5. Chromatic Democracy Revisited

At this juncture, I've already segued from science into philosophy. Please indulge me if I pursue this line of thought a bit further. If some of us had been born spectrally inverted and some not, would all of us see the same colors when placed in the same circumstances? There are those who would reply that we would, for they think of colors as being features of physical objects and other situations outside of our bodies. If so, their view of colors is a bloodless one in which colors do not have the qualitative characteristics that make them interesting in the first place. Others might be of the opinion that in such a world some people would perceive colors correctly, whereas other people would be subject to systematic error. It is difficult to understand how one might in this instance distinguish between the perceptual sheep and the perceptual goats.

I prefer a third alternative, which is that there is no intelligible notion of systematic correctness or incorrectness at work here. Our everyday rough-and-ready pragmatic notions of chromatic veridicality and non-veridicality would continue to be in force for both the invert and the non-invert populations. In ordinary life we would continue to use the same color labels and make the same color discriminations. These practices would be largely useful—otherwise we wouldn't have them in the first place. But if we were to attempt to make them do theoretical work, they would break down under pressure from philosophers, just as they do now.

Individual variation in color perception is one occasion for such a breakdown. Another arises with so-called subjective colors, illusory colors, apparent colors, and the like. What they have in common is that they are products of nervous systems. Consider the optical migraine aura, a hallucination in which the subject sees a slowly expanding arc of vivid flashing prismatic colors. The details of its phenomenology can be readily found on the Internet. Three or four years ago I was privileged to experience this for the first time—privileged, because mine was a purely optical (but not *ocular*) migraine without the ferocious headache that commonly follows in its wake, and seems not generally to be a symptom of underlying brain disease. The ragged flashing colored arc presented itself in precisely the same fashion whether my eyes were open or shut. I conducted my everyday business for the entire half hour of the display. Now were these really *colors* that I saw, or only *color appearances*? If they were appearances, what was it that appeared colored to me? The natural response to the question is, of course, that what appeared to me was an arc composed of shimmering *colors*. It's as if the rainbow shimmered and appeared just to me and without benefit of the suspended droplets of water.[18] Perhaps we should say that regions of space

---

[18] Here are two discussions of migraine auras drawn from the Internet: http://www.migraine-aura. org/content/e27891/index_en.html, and http://brain.oxfordjournals.org/content/130/6/1690.long.

appeared colored. But in this and many other instances it couldn't be physical space. Perhaps we might be better served by invoking a visual space, created by the brain along with the color appearances. Remember that these particular optical migraine effects remain the same whether one's eyes are open or closed. In that respect they are like the phosphenes produced by occluding the blood supply of the retina, or brightly colored and detailed hypnogogic imagery that I, like many others, experience on occasion. Several years ago I spent the better part of the afternoon digging dandelions in the back yard. That night, when I closed my eyes, but before I fell asleep, there were the dandelions, once again growing in the lawn, in exquisite detail and natural colors. More recently I have had memorable experiences of brief but vivid, indeed luminous hypnogogic images of bins of fruits and vegetables, mostly in yellows and greens. These images were unrelated to experiences of the preceding days.

There are many and varied instances of colors, or, if you will, apparent colors, that show themselves in ways that God did not intend. They include the phenomena associated with the Benham disc, the Bidwell disc, the McCullough aftereffect, neon color spreading, Purkinje arcs, and, of course, the Crane-Piantanida display.

All of these color appearances are the products of various components of the normal human color perception system. With their help we can isolate and better understand the operation of those components. In some cases, the connection with everyday visual processing is direct. Colored shadows, for instance, exhibit the same mechanism—simultaneous contrast—that is responsible for the qualitative transformation of orange into brown and back again. Producing color appearances is simply the normal business of the color-vision system. So why not treat all color appearances even-handedly? Overthrow philosophers' chromatic oligarchy in favor of chromatic democracy!

Archimedes famously said, "Give me a fulcrum and a place to stand, and I will move the world!" I say, rather less famously, "Give me a nervous system that generates color appearances, embed it in a physical universe, and I will give you all the colors of the world!"

Oh, never mind. It's already been done.

References

OPPONENT RESPONSES OF LGN CELLS

Derrington, A. M., Krauskopf, J., and Lennie, P. (1984). "Chromatic Mechanisms in Lateral Geniculate Nucleus of Macaque." *Journal of Physiology* 357, 241–265.

Tailby, C., Solomon, S. G., and Lennie, P. (2008). "Functional Asymmetries in Visual Pathways Carrying S-cone Signals in Macaque." *Journal of Neuroscience* 28, 4078–4087.

CENTRAL MECHANISMS OF UNIQUE-HUE PERCEPTION

Stoughton, C. M., and Conway, B. R. (2008). Neural basis for unique hues. *Current Biology* 18, R698–R699.

Mollon, J. D. (2009). "A Neural Basis for Unique Hues?" *Current Biology* 19, R441–R442. (Stoughton and Conway's reply follows immediately after in the same issue.)

Neitz, J. and Neitz, M. (2008). "Colour Vision: The Wonder of Hue." *Current Biology* 18, R700–R702.

THE REDDISH-GREEN EXPERIMENT

Billock, V. A., Gleason, G. A., and Tsou, B. H. (2001). "Perception of Forbidden Colors in Retinally Stabilized Equiluminant Images: An Indication of Softwired Cortical Color Opponency?" *Journal of the Optical Society of America* A 18, 2398–2403.

Crane, H., and Piantanida, T. (1983). "On Seeing Reddish Green and Yellowish Blue." *Science* 221, 1078–1080.

Livitz, G., Yazdanbaksh, A., Rhea, T., Eskew, T., and Mingolla, E. (2011). "Perceiving Opponent Hues in Color Induction Displays." *Seeing and Perceiving* 24, 1–17.

RETINAL POLYMORPHISM AND COLOR MATCHING

Neitz, M., and Neitz J. (1998). "Molecular Genetics and the Biological Basis of Color Vision." In W. G. K. Backhaus, R. Kliegl, and J. S. Werner (eds.), *Color Vision: Perspectives from Different Disciplines* (Berlin: Walter de Gruyter), 101–119.

VARIABILITY OF UNIQUE-HUE CHOICES

Hinks, D., Cardenas, L., Shamey, R., and Kuehni, R. G. (2007). "Unique Hue Stimulus Selection Using Munsell Color Chips." *Journal of the Optical Society of America* A 26, 3371–3378.

Schmidt, B.P., Neitz, M, and Neitz, J. (2014) "Neurobiological Hypothesis of Color Appearance and Hue Perception." *Journal of the Optical Society of America* A 31(4) 195–207.

Webster, M. A. et al. (2002). "Variations in Normal Color Vision. III. Unique Hues in Indian and United States Observers." *Journal of the Optical Society of America* A 19(10), 1951–1962.

ARTIFICIALLY TRICHROMATIC MICE

Jacobs, G. H., Williams, G. A., Cahill, H., and Nathans, J. (2007). "Emergence of Novel Color Vision in Mice Engineered to Express a Human Cone Photopigment." *Science* 315, 1723–1725.

A FUNCTIONALLY TETRACHROMATIC WOMAN

Jordan, G., Deeb, S. S., Bosten, J. M., and Mollon, J. D. (2010). "The Dimensionality of Color Vision in Carriers of Anomalous Trichromacy." *Journal of Vision* 10(8), 12, 1–19.

THE EVOLUTION AND ECOLOGY OF COLOR VISION

Osorio, D., and Vorobyev, M. (2008). "A Review of the Evolution of Animal Colour Vision and Visual Communication Signals." *Vision Research* 48, 2042–2051.

Rowe, M. H. (2002). "Trichromatic Color Vision in Primates." *News Physiological Science* 17, 93–98.

MIGRAINE AURA

http://www.migraine-aura.org/content/e27891/index_en.html.
http://brain.oxfordjournals.org/content/130/6/1690.long.

PHILOSOPHICAL REFLECTIONS ON COLOR

Hardin, C. L. (2008). "Color Qualities and the Physical World." In Edmond Wright (ed.), *The Case for Qualia.* Cambridge, MA: MIT Press.

Hardin, C. L. (1988, 1993), *Color for Philosophers: Unweaving the Rainbow.* Indianapolis, IN: Hackett.

Maund, B. (2006). "Color." Stanford Encyclopedia of Philosophy. http://plato.stanford.edu/entries/color/.

PART VI

Relating the Modalities

16

Morphing Senses
Erik Myin, Ed Cooke, and Karim Zahidi

1. Change and Dependence

Could one, by letting a sense organ react to unusual stimuli, by changing its motricity, by engaging it in unusual tasks, or by a combination of variations in these factors, change the character of the experience that results from perceiving with that sense modality? What would happen, for example, if one identified the stimuli that audition is sensitive to and found a way to give these stimuli properties similar to the properties of stimuli that are normally smelled, and to do this in a way involving exploratory activity and behavioral consequences similar to the behavioral, exploratory, and other consequences involved in smelling? What if, for example, sound stimuli were to acquire the spatial characteristics of olfactory stimuli? What if sound was perceived through sound receptors in the nose by means of a motoric process similar to sniffing? Further, what if sound acquired the broadly affective role that smell seems to play, and what if the sounds began to relate to each other in the way that smells relate to other smells? Would this affect what are normally auditory experiences and turn them into smells? And conversely, what if olfaction became sensitive to an aspect of the world normally perceived through the visual modality, such as color? Suppose we managed to allow the nose to correctly categorize and discriminate between greens, indigos, and reds, as a result of the nose exploring the world similar to the way the eyes explore the world, and leading to the same behaviors (such as discriminating and categorizing colors); if so, could the resulting experience still feel like smell, or would it take on the phenomenal characteristics of vision?

Such questions arise not only in imaginary scenarios but also with respect to the actual phenomenon of sensory substitution. In sensory substitution, stimuli pertaining to aspects of the world normally perceived through one sense are "rerouted" through another sense modality. Well-studied examples of sensory substitution include the tactile-visual sensory substitution (TVSS) system, in which an image captured by a camera is delivered as a tactile "image" to the skin

(Bach-y-Rita et al., 1969) or the vOIce, which transforms visual images into auditory stimuli (Meijer, 1992). If a device such as the TVSS or the vOIce allows a subject to perform tasks that would normally require vision, does that mean that perception with it is visual rather than tactile or auditory?

Regarding both imaginary and real scenarios of modifying a modality, the two most extreme positions that can be taken, are what can be called Change, and its opposite No Change. The first position pronounces that in imaginary or actual cases of modifications in a modality, the source modality changes not only structurally but also in the way in which the experiences acquired though the changed modality would feel to their subjects. The opposite position, No Change, holds that modifying a source modality by adding features of a target modality affects only the level of function and behavior without affecting at least a core of how experience feels to subjects. Experiences would, despite the addition of features of a target modality, retain the phenomenal aspects of the source modality.

The choice between Change and No Change is related to broader theoretical commitments, though these links are, as we attempt to show in this chapter, more subtle than they might seem at first sight. On a fundamental level, one can distinguish between a Dependence View and an Independence View. On the Dependence side of the spectrum stand those who claim that the phenomenal character of a sensory modality is fully determined by the structural features of the modality. By these we mean the physical properties of the eliciting stimuli, the precise motoric ways in which experiences characteristic of that modality are obtained and the ways experiences are related to other experiences and embedded in further behavior.

Dependence of modal character on structural features has been defended prominently by those who advocate a sensorimotor approach to perception and perceptual awareness, as well as by functionalists in the philosophy of mind. Since changes in a modality's structural features go hand in hand with functional changes, functionalism—here understood as the view that functional properties determine phenomenal character—implies that changes in phenomenal character are the result of structural changes. The same goes for sensorimotor theorists. They hold that the character of a modality is determined by the way one interacts with the environment by using the sensory organ associated with that modality. J. Kevin O'Regan writes:

> Why does the feel of colour have a visual nature rather than being like, say, touch or hearing or smell? Colour is a visual-like feel because the laws that describe our interactions with coloured surfaces are laws that are shared with other visual experiences. In particular, when you close your eyes, the stimulation changes drastically (it goes away!). This is one of many facts that govern those interactions with our environment that we call visual. It is a fact that is not shared by, say, auditory interactions, which do not depend on whether you have your eyes open or closed. Other laws that characterize visual interactions concern the way sensory input changes when you move

your eyes, or when you move your head and body, or when you move objects
in such a way as to occlude other objects from view. (O'Regan, 2011, p. 132)

Defenders of the opposite Independence view hold that the phenomenal character of a sensory modality is—in some way—independent of its structural features.
According to this position, there is a core qualitative or phenomenal feature—a
matter of the "what it is like" to have the experience—present in experiences in a
modality, which is independent of its structural features. Independence views come
in two varieties. More detail about this is provided in the next section. Here it suffices to point out how each variety holds that it is possible for a source modality to
be morphed into a target modality without a change in feel. The difference between
the two varieties is to be found in their relationship toward physicalism, the view
that ultimately all properties are physical properties. Type 1 Independence presents
itself as a challenge to physicalism (Chalmers, 1996), holding that the phenomenal
is independent of the physical, and since structural features are a species of physical features, it denies that structural features determine phenomenal character. The
Type 2 Independence view declares itself to be committed to physicalism (Block,
2003). It proclaims that nonfunctional, purely physical features determine phenomenology, and predicts from this that whenever a source modality acquires structural
features of a target modality, no change will occur, as the changes concern only the
level of structural features, and not the level of physical substrate.

In this chapter we engage in an imagined experiment and investigate a real case
of transforming a source modality into a target modality. We examine the relations between the theses of Change and No Change, and the theoretical positions
of Dependence versus Independence. First we consider a thought experiment in
which the functionality normally provided by color vision is achieved instead with
a structurally changed olfactory modality. As we show, while Change has much
going for it, there are different ways in which one could defend the No Change
position. Two of those are Independence views, one physicalist and the other nonphysicalist. We will point out that these positions can be held only at considerable
theoretical and methodological cost. This is not true for the other way in which
No Change can be endorsed, namely, via a Dependence position. Contrary to first
appearances, it is possible to defend such a position and, as we will point out, it
does not carry the heavy price tag of the No Change plus Independence positions.
Then we turn to sensory substitution, to see a similar pattern: both Change and No
Change can be defended within a Dependence framework. Independence leads to
No Change, but again does so only at a considerable cost.

2. Smelling Color

In this section we describe a thought experiment about the structural changes
that would have to be made to make olfaction sensitive to color, so as to acquire
something equivalent to what color perception provides to sighted people. What

should one do to change the structure of olfaction so that it becomes an instrument for color perception? And if those changes were made, would that mean that the olfactory feel would disappear in the process, in order to give way to chromatic feel, as Change predicts. Or would it be possible, or at least conceivable, to smell colors; to have what color perception makes us aware of, but with olfactory phenomenology—confirming No Change? If one thinks about it in an unconstrained way, smelling colors might seem trivially possible. Just imagine color stimuli at one end and smell experiences at the other end. Where normal color perceivers would experience blue, the olfactory see-er would smell the scent of freshly brewed coffee. In fact, such a scenario seems to resemble the well-documented phenomenon of synesthesia—though in synesthesia the novel experience does not replace but rather accompanies the regular experience. But this leaves open whether what is imagined would be a case of smelling color. Would it genuinely be color that was perceived in an olfactory way? Would we have at the same time olfactory phenomenology and as well something like color perception—including, for example, the spatial characteristics of color perception?

Let us then imagine some of the requirements that would have to be met to perceive color through smell. Imagine that Mary, the notorious color-blind super-scientist (Jackson, 1986), despairs for not having sensory access to the color world and decides to subject herself to an experiment. She reckons that she can temporarily do without her normal olfactory modality, thus leaving her a free hand at reshaping it. She wonders what kind of structure should be imposed on olfaction for it to offer her the full functionality that visual color perception provides. She wants to go for the real thing. Her modified olfaction should not only make her capable of identifying colors of individually presented patches but it should also allow her to do such things as pick out the single poppy sprouting from an extended lawn, see the number 25 formed by the orange dots on a background of bluish dots in an Ishihara test, and be overwhelmed by the chromatic abundance of a display of fireworks.

She quickly realizes that to acquire color vision's functionality, her reshaped olfaction should become independent of the motor actions that are usually required for smell. Concretely, she makes sure that it is no way related to inhalation. As Mary wanders around her environment her intake of stimuli does not vary as she varies her way of breathing. Instead of the regular dependence on inhalation, Mary engineers, for her reshaped olfaction, a dependence on eye movements. As a result, her smell perception changes with the way her eyes move: as she flicks her eyes, her "chromatic" smells come and go. Closing her eyes results in an absence of that same experience.

Next, she sets out to mimic the effect that the surrounding environment has on ordinary color vision. She therefore tampers with her olfactory system in such a way that when she is in dark surroundings she barely smells anything, but when the lighting conditions are optimal she enjoys a rich smell experience whenever she fixates a colored surface. As Mary moves around smelling different-colored objects, the smells she experiences co-vary in a systematic way with the reflectance properties of the colored surfaces. For simplicity, let us consider only four possible surface-reflectance properties, corresponding to red, blue, green, and yellow, each of which is consistently perceived with a typical smell. Say red smells like strawberries, blue like coffee, green like a meadow, and yellow like scrambled eggs.

Mary realizes that because of the alacrity of eye movements that usually accompany color vision, she has to make sure that the temporal and spatial resolution of her olfaction is increased drastically. For example, when she is looking at a blue book against a black background, it should be the case that whenever she fixates the black background she experiences the smell of coffee peripherally. When she moves her eyes, however, as soon as they hit the blue book, she should immediately experience the smell of coffee in all its fullness. As her eyes wander over the spine of the blue book, the smell experience of coffee should vary evenly and consistently, shifting in intensity only in response to effects of light and shading. Once her eyes shift back to the black table on which the book is placed, the odor should again fade into the periphery.

The existence of such an ocular-motor-olfactory correlation should be sufficient to afford Mary the capacity to localize the smell on the surface of the book, given that she has retained her black-and-white vision. For a considerable amount of evidence from the study of multisensory integration shows that where an experience, usually tactile or auditory, consistently varies with a visually perceived event, the modality with the greatest spatial acuity—that is, vision—tends to dominate the localization judgment of the combined stimulus (see, e.g., Botvinick & Cohen, 1998, and Spence, 2007). A similar spatial referral of smells to the spatially more acute sense of haptic touch takes place in taste perception: subjects locate taste in the food in their mouths while it is largely determined by retro-nasal odor (Auvray & Spence, 2008). That this tendency would also be found in this case seems reasonable, since the smell experience here co-varies consistently and evenly with the spatially more acute modality of black-and-white vision.

Suppose Mary is able to impose the structural features such as those discussed so far[1] on olfaction, what kind of behavioral repertoire would it open up? To explore this, imagine Mary in a library with a few hundred books on display. True to the simplification introduced earlier, we will assume that the surface reflectance properties of each of these are restricted to red, blue, green, and yellow; each of these is perceived with its typical smell: red smelling like strawberries, blue like coffee, green like a meadow, and yellow like scrambled eggs.

As Mary scans the shelves with her eyes, the smell-experiences should arise and disappear with a frequency that would be bewildering were the smells not so reliably tied to the differentiated spatial locations being serially fixated. Every object should instantaneously express its smell on being sighted, allowing for rapid and

---

[1] Cases such as these can, of course, be much more richly described, as in Cooke and Myin (2011).

precise differentiation. Mary's abilities to perceive shapes, as with normal color vision, would be hugely enhanced through her modified olfactory system. Fine detail marked by color differences would be easily perceivable. Mary would be able to engage in a parallel search for similar colors in a richly chromatically structured environment and be able to differentiate objects identical in all other visual aspects. If, for example, the coffee-smelling books on a shelf were so arranged as to form a rough circle, she would immediately notice this geometrical arrangement standing out against the background smells.

Mary has thus drastically changed the structure of her olfactory system: she can differentiate different colors in a manner that is similar to ordinary vision. The exploratory behavior that is imposed on olfaction is also similar to ordinary vision. The addition of her modified olfactory system to her black and white vision guides her behavior in a way that is similar to the way full color vision would guide her behavior. But what would Mary's experience be like? Would she now finally be able to know what it is like to experience color, as predicted by Change? Or would her experience retain an olfactory phenomenology, despite being like visual color perception in so many respects? And how do those different answers (Change versus No Change) relate to Dependence and Independence?

Let us consider Change first. Recall that Change is the claim that in the process of adding the structural features of color vision to olfaction, the phenomenal quality of Mary's experience changes from olfactory to visual too. The obvious motivation for this position is what was called Dependence in the introduction, or the idea that structural features determine phenomenal quality. Change because of Dependence, can be supported with strong arguments. In linking phenomenology to observable and scientifically investigatable structural changes, it coheres with scientific method and a broadly naturalistic outlook. Moreover, it can point to a vast catalogue of established effects of structural features on phenomenal feel—arguably, much of psychophysics, or much of the experimental psychology of perception.

Though these constitute good reasons to defend the idea that in a thought experiment such as the one sketched, phenomenal character would change, there are complications. For in a thought experiments such as these, whereby a source modality is reshaped toward a target modality, some of the features of the source modality remain in place. In the thought experiment we presented, Mary somehow kept on using her nose to perceive color. We didn't ask to imagine the nose being transformed into a pair of eyes. That seems only fair, for to make olfaction sensitive to color and not simply replace it with vision, we have to retain at least some of the normal structural features of olfaction. Now it might be argued that these remaining characteristics will work to conserve phenomenal character. Thus the possibility opens up for a defense of the No Change position within Dependence. Phenomenal character is then seen as dependent upon structural features, but of the remaining features of the source modality rather than the new ones of the target modality. Mary could go through the process of modification of her olfactory modality, without its character changing from olfactory to visual. Mary's experiences remain olfactory even after the structural changes, not by relying on some form of independence but rather on the simple basis that some of the structural features of olfaction remain. The remaining features of the source modality are tenacious. The Dependence plus No Change position can be called "Tenacity."

If one is already committed to Dependence, how should one decide the issue between Change versus No Change in the context of a thought experiment such as the one presented? More knowledge about the relative weight of different structural features in determining phenomenology would be needed to come to well-supported conclusions. Some structural features might be strongly linked to phenomenal feel; other features might play only a secondary, contingent role. At present, we do not have any well-established, uncontested theory in this area. Without being supplemented by such a theory, Dependence does not offer sufficient guidance to conclusively assess thought experiments such as the one presented here. Depending on whether it is supplemented by theory A or theory B, Dependence can, as we have seen, still lead to either Change or No Change.

No Change could be held for different reasons. It could be motivated by Independence—the view that structural features do not determine the phenomenal character of experience. Independence, as we have seen in the previous section, comes in two varieties. Type 1 Independence opposes the notion that structural features determine phenomenal quality since it rejects physicalism, and thus rejects the idea that physical features, of which structural features are a species, necessarily determine phenomenal features (Chalmers, 1996). Type 1 Independence is often justified by means of conceivability arguments. Such arguments consist in concluding from the alleged conceivability of variation at the phenomenal level without changes in the physical level that the physical does not determine the phenomenal. Standard conceivability arguments concern an Inverted color spectrum (in which the phenomenal characters of color experiences are systematically inverted in some person, who has an experience with the feel of "green" whenever she sees a tomato, and of "red' whenever she sees grass).[2] In the current context, defending Type I independence is to hold that it is conceivable that Mary's experiences would remain olfactory despite the modifications, and to see that as resulting from the failure of physical properties to determine phenomenal properties. There is also a second variant of Independence that could motivate holding No Change. This Type 2 Independence, endorsed by Ned Block (2003), aims to combine physicalism with the rejection of functionalism. According to this position,

---

[2] Defenders of Type 1 Independence can hold that structural features, while not metaphysically determining phenomenal character, determine it nomologically. This implies that phenomenal character is determined, in our world, or a world with our physical laws, by structural features, but that there are logically conceivable possible worlds in which phenomenal character is not determined by structural features. Metaphysically speaking, phenomenal character remains independent of structure.

phenomenal properties are determined by physical properties, but those physical properties are not functional properties—they do not show up in what we have called structural features. In this option, there is a "direct link" from a physical feature to a phenomenal feature, without it having to go through "structural features," thus without it showing up in, for example, function or behavior. As a result, there might be creatures (or artifacts) that would be the same at the level of behavior, function, and structural features, yet different at the level of physical features (carbon-based versus silicon-based, for example), and therefore different at the phenomenal level.

The differences between the Dependence and Independence positions are fundamental. This is particularly conspicuous with respect to Type 1 Independence. For by rejecting physicalism, Type 1 Independence obviously explicitly requires substantive revisions in our metaphysics. Problematically, it does have little to offer in terms of guidelines for how such revision should proceed, and what the consequences would be for scientific method. Type 1 Independence regards all structural features as only contingently related to phenomenal feel. However, as it does not spell out which factors are noncontingently related to phenomenal feel, it fails to provide guidelines for research.

Type 1 Independence is standardly motivated by appeal to intuitions. Thought experiments such as the one we have presented can be used to show that this appeal to intuitions can be turned against rather than for Type 1 Independence (Cooke & Myin, 2011). By adding detail to the imagined situation, they make explicit a tension inherent in holding the No Change position. This tension comes down to imagining a single experience that is simultaneously olfactory, yet has all (or at least many) of the features of a color experience. The only way to achieve that exercise in imagination, it seems to us, is to conceive of the phenomenal character of an experience in a certain modality as a featureless feature. The "what it is like" to have an experience thus becomes a "mere difference" that doesn't seem to be grounded in the modality's specific signature, articulated along a multitude of structural dimensions.

To make clear this difficulty, consider, for example, the spatial characteristics of olfactory experiences versus the spatial characteristics of color experiences. For color, the way color makes shapes stand out is an aspect of the way color is spatially articulated. Olfaction arrives on the scene with a quite different spatiality. Smells haven't got precise boundaries. We can tie them to things and events, though, often by tracing their provenance through movement and by relying on accumulated knowledge about the ways of odors (we know the scent of Chanel No. 5 probably belongs to the lady instead of the tramp both of whom crossed our path, for example). We can simultaneously track two or three smells, as when we seek out the one out of three bottles of milk that has soured by putting our nose to each in turn, but the simultaneous multiplicity offered by vision is completely absent in smell: we can locate no more than one smell at a time as against a whole multitude of spatially distinct colors.

A Dependence position understands such spatial aspects as deriving from the structural aspects of a modality. The specific spatiality of vision, for example, is tied to the reliability inherent in the optics of image forming, as well as shaped by the architecture of the visual system that allows visual exploration to capture a broad gamma of visual features at once, and makes it possible to scan the scene for areas of interest or change with the mere flick of an eye. In contrast, the spatiality of smell is from the start destined to be imprecise because it is grounded in volatile chemicals thrown off from objects, subject to the whims of air movement and diffusion. In the still considerable degree of precision that smell finally obtains, having two nostrils, sniffing, and other forms of olfactory exploration play a major role. For instance, there is such a thing as bi-nasal disparity, thanks to which people can for example weave along winding paths of chocolate scent (Porter et al., 2007).

In denying a necessary link between the structural and the phenomenal, Type 1 Independence has to maintain that it is possible to keep the phenomenal core of olfaction while the structural features of color vision would be added to it. This raises the question of which spatial characteristics the resulting experience would have. Would they be those of olfaction? But then how would the experience allow simultaneous discrimination over a broad field, and thus how would the modified olfaction be a genuine form of color vision?[3] If, on the other hand, the spatial characteristics would be those of vision, how to explain this, if not as deriving from the addition of the structural features of color vision? The only way for the defender of Type 1 Independence to avoid this dilemma is to hold that the phenomenal core of olfaction has no spatial properties whatsoever. However, she should repeat this move with respect to any feature, other than spatiality, as a similar dilemma could be set up with respect to other features as well. What this adds up to is that the defender of a Type 1 Independence view would be left with having to accept phenomenal feel as what we have called a "featureless feature." This doesn't seem a particularly attractive option.

What about Independence of the physicalist variety, Type 2 Independence? Being overtly committed to physicalism, this position doesn't seem to have the heavy metaphysical price tag with which Type 1 Independence comes, as it doesn't require the postulation of kinds of properties entirely different from physical ones, bearing enigmatic relations to them. This type of Independence has costs of its

---

[3] A similar question—though in a different context—was raised by Peter Strawson (1959). He wonders whether it would be possible to translate the spatio-temporal characteristics of color vision into the auditory modality. To answer this question, several ways are discussed in which audition could be used to mimic the spatial relations to which vision has access. But, as Strawson notes, these proposals all falter on the problem that "the momentary states of colour-patches of the visual scene visibly exhibit spatial relations to each other at a moment; whereas the momentary states of the sound-patches of the auditory scene do not audibly exhibit the auditory analogue of spatial relations to each other at a moment". Strawson then discusses the question of whether it is possible to further employ the "formal parallels" that exist between vision and audition in order to make room for such spatio-temporal relations, without thereby turning audition into vision. Although he does not answer the question, he remains sceptical whether this is possible.

own, however. For even if it does not require the postulation of special types of nonphysical properties, it has to postulate the existence of a special mechanism that connects physical properties to phenomenal properties, in a way that excludes behavior, function, and structural properties in general. In the absence of a specification of the link between nonfunctional physical properties and phenomenal properties, Type 2 Independence contains a very crucial lacuna.

Moreover, the very idea of genuinely nonfunctional physical properties is problematic on its own. Defending Type 2 Independence, Ned Block (2003) has argued that phenomenal qualities are a function of the material realizer or physical substrate underlying the experience. According to such a view the phenomenal quality of an experience is determined by the physical properties rather than by the functional role of the physical substrate. What exactly is this opposition between functional role and physical substrate? On the face of it, one way to understand it is in terms of multiple realizability. According to the multiple realizibility thesis, mental states are constituted by their functional role, which can be multiply realized. For example, robots could have something that is functionally equivalent to the human visual system and could therefore be said to see, despite the fact that the robot's system is silicone-based and the human system is carbon-based. Multiple realizability occurs when the relevant functional or causal powers are the same despite different substrates. It is important to realize that multiple realizability does not rest on an absolute opposition between functional and physical properties—the latter being understood as properties of the substrate. It merely pronounces that some of the properties of the substrate are irrelevant with respect to a certain functional or causal profile. It doesn't say that those physical properties are nonfunctional in the sense that they contribute to no causal profile whatsoever. It is quite possible for a functionalist to hold that the properties of some substrate—think about gold or chocolate, for example—are fully functional, yet not multiply realizable. In the context of the mind/body relation, it could be that the human brain/body has unique causal powers that, as a matter of fact, are not replicable in any other substrate—as is perhaps the case for chocolate. What all of this leads to is that the opposition between functional role and causal substrate can, contrary to first appearances, not be understood in terms of multiple realizability. If Block wants to obtain a genuine opposition between functional and physical properties, he has to construe the relevant physical properties as having no functional or causal profile whatsoever—apart from their bringing about phenomenal experience. We do not claim to be able to provide an a priori refutation of such a position. We only note that, in the absence of at least a gesture toward a (nonfunctional!) mechanism that mediates the link between the physical and the phenomenal, it seems rather devoid of positive content. This position agrees with Type 1 Independence that all structural features are only contingently related to phenomenal feel, and, in the absence of the specification of the special physical-to-phenomenal mechanism, it offers no guidance toward finding out about noncontingent factors.

Just like type Type 1 Independence, Type 2 Independence turns out to have little to offer in terms of a positive research program—quite in contrast to Dependence positions, which offer a view of phenomenal qualities that is open to empirical investigation and scientific theorizing.

3. Sensory Substitution

We now turn our attention to a real example of morphing one sense modality into another. Such an example is provided by sensory substitution. Sensory substitution involves the attempt to use an intact sensory modality to restore at least some of the functions of a deficient or lost sensory modality. For example, one can try to use an intact tactile or auditory sense modality to take over (some of the functions of) vision. Visual stimuli are then made available to the ears, or to a patch of skin, and people are trained to perform tasks that normally would require vision, on the basis of these stimuli.

Two well-known sensory substitution devices are the tactile TVSS system and the auditory vOICe system. In both systems, a head-mounted camera captures the stimuli normally registered by the eye. These are then "translated" into the "home format" of the intact modality. In the case of the TVSS, this is a tactile pattern of pressures corresponding to the intensity of the light at various parts in the image.

Subjects are then allowed to explore the environment for a while and are tested on their performance of tasks that would normally require vision. Following such a training period, persons using a sensory substitution device have been found to acquire such capacities as, for example those for locomotor guidance, object localization, pointing and object categorization (see Auvray & Myin, 2009, for further information and pointers to the literature).

Sensory substitution devices are actual cases of modifying a sense by tampering with its structural features. In the TVSS case, the structural features of touch are made more like the structural features of vision, by making changes in the properties of the eliciting stimuli of touch, in the precise motoric ways in which experiences characteristic of touch are obtained and in the ways experiences are embedded in behavior.

But what happens to the modal phenomenal character of the experience in sensory substitution? Does the character of the experience of a TVSS user become visual, as predicted by No Change, or does it remain tactile, as per Change?

This question has been widely discussed. Both functionalists and sensorimotor theorists, on the basis of holding Dependence, have defended change. The functionalist tenet that the character of experience must be determined by the way that experience is related to stimuli, other experiences, and action implies that perception, including its character, becomes visual, to the extent that perception with a sensory substitution device, after the training period, allows subjects to respond "visually" to stimuli that are normally visual. Dennett (1991, pp. 338–344) has defended exactly such a position with respect to the TVSS device. Hurley and Noë (2003) provide another case in defense of the idea that in sensory substitution the modal phenomenal character changes. Their analysis is based on a sensorimotor approach to perception, but it shows convergences with the functionalist position as well. Hurley and Noë point out similarities in exploratory behavior between perception with a sensory substitution device and unaided vision, a similar behavioral/functional potential, and directedness toward similar visual properties. They write:

> What it is like to see is similar to what it is like to perceive with TVSS because seeing and TVSS-perception are similar ways of exploring the environment: they are governed by similar sensorimotor constraints, draw on similar sensorimotor skills, and are directed towards similar visual properties, including perspectivally available occlusion properties such as apparent size and shape. These similarities go beyond just providing spatial information; they extend to the distinctively visual way in which dynamic sensorimotor interactions with the environment provide information to the TVSS-perceiver. (Hurley & Noë, 2003, pp. 144–145)

Various other theorists have opposed the idea that phenomenal character changes, however, thus endorsing No Change. For example, Prinz (2006) holds that the structural changes in cases of sensory substitution do not have any effect on the character of experience. Discussing the TVSS device, he writes, "I have little doubt that subjects master use of the apparatus by adjusting their behavioral dispositions; when their torsos are stimulated, they react by avoiding obstacles in their environment, not by flexing or contracting their abdominal muscles. But I seriously doubt that these subjects experience anything visual" (Prinz, 2006, p. 4).

What happens in sensory substitution, according to Prinz, is not that the phenomenal character of tactile experience changes. Perfectly regular tactile experience just arises as a result of unusual—distal—stimulation, and people learn to react in novel—broadly visual—ways to that perfectly regular tactile stimulation. Changes happen to the input provided to tactile experience and to what actions it leads to, but not to tactile experience itself. It is not clear on what grounds Prinz defends the No Change position. His argument can be read as relying on Independence, but it can also be interpreted as falling within Dependence, and as merely stressing the tenacity of the structural features of the source modality.

Ned Block (2003), however, is very explicit on the underlying reasons for his rejection of the change position. Against functionalist and sensorimotor proposals, Block sees merit in a physicalist form of Independence, according to which the character of experience is determined by properties of the physical substrate of experience, which are not expressed at the functional or sensorimotor level. He writes:

> If a sensory brain state plays an unusual functional role, does the phenomenology go with the role or the brain state? If the phenomenology goes with the functional role, that supports functionalism, which is the view

that phenomenology just is the role. If it goes with the brain state, that supports physicalism, which is the view that phenomenology is what realizes or implements the role....However, I do not think that Hurley and Noë have made it plausible that there are any cases in which phenomenology goes with role when role and realizer conflict. (Block, 2003, pp. 285–286)

To an important degree, this debate is fueled by arguments based on principles rather than by arguments based on evidence. We are told what the character of experience should be, given some theoretical tenets taken to be established already. It is argued that the character of experience when using a sensory substitution device should be visual, given that such use confers visual capacities and comes with sensorimotor interactions typical of vision. Block contests this claim by pointing out the possibility that physical substrate rather than functional role could be what phenomenal character supervenes on. In a preferable situation, rather than attempting to infer what the experienced character is, one would simply ask users of sensory substitution devices about the feel of their experience.

Unfortunately, the limited evidence available is somewhat anecdotal. Take the example of a study from Auvray et al. (2007), which involved blindfolded, sighted participants who were trained for fifteen hours to acquire visual capacities for localization and recognition with the audition-based sensory substitution device vOIce. After having become sufficiently proficient at both tasks (they were, for example, able to localize, recognize, and discriminate between a bottle, a plant, and two different plants), they filled out questionnaires regarding what their experience felt most like in either recognition or localization tasks. The latter were most likely to be categorized as giving rise to visual-like experience. Experience in recognition tasks, on the other hand, tended to be judged as more like audition or touch. Interestingly, some participants likened their experience to having a new sense (in the localization tasks), or compared the use of the sensory substitution device to using a tool (Auvray et al., 2007; Auvray & Myin 2009 for additional discussion).[4]

Although scarce and rather anecdotal, these data seem to support the idea of change and thus the dependence view, as at least in a number of cases, the experience is described as visual. Interestingly, whether subjects describe the phenomenology as visual is a task-dependent affair. If such data can be replicated in a more rigorous way, they seem supportive of the functionalist/sensorimotor position, for, arguably, it is only or especially in the context of specifically visual tasks, such as localization tasks, which require specifically visual interactions, that modal phenomenal character adapts. Moreover, the evidence is in conflict with both varieties of the independence view, since either implies that there would be no report of change in modal phenomenal character. Independence cannot hold in some

---

[4] In total, six subjects took part in the trials. In the localization tasks, half of them described their experience as being visual. None of them described the experience as tactile. In the recognition tasks, half of the subjects described the experience as auditory. Only one person described it as being tactile.

cases but not in others. If the limited available evidence is indicative of the kind of evidence that carefully set up, large-scale studies would yield, the only means to defend Independence would be to hold that participants are systematically deluded about the character of their own experience. Although we do not claim infallible self-knowledge, this avenue seems to us quixotic unless some independent support is provided for the claim that people are systematically deluded about the modal-specific phenomenal character of their experience.[5]

Note however that there is a certain asymmetry in the role the evidence plays with respect to the positions of Independence and Dependence. For even if the evidence were to suggest that there is no change in phenomenal modal character, this in itself does not invalidate the Dependence position. As we have observed earlier, the evidence and the objections might not be pointing toward independence but rather to Tenacity. According to tenacity, remaining features of a modality that undergoes structural changes still imprint phenomenal character after the change. Tenacity can be applied to thought experiments such as the one given in section 2, and to sensory substitution.

Tenacity, so we propose, should be considered to be a case of intermodal dominance. Intermodal dominance occurs when there is a potential conflict between what is perceived through two modalities: one modality would lead to the perception of A, the other modality would lead to the perception of B, and A and B are incompatible perceptions. Whenever such cases occur, actual perception goes the way of one of the modalities, which is called the *dominant* modality.

The theme of intermodal dominance has been widely explored in the psychological literature. A well-known example of such intermodal dominance is the rubber hand illusion (Botvinick & Cohen 1998). In the rubber hand illusion, a person's hand is occluded from his view; instead, he sees a rubber hand. The experimenters stroke both the person's hand and the rubber hand. After a while the person identifies the tactile sensations that arise from stroking his real hand in the rubber hand. The person is thus presented with three sets of stimuli or information—tactile, visual, and proprioceptive—which conflict with each other. This conflict is resolved by the simple fact that one of the modalities is overriding or dominating the other. In the case of the rubber hand illusion, it is the visual modality that dominates the other modalities. Several similar cases are reported in the literature (see, e.g., Hurley & Noë, 2003, and O'Callaghan, 2012). An obvious question is whether there are any general rules that determine which modality overrides which modality. A number of principles exist that try to explain the various examples of intermodal dominance, but none of these is without exception. For example, vision often dominates other senses but it doesn't do so invariably.

---

[5] Eric Schwitzgebel (2012) has argued extensively that there is no incorrigible first-person knowledge about phenomenology. We tend to agree but note that the various examples he gives do not show that we are systematically deluded about the modality in which perception takes place.

Rules for dominance in any other two modalities are not more than rules of thumb (O'Callaghan, 2012, pp. 102–104; for general discussion of dominance, see Stokes & Biggs, this volume).

Tenacity can be construed by analogy with intermodal dominance. In sensory substitution with a TVSS-device there are still some features of tactile perception as well as features of visual perception. These two types of features are in competition as to which determines the character of experience. So there is both something vision-like and tactile-like in perception with TVSS, and the question is which of the two imposes its modal phenomenal character. Defenders of Tenacity will claim that the tactile-like features dominate the vision-like features, whereas the defenders of Change argue for the alternative case of dominance. But, as with regular cases of intermodal dominance, there are no a priori reasons why the tactile-like features should dominate the vision-like features. As a result, one cannot take for granted that tenacity can be established as a matter of principle, so as to imply that in cases of sensory substitution, the source modality (touch, hearing) will dominate over the target modality (vision).

Most important, however, even if Tenacity would apply to some cases of sensory substitution, it is compatible with the general functionalist/sensorimotor outlook that derives from the Dependence view—even if not with the position that has been standardly defended by functionalist/sensorimotor theorists. For no functionalist/sensorimotor theorist needs to deny the obvious truth that sensorimotor substitution builds on an existing modality. Sensory substitution devices add to the functional/sensorimotor repertoire of the source sense, without destroying the repertoire already present. Existing functionality, and existing sensorimotor contingencies, remain in place. If the phenomenal character remains that of the source modality, this can be explained through remaining structural features. The basic functionalist/sensorimotor thesis regarding the dependence of phenomenal character remains standing.

At the same time, this presents challengers of the functionalist/sensorimotor interpretation of sensory substitution with a dilemma. Either they defend Independence of phenomenal character from structural features, or they defend Tenacity. The former position would genuinely endanger the functionalist/sensorimotor position. But it is a quite problematic position, as we have attempted to illustrate with our thought experiment and discussion of sensory substitution. Alternatively, they defend Tenacity. But then, apart from some problems with evidence, they offer no genuine challenge to the functionalist/sensorimotor position, and a fortiori not to Dependence.

4. Conclusion

The aim of this chapter has been to elucidate the discussion concerning the question of whether in real or imagined experiments of morphing a sense the phenomenal character of perception with the modified sense modality changes. The philosophical relevance of this question derives from its being linked with the question of the relationship between the structural features of a sense modality and the phenomenal character of perception through that modality. The latter question is itself part of a whole complex of interrelated questions and problems regarding the relationship between the mental and the physical, which has been a traditional battleground between functionalism, physicalism, and anti-physicalism.

With respect to our starting question we have identified two opposing positions: Change and No Change. Similarly, with respect to the more fundamental question concerning the relationship between structural and phenomenal features, we have identified two opposing positions: Dependence and Independence. It seems natural to think of the first question as an operationalized and experimentally tractable version of the second one. If one adopts this view it is equally natural to map the opposition between Dependence and Independence onto the opposition between Change and No Change—with Dependence mapping onto Change and Independence mapping onto No Change. This is, however, misleading, since Independence is a position that seems problematically related to experimental confirmation or disconfirmation. This is particularly clear in its nonphysicalist version. But, as we have argued, the same is true of the physicalist version of Independence. Contrary to first impressions, perhaps, the physicalist version of Independence seems as yet to have very little to contribute to a positive research program for the study of the mind.

In contrast, and again contrary to first impressions, the Dependence view does not necessarily lead to the Change position. As we have seen, one can be committed to the Dependence view and at the same time defend a No Change position. However, a defender of the Dependence view is not forced to take the No Change or Change position in all possible scenarios: she can consistently, for example, argue for Change in the case of sensory substitution using the vOIce, for No Change in the case of sensory substitution with the TVSS, and for Change in the case of a thought experiment like the one we have presented. The Dependence view is thus responsive to a variety of conditions that might make a differentiated conclusion necessary. As such, the Dependence position offers the possibility to inspire empirical investigations into questions concerning the relationship between structural and phenomenal features.

Acknowledgments

The authors wish to thank, for their excellent advice on earlier versions of this chapter, Jan Degenaar, Victor Loughlin, Bence Nanay, and the editors of this volume.

References

Auvray, M. & Myin, E. (2009). Perception with compensatory devices from sensory substitution to sensorimotor extension. *Cognitive Science* 33, pp. 1036–1058.

Auvray, M., Hanneton, S., & O'Regan, J. K. (2007). Learning to perceive with a visuo-auditory substitution system: Localization and object recognition with The Voice. *Perception* 36, pp. 416–430.

Auvray, M. & Spence, C. (2008). The multisensory perception of flavor. *Consciousness and Cognition* 17, pp. 1016–1031.

Bach-y Rita, P., Collins, C. C., Saunders, F., White, B., & Scadden, L. (1969). Vision substitution by tactile image projection. *Nature* 221, pp. 963–964.

Botvinick, M. & Cohen, J. (1998). Rubber hands "feel" touch that eyes see. *Nature* 391, p. 756.

Block, N. (2003). Tactile sensation via spatial perception. *TRENDS in Cognitive Science* 7, pp. 285–286.

Chalmers, D. (1996). *The Conscious Mind*. Oxford: Oxford University Press.

Cooke, E. & Myin, E. (2011). Is trilled smell possible? How the structure of olfaction determines the phenomenology of smell. *Journal of Consciousness Studies* 18 (No. 11–12), pp. 59–95.

Dennett, D. (1991). *Consciousness Explained*. New York: Little, Brown.

Hurley, S. & Noë, A. (2003). Neural plasticity and consciousness. *Biology and Philosophy* 18, pp. 131–168.

Jackson, F. (1986). What Mary didn't know. *Journal of Philosophy* 83, pp. 291–295.

Meijer, P. B. L. (1992). An experimental system for auditory image representations. *IEEE Transactions Biomedical Engineering* 39, pp. 112–121.

O'Callaghan, C. (2012). Perception and multimodality. In Margolis, E., Samuels, R., & Stich, S., editors, *Oxford Handbook of Philosophy and Cognitive Science*. New York: Oxford University Press, pp. 92–117.

O'Regan, J. K. (2011). *Why Red Doesn't Sound Like a Bell: Understanding the Feel of Consciousness*. New York: Oxford University Press.

Porter, J., Craven, B., Khan, R., Chang, S.-J., Kang, I., Judkewitz, B., & Sobel, N. (2007). Mechanisms of scent tracking in humans. *Nature Neuroscience* 10, pp. 27–29.

Prinz, J. (2006). Putting the brakes on enactive perception. *Psyche* 12, pp. 1–19.

Schwitzgebel, E. (2012). Self-ignorance. In Liu, J. & Perry, J., editors, *Consciousness and the Self. New Essays*. Cambridge: Cambridge University Press.

Spence, C. (2007). Audiovisual multisensory integration. *Science & Technology* 28, pp. 61–70.

Strawson, P. F. (1959). *Individuals*. London: Routledge.

17

A Methodological Molyneux Question

SENSORY SUBSTITUTION, PLASTICITY, AND THE UNIFICATION OF PERCEPTUAL THEORY

Mazviita Chirimuuta and Mark Paterson

1. Introducing the Methodological Molyneux Question

Superficially, vision and touch could not seem more different. If vision shows us distant horizons, touch is limited to the boundaries of our bodies. Whereas vision is synoptic, a tactile picture of the world is built up through a laborious and methodical process of manual exploration. With the oft-noted assumption of visuocentrism in Western philosophy (e.g., Jay 1994; Rorty 1979), visual perception has been esteemed as the paragon of objectivity, and touch the paragon of subjectivity (Jonas 1954). Such well-worn conceits suggest the preeminence of sight in the perception of space and in the apprehension of objects within it.

As we have argued elsewhere, the philosophy of perception has much to benefit from concentrating on commonalities between vision and touch (Paterson 2007; Paterson in press; Chirimuuta 2011), and one strand of debate stretching back to the original Molyneux question[1] certainly has aimed to get a grip on the possible overlap of the visual and tactile, at least in terms of geometric concepts. Simply put, the question asks: if someone born without sight, but who had had direct tactile experience of a solid cube and a sphere, were suddenly able to see, would he or she be able to tell the objects apart by sight alone without touching them? (For further philosophical treatments, see, e.g., Morgan 1977; Evans 1985; Gallagher 2005; Degenaar 1996; Paterson 2006; Paterson in press. For a very recent empirical approach, see Held et al. 2011.)

---

[1] First formulated in a letter to Locke in 1688 that was ignored, William Molyneux posed the question to John Locke for a second time, following the publication of the first edition of Locke's celebrated *An Essay Concerning Human Understanding* of 1690, and subsequently incorporated into the 1692 edition.

Subsequent philosophical discussion between Locke and Berkeley, and later figures such as Reid, pivoted on the possibility of a level of sensory abstraction before perceptions of objects become modality specific (Riskin 2002; Paterson forthcoming). In this vein, one of Berkeley's stated tasks in *New Theory of Vision* was "to consider the difference there is betwixt the ideas of sight and touch, and whether there be any idea common to both senses" (1709 §1). Evans (1985) presents his summary and solution of the Molyneux problem as a lesson in dealing with the senses in more fine-grained bodily terms, considering the integration of vision with other bodily perceptions and sensations including audition and kinesthesia. Evans dismissed psychological interpretations of the problem through Lotze (1885) and later Von Senden (1932/1960), which denied that the blind have any concept of space whatsoever. Even without sight there is, for the blind subject, the possibility of the formation of "simultaneous perceptual representations of his vicinity" writes Evans (1985:382), whether this occurs through acoustics, touch, or any combination of bodily movement and sensation.

Moreover, the dominance of vision in thought concerning the senses has frequently been noted and sometimes lamented (in philosophy, e.g., Jay 1994 and Noë 2004; in perceptual psychology, e.g., Katz 1925/1989 and Gibson 1966; and in the social sciences, e.g., Csordas 1994; Howes 2003; Paterson 2009). Arguments in the philosophy of perception that restrict attention to sight risk not only monotony, but worse, potentially invalid generalization to all senses of proposals holding only for vision. Yet even if a visuocentric stance were dropped and philosophers were to use examples from touch, audition, or smell to illustrate their theories, the question would still arise as to whether it is valid to extend the conclusions back to vision. It may be that we can have no general theory of the senses, only modality-specific accounts,[2] Or it may be that, at some broad level of abstraction, an approach to the senses can be general, but solutions to specific problems must be modality specific. The issue of whether a conceptual framework[3] developed to theorize one sense modality generalizes to other modalities is raised by our *Methodological Molyneux Question* (MMQ). In this chapter we offer a preliminary response, with the expectation that progress can be made in future interdisciplinary work.

---

[2] It pays to clarify terminology at this stage. By *general* theory of the senses, we mean one that is *non*-modal, one that is not dependent on the peculiarity of any one modality for its explanatory impact or intuitive appeal. This is related to—but not to be confused with—questions over *cross*-modality (the extent to which modalities interact with each other); *meta*-modality (the idea that brain areas are specialized to process certain types of information, which are better delivered by some modalities over others, but not exclusive to any modality (Pascual-Leone & Hamilton 2001; Pascual-Leone et al. 2006) and the possibility of *non*-modal representations of geometric shape, as traditionally conceived in the Molyneux debate.

[3] Since a general theory of the senses is something of a remote target, in what follows we speak of a "general conceptual framework." By *conceptual framework* we mean a tool box of concepts that helps philosophers, and possibly also scientists, most usefully frame problems and findings in this area of research. By *general* conceptual framework, we mean one that might be usefully employed across all modalities.

We restrict our attention to vision and touch here because the overt differences between these modalities present an obvious obstacle to a positive
response to the MMQ. A successful program for unifying theories of vision and
touch is grounds for optimism that the challenges presented by other modalities
may be similarly attended, though we do recognize that other modalities, such as
olfaction, may present particular issues not raised by vision and touch. Another
reason for concentrating on these two modalities in particular is that a body of
philosophical and empirical work already exists which analyzes their similarities
and differences, especially with respect to spatial reference frames, the coding
of spatial properties, and the geometric concepts to be derived from them. This
means we are not starting from scratch. We begin with M. G. F. Martin's (1992)
description of a contrast between spatial reference frames employed in vision
and touch, and his negative conclusion regarding the Methodological Molyneux
Question. We argue that his rejection of the possibility of a common account of
these senses is too dismissive, relying on two assumptions that are incompatible with what is known about the complexities of spatial perception in vision
and touch. Martin's treatment assumes first that any difference between vision
and touch is fixed, and second that these modalities do not present a variety
of forms of spatial representation. In sections 2 and 3 we present case studies
of sensory substitution and Braille that undermine both of Martin's assumptions and therefore his conclusion regarding spatial reference frames. We note
that even though the technology of sensory substitution is promising, it is clear
that visual and tactile modalities are not ultimately unified or fully substitutable
through tactile-visual sensory substitution (TVSS). Given significant findings
of disunity within modalities, we observe that some functionally defined visual
submodalities do share common features with certain tactile submodalities. It
is these commonalities that, along with neuroplasticity, allow for substitution of
perceptual functions. So while it is tempting to assume that the only way there
can be an affirmative answer to the MMQ is if there is some arena in which
somehow all sense modalities are unified, this notion of functional substitution
leaves open the possibility of a more unified account, without any strong thesis
of full sensory interchangeability.

In posing the Methodological Molyneux Question, we seek to initiate future
investigation into the possibility of a general conceptual framework that is
not modality specific in its characterization of what perception is and how it
works. One clear motivation for this question is the growing appreciation of
the importance of cross-modal spatial attention (see Spence and Driver 2004;
Streri and Gentaz 2004) and cross-modal sensations, which cannot be understood within modality-specific theories, such as bodily sensations that lie outside of the Aristotelian model of the five distinct or extant senses (e.g., Kemp
and Fletcher 1993; Spelke 1998). Moreover, this work is clearly complementary
to the ongoing debate over how the sense modalities should be categorized and
defined (e.g., Keeley 2002, 2009; Noë 2004; MacPherson 2011). Much empirical

work suggests that each modality is more complex and nonunified than our phenomenology suggests[4]. So it pays to ask what other routes remain open for the theoretical reintegration of the senses.

1.2. MARTIN'S CAUTION REGARDING A UNITARY THEORY OF THE SENSES

Space does not allow a full response to the MMQ in this chapter. Rather, we focus our efforts on removing certain obstacles to a positive response, targeting Michael Martin's swift rejection of any general accounts of visual and tactile modalities. One of the supposed key differences between vision and touch concerns how spatial relations are or are not conveyed (see Millar 2006 for a useful overview). Many discussions have focused on the spatial competencies of the blind. For example, von Senden (1932) went so far as to argue that the congenitally blind lack a concept of space. Révész (1950) observed the performance of blind subjects in spatial tasks such as distance estimation and concluded that touch relies wholly on a body-centered (egocentric) reference frame, whereas visual reference frames utilize external (allocentric) coordinates.

While Millar (2006) presents evidence that external reference cues can indeed be used in haptic tasks, Révész's notion of a fundamental difference is the view more in tune with Martin's (1992) approach. "Sight and Touch" is one of the minority of works in the philosophy of perception that grapples directly with touch.[5] From the phenomenology of these modalities Martin argues that there is a "structural difference between sight and touch" (p. 197). While vision locates objects in an external field, Martin doubts whether touch, which relies on other somatic factors, involves a comparable field: "the visual field plays a role in sight which is not played by any sense field in touch. Touch is dependent on bodily awareness and if, or where, that involves a sense field, it does so in a strikingly different way from that in which visual experience involves the visual field" (p.197). Martin finds the root of the difference in his contention that while the visual field's display of objects is located within it, objects of touch are felt

---

[4] To take the one example of touch, it is not simply a skin-sense but constituted by reafferent feedback at dermal and epidermal levels dealing with pressure (mechanoceptors), temperature (thermoreceptors), along with nerve endings in the muscles dealing with position (proprioceptors) and pain (nociceptors) (Paterson 2007). We use the term "haptics" following Gibson (1966) as a sensory subsystem combining cutaneous pressure sensitivity plus kinesthesis, the sensitivity to muscular movement and load. Note that Fulkerson (2011) argues against the idea that the different functional submodalities of touch are so disunified as to warrant consideration as separate modalities. His case is not problematic for our argument because we posit only that there are functionally dissociable submodalities within the touch modality, concurring with Fulkerson (2011:498) that equivalent dissociations also occur within other modalities including vision.

[5] But see also Berkeley 1709; Merleau-Ponty 1949/1992; O'Shaughnessy 1989; Smith 2002; Fulkerson this volume.

only as impinging on the skin,[6] and therefore not contained by any corporeal sense field:

> The spatial character of bodily awareness will force on us an alternative conception of spatial experience. Central to it will be this contrast between the sense of that which falls within the limits of experience and things feeling to be within a space which extends beyond those limits. (p. 203)

By positing such a distinction between the spatial characters of incommensurable sensory fields, Martin reaffirms Révész's assumption that the visual field is a properly spatial field, involving distance, whereas touch and bodily awareness, insofar as it might constitute a field in itself, is one of contact and proximity, though one that presents objects as extending past the dermal limit. Later, Martin is left "sceptical as to whether one can give one general theory of what perception is, and in particular what it is to perceive the spatial properties of objects" (p. 211) and concludes that "there is no reason to think that any theory adequate to one sense should be adequate to all" (p. 215).

It would seem that Martin is trenchant in his dismissal of our Methodological Molyneux Question, but we believe that a more nuanced appraisal is needed, contesting two assumptions that lie behind his move from observation of certain differences between vision and touch to his general negative conclusion:

A. Each sensory system is fixed in the way it represents objects in space.
B. Each sensory system is uniform in its representation of objects in space, not allowing for functionally specialised subsystems that utilise different kinds of spatial reference frames.

First, we challenge assumption (A) by appeal to a case study on sensory substitution. Sensory substitution is possible only because our brain architecture allows for alteration of the way the substituting modality represents objects in space, such that it takes on some characteristics of the substituted modality. This can occur only because of the underlying phenomenon of neuroplasticity, which allows for reorganization of sensory pathways, even in adulthood (for recent reviews, see Pascual-Leone et al. 2005; Bubic et al. 2010). Martin's account does not consider the possibility of a subject developing a tactile sense field that more greatly resembles

---

[6] See Fulkerson (this volume) for the argument that extends beyond the limits of the body, in cases where probes and tools are actively manipulated by the subject. However, as (Millar 2006:28) describes, views like Martin's are more typical: "The traditional division of sense modalities into 'proximal' and 'distal' senses has had a considerable influence on the view that visuo-spatial concepts differ radically from spatial concepts derived from touch. Touch has typically been considered a proximal sense, because the stimuli arise from direct contact of objects with the body. That seems to be in complete contrast to the distal senses, especially vision, in which stimuli arise from distant objects.... However, as we shall see, this seemingly obvious common sense classification is not actually useful when trying to determine the relation of spatial processes to modality effects." Note that Martin's refinement of the proximal-distal modality distinction does (rightly) consider that touch allows us to perceive objects as lying in space beyond the body, and so is not confined representation of mere dermal stimulation.

a visual field, and as such is consistent with the now outdated tradition positing that sensory systems remain fixed after development (Wiesel & Hubel 1963, 1965).

Second, the assumption of uniformity (B) is undermined by the consideration of parallel processing within sensory systems, which appears to map onto functional differences. The best-known cases of within-modality differentiation are the "what vs. where" streams in vision (Mishkin et al. 1983) characterized by Milner and Goodale (1995) as "vision for conscious representation" versus "vision for action." As we will see in section 3, sensory substitution also relies on a functional heterogeneity within sensory modalities, so that even if two modalities are rather different on first view, particular functions of their submodalities can still be readily substitutable. We illustrate this idea with a case study on Braille, which we term a "functional substitution."

2. Sensory Substitutions

Martin's strong hypothesis is that we cannot give a general account of what it is to perceive the spatial properties of objects. His point is that the geometric curvature of a rubber ball, for example, is *seen* in the context of a visual field, and *felt* as a type of impression on the skin, an impingement on the bodily contour of an object that resides in a space beyond the body's sense field. One tacit assumption (A) is that these contrasting characteristics of the modalities are fixed. But if under certain circumstances the phenomenology of touch can be released from its entanglement with bodily sensation, becoming more distal and vision-like, then Martin's point is undermined. In other words, the changeability of sensory systems and the variety of perceptions they bring about means that Martin cannot have said the final word on visual or tactile spatial perception. An appropriate place to look for such counterevidence is through a case study of sensory substitution.

2.1. THE CASE OF THE "SEEING" TONGUE

The key goal of sensory substitution systems is that in the absence of one modality, another may be repurposed to provide equivalent information. Sensory substitution technologies require fast perceptual learning and, over the long term, substantial cortical remapping. There is a range of such sensory substitution systems, including tactile-audio and tactile-vestibular substitution, but the system most relevant to our meta-Molyneux discussion is tactile-visual sensory substitution (TVSS), as it foregrounds the translation between vision and touch, especially when one is performing spatial tasks. As the pioneer of TVSS from the 1960s until his death in 2006, Paul Bach-Y-Rita, explains: "In a tactile sensory substitution approach, a sensory system previously virtually restricted to contact information must mediate three-dimensional spatial information and integrate spatial cues originating at a distance" (1972:66).

The first devices were largely mechanical, such as the hulking research device built in 1968 that translated a tripod-based low-resolution video feed into patterns of pressure on the skin. Because of the physical size of the tactile array, a 20 × 20 grid spread over ten square inches, the trunk of the body was the only practicable area (Bach-y-Rita 1972:3). Despite such low resolution, with periods of training, congenitally blind individuals could actually discern basic shapes and letters. The transition to a more portable system necessitated a shift from mechanical to electrical systems, and in 1971 a prototype of the Smith-Kettlewell Portable Electrical Stimulation System was demonstrated with blind participants using a head-mounted camera but a lower resolution 8 × 8 array of brass discs held in a plastic grid pressed to the abdomen. An unforeseen outcome of this increased mobility was the new potential for the subject to interact with the environment, so that picking up a telephone, for example, exploited a "hand-sensor" coordination that was technically impossible before. Subsequent versions of these devices unsurprisingly decreased in physical size while increasing the resolution of the vibrotactile array and were later developed for commercial use, marketed in the early 1990s as the VideoTact™ for $45,000 (Visell 2009).

More recently a tongue-based variant known colloquially as the "lollipop" has been tested experimentally and even featured in the media. Developed initially by Bach-y-Rita and his company Wicab Inc. from 1998, the lollipop is a highly portable tongue display unit (TDU) to be marketed as the BrainPort™. A tiny videocamera mounted within spectacles feeds directly into a flexible 25 × 25 electrode array on the tongue, where the patterns of electrical stimulation reportedly feel like champagne bubbles popping. This system outperforms earlier versions of TVSS because the tongue is smaller and more sensitive than the back or abdomen, and saliva in the mouth enhances the electrolytic environment, increasing conductivity (Bach-y-Rita et al. 1998).

The technology has proved successful for allowing users to see shapes and letters, read words, and experience enhanced mobility and spatial awareness without vision. Media coverage and news footage of blind individuals playing games of noughts and crosses, throwing darts at dartboards, and navigating cluttered courses (BrainPort website; "Electronic Lollipop" 2009; Sampaio et al. 2001; Ptito et al. 2005) reveal that the specifications of resolution and refresh rate for the tactile array are good enough to make the device useful in practical tasks.

The Brainport™ and earlier incarnations of TVSS have already attracted much philosophical interest. Morgan (1977), for example, argues that the existence of TVSS implies a positive answer to Molyneux's question. Heil (1983), Hurley and Noë (2003), and Noë (2004) all describe TVSS as endowing a kind of seeing.[7] One of the reasons for claiming that TVSS enables one to see is the "looming" effect of a camera zoom. If the experimenter makes the TVSS camera zoom into an

---

[7] See Prinz (2006) for arguments against this view, and Deroy and Auvray (this volume) for the argument that sensory substitution endows subjects with a new modality distinguishable both from touch and sight.

object, the sudden expansion of the object causes subjects to flinch as if the object is hurtling toward them (Bach-y-Rita 1972:98). This zoom-like effect relies on a characteristically visual stimulus, the expansion of optic flow (Gibson 1979). We emphasize that TVSS enables the modality of touch to respond to spatial cues normally only available to vision, while we remain noncommittal as to whether these particular functional equivalences should rightly be described as sight (hence the scare quotes around the "'seeing' tongue'). Indeed, the debate over whether TVSS perception is seeing is orthogonal to the concerns of this chapter.

An important observation about TVSS is that its benefits are not instantaneous. Switching on the machinery does not immediately endow the subject with this new perceptual capacity. Instead, there is a steady learning process through which the TVSS system becomes a useful means of performing certain perceptual operations (Bach-y-Rita 1972, Sampaio et al. 2001; Ptito et al. 2005; Bubic et al. 2010). The learning rates for different tasks vary. While target detection and spatial orientation are almost immediate, discrimination of horizontal and vertical lines and direction of movement takes some practice. The fast recognition of ordinary objects usually takes ten hours of learning (Lenay et al. 2003:279). A crucial precondition for learning to take place is that the subject must be allowed to manipulate the camera and actively engage with the sequence of image capturing. A series of static forms on the tactile matrix does not facilitate learning, and feedback on discriminatory performance is essential (Sampaio 1995).

Note also that following this process of adaptation TVSS stimulation is not felt as if on the skin, as a kind of bodily sensation, but comes to be "projected" into a reference frame external to the immediate point of vibrotactile contact with the device. The tactile stimulation that conveys information about distal objects is readily distinguished from local irritations on the skin due to the electrode matrix. As Lenay et al. write, "Initially, the subject only feels a succession of stimulations on the skin. But after the learning process...the subject ends up neglecting these tactile sensations, and is aware only of stable objects at a distance, "out there" in front of him" (2003:279).

Thus, TVSS users perceive objects as residing in a space removed from them which, in this regard, is analogous to the visual field. This observation contrasts with Martin's hypothesis that objects felt by touch must appear as impingements on the bodily contour, but not contained within the sense field of that modality. As Lenay et al. (2003:282) continue,

> the subject appears to ignore the position of the tactile stimulations (unless he consciously refocuses his attention on that aspect of the situation) to the benefit of an apprehension of the spatial position of the light source. Conversely, artificial stimuli produced independently of the movement of the finger on which the photoelectric cell is placed are not associated with a distal perception, but continue to be perceived proximally at the level of the skin. Similarly, if the movements [of the perceiver] cease, the distal spatial perception disappears.

These authors describe an entirely pared-down experimental system, using just a single photodiode on the index finger of one hand and a vibrator on the index finger of the other. Once the subject experiences the correlations between exploratory movement, object presence, and tactile stimulation, the vibrations induce perception of a distal object, even when the position of the vibrator on the hand is altered. That the effect requires only a TVSS of a very minimal sort is notable, as it shows that spatial perception of objects within a field comparable to a visual field can arise with sensory capacities that otherwise bear little resemblance to vision.

We now consider what happens during the periods of acclimatization. The learning required for TVSS use is understood to be correlated with structural and physiological changes in the brain, including the visual cortex. In one neuroimaging study Ptito, Moesgaard, and Gjedde (2005) trained eleven early blind participants to discriminate the orientation of a target using the 12×12 electrode TDU (tongue display unit). After one hour of practice, the blind participants showed significantly increased activity in the visual cortex when performing the task, activity not found in the positron emission tomography (PET) scans prior to training. In other words, learning to use TVSS involved the recruitment of new sensory areas of the brain that were not activated initially. It is interesting to compare this study with the long-standing observation that Braille reading involves the recruitment of the visual cortex, even in bindfolded sighted participants undergoing prolonged visual deprivation (Kauffman et al. 2002; Pascual-Leone et al. 2006).

2.2. IMPORTANCE OF NEUROPLASTICITY

The imaging results of Ptito et al. (2005) are unsurprising. Bach-y-Rita and Kercel (2003) state: "Sensory substitution is . . . only possible because of brain plasticity." It is worth pausing here to consider why this is so. The fact that the brain is "plastic" throughout its life span is increasingly recognized to be key to understanding many of its functions, not only in memory and learning but also for perceptual and cognitive processes as well as recovery after injury. Profound changes in the organization of sensory systems occur not only after contact with substitution devices but also as a result of sensory loss or temporary sensory deprivation (Büchel, C. et al. 1998; Kauffman et al. 2002; Pascual-Leone et al. 2006; Merabet and Pascual-Leone 2010; Bubic et al. 2010). It is often noted that the brain of nonsighted individuals "compensates" for the loss by recruiting visual areas of the brain in tactile and auditory tasks, and the extent of compensation does indeed correlate with enhanced behavioral performance. For example, certain blind individuals such as Daniel Kish have learned to navigate through crowded areas using an echolocation technique, making click noises with the tongue and attending to the echoes to sense approaching obstacles. Thaler, Arnott, and Goodale (2011), using functional magnetic resonance imaging (fMRI) data on two individuals who lost sight either in childhood or adolescence, have published results indicating that the primary visual cortex is involved in the utilization of echo information for detecting objects in space. In other words, the self-motivated learning of echolocation has caused the visual cortex to become involved in a nonvisual spatial task.

Neuroplasticity can involve changes in the number and strength of synaptic connections, metabolic changes, and even growth of new neurons (neurogenesis) in the adult brain. What is essential for the effective operation of TVSS is either the growth or reinforcement of peripheral connections from the substituting modality to the central brain areas that typically receive information from the substituted modality.[8] This allows for the substituting sense to receive stimulation in a format that is unusual for that modality—such as the optic flow information in TVSS— and for that stimulus to be interpreted in an appropriate way—in this example, as a "looming" object.

Plasticity also occurs in motor areas of the brain, regions involved in orchestrating the movements of eyes and hands (Ptito et al. 2005). As we have seen, practice in controlling the TVSS camera is crucial to developing proficiency, and this is because perception is at least in part a sensory-motor activity (Findlay and Gilchrist 2003). So for effective use of TVSS the subject must learn a pattern of movements that optimize the capture of visual information and these must become automatic through long-term structural changes in the brain.

We emphasize that the plasticity observed following TVSS is not inherently different from neuroplasticity in other contexts, such as normal development, skill learning, and compensation following brain injury or sensory deprivation (for survey, see Shaw & McEachern 2001). TVSS consequently piggybacks on the pre-existing tendency of the nervous system to reorganize itself in response to changing external stimulation and internal conditions. So even though one might object that we appeal to a sensory system in a technologically modified state in our case against Martin, and that this is irrelevant to discussion of the nature of the sense, our response is that the argument we employ does not depend on TVSS per se, but on the very possibility of neuroplasticity. And this plasticity is also evidenced in other cases of perceptual learning just noted.

We can now recapitulate the case against assumption (A), that the sensory modalities are fixed in the way they represent objects in space. When the sense of touch is presented with optical stimuli and trained to respond to this new type of information, new connections are utilized, linking areas of the brain involved in touch and those normally involved in vision. A consequence is that the touch modality becomes more vision-like, especially in its representation of the spatial location of objects at a distance from the body. Just as a visual image is not felt as a local irritation of the retina, a TVSS image is not felt as a stimulation of the skin. The sense of touch need not literally feel in touch with the objects it perceives. Contra Martin's idea of incommensurate sensory-spatial fields, the sense usually characterized as proximal can indeed become distal.

---

[8] The choice between growth and reinforcement of connections is not exclusive, however.

2.3. OVERSTATING THE TVSS CASE

At this point it might be objected that even in normal touch, perceptions are not felt as local irritations of the skin. In an oft-cited paper on active touch, Gibson (1962) describes the key role of purposeful movement when the sense of touch is used for gathering information about the shape of objects. When subjects were engaged in such "active touch" tasks they were unable to report the flux of sensations on the skin, only the rigid edges of the object felt. He states: "One perceives the object-form but not the skin-form. The latter is, in fact, continually changing as the fingers move in various ways. It is almost completely unreportable, whereas the pattern of physical corners and edges seems to emerge in experience" (Gibson 1962:482). In active touch Martin's proposed body-field is transparent, and the perception lands firmly on the external object. Gibson contrasts these reports with his subjects' observations of passive touch, cases where the experimenter induces the same tactile sensations as would be caused by the subject's manual exploration. In those cases, the cutaneous events become distinct to the subject as something happening to the body surface.

From this, Gibson concludes that there is a mode of touching that is vision-like. He observes: "vision and touch have nothing in common *only when they are conceived as channels for pure and meaningless sensory data*. When they are conceived instead as channels for information-pickup, having active and exploratory sense organs, they have much in common" Gibson (1962:490; original emphasis). So even in sighted subjects and without technological intervention, there is flexibility in whether tactile sensations are felt as patterns of pressure on the skin or contours of external objects, depending on whether the subject is involved in an active perceptual task.

So we must be careful not to overstate the TVSS case. TVSS furnishes us with a quick rebuttal of one obstacle to a general account of perceptual systems, such that we need no longer assume that there is a fundamental, insurmountable difference between the way the modalities of vision and touch represent objects in space. This is because, as we have seen, touch can readily be repurposed to utilize visual information, and there is imaging evidence that cortical plasticity is involved in this process. Yet the discussion of active touch gives us reason to think that vision and touch might not be so different to begin with. We argue in the proceeding section that the successful functioning of TVSS is also due to the inherent complexity of the touch modality in how it represents objects in space. There is more to the story than just cross-modal plasticity.

On the other hand, our case study of TVSS does not by any means demonstrate that vision and touch are completely substitutable, and this leaves room for anyone arguing for a negative response to the MMQ to posit that there is an insurmountable difference between vision and touch other than the distal-cutaneous distinction in spatial perception that we have addressed in this section. Interestingly, some rather strong claims have been made for TVSS as evidencing the substitutability of vision by machine-aided touch. So before moving on to the next section, we should pause briefly to evaluate some of these claims and show why our final case against Martin cannot be made from TVSS alone.

Although somewhat subject to marketing hyperbole, the trademarking and use of the term "Brainport" are significant, heralding a new kind of technology that bypasses peripheral sensory limitations. Among the Wicab company's online promotional material, a short video includes the line: "your brain is what really sees, not your eyes." The implication is that this technology creates a new portal into the brain, bypassing the diseased or damaged eye and optic nerves, thus allowing the subject to see again. Such taglines imply that the process of seeing is straightforwardly a case of directing optical information to the skin through technological means, from where it will be channeled to the brain. Because of neural plasticity, the brain can use information from the tongue as if it came from the eye, resulting in sensory interchange.

There are numerous reasons to be skeptical about such claims for the power of TVSS. A primary issue is that cortical reorganization is limited in adults. Even if a complete rewiring of somatosensory connections to the visual cortex might be possible for the very immature brain, this is beyond the capability of the adult brain. In their review, Bavelier and Neville (2002:446) revisit Hubel and Wiesel's idea of a critical period for forging useful connections to sensory cortices. Although the physiology is more complex than Hubel and Wiesel envisaged, with much plasticity occurring beyond critical periods, it is still true to say that the immature brain has a degree of plasticity that is lost to the adult one. Accordingly, Bubic et al. (2010:368) recommend introduction to sensory substitution devices as early as possible in childhood to maximize the potential benefit. To reiterate, if TVSS could demonstrate that vision and touch were completely interchangeable, even in adulthood, then the case against Martin might be closed. This is not so, but we have indeed seen that the spatial "fields" of vision and touch are subject to alteration with TVSS use, and this challenges Martin's assumption (A) of a fixed difference between these modalities with respect to spatial awareness. In the next section we address the other assumption (B), that each modality uses only one type of spatial representation.

3. Functional Substitution

At the end of section 2 we emphasized that TVSS does not in itself support any strong claims that vision and touch are interchangeable modalities. Consequently, there remains room for our opponent to posit an irreconcilable difference in the spatial representation afforded by vision and by touch, other than the distal-cutaneous distinction that was challenged earlier. It is reasonable to think that the performance of TVSS is restricted by the nature of the sensory systems involved, such that they are never fully substitutable. However, it would be too hasty to concede immediately that no general account of them could ever be formulated. Our task in this section is to question what obstacles to sensory substitution arise from the architecture of vision and touch but also, conversely, to explore how certain kinds of substitution are made possible due to preexisting commonalities across these modalities. In this section we introduce the weaker notion of "functional substitution" and show that even this has positive implications for the MMQ. In other words, there need only be a "weak" functional equivalence rather than a full blown "strong" substitution to undermine both obstacles to a unified sensory philosophy.

One factor limiting sensory substitution is the enormous difference in the spatial resolution of pressure receptors on the skin and photoreceptors in the eye. So even if technological advances deliver TDUs with a far higher resolution than the current 25×25 array available, the device will meet the inherent limits of vibrotactile discrimination and the density of nerve endings in the associated body parts. Regardless of the possibilities of cortical reorganization, the number and distribution of cutaneous nerve endings is not subject to neuroplasticity. Bach-y-Rita and Kercel (2003) argue that such low tactile resolution is not actually an obstacle to TVSS replacing sight, but this is the case only if one constrains the definition of sight to certain coarse discriminations or optically induced responses, such as the recognition of large projected shapes, or the ability to dodge a "looming" object. The acuities attained through earlier incarnations of the "lollipop," as reported by Sampaio et al. (2001), are actually so poor that a person performing at this level would be classified as legally blind.[9]

Another constraint is imposed by the hardware of the body. As noted, the subject's active control of the TVSS camera is a requirement for learning to interpret the vibrotactile patterns. Efficient manipulation of the camera is essential for strong perceptual performance, a sensorimotor skill that develops with prolonged use of TVSS. However, if the subject's viewpoint is controlled through directing the head-mounted eyeglass camera, this involves orienting the head in its entirety and will never be as fluid or rapid as the automatic and largely unconscious control of ocular movements. Saccades, the ballistic type of eye movement used for most tasks such as scanning scenes, examining objects, and reading, are actually the fastest movements made by the human body. An adult engaged in a natural viewing task makes three to five saccades each second, and saccadic reaction times can be as short as 100 milliseconds (Fischer and Weber 1993), whereas the minimum reaction time for a manual response is more than twice as long at 250 milliseconds (Kirchner and Thorpe 2006). Against the assertion within the Brainport™ promotional material, that it is the brain that sees rather than the eyes, the ocular-motor

---

[9] See Loomis et al. (2012) for a detailed discussion of the limitations of TVSS arising from the relative lack of receptor density and neural "bandwidth" in the sensory periphery, when touch is compared to the visual system.

system performs an active—indeed, almost hyperactive—perceptual process that TVSS systems are unlikely to replicate in the near future.[10]

Nevertheless, we know that in some cases, according to certain functional measures such as shape and size discrimination, substitution is deemed successful. What makes it work in those cases, and according to what specific criteria of success? Is it simply the greater degree of neuroplasticity found in those sensory subsystems? Or is it that certain functions or submodalities can be readily substituted because of the existence of corresponding functions in the substituting sense? We now concentrate on this last proposal, but note that plasticity is still crucial even for this limited form of substitution, evidenced by the training periods required. The idea we wish to convey is that these functionally defined systems are channels or streams within which plasticity can most usefully occur in response to TVSS.

Such considerations will give us reason to reject (B), the assumption of the uniformity of individual modalities in their representation of objects in space. This assumption stood behind a negative thesis that there cannot be a general account of the senses. We describe how there is variety in the spatial reference frames employed by individual modalities. As we saw in the TVSS example, touch, as well as vision, may use object-centered (allocentric) rather than body-centered (egocentric) frames of reference for certain tasks, and in fact this is corroborated in the psychology literature (see Millar 2006; Klatzky 1998). Sensory substitution is possible because of such similarities across certain modalities, and can be thought of as expanding the repertoire of tasks for which touch uses object-centered representations. As we will see in the later example that employs minimal technological intervention, the kinds of reference frames available to a particular modality set out the parameters for successful substitution, and some possible explanations for this are discussed. First, a brief account of an example of weak "functional substitution" will set this up.

3.1. LESSONS IN BRAILLE

The ideas developed in this section are best introduced by considering a very different kind of sensory aid—Braille. It is revealing to compare the technology of writing with sensory substitution technologies. Written scripts are means for efficiently converting aural phonemes into visual graphemes or pictograms. Braille, in turn, recodes the visual alphabet into manually perceptible sequences of characters. We refer to this as a "functional substitution" (after Klatzky, personal

---

[10] Hurley (1998) and Noë (2004) have made much of the research on ocular-motor activity to ground the claim that perception is a kind of action, and that motor and sensory systems cannot actually be separated. However, these facts about ocular-motor control stand against their strong claims about TVSS being a kind of vision (Hurley & Noë 2003). Until camera control can even approach the precision and rapidity of normal ocular-motor control, TVSS enhanced touch will never be fully functionally equivalent to vision.

communication) as opposed to a "sensory substitution" because the substitution applies to the specific act of reading and is not a general correspondence between sense modalities.[11] The transfer is possible because both visual and touch modalities are able to represent a sequence of small characters that are individuated by relatively subtle spatial details. These details rely on the consistent application of an allocentric reference frame for their disambiguation, for example, the two slanted lines of a capital A, or top left dot of the Braille A.

In such cases it is useful to characterize the perceptual function non-modally, for example, as the mapping of nearby objects in allocentric coordinates, or the precise localization of lines or dots on a page. Still, one modality may be more capable in this task than another. As Kauffman et al. (2002) report, those sighted individuals who do learn Braille end up relying on visual rather than haptic recognition of the characters. But even if visual input dominates when sight is intact, the reading function need not be thought of as necessarily visual, since when necessary touch can substitute for vision and perform the function. It is a function that is readily substituted for, even if the entire modality is not thereby substituted. This is another reason we talk of Braille as a functional rather than simply a sensory substitution.

It is significant, however, that Braille signs are not just Roman letters raised from a surface. To maximize the capacity of the haptic system, configurations of raised dots are used instead. For example, Loomis (1990) reported that the ability of blindfolded sighted subjects to identify raised letters and digits was poorer (40% accuracy) than their ability in recognizing Braille characters (56% accuracy). This indicates that the difference in the way that spatial information is gathered by the haptic and visual systems is notable, affects discriminatory performance, and is not readily overcome with training and the resultant brain plasticity.

Functional substitution is possible when a task—and potentially some brain region required for it—can be characterized non-modally, and when the substituted and substituting sense share some features in common regarding how they represent objects and space. However, it is critical to acknowledge the variability within each modality in the tasks it performs, and the ways in which it performs them. We replace assumption (B), that each sense is monothematic or uniform in its representation of space, with a picture in which modalities contain within themselves numerous functional streams requiring different spatial reference frames, some of which may be similar to those of other modalities (see Figure 17.1).

Another surprising finding consistent with our picture of partially overlapping functional commonalities is the difficulty in recognizing a two-dimensional raised line drawing of an everyday object by touch alone, a kind of recognition that we

---

[11] Loomis et al. (2012) are not optimistic about the prospects for general purpose sensory substitution technologies that can be used across a range of everyday tasks, and they argue that research efforts should be directed toward new technologies for functional substitution (in their terminology, "special purpose sensory substitution").

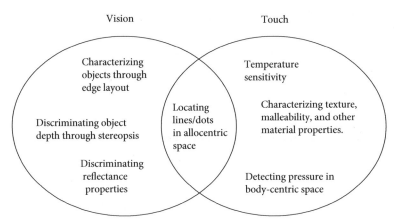

FIGURE 17.1. *A representative but not exhaustive depiction of the functions of visual and tactile modalities. Where functions overlap, the potential for substitution increases.*

do effortlessly and instantaneously by sight (Lederman et al. 1990). Blindfolded subjects are correct only on 34% of trials when given two minutes of exploration time. Subjects achieved up to 100% accuracy at recognizing *actual* objects haptically within just one to two seconds (Klatzky, Lederman, & Metzger 1985). In that case, material cues were present, such as the texture of the surface, and no three-dimensional to two-dimensional projection was involved. Klatzky and Lederman declare that "haptic object identification cannot rely virtually entirely on information about the spatial layout of edges, as appears to be the case in vision," and "material properties were shown to be more available than spatially coded properties under haptic exploration" (2003:116). Put simply, a two-dimensional projection of a three-dimensional object is decoded by the visual system with ease, whereas the haptic system struggles to make sense of this kind of spatial information. Even so, the haptic system is not deficient in all kinds of spatial tasks.

Because neuroanatomical knowledge is incomplete, we can only speculate about the extent to which certain cortical areas are modality specific, cross-modal, or non-modal. When the "input" for a task is provided by one sensory modality or another, the "processing" need not be served by a modality-specific brain region. What we do know is that the anatomical and physiological picture is complex, with neurons and circuits having different levels of task and modality specialization, and all contributing to the execution of these perceptual functions. For instance, Millar (2006:31) writes:

> The specialized sensory, visual, tactile, and movement analyses are not only processed further in dedicated visual, tactile, and motor areas of the brain. Inputs from these areas also converge in multiple, distributed brain areas that are involved in diverse spatial tasks.

Braille, in fact, provides an excellent example of the nonspecialized and distributed nature of sensory and spatial tasks. In oft-cited work, blind Braille experts show activity in areas of the visual cortex during reading (Cohen et al. 1997; Hamilton and Pascual-Leone 1998). Further studies provide evidence that this activity is functionally necessary and not merely epiphenomenenal. Braille readers receiving transcranial magnetic stimulation (TMS) to disrupt activity in the visual cortex find they are temporarily unable to distinguish the characters (Kupers et al. 2007). James et al. (2006) report that an extremely proficient Braille reader who suffered a stroke affecting her visual cortex subsequently lost her ability to interpret Braille. Now, while appropriation of the visual cortex for tactile processing was earlier described as an indication of the power of neuroplasticity, it is necessary to qualify this view. Pascual-Leone and colleagues present an alternative hypothesis, arguing that the visual cortex receives nonvisual inputs even in sighted individuals, and that these are "unmasked" under conditions of visual deprivation:

> A sense-specific brain region like the "visual cortex" may be visual only because we have sight and because the kinds of computations performed by the striate cortex are best suited for retinal, visual information. For example, we might postulate that the "visual cortex" is involved in discriminating precise spatial relations of local, detail [*sic*] features of an object or scene, which might be more advantageously done using visual than other sensory modalities. However, in the face of visual deprivation or well-chosen, challenging tasks, the striate cortex may unmask its tactile and auditory inputs to implement its computational functions on the available nonvisual sensory information.[12] (Pascual-Leone et al. 2006:173)

In support of this view, these authors report that sighted people *can* learn to read Braille haptically, and visual cortical activity is observed, but only if they spend a week under conditions of complete visual deprivation and are provided ample training in Braille use (see also Kauffman et al. 2002). Not only does this haptically evoked visual activity appear rapidly, but it disappears even more rapidly, typically within twenty-four hours of the subjects' blindfolds being removed. The results suggest that the somatosensory input to the visual cortex exists already in the sighted, as there is insufficient time in the course of the experiment for entirely new neural pathways to grow. So, in support of a positive answer to the MMQ, the visual cortex can be thought of not only as a brain region that plastically adapts to receive tactile stimulation but also as one that is somewhat non-modal originally. This provides one reason to think of the functions served by the visual cortex as suitable for general rather than modality-specific analysis.

To sum up, the apparent substitutability of certain sensory functions is not due to unconstrained plasticity but rather to the plastic reinforcement of one aspect of the substituting modality (e.g., fine spatial discrimination in an external spatial reference frame) that was preexistent but overshadowed by the substituted modality.

---

[12] Also described as the "metamodal brain" hypothesis. See note 2 earlier.

This conclusion also gives us grounds to reject the assumption of the uniformity of each sensory modality with respect to spatial representation (B), which was the other reason for dismissing the possibility of a general account of perception. One cannot assert that there is an irreconcilable difference between vision and touch, *tout court*, if within each of these modalities there are various functional streams, some of which do comparable things haptically as are typically done visually. The most obvious counterevidence to (B) is the work showing that the touch modality uses external spatial frames (allocentric coordinates) for certain tasks, just as with vision, and is not restricted to a body-centered space, as Martin assumes.

4. Conclusions

In the last two sections we removed a pair of obstacles to a general account of the senses. But does the material covered in this chapter also provide us with resources for a positive case for unification? Well, the idea that certain functions are substitutable because of the similarity of operation across modalities, and the sharing of neural resources for these tasks (which is enhanced by brain plasticity, even in adults) gives grounds for a tentatively positive response to the MMQ. At this stage we clearly cannot claim to have a general account of all perceptual processes, including ones such as color discrimination that are not mirrored in any modalities other than vision. However, for certain perceptual processes a general, non-modal description is arguably an improvement on a modality-specific one. That is, for a set of subfunctions of touch that have more in common with certain visual functions than with other tactile ones, it makes sense to integrate the theoretical account with the visual cases rather than mix together some rather dissimilar processes all under the unified heading of "touch." Whether the accounts of all perceptual functions can ultimately be integrated is a question for another day. At least we have challenged some assumptions that might otherwise prevent us from even inquiring.

Note that our tentatively positive response to the MMQ comes with an important caveat regarding the relevance of subpersonal neuroscientific data to a theory of perception that is traditionally pitched at the personal level. If there is evidence for general non-modal spatial processing, this suggests a positive answer only insofar as the senses can be theorized at the subpersonal, neurophysiological level. However, this does not necessarily translate into a positive response that would satisfy the requirements of a psychological or philosophical theory of perception because unity at the neural level clearly does not entail unity in any phenomenological aspects. Psychophysical experiments need to be performed to demonstrate that neural commonalities are mirrored in behavior. Our examples of TVSS and Braille fulfill this requirement because they point to cortical activity that is not unique to one modality (e.g., visual cortex activity during TVSS or haptic discrimination tasks) but does indeed correlate with a subject's ability to perform equivalent tasks with different modalities.

We have argued that a general philosophical account of perception is not impossible. This chapter is, by necessity, an overview of a wide range of interlinked issues. A key question remaining is over what purpose any conceptual unification of the senses might serve. Indeed, there is much scope for future work looking specifically at different spatial tasks and the detailed processes of Braille learning, tactile mapping, and spatial navigation. It remains to be seen if this work can only proceed in a case by case basis or if more general principles of non-modal function or cross-modal interaction are likely to emerge.

Acknowledgments

We would like to thank Roberta Klatzky for a fascinating conversation and perceptual demonstration that aided a rethinking of this chapter. We thank the editors of this volume for their valuable comments on an early version, and the reviewer for Oxford University Press for further useful suggestions.

M. C. was supported by a Value in People award from the Wellcome Trust. M. P. wishes to thank Jacki Fisher at the UPMC Sensory Substitution Lab, University of Pittsburgh, for a demonstration of the BrainPort™ TVSS.

References

Bach-y-Rita, P. (1972). *Brain Mechanisms in Sensory Substitution*. New York: Academic Press.

Bach-y-Rita, P., K. A. Kaczmarek, M. E. Tyler, and J. Garcia-Lara. (1998). "Form perception with a 49-point electrotactile stimulus array on the tongue." *Journal of Rehabilitation Research Development* 35: 427–430.

Bach-y-Rita, P. and S. W. Kercel. (2003). "Sensory substitution and the human–machine interface." *TRENDS in Cognitive Sciences* 7: 541–546.

Bavelier, D. and H. Neville (2002). "Cross-modal plasticity: Where and how?" *Nature Reviews Neuroscience* 3: 443–452.

Berkeley, G. (1709/1996). *An Essay towards a New Theory of Vision*. London, Everyman.

BrainPort-Technologies. "BrainPort Vision." 2011, from http://vision.wicab.com/index.php.

Bubic, A., E. Striem-Amit, and A. Amedi. (2010). "Large-Scale Brain Plasticity Following Blindness and the Use of Sensory Substitution Devices." In *Multisensory Object Perception in the Primate Brain*, ed. M. J. Naumer and J. Kaiser. Berlin, Springer.

Büchel, C., C. Price, R. S. J. Frackowiak, and K. Friston. (1998). "Different activation patterns in the visual cortex of late and congenitally blind subjects." *Brain* 121: 409–419.

Chirimuuta, M. (2011). "Touchy-Feely Colour." In *New Directions in Colour Studies*, ed. C. Biggam Hough and D. Simmons. Amsterdam: John Benjamins.

Cohen, L. G., P. Celnik, et al. (1997). "Functional relevance of cross-modal plasticity in blind humans." *Nature* 389: 180–183.

Csordas, T. (1994). *Embodiment and Experience: The Existential Ground of Culture and Self.* Cambridge: Cambridge University Press.

Degenaar, M. (1996). *Molyneux's Problem: Three Centuries of Discussion on the Perception of Forms*. London: Kluwer Academic.

"Electronic lollipop 'allowing blind people to see with their tongues.'" (2009). *Daily Telegraph*, 1 September.

Evans, G. (1985). "Molyneux's Question." In *Gareth Evans: Collected Papers*, ed. A. Phillips. Oxford: Clarendon Press.

Findlay, J. M. and I. D. Gilchrist. (2003). *Active Vision: The Psychology of Looking and Seeing*. Oxford: Oxford University Press.

Fischer, B. and H. Weber. (1993). "Express saccades and visual attention." *Behavioral and Brain Sciences* 16: 553–610.

Fulkerson, M. (2011). "The unity of haptic touch." *Philosophical Psychology* 24(4): 493–516.

Gallagher, S. (2005). *How the Body Shapes the Mind*. Oxford: Clarendon Press.

Gibson, J. J. (1962). "Observations on active touch." *Psychological Review* 69: 477–491.

Gibson, J. J. (1966). *The Senses Considered as Perceptual Systems*. Boston: Houghton Mifflin.

Gibson, J. J. (1979). *The Ecological Approach to Visual Perception*. Hillsdale, NJ: Lawrence Erlbaum.

Hamilton, R. and A. Pascual-Leone. (1998). "Cortical plasticity associated with Braille learning." *Trends in Cognitive Science* 2: 168–174.

Heil, J. (1983). *Perception and Cognition*. Berkeley: University of California Press.

Held, R., Y. Ostrovsky, B. de Gelder, T. Gandhi, S. Ganesh, U. Mathur, and P. Sinha (2011). "The newly sighted fail to match seen with felt." *Nature Neuroscience* 14: 551–553.

Howes, D. (2003). *Sensual Relations: Engaging the Senses in Culture and Social Theory*. Ann Arbor: University of Michigan Press.

Hurley, S. (1998). *Consciousness in Action*. Cambridge, MA: Harvard University Press.

Hurley, S. and A. Noë. (2003). "Neuralplasticity and consciousness." *Biology and Philosophy* 18: 131–168.

James, T. W., K. H. James, K. Humphrey, and M. A. Goodale. (2006). "Do Visual and Tactile Object Representations Share the Same Neural Substrate?" In *Touch and Blindness: Psychology and Neuroscience*, ed. M. A. Heller and S. Ballesteros. Mahwah, NJ: Lawrence Erlbaum.

Jay, M. (1994). *Downcast Eyes*. Berkeley: University of California Press.

Jonas, H. (1954). "The nobility of sight." *Philosophy and Phenomenological Research* 14(4): 507–519.

Katz, D. (1925/1989). *The World of Touch*. Hillsdale, NJ: Lawrence Erlbaum.

Kauffman, T., H. Theoret, and Pascual-Leone, A. (2002). "Braille character discrimination in blindfolded human subjects." *NeuroReport* 13: 1–4.

Keeley, B. L. (2002). "Making sense of the senses: Individuating modalities in humans and other animals." *Journal of Philosophy* 99(1): 5–28.

Keeley, B. L. (2009). "The Role of Neurobiology in Differentiating the Senses." In *Oxford Handbook of Philosophy and Neuroscience*, ed. J. Bickle. Oxford: Oxford University Press.

Kemp, S. and G. J. O. Fletcher. (1993). "The medieval theory of the inner senses." *American Journal of Psychology* 106(4): 559–576.

Kirchner, H. and S. J. Thorpe. (2006). "Ultra-rapid object detection with saccadic eye movements: visual processing speed revisited." *Vision Research* 46:1762–1776.

Klatzky, R. L. (1998). "Allocentric and Egocentric Spatial Representations: Definitions, Distinctions, and Interconnections." *Proceedings, Spatial Cognition, An Interdisciplinary Approach to Representing and Processing Spatial Knowledge*. Berlin: Springer-Verlag: 1–18.

Klatzky, R. L., S. J. Lederman, and V. A. Metzger. (1985). "Identifying objects by touch: An "expert system." *Perception & Psychophysics* 37: 299–302.

Kupers, R., M. Pappens, and A. M. de Noordhout. (2007). "rTMS of the occipital cortex abolishes Braille reading and repetition priming in blind subjects." *Neurology* 68: 691–693.

Lederman, S. J., R. L. Klatzky, C. Chataway, and C. D. Summers. (1990). "Visual mediation and the haptic recognition of two-dimensional pictures of common objects." *Perception & Psychophysics* 47: 54–64.

Lenay, C., O. Gapenne, S. Hanneton, C. Marque, and C. Genouelle. (2003). "Sensory Substitution: Limits and Perspectives." In *Touching for Knowing*, ed. Y. Hatwell, A. Streri, and E. Gentaz. Amsterdam: John Benjamins.

Loomis, J. M. (1990). "A model of character recognition and legibility." *Journal of Experimental Psychology: Human Perception and Performance* 16(1): 106–120.

Loomis J. M., R. L. Klatzky, and N. A. Giudice. (2012) "Sensory Substitution of Vision: Importance of Perceptual and Cognitive Processing." In *Assistive Technology for Blindness and Low Vision*, ed. R. Manduchi and S. Kurniawan. Boca Raton, FL: CRC Press.

Lotze, Rudolf Hermann. (1885). *Microcosmus: An Essay Concerning Man and His Relation to the World*, 2 vols., trans. E. Hamilton and E. E. Constance Jones. Edinburgh: T. & T. Clark.

MacPherson, F. (2011). Taxonomising the senses. *Philosophical Studies* 153(1): 123–142.

Martin, M. G. F. (1992). "Sight and Touch." In *The Contents of Experience*, ed. T. Crane. Cambridge: Cambridge University Press.

Merabet, L. and A. Pascual-Leone. (2010). "Neural reorganization following sensory loss: The opportunity of change." *Nature Reviews Neuroscience* 11: 44–52.

Merleau-Ponty, M. (1992). *The Phenomenology of Perception*. London: Routledge.

Millar, S. (2006). "Processing Spatial Information from Touch and Movement: Implications from and for Neuroscience." In *Touch and Blindness: Psychology and Neuroscience*, ed. M. A. Heller and S. Ballesteros. Mahwah, NJ: Lawrence Erlbaum.

Milner, D. and M. A. Goodale. (1995). *The Visual Brain in Action*. Oxford: Oxford University Press.

Mishkin, M., L. G. Ungerleider, and K. A. Macko. (1983). "Object Vision and Spatial Vision: Two Cortical Pathways." *Trends in Neurosciences* 6: 414–417.

Morgan, M. J. (1977). *Molyneux's Question: Vision, Touch and the Philosophy of Perception*. Cambridge: Cambridge University Press.

Noë, A. (2004). *Action in Perception*. Cambridge, MA: MIT Press.

O'Shaughnessy, B. (1989). "The Sense of Touch." *Australasian Journal of Philosophy* 67(1): 37–58.

Pascual-Leone, A., A. Amedi., F. Fregni, and L. B. Merabet. (2005). "The plastic human brain cortex." *Annual Review of Neuroscience* 28: 377–401.

Pascual-Leone, A. and R. Hamilton. (2001). "The metamodal organization of the brain." *Progress in Brain Research* 134: 427–445.

Pascual-Leone, A., H. Theoret, L. Merabet, T. Kauffmann, and G. Schlaug. (2006). "The Role of Visual Cortex in Tactile Processing: A Metamodal Brain." In *Touch and Blindness: Psychology and Neuroscience,* ed. M. A. Heller and S. Ballesteros. Mahwah, NJ: Lawrence Erlbaum.

Paterson, M. (2006). "Seeing with the hands": Blindness, touch and the Enlightenment spatial imaginary." *British Journal of Visual Impairment* 24(2): 52–60.

Paterson, M. (2007). *The Senses of Touch.* Oxford: Berg.

Paterson, M. (2009). "Haptic geographies: Ethnography, haptic knowledges and sensuous dispositions." *Progress in Human Geography* 33(6): 766–788.

Paterson, M. (in press). *Seeing with the Hands: Philosophy and Blindness after Descartes and Diderot.* London: Reaktion.

Prinz, J. (2006). Putting the brakes on enactive perception. *Psyche* 12: 1–19.

Ptito, M., S. M. Moesgaard, A. Gjedde, and R. Kupers. (2005). "Cross-modal plasticity revealed by electrotactile stimulation of the tongue in the congenitally blind." *Brain* 128: 606–614.

Révész, G. (1950). *Psychology and Art of the Blind.* London: Longmans.

Riskin, J. (2002). *Science in the Age of Sensibility: The Sentimental Empiricists of the French Enlightenment.* Chicago: University of Chicago Press.

Rorty, R. (1979). *Philosophy and the Mirror of Nature.* Princeton, NJ: Princeton University Press.

Sampaio, E. (1995). Les substitutions sensorielles adaptées aux déficits visuels importants. In *Le déficit visuel. Des fondements neurophysiologiques à la réadaptation,* ed. A. B. Safran and A. Assmacopoulos. Paris: Masson.

Sampaio, E., S. Maris, and Bach-y-Rita, P. (2001). "Brain plasticity: 'Visual' acuity of blind persons via the tongue." *Brain Research* 908(2): 204–207.

Shaw, C. A. and J. McEachern, eds. (2001). *Toward a Theory of Neuroplasticity.* Philadelphia: Psychology Press.

Smith, A. D. (2002). *The Problem of Perception.* Cambridge, MA: Harvard University Press.

Spelke, E. S. (1998). "Nativism, empiricism, and the origins of knowledge." *Infant Behavior and Development* 21: 181–200.

Spence, C. and J. Driver. (2004). *Crossmodal Space and Crossmodal Attention.* Oxford: Oxford University Press.

Streri, A. and E. Gentaz. (2004). " Cross-modal recognition of shape from hand to eyes and handedness in human newborns." *Neuropsychologia* 42(10): 1365–1369.

Thaler, L., S. R. Arnott, and M. A. Goodale. (2011). "Neural Correlates of Natural Human Echolocation in Early and Late Blind Echolocation Experts." *PLoS ONE* e20162. DOI: 10.1371/journal.pone.0020162.

Visell, Y. (2009). "Tactile sensory substitution: Models for enaction in HCI." *Interacting with Computers* 21(1–2): 38–53.

von Senden, M. (1960 [1932]). *Space and Sight: The Perception of Space and Shape in the Congenitally Blind before and after Operation,* trans. P. Heath. London: Methuen.

Wiesel, T. and D. Hubel. (1963). "Single-cell responses in striate cortex of kittens deprived of vision in one eye." *Journal of Neurophysiology* 26: 1003–1017.

Wiesel, T. and D. Hubel. (1965). "Comparison of the effects of unilateral and bilateral eye closure on cortical unit responses in kittens." *Journal of Neurophysiology* 28(6): 1029–1040.

18

The Space of Sensory Modalities

Fiona Macpherson

1. Introduction

Is there a space of the sensory modalities? Such a space would be one in which we can represent all the actual, and at least some of the possible, sensory modalities. The relative position of the senses in this space would indicate how similar and how different the senses were from each other. The construction of such a space might reveal unconsidered features of the actual and possible senses, help us to define what a sense is, and provide grounds that we might use to decide what is one token sense rather than multiple token senses.

In this chapter, I explore, refine, and defend the idea that we can construct such a space—an idea that I briefly proposed in earlier work (Macpherson 2011a and 2011b). In doing so, I defend the idea from an objection that Richard Gray (2012) has voiced. Gray claims that the dimensions of the space of sensory modalities must generate a non-arbitrary ordering of the senses. He argues that we cannot find dimensions that do so. I disagree. I identify different ways in which a space could be arbitrary but I argue that we can define a space of the sensory modalities in a non-arbitrary manner. I give examples of what the dimensions might be.

In the next section of this chapter, I outline the background issues. I describe the debate about how we should individuate the senses. I summarise the position that I have argued for elsewhere (Macpherson 2011a and 2011b), namely, that the senses do not form natural kinds. They differ in degree and we should use all of the four standard criteria, which are typically taken to be competing criteria, to individuate the senses in a fine-grained manner. In section 3, I introduce the idea of the space of modalities and describe the role of the criteria for individuating the senses in building the space of sensory modalities. In section 4, I show that we can find dimensions that non-arbitrarily order the senses, focusing particularly on the sensory organ criterion. In section 5, I give examples of dimensions for the other criteria that meet the conditions of non-arbitrariness laid out in section 4. In section 6, I show that if one produces a high-dimensional space, then it is often possible to use principal component analysis (PCA) to produce a second space that has fewer dimensions but preserves all the similarity and difference relationships between the items plotted in the first space. One can also use the analysis to reduce the number of dimensions to any number that one wishes, if one is prepared to lose some similarity and difference data. However, the analysis ensures that as much data as possible is retained, compatible with the reduction. Such a reduction would allow us to reduce the space of the sensory modalities to three dimensions, allowing visualisation of the space of the senses. Finally, in that section, I discuss how this PCA may lead us to identify factors important for individuating the senses that we had not previously considered. And I describe how such analysis might make us reconsider our prior commitments concerning what the senses are, and what we should count as being token instances of senses.

2. Background Issues

There are several questions concerning the individuation of the senses that are distinct. Key among these are the following:

(a) How should we define what a sense is, rather than something that is not a sense? For example, what makes a sense different from an aardvark or an armadillo? Or different from a part of the body, like an arm or an artery? Or different from a bodily process, like arousal or arterisis?

(b) How do we determine what is one sense rather than multiple senses? For example, we know that while most people today think of touch as one sense, Plato held that it was three separate senses on phenomenological grounds: pressure, temperature, and pain (Classen 1993); and some modern scientists think likewise on the grounds that there are three distinctive types of receptors in the skin for detecting pressure, temperature, and pain (Craig 1996).

(c) What kind or type is a token sense, on the assumptions that it is indeed a sense, and that it is one and only one sense?[1]

The key question that is addressed in this chapter is (c), although, as we shall see, the answer to (c) may shed light on answers to (a) and (b).

Traditionally, there have been four main competing philosophical approaches to answering question (c). Each approach has identified a different criterion that should be used to determine what kind of sense a token sense is. The four criteria are these:

---

[1] Types are general sorts of things and tokens are particular concrete instances. (In this respect they are different from occurrences, which need not be concrete.) See Wetzel (2011).

(i)   *Representation*: a sense is the kind it is on account of the objects and
      properties that the experiences associated with that sense represent (or
      present) or about which the brain states associated with the sense carry
      information. For example, vision might be classified as the sense that
      represents three-dimensional coloured objects at a distance from our
      body. Touch might be categorised as the sense that represents the heat,
      texture, and shape of objects that press against our body. Hearing could
      be considered the sense that represents sounds around and in our body,
      and so on.

(ii) *Phenomenal character*: a sense is the kind it is in virtue of the nature of
      "what it is like" (Nagel 1974) for a subject to have the experiences that
      the sense produces. For example, typically, experiences produced by
      vision seem to us to have a certain subjective feel that is different from
      those of touch, which again is different from those of smell, taste, and
      hearing, and so on.

(iii) *Proximal stimulus*: a sense is the kind it is in virtue of the nature of the
      physical stimuli that stimulate the sense organ. For example, vision
      might be characterised as the sense that utilises electromagnetic waves,
      or those of 390–750 nanometres. Hearing could be regarded as that
      which makes use of pressure waves in a medium—or pressure waves
      between 0.0172 and 17.2 metres. Smell might be branded the sense
      whose proximal stimuli are volatile molecules.

(iv) *Sense organs*: a sense is the kind it is on account of the nature of the
      sensory organs and physiology, which may include the relevant parts of
      the brain, associated with it. For example one might claim that vision is
      the sense that uses eyes and, perhaps, the visual cortex. And hearing is
      the sense that utilises ears, and, perhaps, the sort of processing that the
      auditory cortex does, and likewise for the other senses.

I have argued (Macpherson 2011a and 2011b) that the senses cannot be clearly
divided up into a discrete and limited number of different kinds and that the differences between the senses amounts more to a difference of degree than of such
kinds. I will not go into all the details for thinking that here, but one reason is
the large number of actual senses that vary to a greater or lesser degree from the
human senses, and the existence of some that seem to share as many features with
one type of human sense as another. When we also consider the possible senses
that could exist, there seems no good principled way to carve up the senses into a
limited number of discrete kinds.

   Take vision as an example. There is 20/20 normal human vision. Slightly different are various forms of short- and long-sightedness, and the different forms
of colour blindness. More different still are the various forms of visual agnosia.
Then there is what we typically classify as vision in other creatures. For example,
consider bee 'vision' that detects ultra-violet, as well as the light visible to humans,

by means of five eyes of different types. Bee 'vision' is different from our vision in respect of the type of eyes being used. The proximal stimulus overlaps with that of human vision but includes also wavelengths of electromagnetic radiation smaller than those humans can detect. Like human vision, bee 'vision' can represent three-dimensional objects at a distance but, unlike human vision, it is sensitive to differences in surfaces that make them reflect more or less ultra-violet light. Is it similar enough to our vision to warrant the title of vision? And consider senses that are typically not classified as vision but which share features of human vision. For example, some snakes have an infra-red sense that detects electromagnetic waves of longer wavelength than visible light, which, like ordinary human vision, gives them information about three-dimensional objects at a distance from their body. The snakes' infra-red sensitive pits below their eyes are the organs of this sense. The pits are not usually classified as eyes, perhaps because the snakes have a sense that is more similar to our sight than their infra-red sense that utilises organs more like our eyes than their pits. However, it is unclear whether the pits should be thought of as a form of eye. Moreover, the proximal stimulus of their infra-red sense is not visible light but electromagnetic waves of longer wavelength. Is that proximal stimulus similar enough to that of human vision to allow us to count this sense as a form of vision? Consider also bat echo-location, which is like vision in that it detects three-dimensional objects at a distance from the body, yet it involves using organs best thought of as ears sensitive to sound waves. This sense is somewhat like human vision, somewhat like human hearing, and somewhat unique. Then there are possible forms of senses that we can imagine, such as the X-ray 'vision' of Superman, the 'vision' of the Terminator that can analyse something's composition, or a sense that combines features of vision, and other senses. Reflection on these cases suggests that there is no principled way to draw divisions between token instances of senses that carves them up into a limited discrete number of kinds.

If we adopt this view—that the senses do not come in a limited number of discrete kinds—we needn't suppose that the four criteria specified earlier are competing criteria. I've previously argued that the thought that they are competing arises only if we think that we need to pigeonhole each sense into a small number of discrete categories, such as the Aristotelian five: sight, hearing, touch, taste, and smell, or those plus a small number more. It is because the four criteria sometimes differ as to how they would categorise a sense, on the assumption that it has to be one of a fairly limited number, that it seems as if they are in competition. If we reject such a coarse-grained classification then we simply need note what each sense is like with respect to each of the four criteria. Reflecting on the properties that it has, we can note how similar or how different a sense is from one of the Aristotelian senses if we like, but we don't need to categorise it as being one or the other, or as something different altogether.

This view has the advantage that we can then use all the criteria in question to individuate the senses—which rightly allows all the criteria to matter to us practically and to matter to us given philosophical or scientific concerns. For example, suppose that I tell you that I am seeing the pot of green tea in front of me. I might do so because the representational criterion is of import—I want to let you know which properties of the teapot I can detect, such as its colour and shape at a distance from my body. Or the proximal stimulus criterion may be at issue: I may wish to indicate that you should leave the lights on if you want me to notice more about it. Or I may be trying to convey the phenomenal character of my experience to you. Finally, I may wish the sense-organ that is being used to be taken into account by you. I may be informing you that if you want me to continue using the sense that I am using to find out about the teapot then you had better not gouge out my eyes. Contra Nudds (2004), I don't believe that only one of these criteria is what makes the senses significant to us.

Finally, note two things. First, I want to be liberal about the criteria required to individuate the senses. If you think that others are needed and do not fall under those specified, then I would (prima facie) be happy to include them. Second, a problem for those who wish to divide the senses into natural kinds is how to use these criteria. For example, suppose we wanted to use the proximal stimulus criterion to determine which of a variety of candidate senses were vision, and which were not. We would have to decide what the proximal stimulus is in the case of vision. Should we say that vision is any sense that has electromagnetic waves as its proximal stimulus? Or is its proximal stimulus some limited portion of the electromagnetic spectrum, such as those waves detectable by human vision? My view allows us to neatly sidestep this worry. When we no longer need to identify the kind to which a sense belongs, we can simply note for each of the criteria the exact values that the sense takes with respect to it. This is an added advantage of my view.

3. The Role of the Criteria for Individuating the Senses

Suppose that one has noted for each sense the properties it has with respect to the four criteria mentioned: representation, phenomenal character, proximal stimulus, and sensory-organ. The senses, it seems, will be more or less different from one another. If we could construct a space of the sensory modalities, then we would be able to map how similar and how different the senses are from each other. We could place the senses in such a space in a way that recorded their nature vis-à-vis each of the criteria and which compared each to the other with regard to these. In my essay 'Individuating the Senses' (2011a), I expressed this as follows:

> We can think of [the] four criteria as defining a multidimensional space within which we can locate each of the … senses.… Thus, human vision, bee 'vision', snake infrared perception and TVSS perception would each be located at a different place in the multidimensional space.… Plotting the

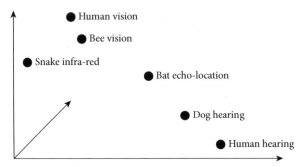

FIGURE 18.1. *An illustration of an imagined desirable space of the sensory modalities.*

actual senses in this space will allow one to see the similarities and connections between them yet, at the same time, to individuate the types in a
nonsparse, fine-grained manner.... [W]e might find that the actual senses
are to be found in clusters in this space. For we will find, for example, that
human vision and bee 'vision' are closer together in this space than human
vision and bat echolocation. Perhaps these clusters would correspond to the
Aristotelian senses or the Aristotelian senses plus a few others. I suspect this
might be the case. This would show us that the folk were trying to reflect
complex facts about the types of senses that we find in the world using an
over-simplistic model, but one whose origin is explicable given the facts.
(2011a: 37–38)

One might hope to get a space of the kind illustrated in Figure 18.1 (whose dimensions are unspecified as yet).

Such a space may shed light on the nature of the different kinds of senses and
may yield insights into our actual commitments concerning what the senses are
and what makes for one or more tokens of a sense or, indeed, suggest revisions to
our prior commitments, in a way that I outline later.

In such space we could plot types of senses like human vision, bee vision,
human smell, and so on. When doing so, we would plot values for normal or ideal
instances of each of these types of senses. Or we could do it for token instances
of each of the senses, such as my vision, your vision, your granny's vision, and
your dog's vision. In this chapter I will suppose that we are doing the former, but
for ease of exposition only. One could easily do either and, indeed, there may be
advantages of doing the latter; nothing I will go on to say will rule out one's so
doing.

This space of sensory modalities was only given a preliminary sketch in my
previous work. My earlier quotation says that the four criteria 'define a multidimensional space'. One might, not unreasonably, have taken this to mean that each
of the criteria forms a dimension of the space. However, it is very hard to see how
one could construct such dimensions, as Richard Gray (2012) has, rightly, com-
plained. More specifically, he claims that if we take the four criteria as dimensions,

then they could not generate a non-arbitrary ordering (that is, they would not generate an ordering that reflected actual similarity). Thus he concludes that such dimensions can't generate a space, that is to say a multidimensional ordering of the senses.

Compare a geometrical model of physical space, as illustrated in Figure 18.2. The x, y, and z dimensions represent orthogonal directions in space away from the common origin point. The value that defines the x dimension is distance in centimetres away from the origin in the x direction—and similarly for the y and z dimensions. These dimensions determine the similarity relations—in this case, distance relations—between all the points. The dimensions do not generate an arbitrary ordering because points that are plotted nearer to each other in the model space correspond to points that are closer together in physical space.

Unlike the dimensions of this Cartesian space, the four criteria for individuating the senses do not constitute suitable dimensions of a space. To illustrate, we might try to specify a proximal stimuli dimension on which we could plot the senses depending on what their proximal stimulus was. But such a dimension would not give us a non-arbitrary ordering. For example, there would be nothing to choose between the two different dimensions illustrated in Figure 18.3.

One might think that we can impose an ordering by just choosing one of the listed dimensions, rather than another. However, while we could just stipulate an ordering along a dimension, the position of any sense on the dimension would be

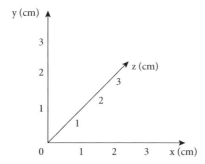

FIGURE 18.2. *Physical space defined by Cartesian coordinates.*

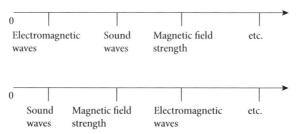

FIGURE 18.3. *Potential proximal stimuli dimensions.*

arbitrary. The space between any two senses would not represent actual similarities and differences between the senses.

Thus, it is clear that the four criteria can't *constitute* the dimensions of the space of the senses. However, instead, we can let the four criteria *determine* the dimensions that do constitute the space. It is in this sense that we should hold that the four criteria define a multidimensional space within which we can locate each of the senses. In other words, we should take each of the four criteria in turn and define a set of dimensions that captures the properties that the criterion identifies as being those that are important for individuating the senses. If we are careful, I believe that we can find suitable non-arbitrary dimensions of that kind that will together define the space of sensory modalities.

In the next section I illustrate at length how to find suitable non-arbitrary dimensions that correspond to the proximal stimulus criterion. One reason for picking this dimension is that it is a particularly tricky case and one that Gray highlights as being problematic. In looking at this criterion, I will identify features, besides non-arbitrariness, that any dimension used to construct the space of the sensory modalities must have. Thus, the lessons learned by considering the dimensions corresponding to the proximal stimulus criterion should be applied to the dimensions corresponding to the other criteria for individuating the senses. In the section after that, section 5, I also indicate, more briefly, how one might construct suitable dimensions for the other criteria.

4. Defining Suitable Dimensions

How do we come up with a set of dimensions that captures the similarities and differences between the senses with respect to their different proximal stimuli? We can look to physics to specify all the nomologically possible kinds of proximal stimuli—for example, different frequencies of electromagnetic waves, sound waves, magnetic field strength; different temperatures and pressures; different amounts of chemicals in the air, chemicals in solution. With these different proximal stimuli identified we can create dimensions on which we can plot sensitivity to these stimuli. However, one has to be very careful in the way that one does this.

It is tempting, but as we will see ultimately wrong, to think that we can specify one dimension corresponding to sensitivity to each of the different kinds of stimuli that physics identifies, to yield a space containing the sort of dimensions depicted in Figure 18.4.

Note that an important and, for our purposes, very helpful fact about creating a space with a number of dimensions is that we don't have to order the dimensions that form a multidimensional space. In other words, if we have three dimensions—call them 1, 2, and 3—it doesn't matter if we make 1 the x dimension, 2 the y dimension, and 3 the z dimension, or whether we make 2 the x dimension, 1 the y dimension, and 3 the z dimension. One ends up with the same space either way. The naming of the dimensions as *x, y,* and *z* (and so on if more are required to form a higher-dimensional space) is purely for convenience of reference. Such naming makes no difference to the space created. In short, we simply need to identify dimensions and specify that they are joined together to form a space. We don't have to sequence the dimensions. This removes what one might have worried was a potential source of arbitrariness in the endeavour of creating the space of the sensory modalities. If there is no choice to be made about the order of the dimensions, there is no arbitrariness that could creep into that choice.

One might have thought that the dimensions in Figure 18.4 could be used to record the sensitivities of each sensory organ to kinds of proximal stimulus. For example, consider the dimension labelled 'sensitivity to electromagnetic waves'. We might think that we could construct a dimension that takes different lengths of electromagnetic wavelengths as its value and then record the sensitivities of the different senses on it. See Figure 18.5 for illustrative purposes, on which I have plotted the following: human vision, which is sensitive to what is often called 'visible light', about 400–700 nanometres; bee vision, which is sensitive to visible light plus some infra-red wavelengths; snake infra-red perception, which is sensitive in the infra-red area of the spectrum; and fictional X-ray and microwave senses. The

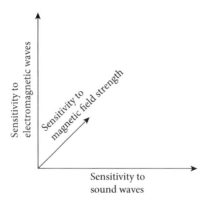

FIGURE 18.4. *Some dimensions one might think could be joined together in space corresponding to the proximal stimulus criterion.*

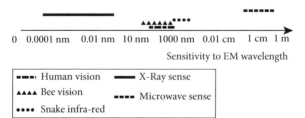

FIGURE 18.5. *A dimension (not to scale) recording sensitivity to electromagnetic wavelength with different senses mapped onto it. The different senses are shown at different heights above the dimension line only so that they can be clearly seen.*

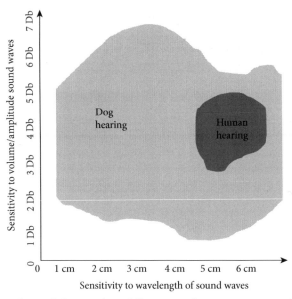

FIGURE 18.6. *A fictional plotting of two different senses' responsiveness to volume and wavelength of soundwaves in air.*

order of values on this dimension are not arbitrary. It is fixed by the specification of the dimension as being one of sensitivity to lengths of electromagnetic waves.

We can imagine joining together such dimensions to record further sensitivities of the senses to different proximal stimuli. Figure 18.6 provides rough illustration (although the values are not accurate). And further, we can imagine joining together yet more similar dimensions. See Figure 18.7, which consists of imagined values for different actual and non-actual senses. Thus, in such spaces we can see that we can plot not only actual senses but also possible senses, as illustrated.

However, as indicated earlier, using these particular dimensions—ones corresponding to sensitivities to different kinds of proximal stimuli—will not work. The reason is that there is not a way to plot at least one value for each sense on these dimensions. To see this, consider the 'sensitivity to electromagnetic wavelength' dimension, along the length of which we mark out the lengths of wavelengths, as in Figure 18.8.

On such a dimension there is no way to plot a value for a sense that is completely insensitive to the presence or absence of any electromagnetic frequencies, such as smell. How do we register a total lack of sensitivity to electromagnetic wavelength? Not by plotting the sense at 'o' for that means 'sensitive to o metres of electromagnetic wavelength', which means sensitive to the absence of electromagnetic wavelength. But smell is not sensitive to that. If it were, it would be able to register when there were no wavelengths present, rather than some. But it cannot do so. It is simply insensitive to both the presence and absence of electromagnetic waves.

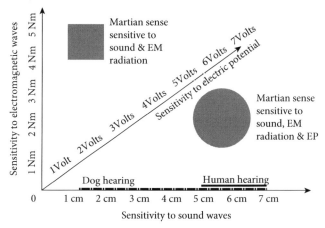

FIGURE 18.7. *Construction of space using dimensions corresponding to the proximal stimulus criterion and fictional values for human and dog hearing plotted together with possible alien senses.*

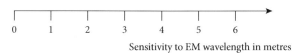

Sensitivity to EM wavelength in metres

FIGURE 18.8. *Sensitivity to EM wavelength dimension.*

To plot something in a multidimensional space, that thing must take at least one value on *each* dimension, for to put it in the space is to plot its position on each and every one of the dimensions that form the space. Thus, we cannot take sensitivities to general kinds of proximal stimuli as dimensions, as this does not allow us to plot on them senses that are not sensitive at all to that kind of proximal stimulus. So, we must find other dimensions that correspond to the proximal stimulus to form our space of sensory modalities.

As we have just seen, we cannot use dimensions corresponding to sensitivity to *kinds* of proximal stimuli, but we can move towards identifying suitable dimensions by considering more specific proximal stimuli. For example, consider a dimension that records the sensitivity of a sense to a specific wavelength of electromagnetic radiation, such as that illustrated in Figure 18.9.

Spectral sensitivity is often expressed as a quantum efficiency—the probability of getting a quantum reaction to a quantum of light. It is also sometimes expressed as a relative response, normalized to a peak value of 1, and quantum efficiency is used to specify the sensitivity at that peak.

On this dimension, the order of the values is not arbitrary. It is fixed by the specification of the dimension. And, importantly, every sense can take a value on the dimension. For example, smell, which is insensitive to 550nm electromagnetic waves, can take a value of zero on this dimension, for zero on this dimension

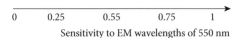

Sensitivity to EM wavelengths of 550 nm

FIGURE 18.9. *A dimension of sensitivity to 550 nanometre electromagnetic waves expressed as the relative response per light energy, normalized to a peak value of 1.*

means that a sense is not sensitive to this wavelength (not that it is sensitive to the absence of this wavelength). Clearly every sense can take a value on the dimension as either it is responsive or not to this wavelength: that exhausts the possibilities. And those facts can be recorded on this dimension.

We can have as many dimensions of this sort as we require—each corresponding to a different wavelength of the electromagnetic spectrum. For example, we can have one corresponding to a wavelength of 550 nm, one to 551 nm, one to 552 nm, or one to 550.5 nm, et cetera. Having infinite dimensions may be problematic for forming a space, but we can have as large a finite number of dimensions as we desire and that we think are required to capture differences between the senses. Similarly, we can have dimensions corresponding to sensitivities to different particular lengths of sound waves, particular strengths of electromagnetic fields, particular temperatures, particular pressures, particular chemicals in solution and in the air, and so on. We can now imagine a highly multidimensional space in which all the senses take a value along each of these dimensions.

But there is a problem with this solution. In constructing a space in which there are different dimensions corresponding to sensitivities to different wavelengths of electromagnetic radiation, we have lost a vital piece of similarity information we want to capture. One attractive feature of the otherwise flawed dimension drawn in Figure 18.5, a dimension recording sensitivity to different wavelengths of electromagnetic radiation, was that it captured the fact that senses that are sensitive to similar electromagnetic wavelengths are more similar to each other than those that are sensitive to different wavelengths. And the more overlap, the more similar they are. The less overlap, and the more they respond to very different wavelengths, the more different they are. For example, human vision is more similar to bee vision than to an X-ray sense, with respect to its sensitivity to electromagnetic wavelength. On the present proposal, however, we simply have a large number of dimensions, on each of which can be recorded sensitivities to a very specific proximal stimulus, all joined together to form a space. But, as they are different dimensions joined to form a space, there is no ordering among them (as explained earlier in this section). Thus we can't capture the similarities and differences between the senses just mentioned. This is a problem, for it is precisely these kinds of similarities and differences that we wish to capture in our space.

Can this problem be solved? One might hope that other dimensions would capture these kinds of similarities and differences, but there is no guarantee of this—and the onus clearly seems to be on me to show that they can be captured. So, at the present point in the dialectic, we have before us two undesirable

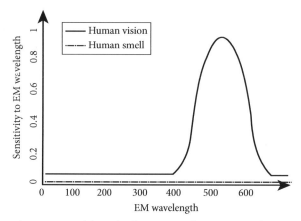

FIGURE 18.10. *A space created from the dimensions of sensitivity to electromagnetic wavelength and length of electromagnetic waves.*

options: dimensions that capture similarity, but on which we can't plot all of the senses, and dimensions on which you can plot all the senses, but not their similarity.

However, there is a way forward. We can construct a space that takes sensitivities to electromagnetic wavelengths as one dimension and electromagnetic wavelengths as another. Figure 18.10 illustrates approximate actual values for the human visual and human smell systems.

In this kind of space, we can register sensitivities to different wavelengths, preserving the order of the wavelengths, thus capturing the sorts of similarities and differences between the senses noted previously. At the same time, we can record a sense, like smell, that is sensitive to no electromagnetic wavelength, including its absence. Moreover, we no longer need a vast number of different dimensions each corresponding to different wavelengths of each type of wave to form our space, for we can capture them all on one wavelength dimension for each type of wavelength. All we need are dimensions corresponding to the different kinds of proximal stimuli conjoined with dimensions corresponding to sensitivity to those stimuli.

Choosing these dimensions provides a solution. However, note that these dimensions are such that a sense cannot take a value on those dimensions if each is considered alone. It does not make sense to ask what value vision or smell takes on a wavelength dimension or on a sensitivity to wavelength dimension. But now we might wonder whether such dimensions are permissible. We might think they are not, as previously I noted that for a dimension to be part of a space in which we can plot the senses, each sense must be able to take at least one value along each dimension. Are we now going back on that?

The answer is 'no'. It is true that each sense must be able to take a value along each dimension if they are to be plotted in a space defined by these dimensions. But it may do so *either* because the dimension is such that just in virtue of its nature alone all senses can take at least one value on it, *or* because the dimension is in a space created by joining it to another particular dimension. Thus, as long as we have both dimensions in our space, each sense can take a value on both dimensions.

One might be worried that it could be problematic to join two such dimensions that depend on each other's presence to other dimensions that we will need to form our space. But it is not. For example, we can join our electromagnetic wavelength dimension and sensitivity to electromagnetic wavelength dimension to unrelated dimensions. To see this, consider the dimension, relevant to the criterion of the nature of the sensory organs, that measures, from 0 to 100, the percentage of the sensory organ made of carbon. One could clearly join this dimension to those under consideration, and plot all the senses in such a space. See Figure 18.11 for how one would do so, supposing that the percentage of carbon in the eyes and the nose was 50%.

And we could join our electromagnetic wavelength dimension and sensitivity to electromagnetic wavelength dimension to other dimensions that depend on one another's presence to form a viable space, such as 'length of sound-wave' and 'sensitivity to sound-wave'. So there is no problem of making a two-dimensional space created from dimensions that depend on one another's presence to form a viable space, a subspace of a larger space.

In this way, we can see clearly how to specify dimensions that characterise the proximal stimulus criterion that generate a non-arbitrary ordering and that capture similarities and differences between the senses. We have also found a constraint that all dimensions that form the space of the sensory modalities must conform to: each sense must be able to take at least one value along each dimension.

However, at this point, one might think that another issue concerning arbitrariness emerges. Gray (2012) raises a problem regarding the arbitrariness of using certain dimensions to form the space of the sensory modalities—dimensions such as 'sensitivities to different frequencies of wavelengths of type X'. He says:

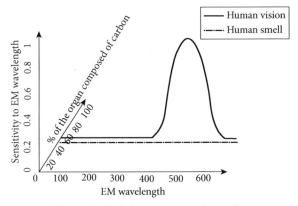

FIGURE 18.11. *Joining different kinds of dimensions together to form a space.*

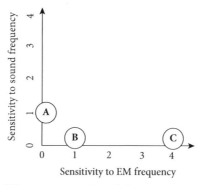

FIGURE 18.12. *Plotting different senses, A, B, and C, on a space created from different dimensions of sensitivities to frequencies of different types of waves.*

Given that the dimensions are based on the values of types of energies, one suggestion might be that the spaces can be united into a single space via their origins at zero energy. However, this cannot be the right way to generate an ordering of all the senses because it would result in the paradoxical outcome that a sense that detects electromagnetic radiation of lower frequencies (for example, human or rat [vision]. . .) would be more similar to human hearing than a sense that detects electromagnetic radiation of higher frequencies (for example, butterfly vision).[2]

Examine Figure 18.12, in which three senses, call them A, B, and C, are plotted. Gray's point, I think, is this: if we create a space using a dimension of sensitivity to sound wave frequency and sensitivity to electromagnetic wave frequency as axes, then the B sense, sensitive to low frequencies, turns out to be closer, and hence more similar, to the A sense than the C sense, which is sensitive to high electromagnetic frequencies. But this is arbitrary, says Gray, for there is no reason to think that the B sense, rather than the C sense, is more similar to the A sense.

However, if this is Gray's point, then it is spurious. *If* the senses can be plotted in the space, that is, *if* they take a value on both dimensions, *then* their place in this space reflects their similarity with respect to these two values. (We should note that this does not mean that their relation in this space reflects the overall similarities and differences of the senses. That will be determined by their place in the highly multidimensional space formed by all the dimensions that we should consider.) But the similarity of the three senses with respect to the values on the two axes is exactly correct. For consider that the A sense takes a zero value on the x-axis so *in this respect* it is more similar to B than C. The B and C senses take a zero value on the y-axis, and so *in that respect* they are equally dissimilar to the A. Overall then, B is more similar to A than C *with respect to these values.*

---

[2] Although Gray says that he thinks a "paradoxical" outcome would result, in fact there would be nothing paradoxical about such an outcome, only something incorrect or puzzling.

The crucial point of the preceding paragraph is the antecedent of the conditional: 'if the sense can be plotted on the above graph'. I think that Gray is confused in part because of a point that I have dealt with already, namely, that dimensions of the sort 'sensitivity to wavelengths of different lengths of type X' or 'sensitivities to different frequencies of wavelengths of type X' are not good dimensions to have as part of the space of the sensory modalities because not all the senses can be plotted on such a dimension. For example, the A sense in Figure 18.12 is represented in this space as being sensitive to a lack of frequency of electromagnetic wavelengths—not as being insensitive to electromagnetic frequencies, as human hearing is. If we want to represent a sense that is insensitive to the presence or absence of frequencies of electromagnetic wavelengths, then we cannot do so in the space in Figure 18.12. However, we have already solved that problem. It is done by ensuring that all senses can take a value on each dimension. So long as we do this we ensure that we do not face the sort of arbitrariness to which Gray refers.

However, two other worries about arbitrariness now arise. The first comes from considering how we join the relevant dimensions together to form our space of sensory modalities. One could think of joining together all the dimensions at their 'zero' value, but one might wonder whether doing so introduces an arbitrary element, for what counts as a zero value on some dimensions is, surely, merely arbitrary, such as zero degrees on the Celsius temperature scale, or zero degrees on the Fahrenheit scale. But, in truth, no such arbitrariness is created for it does not matter which point along each dimension is chosen as the intersection point, so long as there is one common intersection point. This is because the relative distance and relative ordering between the plotted points will remain the same in all cases, wherever the dimensions are joined. One can see this illustrated in Figure 18.13. Thus there is no source of arbitrariness in the joining of the dimensions.

The second additional worry about arbitrariness is, however, more serious. The worry arises because we need to decide on a scale for our dimensions. For example, suppose we have two dimensions each of which measures a different value, x and y,

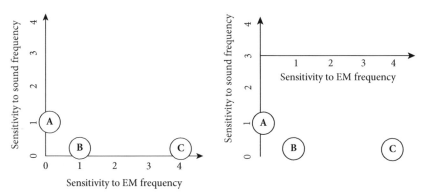

FIGURE 18.13. *Two identical axes joined at different points to make two spaces. Note that the distance between the points plotted is the same in both spaces.*

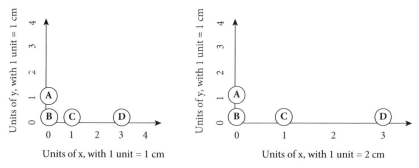

FIGURE 18.14. *Two spaces with points plotted on them, which differ only in the scale of the axes.*

in units of 0, 1, 2, 3... We could choose a scale of 1 unit per one centimetre on both the *x* and *y* axes as is illustrated in the left-hand diagram in Figure 18.14. However, we could also have chosen a scale of 1 unit per one centimetre on the *y*-axis and 1 unit per two centimetres on the *x*-axis, as in the right-hand diagram in Figure 18.14. It seems arbitrary which scale we use for the *x*-axis. However, which one we choose will affect the relative similarities and differences between the points plotted in the spaces. For example, the B and A points remain one centimetre apart in both the left-hand and right-hand space. But the distance between the B and the C points is larger by one centimetre in the right-hand diagram, compared to the left-hand one. Thus, in the left-hand space, B is represented to be as similar to A as it is to C, whilst in the right-hand space B is more similar to A than it is to C. Surely, then, the choice of scale introduces an arbitrary factor that incorrectly determines how similar and how dissimilar different senses will be?

There are three points to be noted that alleviate this worry. The first is that the ordering of points along a dimension will not be affected by issues of scale. Thus, if in the left-hand diagram of Figure 18.14 C is between B and D on the *x* dimension, then this remains the case in the right-hand diagram when we change the scale, and will do so for any change of scale.

The second point is that when scientists create a space in which to plot things by specifying dimensions, they are always faced with choices regarding the scales that they should use, particularly when the units of the dimensions are different. That we face such choices does not reflect a deficiency in our method of space building but reflects mandatory features of such an enterprise that is to be expected. When scientists have no intuitions or a priori knowledge about the relationships between things to be recorded on more than one dimension, then scaling to unit variance (UV) is the standard practice (Eriksson et al. 2006). If this was not done, a dimension that measured a quantity on a scale of 1–100, with each unit represented by one centimetre, would have more influence than a dimension that measured a quantity on a scale of 1–10, with each unit represented by one centimetre, on how similar or how different things were that were plotted in a space created by conjoining those dimensions. Scaling to UV takes the units along a dimension and places them on a scale between zero and one, so that '"long" variables are shrunk and "short" variables are stretched so that all variables will rest on an equal footing'(Eriksson et al. 2006: 208). The scaling weight employed is one divided by the standard deviation of the variable. Such a scaling 'is the most objective way to scale the data', giving each variable an equal opportunity to influence the data analysis. In particular, 'UV-scaling is useful when variables are of different kinds and not directly comparable numerically' (Eriksson et al. 2006: 208).[3]

The third point is that if one has intuitions or knowledge about how different dimensions contribute differently to the relative similarities and differences of the senses, then one can build these into one's model. One way to proceed is to start building the space by selecting one dimension with a particular scale. One can then choose the scale of a second dimension to be added to the space in a way that reflects the sorts of similarities and differences that one believes would hold between the things plotted on them. For example, if it seems to you that two senses that differed by one unit on the y-axis would be just as similar as things that differed by 5 units on the x-axis, then one should set up one's scales to reflect these facts. One could then add a third dimension by comparing it to either the first or the second dimension or to both.

Now a worry arises with this methodology. It is a worry about circularity. One might think that the point of constructing the space of sensory modalities was to discover the similarities and differences between the senses, not just to map out what one's intuitions are. But if we use our intuitions or knowledge about the relationships between the senses to create it, then we are in danger of not finding out anything that we did not know from our model building.

One way forward would be to not use any of one's knowledge and intuitions and simply to give equal weighting to the dimensions using the UV methodology described three paragraphs earlier. However, one could still gain fresh insights into the nature of the senses in two ways even if one used the intuitions and knowledge that one had. First, one could build a model where some dimensions are given an equal and otherwise neutral weighting as per the UV method, while others are given a more substantial or less substantial weighting relative to that, in accord with one's intuitions. Eriksson et al. say

> if prior information about the importance of variables is available, this insight should be reflected in the scaling. Variables that are known to be 'important', for a given problem can be up-weighted, to at least partially

---

[3] This technique is also the standard technique to be done to data prior to principal component analysis, described in section 6, together with mean centering in which 'the average value of each variable is calculated and then subtracted from the data'. In effect, this simply places the intersection of the dimensions at the mean point of the data plotted on each dimension. It is said that 'this improves the interpretability of the model [after PCA]' (Eriksson et al. 2006: 43). I discuss the question of interpreting the dimensions of the model after PCA in section 6.

account for this relevance. Analogously, variables that are noisy, or known to be irrelevant for the problem at hand, can be assigned a lower weight to diminish their contribution to the modeling. (2006: 208)

Further, consider that one could have an intuition of how similar and different a sense was with respect to the values on two dimensions. One might also have an intuition of their similarity and difference with respect to the values on one of those dimensions and a third, and an intuition of their similarity and difference with respect to the values on the third and a fourth. However, one may have no intuition of their similarity and difference with respect to the values on the first and the fourth. But by building a space that reflected these intuitions would one be able to discover their similarity and difference with respect to all the dimensions.

The second way to gain knowledge even by inputting one's intuitions or knowledge into building the space is by performing an analysis of the space that may reveal new dimensions that individuate the senses and which may lead us to revise, reconsider, and hone the scales that we have chosen. Further details of this analysis (principal component analysis) and how it can be used in this way are given in section 6.

In the next section, I consider whether we can identify likely dimensions that correspond to the other criteria, besides the proximal stimulus criterion: the sensory-organ, the representation, and the phenomenal character criteria.

5. Dimensions Corresponding to the Other Criteria

Now that I have given indication of how to construct the dimensions corresponding to the proximal stimulus, I consider how to construct dimensions corresponding to the sensory organ criterion. I believe that the dimensions corresponding to the proximal stimulus may be a subset of the dimensions that correspond to the sense organ criterion. This is because which proximal stimulus an organ is sensitive to will be a property of the sense organ. Figure 18.15 illustrates this.

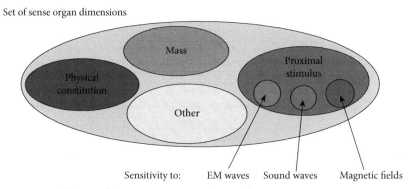

FIGURE 18.15. *The set of dimensions corresponding to the sense organ criterion.*

Thus we already have an idea of some of the dimensions that correspond to the sense organ criterion. But what about sense organ dimensions other than those corresponding to the proximal stimulus?

In the previous section, I mentioned the possibility of having a dimension corresponding to the percentage of the sense organ made up from carbon. Such a dimension creates a non-arbitrary ordering on which every sense organ can take a value. We could create similar dimensions for each of the elements, and, indeed, for molecules or any other important physical feature that we deem to be relevant. See Figure 18.16.

We could also capture the three-dimensional shape of the sense organ. We could create spatial dimensions centred, say, on the centre of mass of the organ. See Figure 18.17. These dimensions establish a non-arbitrary ordering that reflects a real property of the senses. Each sense can be plotted on such dimensions, supposing only

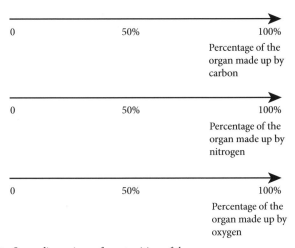

FIGURE 18.16. *Some dimensions of composition of the sense organ.*

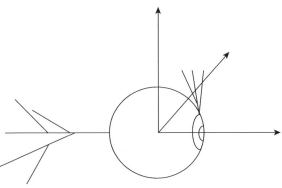

FIGURE 18.17. *An example of spatial dimensions centred on the mass of an eye-like sense organ.*

that it has some sense organ. In fact, there has been some dispute as to whether we must hold that each sense has its own dedicated sense organ. For example, some people have thought that there is a moral sense that has no sense organ associated with it. However, even if there was such a sense, it is reasonable to think that there are brain areas that are active when such a sense is operative. I think it would be reasonable to record the spatial nature of these brain areas on the spatial dimensions. Although such brain areas would not constitute a sense organ in the traditional sense, as they contain no immediate world-facing sensors, nevertheless, because sense organs are increasingly thought of as being constituted not just by external facing organs such as eyes and ears, but also by the nervous system and areas of brain associated with processing information from these organs, it is reasonable to map the associated brain areas on the spatial dimensions proposed to capture what physical structures in the body are associated with a particular sense.

We could also set up dimensions that capture how much of the world a sense is responsive to. For example, as many birds have eyes that point in directions more disparate than our own, they have a much wider field of view than humans, whose eyes both point forward. In an ego-centric framework, typical human vision is just under 180 degrees from left to right, that is, horizontally, and about 100 degrees from top to bottom, that is, vertically. The vision of some birds is nearly 360 degrees horizontally and around 180 degrees vertically. Human hearing is typically sensitive to sounds 360 degrees all around us. Smell is rather limited in its field of perception—at least on some views of smell according to which we can only detect things at our nostrils. (On this view, to the extent that we can determine that a smell is emanating from the left or the right, it is by inference from a series of 'snapshot' smells of different levels of intensity detected in different places in space.) On such views, smell would be plotted as having very small or no degrees of sensitivity in both horizontal and vertical directions. The plotting of these points is illustrated in Figure 18.18.

One could also use dimensions that captured the following properties of sense organs, which would impose a non-arbitrary ordering, and on which each of the senses could be guaranteed to take a value: mass of the organ, number of neurons composing the organ, number of temperature cells in the organ, number of pressure cells in the organ, and so on. Thus, one can see that it will be relatively straightforward to come up with the dimensions corresponding to the sensory-organ criterion.

When it comes to the representation and phenomenal character criteria, those who suppose that these two properties are really the same will claim that there is only one set of dimensions corresponding to these two criteria. Whether this is true or not, finding dimensions corresponding to these dimensions will be, I predict, possible with suitable ingenuity. Finding suitable dimensions for the proximal stimuli and sense organ criteria should, I believe, give us hope. I end this section with just one example of how one might specify some phenomenal character dimensions.

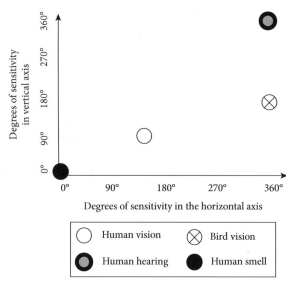

FIGURE 18.18. *Field of view plotted for different senses.*

Consider the colour space created by asking subjects to rank numerous instances of three colour patches *x, y,* and *z* in such a way as to indicate whether *y* or *z* is more similar to *x*, and thereby ordering the patches. We find that such a space can be characterised by three dimensions: lightness, hue, and saturation. White and black are antipodal points, with shades of grey running along the straight line connecting them. These are the achromatic shades. All the other shades have some chroma. Particular shades of red and green, and blue and yellow, respectively, are also antipodal points. See Figure 18.19 for illustration.

To create a phenomenal dimension, consider the straight line in Figure 18.19 leading from the centre of the sphere out to a shade of red, the line labelled as the saturation axis. The point at the start of the line is a shade of grey. All the other points will be increasingly saturated shades of a particular hue of red. Now consider a slightly different line. This one is very similar to the previous one except that the point at the start of the line, which in the previous dimension corresponded to a shade of grey, corresponds simply to a lack of one of the varying shades of differently saturated shades of red. We can imagine taking this as a dimension and plotting whether a sense yields an experience with the phenomenal character that one gets when one looks at the various shades of red along the dimension. Normal human vision will occupy all the points along the line. If there is a sense, such as smell, that yields no experience as of this hue of red, then we can plot it at the zero point that indicates a lack of all such phenomena character. In this way, we can ensure that every sense can be plotted on this dimension. All senses either produce one or more of these phenomenal characters or none of them. We can imagine creating similar phenomenal dimensions for the other colours and for other phenomenal qualities.

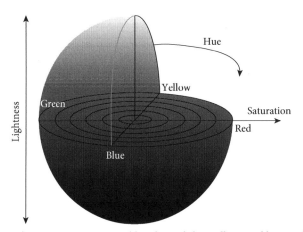

FIGURE 18.19. *The colour space—a roughly spherical shape illustrated here with a section removed to facilitate visualization.*

To summarise this section, the space of the sensory modalities will be created by joining together all the dimensions corresponding to each of the four criteria at a common origin. Each dimension in the space of sensory modalities must be such that each sense can take at least one value on the dimension, and the nature of the dimensions non-arbitrarily fixes the position of the senses in that space. I have indicated likely dimensions that we might use to construct such a space that corresponds to the proximal stimulus, and a few for the sensory-organ and phenomenal character criteria. I believe that with some thought we could go on to identify all that would be required. The goal of this chapter is not to identify all the dimensions that one would need to construct the space of the modalities; rather, it is to alleviate concerns about whether it is in principle possible to construct the space of sensory modalities. The main lesson of the chapter so far is that if there is a dimension along which one wants to record the nature of senses, but that dimension is such that it looks as if placing values along it will be arbitrary or in some other way unsuitable, there are ways of capturing what one wanted to record on that dimension by using instead a combination of other dimensions that are not problematic. I have also suggested ways of constructing dimensions corresponding to aspects of the senses that one might have thought difficult to build.

In the next section I discuss a very powerful technique that allows one to extract information from the space of sensory modalities that I have been considering building, and at the same time refining it.

6. Refining the Space of Sensory with Principal Component Analysis

In this section, I discuss principal component analysis (PCA) and how we can use it to analyse the space of sensory modalities created in the manner indicated previously. Doing so may lead us to refine and alter the space in which we wish to plot the senses. It may yield interesting and important insights into the factors important for individuating the senses and may make us reconsider what we should count as being senses. It may also make us reconsider what we should count as being token instances of senses. In addition, PCA allows us to reduce the dimensions of a multidimensional space, creating spaces with as many dimensions as we please—including a three-dimensional space in which we could visualise the position of the senses.

The space of sensory modalities that we have been considering creating will have many, many dimensions. The idea behind the space is that plotting the senses with respect to their similarity and difference on all the dimensions we consider important will produce a space that captures the similarities and differences between the senses. We might feel that such a highly multidimensional space is in practise of very little use. It does not help us visualise the relationship between the senses because of the high number of dimensions, and we might be concerned about how much new information we will be able to glean from the space that we did not explicitly put into it. Fortunately, however, PCA is a powerful technique developed to analyse multivariate spaces and it promises to yield interesting results. It was first developed by Pearson (1901) but has only come to the fore in the last three decades with the arrival of the massive computing power required to handle the computations on the large data sets that it was designed to analyse.

PCA is a mathematical procedure that is used to analyse a high-dimensional space in which data are plotted. It can be used to produce a number of different things when given a multidimensional space as input:

(1) a space with as few dimensions as possible that still retains all the variability in the data. While the input space may have been constituted by dimensions of correlated variables, the new space will now contain dimensions of linearly uncorrelated variables, called principal components. The number of the dimensions may remain the same, be reduced slightly, or be substantially reduced. The dimensions are also ordered, in the following sense: the dimension that accounts for the most variability in the data is identified as such, the dimension which accounts for the next most variability is identified as such, and so on for all the dimensions of the space.

(2) a space with a specified number of dimensions that retains as much of the variability of the data as it is possible to do with that limited number of dimensions. The new space will now contain dimensions of linearly uncorrelated variables that are ordered as just described. The amount of variability in the data that is retained can vary but, typically, due to the nature of the technique, a very large substantial proportion is retained while reduction to a few dimensions is achieved. The amount of variability retained can be measured.

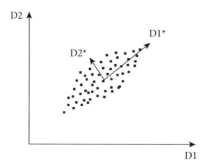

FIGURE 18.20. *An illustration of the results of a PCA of a space with points plotted in it.*

(3) a two- or three-dimensional model that provides a visualisation of
    the space and the data plotted in it. PCA is often used precisely for
    visualisation purposes.

Thus, PCA is a technique of exploratory data analysis that identifies hidden patterns in the data of a high multidimensional space and classifies the newly produced dimensions according to how much of the information, stored in the data,
they account for. This means that the dimensions of the newly created space are
typically not the dimensions that constitute the space that is analysed.[4]

To illustrate with a simple example of a PCA, consider Figure 18.20. The points
plotted in the space given by the dimensions D1 and D2 can be re-plotted in a
space with dimensions D1* and D2*, where D1* and D2* are uncorrelated dimensions, and D1* is the dimension that accounts for most variability between the
items plotted, and D2* the next most. Moreover, the space created by D1* and D2*
preserves all the similarity and difference information as was in the space created
by D1 and D2. Also, the dimensions D1* and D2* represent different values from
those represented by D1 and D2.

In the space of sensory modalities that I have suggested creating, we could plot
various categories of senses. For example we could plot the following senses:

- all human senses
- all actual senses
- the senses that folk-psychology recognises
- all nomologically possible senses
- all metaphysically possible senses.

Then, using PCA, we could work out the smallest number of dimensions needed
to capture all the similarity and difference information for each of these groups of
senses.[5] This technique is used all the time in science for taxonomical purposes.

---

[4] PCA is described at length in Eriksson et al. (2006).

[5] In fact, you could plot whatever group of senses interests you. For example, someone might think
that creating the space of all the sensory modalities is too difficult and of little value and may just want

To illustrate with just one of many examples, consider Crescenzi's and Giuiani's (2001) construction of their taxonomy of tumours. They first selected 1,416 dimensions corresponding to different gene expression levels—properties that tumours may have. They then conjoined these dimensions to form a high-dimensional space and plotted 60 tumours in it. They then performed a PCA and discovered that only five dimensions were required to explain the vast majority of the variance among the tumours. These five dimensions were different to each of the dimensions that formed their original highly multidimensional space. Interestingly, and importantly, they could *interpret* the new dimensions and work out what characteristics of tumours they corresponded to—characteristics that they had not considered prior to doing the PCA.

Crescenzi and Giuiani state a fact that is always noted about this technique, 'From the interpretive point of view, the major merit of PCA resides in the possibility to attach a biological meaning to the components' (2001: 117). In other words, when one performs a PCA, one finds the principal components, which can turn out to be new dimensions—dimensions different from those that one puts into the space on which one performed the analysis. These new dimensions can often be given an interpretation in terms we are familiar with, so that they turn out to represent biological, physical, or psychological properties that we had not previously considered.

Importantly, when performing PCA, scientists often tinker with

- which dimensions to use to form the initial space on which the PCA is performed,
- the scale of the dimensions, and
- the examples to plot,

until PCA

- reduces the dimensions greatly while not losing too much similarity and difference information,
- produces dimensions that account for much variability in the data that were not used to construct the original space, and
- produces dimensions that can be identified with biological, physical, psychological, or other natural or scientific properties.

Hence, PCA can yield insights into whatever is being taxonomised.

---

to create the space of visual senses: human vision, octopus vision, bee vision, and so on. As I stated in the first section of the chapter, I've argued elsewhere (Macpherson 2011a and 2011b) that I don't think the senses fall into a small discrete number of natural kinds like vision, audition, and so on. I think there is no non-arbitrary answer to whether snake infra-red, bee 'vision', X-ray 'vision', bat echo-location, or the sense used in tactical visual sensory substitution should count as vision or not. I believe that all the senses are simply more or less different along a number of different dimensions. Thus, I don't see any value in trying to plot a subset of senses, like those someone might be tempted to call the 'visual' ones. However, if others were to disagree, they could nonetheless plot whichever senses they liked using the techniques I've described in this chapter.

Note that the issue of which scale to use for the dimensions is included in what one might alter to produce an interesting analysis. As mentioned in section 4, this is one way, in addition to others mentioned there, in which choices about the appropriate scales to use for dimensions can be made.

Tinkering with the PCA in the way just described might include toying with which things we take to be senses, and what properties we believe something must have to be a sense, for excluding or including certain cases might produce the best analyses. For example, does excluding or including the interoceptive senses alter the analysis? Does excluding vomeronasal reception produce a more simple or elegant PCA? We might also consider whether to count, for example, touch as one sense or as multiple senses, for it might turn out that we produce the best analysis if we treat it as one, rather than three separate senses of pressure, temperature, and pain. We might also see whether it is best to do the analysis on types of normally functioning senses in each species, or whether to plot for token individual normal and non-normal instances of senses.

The PCA might also yield interesting results about which properties really matter for individuating the senses. For example, it might turn out that a PCA allows one to identify a small number of dimensions that are required to characterise the space of sensory modalities while retaining most of the variability data, and that we can interpret these dimensions as corresponding to certain properties of the senses. For all we know, we might even end up with four dimensions, the best interpretation of which might be a property of each of the four criteria that we started with, namely, the proximal stimulus, the sense organ, the representational, and the phenomenal character criterion. Thus, it is possible that we might end up with a space with four dimensions corresponding to properties of the four criteria that we initially might have thought formed the space of sensory modalities. Or we may end up with an elegant three-dimensional space that allows us to visualise the space of the sensory modalities. We can certainly forcibly reduce the number of dimensions to three to see such a space while noting how much, if any, variance data we lose when we do so.

What exactly we will find remains to be seen. However, let me emphasise most strongly that tinkering with the model on which one conducts the PCA is often done *until* a useful analysis is yielded in which the principal components can be identified with certain biological, physiological, or psychological properties.

This kind of tinkering with data sets with respect to which examples to plot, which dimensions of which scales to use, the number of dimensions to which one will reduce the space, and the tolerance for data variance loss is often the subject of debate within a community of taxonomists spanning many years. See, for example, Noy-Meir and Whittaker (1977) who summarise and contribute to the debate concerning patterns of variation in the composition of species of vegetation at different places.[6]

---

[6] Using different axes, or plotting different points, one might end up with two (or more) spaces that each is reducible to a small number of axes using PCA while not losing much information. One might

In short, when constructing a space of the sensory modalities, one hopes to produce a space in which the senses are plotted that reveals more about the relationships between the senses than one explicitly put in. The high-dimensional space that we have considered creating will contain such information. However, PCA is an incredibly powerful tool that is likely to allow us to extract more and different information still—an extra deep layer of information hidden within that created when building the high-dimensional space. And results of PCA can feed back to inform the sorts of choices that we should be making when choosing the initial dimensions of the space of sensory modalities and the senses to plot within it.

7. Summary

I believe I have laid out, in a programmatic way, what would be required to create a space of the sensory modalities. And I have shown that completion of such a task, while large and difficult, should be possible.

For each of the four criteria that we should use to individuate the senses—the proximal stimulus, the sense organ, the representational, and the phenomenal character criterion—we need to specify a set of dimensions that captures the nature of each. These may overlap, some may be subsets of the others, et cetera. We then use these dimensions to form a space of the sensory modalities that captures the similarities and differences between them. However, in order to ensure that these dimensions really form an appropriate space we need to choose dimensions that do not generate an arbitrary ordering and ensure that each sense can take at least one value on each dimension. We need to consider the scale that should be used for the dimensions. We can blindly suppose that they all contribute the same to the space and scale them to unit variance. Or we can deviate from this and feed in our intuitions about the relative significance of the dimensions, and feed in our limited intuitions or knowledge about how similar the senses are with respect to a limited number of dimensions.

I have tried to show that it is plausible to think that we can find suitable dimensions in the case of the proximal stimulus criterion and, to a lesser degree, in the case of the sense organ, phenomenal character and representational criteria. These dimensions will then define a space in which the actual senses can be plotted and where at least many (nomologically and metaphysically) possible senses could be

---

find that the dimensions in the different spaces are identified with different properties. In such a situation arguments would have to be had about which space was preferable and why—as occurs at present in certain cases of taxonomy such as the one concerning patterns of vegetation. However, both sets of properties identified with the two different spaces could be ones that are philosophically illuminating when considering the nature of the senses.

plotted too. Such a space should reveal the similarities and differences between the senses.

When we have created such a space, we can then carry out a principal component analysis on it, in the hope, and reasonable expectation, that such an analysis will lead us to refine the space, reduce the dimensions, and identify new properties crucial for individuating the sensory modalities, and give us further insight into the relationships between the senses.

It is interesting to consider whether construction of a multidimensional space, and a principal component analysis of it, could help to determine the nature, individuation, and taxonomy of other objects, states, events, and properties that philosophers are interested in. To my knowledge, to date, philosophers have not used this methodology. However, I predict that there are cases, in addition to that of the sensory modalities, in which it will be illuminating.

Acknowledgments

I would like to thank Clare Batty, Jon Bird, Adam Rieger, and Barry Smith for discussing the ideas in this chapter with me, and Craig French, and the editors of this volume, for helpful comments on a draft of the chapter. This work was supported by two grants from the Arts and Humanities Research Council (grant numbers AH/I027509/1 and AH/L007053/1).

References

Classen, C. (1993) *Worlds of Sense: Explaining the Senses in History and across Cultures.* London: Routledge.

Craig, A. D. (1996) 'Pain, Temperature, and the Sense of the Body', in O. Franzén, R. Johansson, and L. Y. Terenius (eds.), *Somesthesis and the Neurobiology of the Somatosensory Cortex.* Basel: Birkhäuser, 27–39.

Crescenzi, M. and Giuiani, A.. (2001) 'The main biological determinants of tumor line taxonomy elucidated by a principal component analysis of microarray data', *FEBS Letters*, 507:114–118.

Eriksson, L., Johansson, E., Kettaneh-Wold, N., Trygg, J., Wikström, C., and Wold, S. (2006) *Multi- and Megavariate Data Analysis, Part I,* 2nd revised and enlarged edition. Umeå: Umetrics AB.

Gray, R. (2012) 'Is There a Space of Sensory Modalities?' *Erkenntnis,* published online first, DOI 10.1007/s10670-012-9409-0.

Macpherson, F. (2011a) 'Individuating the Senses', in F. Macpherson (ed.), *The Senses: Classical and Contemporary Readings.* Oxford: Oxford University Press, 3–36.

Macpherson, F. (2011b) 'Taxonomising the senses', *Philosophical Studies,* 153(1): 123–142.

Nagel, T. (1974) 'What is it like to be a bat?' *Philosophical Review,* 83: 435–450.

Noy-Meir, I. and Whittaker, R. H. (1977) 'Continuous multivariate methods in community analysis: Some problems and developments'. *Vegetatio*, 33(2–3): 79–98.

Nudds, M. (2004) 'The significance of the senses'. *Proceedings of the Aristotelian Society*, 104(1): 31–51.

Pearson, K. (1901) 'On lines and planes of closest fit to systems of points in space'. *Philosophical Magazine*, 2(11): 559–572.

Wetzel, L. (2011) 'Types and Tokens', E. N. Zalta (ed.) *The Stanford Encyclopedia of Philosophy* (Spring 2011 edition), http://plato.stanford.edu/archives/spr2011/entries/types-tokens.

19

Distinguishing the Commonsense Senses

Roberto Casati, Jérôme Dokic, and François Le Corre

1. Introduction

Common sense distinguishes five senses or modalities of sensory experiences of the environment: sight, touch, hearing, smell, and taste. Such a classification appears to be a cultural invariant.[1] But where does this classification come from, and is it a valid one? The theoretical question of the individuation or classification of the senses can be construed in at least two different ways: on the one hand, one may investigate the naive or ordinary criteria for distinguishing among the senses, as well as wonder why we ordinarily recognize five senses rather than, say, four or six. This might be called the "anthropological project." On the other hand, one may try to understand the very nature of the senses and study in particular the question of whether the senses are natural kinds— that is to say, whether our ordinary classification "carves nature at its joints," to use an expression by Plato (*Phaedrus* 265d–266a). This might be called the "psychological project."

Now, the anthropological project can be pursued in two ways: first, one may look at the historical or cultural records, that is to say at the way people *explicitly* did or do classify the (traditional five) senses; second, one may be interested in the way people *implicitly* classify the senses (whatever their nature and number)—a subproject that may be handled by experimental philosophers. With regard to the psychological project, there is a debate concerning how we should pursue it: some philosophers argue that this project needs scientific support; where the sciences involved are essentially the empirical sciences of perception, (neuro-)psychology, and (neuro-)ethology (Keeley, 2002:6). Others argue that this strategy looks like a subject-shift and that the psychological project just consists in taking as its starting point the commonsensical understanding of the senses (Nudds, 2004: fn11; see also Nudds, 2011). And then, if it happens that our ordinary classification does

---

[1] Jütte (2005). But see also Howes (1991, 2003) for the claim that such a classification is a cultural variant.

not rely on sound psychological bases, then it could be necessary, for the purposes of science, to replace our naive concept of the senses with a more technical one, which is likely to admit, maybe, more than five sensory modalities—or maybe fewer than five.[2]

In what follows, we propose to explore some aspects of the relations between the scientific and commonsensical projects for individuating the senses.[3] We start by offering a guide through different philosophical approaches about (some of) the criteria of individuation. In particular, we shall ask for each criterion to what extent it can be useful for both projects. Then we pay special attention to the faculty of hearing, which offers promising examples of the strategy we pursue of combining common sense and science.

We consider this discussion as subserving a much larger project concerning the interactions between philosophy and the empirical sciences. Deciding whether commonsense classifications are adequate is certainly an interesting project in itself. However, something more can be said. How can philosophical inquiry inform the scientific study of the senses? Biologists, psychologists, and ethologists are confronted with the problem of characterizing the various ways in which humans and animals are able to extract and use information from their environment (here construed widely as to include animals' own bodies). Borderline questions have reshaped the theoretical landscape. These may involve the discovery of human capabilities that have so far escaped the commonsense classification (Are the postural and the vomeronasal senses senses? Is visuo-tactile sensory substitution a form of vision or a form of touch?) or the discovery of capabilities in animals that defy the commonsense classification (echolocation in bats, the use of the star-shaped nose in the star-nosed mole). What theoretical commitments are we making when we credit these capabilities with the "sense" label?

2. Four Criteria for Classifying the Senses

In a classic article in 1962, the philosopher Paul Grice proposed four possible criteria for classifying the senses. In this section, we will present (some of) the pros and cons of these criteria, with regard to their explanatory potential for the commonsensical and/or scientific point of views on the individuation of the senses.[4]

---

[2] From this point of view, acknowledging fewer than five senses is no less revisionary than postulating more than five ones. See Stoffregen and Bardy (2001).

[3] Our attention will then be focused on the psychological project. But it is worth indicating that those who argue in favor of the commonsensical point of view may rely upon research from the anthropological project.

[4] See Casati and Dokic (1994, chap. 2).

2.1. THE CRITERION OF QUALIA

The term "qualia" refers to qualitative or phenomenal properties of a sensory experience that determine "what it is like" to have this experience (Nagel, 1974). It is assumed here that visual experience, for example, has a proprietary "phenomenal character," distinct from the phenomenal character of auditory experience. What it is like to see the world is subjectively different from what it is like to hear it.

Grice has notably defended this criterion by arguing for its ineliminability (as opposed to the eliminability of the other criteria) on the basis of a thought experiment.[5] He imagines a creature that possesses two pairs of organs, more or less like our eyes in as much as both pairs are light-sensitive. According to Grice, if the creature claims, on the basis of her own experience, that there is a difference between the use of one pair and the use of the other, then we would be inclined to judge that each pair refers to a different sensory modality (Grice, 1962:260–261). Consequently, if all sensory experiences are associated with specific qualia, accessible by introspection, then this criterion might be a good candidate for being the naive or ordinary criterion, because anyone could use phenomenal differences for distinguishing her own experiences.

However, this criterion has been challenged from many directions. First, one may turn Grice's thought experiment against the criterion of qualia. For instance, O'Dea (2011) proposes a variation in which a creature has not two but just one pair of eye-like organs. Under these circumstances, the creature can still claim that there is a difference between using its eyes in the *morning* and using them in the *afternoon* (302). According to O'Dea, in such a situation we would not be inclined to consider that sight morning and sight afternoon are different sensory modalities, only because of a qualitative difference. This shows that Grice has given no positive reason in favor of a qualia-based interpretation of his own thought experiment, rather than, for example, a sensory organ-based interpretation—notably because there is an analogy, in Grice's thought experiment, between the difference in qualitative experience and different (pairs of) organs.

Second, one may criticize Grice's proposal in the light of recent scientific research. For instance, one may deny that *all* sensory modalities are associated with qualia. As Keeley (2002) says:

> While the science is admittedly controversial here, the possibility of a human vomeronasal system stands as a potentially interesting case of a modality without a special introspectible experiential character. Women who can guess the gender of breath do not report that they experience "male" versus "female" qualia associated with the breaths. Indeed, subjects are generally surprised to be informed that they are so good at distinguishing the smells. (25)

---

[5] Another defense of this criterion may be found in Leon (1988) and in Lopes (2000).

If scientists are right to make a place for a human vomeronasal system,[6] and if ordinary people are willing to accept the vomeronasal sense as an actual sense (and casual conversations suggest that they are), then the criterion of qualia turns out to be inadequate, as there are no qualia here to rely upon.

Third, one may also deny that the criterion of qualia is of any help in explaining experimental results and for making clear predictions, notably with regard to multimodal or cross-modal interactions. For instance, in the McGurk Effect experiment (McGurk & MacDonald 1976), (some) participants claim to have an auditory experience of a particular phoneme, /da/—in the original experiment—even though the actual emitted phoneme was /ba/. Why are they confused? Likely, because when the sound is displayed, participants are, at the same time, looking at a person (on a screen) who articulates with his lips the phoneme /ga/. There is an interaction between the visual information (/ga/) and the auditory information (/ba/) that culminates in the perceptual experience of yet another phoneme (/da/), which is actually neither visually nor audibly displayed. Here, the defenders of the criterion of qualia could only predict that the participants in the McGurk experiment should have an auditory experience of /ba/, corresponding to the auditory stimulation. This illustrates the fact that it might be quite hard to specify an experience as an auditory experience as opposed to a visual experience.

Finally, in a more general way, one could go as far as to deny the very existence of qualia. And of course, the ontological status of qualia is notoriously controversial. Philosophers of perception are divided into "qualiaphiles" and "qualiaphobes." Qualiaphobes (Dennett, 1991) often argue that sensory experience is phenomenally transparent. When we try to demonstrate, through introspection, the properties of our experience of a red cube—for example, to try to identify a specific chromatic quale—we fall back on the very property of the redness of the cube that is represented in our experience (see Tye, 2009). If one does not accept qualia, the criterion of qualia is clearly pointless.

2.2. THE CRITERION OF CONTENT

While the criterion of qualia depends on the identification of properties of the experience itself, the criterion of content is focused on the properties represented in experience, that is to say, on its intentional or informational content. The defender of this criterion may take inspiration from Aristotle, who distinguished between two kinds of objects of the senses: (1) the proper sensible, specified as "what is special to a single sense"; (2) the common sensibles, specified as "what is common to any and all of the senses." According to him, "colour is the special object of sight, sound of hearing, flavor of taste.... [M]ovement, rest, number, figure, magnitude ... are common to all" (see *De Anima*, Book II, chap. 6).[7]

---

[6] The claim is actually controversial. See Hughes (1999, chap. 19).

[7] On Aristotle's theory, see Sorabji (1971).

The main task for a defender of the criterion of content is twofold: on the one hand, she needs to offer a non-arbitrary determination of those properties that could be perceptible only by a single modality (e.g., why is color and not shape the special object of sight?), and on the other hand, she needs to account for the possibility of the "double determinability of properties" (Coady, 1974:118) (e.g., why is it acceptable to say (1) "I *feel* that this is round" as well as (2) "I *see* that this is round"?).

In order to tackle the task, philosophers sometimes use the notion of a "key feature" or "key property," which was introduced and defended by Roxbee Cox in 1970. According to Roxbee Cox, a key property is a property that one can directly perceive, where "directly perceive" means that the perception of the property does not require or involve the perception of another property (535).

Thus, although the perception of shape might require the perception of color, it is not the case, according to Roxbee Cox, that the perception of color requires the perception of shape—and neither does it require the perception of shade, nor the perception of spatial relations, and so on. He concludes that given that the perception of color does *not* require or involve the perception of any other property, then "having some colour property" must be the key property for sight (537).

Furthermore, this notion of "key property" also explains why one may utter sentences like (1) "I *feel* that this is round" and (2) "I *see* that this is round." One may utter (2) because here, the perception of color *is* required for the perception of shape; the perception of color is what makes the perception of shape possible. And one may utter (1) in those situations where one is blindfolded; in such situations the perception of shape only requires that the object has some feel to the touch, where "having some feel to the touch" (538) is, according to Roxbee Cox, the key property for touch.

Nonetheless, this criterion faces numerous difficulties. First, as Heil (1983) suggests, it is not obvious that colors might be directly perceived by sight *only*:

> A creature equipped [with sonar devices, e.g.] might, I am suggesting, best be described as hearing the colours of objects.... That colors are detectable "directly" only by sight is—at best—a contingent fact, not a necessary truth about vision. (1983:149)[8]

Second, even if colors are directly perceived only by sight, this criterion seems to imply that each and every visual experience is an experience of chromatic properties. But what about the experience had by subjects who suffer from one form of achromatopsia, a condition affecting just the perception of color? These people perceive the world in black and white (or, more accurately, in bright and dark)

---

[8] References to Heil (1983) are taken from Macpherson (2011). In the same spirit of Heil criticism, we might also imagine a device that helps blind people to discriminate between colors, using some kind of thermal display. Here, one will be inclined to say that blind people are directly perceiving colors by touch.

and cannot establish, on the sole basis of their visual experience, the distinctions we make among most of our different color shades, but no one would intuitively deny them the ability to *see* the world. Linking sight not only to the perception of chromatic colors, but also to the "achromatic" colors (black and white and all shades of gray), which would be preserved in achromatopsia, could circumvent this difficulty.

Third, however, the defender of the criterion of content should address an even broader challenge. The criterion implies that it is possible to identify a key property without making essential reference to the sensory modality that one seeks to define. If such an independent identification was impossible, the definition would immediately be circular: for example, sight would be defined as the perception of a colored object, and color would in turn be defined as a type of property that is revealed only to sight. But if no independent identification is possible, then it is not clear what makes an alleged key property a *key* property precisely.

2.3. THE CRITERION OF THE STIMULUS

The criterion of qualia and the criterion of content mainly refer to the way people experience the world, subjectively. Macpherson classifies these criteria as "experiential criteria" for individuating the senses, as opposed to the "physical criteria."[9] The criterion of the stimulus is a physical criterion, because it invokes the natural structure of our sensory experience. In particular, it individuates the senses by the type of sensory stimulation that is the causal source of the experience.

One defense of this criterion may be found in Heil's 1983 book and in a recent paper in 2011. In these texts, Heil's aim is to build a general theory of perception that "ties perceiving to the acquiring of beliefs" (Heil, 1983:137), and for that purpose he starts by giving an (independent) account of the senses. According to him, perception depends upon a causal process, which begins with a physical stimulation and ends with the production of a belief (Heil, 2011:146).

For instance, in order to entertain a visual belief it is necessary to have visual access to a source of information, and such an access depends in turn on a kind of physical stimulation that is, in the case of vision, light radiation. In order to entertain an auditory belief it is necessary to have auditory access to a source of information, and such an access depends in turn on pressure waves. And so on and so forth for the other senses (see Heil, 1983:140).

According to Heil, his defense of the criterion of the stimulus is supported by experiments involving a tactile visual substitution system (henceforth, TVSS; Bach-Y-Rita et al., 1969). Subjects using a TVSS have a camera mounted on their head, which collects information about their surroundings. Thanks to a mechanism that converts the visual image produced by the camera in tactile information

---

[9] Macpherson (2011:23).

displayed on different parts of the body (back, stomach, tongue, fingertip, etc.), these subjects become able to identify, in particular, the shape of distal objects, or to avoid obstacles (Auvray & Myin, 2009). Heil then argues that if the senses were not distinguished by physical stimuli, then we could not describe the experience of a blind individual who is using a TVSS device as an experience of *seeing*, rather than an experience of *feeling* (the vibrating pins on the back, stomach, or tongue of the subject). Now the seeing-interpretation seems to win because in making discrimination between distal objects possible, a TVSS-equipped subject and a sighted one "would *describe* their experiences in exactly the same way; both would be unable to detect the presence of objects if the lights were switched off or if an opaque screen were placed in front of the objects scanned" (Heil, 2011:289). Indeed, Heil quotes a TVSS-trained (congenitally blind) subject who describes his own experience as "seeing with the skin" (Heil, 2011:288).

From a naturalist point of view, it is obvious that the study of the type of stimuli to which visual (auditory, etc.) processes are sensitive is an important part of our scientific understanding of the nature of our sensory experience. What is less obvious is (1) that the TVSS users should be said to have an experience of *seeing*; (2) that the criterion of the stimulus is able to predict distinctions among the senses that are close to that of common sense.

Concerning (1), Keeley (2002) argues that Heil's account makes a confusion between two kinds of abilities: "detection" and "reception":

> The suffix -*detection* [e.g., as in "visual detection"] is applied to any organism that is capable of responding, by any means, to the presence of a particular type of stimulation in the environment. The suffix -*reception* is reserved for those organisms that carry out such sensory discriminations through the use of a dedicated anatomical system of structures. (2002:17)

Keeley argues that a congenitally blind TVSS user is capable of visual detection—in as much as she is able, for example, to avoid obstacles—but that she is not capable of visual reception, precisely because of the absence of a functional visual anatomical system. As Keeley states, it is not because we can detect electricity with our tongues that we possess an electrical modality. Against Keeley, a defender of the criterion of the stimulus could claim that her purpose is to account for people's intuitions, and that people would ordinarily describe a TVSS user as seeing rather than as feeling—especially as some users claim to forget the vibrating pins after a few hours of training while being still able to recognize the shape of distant objects. But there is still reason to question the explanatory power of commonsensical intuitions proclaimed by the defenders of the criterion of the stimulus. Indeed, concerning (2), it is worth noting that, on the one hand, the same sense may relate to different types of stimuli, as in the case of pressure and heat, which, broadly, fall within the province of touch, and, on the other hand, that two different senses can share the same type of stimulus specified in physical terms—for example, chemical stimulations for both gustatory and olfactory perceptions; yet people would likely talk about different senses here.

2.4. THE CRITERION OF THE SENSORY ORGAN

The last criterion discussed by Grice is another physical criterion, namely, the criterion of the sensory organ. Indeed, it seems plausible to consider that each sense corresponds to a sense organ, which from a functional point of view transduces packages of physical energy of a certain type—specified via the criterion of the stimulus—into perceptual states and representations.

But what may count as a sensory organ? There are at least two possible strategies to answer that question. On the one hand, one's specifications may speak to commonsensical intuitions. On the other hand, one may try to specify a sensory organ within a scientific framework, that is to say, in neurobiological terms.

According to the first strategy, it is out of doubt that the ordinary explicit classifications of the senses equate the five senses with the five external sensory organs, such as eyes, ears, the skin, nose, and mouth, which are intuitively organs for sight, hearing, touch, smell, and taste, respectively.[10] The challenge for the defenders of this approach is then to explain why people from various cultures do not seem to take into account other possible senses such as, for example, proprioception.[11] One way of defining a sensory organ that could meet this challenge may be borrowed from David Armstrong's idea, according to which a sensory organ is "a portion of the body which we. . . move at will with the object of perceiving what is going on in. . . our environment" (1968:213). By virtue of its reference to the will, this definition implies that a sensory organ is only what we can voluntarily engage in order to transform our relationship to the sensory world: say, the eyes that follow a moving object, our head that we can direct toward the sounds we hear, or our hands as they move on the surface we are exploring. Such a definition might have the advantage of explaining why common sense does not recognize as a sense certain sensory modalities such as vomeronasal sense or the ones revealed by cognitive science, such as proprioception or the sense of balance (Berthoz, 2000), simply because it does not seem as if we can directly influence these senses to adjust our relationship to the sensory world.

However, the commonsensical criterion of the sensory organ encounters some difficulties. Prima facie, it is a bit odd to consider the head as the organ of audition. Indeed, if the head is thought of as an organ that we can move at will, it also seems that the head is an organ that helps us to see, smell, touch, and so on, and not only to hear.[12]

Furthermore, it is not at all clear that we do not or cannot act on these (non-traditional) senses somehow. For instance, if we consider the entire body as a sensory organ—as perhaps some dancers might be willing to accept—this could

---

[10] See Jütte (2005) for examples and references.

[11] For a potential exception, see Geurts (2002).

[12] Not to mention that not only the orientation but also the overall shape of the head influences what is heard as well.

explain why we have a sense like the sense of balance. But then, this makes it difficult to explain why folk ordinarily count five senses and not six instead.[13]

What about the second strategy? According to it, a sensory organ must be understood as a neurobiological substrate. One prominent defender of this neurobiological criterion of the sensory organs is Keeley:

> On my account, to possess a genuine sensory modality is to possess an appropriately wired-up sense organ that is historically dedicated to facilitating behavior with respect to an identifiable physical class of energy. (2002:6)

Now, Keeley's approach to the individuation of the senses is meant to help scientists—biologists and ethologists—that might encounter difficulties in determining whether a particular sense organ is an entirely new one, or, if it is not, in determining the type of sensory modality it belongs to. For instance, there is a controversy about the star-shaped nose of the star-nosed mole. Such a creature looks like an ordinary mole except that it has numerous pink fleshy appendages around its snout, with which the star-nosed mole can touch various things. The question is, is this star-shaped organ sensitive to chemical stimuli (as the nose is) or to tactile stimuli (as the skin is)? Keeley claims that the star-shaped nose of the mole should be described as a tactile sense (2002:26). And this is because scientists have shown that the star-shaped organ (1) is sensitive to the same kinds of sensory stimuli as our skin, (2) is wired up as the tactile sense organs of other species of moles is, (3) gives rise to certain behaviors that can only be accomplished by the tactile sense—such as grasping a prey and bringing it toward the mouth. And all this leads to the hypothesis that the function of this organ has been dedicated to the detection of tactile stimuli.[14] Now, Keeley argues that the same strategy should be used in other occasions, such as, for instance, when we look for the presence or absence of a magnetic sense in migratory birds (2002:27).[15]

Nonetheless, in addition to the fact that this neurobiological criterion might be of no help for a commonsensical approach, as it cannot, by itself, predict an intuitive division among the senses, it might be more awkward for Keeley's purposes to point that this criterion may also be unhelpful for science as well. We

---

[13] Concerning the case of the vomeronasal sense, one might think here of the phenomenon called "Fhlemen response." Ethologists have shown that, for example, equines often turn their lips up in order to perceive some odors and pheromones in particular (thanks to the Jacobson's organ) of other conspecifics and/or of ordinary or new objects. The situation is more complicated for humans, precisely because it is still unclear whether we do or do not possess such a vomeronasal sense and where it (if any) is located. But this lack of data is insufficient to preclude the existence of such a sense as well as the possibility of interacting with it (perhaps do we interact with it in some unconscious way(s)). Here we take our inspiration from Keeley (2009).

[14] See Keeley (2002:27) and Hughes (1999:30–32), who both refer to Catania and Kaas (1996), "The Unusual Nose and Brain of the Star-nosed Mole," *BioScience* 86(8): 578–586.

[15] This strategy might also help to preclude certain apparent senses as actual senses.

saw that Keeley is aware that there is no positive reason to assert the existence of a specific organ for the vomeronasal sense yet. Here is how he deals with this difficulty: "It seems pretty clear that we don't have a spatially distinct vomeronasal organ (VNO), as other animals do; but perhaps pheromone sensitive cells are mixed in with other sensory cells in the olfactory bulbs. VNO-type cells might be a distinct subset of chemosensory cells in the human olfactory bulb" (2009a: 235). If the vomeronasal sense is implemented in these VNO-type cells, then VNO-type cells *are* the organ of the vomeronasal sense.

However, this does not come without problems. Indeed, such a strategy might be unhelpful because if VNO-type cells are instances of multimodal cells, nothing could prevent scientists from considering that any token of multimodal cells actually is a token of an entirely distinct *type* of sense, rather than a token of a multisensory process between two different sensory modalities.[16] One possible reason is that scientists determine the specificity of some cells with regard to their own way of distinguishing among the senses, which likely is nothing but a commonsensical way. Why should we consider that the mix of different kinds of cells might create a new type of sense in some occasions but not in others? In other words, why do cognitive scientists speak about "multimodal convergence" or "multimodal transformation," and so forth, rather than speaking about radically different types of senses? Keeley needs to address this challenge, on pain of rendering his theory no more helpful for science than any commonsensical approaches.

In summary, we have shown that each criterion faces various difficulties. In particular, no criterion seems to be able to account for our commonsensical intuitions and at the same time to explain some recent scientific data on sensory perception. At this point, one might favor different strategies. For instance, one might argue that the search for a scientific criterion leads to a dead end and then focus only on making sense of commonsensical intuitions, as Nudds (2004) suggests; or, one might argue that all these four criteria need to be taken into account and mixed somehow, as Macpherson (2011) suggests. Or still, one might argue that scientific investigation is the only way for individuating the senses. We, however, shall pursue the search for a criterion of individuation—that does not need to involve each of the four proposed criteria—while still giving to commonsensical intuitions an important role to play, as we try to give as wide as possible an offer of conceptual instruments for addressing the classification question that may arise in the empirical study of the senses. We focus our attention in what follows on the case of audition.

---

[16] And why should we consider that pheromones are a specific *class* of physical stimulation after all? It is maybe because we do have a sense like the sense of olfaction that we can detect pheromones as well as other odors.

3. In Search of Auditory Qualia: Martians versus Venusians

Let us start with the criterion of qualia and distinguish two aspects of normal auditory perception: on the one hand, the informational *content* of the experience, which determines the beliefs the subject is likely to form on the basis of her experience, and more generally the experience's behavioral consequences; on the other hand, the *qualia* associated with the experience itself. Beliefs related to hearing have a characteristic spatial signature: when we hear a sound, we can form a hypothesis about the activity of a material sound source, generally perceived as being in a certain direction and at a distance (even approximate) from us. The sound source itself need not be visible; it can be hidden by another material object, or even lie within it.

Now two thought experiments suggest that the auditory qualia do not play an essential role in the individuation of hearing.[17] Imagine that a certain event occurs—say, an explosion. Suppose that Martians form the same beliefs that we form spontaneously on the basis of our auditory experience; they might declare: "An explosion just occurred"; or they might just move their heads in the direction of the sound source. However, their experience is devoid of the qualia associated with our experience. Either there is no qualitative effect that hearing an explosion has on them or this effect is not the same; for instance, it might be the qualitative effect that, say, seeing a rainbow has on us. In other words, the experience of Martians has the same informational content as our auditory experience but is associated with no qualia or with qualia that are associated in us with different types of experiences.

On the other hand, Venusians do not form the same beliefs that we do, nor do they declare: "An explosion just occurred" or move their heads accordingly toward the source of the event, which means that their experience does not have the same type of informational content as our auditory experience. However, given such an event, namely, the explosion, they enjoy the same type of qualia as we do when we, as humans, hear the explosion. In other words, they feel the qualitative effect of hearing an explosion.[18]

Common sense makes us say, probably, that the Martians, unlike the Venusians, hear external events. Why? Because, given what we said about auditory beliefs, the exercise of the faculty of hearing consists in part of being able to localize the sound source, that is to say, to grasp the relevant content through the formation of appropriate spatial beliefs or more generally appropriate behavior; and given that Venusians fail to do that, then it seems as if their experience of the explosion might not be an auditory experience at all. It follows that in order to determine the very auditory nature of the experience, the type of informational content of

---

[17] In this section, we build on thought experiments designed by Nelkin (1990).

[18] The situation here is analogous to the madman described by Lewis (1978: 122): "he feels pain but his pain does not at all occupy the typical causal role of pain."

the experience is more relevant than the qualia associated with it. Venusians, and not Martians, perhaps, are able to enjoy music, but then their experience of music as we know it is not necessarily an auditory experience; it might be a visual or a tactual experience.

It may be objected that the dissociation between the informational content and the auditory experience of qualia is questionable. Indeed, for qualiaphobes, auditory qualia are determined by what you hear and do not just "float" next to the informational content of the experience. Insofar as common sense is not disturbed by the alleged unintelligibility of the foregoing scenarios, it would be guilty of tolerating a double dissociation between the content of experience and its phenomenal or qualitative character in Martians and Venusians.

To assess this objection, we should look for more realistic cases of experiences that come close, at least in some respects, to those of Martians and Venusians. Consider, once again, the possibility of sensory substitution devices involving the auditory modality. We already mentioned that there are devices for visuo-tactile substitution that allow congenitally blind people to have an experience whose information content is similar to that of visual perception, so that they can evaluate the shape of distant objects and learn how to avoid obstacles. What that means is that they are inclined to form beliefs of a visual type. In addition, it is interesting to note that at least some of them deplore the lack of emotional contour associated with the exercise of their new sensory faculty, as if their experience lacked visual qualia (Bach-y-Rita, 1997). It is then possible to imagine devices for haptic hearing or for visual hearing, capable of translating auditory stimuli into visual or tactile stimuli.[19] Here, subjects who would use an auditory-visual sensory substitution devices (let us call it AVSS) would have an experience similar to that of the Martians, namely, a type of auditory information content in the absence of auditory qualia.

As for Venusians, a hypothesis is that their sensory experience is similar, in some respects, to the situation of spatially deaf patients.[20] These patients can recognize sounds and their sources but are unable to locate them in egocentric space. They may declare hearing the sound of a violin, for example, without being able to tell if the sound comes from the left or from the right, or if the sound source is in front of or behind them. In that sense, they are unable to form spatial auditory beliefs on the basis of their experience.[21]

---

[19] A device that would be the reverse of, for instance, *The Prosthesis Substituting Vision by Audition*, which translates black-and-white images from a head-mounted video camera into sounds that the subject hears through headphones in real time (Capelle et al., 1998).

[20] See Clarke et al. (2002). Spatial deafness is the mirror image of auditory agnosia, in which patients can localize sounds without being able to categorize them, for instance, as the sound of a violin.

[21] Note that since presumably the spatially deaf patients have some non-spatial auditory beliefs, such as the belief that a violin is playing, we would need to envisage a subject with both spatial deafness and auditory agnosia to illustrate the double dissociation between informational content and qualitative character.

Our aim in this section was not to defend the intelligibility of the scenarios involving Martians and Venusians but to point to a dilemma that defenders of the criterion of qualia have to face. Either qualia are conceived as nonrepresentational, that is, as being able to vary independently of informational content, or they are not. In the first case, our scenarios are intelligible, and the criterion of qualia can be shown to be faulty; what counts as hearing does not depend on the presence of auditory qualia. In the second case, the scenarios are not metaphysically possible, and the informational content of the AVSS user's experience will be deemed very different from the informational content of the normal hearing person. However, the criterion of qualia has no bite independently of the criterion of content; indeed, it fully reduces to the latter.

4. The Content of Auditory Experience: Saturnians versus Mercurians

As the criterion of qualia does not appear to be able to reveal the nature of the auditory experience (at least if qualia are nonrepresentational), let us turn to the criterion of content. Hearing gives us access to sounds, construed as dynamic entities, or events, typically produced by an object or a sonorous material (e.g., a bell). But what exactly is the relationship between auditory perception and sound? Two theories can be envisaged at this stage:

Jealousy: sounds are the jealous objects of auditory perception in the sense that a sound can be perceived only by hearing.
Necessity: any type of auditory experience is necessarily, at least, about some sound.

At first glance, *Jealousy* does not sit well with at least some naturalistic conceptions of sound. Suppose, for example, that sounds are vibratory events that affect a sonorous object or physical piece of matter (Casati & Dokic, 1994, 2005). This assumption leaves the possibility open that sounds can be discernible through other sensory modalities, such as touch. Indeed, in a rock concert, the bass can be heard but it can also be felt in the form of vibrations in our body. As for *Necessity*, it must be at least amended to reflect the auditory experience of silence. Hearing silence is not ceasing to hear, in the sense of a (temporary) loss of the faculty of hearing. In the experience of silence, the faculty of hearing is actually engaged, but no sound is heard.[22]

However, the situation is more complex, and we should look a little further into the nature of the content of auditory perception. First, let us distinguish two concepts of sound. In a broad sense, sounds are events that can be heard directly.

---

[22] See also Sorensen (2009).

In this sense, sounds may possess a given tonal quality (pitch), but can also be noises (humming, clicking, hitting, etc.). In a narrow sense, sounds are necessarily provided with a tonal quality and therefore must be distinguished from noise.

Clearly, auditory perception does not necessarily target sounds in the narrow sense. Within the field constituted by the possible immediate objects of hearing, something emerges that can be called a "tonal window," that is to say, an ordered space of sounds, in the narrow construal. Here is a standard physicalist definition of the range of the tonal window in humans:

> The frequency range for tonal hearing is usually placed between 20 Hz and 15,000 Hz. Below 20 Hz, the sound no longer has a continuous tonal quality; we do hear sounds below 20 Hz, but they resemble a series of independent thumps. (Handel, 1993: 65)

The technical definition highlights two interesting philosophical points. First, it admits that we can hear sounds below 20 Hz. Only we do not hear such sounds as tones, in the narrow sense, but as a set of rattlings structured as a rhythm, a pulse, or a measure.

The second point concerns the boundary between the tonal sounds and the other sounds located around 20 Hz. Several questions arise. What is the status of the border? Does its actual location correspond to any physical or psychological constraint? Couldn't we imagine that it be set at a different point and that our tonal window had a different extension than it has in fact?

To help answer these questions, consider, as a thought experiment, two species of creatures whose sensory apparatus is somewhat different from ours. The Saturnians perceive a steady pulse above 1 Hz (one beat per second) as a sound of a given pitch. In other words, they perceive as tones many things we perceive as a meter, such as a meter of ten beats per second. Mercurians, on the other hand, have a tonal window whose lower limit is 1 kHz (one thousand beats per second). What is for us a middle C, they perceive as an ultra fast pace.

These two imaginary scenarios pinpoint a potential conflict between two rather different ontological conceptions of sounds. The first conception is largely consensual in the philosophical tradition and it appears to correspond to some commonsense intuitions. It states that sounds are defined by their qualitative properties, in particular their tonal properties. It thus implies either that noises are not sounds, or that their sound essence is radically different from that of "tonal" sounds.

The second conception decrees that the tonal quality of sound is not part of its essence or its constitution as a physical entity. It follows that the true nature of sounds, consisting of sequences of pulses, is revealed in the experience precisely below the limit of 20 Hz. By contrast, the hearing of mechanical vibrations above 20 Hz does not constitute any more an experience of sounds as they really are, namely, as common sensibles, potentially accessible to other sensory modalities, but as they appear to us in a qualitative (tonal) mode of presentation.

The fact that mechanical vibrations in a range of frequencies can be heard in one case as a meter and in another as a tone has potentially far-reaching consequences. At a minimum, the criterion of qualia proves too strong here. Moreover, note that meters are traditionally considered primary qualities, whereas tones are traditionally considered secondary qualities—the challenge for traditional theories of the distinction between two types of qualities is worth exploring.

To sum up, defenders of the criterion of content face a dilemma. Either sounds are audibilia, that is, accessible only through the auditory modality (Jealousy), or they are not. The first horn of the dilemma is congenial to the narrow concept of sound, according to which sounds are necessarily provided with tonal qualities. However, it raises the general worry that sounds are individuated too tightly in terms of phenomenal characteristics of our auditory experience. As a consequence, the application of the criterion of content might be saddled with vicious circularity (individuation of what is heard would necessarily involve some reference to hearing). A more specific worry is that the narrow concept of sound leaves unexplained the nature of the boundary between tonal sounds and noises, which is internal to our auditory experience. Our scenarios involving Saturnians and Mercurians suggest that the same fragment of perceived reality can be heard as a tone or as a meter. Since meters are clearly primary qualities, they cannot be identical with mere audibilia. This leads us to the second horn of the dilemma, which we already found problematic (section 2). What we have suggested in this section is that even "key" properties such as sounds might turn out to be common sensibles after all, pace Jealousy.

5. Combining Common Sense and Science

We have seen that the problem of the individuation of the senses can be approached in two ways, according to the importance given to commonsense classification. In this discussion, we paid special attention to those criteria that claim to justify, at least to some extent, our intuitive classification. We explored in detail, in the case of auditory experience, the criterion of qualia and the criterion of content.

If we began by dismissing the idea that one can define the auditory modality by reference to "floating" auditory qualia, that is to say, qualia that are separated from the informational content of experience, our discussion of the criterion of content showed the interest of introducing the concept of a qualitative mode of presentation of sound, which, in the normal auditory experience, construes sound as a given tonal quality (the sound in the narrow sense).

In other words, our strategy here has consisted in introducing a distinction between two kinds of qualitative modes of presentation: on the one hand, a qualitative *mechanical* mode of presentation, thanks to which sounds, as mechanical vibrations, can be discerned by other sensory modalities, and, on another hand, a qualitative *tonal* mode of presentation, thanks to which only the auditory modality gives us access to the particular qualitative tonal property of a sound. The same sound could in principle be heard under one or the other auditory mode of presentation, namely, as a mechanical vibration or as a sound in the narrow sense. One might think that human auditory experience reveals a given sound either as a mechanical vibration or under a tonal mode of presentation, but not both at the same time. However, we have also suggested that there are human experiences that can be conceived as ambiguous in this respect, as for instance when we hear events at the boundary between tonal sounds and noises. Furthermore, one could even claim that the same sound can be perceived under both (mechanical and tonal) modes of presentation. Suppose for instance that one is touching a sounding object. One has tactile access to vibratory events that are in fact identical with the sound made by the object. Given that the mechanical mode of presentation is common to our tactile and auditory experiences, the same sound is perceived both mechanically and tonally.[23]

If both conceptual analysis and science motivate the construal of sound as a physical entity in the realm of mechanical vibrations, common sense is closer to what we called the Jealousy thesis that certain dynamic entities, that is, sounds in the narrow sense, are audibilia, in the sense that they are only perceptible through hearing. We can then propose the following synthesis. Both conceptual analysis and science are right about the ontology of sound, which by its mechanical nature is in principle available to sensory modalities other than hearing. But, possibly, only hearing can represent certain sounds as having a given tonal quality. Therefore, sounds in the narrow sense do not form a physical natural kind; they are at best an important subjective aspect of our sensory experience that common sense tends to regard as characteristic of hearing.

It does not follow that the criterion of content, even supplemented by the notion of qualitative modes of presentation, is sufficient for the individuation of the senses. Indeed, no criterion taken in isolation seems entirely adequate. As Nelkin (1990) says, "each criterion by itself might explain part of the truth; none by itself explains the whole truth" (191). It would thus be appropriate to explore the possibility that the naive concept of sense modality is actually complex, and that several relatively independent criteria must be combined to approximate the commonsense classification. Even if we cannot defend this theoretical option here, we may suggest combining the criterion of content and the criterion of the sensory organ, construed in relational terms.[24] Common sense associates each sensory modality with a bodily organ on which we can act directly to indirectly modify the content of our experience. It is thus the activity related to listening, as it is capable of producing (among others) the experience of sound in a narrow sense, which would

---

[23] More speculatively, if the mechanical mode of presentation is conceived as being literally common to one's tactile and auditory experiences, a given sound could even be *heard* as both a vibratory event and a tone.

[24] Here we take our inspiration from Nelkin (1990).

specifically characterize the experience of hearing. The question of whether such a combination of criteria is adequate must also certainly be explored in relation to other sensory modalities, but we must postpone this project to another occasion.

References

Armstrong D. M., 1968, *A Materialist Theory of the Mind*, London, Routledge & Kegan Paul.

Auvray M., & Myin E., 2009, "Perception with compensatory devices. From sensory substitution to sensorimotor extension," *Cognitive Science*, 33, 1036–1058.

Berthoz A., 2000, *The Brain's Sense of Movement*, Cambridge, MA, Harvard University Press.

Bach-y-Rita P., Collins C. C., Saunders F. A., White B., & Scadden, L., 1969, "Vision substitution by tactile image projection," *Nature*, 221, 963–964.

Bach-y-Rita P., 1997, "Substitution sensorielle et qualia," in Proust J. (dir.), *Perception et intermodalité, approches actuelles de la question de Molyneux*, Paris, Presses Universitaires de France.

Casati R., & Dokic J., 1994, *La Philosophie du son*, Nîmes, Éditions Chambon.

Casati R., & Dokic J., 2005, "Sounds," in Zalta E. N. (Ed.), *The Stanford Encyclopedia of Philosophy*, http://plato.stanford.edu/archives/fall2005/entries/sounds/.

Clarke S., Bellmann Thiran A., Maeder P., Adriani M., Vernet O., Regli L., Cuisenaire O., & Thiran J.-P., 2002, "What and where in human audition: Selective deficits following focal hemispheric lesions," *Experimental Brain Research*, 147, 8–15.

Coady C. A. J., 1974, "The senses of Martians," *Philosophical Review*, 83(1), 107–125.

Dennett D., 1991, *Consciousness Explained*, Boston: Little, Brown.

Geurts, K. L., 2002, *Culture and the Senses: Bodily Ways of Knowing in an African Community*, Berkeley, University of California Press.

Grice H. P., 1962, "Some remarks about the senses," in Grice H. P., *Studies in the Way of Words*, Cambridge, MA, Harvard University Press, 1989, pp. 248–268.

Handel S., 1993, *Listening. An Introduction to the Perception of Auditory Events*, Cambridge, MA, MIT Press.

Heil J., 1983, "The senses," in Heil J., *Perception and Cognition*, Berkeley, University of California Press; reprinted in Macpherson F. (Ed.), 2011, *The Senses: Classical and Contemporary Philosophical Perspectives*, Oxford, Oxford University Press, pp. 136–155.

Heil J., 2011, "The senses," in Macpherson F. (Ed.), 2011, *The Senses: Classical and Contemporary Philosophical Perspectives*, Oxford, Oxford University Press, pp. 284–296.

Howes D. (Ed.), 1991, *The Varieties of Sensory Experience: A Sourcebook in the Anthropology of the Senses*, Anthropological Horizons, 1, Toronto, University of Toronto Press.

Howes D., 2003, *Sensual Relations: Engaging in the Senses in Culture and Social Theory*, Ann Arbor, University of Michigan Press, 4th ed.

Hughes H. C., 1999, *Sensory Exotica: A World beyond Human Experience*, Cambridge, MA, MIT Press, 2nd ed.

Jütte R., 2005, *A History of the Senses: From Antiquity to Cyberspace*, Cambridge, Polity Press.

Keeley B., 2002, "Making Sense of the Senses: Individuating Modalities in Humans and Other Animals," *Journal of Philosophy*, 99(1), 5–28; reprinted in Macpherson F. (Ed.),

2011, *The Senses: Classical and Contemporary Philosophical Perspectives*, Oxford, Oxford University Press, pp. 220–240.

Keeley B., 2009, "The Role of Neurobiology in Differentiating the Senses," in John Bickle (Ed.), *The Oxford Handbook of Philosophy and Neuroscience*, Oxford, Oxford University Press, pp. 226–250.

Leon M., 1988, "Characterising the Senses," *Mind and Language*, 3(4), 243–270; reprinted in Macpherson F. (Ed.), 2011, *The Senses: Classical and Contemporary Philosophical Perspectives*, Oxford, Oxford University Press, pp. 156–183.

Lewis D., 1978, "Mad Pain and Martian Pain," in *Philosophical Papers*, Vol. II, New York, Oxford University Press.

Lopes Dominic, 2000, "What is it like to see with your ears? The representational theory of mind," *Philosophy and Phenomenological Research*, 60(2), 439–453.

Macpherson F. (Ed.), 2011, *The Senses: Classical and Contemporary Philosophical Perspectives*, Oxford, Oxford University Press.

Macpherson F., 2011, "Introduction: Individuating the Senses," in Macpherson F. (Ed.), *The Senses: Classical and Contemporary Philosophical Perspectives*, Oxford, Oxford University Press, pp. 3–43.

McGurk H., & MacDonald J., 1976, "Hearing lips and seeing voices," *Nature*, 264(5588), 746–748.

Nagel T., 1974, "What is it like to be a bat?" *Philosophical Review*, 83, 435–450.

Nelkin N., 1990, "Categorising the senses," *Mind and Language*, 5, 149–165; reprinted in Macpherson F. (Ed.), 2011, *The Senses: Classical and Contemporary Philosophical Perspectives*, Oxford, Oxford University Press, pp. 184–200.

Nudds M., 2004, "The Significance of the Senses," *Proceedings of the Aristotelian Society* 104(1), 31–51.

Nudds M., 2011, "The senses as psychological kinds," in Macpherson F. (Ed.), 2011, *The Senses: Classical and Contemporary Philosophical Perspectives*, Oxford, Oxford University Press, pp. 311–340.

O'Dea J. 2011, "A proprioceptive account of the sense modalities," in Macpherson F. (Ed.), 2011, *The Senses: Classical and Contemporary Philosophical Perspectives*, Oxford, Oxford University Press, pp. 297–310.

Roxbee-Cox J. W., 1970, "Distinguishing the senses," *Mind*, 79, 1530–1550.

Sorensen R., 2009, "Hearing silence: The perception and introspection of absences," in Nudds M., & O'Callaghan C., (Eds.), 2009, *Sounds and Perception, New Philosophical Essays*, Oxford, Oxford University Press, 126–145.

Stoffregen T. A., & Bardy B. G., 2001, "On specification and the senses," *Behavioral and Brain Sciences*, 24, 195–213.

Tye M., 2009, *Consciousness Revisited: Materialism without Phenomenal Concepts*. Cambridge, MA, MIT Press.

{ INDEX }

infrared radiation, 283, 436
inhomogeneities, spatial and temporal, 215–16
inner sense, 8, 17, 277–79, 281, 283, 285–94, 429
  as a higher-order sense, 278, 287, 290–91
  considered as a genuine sense, 286–91
  contrasted with first-order senses, 278
  organ of, 289–90
  time as the form of, 44
integration, of information from the senses, 14–15,
      67, 95, 106–8, 110, 113, 166–69, 172–74,
      176–77, 179–84, 186, 201–2, 250, 254, 268,
      334, 397, 411, 413. *See also* cross-modality;
      inter-modality; multi-modality
  impairments to, 139
  and ventriloquism, 154
interaction, of the senses, 8, 13–15, 95, 97,
      99, 106–13, 122, 168, 174–79, 183. *See
      also* cross-modality; inter-modality;
      multi-modality
  definition of, 85
  of taste and smell, 256
  within touch, 200–3
  of vision and audition, 168, 465
  of vision and smell, 14n6
interoceptive senses, 458
inter-modality, 97, 138–41, 152–56, 200. *See also*
      cross-modality; multi-modality
  definition, 138
  dominance, 406–7
inter-modal causality, 172
inter-modal dominance, 406–7
inter-modal meter. *See* inter-modal rhythm
inter-modal relation perception, 153–56
inter-modal rhythm, 139, 154
Intons-Peterson, M.J., 373n27
introspection, 162, 290, 464–65
  as providing support for the multi-sensory
      view of consciousness, 103–5, 122, 143–45
isotropic perceptual models, 58–61, 63, 67, 70
  definition of, 58
itches, 8, 69, 191–95, 199–200, 203
Izmailov, Ch. A., 50n9

Jackson, F., 396
Jacobs, G.H., 385
James, T. W. 14, 198, 426
James, W., 54
Jansson, G., 329
Jay, M., 410–11
Jiang, Y., 101
Johnson, J.A., 123
Jolicoeur, P., 114–15
Jonas, H., 410
Jones, L.A., 198
Jordan, G., 386
Jordan, K.E., 119, 184n38

Kahneman, D., 118–19, 170
Kandel, E.R., 321
Kant, I., 4, 44–55, 69–71
  a priori intuitions, 47, 49–51, 70
  on the cognitive necessity of perceiving space
      as three-dimensional, 49–51
  on non-Euclidean geometry, 49n7
  on the outerness of appearances, 44, 46–49
  on space, 44–45, 69–70
  on time, 52–56, 70
Kappers, A.M., 49
Kappes, S.M., 256n8
Karns, C.M., 133n1
Katz, D., 411
Kawamata, T., 363–64, 366, 372
Kawamura, Y., 251
Keeley, B.L., 16, 192–93, 251n3, 278n3, 279, 283–84
Kelly, D.H., 304
Kemp, S., 412
Kentridge, R.W., 101
Kepler, J., 3
Kilgard, M.P., 319
Kim, J.-K., 329, 336
Kirchner, H., 422
Klatzky, R.L., 198, 201–2, 204, 329, 348, 360, 376,
      423, 425, 429–30
Kluver, H., 307
Ko, Y., 318
Kobayashi, M., 373n27
Koch, C., 30–32, 97, 101
Koffka, K., 3
Kohler, W., 3
Kohn, A., 77
Koppen, C., 108
Korsmeyer, C., 249
Kosslyn, S.M., 59, 100, 123n23, 289, 360
Kourtzi, Z., 361
Kristofferson, A.B., 97, 102, 104–5
Kubovy, M., 117–19, 138n9, 232n31
Kulvicki, J., 7–8, 168, 205, 207–10, 214n5, 217, 219
Kupers, R., 343, 426

Labbe, D., 262
Lakatos, S., 112
Lamme, V.A.F., 101
Langer, K., 313
Larsen, A., 114
Lashley, K.S., 319
Laughlin, Z., 259
Lawless, H.T., 251–52, 254n8, 258–60, 265
Lawrence, G., 261
learning, 17, 25–29, 77–79, 81, 193, 207
  in olfactory discrimination, 228, 233, 235, 243
  how to perceive using SSD systems, 330, 335
  how to perceive using TVSS systems, 417–19
Le Corre, F., 13, 462

Printed in Great Britain
by Amazon.co.uk, Ltd.,
Marston Gate.